4.

W9-BII-337

NFPA HANDBOOK
OF THE NATIONAL ELECTRICAL CODE

Other McGraw-Hill Handbooks of Interest

NFPA HANDBOOK
OF THE NATIONAL ELECTRICAL CODE

Based on the Current 1971 Code

JOHN H. WATT

Previously Edited by FRANK STETKA

Third Edition

SPONSORED BY THE NATIONAL FIRE PROTECTION ASSOCIATION

McGRAW-HILL BOOK COMPANY

New York   St. Louis   San Francisco   Düsseldorf   Johannesburg
Kuala Lumpur   London   Mexico   Montreal   New Delhi
Panama   Rio de Janeiro   Singapore   Sydney   Toronto

34567890 MUBP 76543

Foreword

The National Electrical Code, as its name implies, is a nationally accepted guide to the safe installation of electrical wiring and equipment.

This NFPA Handbook of the National Electrical Code has, as its purpose, aiding those concerned with electrical safety in understanding the scope and intent of the 1971 Edition of the Code. Included is a verbatim reproduction of the official 1971 National Electrical Code as published by its sponsor, the National Fire Protection Association, and as approved by the American National Standards Institute (formerly the United States of America Standards Institute, and prior to that the American Standards Association). Added, where necessary or considered desirable, are comments, diagrams, and illustrations, supplied by the author, to facilitate understanding of the Code rules.

The author wishes it clearly understood that the National Electrical Code is prepared by the cooperative effort of representatives of every segment of the electrical industry with the sole purpose of safeguarding the public in its utilization of its great servant—electricity. The development of this Handbook is likewise a cooperative effort incorporating the knowledge and ideas of the over 200 members of the National Electrical Code Committee, and the guidance given herein taps experience in the application and interpretation of the Code developed over the more than half a century since it first appeared.

The McGraw-Hill Book Company has been publishing a Handbook on the National Electrical Code since 1932. Originally developed by Arthur L. Abbott in that year and carried on in seven successive editions until the time of his death in 1952, each subsequent issue has been authored by the Electrical Field Engineer of the National Fire Protection Association. The late Charles L. Smith prepared the editions based on the 1953 and 1956 Codes while he served as the NFPA Electrical Specialist. Frank Stetka took on the responsibility upon assuming the position and edited the Handbooks based on the 1959, 1962, 1965, and 1968 Codes. Mr. Merwin M. Brandon, Chairman of the National Electrical Code Committee from 1950 to 1961, assisted in a previous Handbook (based on the 1965 Code). Following the retirement of Mr. Stetka at the end of 1968, John Watt assumed the position of Electrical Field Engineer for the NFPA. This edition has been prepared by Mr. Watt, based on the 1971 National Electrical Code.

Changes in the 1971 National Electrical Code (as compared with the 1968

Code) are indicated by vertical marginal rules on the affected pages. In certain cases, minor editorial changes are not so indicated.

This edition of the NFPA Handbook of the National Electrical Code replaces the edition published in 1969 by the McGraw-Hill Book Company.

The author wishes to give particular acknowledgment to the assistance of Mr. Richard L. Lloyd, Chairman of the National Electrical Code Committee; and to the chairmen of the various Code-Making Panels of the National Electrical Code Committee, many of whom were consulted by the author in the preparation of this Handbook. The contributions of the manufacturers who provided illustrations and information about their products are greatly appreciated. The aid and assistance given by the staff of the McGraw-Hill Book Company made this book possible, and their cooperative attitude assisted the author in overcoming many technical problems in connection with the preparation of this text.

John Watt assumed the position of Electrical Field Engineer of the National Fire Protection Association and Secretary of the National Electrical Code Committee in January, 1969. His previous experience of 30 years in the electrical construction industry provides an excellent background. He was supervising electrical inspector for the City of Seattle and the New York Board of Fire Underwriters. He was also an electrical contractor and trade school instructor. Mr. Watt is well known for his ten-year career as Associate Editor for *Electrical Construction and Maintenance,* and for his numerous articles on electrical construction. He is the author of the ninth edition of the popular American Electricians' Handbook. He is also the Secretary of the NFPA Electrical Section, and he is a corporate member of the Underwriters' Laboratories, member of the UL Electrical Council as a Safety Expert, and holds membership in the International Association of Electrical Inspectors, Institute of Electrical and Electronics Engineers, and the International Brotherhood of Electrical Workers.

National Electrical Code

This NFPA Handbook of the National Electrical Code is based on the 1971 Edition of the National Electrical Code as developed by the National Electrical Code Committee of the American National Standards Institute (ANSI), sponsored by the National Fire Protection Association (NFPA). The National Electrical Code is identified by the designation NFPA No. 70-1971 and ANSI C 1-1971. The NFPA adopted this 1971 Code at the NFPA Annual Meeting held in San Francisco, Ca., May 17–21 and approval was given by ANSI on June 25, 1971.

The National Electrical Code, as its name implies, is a nationally accepted guide to the safe installation of electrical wiring and equipment. The committee sponsoring its development includes all parties of interest having technical competence in the field, working together with the sole objective of safeguarding the public in its utilization of electricity. The procedures under which the Code is prepared provide for the orderly introduction of new developments and improvements in the art, with particular emphasis on safety from the standpoint of its end use. The rules of procedure under which the National Electrical Code Committee operates are published in each official edition of the Code and in separate pamphlet form so that all concerned may have full information and free access to the operating procedures of the sponsoring committee. The Code has been a big factor in the growth and wide acceptance of the use of electrical energy for light and power and for heat, radio, television, signaling, and other purposes from the date of its first appearance (1897) to the present.

The National Electrical Code is primarily designed for use by trained electrical people and is necessarily terse in its wording. As a consequence, some sections are clearer if explained from the standpoint of the background intent of the Code writers, and giving these explanations is the first purpose of this NFPA Handbook of the National Electrical Code.

The sponsoring National Electrical Code Committee is composed of a Correlating Committee and seventeen Code-Making Panels, each responsible for one or more Articles in the Code. Each Panel is composed of experienced men representing balanced interests of all segments of the industry and the public concerned with the subject matter. The present Chairman of the National Electrical Code

Committee is Richard L. Lloyd, Assistant to the President, Codes and Standards of the Underwriters' Laboratories, Inc. and the Vice-Chairman is Baron Whitaker, President of the Underwriters' Laboratories, Inc. John Watt, author of this Handbook, has been the Secretary of the National Electrical Code Committee and Electrical Field Engineer of the NFPA since January, 1969. The internal operations of the sponsoring committee are guided by a "Manual of Procedure for Code-Making Panels." This Manual is published in pamphlet form, and copies are available from the NFPA, 60 Batterymarch Street, Boston, Massachusetts, 02110.

The National Fire Protection Association also has organized an Electrical Section to provide the opportunity for NFPA members interested in electrical safety to become better informed and to contribute to the development of NFPA electrical standards. This new Handbook reflects the fact that the National Electrical Code was revised in 1971, requiring an updating of the previous Handbook which was based on the 1968 Edition of the Code. The established schedule of the National Electrical Code Committee contemplates a new edition of the National Electrical Code every three years. The "Timetable for the 1974 National Electrical Code" has been announced and is published in all official copies of the 1971 National Electrical Code as well as in this volume. Provision is made under the rules of procedure for handling urgent emergency matters through a Tentative Interim Amendment Procedure. The Committee also has established rules for rendering Official Interpretations. Two general forms of findings for such Interpretations are recognized: (1) those making an interpretation of literal text and (2) those making an interpretation of the intent of the National Electrical Code when a particular rule was adopted. All Tentative Interim Amendments and Official Interpretations are published by the NFPA as they are issued, and notices are sent to all interested trade papers in the electrical industry.

Those interested in further details on the processing of each new edition of the National Electrical Code should be advised that the schedule includes a final date for receipt of proposals for changes from the public. For the 1974 Code, this date is December 1, 1972. In July of 1973, following processing of all proposals received, the Association will issue the "Proposed Amendments for the 1974 National Electrical Code." Public announcement will be made of the issuance of this document, and a period of study is included so that all interested persons may comment on the Proposed Amendments. In April 1974, the Association will issue the final agreed upon Proposed 1974 National Electrical Code (with revisions to the 1971 Code indicated) which will be presented at the Annual Meeting of the Association in that year (now scheduled for May 20–24 at the Fountainbleau Hotel, Miami Beach, Florida) for action. All interested persons may attend this meeting and participate in any discussions on the proposed 1974 Code that are pertinent to the adoption procedures. Further details with regard to procedures are available from the Association upon request.

As is indicated in the Foreword, the 1971 National Electrical Code is published verbatim in this Handbook. The NFPA also publishes the Code in separate pamphlet form, single copy price $3.50 (soft cover), $4.95 (hard cover-HC), and in Volume 5 of the National Fire Codes (issued annually; $5.00 per copy).

The National Electrical Code had its origin in 1897 as a result of united efforts of various insurance, electrical, architectural, and allied interests. The original

Code, prepared by the National Conference on Standard Electrical Rules, was issued in successive editions until the National Conference was disbanded in 1911. Since then the National Fire Protection Association has been sponsor. The text for editions up to 1947 was prepared by the NFPA Electrical Committee. In 1949 the NFPA Electrical Section was organized and the National Electrical Code Committee created.

The National Electrical Code is purely advisory as far as the National Fire Protection Association is concerned but is very widely used as the basis of law and for legal regulatory purposes. The Code is administered by various local inspection agencies, whose decisions govern the actual application of the National Electrical Code to individual installations. Local inspectors are largely members of the International Association of Electrical Inspectors, 201 East Erie Street, Chicago, Illinois, 60611. This organization, the National Electrical Manufacturers Association, the National Electrical Contractors Association, the Edison Electric Institute, the Underwriters' Laboratories, governmental groups and independent experts—all contribute to the development and application of the National Electrical Code.

Determination of the suitability of devices and materials for installation in accordance with the National Electrical Code is the responsibility of the electrical-inspection authority, which, under the terms of the Code, must approve the devices and materials used. Many such "approvals" are based upon tests and listings of Underwriters' Laboratories, Inc., 207 East Ohio Street, Chicago, Illinois, 60611. This nationally recognized testing laboratory maintains facilities for testing electrical equipment and checking manufacturers' production to assure maintenance of proper standards, evidenced by a label or reexamination marker on each individual product. Underwriters' Laboratories, Inc., publishes annually (with bi-monthly supplements) three pamphlets indicating electrical appliances and materials which have been examined and listed by them entitled: "Electrical Appliance and Utilization Equipment List," "Electrical Construction Materials List," and "Hazardous Location Equipment List." These Lists may be secured from local representatives of the Laboratories in principal cities of the United States. Standards for design and testing of various types of electrical equipment developed by Underwriters' Laboratories, Inc., may be obtained from their main office at 207 East Ohio Street, Chicago, Illinois, 60611.

Brief History of the National Electrical Code

The National Electrical Code was originally drawn in 1897 as a result of the united efforts of various insurance, electrical, architectural, and allied interests. The original Code was prepared by the National Conference on Standard Electrical Rules, composed of delegates from various interested national associations. Prior to this, acting on an 1881 resolution of the National Association of Fire Engineers' meeting in Richmond, Virginia, a basis for the first Code was suggested to cover such items as identification of the white wire, the use of single disconnect devices, and the use of insulated conduit.

In 1911, the National Conference of Standard Electrical Rules was disbanded, and since that year, the National Fire Protection Association (NFPA) has acted as sponsor of the National Electrical Code. Beginning with the 1920 edition, the National Electrical Code has been under the further auspices of the American National Standards Institute (and its predecessor organizations, United States of America Standards Institute, and the American Standards Association), with the NFPA continuing in its role as Administrative Sponsor. Since that date, the Committee has been identified as "ANSI Standards Committee C1" (formerly "USAS C1" or "ASA C1").

Major milestones in the continued updating of successive issues of the National Electrical Code since 1911 appeared in 1923, when the Code was rearranged and rewritten; in 1937 when it was editorially revised so that all the general rules would appear in the first chapters followed by supplementary rules in the following chapters; and in 1959 when it was editorially revised to incorporate a new numbering system under which each Section of each Article is identified by the Article Number preceding the Section Number.

For many years the National Electrical Code was published by the National Board of Fire Underwriters (now American Insurance Association) and this public service of the National Board helped immensely in bringing about the wide public acceptance which the Code now enjoys. It is recognized as the most widely adopted Code of standard practices in the U.S.A. Over 700,000 copies of the 1971 Code were printed to fill orders within the first six months of issue. The National Fire Protection Association first printed the document in pamphlet form in 1951 and has, since that year, supplied the Code for distribution to the public through its own office and through the American National Standards Institute. The National Electrical Code also appears in Volume 5 of the National Fire Codes, issued annually by the National Fire Protection Association. This Volume 5 (available for $5.00 per copy) also includes the following NFPA related electrical Standards: Protection of Electronic Computer/Data Processing Equipment (NFPA No. 75-1968), Essential Electrical Systems for Hospitals (NFPA No. 76A-1971), Metalworking Machine Tools (NFPA No. 79-1971) and Purged Enclosures for Electrical Equipment in Hazardous Locations (NFPA No. 496-1971).

It has been the practice of the NFPA as sponsor of the National Electrical Code to include in each edition a list of the personnel of the Committee, and each NFPA edition of the Code carries this roster. Also in each printing of the text of the National Electrical Code and in the Appendix of this Handbook, the Rules of Procedure for the NFPA Electrical Section and for the National Electrical Code Committee are published, together with the Time Schedule for the next edition of the Code. To further facilitate improvements in the Code, the Appendix contains a special section on the "Method of Submitting a Proposal to Revise the National Electrical Code." The publication of this information is consistent with the operating procedures of the American National Standards Institute and the National Fire Protection Association to assure that all interested parties may participate in the work of the sponsoring committee and that there is an orderly procedure for processing the many changes that flow from the expanding use of electricity and the many new materials, methods, and systems that characterize the growth of the electrical industry.

Contents

Chapter 4. EQUIPMENT FOR GENERAL USE

Principal Tables

Chapter 9

Resume of Code Changes

The following list indicates deletions, significant revisions, and new items that are reflected in the 1971 National Electrical Code through changes to the 1968 edition. In all cases, revisions or additions that appear in the 1971 Code are indicated by vertical marginal lines on pages where such changes have been made.

Art. 100. Definitions. Deleted. (1) Common Main Grounding Conductor; **(2)** Main Grounding Conductor.

New. (1) Grounding Electrode Conductor; **(2)** Rainproof.

Revised. (1) Accessible (As applied to wiring methods); **(2)** Equipment Grounding Conductor; **(3)** Exposed (As applied to wiring methods); **(4)** Receptacle (single and multiple); **(5)** Service Equipment.

Art. 110. Deleted. (1) 110-15. Now in 110-14; **(2)** 110-17(a) (3). (4) and (5) now (3) and (4).

Art. 200. New. (1) 200-4, Exc.; **(2)** 200-7, Exc. 4.

Art. 210. New. (1) 210-6(c). Old (c) now (d); **(2)** 210-7 last paragraph; **(3)** 210-22(b) last sentence in 1st paragraph, 2nd paragraph, and last sentence in 3rd paragraph; **(4)** 210-22(c), Exc.; **(5)** 210-22(d); **(6)** 210-22(e); **(7)** Table 210-25 2nd fineprint note.

Revised. (1) 210-5; **(2)** 210-6(a), Exc. 1.

Art. 215. New. 215-8.

Art. 220. New. (1) 220-2 2nd paragraph; **(2)** 220-2(b) last sentence of 1st paragraph; **(3)** 220-4, Exc.; **(4)** 220-4(a). Old (a), Table 220-4(a), (b) thru (m) now (b), Table 220-4(b), (c) thru (n); **(5)** 220-4(o); **(6)** 220-9(c).

Revised. Table 220 7.

Art. 230. Deleted. 230-44 fineprint note.

New. (1) 230-2, Exc. 7; **(2)** 230-31(a) last sentence of 1st paragraph; **(3)** 230-90(a), Exc. 5; **(4)** 230-94(f); **(5)** 230-95; **(6)** 230-96; **(7)** 230-98.

Revised. (1) 230-2, Exc. 4; **(2)** 230-30; **(3)** 230-40(a), Exc.; **(4)** 230-70(e); **(5)** 230-70(g).

Art. 240. Deleted. (1) 240-4; **(2)** 240-5(a), Exc. 2 Note; **(3)** 240-5(a), Exc. 2. Exc. 3, 4, and 5 now 2, 3 and 4; **(4)** 240-9; **(5)** 240-G (240-24). Parts H and I now G and H; **(6)** 240-25(b). (c) thru (f) now (b) thru (e).

New. (1) 240-5(a), Exc. 5 and 6; **(2)** 240-15, Exc. 7; **(3)** 240-16(d).

Revised. (1) 240-5(a), Exc. 4; **(2)** 240-23(c); **(3)** 240-25(e).

Art. 250. Deleted. (1) 250-4; **(2)** 250-6. Now in 250-5(b), Exc.; **(3)** 250-8. Now in 250-5(a); **(4)** 250-25(e) last sentence; **(5)** 250-34. Now in 250-46; **(6)** 250-77 2nd sentence; **(7)** 250-85; **(8)** 250-112(a), (b), (c).

New. (1) 250-44(e); **(2)** 250-50; **(3)** 250-62; **(4)** 250-70; **(5)** 250-79(c) and (d); **(6)** 250-80; **(7)** 250-82(d); **(8)** 250-95 2nd paragraph and exceptions.

Revised. (1) 250-1; **(2)** 250-5; **(3)** 250-23(a) and (b); **(4)** 250-24; **(5)** 250-26; **(6)** 250-42; **(7)** 250-45(c), Exc.; **(8)** 250-45(d), Exc. 2; **(9)** 250-53; **(10)** 250-61; **(11)** 250-79; **(12)** 250-91(b); **(13)** 250-92(a) and (b); **(14)** 250-112.

Art. 300. Deleted. (1) 300-1(a) and (c). (b) and (d) now (a) and (b); **(2)** 300-22(c) (2) and (c) (3); **(3)** 300-23. Now in new Art. 305.

New. 300-13 2nd paragraph.

Revised. (1) 300-19(a); **(2)** 300-21; **(3)** 300-22(b) and (d).

Art. 305. New Article.

Art. 310. Deleted. (1) 310-2(c) thru (f). Most of this material now in new Section 310-12. (g) thru (i) now (c) thru (e) and Tables 310-2(i) (1) thru (i) (4) now (e) (1) thru (e) (4); **(2)** Tables 310-2(a) and (b), Type THW-MTW; **(3)** Notes 9 and 13 to Tables 310-12 thru 310-15. Notes 10, 11, 12, 14 and 15 now 9, 10, 11, 12 and 13.

New. (1) Table 310-2(a), Types PTF, PTFF, and TFE: **(2)** Table 310-2(b), Type TFE; **(3)** 310-2(c), Exc. 4; **(4)** Section 310-12; **(5)** Table 310-12*** Note.

Revised. (1) Table 310-2(a), Type THW; **(2)** Table 310-2(e) (1); **(3)** 310-9; **(4)** Table 310-14* Note.

Art. 318. New. 318-2(a) (8).

Art. 328. Entire Article deleted.

Art. 334. New. 334-6(b) last sentence.

Art. 337. New Article.

Art. 346. Deleted. 346-6(a) and (b).

Revised. 346-6.

Art. 347. Deleted. (1) 347-3(b) and (h). (c) thru (g) now (b) thru (f); **(2)** 347-11(a) and (b). (a) (3) now in 347-4.

Revised. (1) 347-2(b); **(2)** Table 347-8; **(3)** 347-11.

Art. 350. New. 350-5, Exc.

Revised. (1) 350-3(3); **(2)** Table 350-3.

Art. 351. Extensively revised.

Art. 352. New. 352-7. Old 352-7 now 352-8.

Revised. 352-1.

Art. 363. New Article.

Art. 370. New. (1) 370-1 2nd paragraph; **(2)** 370-13 last paragraph.

Revised. (1) 370-6; **(2)** 370-17.

Art. 373. New. 373-11(d) last sentence.

Revised. (1) Table 373-6(a); **(2)** 373-8.

Art. 374. Revised. 374-5.

Art. 380. Revised. (1) 380-8; **(2)** 380-10; **(3)** 380-14.

Art. 384. New. 384-3(d).

Art. 400. New. (1) Table 400-9(b), Types ETT and ETLB; **(2)** Table 400-11, Types ETT and ETLB.

Art. 402. New. (1) Table 402-4, Types PTF and PTFF; **(2)** Table 402-6, Types PTF and PTFF; **(3)** 402-7.

Art. 410. Deleted. (1) 410-53. Now in 370-17; **(2)** 410-93, Exc. 2.

New. (1) 410-4(c); **(2)** 410-14 2nd paragraph; **(3)** 410-52(c) and (d); **(4)** 410-55(b) (3) last 3 sentences; **(5)** 410-55(b) (4).

Revised. (1) 410-8; **(2)** 410-14; **(3)** 410-54; **(4)** 410-65(b) (2) last sentence; **(5)** 410-71(e).

Art. 422. Deleted. 422-6, Exc. 1. Now in 422-27(e). Exc. 2 now a 2nd paragraph.

New. (1) 422-1 2nd sentence; **(2)** 422-7; **(3)** 422-14 2nd and 3rd sentences and Exc.; **(4)** 422-18; **(5)** 422-27(e).

Revised. (1) 422-26; **(2)** 422-32; **(3)** 422-43.

Art. 424. Deleted. (1) 424-20. Now in 424-19(c). 424-21 thru 424-23 now 424-20 thru 424-22; **(2)** Part G (424-71 thru 424-80). Now in new Art. 426.

New. (1) 424-3(b) 3rd paragraph; **(2)** 424-28(b).

Revised. (1) 424-3; **(2)** 424-19(c). Formerly 424-20; **(3)** 424-22(c); **(4)** 424-63.

Art. 426. New Article.

Art. 430. Deleted. (1) 430-6(b). (c) now (b); **(2)** 430-7(c). (d) and (e) now (c) and (d); **(3)** 430-53(d); **(4)** 430-60. Now in 2nd paragraph of 430-52; **(5)** 430-72, Exc. (2). Exc. (3) now (2); **(6)** 430-83, Exc. 3. Exc. 4 now 3; **(7)** 430-109, Exc. 6; **(8)** 430-110(b). (c) and (d) now (b) and (c); **(9)** 430-122; **(10)** Table 430-153. Now in Table 430-152.

New. (1) 430-7(a). New (3) and (10). Old (3) thru (8) now (4) thru (9); **(2)** 430-32(a) (3). Old (3) now (4); **(3)** 430-53(c) (4) 2nd sentence; **(4)** 430-110(c) (4).

Revised. (1) 430-32(a) (2); **(2)** 430-32 (c) (3) and (c) (4); **(3)** Table 430-37; **(4)** 430-40; **(5)** 430-52; **(6)** 430-106; **(7)** 430-109, Exc. 3 and 4.

Art. 440. New Article.

Art. 450. Deleted. (1) 450-1 fineprint note; **(2)** 450-44. Now 450-8.

New. (1) 450-2, Exc. 1 and 2; **(2)** 450-3(b) (1) and (b) (2). Old 450-3(a) and (b) now (a) (1) and (a) (2); **(3)** 450-8. Formerly 450-44. Old 450-8 and 450-9 now 450-9 and 450-10; **(4)** 450-22.

Revised. 450-45(e).

Art. 500. New. 500-2(a), (b) and (c); **(2)** Tables 500-2(b) and (c).

Revised. 500-2.

Art. 501. New. (1) 501-5(a) (3), Exc.; **(2)** 501-5(b) (2), Exc.

Art. 511. New. 511-2(e).

Art. 514. New. (1) 514-2(e). Old (e) and (f) now (f) and (g); **(2)** 514-8, Exc.

Art. 516. Extensively revised.

Art. 517. Extensively revised and Title Change.

Art. 530. New. 530-18(a). Old (a) now lead paragraph.

Art. 550. (Title Changed). Deleted. 550-9(b) (2). Now in 550-9(c). (b) (3) and (b) (4) now (b) (2) and (b) (3).

New. (1) 550-2 (6 new definitions); **(2)** 550-3. Old (a) thru (c) replaced with (b) thru (k). First two paragraphs and Exception now (a); **(3)** 550-4 3rd sentence of 1st paragraph; **(4)** 550-4(a) last sentence of 1st paragraph and last paragraph; **(5)** 550-4(c). Formerly 2nd paragraph of (b). Old (c) now (d); **(6)** 550-7(c); **(7)** 550-8(e) fineprint note; **(8)** 550-8(j) and (k); **(9)** 550-12; **(10)** 550-13; **(11)** Part B, 550-21 thru 550-23.

Revised. (1) 550-1(a); **(2)** 550-5(b); **(3)** 550-6(c) (1); **(4)** 550-7(a); **(5)** 550-8(i) (1); **(6)** 550-9(c).

Art. 551. Completely revised and Title Change.

Art. 555. Completely revised and Title Change.

Art. 610. Deleted. (1) 610-1 fineprint note; **(2)** 610-21(c) fineprint note; **(3)** 610-21(d) last sentence; **(4)** 610-31 exception in 2nd sentence.

Art. 620. Deleted. (1) 620-52. Now 620-38; **(2)** 620-72(a). (b) now 2nd and 3rd paragraphs; **(3)** 620-84.

Art. 620 (*Continued*)

New. (1) 620-1 fineprint note; **(2)** 620-38; **(3)** 620-39.

Revised. (1) 620-33; **(2)** 620-37; **(3)** 620-71.

Art. 630. New. (1) 630-22; **(2)** 630-23; **(3)** 630-24.

Revised. 630-21.

Art. 660. New. (1) Fig. 660-3(b); **(2)** 660-8. Old 660-8 and 660-9 now 660-9 and 660-10.

Art. 660. Revised. 660-7.

Art. 665. Deleted. (1) 665-9 last sentence; **(2)** 665-17 last sentence.

Art. 670. Revised. 670-2 2nd paragraph. Replaces old (a) and (b).

Art. 680. Extensively revised and Title Change.

Art. 700. New. 700-17, Exc. 3.

Revised. (1) 700-7; **(2)** 700-10; **(3)** 700-22 1st two sentences of 1st paragraph.

Art. 710. New. (1) 710-12 last sentence; **(2)** 710-21(b) (2) 2nd paragraph.

Revised. 710-11(a) and (b). Replaces old 710-11.

Art. 725. Revised. 725-14.

Art. 730. Deleted. 730-8(a) and (b). Replaced with one sentence.

Revised. (1) 730-1; **(2)** 730-7(c).

Art. 800. Deleted. (1) 800-2(a) last sentence; **(2)** 800-2(d). Now in 800-2(c).

New. (1) 800-3(c); **(2)** 800-31(b) (7).

Revised. (1) 800-2; **(2)** 800-31(b) (5).

Art. 820. Deleted. 820-3(b). (a) is now 2nd paragraph.

New. 820-8(a) (8).

Revised. 820-8(a) (6).

Chap. 9. Deleted. (1) Tables 1 thru 3, See **New; (2)** Table 4 25% and 35% columns; **(3)** Example 1 to 8 references to conductor sizes based on calculations.

New. Tables 1, 2, 3A, 3B, and 3C replace Tables 1 thru 3.

Revised. (1) Notes to Tables preceding Table 1; **(2)** Table 5.

Appendix. Time Schedule for 1974 Code.

Introduction to the Code

ARTICLE 90. INTRODUCTION

90-1. Purpose.

(a) The purpose of this Code is the practical safeguarding of persons and of buildings and their contents from hazards arising from the use of electricity for light, heat, power, radio, signalling and for other purposes.

▶ This is a clear-cut statement of the intent of the Code and is of particular importance wherever enforcement of the Code is made mandatory by law.

(b) This Code contains provisions considered necessary for safety. Compliance therewith and proper maintenance will result in an installation essentially free from hazard, but not necessarily efficient, convenient, or adequate for good service or future expansion of electrical use.

Hazards often occur because of overloading of wiring systems by methods or usage not in conformity with the Code. This occurs because initial wiring did not provide for increases in use of electricity. For this reason it is recommended that the initial installation be adequate and that reasonable provisions for system changes be made as may be required for future increase in the use of electricity.

(c) This Code is not intended as a design specification nor an instruction manual for untrained persons.

▶ The National Electrical Code contains provisions considered necessary for safety, but does not provide information of a design nature and should not be used to insure adequate or efficient forms of installation. These latter features should be obtained from design manuals or through the services of a competent consulting engineer or electrical contractor.

90-2. Scope.

(a) Covered. It covers the electric conductors and equipment installed within or on public and private buildings and other premises, including yards, carnival

1

and parking lots, and industrial substations; also the conductors that connect the installations to a supply of electricity, and other outside conductors adjacent to the premises; also mobile homes and recreational vehicles.

(b) Not Covered.   It does not cover.

(1)   Installations in ships, watercraft, railway rolling stock, aircraft or automotive vehicles (except mobile homes and recreational vehicles).

(2)   Installations underground in mines.

(3)   Installations of railways for generation, transformation, transmission or distribution of power used exclusively for operation of rolling stock or installations used exclusively for signaling and communication purposes.

(4)   Installations of communication equipment under exclusive control of communication utilities, located outdoors or in building spaces used exclusively for such installations.

(5)   Installations under the exclusive control of electric utilities for the purpose of communication, metering or for the generation, control, transformation, transmission and distribution of electric energy located in buildings used exclusively by utilities for such purposes or located outdoors on property owned or leased by the utility or on public highways, streets, roads, etc., or outdoors by established rights on private property.

(c) Special Permission.   The authority having jurisdiction for enforcing the Code may grant exception for the installation of conductors and equipment, not under the exclusive control of the electric utilities and used to connect the electric utility supply system to the service entrance conductors of the premises served, provided such installations are outside a building or terminate immediately inside a building wall.

90-3. Code Arrangement.   This Code is divided into nine chapters. Chapters 1, 2, 3 and 4 apply generally; Chapters 5, 6 and 7 apply to special occupancies, special equipment, or other special conditions. The latter chapters supplement or amend the general rules. Chapters 1–4 apply except as amended by Chapters 5, 6 and 7 for the particular conditions.

Chapter 8 covers communications systems and is independent of the other chapters except where they are specifically referenced therein.

Chapter 9 consists of tables and examples.

90-4. Definitions.   Article 100 contains definitions of a number of terms that are used in two or more Articles. In general, terms used only in a single Article are defined in the Article concerned. For electrical terms not defined in the Code, refer to the ANSI Standard Definitions of Electrical Terms, ANSI C-42-series.

▶   It is the intention that, so far as practicable, the Code definitions shall be in agreement with the latest revision of the American National Standards Institute C-42, "Definitions of Electrical Terms." The Standard contains definitions of most electrical terms that are in use at the present time. Copies may be obtained from the American National Standards Institute, 1430 Broadway, New York, N.Y. 10018.

90-5. Fundamental Rules.   Throughout the Code are paragraphs which state only fundamentals or objectives of safeguarding. These are followed by paragraphs setting forth the recognized methods and detail by which the purpose and intent of the fundamental may be satisfied. Accordingly, when employed, the rules stating a fundamental only will appear as the first paragraph of an Article or Section.

90-6. Interpretation. In order to promote uniformity of interpretation and application of this Code, the National Electrical Code Committee of the National Fire Protection Association has established a formal procedure for rendering interpretations in case of question. Applications for interpretations should be addressed to the National Fire Protection Association (see procedure for securing official interpretations of Code appearing in the Appendix).

▶   Official interpretations of the National Electrical Code are based on specific sections of specific editions of the Code. In most cases such official interpretations apply to the stated conditions on given installations. Accordingly, they would not necessarily apply to other situations that vary slightly from the statement on which the official interpretation was issued.

As official interpretations of each edition of the Code are issued they are published in the NFPA Fire News and press releases are sent to interested trade papers.

All official interpretations issued on a specific code edition are reviewed by the appropriate code-making panel during the period when the specific code edition is being revised. In reviewing an interpretation a code panel may agree with the interpretation findings and clarify the code text to avoid further misunderstanding of intent, or the panel may reject the findings of the interpretation and alter the code text to clarify the code panel's intent. On the other hand, the code panel may not recommend any change in the code text because of the special conditions described in the official interpretation. For these reasons the NFPA does not catalog official interpretations issued on previous editions of the Code. And in reviewing all previous interpretations it can be stated that practically none of them would apply to the present edition of the Code because of revised code wording that materially changes the intent.

If anyone feels that a past interpretation applies to the present text they should submit it in the form of a proposed code change when revisions for the next edition of the Code are being considered.

With the wide adoption of the Code throughout the country the authority having jurisdiction has the prime responsibility of interpreting code rules in its area, and disagreements on the intent of particular code rules should be resolved at the local level if at all possible. There is no guarantee that the authority having jurisdiction will accept the findings of an official interpretation processed in accordance with Part D in the Appendix of the Code in this Handbook.

90-7. Enforcement. This Code is intended to be suitable for mandatory application by governmental bodies exercising legal jurisdiction over electrical installations and for use by insurance inspectors. The administrative authority supervising such enforcement of the Code will have the responsibility for making interpretations of the rules, for deciding upon the approval of equipment and materials, and for granting the special permission contemplated in a number of the rules.

▶ The local authority having jurisdiction is responsible for the enforcement of Code requirements and is charged with making any interpretations that may be necessary in regard to specific installations or rules.

Even where there may be no enforcement by a local authority, an installer should be concerned as to his legal liability in any construction which may present a fire or accident hazard. Compliance with the latest edition of the Code will minimize the risk of legal actions.

90-8. Examination of Equipment for Safety. For approval of specific items of equipment and materials covered by the Code, examinations for safety should be made under standard conditions, and the record made generally available through promulgation by organizations properly equipped and qualified for experimental testing, inspections of the run of goods at factories, and service-value determination through field inspections. This avoids the necessity for repetition of examinations by different examiners, frequently with inadequate facilities for such work, and the confusion that would result from conflicting reports as to the suitability of devices and materials examined for a given purpose. It is the intent of the Code that factory-installed internal wiring or the construction of equipment need not be inspected at the time of installation of the equipment except to detect alterations or damage if the equipment has been listed by an electrical testing laboratory, which is nationally recognized as having the facilities described above and which requires suitability for installation in accordance with the Code.

▶ It is not the intent of the National Electrical Code to include the detailed requirements for electrical equipment. Such information is usually contained in individual standards for the equipment concerned.

The last sentence does not intend to take away the authority of the local inspector to examine and approve equipment, but rather to indicate that the requirements of the National Electrical Code did not generally apply to the internal construction of devices which had been listed by a nationally recognized electrical testing laboratory.

90-9. Wiring Planning.

(a) It is recommended that electrical engineers and others when drawing plans and specifications make provision for ample raceways for wiring, spaces for equipment, and allowances for future increases in the use of electricity. In laying out an installation for constant-potential systems, provision should be made for distribution centers located in easily accessible places for convenience and safety of operation.

▶ Space should always be provided for the equipment required for future extensions of the wiring installation. Failure to provide this space is short-sighted economy for the user.

(b) It is elsewhere provided in this Code that the number of wires and circuits confined in a single enclosure be varyingly restricted. It is strongly recommended that electrical engineers and others who are planning installations provide similar restrictions wherever practicable, to the end that the effects of breakdowns from short-circuits or grounds, even though resulting fire and similar damage are confined to wires, their insulation and enclosures, may not involve entire services to premises nor interruptions of essential and independent services.

90-10. Revisions. It is customary to revise this Code periodically to conform with developments in the art and the result of experience, and the latest edition of the Code should always be used.

CHAPTER ONE ──────────────

General

ARTICLE 100. DEFINITIONS

General guides for this Article on Definitions include: (1) for simplicity, only definitions essential to the proper use of this Code are included; (2) only those terms used in two or more Articles are defined in full in Article 100, other definitions being defined in the individual Article where they apply; (3) in general, NEC definitions will be the same as definitions in the latest revision of ANSI C-42-series, "Definitions of Electrical Terms," and are so identified by an asterisk*.

▶ Frequent reference to the definitions listed in Article 100 should be made to provide a clearer understanding of the intent of various code requirements.

Accessible: (As applied to wiring methods.) Capable of being removed or exposed without damaging the building structure or finish, or not permanently closed in by the structure or finish of the building. (See "Concealed" and "Exposed.")

▶ See comments following "Exposed: (As applied to wiring methods.)"

*Accessible: (As applied to equipment.) Admitting close approach because not guarded by locked doors, elevation or other effective means. (See "Readily Accessible.")

Ampacity: Current-carrying capacity expressed in amperes.

Anesthetizing Location: See Section 517-2.

Appliance: An appliance is utilization equipment, generally other than industrial, normally built in standardized sizes or types, which is installed or connected as a unit to perform one or more functions such as clothes washing, air conditioning, food mixing, deep frying, etc.

6

Appliance—Fixed: An appliance which is fastened or otherwise secured at a specific location.

Appliance—Portable: An appliance which is actually moved or can easily be moved from one place to another in normal use.

▶   For example: toasters, coffee-makers, etc.

Appliance—Stationary: An appliance which is not easily moved from one place to another in normal use.

▶   For example: Clothes washers, dryers, refrigerators, freezers, window-type air-conditioners, etc.

Approved: Acceptable to the authority enforcing this Code.

▶   See paragraphs "Interpretation" and "Enforcement" in the Introduction, also Section **110-2**.

*Askarel: A synthetic nonflammable insulating liquid which, when decomposed by the electric arc, evolves only nonflammable gaseous mixtures.

▶   This is a word used in Art. **450** to indicate transformer liquid that will not burn.

*Attachment Plug (Plug Cap) (Cap):   An attachment plug is a device which, by insertion in a receptacle, establishes connection between the conductors of the attached flexible cord and the conductors connected permanently to the receptacle.

*Automatic: Automatic means self-acting, operating by its own mechanism when actuated by some impersonal influence, as for example, a change in current strength, pressure, temperature, or mechanical configuration. (See "Non-automatic.")

Block (City, Town, or Village):   See Section 800-2.

Bonding Jumper: A reliable conductor to assure the required electrical conductivity between metal parts required to be electrically connected.

Bonding Jumper, Circuit: The connection between portions of a conductor in a circuit to maintain required ampacity of the circuit.

Bonding Jumper, Equipment: The connection between two or more portions of the equipment grounding conductor.

Bonding Jumper, Main: The connection between the grounded circuit conductor and the equipment grounding conductor at the service.

Branch Circuit: A branch circuit is that portion of a wiring system between the final overcurrent device protecting the circuit and the outlet(s).

A device not approved for branch circuit protection such as a thermal cutout or motor overload protective device is not considered as the overcurrent device protecting the circuit.

*Branch Circuit—Appliance: An appliance branch circuit is a circuit supplying energy to one or more outlets to which appliances are to be connected; such circuits to have no permanently connected lighting fixtures not a part of an appliance.

Branch Circuit—General Purpose: A branch circuit that supplies a number of outlets for lighting and appliances.

Branch Circuit—Individual: A branch circuit that supplies only one utilization equipment.

▶   *Example:* Only one heater, as a single unit, may be placed on an individual branch circuit. Where more than a single unit is used on a branch circuit, the circuit needs to conform with the requirements of Section 210-24. See also Section 424-3.

An individual branch circuit supplying a receptacle may only supply a "single" receptacle.

A branch circuit supplying two or more single receptacles or one or more duplex receptacles needs to conform to Section 210-24.

A duplex receptacle without a split bus is actually two devices (receptacles) on the same yoke and is not intended to be used on an individual branch circuit. See the definition of "Receptacle" in this Article.

Branch Circuit, Multiwire: A multiwire branch circuit is a circuit consisting of two or more ungrounded conductors having a potential difference between them, and an identified grounded conductor having equal potential difference between it and each ungrounded conductor of the circuit and which is connected to the neutral conductor of the system.

Branch-Circuit Selection Current: See Section 440-3(c) Note.

Building: A structure which stands alone or which is cut off from adjoining structures by fire walls with all openings therein protected by approved fire doors.

▶   Most areas have building codes to establish the requirements for buildings, and such codes should be used as a basis for deciding the use of the definition given in the National Electrical Code. The use of the term "fire walls" in this definition has resulted in differences of opinions among electrical inspectors and others, and a request for a clarification has been frequently proposed. Since the definition of a fire wall may differ in each jurisdiction, the processing of an interpretation of a "fire wall" has been studiously avoided in the National Electrical Code because this is a function of Building Codes and not a responsibility of the National Electrical Code.

*Cabinet: An enclosure designed either for surface or flush mounting, and provided with a frame, mat or trim in which swinging doors are hung.

▶   The door of a cabinet is hinged to a trim covering, wiring space, or gutter; the door of a cutout box is hinged directly to the side of the box. Cabinets usually contain panelboards, while cutout boxes contain cutouts, switches, or miscellaneous apparatus.

Cell (As Applied to Raceways):   See Sections 356-1 and 358-1.

Circuit Breaker: A device designed to open and close a circuit by nonautomatic means, and to open the circuit automatically on a predetermined overload of current, without injury to itself when properly applied within its rating.

Communication Circuit: See Section 800-1.

Concealed: Rendered inaccessible by the structure or finish of the building. Wires in concealed raceways are considered concealed, even though they may become accessible by withdrawing them. [See "Accessible—(As applied to wiring methods)."]

▶   Wires run in an unfinished basement or an accessible attic on knobs or through tubes are not "rendered inaccessible by the structure or finish of the building," and are therefore considered as open work rather than knob and tube work, which is a concealed type of wiring.

Conductor:

Bare: A bare conductor is one having no covering or insulation whatsoever. (See "Conductor, Covered.")

Covered: A covered conductor is one having one or more layers of nonconducting materials that are not recognized as insulation under the Code. (See "Conductor, Bare.")

Insulated: An insulated conductor is one covered with material recognized as insulation.

▶   A covered conductor is one that is neither bare nor insulated as would be the case where a nonstandard insulating material were used or where the thickness of insulation was below that required for a specific type of insulated conductor. In other words a conductor with insulation is not an "insulated conductor" unless constructed to meet the requirements for a specific recognized conductor type and so identified.

An insulated conductor is one which is provided with insulating material of the type and thickness described in Table **310-2***b* and otherwise meeting the requirements for the specific type designations which are applicable.

*Connector, Pressure (Solderless): A pressure wire connector is a device which establishes the connection between two or more conductors or between one or more conductors and a terminal by means of mechanical pressure and without the use of solder.

Continuous Load: A load where the maximum current is expected to continue for three hours or more.

Control Circuit: See Section 430-71.

Controller: A device, or group of devices, which serves to govern, in some predetermined manner, the electric power delivered to the apparatus to which it is connected. See also Section 430-81(a).

▶   See "Motor Controllers," Art. **430**, Part G.

Cooking Unit, Counter-Mounted: An assembly of one or more domestic surface heating elements for cooking purposes designed for flush mounting in, or supported by, a counter, and which assembly is complete with inherent or separately mountable controls and internal wiring. (See "Oven, Wall-Mounted.")

Current Limiting Overcurrent Protective Device: (See Section 240-27.)

*Cutout Box: An enclosure designed for surface mounting and having swinging doors or covers secured directly to and telescoping with the walls of the box proper. (See "Cabinet.")

*Demand Factor: The demand factor of any system, or part of a system, is the ratio of the maximum demand of the system, or part of a system, to the total connected load of the system, or of the part of the system under consideration.

Device: A unit of an electrical system which is intended to carry but not utilize electric energy.

▶   Switches, fuses, circuit breakers, controllers, receptacles, and lampholders are "devices."

Disconnecting Means: A device, or group of devices, or other means whereby the conductors of a circuit can be disconnected from their source of supply.

▶   Manually operable switches and circuit breakers are examples, and under certain conditions (see Articles **422, 424, 430** and **440**) branch-circuit overcurrent devices or attachment plugs can serve as the disconnecting means.

Dry: (See "Location—Dry.")

Dust-Ignition-Proof: See Section 502-1.

*Dustproof: So constructed or protected that dust will not interfere with its successful operation.

*Dust-tight: So constructed that dust will not enter the enclosing case.

Duty:

   *Continuous: Continuous duty is a requirement of service that demands operation at a substantially constant load for an indefinitely long time.

   *Intermittent: Intermittent duty is a requirement of service that demands operation for alternate intervals of (1) load and no load; or (2) load and rest; or (3) load, no load and rest.

   *Periodic: Periodic duty is a type of intermittent duty in which the load conditions are regularly recurrent.

   *Short Time: Short time duty is a requirement of service that demands operation at a substantially constant load for a short and definitely specified time.

   *Varying: Varying duty is a requirement of service that demands operations at loads, and for intervals of time, both of which may be subject to wide variation.

See Table 430-22 (a—Exception) for illustrations of various types of duty.

▶   See also Section **430-33.**

Duty Cycle (Welding):   (See Section 630-31(c).)

*Electric Sign: A fixed, stationary or portable, self-contained, electrically illuminated utilization equipment with words or symbols designed to convey information or attract attention.

*Enclosed: Surrounded by a case which will prevent a person from accidentally contacting live parts.

Equipment: A general term including material, fittings, devices, appliances, fixtures, apparatus and the like used as a part of, or in connection with, an electrical installation.

*Explosion-proof Apparatus: Apparatus enclosed in a case which is capable of withstanding an explosion of a specified gas or vapor which may occur within it and of preventing the ignition of a specified gas or vapor surrounding the enclosure by sparks, flashes, or explosion of the gas or vapor within, and which operates at such an external temperature that a surrounding flammable atmosphere will not be ignited thereby.

▶   See Arts. 500 to 517.

Exposed: (As applied to live parts.) Exposed means that a live part can be inadvertently touched or approached nearer than a safe distance by a person. It is applied to parts not suitably guarded, isolated or insulated. (See "Accessible" and "Concealed.")

Exposed: (As applied to wiring methods.) On or attached to the surface or behind panels designed to allow access. [See "Accessible—(As applied to wiring methods)."]

▶   Any wiring method, together with associated equipment such as outlet boxes and conduit fittings, is considered "exposed" when installed in the open on surfaces. Such systems are also considered "exposed" if they are installed behind "lift-out" ceiling, wall or floor panels that are designed to allow access. Since wireways and busways are approved only for exposed work (Sections 362-2 and 364-2), they are permitted behind panels designed to allow access if the space is not used for air-handling purposes. (See Section 300-22c.)

*Externally Operable: Externally operable means capable of being operated without exposing the operator to contact with live parts.

This term is applied to equipment such as a switch, that is enclosed in a case or cabinet.

▶   Switches and circuit breakers are in many cases required to be externally operable.

If a switch or circuit breaker is mounted in a cabinet or box so that it cannot be operated until the door is opened, the device may still be considered as externally operable if no live parts are exposed when the door is opened.

Feeder: A feeder is the circuit conductors between the service equipment, or the generator switchboard of an isolated plant, and the branch circuit overcurrent device.

Festoon Lighting: See Section 730-6(b).

Fitting: An accessory such as a locknut, bushing or other part of a wiring system which is intended primarily to perform a mechanical rather than an electrical function.

Garage: A building or portion of a building in which one or more self-propelled vehicles carrying volatile, flammable liquid for fuel or power are kept for use, sale, storage, rental, repair, exhibition or demonstrating purposes, and all that portion of a building which is on or below the floor or floors in which such vehicles are kept and which is not separated therefrom by suitable cutoffs.

▶   See Chap. 5, Arts. 511 and 512.

Ground: A ground is a conducting connection, whether intentional or accidental, between an electrical circuit or equipment and earth, or to some conducting body which serves in place of the earth.

Grounded: Grounded means connected to earth or to some conducting body which serves in place of the earth.

Grounded (Effectively Grounded Communication System): See Section 800-2(c)(1).

Grounded Conductor: A system or circuit conductor which is intentionally grounded.

Grounding Conductor: A conductor used to connect equipment or the grounded circuit of a wiring system to a grounding electrode or electrodes.

Grounding Conductor, Equipment: The conductor used to connect noncurrent-carrying metal parts of equipment, raceways, and other enclosures to the system grounded conductor at the service and/or the grounding electrode conductor.

Grounding Electrode Conductor: The conductor used to connect the grounding electrode to the equipment grounding conductor and/or to the grounded conductor of the circuit at the service.

▶   **This new definition takes the place of the two former definitions of common main and main grounding conductors. Accordingly, it applies to the grounding conductor that extends to a grounding electrode for either grounded or ungrounded systems. See Tables 250-94(a) and (b).**

Guarded: Covered, shielded, fenced, enclosed or otherwise protected, by means of suitable covers or casings, barriers, rails or screens, mats or platforms, to remove the liability of dangerous contact or approach by persons or objects to a point of danger.

▶   See Arts, 110, 430, 450, and 710.

Hazardous Locations: See Article 500.

Header: See Section 356-1.

Header Ducts: See Section 358-1.

Hoistway: Any shaftway, hatchway, wall hole, or other vertical opening or space in which an elevator or dumbwaiter is designed to operate.

▶   See Art. 620.

Identified: Identified, as used in this Code in reference to a conductor or its terminal, means that such conductor or terminal is to be recognized as grounded. See Article 200.

*Isolated: Isolated means that an object is not readily accessible to persons unless special means for access are used.

▶   See Sections **710-11** and **710-22.** Oil circuit breakers and switches should be isolated from other electrical apparatus where practicable.

*Lighting Outlet: An outlet intended for the direct connection of a lampholder, a lighting fixture or a pendant cord terminating in a lampholder.

Location:

Damp Location: Partially protected locations under canopies, marquees, roofed open porches, and like locations, and interior locations subject to moderate degrees of moisture, such as some basements, some barns, and some cold-storage ware-houses.

Dry Location: A location not normally subject to dampness or wetness. A location classified as dry may be temporarily subject to dampness or wetness, as in the case of a building under construction.

Wet Location: Installations underground or in concrete slabs or masonry in direct contact with the earth, and locations subject to saturation with water or other liquids, such as vehicle washing areas, and locations exposed to weather and unprotected.

Low-Energy Power Circuit: A circuit which is not a remote-control or signal cir-cuit but which has the power supply limited in accordance with the requirements of Class 2 remote control circuits. See Article 725.

Such circuits include electric door openers and circuits used in the operation of coin operated phonographs.

Multioutlet Assembly: A type of surface or flush raceway designed to hold conductors and attachment plug receptacles, assembled in the field or at the factory.

▶   Multioutlet assemblies may be metallic or nonmetallic. They are intended for surface mounting except that the metal type may be surrounded by the building finish or recessed so long as the front is not covered, and the non-metallic type may be recessed in baseboards. (See Art. **353.**)

*Nonautomatic: Nonautomatic means that the implied action requires personal intervention for its control. (See "Automatic.")

As applied to an electric controller, nonautomatic control does not necessarily imply a manual controller, but only that personal intervention is necessary.

*Outlet: A point on the wiring system at which current is taken to supply utilization equipment.

*Outline Lighting: An arrangement of incandescent lamps or gaseous tubes to outline and call attention to certain features such as the shape of a building or the decoration of a window.

▶   See Art. **600.**

Oven, Wall-Mounted: A domestic oven for cooking purposes designed for mounting in or on a wall or other surface.

Panelboard: A single panel or group of panel units designed for assembly in the form of a single panel; including buses, and with or without switches and/or automatic overcurrent protective devices for the control of light, heat or power circuits of small individual as well as aggregate capacity; designed to be placed in a cabinet or cutout box placed in or against a wall or partition and accessible only from the front. (See "Switchboard.")

Projector, Nonprofessional: See Section 540-30.

Projector, Professional: See Section 540-10.

Qualified Person: One familiar with the construction and operation of the apparatus and the hazards involved.

Raceway: Any channel for holding wires, cables or busbars, which is designed expressly for, and used solely for, this purpose.

Raceways may be of metal or insulating material and the term includes rigid metal conduit, rigid nonmetallic conduit, flexible metal conduit, electrical metallic tubing, underfloor raceways, cellular concrete floor raceways, cellular metal floor raceways, surface raceways, structural raceways, wireways and busways.

Rainproof: So constructed, protected or treated as to prevent rain from interfering with successful operation of the apparatus.

*Raintight: So constructed or protected that exposure to a beating rain will not result in the entrance of water.

▶   In Sections **230-52** and **730-23,** *raintight* is applied to raceways on the exterior of buildings.

Rated-Load Current: See Section 440-3(a) Note.

*Readily Accessible: Capable of being reached quickly, for operation, renewal, or inspections, without requiring those to whom ready access is requisite to climb over or remove obstacles or to resort to portable ladders, chairs, etc. (See "Accessible.")

▶   The term *readily accessible* implies a need for performing promptly an indicated act, for example, to reach quickly a disconnecting switch or circuit breaker without the use of ladders, chairs, etc. The installation of such a switch or circuit breaker at a height above 7 ft from a standing level is not considered "readily accessible."

Receptacle: A receptacle is a contact device installed at the outlet for the connection of a single attachment plug.

A single receptacle is a single contact device with no other contact device on the same yoke. A multiple receptacle is a single device containing two or more receptacles.

▶   Only a single receptacle can be served by an individual branch circuit. See Sections **210-21***b* and **555-3.**

*Receptacle Outlet: An outlet where one or more receptacles are installed.

Remote-Control Circuit: Any electrical circuit which controls any other circuit through a relay or an equivalent device.

Sealable Equipment: Equipment enclosed in a case or cabinet that is provided with means of sealing or locking so that live parts cannot be made accessible without opening the enclosure. The equipment may or may not be operable without opening the enclosure.

▶   See Section 230-62.

Sealed (Hermetic Type) Motor Compressor: A mechanical compressor consisting of a compressor and a motor, both of which are enclosed in the same sealed housing, with no external shaft nor shaft seals, the motor operating in the refrigerant atmosphere.

Service: The conductors and equipment for delivering energy from the electricity supply system to the wiring system of the premises served.

*Service Cable: The service cable is the service conductors made up in the form of a cable.

Service Conductors: The supply conductors which extend from the street main, or from transformers to the service equipment of the premises supplied.

▶   In an overhead distribution system, the service conductors begin at the line pole where connection is made. If a primary line is extended to transformers installed outdoors on private property, the service conductors to the building proper begin at the secondary terminals of the transformers. See Section 230-100.

Where the supply is from an underground distribution system, the service conductors begin at the point of connection to the underground street mains.

In every case the service conductors terminate at the service equipment.

Service Drop: The overhead service conductors from the last pole or other aerial support to and including the splices, if any, connecting to the service-entrance conductors at the building or other structure.

Service-Entrance Conductors, Overhead System: The service conductors between the terminals of the service equipment and a point usually outside the building, clear of building walls, where joined by tap or splice to the service drop.

Service-Entrance Conductors, Underground System: The service conductors between the terminals of the service equipment and the point of connection to the service lateral.

Where service equipment is located outside the building walls, there may be no service-entrance conductors, or they may be entirely outside the building.

Service Equipment: The necessary equipment, usually consisting of a circuit breaker or switch and fuses, and their accessories, located near the point of entrance of supply conductors to a building or other structure, or an otherwise defined area, and intended to constitute the main control and means of cutoff of the supply.

▶   A meter is not considered a part of the service equipment.

Service Lateral: The underground service conductors between the street main, including any risers at a pole or other structure or from transformers, and the first point of connection to the service entrance conductors in a terminal box or meter or other enclosure with adequate space, inside or outside the building wall. Where there is no terminal box, or meter or other enclosure with adequate space, the point of connection shall be considered to be the point of entrance of the service conductors into the building.

Service Raceway: The rigid metal conduit, electrical metallic tubing, or other raceway, that encloses the service-entrance conductors.

▶   The term *service raceway* also includes wireways, auxiliary gutters, and busways. See Sections **230-44a** and *b*.

Setting: (Of Circuit Breaker.)   The value of the current at which it is set to trip.

Show Window: A show window is any window used or designed to be used for the display of goods or advertising material, whether it is fully or partly enclosed or entirely open at the rear, and whether or not it has a platform raised higher than the street floor level.

Sign: See "Electric Sign."

Signal Circuit: Any electrical circuit which supplies energy to an appliance which gives a recognizable signal.

Such circuits include circuits for door bells, buzzers, code-calling systems, signal lights, and the like.

Special Permission: The written consent of the authority enforcing this Code.

▶   See paragraphs entitled "Interpretation" (Section **90-6**) and "Enforcement" (Section **90-7**) in the Introduction of the Code.

Switchboard: A large single panel, frame, or assembly of panels, on which are mounted, on the face or back or both, switches, overcurrent and other protective devices, buses and usually instruments. Switchboards are generally accessible from the rear as well as from the front and are not intended to be installed in cabinets. (See "Panelboard.")

▶   In most modern installations switchboards are completely enclosed in metal.

Switches:

   *General Use Switch: A general use switch is a switch intended for use in general distribution and branch circuits. It is rated in amperes, and it is capable of interrupting its rated current at its rated voltage.

   General Use Snap Switch: A form of general use switch so constructed that it can be installed in flush device boxes, or on outlet box covers, or otherwise used in conjunction with wiring systems recognized by this Code.

   AC General Use Snap Switch: A form of general use snap switch suitable only for use on alternating current circuits for controlling the following:

   (a) Resistive and inductive loads (including electric discharge lamps) not exceeding the ampere rating at the voltage involved.

   (b) Tungsten filament lamp loads not exceeding the ampere rating at 120 volts.

(c) Motor loads not exceeding 80 per cent of the ampere rating of the switches at the rated voltage.

All AC general use snap switches are marked "AC" in addition to their electrical rating.

AC-DC General Use Snap Switch: A form of general use snap switch suitable for use on either direct or alternating current circuits for controlling the following:

(a) Resistive loads not exceeding the ampere rating at the voltage involved.

(b) Inductive loads not exceeding one-half the ampere rating at the voltage involved, except that switches having a marked horsepower rating are suitable for controlling motors not exceeding the horsepower rating of the switch at the voltage involved.

(c) Tungsten filament lamp loads not exceeding the ampere rating at 125 volts, when marked with the letter "T".

AC-DC general use snap switches are not generally marked AC-DC, but are always marked with their electrical rating.

*Isolating Switch: An isolating switch is a switch intended for isolating an electric circuit from the source of power. It has no interrupting rating, and it is intended to be operated only after the circuit has been opened by some other means.

Motor Circuit Switch: A switch, rated in horsepower, capable of interrupting the maximum operating overload current of a motor of the same horsepower rating as the switch at the rated voltage.

Thermal Cutout: An overcurrent protective device which contains a heater element in addition to and affecting a renewable fusible member which opens the circuit. It is not designed to interrupt short circuit currents.

Thermally Protected: (As applied to motors.) The words "Thermally Protected" appearing on the nameplate of a motor or motor-compressor indicate that the motor is provided with a thermal protector.

Thermal Protector: (As applied to motors.) A thermal protector is a protective device for assembly as an integral part of a motor or motor-compressor and which, when properly applied, protects the motor against dangerous overheating due to overload and failure to start.

The thermal protector may consist of one or more sensing elements integral with the motor or motor-compressor and an external control device.

*Utilization Equipment: Utilization equipment is equipment which utilizes electric energy for mechanical, chemical, heating, lighting, or similar useful purposes.

*Ventilated: Provided with a means to permit circulation of air sufficient to remove an excess of heat, fumes or vapors.

Volatile Flammable Liquid: A flammable liquid having a flash point below 100°F or whose temperature is above its flash point.

*Voltage (of a circuit): Voltage is the greatest root-mean-square (effective) difference of potential between any two conductors of the circuit concerned.

On various systems such as 3-phase 4 wire, single phase 3 wire and 3 wire direct current, there may be various circuits of various voltages.

▶   On a three-phase four-wire wye system or on any d-c or single-phase three-wire system there are two voltages. If the "circuit concerned" is a feeder including all the conductors of the system, the *voltage of the circuit* is the highest voltage between any two of the conductors. A two-wire subfeeder or branch circuit supplied by such a system may have only the lower voltage between the two conductors, in which case this lower voltage is the voltage of the circuit. (See Section 110-5.)

Voltage to Ground: In grounded circuits the voltage between the given conductor and that point or conductor of the circuit which is grounded; in ungrounded circuits, the greatest voltage between the given conductor and any other conductor of the circuit.

▶ The voltage to ground on a three-phase, three wire 480-volt ungrounded supply system would be 480 volts. The term *circuit* means the entire system —not merely *branch* circuits.

Watertight: So constructed that moisture will not enter the enclosing case.
*Weatherproof: Weatherproof means so constructed or protected that exposure to the weather will not interfere with successful operation.

Rainproof, raintight or watertight equipment may fulfill the requirements for "weatherproof." However, weather conditions vary and consideration should be given to conditions resulting from snow, ice, dust, or temperature extremes.

Welder, Electric:
  Rated Primary Current: Section 630-31(c).
  Actual Primary Current: Section 630-31(c).
Wet: (See "Location—Wet.")
X-ray:
  Long Time Rating: Section 660-1.
  Momentary Rating: Section 660-1.

ARTICLE 110. GENERAL

110-1. Scope. This Article provides the general requirements for electrical installations.
110-2. Approval. The conductors and equipment required or permitted by this Code shall be acceptable only when approved. See definition of "Approved" in Article 100.

▶ The definition of "approved" states that this term means "acceptable to the authority enforcing this Code," such authority usually being a municipal, state, or Federal inspection department or an Underwriters' inspection or rating bureau. In most cases it is assumed that the approval of the inspection department will be based upon listings by Underwriters' Laboratories, Inc., where there are UL standards for specific equipment.

Since by definition the term "equipment" includes all the materials, devices, and apparatus used in an electrical installation, the effect is to require that only approved material, devices, and apparatus shall be used.

110-3. Mandatory and Advisory Rules. Mandatory rules of this Code are characterized by the use of the word, "shall." Advisory rules are characterized by the use of the word, "should," or are stated as recommendations of that which is advised but not required.

110-4. Examination of Equipment. Materials, devices, fittings, apparatus and appliances designed for use under this Code shall be judged chiefly with reference to the following considerations which also determine the classification by types, size, voltages, current capacities, and specific use.

(a) Suitability for installation and use in conformity with the provisions of this Code.

(b) Mechanical strength and durability, including, for parts designed to enclose and protect other equipment, the adequacy of the protection thus provided.

(c) Electrical insulation.

(d) Heating effects under normal conditions of use and also under abnormal conditions likely to arise in service.

(e) Arcing effects.

110-5. Voltages. Throughout this Code the voltage considered shall be that at which the circuit operates, whether the current is supplied by a battery, generator, transformer, rectifier, or a thermopile.

▶   See definitions "Voltage (of a circuit)" and "Voltage to Ground."

110-6. Conductor Gages. Conductor sizes are given in American Wire Gage (AWG).

▶   In this country, the American Wire Gage is the standard for copper wire and for aluminum wire used for electrical conductors. The American Wire Gage is the same as the Brown & Sharpe (B. & S.) gage. The largest gage size is No. 0000; above this size the sizes of wires and cables are stated in circular mils.

The circular mil is a unit used for measuring the cross-sectional area of the conductor, or the area of the end of a wire which has been cut square across. One circular mil (commonly abbreviated cir mil or cm) is the area of a circle 1/1,000 in. in diameter. The area of a circle 1 in. in diameter is 1,000,000 cir mils, also, the area of a circle of this size is 0.7854 sq in.

To convert square inches to circular mils, multiply the square inches by 1,273,200.

To convert circular mils to square inches, divide the circular mils by 1,273,200 or multiply the circular mils by 0.7854 and divide by 1,000,000.

In interior wiring the gage sizes 14, 12, and 10 are usually solid wire; No. 8 as commonly used may be either solid or stranded; and all sizes larger than No. 8 are usually stranded. No. 8 and larger conductors in raceways are required to be stranded. (See Section 310-9.)

A cable (if not larger than 1,000,000 cir mils) will have one of the following numbers of strands: 7, 19, 37, or 61. In order to make a cable of any standard size, in nearly every case the individual strands cannot be any regular gage number but must be some special odd size. For example, a

No. 00 cable must have a total cross-sectional area of **133,100** cir mils and is usually made up of 19 strands. No. 12 has an area of **6,530** cir mils and No. 11, an area of **8,234** cir mils, therefore each strand must be a special size between Nos. 12 and 11.

110-7. Conductors.   Conductors normally used to carry current shall be of copper unless otherwise provided in this Code. Where the conductor material is not specified, the sizes given in this Code shall apply to copper conductors. Where other materials are used, the size shall be changed accordingly.

For aluminum and copper-clad aluminum conductors, see Tables 310-14 and 310-15.

110-8. Wiring Methods.   Only wiring methods recognized as suitable are included in this Code. The recognized methods of wiring may be installed in any type of building or occupancy except as otherwise provided in this Code.

▶   **See Art. 300.**

110-9. Interrupting Capacity.   Devices intended to break current shall have an interrupting capacity sufficient for the voltage employed and for the current which must be interrupted.

110-10. Circuit Impedance and Other Characteristics.   The overcurrent protective devices, the total impedance and other characteristics of the circuit to be protected shall be so selected and coordinated as to permit the circuit protective devices used to clear a fault without the occurrence of extensive damage to the electrical components of the circuit. This fault may be assumed to be between two or more of the circuit conductors; or between any circuit conductor and the grounding conductor or enclosing metal raceway.

▶   It is the intent of Sections 110-9 and 110-10 that overcurrent devices have interrupting capacity ratings not less than the short-circuit current available at the line terminals of each overcurrent device. See Sections **240-23c** and **240-25e** for common I. C. ratings of fuses and circuit breakers (up to 10,000 amp).

If overcurrent devices with a specific I. C. rating are inserted at a point on a wiring system where the available short-circuit current exceeds the I. C. rating of the device, a resultant downstream solid short circuit between conductors or between one ungrounded conductor and ground (in grounded systems) could cause serious damage to life and property.

Since each electrical installation is different, the selection of overcurrent devices with proper I. C. ratings is not always a simple task. To begin with, the amount of available short-circuit current at the service equipment must be known. Such short-circuit current depends upon the capacity rating of the utility primary supply to the building, transformer impedances, and service conductor impedances. Most utilities will provide this information.

Downstream from the service equipment I. C. ratings of overcurrent devices may be reduced to lower than those at the service, depending on lengths and sizes of feeders, line impedances and other factors. However, large motors and capacitors, while in operation, will feed additional current into a fault, and this must be considered when calculating short-circuit currents.

Manufacturers of overcurrent devices have excellent literature on figuring short-circuit currents, including graphs, charts, and one-line-diagram layout sheets to simplify the selection of proper overcurrent devices.

See comments on Section 230-95, which concerns ground-fault protection of 480Y/277-volt systems.

110-11. Deteriorating Agencies.   Unless approved for the purpose, no conductors or equipment shall be located in damp or wet locations; where exposed to gases, fumes, vapors, liquids or other agents having a deteriorating effect on the conductors or equipment; nor where exposed to excessive temperatures.

Control equipment, utilization equipment and busways approved for use in dry locations only, should be protected against permanent damage from weather during building construction.

110-12. Mechanical Execution of Work.   Electrical equipment shall be installed in a neat and workmanlike manner.

▶   This statement has been the source of many conflicts because opinions differ as to what is a neat and workmanlike manner.

The Code places the responsibility for determining what is acceptable on the authority having jurisdiction and how it is applied in the particular jurisdiction. This basis in most areas is the result of:

1. Competent knowledge and experience of installation methods;

2. What has been the established practice by the qualified journeyman in the particular area;

3. What has been taught in the trade schools having certified electrical training courses for apprentices and journeymen.

There should be an understanding that individual inspectors will not make an arbitrary ruling of their own but will apply in a uniform manner the practice established by the organization having responsibility for enforcement of electrical requirements.

Examples which generally would not be considered as "neat and workmanlike" include nonmetallic cables installed with kinks or twists; unsightly exposed runs; wiring improperly trained in enclosures; slack in cables between supports; flattened conduit bends; or improvised fittings, straps, or supports.

110-13. Mounting of Equipment.   Electrical equipment shall be firmly secured to the surface on which it is mounted. Wooden plugs driven into holes in masonry, concrete, plaster or similar materials shall not be depended on for security.

▶   Knowledge of the proper selection and use of fasteners, such as Rawl plugs, toggle bolts, and expansion shields, will avoid faulty methods of support. Manufacturers of fastening devices should be freely consulted to assure proper mounting of equipment.

110-14. Electrical Connections.   Because of different characteristics of copper and aluminum, devices such as pressure terminal or pressure splicing connectors and soldering lugs shall be suitable for the material of the conductor and shall be properly installed and used. Conductors of dissimilar metals shall not be inter-mixed in a terminal or splicing connector where physical contact occurs between dissimilar conductors (such as copper and aluminum, copper and copper-clad aluminum, or aluminum and copper-clad aluminum), unless the device is suitable for the purpose and conditions of use. Materials such as solder, fluxes, inhibitors, and compounds, where employed, shall be suitable for the use and shall be of a type which will not adversely affect the conductors, installation, or equipment.

(a) **Terminals.**   Connection of conductors to terminal parts shall insure a thor-oughly good connection without damaging the conductors and shall be made by means of pressure connectors (including set-screw type), solder lugs or splices to flexible leads except that No. 8 or smaller solid conductors and No. 10 or smaller stranded conductors may be connected by means of wire-binding screws or studs and nuts having upturned lugs, or the equivalent. Terminals for more than one conductor and terminals used to connect aluminum shall be of a type suitable for the purpose.

(b) **Splices.**   Conductors shall be spliced or joined with splicing devices suitable for the use or by brazing, welding, or soldering with a fusible metal or alloy. Soldered splices shall first be so spliced or joined as to be mechanically and electrically secure without solder and then soldered. All splices and joints and the free ends of conductors shall be covered with an insulation equivalent to that of the conductors or with an insulating device suitable for the purpose.

▶   Proper electrical connections at terminals and splices are absolutely es-sential to insure a safe installation. Improper connections are the causes of many failures of wiring devices, equipment burndowns, and electrically-oriented fires.

Many years ago soldered splices and lugs were widely used in the elec-trical industry, but in modern practice such methods have been replaced with solderless-type lugs, terminals and splicing devices. These modern solderless devices have overcome most of the flaws inherent in soldered splices and lugs. However, solderless devices are only as good as they are selected and used, and misapplications or poor workmanship account for many failures.

Proper connections for all types of solderless devices can be assured if suitable wire combinations, types of conductor material (copper, copper-clad aluminum or aluminum), and proper torque-tightening of screws are used with specific devices. In general, approved pressure-type wire splicing lugs or connectors bear no marking if approved for only copper wire. If approved for copper, copper-clad aluminum, and/or aluminum they are marked *CU/AL;* and if approved for aluminum only they are marked *AL.* Devices listed by Underwriters' Laboratories, Inc., indicate the range or combination of wire sizes for which such devices have been listed.

Where solderless terminals are not suitable for aluminum (or copper-clad aluminum) conductors, a short piece of copper wire can be attached to the terminal, and the other end is then connected to the aluminum wire with a pressure-type splicing device approved for joining copper and aluminum (straight types for larger conductors and pig-tail types for smaller conductors). In such cases consideration must be given to available space in enclosures.

Reports have been made of field failures where aluminum conductors have been connected to the screw terminals of wiring devices. These failures have been largely due to poor workmanship and the use of minimum-quality wiring devices. To avoid such problems, aluminum conductors should be formed with a three-fourths loop around the terminals (in the tightening direction); the screws should be properly tightened; and high-quality wiring devices with wider, more rugged screws should be used. To date Underwriters has not listed any wiring device *push-in* terminals for use with aluminum conductors. At present, Underwriters and the manufacturers of conductors and wiring devices are reviewing the problem of aluminum terminations at wiring devices, and revised standards may be forthcoming in the near future.

110-16. Working Space about Electrical Equipment (600 Volts or Less).
Sufficient access and working space shall be provided and maintained about all electrical equipment to permit ready and safe operation and maintenance of such equipment.

(a) Working Clearances. Except as elsewhere required or permitted in this Code, the dimension of the working space in the direction of access to live parts, operating at not more than 600 volts, which are likely to require examination, adjustment, servicing or maintenance while alive, shall not be less than indicated in Table 110-16(a). In addition to the dimensions shown in Table 110-16(a) the work space shall be at least 30 inches wide in front of the electrical equipment. Distances are to be measured from the live parts if such are exposed or from the enclosure front or opening when such are enclosed. Concrete, brick or tile walls shall be considered as grounded.

Table 110-16(a). Working Clearances

Voltage to Ground		Minimum clear distance		
	Condition:	1	2	3
0–150		2½ ft.	2½ ft.	3 ft.
151–600		2½	3½	4

Where the "Conditions" are as follows:

1. Exposed live part on one side and no live or grounded part on the other side of the working space or exposed live parts on both sides effectively guarded by suitable wood or other insulating materials. Insulated wire or insulated bus bars operating at not more than 300 volts shall not be considered live parts.
2. Exposed live parts on one side and grounded parts on the other side.
3. Exposed live parts on both sides of the work space (not guarded as provided in Condition 1) with the operator between.
Exception No. 1: Working space is not required in back of assemblies such as

dead-front switchboards or control centers when there are no renewable or adjustable parts such as fuses or switches on the back and when all connections are accessible from other locations than the back.

Exception No. 2: Smaller spaces may be permitted by the authority having jurisdiction where it is judged that the particular arrangement of the installation will provide adequate accessibility.

(b) Clear Spaces.   Working space required by this Section shall not be used for storage. When normally enclosed live parts are exposed for inspection or servicing, the working space, if in a passageway or general open space, shall be suitably guarded.

(c) Access and Entrance to Working Space.   At least one entrance of sufficient area shall be provided to give access to the working space about electrical equipment.

(d) Front Working Space.   In all cases where there are live parts normally exposed on the front of switchboards or control centers, the working space in front of such boards or panels shall be not less than 3 feet.

(e) Illumination.   Adequate illumination shall be provided for all working spaces about switchboards and control centers.

(f) Headroom.   The minimum headroom of working spaces about switchboards or control centers where there are live parts exposed at any time, shall be 6¼ feet.

For higher voltages, see Article 710.

▶   These important requirements are necessary to provide safe access and working space around switchboards and control centers. E. E. Carlton of the State of California is responsible for initiating these rules as a result of field experiences in his state.

110-17. Guarding of Live Parts.   (Not more than 600 Volts)

(a)   Except as elsewhere required or permitted by this Code, live parts of electrical equipment operating at 50 volts or more shall be guarded against accidental contact by approved cabinets or other forms of approved enclosures, or any of the following means:

(1)   By location in a room, vault, or similar enclosure which is accessible only to qualified persons.

(2)   By suitable permanent, substantial partitions or screens so arranged that only qualified persons will have access to the space within reach of the live parts. Any openings in such partitions or screens shall be so sized and located that persons are not likely to come into accidental contact with the live parts or to bring conducting objects into contact with them.

(3)   By location on a suitable balcony, gallery, or platform so elevated and arranged as to exclude unqualified persons.

(4)   By elevation at least 8 feet above the floor or other working surface.

(b)   In locations where electrical equipment would be exposed to physical damage, enclosures or guards shall be so arranged and of such strength as to prevent such damage.

(c)   Entrances to rooms and other guarded locations containing exposed live parts shall be marked with conspicuous warning signs forbidding unqualified persons to enter.

For motors see Sections 430-132 and 430-133. For additional requirements at voltages over 600 see Article 710.

▶   Live parts of equipment should in general be protected from accidental contact by complete enclosure, *i.e.,* the equipment should be "dead-front." Such construction is not practicable in some large control panels, and in such cases the apparatus should be isolated or guarded as required by these rules.

110-18. Arcing Parts. Parts of electrical equipment which in ordinary operation produce arcs, sparks, flames or molten metal, shall be enclosed unless separated and isolated from all combustible material. For hazardous locations see Articles 500–517 inclusive. For motors see Section 430-14.

▶   The same considerations apply here as in the case covered in Section 110-17. Full enclosure is preferable, but where this is not practicable, all combustible material must be kept well away from the equipment.

110-19. Light and Power from Railway Conductors. Circuits for lighting and power shall not be connected to any system containing trolley wires with a ground return, except in electric railway cars, car houses, power houses, or passenger and freight stations operated in connection with electric railways.
110-20. Insulation Resistance. All wiring shall be so installed that when completed the system will be free from short circuits and from grounds other than as provided in Article 250.

▶   Previous editions of the Code (e.g., 1965) contained *recommended* values for testing insulation resistance. It was found that those values were incomplete and not sufficiently accurate for use in modern installations, and the recommendation was deleted from the Code. However, basic knowledge of insulation-resistance testing is important.

Measurements of insulation resistance can best be made with a megohmmeter insulation tester. As measured with such an instrument, insulation resistance is the resistance to the flow of direct current (usually at 500 or 1000 volts for systems of 600 volts or less) through or over the surface of the insulation in electrical equipment. The results are in ohms or megohms, but insulation readings will be in the megohm range.

The insulation resistance test is nondestructive, quite different from a high-voltage or *breakdown* test. It is made with direct-current rather than alternating-current, and is not a measure of dielectric strength as such. However, insulation-resistance tests assist greatly in determining when and where not to apply high voltage.

In general, insulation resistance decreases with increased size of a machine or length of cable, because there is more insulating material in contact with conductors and frame, ground, or sheath.

Insulation resistance usually increases with higher voltage rating of apparatus because of increased thickness of insulating material.

Insulation-resistance readings are not only *quantitative,* but are *relative* or *comparative* as well, and since they are influenced by moisture, dirt, and deterioration, they are reliable indicators of the presence of those conditions.

Cable and conductor installations present a wide variation of conditions from the point of view of the resistance of the insulation. These conditions result from the many kinds of insulating materials used, the voltage rating or insulation thickness, and the length of the circuit involved in the measurement. Furthermore, such circuits usually extend over great distances, and may be subject to wide variations in temperature, which will have an effect on the insulation resistance values obtained. The terminals of cables and conductors will also have an effect on the test values unless they are clean and dry, or guarded.

It is important to understand the correct use of insulation testers. The use of an insulation tester is not complicated. However, temperature correction, humidity, temporary dampness during construction, types of conductor insulation, lengths of runs, and the proper *interpretation* of readings are major factors that must be considered. The important thing is to make an insulation test and to record the results for immediate and future attention.

Excellent manuals on this subject are available from instrument manufacturers, such as the James G. Biddle Co., Plymouth Meeting, Pa., and thorough knowledge in the use of insulation testers is essential if the test results are to be meaningful.

See Fig. 110-1 for a typical megohmmeter insulation tester.

FIG. 110-1. Multivoltage multirange Megger insulation tester. (*James G. Biddle Co.*)

110-21. Marking. The manufacturer's name, trademark, or other descriptive marking by which the organization responsible for the product may be identified, shall be placed on all electrical equipment. Other markings shall be provided giving voltage, current, wattage, or other ratings as are prescribed elsewhere in this Code. The marking shall be of sufficient durability to withstand the environment involved.

▶ The marking required in Section 110-21 should be done in a manner which will allow inspectors to examine such marking without removing the equipment from a permanently installed position.

110-22. Identification. Each disconnecting means required by this Code for motors and appliances, and each service, feeder or branch circuit at the point where it originates, shall be legibly marked to indicate its purpose unless located and arranged so the purpose is evident. The marking shall be of sufficient durability to withstand the environment involved.

CHAPTER TWO ———————————————

Wiring Design and Protection

ARTICLE 200. USE AND IDENTIFICATION OF GROUNDED CONDUCTORS

200-1. Scope. This Article provides requirements for the use and identification of a grounded conductor in interior wiring systems. (See definitions of "grounded conductor" and "grounding conductor" in Article 100.)

200-2. General. All interior wiring systems shall have a grounded conductor which is continuously identified throughout the system except as follows:

Exception No. 1: A grounded conductor is not required in certain circuits or systems as provided in Sections 200-5, 250-3, 250-5, 250-7, 503-13, and 517-63.

Exception No. 2: Continuous identification throughout a length of a conductor between terminals is not required for certain conductors under Section 200-6 (a and b).

▶   Ungrounded circuits are required in anesthetizing locations such as hospital operating rooms. (See Section **517-63.**) Such circuits must be connected to a system which is provided with a line isolation monitor. (See pamphlet No. **56A-1971,** National Fire Protection Association, "Inhalation Anesthetics Standard.")

200-3. Connection to Grounded System. No interior wiring shall be electrically connected to a supply system unless the latter contains, for any grounded conductor of the interior system, a corresponding conductor which is grounded.

Electrically connected implies connection capable of carrying current as distinguished from connection through electromagnetic induction.

▶   The interior wiring grounded conductor and the system grounded conductor must be connected together, in order to assure a completely grounded system.

200-4. Circuits Derived from Autotransformers. Branch circuits as described in Article 210 shall not be supplied through autotransformers (transformers in which a part of the winding is common to both primary and secondary circuits) unless the system supplied has an identified grounded conductor which is solidly connected to a similar identified grounded conductor of the system supplying the autotransformer.

Exception: An autotransformer may be used to extend or add an individual branch circuit in an existing installation for an equipment load without the connection to a similar identified grounded conductor when transforming from a nominal 208 volts to a nominal 240 volts supply or similarly from 240 volts to 208 volts.

▶   Figure 200-1 shows how a 110-volt system for lighting may be derived from a 220-volt system by means of an autotransformer. The 220-volt system either may be single phase or may be one leg of a three-phase system.

In Fig. 200-2 an autotransformer is used to derive a three-wire 110/220-volt system for lighting from a 220-volt system.

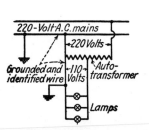

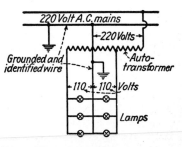

Fig. 200-1. Autotransformer used to derive a two-wire 110-volt system for lighting from a 220-volt power system.

Fig. 200-2. Autotransformer used to derive a three-wire 110/220-volt system for lighting from a 220-volt system.

In both of the cases illustrated by Figs. 200-1 and 200-2 the "supplied" system has a grounded wire solidly connected to a grounded wire of the "supplying" system; 220-volt single-phase systems with one conductor grounded and 220-volt three-phase three-wire systems with one conductor grounded are not commonly used, hence it is not often possible to make use of either one of the arrangements shown in the figures.

Autotransformers are commonly used to supply reduced voltage for starting induction motors.

The exception permits the use of an autotransformer in existing installations for an individual branch circuit without connection to a similar identified grounded conductor where transforming from 208 to 240 volts or vice versa. Typical applications are with cooking equipment, heaters, motors, and air-conditioning equipment. For such applications *buck or boost* transformers are commonly used.

Buck or boost transformers are designed for use on single- or three-phase circuits to supply 12/24- or 16/32-volt secondaries with a 120/240-volt primary. When connected as autotransformers the kva load they will handle

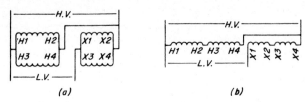

Fig. 200-3. Typical buck or boost transformers connected as auto-transformers for changing 240 volts single phase to 208 volts or vice versa.

is large in comparison to their physical size and relative cost. Figures 200-3 and 200-4 show typical autotransformer connections for single- and three-phase loads. As shown in Fig. 200-3, a 5-kva buck or boost transformer will handle equipment rated up to 32 kva. For open-delta connections, as shown in Fig. 200-4, two 5-kva buck or boost transformers will handle equipment rated up to 56 kva.

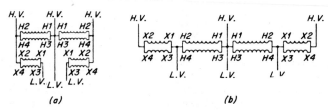

Fig. 200-4. Typical buck or boost transformers connected in three-phase open delta as autotransformers for changing 240 volts to 208 volts or vice versa.

Complete information on buck or boost transformers may be obtained from manufacturers of such equipment.

200-5. Unidentified Circuits.

(a) Two-wire branch circuits and AC circuits of two or more conductors may be tapped from the ungrounded conductors of circuits having identified grounded neutrals. Switching devices in each tapped circuit shall have a pole in each ungrounded conductor. These poles shall manually switch together where the switching devices serve as the disconnecting means required by Sections 422-21 and 422-23.

Exception: For motor controllers see Section 430-84, for heating equipment see Section 424-20, and for de-icing equipment, see Section 426-21.

(b) Polyphase circuits need not have one conductor grounded and identified, except as required by Section 250-5, but where one conductor is grounded it shall be identified.

(c) Other unidentified ungrounded systems or circuits may be used only by special permission.

▶ This permits the use of two-wire branch circuits tapped from the outside conductors of any of the following systems, where the neutral is grounded: three-wire d-c or single-phase, four-wire three-phase, and five-wire two-phase systems.

Figures 200-5 and 200-6 illustrate the use of unidentified two-wire branch circuits to supply small motors, the circuits being tapped from the outside conductors of a three-wire d-c or single-phase system (**Fig. 200-5**) and a four-wire three-phase wye system (**Fig. 200-6**).

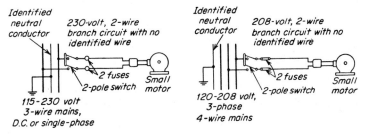

FIG. 200-5.   FIG. 200-6.

FIGS. 200-5 and 200-6. Unidentified branch circuits tapped from the outside conductors of multiwire systems.

All poles of the disconnecting means used for branch circuits supplying stationary appliances shall be operated at the same time. This requirement applies where the circuit is supplied by either circuit breakers or switches.

In the case of fuses and switches, when a fuse blows in one pole, the other pole may not necessarily open and the requirement to "manually switch together" only involves the manual operation of the switch. Similarly, when a pair of circuit breakers is connected with handle ties, an overload on one of the conductors with the return circuit through the neutral may open only one of the circuit breakers; but the manual operation of the pair when used as a disconnecting means will open both poles. The words "manually switched together" should be considered as "operating at the same time," that is, during the same operating interval, and apply to the equipment used as a disconnecting means and not as an overcurrent protective device. While there may be some slight difference in the opening instant for circuit breakers connected by handle ties, this is of no consequence, and even where a two-pole breaker may have a common trip, both poles may not open at exactly the same instant.

Circuit breakers with handle ties are, therefore, considered as providing the disconnection required by this Section.

The requirement in paragraph *a* to "manually switch together" can be achieved by a "master handle" or "handle tie" since the operation is intended to be effected by manual operation. The intent was not to require a common trip for the switching device but to require that it have the ability to disconnect ungrounded conductors by one movement of the hand. For service disconnecting means see Section **230-70***g*.

200-6. Means of Identification of Grounded Conductors.   Identification for grounded conductors shall be as follows:

(a)   Insulated conductors of No. 6 or smaller, except conductors of Type MI cable, shall have an outer identification of white or natural gray color as specified in 310-2(c). The grounded conductors of Type MI cable shall be identified by distinctive marking at the terminals during the process of installation.

(b)   Insulated conductors larger than No. 6, shall have an outer identification of white or natural gray color, or shall be identified by distinctive white marking at terminals during process of installation.

(c)   Where, on a 4-wire delta-connected secondary, the midpoint of one phase is grounded to supply lighting and similar loads, that phase conductor having the higher voltage to ground shall be orange in color or be indicated by tagging or other effective means at any point where a connection is to be made if the neutral conductor is present.

▶   The general requirements on identification of conductors are contained in Art. 200 of the Code and concern primarily the grounded circuit conductor which is required to be the identified conductor. Where a system consists of a four-wire three-phase delta with midpoint of one phase grounded, Section 200-6c requires that the phase having the higher voltage to ground be orange in color or be identified by tagging or other effective means at any point where a connection is to be made if the neutral is present. The *high leg* of a 120/240-volt, four-wire, three-phase delta system is 208 volts to ground and to neutral (120 volts $\times$ 1.73).

For many years, it has been the practice to use black-colored conductors for large feeders, with only the neutral grounded conductor identified. Although plastic insulation is now available in colors, even in the larger sizes, there is no requirement for the use of such color coding for feeders other than for the neutral, which is to be identified by white or natural gray. The color coding mentioned in Section 210-5 concerns branch circuits and not feeders. Definitions for "branch circuits" and for "multiwire branch circuits" are given in Art. 100.

200-7. Identified Conductor in Grounded Circuits Only.   Conductors having white or natural gray covering shall not be used other than as conductors for which identification is required by Section 200-2, except under the following conditions, and then only where they are, in other respects, suitable for use as ungrounded conductors in the circuit:

Exception No. 1: Identified conductors, rendered permanently unidentified by painting or other effective means at each outlet where the conductors are visible and accessible, may be used as unidentified conductors.

Exception No. 2: Cable containing an identified conductor may be used for single-pole, three-way or four-way switch loops where the connections are so made that the unidentified conductor is the return conductor from the switch to the outlet.

This exception makes it unnecessary to paint the terminal of the identified conductor at the switch outlet.

Exception No. 3: A flexible cord for connecting a portable or stationary appliance, having one conductor identified with a white or natural gray outer finish or by any other means permitted by Section 400-13, may be used whether or not the outlet to which it is connected is supplied by a circuit having a grounded conductor.

Exception No. 4: A white or natural gray conductor of circuits less than 50 volts need only be grounded as required by Section 250-5(a).

200-8. Connections to Screw Shells.   An identified conductor, where run to a screw-shell lampholder, shall be connected to the screw shell.

200-9. Means of Identification of Terminals.   The identification of terminals to which a grounded conductor is to be connected shall be by means of a metallic plated coating substantially white in color, such as nickel or zinc, or the terminals may be of material substantially white in color. The other terminals shall be of a readily distinguishable different color.

200-10. Identification of Terminals.

(a) Device Terminals.   All devices provided with terminals for the attachment of conductors and intended for connection to more than one side of the circuit shall have terminals properly marked for identification except as follows:

Exception No. 1: Marking may be omitted where the electrical connection of a terminal intended to be connected to the grounded conductor is clearly evident.

Exception No. 2: Single-pole Devices. Devices to the terminals of which only one side of the line is connected need not have terminals marked for identification.

Exception No. 3: Panelboards and Devices. The terminals of lighting panelboards and of devices having a normal current rating of over 30 amperes need not be marked for identification, except as required in Section 200-10(b) for polarized receptacles for attachment plugs and polarized attachment plugs.

(b) Plugs, Receptacles, and Connectors.   Polarized attachment plugs, receptacles and cord connectors for plugs and polarized plugs shall have the terminal intended for connection to the grounded (white) conductor identified by a metal or metal coating substantially white in color.

If the terminal for the grounded conductor is not visible, the conductor entrance hole for the connection shall be marked with the word "white."

The terminal for the connection of the equipment grounding conductor shall be identified by: (1) A green colored, not readily removable terminal screw with hexagonal head; or (2) A green colored hexagonal, not readily removable terminal nut; or (3) A green colored pressure wire connector. If the terminal for the grounding conductor is not visible, the conductor entrance hole shall be marked with the word "green" or otherwise identified by a distinctive green color.

Exception: Two-wire attachment plugs, unless of the polarity type, need not have their terminals marked for identification.

(c) Screw Shells.   In the case of devices with screw shells, the identified terminal shall be the one connected to the screw shell. This does not apply to screw shells which serve as fuseholders.

(d) Screw-Shell Devices with Leads.   In the case of screw-shell devices with attached leads, the conductor attached to the screw shell shall have white or natural gray finish. The outer finish of the other conductor shall be of a solid color that will not be confused with the white or natural-gray finish which is to identify the grounded conductor.

(e) **Fixed Appliances.** The terminals of fixed appliances need not be marked to indicate the proper connection to the grounded conductor unless a single-pole switch forms an integral part, then the terminal connected to the switch shall be the unidentified terminal.

(f) **Portable Appliances.** The terminals of portable appliances need not be marked for identification.

ARTICLE 210. BRANCH CIRCUITS

210-1. Scope. The provisions of this Article shall apply to branch circuits supplying lighting or appliance loads or combinations of such loads. Where motors, or motor-operated appliances, are connected to any circuit supplying lighting or other appliance loads, the provisions of both this Article and Article 430 shall apply. Article 430 shall apply where branch circuit supplies only motor loads.

210-2. Specific Purpose Branch Circuit. The provisions applying to branch circuits referred to in the following list are exceptions to the provisions of this Article or are supplementary thereto, and shall apply to branch circuits supplying the loads referred to therein:

Air-Conditioning and Refrigerating Equipment.....	Sections 440-5, 440-31, 440-32
Busways...	Section 364-8
Cranes and Hoists.......................................	Section 610-42
Data Processing Systems.................................	Section 645-2
Elevators, Dumbwaiters and Escalators....................	Section 620-61
Fixed Electric Space Heating Equipment..................	Section 424-3
Fixed Outdoor De-icing and Snow Melting Equipment...........	Section 426-3
Infrared Industrial Heating Equipment..................	Sections 422-15, 424-3
Induction and Dielectric Heating Equipment....................	Article 665
Instruments...	Section 384-22
Marinas and Boatyards...................................	Section 555-4
Mobile Homes and Parks..................................	Article 550
Motion Picture Studios and Similar Locations....................	Article 530
Motors and Motor Controllers...............................	Article 430
Organs...	Section 650-6
Recreational Vehicles and Parks............................	Article 551
Remote-Control, Low-Energy Power, Low-Voltage Power and Signal Circuits...	Article 725
Signs and Outline Lighting................................	Section 600-6
Sound Recording and Reproduction..........................	Section 640-6
Systems over 600 Volts..................................	Article 710
Systems under 50 Volts..................................	Article 720
Theaters and Assembly Halls...............	Sections 520-41, 520-51, and 520-62
Welders..	Article 630
X-ray Equipment.......................................	Section 660-3

210-3. Classifications. Branch circuits recognized by this Article shall be classified in accordance with the maximum permitted rating or setting of the overcurrent device, and the classification for other than individual branch circuits shall be 15, 20, 30, 40 and 50 amperes. When conductors of higher capacity are used for any reason, the rating or setting of the specified overcurrent device shall determine the circuit classification.

▶ The size of conductor does not determine the circuit rating. For example: A circuit with 30-amp conductors protected by 15-amp fuses or circuit breakers is still a 15-amp circuit. For the 15-, 20-, 30-, 40-, and 50-amp circuits referred to above, see Section 210-24.

A. General Provisions

210-4. Multiwire Branch Circuits.   Branch circuits recognized by this Article may be installed as multiwire circuits.

See Article 100 for Definition.

▶ Multiwire branch circuits are most commonly three-wire circuits taken from a three-wire single-phase system.

The advantages of three-wire circuits are, first, that only three wires are required to supply a load that would require four wires if two-wire circuits were used; and, second, that, other conditions being the same, the percentage voltage drop is only one-half as great in a three-wire as in a two-wire circuit.

Three-wire circuits may be used to good advantage in simple wiring layouts in large spaces, where each circuit supplies only a few outlets. In most localities three-wire circuits are commonly used in house wiring but, where this practice is followed, special care must be taken to see that the circuits are properly balanced.

Three-phase four-wire circuits and two-phase five-wire circuits are also permissible. In a four-wire circuit the neutral wire can never be called on to carry a current heavier than the heaviest current carried by any one of the outside or phase wires, and therefore all four wires may be of the same size. In a three-wire two-phase circuit the neutral must have a carrying capacity of at least 1.41 times the ampere rating of the circuit.

210-5. Color Code for Branch Circuits.
(a) Grounded Conductor.   The grounded conductor of a branch circuit shall be identified by a continuous white or natural-gray color. Where conductors of different systems are installed in the same raceway, box, gutter or other types of enclosures, one system shall have a neutral, if required, having an outer covering of white or natural gray. Each other system having a neutral, if required, shall have an outer covering of white with an identifiable colored stripe (not green) running along the insulation or other suitable and different means of identification.

Exception: The grounded conductors of Type MI cable shall be identified by distinctive marking at the terminals during the process of installation.

(b) Grounding Conductor.   The grounding conductor of a branch circuit shall be identified by a continuous green color or a continuous green color with one or more yellow stripes unless it is bare.

The above is not intended to prohibit the use of a conductor having a continuous green color or a continuous green color with one or more yellow stripes as insulation for internal wiring of equipment, except where such wiring serves as the lead wires to which the branch-circuit conductors attach.

(c) Ungrounded Conductor. Where installed in raceways, as open work or as concealed knob-and-tube work, the ungrounded conductor shall be identified by any color other than as specified in (a) and (b) above. All ungrounded conductors of the same color shall be connected to the same ungrounded feeder conductor and the conductors for systems of different voltages shall be of different colors.
Exception: As permitted in Section 200-7.

It is recommended for a basic single wiring system that the following colors be used: 3-wire circuits, 1 black, 1 white and 1 red; 4-wire circuits, 1 black, 1 white, 1 red, and 1 blue.

▶   Section **210-5** divides color coding of branch-circuit conductors into three categories: (a) grounded conductor; (b) grounding conductor; and (c) ungrounded conductor. The major item in paragraph (a) is the requirement concerning the use of two grounded neutral conductors from different systems in the same enclosure, such as a conduit containing a **480Y/277**-volt circuit and a **208Y/120** or similar lower voltage circuit. In such instances one system would use the conventional white or natural gray color for the neutral, while the other system neutral would have to be identified by the use of a white color with a colored stripe (not green) or other suitable and different means (such as labels).

An entirely new concept of identifying ungrounded conductors is expressed in paragraph (c). First, color coding applies only where such conductors are used for open work, concealed knob-and-tube work, or in raceways. Second, you can pick the color code on a given installation, and once established, each specific color must be connected to the same ungrounded feeder conductor. Third, where different voltage systems, such as **480Y/277** and **208Y/120** are used in the same premises, the color codes for both systems cannot be the same. Pick one color scheme for one system and a different one for the second one. Furthermore, any additional systems at other voltage levels will require separate color coding schemes. There is a recommendation for a basic color scheme where a basic single system is used.

210-6. Voltage.

(a) Voltage to Ground. The voltage to ground on branch circuits supplying lampholders, fixtures, or standard receptacles of 15-ampere or less rating shall not exceed 150 volts, except as follows:

Exception No. 1: In industrial establishments where the conditions of maintenance and supervision assure that only competent individuals will service the lighting fixtures, the voltage of branch circuits may be as high as 300 volts to ground provided that such branch circuits:

(1) Supply only lighting fixtures which are equipped with mogul-base screw-shell lampholders or with lampholders of other types approved for the application.

(2) The lighting fixtures are mounted not less than 8 feet from the floor, and

(3) The lighting fixtures do not have switch control as an integral part of the fixture.

Exception No. 2: In industrial establishments, office buildings, schools, stores, and public and commercial areas of other buildings, such as hotels or transportation terminals, the voltage of branch circuits which supply only the ballasts for electric discharge lamps mounted in permanently installed fixtures, by other than screw-shell type lampholders, which do not have manual switch control as an integral part of the fixture shall not exceed 300 volts to ground. Where screw-shell type lampholders are used for electric discharge lamps the fixtures shall be installed not less than eight feet from the floor.

Exception No. 3: For infrared industrial heating appliances as described in Section 422-15;

Exception No. 4: In railway properties as described in Section 110-19;

Exception No. 5: The branch circuits supplying the ballasts for electric discharge lamps mounted in permanently installed fixtures on poles for the illumination of areas such as highways, bridges, athletic fields, parking lots, at a height not less than 22 feet, or on other structures such as tunnels at a height not less than 18 feet, shall not exceed 500 volts between conductors when installed as provided in Section 730-7(c).

▶ In other than residential occupancies, 230-volt or 208-volt two-wire circuits may be used to supply lampholders of all standard types if the circuits are taken from a 115/230-volt single-phase three-wire system or a 208Y/120-volt three-phase four-wire system having a grounded neutral. In industrial establishments, office buildings, schools and stores, and public and commercial areas of other buildings such as hotels or transportation terminals, the voltage to ground of lighting circuits may be as much as 300 volts. This permits the use of electric-discharge ballasts at line-to-line or line-to-neutral voltages (254 to 277 volts) of a three-phase four-wire 480Y/277-volt system, and makes it unnecessary to use separate transformers to supply the lighting load.

Exception 1. Where the inspection authority having jurisdiction is satisfied that all repairs and maintenance of fixtures will be performed by qualified persons, fixtures approved for the application may be installed on 480Y/277-volt circuits, provided they are at least 8 ft from the floor and are controlled by switches entirely separate and apart from the fixtures, *i.e.*, by panelboard or wall switches. Fixtures approved for the application could include medium-base lampholders.

Exception 2. This permits the use of electric discharge lamps, other than screw-shell types, on a 480Y/277-volt system at less than 8 ft from the floor, provided that the fixtures are controlled by switches entirely separate and apart from the fixtures, *i.e.*, by panelboard or wall switches.

(b) Voltage Between Conductors—Dwellings. In dwelling occupancies, the voltage between conductors supplying lampholders of the screw-shell type, receptacles, or appliances, shall not exceed 150 volts, except as follows:

Exception: The voltage between conductors may exceed 150 volts when supplying only:

(1) Permanently connected appliances,

(2) Portable and stationary appliances of more than 1,380 watts,

(3) Portable motor-operated appliances of ¼ horsepower or greater rating.

▶ In residential occupancies 230-volt two-wire circuits may be used to supply lampholders of other than the screw-shell type, permanently connected appliances, or portable appliances of more than 1,380 watts rating. Since the lampholders for fluorescent lamps are not of the screw-shell type, 230-volt lamps of this type may be used in residential occupancies.

(c) Voltage Between Conductors—Nondwelling Occupancies. In nondwelling occupancies other than the industrial establishments referred to in Exception No. 1 of Section 210-6(a) the voltage between conductors of branch circuits that supply screw-shell lampholders of the medium size shall not exceed 150 volts.

(d) Voltage Drop. The size of the conductors for branch circuits as defined in Article 100 should be such that the voltage drop would not exceed 3 per cent to the farthest outlet for power, heating, lighting, or combinations thereof. Providing further that the maximum total voltage drop for feeders and branch circuits should not exceed 5 per cent over all.

210-7. Grounding-Type Receptacles and Protection. Receptacles and cord connectors equipped with grounding contacts shall have those contacts effectively grounded. The branch circuit or branch circuit raceway shall include or provide a grounding conductor to which the grounding contacts of the receptacle or cord connector shall be connected. Acceptable grounding means are outlined in Section 250-91(b).

Exception: For extensions only in existing installations which do not have a grounding conductor in the branch circuit, the grounding conductor of a grounding type receptacle outlet may be grounded to a grounded cold water pipe near the equipment.

All 15- and 20-ampere receptacle outlets on single-phase circuits for construction sites shall have approved ground-fault circuit protection for personnel. This requirement shall become effective on January 1, 1974.

▶   In all cases where a grounding-type receptacle is installed it shall be grounded. For nonmetallic-sheathed cable the grounding conductor is run with the branch-circuit conductors. The armor of Type AC metal-clad cable, the sheath of ALS cable, and certain metallic raceways are acceptable as grounding means. The exception applies only to extensions to existing installations which do not provide a grounding conductor.

The last paragraph of Section 210-7 calls for personnel ground-fault circuit protection for all single-phase, 15- and 20-ampere receptacle outlets, installed on construction sites. An enforcement date of January 1, 1974 has been established to permit a detailed study of selected construction sites that are using ground-fault circuit interrupters. This study will help to determine the proper GFI current trip level (e.g., 5, 10 or 20 milliamperes) for such applications, and will permit manufacturers enough time to produce the necessary equipment with any needed refinements.

One logical place to introduce ground-fault protection is on construction sites where many portable tools are plugged into single-phase receptacle outlets. For such tools, equipment grounding cannot be assured, and many accidents have been attributed to *line-to-ground* faults where grounding was omitted or disconnected. Figure 210-1 shows a typical arrangement of a personnel ground-fault circuit-interrupter. The incoming two-wire circuit is connected to a two-pole, shunt-trip overload circuit breaker. The load-side conductors pass through a toroidal coil onto the outgoing circuit. As long as the current in both load wires is equal the circuit functions normally. If one of the conductors becomes in contact with a grounded condition or passes through a person's body to ground, an unbalanced current is established.

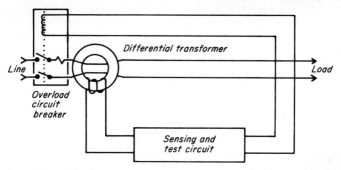

Fig. 210-1. Circuit arrangement of a typical ground-fault circuit-interrupter for personnel protection. (*Pass & Seymour, Inc.*)

This unbalanced current is picked up by the differential transformer, and a circuit is established through the sensing circuit to energize the shunt trip of the overload circuit breaker and quickly open the main circuit. Present settings are set to operate when line-to-ground currents reach 5 milliamperes or greater, which is in line with present standards of Underwriters' Laboratories, Inc. Depending on the detailed studies previously mentioned, the 5 ma level could be raised slightly for construction-site applications. On the other hand, the 5 ma level may prove to be entirely satisfactory. Even at trips of 5 ma, it should be clearly understood that instantaneous current will be higher and any shock during the time the fault is being cleared will not feel comfortable. A shock at 5 ma is not pleasant either. The key to the

Fig. 210-2. A ground-fault circuit-interrupter for personnel protection. See Fig. 210-1 for circuit arrangement. (*Pass & Seymour, Inc.*)

ground-fault circuit-interrupter is the time-current characteristic. Trip-out time is about 1/40 of a second (25 milliseconds) when the fault reaches or exceeds 5 ma.

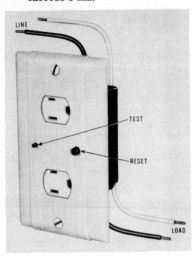

FIG. 210-3. Duplex receptacle, rated 15 amps, 125 volts, with built-in ground-fault circuit interrupter. Load wires are also protected by GFCI. (*Pass & Seymour, Inc.*)

Figures 210-3 and 210-4 show receptacles and branch-circuit breakers with built-in ground-fault protection. Current UL-listed GFCI's are presently available in the units shown in Figs. 210-2, 210-3 and 210-4. Such units

FIG. 210-4. Plug-in circuit breaker (15, 20 or 30 amp single pole) with built-in ground-fault circuit-interrupter. Jumper lead connects to neutral bar in panelboard. (*Square D Co.*)

contain a *test switch* so that the unit can be checked periodically to insure continued safety.

210-8. Heavy-Duty Lampholders.   Heavy-duty lampholders referred to in this Article shall include lampholders rated at not less than 750 watts.

Exception: Admedium lampholders rated at 660 watts shall be considered to be heavy-duty types.

▶   The intent is to limit the rating of lighting branch circuits supplying fluorescent fixtures to 20 amp. The ballast is connected to the branch circuit rather than the lamp, but by controlling the lampholder rating, a 20-amp limit is established for the ballast circuit. Most lampholders manufactured and intended for use with electric-discharge lighting for illumination purposes are rated less than 750 watts, and are not classified as heavy-duty lampholders.

B. Specific Requirements

210-19. Conductors.   Circuit conductors shall conform to the following:

(a) Ampacity.   Shall have an ampacity of not less than the rating of the branch circuit and not less than the maximum load to be served.

(b) Minimum Size.   Shall not be smaller than No. 8 for ranges of 8¾ kw or more rating, nor smaller than No. 14 for other loads.

(c) Exceptions:

Exception No. 1: Range Loads. See Note 5 of Table 220-5. Where the maximum demand of a range of 8¾ kw or more rating is computed according to Column A of Table 220-5, the neutral conductor of a three-wire branch circuit supplying a household electric range, a wall-mounted oven or a counter-mounted cooking unit may be smaller than the ungrounded conductors but shall have an ampacity at least 70 per cent of the ampacity of the ungrounded conductors and shall not be smaller than No. 10.

Cable assemblies with the neutral conductor smaller than the ungrounded conductors shall be so marked.

▶   The maximum demand for a range of 12 kw rating or less may be considered as 8 kw. 8,000 watts divided by 230 volts is approximately 35 amp. Therefore, No. 8 conductors may be used for the range branch circuit. On modern ranges the heating elements of surface units are controlled by five-heat unit switches. The surface-unit heating elements will not draw current from the neutral unless the unit switch is in one of the low-heating positions. This is also true to a greater degree as far as the oven-heating elements are concerned, so that the maximum current in the neutral of the range circuit seldom exceeds 20 amp. Exception 1 permits a smaller-size neutral than the ungrounded conductors, but not smaller than No. 10.

Exception No. 2: Tap Conductors. Tap conductors may be of less capacity than the branch circuit rating provided no tap conductor is of less capacity than the load to be served and provided the rating is not less than 20 amperes for 40 or 50 ampere circuits or 15 amperes for circuits rated less than 40 amperes and only when these tap conductors supply either:

(a) *Individual lampholders or fixtures with taps extending not longer than 18 inches beyond any portion of the lampholder or fixture, except as required in Section 410-65 (b-2); or,*

(b) *Individual outlets with taps not over 18 inches long; or,*

(c) *Infra-red lamp industrial heating appliances.*

(d) *Nonheating leads of snow and de-icing cables and mats.*

▶   **No. 14 wire, not longer than 18 in., may be used to supply an outlet unless the circuit is a 40- or 50-amp branch circuit, in which event the minimum size of the tap conductor must be No. 12.**

Exception No. 3: Fixture Wires and Cords. Fixture wires and cords may be of smaller size, but not less than the size specified in Exception No. 2 of Section 240-5(a).

See Tables 400-9(b) and 402-4.

Exception No. 4: Outlet Devices. Outlet devices may have less carrying capacity than the branch circuit rating, but not less than the types and ratings specified in Sections 210-21(a–c).

Exception No. 5: Where tap conductors supply electric ranges, wall-mounted electric ovens and counter-mounted electric cooking units from 50 ampere branch circuits they shall be of suitable capacity for the load to be served, not less than 20 amperes in rating and no longer than necessary for servicing the appliance.

▶   **This would permit a 50-amp branch circuit to be run to counter-mounted electric cooking units and wall-mounted electric ovens. The tap to each unit must be as short as possible and should be made in a junction box immediately adjacent to each unit. The words "no longer than necessary for servicing the appliance" mean that it should be necessary only to move the unit to one side in order that the splices in the junction box be accessible.**

210-20. Overcurrent Protection.   The rating or setting of overcurrent devices shall conform to the following:

(a) Rating.   Shall not be in excess of the value specified in Section 240-5.

Exception: Tap Conductors and Fixture Wires. Tap conductors, fixture wire and cords as permitted in Section 210-19(c) may be considered as protected by the circuit overcurrent device.

(b) Single Appliance.   Shall not exceed 150 per cent of the rating of the appliance, where the circuit supplies only a single appliance of 10-ampere or more rating.

(c) Continuous Loads.   Where loads other than motor loads will constitute continuous loads see Sections 210-23(b), 220-2 and 240-2.

210-21. Outlet Devices.   Outlet devices shall have a rating not less than the load to be served and shall conform to the following:

(a) Lampholders.   Lampholders when connected to circuits having a rating of over 20 amperes shall be of the heavy-duty type.

▶   **See comments following Section 210-8.**

(b) Receptacles. Receptacles installed on 15 ampere and 20 ampere branch-circuits shall be of the grounding type and they shall be installed in accordance with Section 210-7. Grounding type receptacles which are of a type that rejects nongrounding-type attachment plugs or which are of the locking type may be used for specific purposes or in special locations.

▶ **The 15- and 20-amp grounding-type receptacle requirement applies to all buildings regardless of type of occupancy.**

A single receptacle installed on an individual branch circuit shall have a rating of not less than the rating of the branch circuit.

▶ **See comments following the definitions of "Branch Circuit—Individual" and "Receptacle" in Article 100.**

Grounding-type receptacles shall be used as replacements for existing non-grounding types and shall be connected to a grounding conductor installed in accordance with Section 250-57.

Exception: If it is impractical to reach a source of ground, a nongrounding-type receptacle shall be used.

The installation of grounding type outlets shall not be used as a requirement that all portable equipment be of the grounded type. See Article 250 for requirements for the grounding of portables.

▶ **The purpose here is to make certain that grounding-type receptacles are used and grounded where a ground is available, and nongrounding-type receptacles are used where grounding is impractical so that no one will be deceived as to the availability of a grounding means for appliances.**

In order to prevent the improper interpretation of the intent of this requirement, some explanatory wording was included, which reads, "the installation of grounding type outlets shall not be used as a requirement that all portable equipment be of the grounding type."

There are some appliances, such as a toaster, in which grounding of the enclosure could introduce an additional hazard. For example, where a fork is used to retrieve a small-diameter bread slice or English muffin that cannot easily be lifted out by hand, the possibility is present that the "live" element may be contacted, and if the person and the enclosure are not grounded, no shock or electrical fault will result. If the enclosure is grounded, the possibility of a shock or burn from a fault becomes substantial.

This approach to providing adequate grounding only where needed is based on the recommendations of a technical subcommittee of the National Electrical Code Committee made up of a membership representing all of the major segments of the electrical industry.

One of the major problems in reducing electric-shock accidents is the education of users of electrical equipment to understand the causes of electric shock, the functioning of a grounding conductor, and the need to maintain its integrity. Misuse of electrical equipment is one of the leading causes of electric shock.

It should be recognized that the replacement of an attachment plug or flexible cord on a grounded-type portable appliance necessitates a knowledge of the conductor identification in order to avoid connections that create a shock hazard rather than provide the intended protection.

Section 250-45 indicates the conditions under which cord-connected equipment needs to be grounded.

The obvious purpose is to have grounding-type receptacles conveniently located for general use so that any appliance which needs to be grounded can be grounded by simply connecting the attachment plug to the receptacle. It is realized that there are millions of receptacles in current use which are not of the grounded type and that it will take a long time to arrive at the point where even most of the general-use receptacles on 15- and 20-amp circuits are of the grounded type. In the interim, it will be necessary to use an adapter or other means to achieve grounding of a cord-connected appliance which is supplied from a nongrounded-type receptacle.

Double-insulated tools and appliances, and ground-fault protection for personnel offer a high degree of protection from shock hazards.

Receptacles required in Sections 517-61(d) and 517-62(e) are considered as meeting the requirements of this Section.

When connected to circuits having two or more outlets, receptacles shall conform to the following:

15-amp circuits............Not over 15-amp rating
20-amp circuits..............15- or 20-amp rating
30-amp circuits.....................30-amp rating
40-amp circuits..............40- or 50-amp rating
50-amp circuits.....................50-amp rating

For receptacle rating of cord-connected electric-discharge lighting fixtures see Section 410-14.

Receptacles connected to circuits having different voltages, frequencies or types of current (AC or DC) on the same premises shall be of such design that attachment plugs used on such circuits are not interchangeable.

Grounding type receptacles shall be installed only on circuits of the voltage class and current for which they have been approved.

Receptacles rated at 15 amperes connected to 15 or 20 ampere branch circuits serving two or more outlets shall not supply a total load in excess of 12 amperes for portable and stationary appliances. Receptacles rated at 20 amperes connected to 20 ampere branch circuits serving two or more outlets shall not supply a total load in excess of 16 amperes for portable and stationary appliances.

(c) Capacity of range receptacles may be based on single range loads as computed from Table 220-5.

210-22. Receptacle Outlets Required. Receptacle outlets shall be installed as follows:

(a) **General.** Where portable cords are used, except where the attachment of cords by other means is specifically permitted.

A cord connector that is supported by a permanently connected cord pendant is considered a receptacle outlet.

► Plugging a portable cord into a lampholder is not permissible. See Section 410-41.

(b) Dwelling-Type Occupancies.   In every kitchen, family room, dining room, breakfast room, living room, parlor, library, den, sun room, recreation room and bedroom, receptacle outlets shall be installed so that no point along the floor line in any wall space is more than six feet, measured horizontally, from an outlet in that space, including any wall space two feet wide or greater and the wall space occupied by sliding panels in exterior walls. The wall space afforded by fixed room dividers, such as free-standing bar-type counters, shall be included in the 6-foot measurement.

In kitchen and dining areas a receptacle outlet shall be installed at each counter space wider than 12 inches. Counter top spaces separated by range tops, refrigerators or sinks shall be considered as separate counter top spaces. Receptacles rendered inaccessible by the installation of stationary appliances will not be considered as these required outlets.

Receptacle outlets shall, insofar as practicable, be spaced equal distances apart. Receptacle outlets in floors shall not be counted as part of the required number of receptacle outlets unless located close to the wall. At least one wall receptacle outlet shall be installed in the bathroom adjacent to the basin location.

► In determining the location of a receptacle outlet, the measurement is to be made along the floor line of the wall and is to continue around corners of the room, but is not to extend across doorways, archways, fireplaces, passageways, or other space unsuitable for having a flexible cord extended across it.

Outlets in other sections of the dwelling for special appliances, such as laundry equipment, shall be placed within 6 feet of the intended location of the appliance. At least one outlet shall be installed for the laundry.

► The location of outlets for special appliances within 6 feet of the appliance does not affect the spacing of general-use convenience outlets but merely adds a requirement for special-use outlets.

Figure 210-5 shows two wall sections 9 ft and 3 ft wide extending from the same corner of the room. The receptacle shown located in the wider section of the wall will permit the plugging in of a lamp or appliance located within 6 ft of either side of the receptacle. The same rule would apply to the other wall shown.

Receptacle outlets shall be provided for all wall space within the room except individual isolated sections which are less than 2 ft in width. For example, a wall space 23 in. wide and located between two doors would not need a receptacle outlet.

Sliding panels in exterior walls are counted the same as regular wall space, and a floor-type receptacle can be used to meet the required spacing.

It is considered more desirable and safer to have an outlet at these locations than to run extension cords which may in many instances have to cross a passageway used in connection with the sliding glass door or panel.

The reference to "sliding panels" in exterior walls is not based on whether or not the structure is called a wall, but rather on the less-defined term *wall space*. This was intended to convey the thought of locations wherein

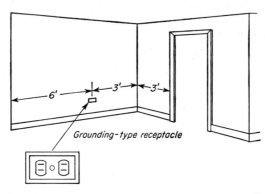

Grounding-type receptacle

FIG. 210-5. Location of the receptacle as shown will permit the plugging in of a lamp or appliance located 6 ft on either side of the receptacle.

portable lamps and other electrical appliances might be used in normal occupancy conditions where these lamps or appliances could be connected by means of the normally supplied 6-ft flexible cord without requiring the use of extension cords.

In residential bathrooms a wall receptacle outlet must be installed adjacent to the wash basin. Fixtures that contain a receptacle are not considered to be a "wall receptacle outlet," and where used in the past, have been highly undesirable and inconvenient for the user.

Receptacles installed behind stationary appliances, such as refrigerators or freezers, are inaccessible to the user, and they are not counted as one of the *required* receptacles in determining the minimum number in a given room.

Exception No. 1: A dwelling unit that is an apartment or living area in a multi-family building where laundry facilities are provided on the premises that are available to all building occupants need not be provided with a laundry receptacle.

Exception No. 2: In other than single family dwellings where laundry facilities are not to be installed or permitted, a laundry receptacle need not be provided.

Exception No. 3: A dwelling that is a unit in a hotel, motel, motor court, or motor hotel, need not be provided with a laundry receptacle.

(c) Guest Rooms in Hotels, Motels, and Similar Occupancies.   These shall have receptacles installed in accordance with Section 210-22(b).

Exception: In rooms of hotels and motels receptacles may be located convenient for the permanent furniture layout.

(d) Ground-Fault Circuit Protection.   For residential occupancies all 120-volt, single-phase, 15- and 20-ampere receptacle outlets installed outdoors shall have approved ground-fault circuit protection for personnel. The effective date of this requirement shall be January 1, 1973.

Such ground-fault circuit protection may be provided for other circuits, locations and occupancies, and where used will provide additional protection against line-to-ground shock hazard. See Section 215-8.

▶ Effective January 1, 1973 all 120-volt, single-phase, 15- and 20-amp receptacle outlets installed outdoors on residential properties must have approved personnel ground-fault circuit protection. Such protection can be installed at the panelboard, or may be built into the receptacle.

With increased use of electrical appliances outdoors, such as lawn mowers, hedge trimmers, portable radios and hi-fi equipment, portable tools and various appliances, shock hazards have been greatly increased in such areas. Ground-fault protection for outdoor receptacles serving such equipment will prevent serious shock hazards and fatalities when faulty equipment is encountered by users.

Because of wide exposure to the earth, outdoor locations represent a severe danger to users of electrical equipment, and the requirement for ground-fault protection of outdoor receptacles is fully justified. For a description of typical ground-fault protection see comments following Section 210-7 and Figs. 210-1, 210-2, 210-3 and 210-4.

The second paragraph of Section 210-22d *permits* the use of ground-fault protection for other circuits, locations, and occupancies. A wider use of such protection should be promoted to reduce line-to-ground shock hazards, which are common with cord- and plug-connected appliances and tools.

(e) Show Windows. At least one receptacle shall be installed directly above a show window for each 12 linear feet or major fraction thereof of show window area, measured horizontally at the base.

▶ The requirement for receptacles in show windows is to accommodate portable signs and similar displays. A show window measuring 32 ft along the horizontal base would require three receptacles (32/12 = 2.66 or 3), spaced not more than 12 linear feet apart directly above the show window.

210-23. Maximum Load. The maximum load shall conform to the following:

(a) Appliances Consisting of Motors and Other Loads. Where a circuit supplies only motor operated appliance loads, Article 430 shall apply. Where a circuit supplies only air conditioning and/or refrigerating equipment, Article 440 shall apply. For other than a portable or stationary appliance, the branch circuit size shall be calculated on the basis of 125 per cent of motor load where the motor is larger than $\frac{1}{8}$ hp plus the sum of the other loads.

(b) Other Loads. The total load shall not exceed the branch circuit rating, and shall not exceed 80 per cent of the rating when load will constitute a continuous load such as store lighting and similar loads. In computing the load of lighting units which employ ballasts, transformers or autotransformers, the load shall be based on the total of the ampere rating of such units and not on the wattage of the lamps.

▶ Where the load of a branch circuit is expected to be continuous, such as in stores, hotel lobbies, and places of public gathering, such loads must not exceed 80 per cent of circuit rating unless Exception No. 1 below is applied. The term "Continuous Load" is defined as three hours or more in Art. 100, Definitions.

Exception No. 1: When the assembly including the overcurrent device protecting the branch circuit is approved for continuous operation at 100 per cent of its rating, the total load may equal the branch circuit rating.

Exception No. 2: Where branch circuits are derated in accordance with Note 8 to Tables 310-12 through 310-15 an additional derating factor for continuous loading shall not apply.

Exception No. 3: Range Loads. See Note 5 of Table 220-5.

210-24. Permissible Loads.   Individual branch circuits may supply any loads. Branch circuits having two or more outlets may supply only loads as follows:

(a) 15- and 20-Ampere Branch Circuits.   Lighting units and/or appliances. The rating of any one portable or stationary appliance shall not exceed 80 per cent of the branch circuit rating. The total rating of fixed appliances shall not exceed 50 per cent of the branch circuit rating when lighting units or portable or stationary appliances are also supplied. Small appliance branch circuits shall supply only the loads stipulated in Section 220-3(b).

▶ *Example:* 50 per cent of a 15-amp branch circuit = 7.5 amp. A room-air-conditioning unit fastened in place, with a rating not in excess of 7.5 amp may be installed on a 15-amp circuit having two or more outlets. Such units may not be installed on one of the small-appliance branch circuits required in Section 220-3*b*.

(b) 30-Ampere Branch Circuits.   Fixed lighting units with heavy duty lampholders in other than dwelling occupancies; or appliances in any occupancy. The rating of any one portable or stationary appliance shall not exceed 24 amperes.

(c) 40-Ampere Branch Circuits.   Fixed lighting units with heavy duty lampholders in other than dwelling occupancies; or fixed cooking appliances; or infrared heating units.

(d) 50-Ampere Branch Circuits.   Fixed lighting units with heavy duty lampholders in other than dwelling occupancies; or fixed cooking appliances; or infrared heating units.

The term "fixed" as used in this Section recognizes cord connections where otherwise permitted.

Fixed outdoor electric snow melting and deicing installations may be supplied by any of the branch circuits described herein provided the circuit supplies no other load.

▶ Except as permitted in Section 660-3 for portable, mobile, and transportable medical X-ray equipment, branch circuits having two or more outlets may supply only the loads specified in each of the above categories. It should be noted that any other circuit is not permitted to have more than one outlet and would be an individual branch circuit.

The special receptacle circuits for the small-appliance load in kitchen, laundry, etc., called for in Section **220-3***b* must be **20**-amp circuits.

The **30**-amp circuit may be used as a special circuit to supply receptacles rated at **30** amp, but cannot be used for the supply of lighting outlets in a dwelling. **30**-amp circuits are suitable for use as lighting circuits in occupancies such as stores, offices and industrial plants.

The principal application of the **40**- and **50**-amp circuits are for use as lighting circuits in large buildings and for range circuits in any occupancy. These circuits are not permitted in dwellings as lighting circuits. They may be used to supply a group of fixed cooking appliances, as in a hotel kitchen, though several circuits of lower capacity would usually be more practical for this purpose. These circuits may also be used to supply wall-mounted ovens and counter-mounted cooking units in a dwelling or elsewhere. When fixed or stationary cooking appliances are installed in other than dwelling occupancies, Table **220-5** does not apply. See Note **3** of Table **220-5**. See comments following "Branch Circuit—Individual" in Art. 100, Definitions.

210-25. Table of Requirements. The requirements for circuits having two or more outlets [other than the receptacle circuits of Section 220-3(b)] as specifically provided for above are summarized in Table 210-25.

Table 210-25
Branch Circuit Requirements

(Type FEP, FEPB, RUW, SA, T, TW, RH, RUH, RHW, RHH, THHN, THW, THWN, and XHHW conductors in raceway or cable.)

CIRCUIT RATING	15 Amp.	20 Amp.	30 Amp.	40 Amp.	50 Amp.
CONDUCTORS: (Min. Size)					
Circuit Wires*	14	12	10	8	6
Taps	14	14	14	12	12
Fixture Wires and Cords	Refer to Section 240-5(a), Exception No. 2				
OVERCURRENT PROTECTION	15 Amp.	20 Amp.	30 Amp.	40 Amp.	50 Amp.
OUTLET DEVICES:					
Lampholders Permitted	Any Type	Any Type	Heavy Duty	Heavy Duty	Heavy Duty
Receptacle Rating**	15 Max. Amp.	15 or 20 Amp.	30 Amp.	40 or 50 Amp.	50 Amp.
MAXIMUM LOAD	15 Amp.	20 Amp.	30 Amp.	40 Amp.	50 Amp.
PERMISSIBLE LOAD	Refer to Section 210-24(a)	Refer to Section 210-24(a)	Refer to Section 210-24(b)	Refer to Section 210-24(c)	Refer to Section 210-24(d)

* These ampacities are for copper conductors where derating is not required. See Tables 310-12 through 310-15.

** For receptacle rating of cord-connected electric-discharge lighting fixtures see Section 410-14.

ARTICLE 215. FEEDERS

215-1. Scope. This Article deals with installation requirements for, and, the size of conductors in the feeders needed to supply power to branch circuits and, the loads as calculated under Article 220.

215-2. Conductor Size. Feeder conductors shall have a current rating not smaller than the feeder load as determined by Section 220-4. A 2-wire feeder supplying two or more 2-wire branch circuits, or a 3-wire feeder supplying more than two 2-wire branch circuits, or two or more 3-wire branch circuits, shall be not smaller than No. 10. Where a feeder carries the total current supplied by the service-entrance conductors, such feeder, for services of No. 6 and smaller, shall be of the same size as the service-entrance conductors.

Where at any time it is found that feeder conductors are, or will be, overloaded, the feeder conductors shall be increased in capacity to accommodate the actual load served.

See Examples Nos. 1 to 7 of Chapter 9.

▶   This Article deals with the determination of the minimum sizes of feeder conductors necessary for safety. Overloading of conductors may result in insulation breakdowns due to overheating; overheating of switches, busbars, and terminals; the blowing of fuses and consequent overfusing; excessive voltage drop and excessive copper losses. Thus the overloading will in many cases create a fire risk and is sure to result in very unsatisfactory service.

The actual maximum load on a feeder depends upon the total load connected to the feeder and the demand factor. If at certain times the entire connected load is in operation, the demand factor is 100 per cent; *i.e.*, the maximum load, or maximum demand, is equal to the total connected load. If the heaviest load ever carried is only one-half the total connected load, the demand factor is 50 per cent. The actual load on a feeder can best be determined by a recording ammeter.

A feeder must not be smaller than No. 10 under any of the following conditions:

Feeder	Branch circuits supplied
Two-wire............	Two or more two-wire circuits
Three-wire..........	Three or more two-wire circuits
Three-wire..........	Two or more three-wire circuits

Nominal Voltage

For uniform application of the provisions of Arts. 210 and 220, a nominal voltage of 115 and 230 volts shall be used in computing the ampere loads on conductors.

There are two steps in the process of predetermining the maximum load

that a feeder will be required to carry: first, a reasonable estimate must be
made of the probable connected load; and, second, a reasonable value for
the demand factor must be assumed.   From a survey of a large number of
buildings, the average connected loads and demand factors have been
ascertained for lighting and small-appliance loads in buildings of the more
common classes of occupancy and these data are presented in Sections
220-2 and 220-4 as minimum requirements.

The load is specified in terms of watts per square foot for certain occupancies. These loads are here referred to as standard loads, because they
are minimum standards established by the Code in order to provide that
the feeders and branch circuits shall have sufficient carrying capacity for
safety.

Feeder loads may consist of lamps, motors, appliances that are not motor-
driven, or of any combination of such loads.

In addition to lighting loads, standard loads are set up for small appliances
in dwelling occupancies. These small appliances are, in general, those that
may be supplied by the 20-amp branch circuits described in Art. 220.

In the case of large appliances and motors that are not incorporated in
appliances, it is assumed that the number of appliances or motors and the
current rating of each are definitely known before the wiring is installed,
and the feeder sizes are to be based upon these definitely known loads,
termed in the Code "specific" loads.

215-3. Voltage Drop.   The size of the conductors for feeders should be such
that the voltage drop for the load as computed by Section 220-4 would not be
more than 3% for power, heating or lighting loads or combinations thereof.
Providing further that the maximum total voltage drop for conductors for
feeders and branch circuits should not exceed 5% over all.

▶   This Section indicates not more than 3% for feeders supplying power,
heating, or lighting loads. It also provides for a maximum drop of 5% for the
conductors between the service entrance equipment and the connected load.
If the feeders have an actual voltage drop of 3%, then only 2% is left for the
branch circuits. If a lower voltage drop is obtained in the feeder, then the
branch circuit has more voltage drop available, provided that the total drop
does not exceed 5%. For any one load, the total voltage drop is made up of the
voltage drop in the one or more feeders plus the voltage drop in the branch
circuit supplying that load.

The values stated in Section **215-3** are recommended values and are not
intended to be enforced as a requirement.

Convenient voltage-drop tables and slide calculators are available from
various electrical equipment manufacturers. Voltage-drop calculations will
vary according to the actual circuit parameters, e.g., AC or DC, single or
multiphase, power-factor, circuit impedance, line reactance, types of enclosures (nonmetallic or metallic), length and size of conductors, and conductor material (copper, copper-clad aluminum, or aluminum).

The following voltage-drop formula can be used to provide fairly accurate results for most applications.

$$VD = \frac{2K \times L \times I}{CM}$$

$$CM = \frac{2K \times L \times I}{VD}$$

where: VD = voltage drop
$\quad\quad CM$ = area of conductor in circular mils (See Table 8, Chapter 9)
$\quad\quad I$ = current in amperes
$\quad\quad L$ = length one way of circuit in feet
$\quad\quad K$ = resistivity of conductor material in ohms per ft per cm-ft = 12
$\quad\quad\quad$ for copper and 18 for aluminum or copper-clad aluminum

This formula is for two-wire AC (when inductance can be neglected) and DC circuits. On three-wire single-phase or DC systems with balanced loads, measure voltage drop across the outside wires (e.g., 230 volts instead of 115 volts). For three-phase, three- or four-wire systems, multiply the voltage drop in the two-wire formula by 0.866.

Example: 230-volt, two-wire heating circuit. Load is 24 amperes. Circuit size is No. 10 AWG copper, and the one-way circuit length is 200 ft.

$$VD = \frac{24 \times 200 \times 24}{10,380} = \frac{115,200}{10,380} = 11$$

An 11-volt drop on a 230-volt circuit is about a 5% drop (11/230 = .0478). No. 8 AWG copper conductors would be needed to reduce the voltage drop to 3% on the branch circuit and allow 2% more on the feeder.

215-4. Overcurrent Protection.   Feeders shall be protected against overcurrent in accordance with the provisions of Article 240.

215-5. Common Neutral Feeder.   A common neutral feeder may be employed for two or three sets of 3-wire feeders, or two sets of 4-wire or 5-wire feeders. When in metal enclosures, all conductors of feeder circuits employing a common neutral feeder shall be contained within the same enclosure as provided in Section 300-20.

▶   The neutral conductor of a feeder is one of the conductors of the circuit and for an a-c system all of the conductors, including the neutral, must be contained in the same metal raceway. With a three-phase four-wire system, a single feeder is often used to supply a combination lighting and motor load. Assume 208Y/120 volts and a load of 200 amp for motors and 100 amp for lighting. The total load on the feeder is 300 amp. None of the motor load will cause current in the neutral conductor. Therefore the maximum current that the neutral will carry is 100 amp, and the neutral conductor can be sized accordingly.

Where a feeder supplies only a lamp load on a three-wire d-c, three-wire single-phase, or four-wire three-phase, the neutral conductor must be of such a size as to carry the maximum current on any one of the outside conductors, except that if this current is in excess of 200 amp the neutral must have a carrying capacity of only 200 amp plus 70 per cent of the excess over 200 amp. There may, however, be no reduction in neutral capacity for any portion of the load supplying electric-discharge lighting. See Section 220-4e and Example 4 in Chap. 9.

Inasmuch as the maximum current in the neutral of a range is generally much less than the current in the ungrounded conductors, the branch-circuit neutral is permitted to have a minimum ampacity of only 70 per cent of that of the ungrounded conductors, except that it shall not be smaller than No. 10.

If two three-wire feeders use a common neutral, the opening of a fuse in one of the supply conductors would force the current of both feeders through the common neutral, so theoretically the neutral should be large enough to carry the total current of both feeders. The likelihood of having this condition with both feeders fully loaded is remote, so the Code permits a demand factor of 70 per cent to that portion of the possible load in excess of 200 amp. Thus, if the maximum possible load were 400 amp, the neutral would need to be only large enough to carry 200 amp plus 70 per cent of 200 amp, or 340 amp.

215-6. Diagram of Feeders.   If required by the authority having jurisdiction, a diagram showing feeder details shall be supplied previous to installation. This diagram should show: Area in square feet; load (before applying demand factors); demand factors selected; computed load (after applying demand factors); and the size of conductors.

215-7. Installation Requirements.   Where a feeder supplies branch circuits in which grounding conductors are required, the feeder shall include or provide a grounding means to which the grounding conductor of the branch circuit shall be connected.

▶   A feeder must include or provide the same means for grounding as is required in Section 210-7 for a branch circuit.

215-8. Ground-Fault Personnel Protection.   Feeders supplying power to 15- and 20-ampere receptacle branch circuits may be protected by a ground-fault circuit-interrupter approved for the purpose in lieu of the provisions of Section 210-22(d).

▶   A ground-fault circuit-interrupter may be located in the feeder and protect all branch circuits connected to that feeder. In such cases the provisions of Section 210-22(d) will be satisfied and additional *downstream* ground-fault protection would not be required. It should be mentioned, however, that downstream ground-fault protection is more desirable than ground-fault protection in the feeder because less equipment will be de-energized when the ground-fault circuit-interrupter opens the supply in response to a line-to-ground fault.

ARTICLE 220. BRANCH CIRCUIT AND FEEDER CALCULATIONS

220-1. Scope. This Article provides the basis for calculating the expected branch circuit and feeder loads and for determining the number of branch circuits required.

220-2. Calculation of Branch Circuit Loads. The load for branch circuits shall be computed in accordance with the provisions of this Section.

The continuous load supplied by a branch circuit shall not exceed 80 per cent of the branch-circuit rating.

Exception No. 1: Where the assembly, including the overcurrent devices protecting the branch circuit and feeder is approved for operation at 100 per cent of their rating, the continuous load supplied by the branch circuit may equal the ampacity of the branch-circuit conductors.

Exception No. 2: Where branch circuits are derated in accordance with Note 8 to Tables 310-12 through 310-15, branch-circuit loads shall not exceed the derated ampacity of the conductors.

(a) General Lighting Load.

(1) In Listed Occupancies. In the occupancies listed in Table 220-2(a), a load of not less than the unit load specified shall be included for each square foot of floor area.

In determining the load on the "watts per square foot" basis, the floor area shall be computed from the outside dimensions of the building, apartment or area involved, and the number of floors; not including open porches, garages in connection with dwelling occupancies, nor unfinished spaces and unused spaces in dwellings unless adaptable for future use.

The unit values herein are based on minimum load conditions and 100 per cent power factor, and may not provide sufficient capacity for the installation contemplated.

In view of the trend toward higher intensity lighting systems and increased loads due to more general use of fixed and portable appliances, each installation should be considered as to the load likely to be imposed and the capacity increased to insure safe operation.

Where electric discharge lighting systems are to be installed, high power-factor type should be used or the conductor capacity may need to be increased.

(2) In Other Occupancies. In other occupancies, a load of not less than the unit load specified in Section 220-2(b) shall be included for each outlet.

(b) Other Loads. For lighting other than general illumination and for appliances other than motors, a load of not less than the unit load specified below shall be included for each outlet. The loads indicated below are based on nominal branch-circuit voltages.

*Outlets supplying specific appliances and other loads . . . .
. . . . .Ampere rating of appliance

Outlets supplying heavy-duty lampholders . . . . .600 volt-amperes

‡Other outlets . . . . .180 volt-amperes

* For motors, see Sections 430-22 amd 430-24.

‡ This provision shall not be applicable to receptacle outlets connected to the circuit specified in Section 220-3(b) nor to receptacle outlets provided for the connection of stationary equipment as provided for in Section 400-3.

(c) Exceptions. The minimum load for outlets specified in Section 220-2(b) shall be modified as follows:

Exception No. 1: Ranges. For household electric ranges, the branch circuit load may be computed in accordance with Table 220-5.

Exception No. 2: Show-Window Lighting. For show-window lighting a load of not less than 200 watts for each linear foot of show-window, measured horizontally along its base, may be allowed in lieu of the specified load per outlet.

Exception No. 3: Multioutlet Assemblies. Where fixed multioutlet assemblies are employed, each five feet or fraction thereof of each separate and continuous length shall be considered as one outlet of not less than 1½ ampere capacity; except in loca-

Table 220-2(a). General Lighting Loads by Occupancies

Type of Occupancy	Unit Load per Sq. Ft. (Watts)
Armories and Auditoriums	1
Banks	5
Barber Shops and Beauty Parlors	3
Churches	1
Clubs	2
Court Rooms	2
*Dwellings (Other Than Hotels)	3
Garages—Commerical (storage)	½
Hospitals	2
*Hotels and Motels, including apartment houses without provisions for cooking by tenants	2
Industrial Commercial (Loft) Buildings	2
Lodge Rooms	1½
Office Buildings	5
Restaurants	2
Schools	3
Stores	3
Warehouses Storage	¼
In any of the above occupancies except single-family dwellings and individual apartments of multifamily dwellings:	
Assembly Halls and Auditoriums	1
Halls, Corridors, Closets	½
Storage Spaces	¼

* All receptacle outlets of 15-ampere or less rating in single-family and multifamily dwellings and in guest rooms of hotels and motels [except those connected to the receptacle circuits specified in Section 220-3(b)] may be considered as outlets for general illumination, and no additional load need be included for such outlets.

tions where a number of appliances are likely to be used simultaneously, when each one foot or fraction thereof shall be considered as an outlet of not less than 1½ amperes. The requirements of this Section are not applicable to dwellings or the guest rooms of hotels.

Exception No. 4. Telephone Exchanges. Shall be waived for manual switchboards and switching frames in telephone exchanges.

The provisions of Section 220-2(b) shall apply to all other receptacle outlets.

(d) Existing Installations.   Additions to existing installations shall conform to the following:

(1) Dwelling Occupancies.   New circuits or extensions to existing circuits may be determined in accordance with Sections 220-2(a or b); except that portions of existing structures not previously wired, or additions to the building structure, either of which exceeds 500 square feet in area, shall be determined in accordance with Section 220-2(a).

(2) Other Than Dwelling Occupancies.   When adding new circuits or extensions to existing circuits in other than dwelling occupancies, the provisions of Section 220-2(a or b) shall apply.

220-3. Branch Circuits Required.   Branch circuits shall be installed as follows:

(a) Lighting and Appliance Circuits.   For lighting, and for appliances, including motor-operated appliances, not specifically provided for in Section 220-3(b), branch circuits shall be provided for a computed load not less than that determined by Section 220-2.

The number of circuits shall be not less than that determined from the total computed load and the capacity of circuits to be used. In every case the number shall be sufficient for the actual load to be served, and the branch circuit loads shall not exceed the maximum loads specified in Section 210-23.

Where the load is computed on a "watts per square foot" basis, the total load, in so far as practical, shall be evenly proportioned among the branch circuits according to their capacity.

When lighting units to be installed operate at other than 100 per cent power factor, see Section 210-23(b) for maximum ampere load permitted on branch circuits.

For general illumination in dwelling occupancies, it is recommended that not less than one branch circuit be installed for each 500 square feet of floor area in addition to the receptacle circuits called for in Section 220-3(b).

See Examples No. 1, 1a, 1b, 1c, and 4, Chapter 9.

(b) Small Appliance Branch Circuits, Dwelling Occupancies.   For the small appliance load, including refrigeration equipment, in kitchen, pantry, family room, dining room, and breakfast room of dwelling occupancies, two or more 20-ampere appliance branch circuits in addition to the branch circuits specified in Section 220-3(a) shall be provided for all receptacle outlets in these rooms, and such circuits shall have no other outlets.

Receptacle outlets supplied by at least two appliance receptacle branch circuits shall be installed in the kitchen.

▶   This provision is intended to require that at least two appliance receptacle circuits be installed in the kitchen. They may be installed on the circuits which also supply the receptacles in the pantry, family room, dining room and breakfast room or on separate appliance circuits. The important point is that there be receptacle outlets on each of two appliance branch circuits in the kitchen.

It should be noted that all of the rooms listed are areas in dwelling occupancies where cooking or food-preparing appliances may be expected to be used.

At least one 20-ampere branch circuit shall be provided for laundry receptacle(s) required in Section 210-22(b).

Receptacle outlets installed solely for the support of and the power supply for electric clocks may be installed on lighting branch circuits.

A three wire 115/230 volt branch circuit is the equivalent of two 115 volt receptacle branch circuits.

(c) Other Circuits.   For specific loads not otherwise provided for in Section 220-3(a or b), branch circuits shall be as required by other sections of the Code.
220-4. Calculation of Feeder Loads.   The computed load of a feeder shall be not less than the sum of all branch circuit loads supplied by the feeder, as determined by Section 220-2, subject to the following provisions:

Exception: When the calculated load for multi-family dwellings under this Section without electric cooking exceeds that calculated under Section 220-9 for the identical load plus electric cooking (based on 8 kw per unit), the lesser of the two loads may be used.

▶   This exception permits equitable load calculation for multi-family dwellings that have gas ranges and electric air-conditioning units. In figuring the load for such units by the standard method specified in Sections **220-4**b through k the net load usually exceeds that permitted in Section **220-9** with the same loads plus "electric" cooking. The exception permits the use of Section 220-9 if the previously mentioned gas ranges are assumed to be "electric" and are based on 8 kw per unit. Then in comparing the *standard* method of calculation to the Section **220-9** *optional* calculation, the lesser of the two loads may be used.

(a) Continuous and Noncontinuous Loads.   When a feeder supplies continuous loads or any combination of continuous and noncontinuous load the rating of the overcurrent devices shall not be less than the noncontinuous load plus 125 per cent of the continuous load.

Exception: When the assembly including the overcurrent devices protecting the feeder(s) are approved for operation at 100 per cent of their rating, the ampacity of the feeder may equal the sum of the continuous load plus the noncontinuous load.
(b) General Lighting.   The demand factors listed in Table 220-4(b) may be applied to that portion of the total branch circuit load computed for general illumination. These demand factors shall not be applied in determining the number of branch circuits for general illumination supplied by the feeders.

See Section 220-4(h and i).
The demand factors herein are based on minimum load conditions and 100 per cent power factor, and in specific instances may not provide sufficient capacity for the installation contemplated. In view of the trend toward higher intensity lighting systems and increased loads due to more general

use of fixed and portable appliances, each installation should be considered as to the load likely to be imposed and the capacity increased to insure safe operation. Where electric discharge lighting systems are to be installed, high power-factor type should be used or the conductor capacity may need to be increased.

Table 220-4(b). Calculation of Feeder Loads by Occupancies

Type of Occupancy	Portion of Lighting Load to which Demand Factor Applies (wattage)	Feeder Demand Factor
Dwellings—other than Hotels	First 3000 or less at	100%
	Next 3001 to 120,000 at	35%
	Remainder over 120,000 at	25%
*Hospitals	First 50,000 or less at	40%
	Remainder over 50,000 at	20%
*Hotels and Motels—including Apartment Houses without provision for cooking by tenants	First 20,000 or less at	50%
	Next 20,001 to 100,000 at	40%
	Remainder over 100,000 at	30%
Warehouses (Storage)	First 12,500 or less at	100%
	Remainder over 12,500 at	50%
All Others	Total Wattage	100%

* The demand factors of this Table shall not apply to the computed load of sub-feeders to areas in hospitals, hotels and motels where entire lighting is likely to be used at one time; as in operating rooms, ballrooms, or dining rooms.

(c) Show-Window Lighting. For show-window lighting, a load of not less than 200 watts shall be included for each linear foot of show window measured horizontally along its base.

▶ In computing the feeder size, a load of not less than 200 watts per linear foot must be included, but branch circuits for show-window lighting need be provided only as required for the actual lighting equipment to be used.

(d) Motors. For motors, a load computed according to the provisions of Sections 430-24, 430-25 and 430-26 shall be included.

(e) Feeder Neutral Load. The feeder neutral load shall be the maximum unbalance of the load determined by Section 220-4. The maximum unbalanced load shall be the maximum connected load between the neutral and any one ungrounded conductor; except that the load thus obtained shall be multiplied by 140 per cent for 5-wire, 2-phase systems. For a feeder supplying household electric ranges, wall-mounted ovens and counter-mounted cooking units, the maximum unbalanced load shall be considered as 70 per cent of the load on the ungrounded conductors, as determined in accordance with Table 220-5. For 3-wire DC or single-phase AC, 4-wire 3-phase and 5-wire 2-phase systems, a further demand-factor of 70 per cent may be applied to that portion of the unbalanced load in excess of 200 amperes. There shall be no reduction of the neutral capacity for that portion of the load which consists of electric discharge lighting.

See Examples 1, 1a, 1b, 1c, 2, 3, 4 and 5, Chapter 9.

(f) Fixed Electrical Space Heating. The computed load of a feeder supplying fixed electrical space heating equipment shall be the total connected load on all branch circuits.

Exception No. 1: Where reduced loading of the conductors results from units operating on duty-cycle, intermittently, or from all units not operating at one time, the authority enforcing this code may grant permission for feeder conductors to be of a capacity less than 100 per cent, provided the conductors are of sufficient capacity for the load so determined.

Exception No. 2: Section 220-4(f) does not apply when feeder capacity is calculated in accordance with the optional methods in Section 220-7 for a single-family dwelling or an individual apartment of a multi-family dwelling and in Section 220-9 for multi-family dwellings.

(g) Noncoincident Load. In adding the branch circuit loads to determine the feeder load, the smaller of two dissimilar loads may be omitted from the total where it is unlikely that both of the loads will be served simultaneously.

(h) Small Appliances. The computed branch circuit load for receptacle outlets in other than dwelling occupancies, for which the allowance is not more than 1½ amperes per outlet, may be included with the general lighting load and subject to the demand factors in Section 220-4(b).

Dwelling Occupancies

The requirements in following Sections 220-4(i) through (l) apply to dwelling type occupancies and are supplemental to the preceding Sections 220-4(a) through (h).

(i) 1. Small Appliances. In single-family dwellings, in individual apartments of multi-family dwellings having provisions for cooking by tenants, and in each hotel suite having a serving pantry, a feeder load of not less than 1500 watts for each two-wire circuit installed as required by Section 220-3(b) shall be included for small appliances (portable appliances supplied from receptacles of 15 or 20 ampere rating) in kitchen, pantry, family room, dining room, and breakfast room. Where the load is subdivided through two or more feeders, the computed load for each shall include not less than 1500 watts for each two-wire circuit for small appliances. These loads may be included with the general lighting load and subject to the demand factors in Section 220-4(b).

2. Laundry Circuit. A feeder load of not less than 1500 watts shall be included for each 2-wire laundry circuit installed as required by Section 220-3(c). This load may be included with the general lighting load and subject to the demand factors in Section 220-4(b).

(j) Electric Ranges. The feeder load for household electric ranges and other cooking appliances, individually rated more than 1¾ kw, may be calculated in accordance with Table 220-5.

In order to provide for possible future installation of ranges of higher ratings, it is recommended that where ranges of less than 8¾ kw ratings or wall-mounted ovens and counter-mounted cooking units are to be installed, the feeder capacity be not less than the maximum demand value specified in Column A of Table 220-5.

Where a number of single-phase ranges are supplied by a 3-phase, 4-wire feeder, the current shall be computed on the basis of the demand of twice the maximum number of ranges connected between any two phase wires.

See Example 7, Chapter 9.

▶   The load for one or more household electric ranges or other household cooking appliances which are individually rated at more than 1.75 kw and are all of the same rating may be calculated in accordance with the following:

For ranges individually rated at 8.75 kw or more but not more than 12 kw, the load on the feeder may be considered as the maximum demand value specified in column A in Table 220-5 for the given number of ranges.

For range, wall-mounted oven, or counter-mounted cooking unit branch circuits, see Note 5 of Table 220-5.

For commercial ranges see Note 3 of Table 220-5.

(k) Fixed Electrical Appliances (Other than Ranges, Clothes Dryers, Air Conditioning Equipment or Space Heating Equipment). Where four or more fixed electrical appliances other than electric ranges, clothes dryers, air conditioning equipment or space heating equipment are connected to the same feeder in a single- or multi-family dwelling, a demand factor of 75 per cent may be applied to the fixed appliance load.

▶   *Example:* 115/230-volt service, single-family dwelling.

Water heater.....	2,500 watts, 230 volts =	11.0 amp
Kitchen disposal.... ½hp	115 volts = 6.5 amp + 25 per cent =	8.1 amp
Furnace motor...... ¼hp	115 volts =	4.6 amp
Attic fan........ ¼hp	115 volts = 4.6 amp	0.0 amp
Water pump.. ½hp	230 volts =	3.7 amp
Load in amperes on each ungrounded leg of feeder		= 27.4 amp

To comply with Section 430-24, 25 per cent is added to the full-load current of the ½-hp 115-volt motor because it is the highest-rated motor in the group. Since it is assumed that the load on the 115/230-volt feeder will be balanced and each of the ¼-hp motors will be connected to different ungrounded conductors, only one is counted in the above calculation. Except for the 115-volt motors, all the other appliance loads are connected to both ungrounded conductors and are automatically balanced. Since there are four or more fixed appliances in addition to a range, clothes dryer, etc., a demand factor of 75 per cent may be applied to the total load of these appliances. 75 per cent of 27.4 = 20.5 amp, which is the current to be added to that computed for the lighting and other loads to determine the total current to be carried by the ungrounded (outside) service-entrance conductors.

The above demand factor may also be applied to similar loads in multi-family dwellings.

(l) Space Heating and Air Cooling. In adding branch circuit loads for space heating and air cooling in dwelling occupancies, the smaller of the two loads may be omitted from the total where it is unlikely that both of the loads will be served simultaneously.

(m) Farm Buildings. Feeders supplying farm buildings (excluding dwellings) or loads consisting of two or more branch circuits shall have minimum capacity computed in accordance with the following table:

Table 220-4(m). Demand Computation for Farm Buildings or Loads

Load in Amperes at 230 Volts	Per Cent of Connected Load
Loads expected to operate without diversity, but not less than 125% full load current of the largest motor and not less than first 60 amperes.	100%
Next 60 Amperes of all other loads	50%
Remainder of other load	25%

Note 1: For services to farm dwellings, see Sections 220-2 through 220-7.
Note 2: For service at main point of delivery to farmstead, see Section 220-4(n).

(n) Farm Services.

(1) Service equipment and service entrance conductors for individual farm buildings (excluding dwellings) shall have minimum capacity computed in accordance with Section 220-4(m).

(2) Minimum capacity of service conductors and service equipment, if any, at the main point of delivery to farms (including dwellings) shall be determined in accordance with the following formula:

100 per cent of the largest demand computed in accordance with Section 220-4(m).

75 per cent of the second largest demand computed in accordance with Section 220-4(m).

65 per cent of the third largest demand computed in accordance with Section 220-4(m).

50 per cent of the demands of remaining loads computed in accordance with Section 220-4(m).

Note 1: Consider as a single computed demand the total of the computed demands of all buildings or loads having the same function.
Note 2: The demand of the farm dwelling, if included in the demands of this formula, should be computed in accordance with Note 1 of Table 220-4(m).

(o) Electric Clothes Dryers. When feeder capacity and circuits are installed for one or more electric clothes dryers, a feeder load of 5,000 watts or the nameplate rating of the appliance, whichever is larger, shall be included for each dryer, subject to the demand factors of Table 220-6(b).

▶   Section 220-4(o) prescribes a *minimum* demand of 5 kw for *120/240-volt* electric clothes dryers in determining branch-circuit and feeder sizes. Feeder demands are subject to Table 220-6(b). This rule is helpful because the ratings of electric clothes dryers are not usually known in the planning stages when feeder calculations must be determined.

Table 220-5. Demand Loads for Household Electric Ranges, Wall-Mounted Ovens, Counter-Mounted Cooking Units and Other Household Cooking Appliances Over 1¾ kw Rating

Column A to be used in all cases except as otherwise permitted in Note 4 below.

NUMBER OF APPLIANCES	Maximum Demand (See Notes) COLUMN A (Not over 12 kw Rating)	Demand Factors (See Note 4) COLUMN B (Less than 3½ kw Rating)	COLUMN C (3½ kw to 8¾ kw Rating)
1	8 kw	80%	80%
2	11 kw	75%	65%
3	14 kw	70%	55%
4	17 kw	66%	50%
5	20 kw	62%	45%
6	21 kw	59%	43%
7	22 kw	56%	40%
8	23 kw	53%	36%
9	24 kw	51%	35%
10	25 kw	49%	34%
11	26 kw	47%	32%
12	27 kw	45%	32%
13	28 kw	43%	32%
14	29 kw	41%	32%
15	30 kw	40%	32%
16	31 kw	39%	28%
17	32 kw	38%	28%
18	33 kw	37%	28%
19	34 kw	36%	28%
20	35 kw	35%	28%
21	36 kw	34%	26%
22	37 kw	33%	26%
23	38 kw	32%	26%
24	39 kw	31%	26%
25	40 kw	30%	26%
26-30	15 kw plus 1 kw for each range	30%	24%
31-40		30%	22%
41-50	25 kw plus ¾ kw for each range	30%	20%
51-60		30%	18%
61 & over		30%	16%

▶   The likelihood of one range having all the surface units and ovens on simultaneously for any length of time is small. As the number of ranges increases, the likelihood of full loading of all of them decreases. This was checked by recording meters for range installations over wide areas and formed the basis for the diversity factors included in the Code.

Note 1. Over 12 kw to 27 kw ranges *all of same rating.* For ranges, individually rated more than 12 kw but not more than 27 kw, the maximum demand in Column A shall be increased 5 per cent for each additional kw of rating or major fraction thereof by which the rating of individual ranges exceeds 12 kw.

Note 2. Over 12 kw to 27 kw ranges *of unequal ratings.* For ranges individually rated more than 12 kw and of different ratings but none exceeding 27 kw an average value of rating shall be calculated by adding together the ratings of all ranges to obtain the total connected load (using 12 kw for any range rated less than 12 kw) and dividing by the total number of ranges; and then the maximum demand in Column A shall be increased 5 per cent for each kw or major fraction thereof by which this average value exceeds 12 kw.

Note 3. This table does not apply to commercial ranges. See Table 220–6(a) for demand factors for commercial cooking equipment.

Note 4. Over 1¾ kw to 8¾ kw. In lieu of the method provided in Column A, loads rated more than 1¾ kw but not more than 8¾ kw may be considered as the sum of the nameplate ratings of all the loads, multiplied by the demand factors specified in Columns B or C for the given number of loads.

Note 5. Branch Circuit Load. Branch circuit load for one range may be computed in accordance with Table 220-5. The branch circuit load for one wall-mounted oven or one counter-mounted cooking unit shall be the nameplate rating of the appliance. The branch circuit load for a counter-mounted cooking unit and not more than two wall-mounted ovens, all supplied from a single branch circuit and located in the same room shall be computed by adding the nameplate ratings of the individual appliances and treating this total as equivalent to one range.

▶   Where a counter-mounted cooking unit and not more than two wall-mounted ovens are installed on one branch circuit in the same room, the last sentence in Note 5 requires that the nameplate ratings of the individual appliances be added together and this total be treated as equivalent to one range.

Example:

1 counter-mounted cooking unit . . . .   **7 kw**
1 wall-mounted oven . . . .   **6 kw**
1 wall-mounted oven . . . .   **5 kw**

   Total . . . .   **18 kw**

From column A, the maximum demand for 1 range of 12 kw rating is 8 kw. 18 kw exceeds 12 kw by 6 (see Note 1).

5 per cent × 6 = 30 per cent (5 per cent increase for each kilowatt in excess of 12).

8 kw × 30 per cent = 2.4 kw increase.

8 kw + 2.4 kw = 10.4 kw-value to be used in selection of branch circuit.

10,400 watts ÷ 230 volts = 45 amp.

Table 220-6(a). Feeder Demand Factors for Commercial Electric Cooking Equipment; including Dishwasher Booster Heaters, Water Heaters, and Other Kitchen Equipment

Number of Units of Equipment	Demand Factors (per cent)
1	100
2	100
3	90
4	80
5	70
6 & over	65

Table 220-6(b). Demand Factors for Household Electric Clothes Dryers

Number of Dryers	Demand Factor (per cent)
1	100
2	100
3	100
4	100
5	80
6	70
7	65
8	60
9	55
10	50
11-13	45
14-19	40
20-24	35
25-29	32.5
30-34	30
35-39	27.5
40 up	25

220-7. Optional Calculation for Single Family Dwelling or Individual Apartment of Multi-Family Dwelling. For a single family dwelling or individual apartment of a multifamily dwelling served by a 115/230 volt, 3-wire, 100 ampere or larger service where the total load is supplied by one feeder or one set of service entrance conductors, the percentages shown in Table 220-7 may be used in lieu of the method of determining feeder (and service) loads detailed in Section 220-4.

All other load shall include 1500 watts for each 20 ampere appliance circuit [Section 220-3(b)]; lighting and portable appliances at 3 watts per square foot; all fixed appliances, (including four or more separately controlled space heating units [see Section 220-4(l)], ranges, wall-mounted ovens and counter-mounted cooking units) at nameplate rated load (kva for motors and other low power-factor loads).

See Examples 1(b) and 1(c) of Chapter 9.

▶   This optional method of calculations is restricted to a single-family residence or an individual apartment of a multi-family dwelling.

Examples of how these calculations are applied are also given in Chap. 9 in Examples 1*b* and *c*.

Table 220-7. Optional Calculation for Single-Family Dwelling or Individual Apartment of Multi-Family Dwelling

LOAD (in kw or kva)	Per Cent of Load
Air conditioning and cooling including heat pump compressors*...........	100%
Central electrical space heating or less than 4 separately controlled electric space heating units...	65%
First 10 kw of all other load..	100%
Remainder of other load...	40%

* Use the larger of the air-conditioning load or the diversified demand of the heating load when applying Section 220-4(l).

The required demand load for each feeder and for the service-entrance conductors shall not be less than the connected load of the space heating or air conditioning, whichever is greater.

220-8. Optional Calculation for Additional Loads in Existing One-Family Dwelling Occupancy.

Load calculations for an existing one-family dwelling occupancy now served by an existing 115/230-volt or 120/208-volt, 3-wire, 60-ampere service may be computed as follows:

Load in kw or kva	Per Cent of Load
First 8 kw of load at	100%
Remainder of load at	40%

Load calculation shall include lighting and portable appliances at 3 watts per square foot; 1500 watts for each 20-ampere appliance circuit; range or wall-mounted oven and counter-mounted cooking unit, and other fixed or stationary appliances, at nameplate rating.

If air conditioning equipment or electric space heating equipment is to be installed the following formula shall be applied to determine if the existing service is of sufficient size.

Air conditioning equipment* 100%
Central electrical space heating* 100%
Less than four separately controlled space heating units* 100%
First 8 KW of all other load 100%
Remainder of all other load 40%

Other loads shall include:
1500 watts for each 20 ampere appliance circuit.
Lighting and portable appliances at 3 watts per sq. ft.
Household range or wall-mounted oven and counter-mounted cooking unit.
All other fixed appliances including four or more separately controlled space heating units, at nameplate rating.

* Use larger connected load of air conditioning and space heating, but not both.

▶   The purpose of Section 220-8 is to permit the maximum possible load on an existing 60-amp service. The calculations are based on numerous load surveys and tests made by local utilities throughout the country. This optional method would seem to be particularly advantageous when *smaller* loads such as window air conditioners or bathroom heaters are to be installed in a dwelling with an existing 60-amp service. If there is an existing electric range, say 12 kw (and no electric water heater), it would not be possible to add any load of substantial rating. The total *gross load* that can be connected to an existing 115/230-volt 60-amp service would be **22,500 watts (X)**, based on the formula: **13,800 watts (230V × 60A) = 8000 + .4(X − 8000)**.

Thus, an existing 1000-sq ft dwelling with a 12-kw electric range, two 20-amp appliance circuits, a 750-watt furnace circuit and a 60-amp service would have a gross load of:

	Watts
1000 sq ft $\times$ 3 watts/sq ft	3,000
Two 20-amp appliance circuits @ 1500 watts each	3,000
One electric range @	12,000
Furnace circuit @	750
Gross watts	18,750

Since the *maximum* permitted gross load is 22,500 watts, an appliance not exceeding *3750 watts* could be added to this existing 60-amp service. However, Section 220-8 lists air conditioning equipment, central space heating, and less than four separately controlled space heating units at 100% demands, and if the appliance to be added is one of these, then it would be limited to *1500 watts*. From the 18,750-watt gross load we have 8000 watts @ 100% demand + [10,750 watts (18,750 − 8000) × .40] or 12,300 watts. Then, 13,800 watts (60A × 230V) − 12,300 watts = *1500 watts* for an appliance listed at 100% demand.

220-9. Optional Calculation for Multi-Family Dwellings.

(a) For multi-family dwellings equipped with electric cooking equipment, and electric space heating or air conditioning or both, the required demand load for each feeder and for the service entrance conductors may be determined by the following method in lieu of the method of determining feeder (and service) loads detailed in Section 220-4, provided that no individual dwelling unit is supplied by more than one feeder. Any house loads on such feeders shall be calculated in accordance with applicable Sections of Article 220 and shall be added to loads as determined by this Section.

(b) The connected load to which the demand factor applies shall include:

(1) 1500 watts for each 2-wire 20 ampere appliance circuit required by Section 220-3(b) and 1500 watts for each 2-wire 20 ampere laundry circuit installed in accordance with Section 220-3(b).

(2) Lighting and portable appliances at 3 watts per square foot.

(3) All fixed or stationary appliances including ranges, wall-mounted ovens, counter-mounted cooking units, and laundry dryers at nameplate rated load (kva for motors and other low power-factor loads).

(4) Water heaters at nameplate rated load, using only the maximum possible at one time in the case of a water heater with interlocked elements.

(5) The larger load of all space heating units or all air conditioning units, per Section 220-4(1).

(c) The required demand load for each feeder and for the service-entrance conductors shall not be less than the connected load of the space heating or air conditioning, whichever is greater.

▶   See Example 4*a* in Chapter 9.

Table 220-9. Demand Factors for Feeders and Service Entrance Conductors for Multi-Family Dwelling

Number of Dwelling Units	Demand Factor (per cent)
3–5	45
6–7	44
8–10	43
11	42
12–13	41
14–15	40
16–17	39
18–20	38
21	37
22–23	36
24–25	35
26–27	34
28–30	33
31	32
32–33	31
34–36	30
37–38	29
39–42	28
43–45	27
46–50	26
51–55	25
56–61	24
62 & over	23

ARTICLE 230. SERVICES

A. General Requirements

230-1. Scope.   The provisions of this Article shall apply to the conductors and equipment for control and protection of services—circuits that conduct electric power from the supply system or plant to the premises to be served.

230-2. Number of Services to a Building or Other Premises Served.   In general, a building or other premises served shall be supplied through only one set of service conductors, except as follows:

Exception No. 1: Fire Pumps. Where a separate service is required for fire pumps.

Exception No. 2: Emergency Lighting. Where a separate service is required for emergency lighting and power purposes.

Exception No. 3: Multiple-Occupancy Buildings.

(a) By special permission, in multiple-occupancy buildings where there is no available space for service equipment accessible to all the occupants.

▶   The granting of special permission is a responsibility of the local authority having jurisdiction as covered by Section 90-7.

(b) Buildings of multiple occupancy may have two or more separate sets of service-entrance conductors which are tapped from one service drop or lateral, or two or more sub-sets of service-entrance conductors may be tapped from a single set of main service-entrance conductors.

DEFINITION: Sub-sets of service-entrance conductors are taps from main service conductors run to service equipment.

Exception No. 4: Capacity Requirements. By special permission, or where capacity requirements are in excess of 3,000 amperes, two or more services may be installed.

Exception No. 5: Buildings of Large Area. By special permission, where more than one service is necessary due to the area over which a single building extends.

Exception No. 6: Different Characteristics or Classes of Use. Where additional services are required for different voltages, frequency, or phase, or different classes of use. Different classes of use could be because of needs for different characteristics, or because of rate schedule as in the case of controlled water heater service.

Exception No. 7: Separate Enclosures. Where two to six service disconnecting means in separate enclosures supply separate loads from one service drop or lateral, one set of service-entrance conductors may supply each or several such service enclosures.

▶   It is generally the rule that a small building be supplied through one service.

Because of the type or size of occupancy or the need for different classes of use, it is sometimes necessary to supply a building with more than one set of service conductors.

Example: Exceptions 1 and 2 recognize additional separate services to supply fire pumps or emergency lighting. Each separate service is limited to not more than six disconnecting means, as described in Section **230-70g**. This would mean that the service could consist of the regular service equipment with six two- or three-pole circuit breakers or switches and separate service equipment to supply a fire pump, emergency lighting, etc.

Exception No. **3** pertains to multiple-occupancy buildings, and 3(a) requires special permission. The provisions of 3(b) permit two or more sub-sets of service-entrance conductors to be tapped from a single set of main service-entrance, and this rule should be coordinated with Section **230-70**(b).

Exception No. **4** allows two or more services without special permission where a calculated service load exceeds **3000** amp. For lesser loads special permission is required to install more than one service.

Exception No. **5** requires special permission to install more than one service to buildings of *large area*. Examples of large-area buildings are high-rise buildings, shopping centers, and major industrial plants. In granting special permission the authority having jurisdiction must examine the availability of utility supplies for a given building, load concentrations within the building, and the ability of the utility to supply more than one service. Any of the special permission clauses in the exceptions in Section **230-2** require close cooperation and consultation between the authority having jurisdiction and the serving utility.

Exception No. **6** pertains to different classes of service some of which are described in Figs. **230-2** and **230-4** and in the comments on Section **230-21**.

Exception No. **7** permits two to six disconnecting means to be supplied from a single service drop or lateral where each disconnecting means supplies separate loads. Examples would be services to multi-family dwellings where six 400-amp service entrances could be used in lieu of a single main 2,400-amp entrance. Another application would be in a single-occupancy building where up to six subdivided loads can extend from a single drop or lateral, and in such cases, doughnut-type CT's would be installed at the service drop where single metering is required. This same approach can be used in subdividing service entrances into smaller load blocks to avoid the use of the equipment ground-fault circuit protection indicated in Section **230-95**. The real importance of this rule is to avoid "paralleling" conductors with large-capacity services where this is desired. Another benefit concerns services added to an existing installation, and would allow a new additional service entrance in many instances without replacing the original one.

230-3. Supply to a Building from Another.   The service conductors supplying each building or structure shall not pass through the inside of another building unless these buildings are under single occupancy or management. See Section 230-45.

B. Insulation and Size of Service Conductors

230-4. Insulation of Service Conductors.   Service conductors shall normally withstand exposure to atmospheric and other conditions of use without detrimental leakage of current to adjacent conductors, objects, or the ground.

For Service Drops—See Section 230-22.
For Service Entrance Conductors—See Section 230-40.
For Underground Services—See Section 230-30.

▶   It is not necessary to insulate the neutral conductor, because it is solidly tied to the service conduit, tubing, or cable armor at the service-equipment enclosure.

230-5. Size of Service Conductors.   Service conductors shall have adequate ampacity to safely conduct the current for the loads supplied without a temperature rise detrimental to the insulation or covering of the conductors, and shall have adequate mechanical strength.

Minimum sizes are given in the following references:
For Service Drops—Section 230-23.
For Service Entrance Conductors—Section 230-41.
For Underground Service Conductors—Section 230-31.
For Farmstead Service Conductors—See Section 220-4(n).

C. Service Drops

230-21. Number of Drops.   No building shall be supplied through more than one service drop, except for the purposes listed in Section 230-2.

▶   A building as defined in Art. **100** is a structure which stands alone or is cut off from adjoining structures by fire walls with all openings therein protected by approved fire doors. A building divided into four units by such fire walls may be supplied by four separate service drops, but a similar building without the fire walls may be supplied by only one service drop except as permitted in Section **230-2**.

A commercial building may be a single building but may be occupied by two or more tenants whose quarters are separate, in which case it might be undesirable to supply the building through one service drop. Under these conditions special permission may be given to install more than one service drop.

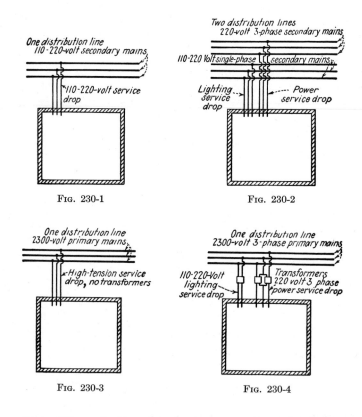

Fɪɢ. 230-1   Fɪɢ. 230-2

Fɪɢ. 230-3   Fɪɢ. 230-4

Some of the applications of service drops are shown in Figs. **230-1** through **230-4**. A secondary lighting main and a secondary power main run on the same pole line should be considered as different classes of use, so conductors from each main may be carried into one building. If the distribution line consists only of a high-voltage primary as in **Fig. 230-4,** two service drops, one for light and one for power, may be run to one building if the lighting service drop and the power service drop are supplied through different transformers.

230-22. Service Drop Conductors.

(a) Cable.   Individual conductors of multi-conductor cable shall be insulated or covered with thermoplastic, rubber or other vulcanizable material.

Exception: A grounded conductor may be bare.

(b)   All open, individual conductors shall be insulated or covered.

230-23. Minimum Size of Service Drop Conductors.   Conductors shall have sufficient ampacity to carry the load. They shall have adequate mechanical strength and shall not be smaller than No. 8 copper or No 6 aluminum.

Exception: For installations to supply only limited loads of a single branch circuit such as small polyphase power, controlled water heaters and the like, they shall not be smaller than No. 12 hard drawn copper or equivalent.

Overhead conductors to a building or other structure from another building or other structure (such as a pole) on which a meter or disconnecting means is installed shall be considered as a service drop and installed accordingly.

The grounded conductor shall not be less than the minimum size required by Section 250-23(b).

Conductors having extruded covering used for service drops have the same ampacities as covered conductors listed in Tables 310-13 and 310-15.

230-24. Clearance of Service Drops.   Service drop conductors shall not be readily accessible and when not in excess of 600 volts, shall conform to the following:

(a) Clearance Over Roof.   Conductors shall have a clearance of not less than 8 ft. from the highest point of roofs over which they pass with the following exceptions:

Exception No. 1: Where the voltage between conductors does not exceed 300 and the roof has a slope of not less than 4 inches in 12 inches the clearance may be not less than 3 feet.

▶   The intent of Exception 1 is that where the roof has a slope greater than 4 in. in 12 in. it is considered difficult to walk upon and the height of conductors could then be less than 8 ft from the highest point over which they pass but in no case less than 3 ft except as permitted in Exception 2. See Figs. 230-5 and 230-6.

Exception No. 2: Service drop conductors of 300 volts or less which do not pass over other than a maximum of 4 feet of the overhang portion of the roof for the purpose of terminating at a (through-the-roof) service raceway or approved support may be maintained at a minimum of 18 inches from any portion of the roof over which they pass.

▶   See Figs. 230-5 and 230-6.

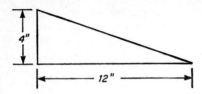

FIG. 230-5. Roof having a slope of not less than 4 in. in 12 in.

(b) Clearance from Ground.   Service drop conductors when not in excess of 600 volts, shall have the following minimum clearance from ground.

    10 feet—above finished grade, sidewalks or from any platform or projection from which they might be reached;

    12 feet—over residential driveways and commercial areas such as parking lots and drive-in establishments not subject to truck traffic;

    15 feet—over commercial areas, parking lots, agricultural or other areas subject to truck traffic;

    18 feet—over public streets, alleys, roads and driveways on other than residential property.

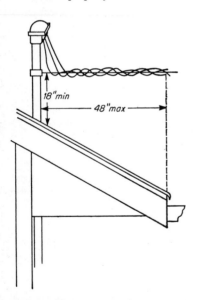

FIG. 230-6. Service-drop conductors passing over the overhang portion of the roof. Section 230-24, Exception No. 2.

(c) Clearance from Building Openings.   Conductors shall have a clearance of not less than 36 inches from windows, doors, porches, fire escapes, or similar locations.

Conductors run above the top level of a window are considered out of reach from that window. For clearance of conductors of over 600 volts see National Electrical Safety Code ANSI C2-1960. (Available from Superintendent of Documents, Government Printing Office, Washington, D.C. 20401.)

▶   The intent here is to provide the clearance specified and to prevent mechanical damage to and accidental contact with service conductors.

230-25. Supports Over Buildings.   Where practicable, conductors passing over a building shall be supported on structures which are independent of the building. Where necessary to attach conductors to roof they shall be supported on substantial structures.

230-26. Point of Attachment.   The point of attachment of a service drop to a building or other structure shall be not less than 10 feet above finished grade and shall be at a height to permit the minimum clearance requirements of Section 230-24.

In the event a mast type riser is required to attain the required height, it shall be of such construction and so supported that it will withstand the strain imposed by the service drop. Raceway fittings shall be of a type approved for the purpose.

▶   The clearances required in Sections **230-24** through **230-26** are based on safety-to-life considerations in that wires are required to be kept a reasonable distance from people who stand, reach, walk, or drive under service-drop conductors.

230-27. Means of Attachment.   Multiple-conductor cables used for service drops shall be attached to buildings or other structures by fittings approved for the purpose. Open conductors shall be attached to noncombustible, nonabsorptive insulators securely attached to the building or other structure or by fittings approved for the purpose.

▶   See Section **230-50** for support of cable.

D. Underground Services

230-30. Insulation.   Service lateral conductors shall be insulated for the applied voltage.

Exception: A grounded conductor may be:

(1) Bare copper used in a raceway.

(2) Bare copper for direct burial where bare copper is judged to be suitable for the soil conditions.

(3) Bare copper for direct burial without regard to soil conditions where part of an approved cable assembly with a moisture- and fungus-resistant outer covering.

(4) Aluminum or copper-clad aluminum without individual insulation or covering used in a raceway or for direct burial when:

a. Part of an approved cable assembly with a moisture- and fungus-resistant outer covering, and when:

b. The nominal voltage to ground of any conductor is not over 300 volts.

▶   Section **230-30** Exception concerns the use of aluminum, copper-clad aluminum, and bare copper conductors where used as grounded conductors in underground and direct-burial situations. The restriction for limiting the use of uninsulated grounded conductors to 300 volts to ground or less applies only to aluminum or copper-clad aluminum conductors.

230-31. Size of Underground Service Conductors.

(a) Size of Underground Service Lateral. Conductors shall have sufficient ampacity to carry the load. They shall not be smaller than No. 8 copper or No. 6 aluminum or copper-clad aluminum. The grounded conductor shall be not less than the minimum size required by Section 250-23(b).

Exception: For installations to supply only limited loads of a single branch circuit such as small polyphase power, controlled water heaters and the like, they shall not be smaller than No. 12 copper or No. 10 aluminum or copper-clad aluminum.

(b) Size of Underground Service Entrance Conductors. Same as required for overhead service entrance conductors. See Section 230-41.

(c) Number of Service Laterals. No building or other structure shall be supplied through more than one service lateral, except for the purposes listed in Section 230-2.

230-32. Protection Against Damage.

(a) In the Ground. Underground service conductors shall be protected against physical damage by being installed:

(1) in duct;

(2) in rigid metal conduit or electrical metallic tubing made of a material suitable for the condition, or provided with corrosion protection suitable for the condition;

(3) in rigid nonmetallic conduit if installed in accordance with Sections 347-2 and 347-3.

(4) by direct burial in the earth. Conductors buried directly in the earth, whether as single conductors or as multi-conductor cable, shall be of a type approved for the purpose. Where necessary to prevent physical damage to the conductors from rocks, slate, etc., or from vehicular traffic, etc., direct buried conductors shall be provided with supplementary protection, such as sand, sand and suitable running boards, suitable sleeves, or other approved means. Conductors under a building shall be in a raceway that is extended to the outer perimeter of the building.

(5) other approved means.

▶ Type USE cable is approved for underground installation including burial directly in the earth.

(b) On Poles. Where underground service conductors are carried up a pole the mechanical protection shall be installed to a point at least 8 feet above the ground. Such mechanical protection may be provided by the use of approved cable, pipe, or other approved means.

▶ Where a direct-burial cable is carried up a pole, a conduit or steel-pipe "sleeve" may be used to protect the cable from physical damage.

(c) Where Entering Building. Underground service conductors shall have mechanical protection in the form of rigid or flexible conduit, electrical metallic tubing, auxiliary gutters, the metal tape of an approved service cable, or other approved means. The mechanical protection shall extend to the enclosure for the service equipment unless the service switch is installed on a switchboard, in which case a bushing shall be provided which, except where lead-covered conductors are used, shall be of the insulating type.

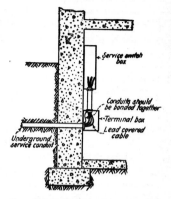

▶ An underground service conduit usually terminates at the inside of the building wall unless the building has no basement. A metal conduit or a service cable may terminate at this point or may be run directly to the service equipment, as shown in Fig. 230-7.

From the terminal box, the conductors are run to the service equipment

Fig. 230-7. Terminal box used at the end of an underground service conduit.

in rigid or flexible metal conduit or electrical metallic tubing or in an auxiliary gutter, and may terminate at any suitable point behind the switchboard. If the conductors are lead-covered, the end of the conduit or tubing is to be fitted with an ordinary bushing. If the conductors are not lead-covered, an insulating bushing must be used.

230-33. Raceway Seal. Where a service raceway or duct enters from an underground distribution system, the end within the building shall be sealed with suitable compound so as to prevent the entrance of moisture or gases. Spare or unused ducts shall also be sealed.

▶ This is not a requirement for a sealing fitting but for merely a putty-like compound stuffed into the end of the raceway.

E. Service-Entrance Conductors

230-40. Insulation of Service-Entrance Conductors.

(a) Service-entrance conductors entering buildings or other structures shall be insulated. Where only on the exterior of buildings or other structures the conductors shall be insulated or covered.

Exception: A grounded conductor may be:

(1) Bare copper used in a raceway.

(2) Bare copper for direct burial where bare copper is judged to be suitable for the soil conditions.

(3) Bare copper for direct burial without regard to soil conditions where part of an approved cable assembly with a moisture- and fungus-resistant outer covering.

(4) Aluminum or copper-clad aluminum without individual insulation or covering used in a raceway or for direct burial when:

a. Part of an approved cable assembly with a moisture- and fungus-resistant outer covering, and when:

b. The nominal voltage to ground of any conductor is not over 300 volts.

(b) Open individual conductors which enter the building or other structure shall be rubber-covered or thermoplastic-covered.

230-41. Size of Service-Entrance Conductors, Overhead System and Underground System. Service-entrance conductors shall have sufficient ampacity to carry the load as determined by Article 220 and in accordance with Tables 310-12, 310-13, 310-14, 310-15. Service entrance conductors shall not be smaller than No. 6 except:

Exception No. 1: For single family residences with an initial load of 10 kw or more computed in accordance with Article 220, or if the initial installation has more than five 2-wire branch circuits, the service-entrance conductors shall have an ampacity of not less than 100 amperes 3-wire.

It is recommended that a minimum of 100 ampere 3-wire service be provided for all individual residences.

Exception No. 2: For installations consisting of not more than two 2-wire branch circuits they shall not be smaller than No. 8.

Exception No. 3: By special permission due to limitations of supply source or load requirements they shall not be smaller than No. 8.

Exception No. 4: For installations to supply only limited loads of a single branch circuit, such as small polyphase power, controlled water heaters and the like, they shall not be smaller than the conductors of the branch circuit and in no case smaller than No. 12.

Exception No. 5: The grounded (neutral) conductor shall have an ampacity in conformity with Section 220-4(e), and shall not be less than the minimum size required by Section 250-23(b).

230-42. Service-Entrance Conductors without Splice. Service-entrance conductors shall be without splice except as follows:

Exception No. 1: Clamped or bolted connections in a meter enclosure are permitted.

Exception No. 2: Taps to main service conductors are permitted as provided in Section 230-2 Exception No. 3(b) or to individual sets of service equipment as provided in Section 230-70(g).

► **See Fig. 230-16.**

Exception No. 3: At a properly enclosed junction point where an underground wiring method is changed to another type of wiring method.

► **See Fig. 230-7.**

Exception No. 4: A connection is permitted where service conductors are extended from a service drop to an outside meter location and returned to connect to the service-entrance conductors of an existing installation.

▶   Where the meter is placed on the line side of the service equipment, splices are necessary in order to connect the meter, and the forms of connections used in the meter base shown in Fig. 230-17 are satisfactory.

Where an underground service conduit terminates in a terminal box as shown in Fig. 230-7, the service conductors may be spliced in the box, provided the run is continued in a different type of raceway or as a suitable type of cable.

Figure 230-8 shows a form of construction sometimes employed where the inside meter of an existing installation is removed and an outdoor meter is installed. New service-entrance conductors are connected to the service drop and are carried down to a meter fitting in raceway or cable. From the meter, the outside service conductors return in the raceway or cable and are spliced to the old service-entrance conductors. These splices are permitted by Exception No. 4.

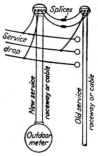

230-43. Other Conductors in Service Raceway. Conductors other than service conductors, grounding conductors, or control conductors from time switches having overcurrent protection, shall not be installed in the same service raceway or service entrance cable.

Fig. 230-8. Splices in service-entrance conductors where an outdoor meter is installed in place of an indoor meter for an existing installation.

▶   See Fig. 230-9.

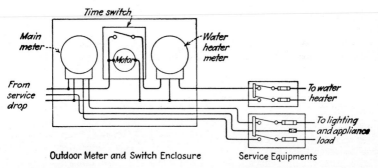

Fig. 230-9. A time switch with its control circuit connected on the supply side of the service equipment.

F. Installation of Service-Entrance Conductors

230-44. Wiring Methods. Service-entrance conductors extending along the exterior, or entering buildings or other structures may be installed as follows:

(a) As separate conductors, in cables approved for the purpose, cablebus, or enclosed in rigid conduit;

(b) For circuits not exceeding 600 volts the conductors may be installed in electrical metallic tubing, wireways, auxiliary gutters, or busways.

▶   Paragraph *a* concerns services at all voltages (see Section **230-101***b* also), while paragraph *b* concerns services **600** volts or less.

230-45. Conductor Considered Outside Building. Conductors placed under at least two inches of concrete beneath a building, or conductors within a building in conduit or duct and enclosed by concrete or brick not less than two inches thick shall be considered outside the building.

230-46. Mechanical Protection. Individual open conductors or cables other than approved service-entrance cables, shall not be installed within 8 feet of the ground or where exposed to physical damage. Service-entrance cables, where liable to contact with awnings, shutters, swinging signs, installed in exposed places in driveways, near coal chutes or otherwise exposed to physical damage, shall be of the protected type or be protected by conduit, electrical metallic tubing or other approved means.

230-47. Individual Open Conductors Exposed to Weather. Individual open conductors exposed to weather shall be supported on insulators, racks, brackets, or other means, placed at intervals not exceeding 9 feet and separating the conductors at least 6 inches from each other and 2 inches from the surface wired over; or at intervals not exceeding 15 feet if they maintain the conductors at least 12 inches apart. For 300 volts or less, conductors may have a separation of not less than 3 inches where supports are placed at intervals not exceeding 4½ feet and conductors are not less than 2 inches from the surface wired over.

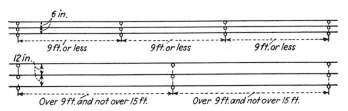

Fig. 230-10. Either of the above arrangements may be employed in supporting outside service conductors exposed to the weather.

230-48. Individual Open Conductors Not Exposed to Weather. Individual open conductors not exposed to the weather may be supported on glass or porcelain knobs placed at intervals not exceeding 4½ feet and maintaining the conductors at least one inch from the surface wired over and a separation of at least 2½ inches between conductors.

230-49. Individual Conductors Entering Buildings or Other Structures. Where individual open conductors enter a building or other structure, they shall enter through roof bushings or enter through the wall in an upward slant through individual, noncombustible, nonabsorptive, insulating tubes. Drip loops shall be formed on the conductors before they enter the tubes.

230-50. Service Cables.
(a) **Approved Service-Entrance Cables.** Approved service-entrance cables shall

be supported by straps or other approved means within 12 inches of every service head, gooseneck, or connection to a raceway or enclosure and at intervals not exceeding 4½ feet.

(b) Other Cables. Cables that are not approved for mounting in contact with a building or other structure shall be mounted on insulating supports installed at intervals not exceeding 15 feet and in a manner that will maintain a clearance of not less than 2 inches from the surface over which they pass.

230-51. Connections at Service Head.

(a) Service raceways shall be equipped with a raintight service head.

(b) Service cables, unless continuous from pole to service equipment or meter, shall be either:

(1) equipped with a raintight service head or

(2) formed in a gooseneck, taped and painted or taped with a self-sealing weather-resistant thermoplastic.

(c) Service heads and goosenecks in service-entrance cables shall be located above the point of attachment of the service-drop conductors to the building or other structure.

Exception: Where it is impracticable to locate the service head above the point of attachment, the service head may be located not farther than twenty-four inches from the point of attachment.

(d) Service cables shall be held securely in place by connection to service-drop conductors below the gooseneck or by a fitting approved for the purpose.

(e) Service heads shall have conductors of opposite polarity brought out through separately bushed holes.

(f) Drip loops shall be formed on individual conductors. To prevent the entrance of moisture, service-entrance conductors shall be connected to the service-drop conductors either:

(1) below the level of the service head, or

(2) below the level of the termination of the service-entrance cable sheath.

(g) Service-drop conductors and service-entrance conductors shall be so arranged that water will not enter service raceway or equipment.

▶   See Fig. 370-1 for service head.

Where no service head is used at the upper end of a service cable, the cable should be bent over so that the individual conductors leaving the cable will extend in a downward direction and the end of the cable should be carefully taped and painted to exclude moisture.

Figure 230-11 shows a service cable

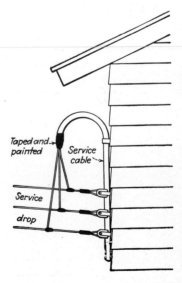

Fig. 230-11. Service-entrance cable terminating in a gooseneck.

terminating in a gooseneck above the service drop. The connections to the conductors of the service drop tend to hold the gooseneck in shape.

By using the fitting shown in Fig. 230-12 the gooseneck is held in place securely without depending upon the connections to the service drop conductors.

Where the pole connection is higher than the connection of the service-entrance conductors at the service head, the connections at the pole should be made in such a manner that moisture will not enter the conductor.

In many cases the connection at the utility pole is higher than the connection at the building. Any stranded service-drop conductors act as a hose and the moisture is forced up through the service-entrance conductors by this head pressure and down into the meter or service equipment.

230-52. Raceways to Drain.   Where exposed to the weather, raceways enclosing service-entrance conductors shall be raintight and arranged to drain. Where embedded in masonry, raceways shall be arranged to drain.

Fig. 230-12. Fitting for use with service-entrance cable. (*Kwik-on Co.*)

▶   It is difficult to keep water vapor from entering metal raceways, but most of the trouble from this source can be prevented by avoiding low points in the raceway where water can collect.

230-53. Termination at Service Equipment.   Any service raceway or cable shall terminate at the inner end in a box, cabinet, or equivalent fitting that effectively encloses all live metal parts.

Exception: Where the service disconnecting means is mounted on a switchboard having exposed bus-bars on the back, a raceway may terminate at a bushing.

G. Service Equipment

230-60. Hazardous Locations.   Service equipment installed in hazardous locations shall comply with the requirements of Articles 500 through 517.

230-61. Service Equipment Grouped.   Where supplied at the same side of the building by more than one overhead service drop or more than one set of underground service conductors, the service equipment, except for services as permitted in Section 230-2, shall be grouped and equipment marked to indicate the load it serves.

The one or more additional service disconnecting means for fire pumps or for emergency services shall be installed sufficiently remote from the one to six service disconnecting means for normal services to minimize the possibility of simultaneous interruption of supply.

See Sections 700-9 and 700-10 for emergency system services.

▶   The special or emergency service equipments permitted by Section 230-21 do not have to be grouped with the regular service equipment. It should also be noted that Section **700-9** requires emergency services to be widely separated from the other services.

The service equipment should be identified on the enclosures by such designations as "Light—115/230 Volts" and "Power—220 Volts."

H. Grounding and Guarding

230-62. Guarding. Live parts of service equipment shall be enclosed so that they will not be exposed to accidental contact, unless mounted on a switchboard, panelboard or controller accessible to qualified persons only and located in a room or enclosure free from easily ignitible material. Such an enclosure shall be provided with means for locking or sealing doors giving access to live parts.

230-63. Grounding and Bonding. Service equipment shall be grounded as follows:

(a) Equipment. The enclosure for service equipment shall be grounded in the manner specified in Article 250, unless (1) the voltage does not exceed 150 volts to ground and such enclosures are (2) isolated from conducting surfaces, and (3) unexposed to contact by persons or materials that may also be in contact with other conducting surfaces.

(b) Raceways and Cable Armor. Service raceways, cable armor and the metal sheath of service cables, shall be grounded. Conduit and metal pipe from underground supply shall be considered sufficiently grounded where containing lead-sheathed cable bonded to a continuous underground lead-sheathed cable system.

(c) Flexible Metal Conduit. Where a rigid metal raceway containing service conductors is interrupted by flexible metal conduit, whether between two sections of the raceway or between the end of the raceway and the service-equipment enclosure, the sections of raceway and the equipment enclosure so interrupted

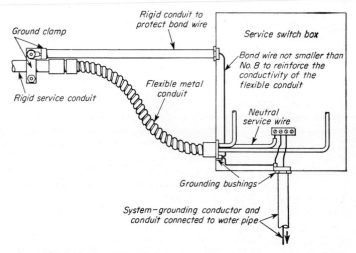

FIG. 230-13. Illustration of bonding around a short length of flexible conduit in a service run as described in Section 230-63c.

shall be bonded together by an equipment bonding jumper sized in accordance with Table 250-94(a) and attached by means of pressure connectors, clamps, or other approved means. The bonding jumper and attachment means shall be protected from physical damage.

J. Disconnecting Means

230-70. General.

(a) Disconnection from Service Conductors.   Means shall be provided for disconnecting all conductors in the building or other structure from the service entrance conductors.

(b) Location.   The disconnecting means shall be located at a readily accessible point nearest to the entrance of the conductors, either inside or outside the building or structure. Sufficient access and working space shall be provided about the disconnecting means.

In a multiple occupancy building, each occupant shall have access to his disconnecting means. A multiple occupancy building having individual occupancy above the second floor shall have service equipment grouped in a common accessible place, the disconnecting means consisting of not more than six switches or six circuit breakers. Multiple occupancy buildings that do not have individual occupancy above the second floor may have service conductors run to each occupancy in accordance with Section 230-2, Exception No. 3 and each such service may have not more than six switches or circuit breakers.

▶   The first paragraph states that the disconnecting means shall be located at a readily accessible point nearest to where the service conductors enter the building. No specific distance is stated, and approval of a specific installation is based on many existing factors and is a responsibility of the local inspection authority, as indicated in Section 90-7 of the Code.

The reason for keeping service conductors to a minimum length is that they do not have overcurrent protection and thus could become badly overheated in the event of an electrical breakdown or fault. The interior of the building presents more readily ignitible material than the outside, greater delay in the detecting of a fire, and greater life hazard to persons within the building in the event of a fire. For these and other reasons, the run of service conductors within the building should be kept to a minimum. See comments following Section 230-90a.

In the second paragraph, "individual occupancy" means any space such as an office or living apartment that is independent of any other occupancy in the building. Generally each such space is supplied through a separate meter.

Each apartment intended for use as living quarters by one family is an individual occupancy. Each apartment might be supplied through a separate meter, or all might be supplied through one meter.

It should be noted that the access for each occupant as required by paragraph b would not apply where the building was under the management of a building superintendent or the equivalent and where electrical service and maintenance was furnished. See Section 240-16d, Exception.

Where there *is* individual occupancy above the second floor, the dis-

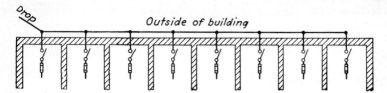

FIG. 230-14. Multiple-occupancy building having eight occupancies but no individual occupancy above the second floor. The service equipment for each occupancy may consist of any number of fusible switches or circuit breakers not exceeding six.

connecting means shall be located in a commonly accessible place, as shown in Fig. 230-15.

Where there is *no* individual occupancy above the second floor, a separate set of service-entrance conductors may be run to each occupancy, as shown in Fig. 230-14.

In order to comply with Section **230-70b**, the conductors should either be run on the outside of the building to each occupancy or, if run inside the building, be encased in 2 in. of concrete or masonry in accordance with Section **230-45**. In either case the service equipment should be located "nearest to the entrance of the conductors inside the building," and each occupant would have access to his disconnecting means.

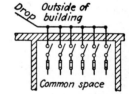

FIG. 230-15. Multiple-oc-cupancy building having one or more individual occupancies above the second floor.

Any desired number of sets of service-entrance conductors may be tapped from the service drop or lateral, or two or more subsets of service-entrance conductors may be tapped from a single set of main service conductors.

(c) Approval.   The disconnecting means shall be of a type approved for service equipment and for prevailing conditions.

(d) Types Permitted.   The disconnecting means for ungrounded conductors shall consist of either:

(1)   A manually operable switch or circuit breaker equipped with a handle or other suitable operating means positively identified and marked for mechanical operation by hand.

(2)   An electrically operated switch or circuit breaker provided the switch or circuit breaker can be opened by hand in event of a failure of the power supply and the open and closed positions are clearly indicated to the operator.

(e) Externally Operable.   An enclosed service disconnecting means shall be externally operable without exposing the operator to contact with live parts.

Exception: An electrically operated switch or circuit breaker need not be capable of being externally operable by hand to the closed position.

▶   If a switch can be opened and closed without exposing the operator to contact with live parts, it is an externally operable switch, even though access to the switch handle requires opening the door of a cabinet. The exception pertains to electrically operated switches and circuit breakers.

(f) Indicating.   The disconnecting means shall plainly indicate whether it is in the open or closed position.

(g) Switch and Circuit Breaker.   The service disconnecting means for each set or for each sub-set of service-entrance conductors shall consist of not more than six switches or six circuit breakers mounted in a single enclosure, grouped together in separate enclosures, or in or on a switchboard. Where two to six service disconnects are installed at one service location, each such disconnecting device shall be permanently marked to identify it as a service disconnecting means.

Two or three single-pole switches or breakers, capable of individual operation, may be installed on multiwire circuits, one pole for each ungrounded conductor, as one multipole disconnect provided they are equipped with "handle ties" or a "master handle" to disconnect all conductors of the service with no more than six operations of the hand.

See Section 384-16(a) for service equipment in panelboards.

▶   The intent in paragraph *g* is to limit to six operations of the hand the disconnection of all conductors of the service. The limitation is applicable to all of the service disconnecting means located in one place or "grouped" as required in Section 230-61. It does not include the "separate" services for fire pumps, emergency lighting, etc., which are recognized in Section 230-2 as being separate services for specific purposes.

See comments following Section 200-5. The cross reference to Section 384-16*a* calls attention to the requirement of over 20 amp rating for service disconnect means and overcurrent protection.

(h) Simultaneous Openings.   Each disconnecting means shall simultaneously disconnect all ungrounded conductors.

See Section 200-5(a).

(i) Disconnection of Grounded Conductor.   Where the switch or circuit breaker does not interrupt the grounded conductor, other means shall be provided in the service cabinet or on the switchboard for disconnecting the grounded conductor from the interior wiring.

▶   In paragraph *i* the other means for disconnecting the grounded conductor from the interior wiring may be a screw or bolted lug on the neutral terminal block.

The grounded conductor must not be run straight through the service switch box with no means of disconnection.

230-71. Rating of Service Equipment.

(a)   The service equipment shall have a rating not less than the load to be carried determined in accordance with Article 220. The service disconnecting means shall have a rating of not less than 60 amperes except:

Exception No. 1: For single family residences with an initial load of 10 kw or more computed in accordance with Article 220, or if the initial installation has more than five 2-wire branch circuits, the service equipment shall have a rating of not less than 100 amperes 3-wire.

▶   **See Examples 1(b) and (c), Chap. 9.**

Exception No. 2: For installations consisting of not more than two 2-wire branch circuits a service equipment of 30-ampere minimum rating may be used.

(b) Where multiple switches or circuit breakers are used in accordance with Section 230-70(g) the combined rating shall not be less than required for a single switch or breaker.

230-72. Connection to Terminals. The service conductors shall be attached to the disconnecting means by pressure connectors, clamps or other approved means, except that connections which depend upon solder shall not be used.

230-73. Equipment Connected to the Supply Side of Service Disconnect. Equipment shall not be connected to the supply side of the service disconnecting means.

Exception No. 1: Service fuses.

Exception No. 2: Fuses and disconnecting means or circuit breakers, in meter pedestals, connected in series with the ungrounded service conductors and located away from the building supplied.

Exception No. 3: Meters nominally rated not in excess of 600 volts, provided all metal housings and service enclosures are grounded in accordance with Article 250.

Exception No. 4: Instrument transformers (current and potential), high-impedance shunts, surge-protective capacitors, time switches and lightning arresters.

Exception No. 5: Taps used only to supply time switches, circuits for emergency systems, fire pump equipment, fire and sprinkler alarms if provided with service equipment and installed in accordance with requirements for service-entrance conductors.

▶   Emergency-lighting circuits, surge protective capacitors, and fire alarm and other protective signaling circuits, when placed ahead of the regular service disconnecting means, must have separate disconnects and overcurrent protection.

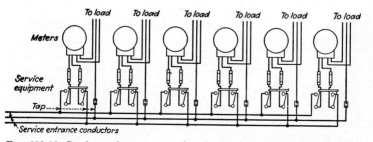

Fig. 230-16. Service equipment grouped at the point of entrance of the service conductors. No main switch is required. This could consist of six sets of fuses and switches or six circuit breakers as shown in Fig. 230-17. They could be in one enclosure or in separate enclosures.

230-74. Safeguarding Emergency Supply. Where an emergency supply is provided to feed the conductors controlled by the service disconnecting means, the disconnector shall be of a design that will open all ungrounded conductors from the usual supply before connection is made to the emergency supply, unless agreed upon arrangements have been made for parallel operation and suitable automatic control equipment provided. See Article 700.

▶ This is intended to prevent an on-site generating plant for emergency service from feeding back into the utility company's supply.

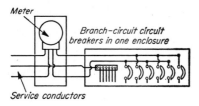

FIG. 230-17. Six circuit breakers in one enclosure suitable for use as service equipment.

Figures 230-16 and 230-17 comply with Sections 230-70g and 230-90a Exception 3, which provide that any number of circuit breakers or fusible switches up to and including six may be used as the service equipment.

230-76. More than One Building or Other Structure.
(a) Disconnect Required for Each. Where more than one building or other structure is on the same property and under single management, each building or other structure served shall be provided with a readily accessible disconnecting means within, on, or adjacent to the building or other structure for disconnecting all ungrounded conductors.

(b) Suitable for Service Equipment. The disconnecting means specified in (a) above shall be suitable for service equipment.

Exception: For garages and outbuildings on residential property, the disconnecting means may consist of a snap switch or of a set of 3-way or 4-way snap switches suitable for use on branch circuits.

▶ Applications of this rule to two buildings under single management and to three buildings under single management are shown in Figs. 230-18 and and 230-19.

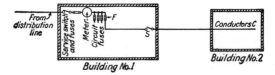

FIG. 230-18. With two buildings under single management, a switch, *S*, must be installed to control conductors *C*. This switch may be in building No. 1 if that building is adjacent to building No. 2.

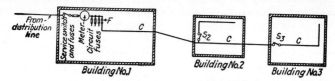

Fig. 230-19. Three buildings under single management. A switch S_2 must be provided to control the wiring in building No. 2, and a switch S_3 to control the wiring in building No. 3. Switch S_3 may be in either building No. 1 or building No. 2 if these buildings are adjacent to building No. 3.

Where outlets in a detached garage are supplied from a dwelling on the same premises, the garage circuit must be controlled by a switch; this may be a snap switch and may be either in the house or in the garage. (Three-way switches would provide greater convenience.) Disconnecting means must be provided for the wiring in each farm building.

K. Overcurrent Protection

230-90. Where Required.   Each ungrounded service-entrance conductor shall have overcurrent protection.

(a) Ungrounded Conductor.   Such protection shall be provided by an overcurrent device in series with each ungrounded service conductor, having a rating or setting not higher than the allowable ampacity of the conductor, except as follows:

▶   The intent in paragraph *a* is to assure that the overcurrent protection required in the service-entrance equipment protects the service-entrance conductors from "overload." It is obvious that these overcurrent devices cannot provide "fault" protection for the service-entrance conductors if the fault occurs in the service-entrance conductors, but can protect them from overload where so selected as to have proper rating. Conductors on the load side of the service equipment are considered as feeders or branch circuits and are required by the Code to be protected as described in Arts. 210, 215, and 240.

Assume that the load of a building computed in accordance with Art. 220 is 255 amp. Under Section 240-5a, Exception 1, a 300-amp fuse or circuit breaker may be considered as the proper-size overcurrent protection for service conductors rated between 255 and 300 amp.

If the load could be separated in such a manner that six circuit breakers could be used instead of a single service disconnect means, total rating of the circuit breakers should be as near the ampacity of the service-entrance conductors as practicable based on standard ampere rating. See Section 240-5 and comments for Section 230-90a, Exception 3.

Example: Six feeders supplied by six circuit breakers. If copper service-entrance conductors are 250,000-cir mil Type THW (255 amp), six 50-amp circuit breakers with a total rating of 300 amp would be considered reasonable. This applies also to fused switches. It will be noted that the requirement is based on the fuse in the switch and not the rating of the switch; for example, for the above purpose a **60**-amp switch with a **50**-amp fuse is counted the same as a **50**-amp circuit breaker. In all the above cases the ungrounded service-entrance conductors are considered as being properly protected in accordance with Section **230**-90a.

Exception No. 1: For motor-starting currents, ratings in conformity with Sections 430-52, 430-62, or 430-63 may be used.

▶   For motor branch circuits and feeders, Arts. **220** and **430** permit the use of overcurrent devices having ratings or settings higher than the capacities of the conductors. Article **230** makes similar provisions for services where the service supplies a motor load or a combination load of both motors and other loads.

Exception No. 2: Fuses and circuit breakers may have a rating or setting in conformity with Section 240-5(a), Exception No. 1, and Section 240-5(b).

Exception No. 3: Not more than six circuit breakers or six sets of fuses may serve as the overcurrent device.

▶   For residential occupancies, the most widely accepted interpretation of Exception **3** by authorities having jurisdiction is to compute the total load of the building according to Art. **220**. This will provide the minimum size of the service-entrance conductors. Then, if multiple overcurrent devices (two to six sets of fuses or circuit breakers) are used, the total rating of the multiple overcurrent devices need *not* match the ampacities of the service-entrance conductors within the limits of Exception **2**. The logic to this interpretation is the nature of loads in residential occupancies where basic laws of diversity will prevent any serious or prolonged overload on the service-entrance conductors.

Exception No. 4: In a multiple occupancy building each occupant shall have access to his overcurrent protective devices. A multiple occupancy building having individual occupancy above the second floor shall have service equipment grouped in a common accessible place, the overcurrent protection consisting of not more than six circuit breakers or six sets of fuses. Multiple occupancy buildings that do not have individual occupancy above the second floor may have service conductors run to each occupancy and each such service may have not more than six circuit breakers or six sets of fuses.

Exception No. 5: Fire Pumps. Where the service to the fire pump room is judged to be outside of buildings, these provisions shall not apply. Service equipment for fire pump services shall be selected or set to carry locked-rotor current of the motor(s) indefinitely (See NFPA No. 20—1970, Standard for Centrifugal Fire Pumps).

▶   In the interest of fire protection, fire pump motors are permitted to have much larger overcurrent protection than normal motor applications since the purpose of fire pumps is to aid in putting out fires. It should also be noted that Section **430-31***b* does not require motor-running protection for fire pumps for this same reason.

A set of fuses is all the fuses required to protect all the ungrounded conductors of a circuit. Single pole breakers may be grouped as in Section 230-70(g) as one multiple protective device.

▶   See comments following Section **230-70(b)**.

(b) Not in Grounded Conductor.   No overcurrent device shall be inserted in a grounded service conductor except a circuit breaker which simultaneously opens all conductors of the circuit.

(c) More Than One Building.   In a property comprising more than one building under single management, the ungrounded conductors supplying each building served shall be protected by overcurrent devices, which may be located in the building served or in another building on the same property, provided they are accessible to the occupants of the building served.

230-91. Location.   The service overcurrent device shall be an integral part of the service disconnecting means or shall be located immediately adjacent thereto, unless located at the outer end of the entrance.

▶   The overcurrent devices, if inside the building, shall be close to the point at which the service conductors enter the building, because the service conductors are not fully protected against overcurrent and any run of service conductors inside a building is more or less hazardous and hence should be as short as possible. If the disconnecting means and overcurrent device are installed outside the building, it is not of great importance, from a safety standpoint, that this equipment be mounted close to the point at which the load-side conductors enter the building.

230-92. Location of Branch-Circuit Overcurrent Devices.   Where the service overcurrent devices are locked or sealed, or otherwise not readily accessible, branch-circuit overcurrent devices shall be installed on the load side, shall be mounted in an accessible location and shall be of lower rating than the service overcurrent device.

230-93. Protection of Specific Circuits.   Where necessary to prevent tampering, an automatic overcurrent device protecting service conductors supplying only a specific load such as a water heater, may be locked or sealed where located so as to be accessible.

230-94. Relative Location of Overcurrent Device and Other Service Equipment.   The overcurrent device shall protect all circuits and devices except as follows:

(a)   The service switch may be placed on the supply side.

(b)   High impedance shunt circuits, lightning arresters, surge protective capacitors, instrument transformers, (current and potential), may be connected and installed on the supply side of the service disconnecting means as permitted in Section 230-73.

(c)   Circuits for emergency supply and time switches may be connected on the supply side of the service overcurrent device where separately provided with overcurrent protection.

(d) Circuits used only for the operation of fire alarm, other protective signalling systems, or the supply to fire pump equipment may be connected on the supply side of the service overcurrent device where separately provided with overcurrent protection.

(e) Meters nominally rated not in excess of 600 volts, provided all metal housings and service enclosures are grounded in accordance with Article 250.

(f) Where service equipment is operated electrically, the control circuit may be connected ahead of the service equipment if suitable overcurrent protection and disconnecting means are provided.

230-95. Ground-Fault Protection of Equipment. Ground-fault protection of equipment shall be provided for grounded wye electrical services of more than 150 volts to ground, but not exceeding 600 volts phase-to-phase for any service disconnecting means rated 1000 amperes or more. The ground-fault protection may consist of overcurrent devices or combination of overcurrent devices and current transformers or other equivalent protective equipment which shall operate to cause the service disconnecting means to open all ungrounded conductors of the faulted circuit at fault current values of 1200 amperes or more.

When a switch and fuse combination is used, the fuses employed shall be capable of interrupting any current higher than the interrupting capacity of the switch during a time when the ground-fault protective system will not cause the switch to open.

It is recognized that ground-fault protection is desirable for service disconnecting means rated less than 1000 amperes on grounded systems having more than 150 volts to ground, not exceeding 600 volts phase-to-phase.

Ground-fault protection that functions to open the service disconnecting means will not protect service conductors or the service disconnecting means but will limit the damage to conductors and equipment on the load side of the ground-fault protection.

This added protective equipment at the service equipment will make it necessary to review the over-all wiring system for proper selective overcurrent protection coordination. Additional installations of ground-fault protective equipment will be needed on feeders and branch circuits where maximum continuity of electrical service is necessary.

▶   Section **230-95** is aimed mainly at **480Y/277**-volt services. The purpose is to prevent *burndowns* of such services where line-to-ground faults occur on the load side of any service disconnecting means rated 1000 amp or more. Any disconnecting means rated less than 1000 amp, such as the use of five 800-amp disconnecting means in lieu of a single 4000-amp disconnect, would not require ground-fault protection as described in this Section.

Data have shown that arcing to ground from an ungrounded conductor of a 480Y/277-volt system is sustained at voltages from 70 to 140 volts.

With larger conventional fuses and circuit breakers the line-to-ground arc is seen only as a moderate *load* current. Hence, such devices may not operate and serious burndowns and fires may result. Voltages below 150 volts to ground generally do not sustain line-to-ground arcs because the arc voltage is low. Higher voltage systems, such as 4160Y/2400 volts, will usually provide enough ground fault current in line-to-ground arcing faults to clear conventional overcurrent devices used with such systems, and this is the major reason why ground-fault equipment protection is not required for systems of over 600 volts phase to phase.

The selection of ground-fault equipment protection for **480Y/277**-volt systems requires a careful analysis of each particular installation—much the same as short-circuit studies to determine the interrupting capacity of overcurrent devices throughout a given installation (see comments following Sections 110-9 and 110-10).

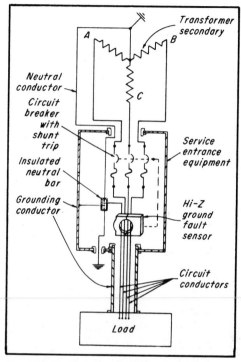

FIG. 230-20. Ground-fault sensor installed around all conductors. (*O. Z. Electrical Mfg. Co., Inc.*)

Figures **230-20** and **230-21** show two basic types of ground-fault equipment protectors presently available. The ground-fault sensor in Fig. **230-20** encircles all circuit conductors (phase conductors and the neutral). Under normal conditions the sum of all currents flowing through the circuit conductors will be zero. However, if one ungrounded conductor arcs to ground downstream from the ground fault sensor, such as to metallic conduits or cabinets, a *stray* current will return to the neutral bar through the metallic enclosures. This sets up a flux in the ground fault sensor toroid in proportion to the amount of current in the grounding conductor. When this current exceeds the trip rating of the unit the circuit breaker shunt trip will operate and open the ungrounded conductors.

The ground-fault sensor shown in Fig. **230-21** is placed only over the bonding jumper (from the metal enclosure to the insulated neutral bar) and

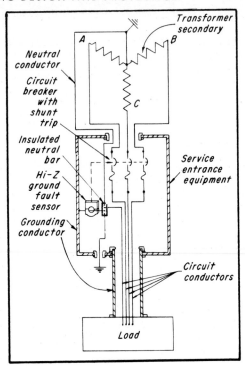

Fig. 230-21. Ground-fault sensor installed around the grounding-conductor bonding jumper only. (*O. Z. Electrical Mfg. Co., Inc.*)

directly measures the line-to-ground current in the grounding conductor. When this current exceeds the trip rating of the unit it will operate the circuit breaker trip unit as explained in the description of Fig. 230-20.

The 1200-amp value mentioned in Section 250-95 is the *maximum* trip setting to clear ground-faults. Lower settings are permitted, and there are no minimum or maximum *time values* because of differing needs for each installation. If ground-fault settings are too low, an unnecessary outage may occur.

The fine print notes in Section **230-95** outline the basic considerations in selecting the number and locations of ground-fault protectors. Manufacturers of such equipment provide excellent literature on this subject, and consultation with these manufacturers will avoid costly misapplications.

230-96. Working Space. Sufficient working space shall be provided in the vicinity of the service overcurrent devices to permit safe operation, replacements, inspection, and repairs. In no case shall this be less than that specified by Section 110-16.

230-98. Available Short-Circuit Current. Service equipment and its overcurrent protective devices shall have short-circuit current rating equal to or not less than the available short-circuit current at its supply terminal.

▶   See comments following Sections 110-9 and 110-10.

L. Services Exceeding 600 Volts

230-100. Scope. Service conductors and equipment used on circuits exceeding 600 volts shall comply with the applicable provisions of the preceding Sections of this Article and with the following Sections which are additions to or modifications of the preceding Sections.

Secondary conductors, not the primary conductors, are the service conductors to the building proper in the following cases:

1. Where step-down transformers are located outdoors.
2. Where step-down transformers are located in a separate building from the one served.
3. Where step-down transformers are located in the building served in transformer vaults, locked rooms or locked enclosures in accordance with Article 450 and accessible only to qualified persons.

In all other cases, the primary conductors are the service conductors.

In no case will the provisions of this Article apply to equipment connected ahead of the service conductors.

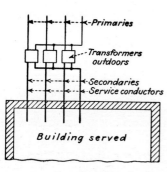

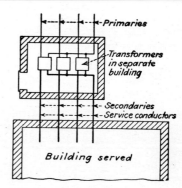

Fig. 230-22   Fig. 230-23

▶   In the cases shown in Figs. 230-22 through 230-25, the secondary conductors are considered as the service conductors. The transformers in vaults are assumed to be accessible only to qualified persons.

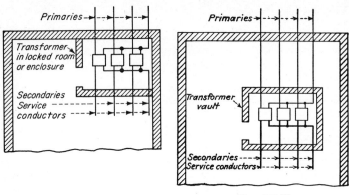

FIG. 230-24   FIG. 230-25

230-101. Service-Entrance Conductors.

(a) **Conductor Size.** Service conductors shall be not smaller than No. 6 unless in cable. Conductors in cable shall be not smaller than No. 8.

(b) **Wiring Methods.** Service-entrance conductors shall be installed by means of one of the following wiring methods:

(1) In rigid metal conduit.

(2) In rigid nonmetallic conduit where encased in not less than 2 inches of concrete.

(3) As multi-conductor cable approved for the purpose.

(4) As open conductors where supported on insulators approved for the purpose and where either accessible only to qualified persons or where effectively guarded against accidental contact.

(5) In cablebus.

Where surface contamination cannot be prevented and high surface resistivity cannot be maintained, metallic shielding shall be used at over 3 kv. See Table 710-5 for shielding of solid dielectric-insulated conductors.

(c) **Open Work.** Open wire services over 600 volts shall be installed in accordance with the provisions of Article 710, Part D.

(d) **Supports.** Service conductors and their supports, including insulators, shall have strength and stability sufficient to insure maintenance of adequate clearance with abnormal currents in case of short circuits.

(e) **Guarding.** Open wires shall be guarded where accessible to unqualified persons.

(f) **Service Cable.** Where cable conductors emerge from a metal sheath or raceway, the insulation of the conductors shall be protected from moisture and physical damage by a pothead or other approved means.

(g) **Draining Raceways.** Unless conductors specifically approved for the purpose are used, raceways embedded in masonry, or exposed to the weather, or in wet locations shall be arranged to drain.

(h) **Over 15,000 Volts.** Where the voltage exceeds 15,000 volts between conductors they shall enter either metal enclosed switchgear or a transformer vault conforming to the requirements of Section 450-41 through 450-48.

(i) Conductor Considered Outside Building. Conductors placed under at least two inches of concrete beneath a building, or conductors within a building in conduit or duct and enclosed by concrete or brick not less than two inches thick shall be considered outside the building.

230-102. Warning Signs. High voltage signs shall be posted where unauthorized persons might come in contact with live parts.

230-103. Disconnecting Means. The circuit breaker or the alternatives for it specified in Section 230-106 will constitute the disconnecting means required by Section 230-70 and shall comply with Section 230-70(h). The disconnecting means shall be capable of being closed on a fault within the maximum interrupting rating of the overcurrent protection.

▶   Section 230-70 requires a disconnect means for every service. This requirement is met by the use of circuit breakers or switches, or fuses alone as permitted in Section 230-106*a*.

230-104. Isolating Switches. Isolating switches shall be provided as follows:

(a) Air-break isolating switches shall be installed between oil switches or air or oil circuit breakers used as service switches and the supply conductor, except where such equipment is mounted on removable truck panels or metal-enclosed switchgear units which cannot be opened unless the circuit is disconnected, and which, when removed from the normal operating position, automatically disconnect the circuit breaker or switch from all live parts.

(b) When the fuses used with nonautomatic oil switches in accordance with Section 230-106 are of a type that may be operated as a disconnect switch, they may serve as the isolating switch when they completely disconnect the oil switch and all service equipment from the source of supply.

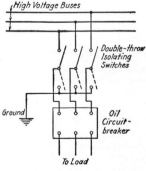

Fig. 230-26. High-voltage fuses and isolating switches. (*Westinghouse Electric Corp.*)

Fig. 230-27. A method of grounding the load side of isolating switches while the switches are open.

(c) Air-break isolating switches shall be accessible to qualified attendants only. They shall be arranged so that a grounding connection on the load side can readily be made. Such grounding means need not be provided for duplicate isolating switches, if any, installed and maintained by the supply company.

230-105. Equipment in Secondaries. Where the primary service equipment supplies one or more transformers whose secondary windings connect to a single set of mains, and the primary load-interrupter switch or circuit-breaker is capable of being opened and closed from a point outside the transformer vault, the disconnecting means and overcurrent protection may be omitted from the secondary circuit provided the primary fuse or circuit-breaker is rated or set to protect the secondary circuit.

230-106. Overcurrent Protection. Overcurrent devices shall be provided in accordance with the following:

(a) In Vault or Consisting of Metal-Enclosed Switchgear. Where the service equipment is installed in a transformer vault meeting the provisions of Sections 450-41 through 450-48, or consists of metal-enclosed switchgear, the requirements for overcurrent protection and disconnecting means may be fulfilled by the following:

(1) A non-automatic oil switch, oil fuse cutout, air load-interrupter switch, or other approved switch, capable of interrupting the rated circuit load, and suitable fuses may be used.

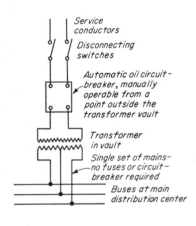

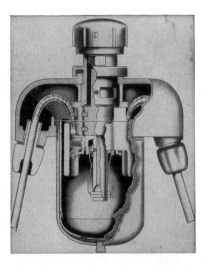

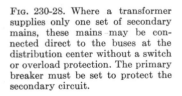

Fig. 230-28. Where a transformer supplies only one set of secondary mains, these mains may be connected direct to the buses at the distribution center without a switch or overload protection. The primary breaker must be set to protect the secondary circuit.

Fig. 230-29. Oil-fuse cutout. (*General Electric Co.*)

(2) An automatic trip circuit breaker of suitable current carrying and interrupting capacity with an overcurrent unit in each ungrounded conductor may be used.

(3) A switch capable of interrupting the no-load current of the transformer supplied through the switch and suitable fuses may be used, provided the switch is interlocked with a single switch or circuit breaker on the secondary circuit of the transformer so that the primary switch cannot be opened when the secondary circuit is closed.

(4) Metal-enclosed switchgear shall consist of a substantial metal structure and a sheet metal enclosure. Barriers between adjacent switchgear units and internal metal barriers shall be not less than ⅛ inch of metal or No. 11 MSG. All other covers, panels and doors shall be not less than No. 14 MSG. Where installed over a wood floor, suitable protection thereto shall be provided.

(b) Not in Vault or Not Consisting of Metal-Enclosed Switchgear. Where the service equipment is not in a vault or metal-enclosed switchgear, the requirements for the overcurrent protection and disconnecting means may be fulfilled by the following:

(1) Air load-interrupter switches, or other approved switches, capable of

Fig. 230-30. Group-operated interrupter-switch and power-fuse combination for use in metal-enclosed switchgear. Shown in open position. Switch rating: 14.4 kv, 600 amp continuous and interrupting, 40,000 amp momentary, 40,000 amp fault closing. Fuse rating: 400 E amp max continuous, 40,000 amp RMS asym. interrupting. (*S and C Electric Company.*)

interrupting the rated circuit load may be used with suitable fuses on a pole or elevated structure outside the building provided the switch may be operated by persons using the building.

(2) On circuits of any voltage, an automatic trip circuit breaker of suitable ampacity and interrupting capacity with an overcurrent unit in each ungrounded conductor may be used. The circuit breaker shall be located outside the building as near as practicable to where the service conductors enter the building. The location may be on a pole, roof, foundation, or other structure.

(c) Fuses.   Fuses shall have an interrupting rating at least equal to the maximum short-circuit current possible in the circuit.

(d) Circuit Breakers.   Circuit breakers shall be free to open in case the circuit is closed on an overload. This can be accomplished by means such as trip-free breakers or by multiple breakers having an operating handle per pole. A service circuit breaker shall indicate clearly whether it is open or closed, and shall be capable of interrupting the maximum short-circuit current to which it may be subjected.

(e) Enclosed Overcurrent Devices.   The restriction to 80 per cent of rating for an enclosed overcurrent device on continuous loads shall not apply to overcurrent devices installed in services operating at over 600 volts.

▶   Suitable ampacity as mentioned in Section **230-106**b **(2)** is the ability of the circuit breaker to carry the connected load without overheating.

FIG. 230-31. Exploded view of indoor solid-material (SM) power fuseholder (boric-acid arc-extinguishing type). Shows spring and cable assembly, refill unit, holder, and muffler. Rated 14.4 kv, 400 E amp max., 40,000 amp RMS asym. interrupting. (*S and C Electric Company.*)

Suitable interrupting capacity is the ability of the circuit breaker to interrupt overloads and short circuits without injury to the circuit breaker.

Fuses designed for use under the conditions stated in Section 230-106a (1) are illustrated in Figs. 230-26, 230-29, 230-30, and 230-31.

230-107. Lightning Arresters. Lightning arresters installed in accordance with the requirements of Article 280 shall be placed on each ungrounded overhead service conductor on the supply side of the service equipment, when called for by the authority having jurisdiction.

ARTICLE 240. OVERCURRENT PROTECTION

A. Installation

240-1. Scope. This Article provides the general requirements for the application of overcurrent protective devices.

240-2. Purpose of Overcurrent Protection. Overcurrent protection for conductors and equipment is provided for the purpose of opening the electric circuit if the current reaches a value which will cause an excessive or dangerous temperature in the conductor or conductor insulation.

240-3. Protection of Equipment. Equipment shall be protected against overcurrent as specified in the references in the following list:

Equipment	Article No.
Air-Conditioning and Refrigerating Equipment	440
Appliances	422
Capacitors	460
Cranes and Hoists	610
Electric Signs and Outline Lighting	600
Electric Welders	630
Elevators, Dumbwaiters, Escalators, and Moving Walks	620
Emergency Systems	700
Fixed Electric Space Heating Equipment	424
Fixed Outdoor Electric De-Icing and Snow Melting Equipment	426
Generators	445
Induction and Dielectric Heating Equipment	665
Metalworking Machine Tools	670
Motion Picture Studios and Similar Locations	530
Motors, Motor Circuits and Controllers	430
Organs	650
Over 600 Volts—General	710
Remote-Control, Low-Energy Power, Low-Voltage Power and Signal Circuits	725
Services	230
Sound-Recording and Similar Equipment	640
Switchboards and Panelboards	384
Theaters and Assembly Halls	520
Transformers and Transformer Vaults	450
X-ray Equipment	660

240-5. Overcurrent Protection.

(a) Conductors. Conductors shall be protected in accordance with their ampacities, as given in Tables 310-12 through 310-15, except as follows:

Exception No. 1: Rating of Nonadjustable Overcurrent Protection of 800 Amperes or Less. Where the standard ampere ratings of fuses and nonadjustable circuit breakers do not correspond with the allowable ampacities of conductors, the next higher standard rating may be used, only where the rating is 800 amperes or less.

Exception No. 2: Fixture Wires and Cords. Fixture wire or flexible cord, Size No. 16 or No. 18, and tinsel cord shall be considered as protected by 20 ampere overcurrent devices except as provided in Section 620-61. Fixture wires of the sizes permitted for taps in Section 210-19 (c-2) shall be considered as protected by the overcurrent protection of the 30, 40, and 50 ampere branch circuits of Article 210. Flexible cord approved for use with specific appliances shall be considered as protected by the overcurrent device of the branch circuit of Article 210 when conforming to the following:

20 ampere circuits, No. 18 cord and larger.

30 ampere circuits, cord of 10 ampere capacity and over.

40 ampere circuits, cord of 20 ampere capacity and over.

50 ampere circuits, cord of 20 ampere capacity and over.

Exception No. 3: Motor Circuits. Motor and motor-control circuit conductors protected in accordance with Parts C, D, E, and F of Article 430. Motor-operated appliance circuit conductors protected in accordance with Parts B and D of Article 422. Air-conditioning and refrigerating equipment circuit conductors protected in accordance with Parts C and F of Article 440.

Exception No. 4: Control Circuits. Where not in the same cable with communication circuits, as provided in Section 725-7, conductors of control circuits other than motor-control circuits shall be considered as protected by overcurrent devices that are rated or set at not more than 300 per cent of the ampacity of the remote-control conductors.

Exception No. 5: Transformer Secondary Conductors. Conductors supplied by the secondary side of a single-phase transformer having a 2-wire (single-voltage) secondary shall be considered as protected by overcurrent protection provided on the primary (supply) side of the transformer, provided this protection is in accordance with Section 450-3(a)(1) or (b)(1) and does not exceed the value determined by multiplying the secondary conductor ampacity by the secondary-to-primary transformer voltage ratio.

▶   *Example:* A 10-kva dry-type transformer has a two-wire 480-volt primary and a two-wire 240-volt secondary (a 2:1 ratio). The full-load primary current is 20.8 amp. The full-load secondary current is 41.6 amp. The primary conductors are No. 10 AWG copper conductors, Type TW. The secondary conductors are No. 6 AWG copper conductors, Type TW, which extend to a 10-kw heater. Primary protection consists of two 25-amp fuses. This arrangement satisfies Exception 5 in that (1) the primary of the transformer is protected to satisfy Section 450-3*b1* (20.8 amp × 125% is more than 25 amp); (2) the No. 10 primary conductors have an ampacity of 30 amp and are properly protected; (3) the No. 6 secondary conductors have an ampacity of 55 amp, which times ½ (*the secondary-to-primary voltage ratio*) = 27.5 amp and is properly protected by the 25-amp primary fuse. Accordingly, no overcurrent protection is required in the secondary, and the length of secondary conductors is not limited.

For other than two-wire to two-wire transformations complying with Exception 5, secondary conductors must be protected on the secondary side, except as permitted for limited tap lengths in Exceptions 5 and 7 of Section 240-15.

Where transformers have more than two wires on the secondary, unbalanced currents in the secondary will cause an overload on part of the secondary circuit and transformer winding and go unnoticed by the primary overcurrent device.

If, in the previous example, the secondary was three-wire, 120/240-volts, one secondary transformer winding could carry 100 amp (line-to-neutral with no load on the other 120-volt winding). In this case the 25-amp primary fuse sees the 100-amp secondary load as only 25 amp as the result of a 4:1 ratio (480:120), and one 120-volt secondary winding and two of the three No. 6 secondary conductors would be seriously overloaded.

Main secondary protection will protect against such unbalances, except for a line-to-ground fault that could occur between the transformer secondary connection and the secondary overcurrent devices; however this risk is inherent in the 10- and 25-ft tap rule exceptions of Section 240-15.

Exception No. 6: Tap Conductors. Tap conductors as permitted in Sections 210-19(c); 240-15, Exception Nos. 3, 5, 6 and 7; 364-9 and 364-10; and Part D of Article 430.

(b) Standard Ratings. Standard ampere ratings for fuses and nonadjustable circuit breakers are 15, 20, 25, 30, 35, 40, 45, 50, 60, 70, 80, 90, 100, 110, 125, 150, 175, 200, 225, 250, 300, 350, 400, 450, 500, 600, 700, 800, 1000, 1200, 1600, 2000, 2500, 3000, 4000, 5000, and 6000.

240-6. Fuses.

(a) Plug fuses and fuseholders shall not be used in circuits exceeding 125 volts between conductors except in circuits supplied from a system having a grounded neutral and no conductor in such circuits operating at more than 150 volts to ground.

(b) Cartridge fuses and fuseholders rated at 300 volts shall not be used in circuits exceeding 300 volts between conductors except in circuits supplied from a system having a grounded neutral and no conductor in such circuits operating at more than 300 volts to ground.

(c) The screw shell of plug-type fuseholders shall be connected to the load side of the circuit.

240-8. Thermal Devices. Thermal cutouts, thermal relays and other devices not designed to open short circuits, shall not be used for protection of conductors against overcurrent due to short circuits or grounds but may be used to protect motor branch circuit conductors from overload if protected in accordance with Section 430-40.

▶   Thermal cutouts and thermal and magnetic relays are used to protect the motors as well as the motor circuit conductors against excessive overloads, but they must be backed up by fuses or circuit breakers that provide short circuit protection.

240-11. Ungrounded Conductors.

(a) An overcurrent device (fuse or overcurrent trip unit of a circuit breaker) shall be placed in each ungrounded conductor. For motor circuits see Article 430.

(b) Circuit breakers shall open all ungrounded conductors of the circuit, except as follows:

Exception: Individual single-pole circuit breakers may be used for the protection of each conductor of ungrounded 2-wire circuits, each ungrounded conductor of 3-wire direct-current or single-phase circuits, or for each ungrounded conductor of lighting or appliance branch circuits connected to 4-wire 3-phase systems, or 5-wire 2-phase systems, provided such lighting or appliance circuits are supplied from a system having a grounded neutral and no conductor in such circuits operates at a voltage greater than permitted in Section 210-6.

240-12. Grounded Conductor. No overcurrent device shall be placed in any permanently grounded conductor, except as follows:

Exception No. 1: Where the overcurrent device simultaneously opens all conductors of the circuit.

Exception No. 2: For motor-running protection as provided in Sections 430-36 and 430-37.

▶ **Many years ago fused neutrals were in use, but it was found that damage resulted from an unbalanced voltage when only the neutral fuse opened.**

240-13. Change in Size of Grounded Conductor. Where a change occurs in the size of the ungrounded conductor, a similar change may be made in the size of the grounded conductor.

▶ **In effect, this recognizes the fact that if the neutral is the same size as the ungrounded conductor, it will be protected wherever the ungrounded conductor is protected. One of the most obvious places this is encountered is in a distribution center where a small grounded conductor may be connected directly to a large grounded feeder conductor.**

240-14. Fuses or Circuit Breakers in Parallel. Overcurrent devices consisting of fuses and/or circuit breakers shall not be arranged or installed in parallel.

Exception: Circuit breakers assembled in parallel which are tested and approved as a single unit.

B. Location

240-15. Location in Circuit. Overcurrent devices shall be located at the point where the conductor to be protected receives its supply, except as follows:

Exception No. 1: Service Conductors. An overcurrent protective device for service conductors may be located as specified in Section 230-91.

Exception No. 2: Smaller Conductor Protected. Where the overcurrent device protecting the larger conductors also protects the smaller conductors in accordance with Tables 310-12 through 310-15.

Exception No. 3: Branch Circuits. Taps to individual outlets and circuit conductors supplying a single household electric range shall be considered as protected by the branch circuit overcurrent devices when in accordance with the requirements of Sections 210-19, 210-20 and 210-25.

Exception No. 4: Feeder Taps. A conductor tapped from a feeder shall be considered as properly protected from overcurrent when installed in accordance with Sections 364-8 and 430-59.

Exception No. 5: Feeder Taps Not Over 10 Feet Long. For conductors tapped to a feeder where all of the following conditions are met:

(a) The length of each tap conductor does not exceed 10 feet; (b) the ampacity of the tap conductors is (1) not less than the combined computed loads of the circuits supplied by the tap conductors, and (2) not less than the ampere rating of the switchboard or panelboard supplied by the tap conductors; (c) the tap conductors do not extend beyond the switchboard, panelboard, or control devices they supply; (d) except at the point of connection to the feeder the tap conductors are enclosed in a raceway, which shall extend from the tap to the enclosure of an enclosed switchboard, panelboard, or control devices or to the back of an open switchboard.

Exception No. 6: Feeder Taps Not Over 25 Feet Long. Where the smaller conductor has an ampacity at least one-third that of the conductor from which it is supplied, and provided the tap is suitably protected from physical damage, is not over 25 feet long, and terminates in a single circuit breaker or set of fuses which will limit the load on the tap to that allowed by Tables 310-12 through 310-15. Beyond this point the conductors may supply any number of circuit breakers or sets of fuses.

Exception No. 7: Transformer Feeder Taps with Primary Plus Secondary Not Over 25 Feet Long. Where all of the following conditions are met: (1) the conductors supplying the primary of a transformer have an ampacity at least one-third that of the conductors or overcurrent protection from which they are tapped, and (2) the conductors supplied by the secondary of the transformer have an ampacity that, when multiplied by the ratio of the secondary-to-primary voltage, is at least one-third the ampacity of the conductors or overcurrent protection from which the primary conductors are tapped, and (3) the total length of one primary plus one secondary conductor, excluding any portion of the primary conductor that is protected at its ampacity, is not over 25 feet, and (4) the primary and secondary conductors are suitably protected from physical damage, and (5) the secondary conductors terminate in a single circuit breaker or set of fuses which will limit the load to that allowed in Tables 310-12 through 310-15.

▶   Exception 2 is illustrated by **Fig. 240-1**. A No. 00 feeder is run from a main switchboard where it is protected by **125-amp** fuses. No. 0 conductors are tapped to the feeder conductors.

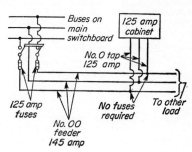

Fig. 240-1. Feeder tap where the tap conductors are protected by the feeder fuses.

Exception **5** concerns a 10-ft feeder tap to a switchboard, panelboard, single fusible switch or single circuit breaker. If the tap extends to a switchboard or panelboard the tap must have an ampacity not less than the switchboard or panelboard rating. Furthermore if the panelboard is a lighting and appliance type (see definition in Section **384-14**) the tap must terminate in an overcurrent device complying with Section **384-16a**. Taps to a fusible switch or circuit breaker must be sized not less than the calculated load supplied by the switch or breaker, in which case, the tap would be of a size not less than the load conductors of the switch or breaker.

In extending to equipment the tap must be enclosed in a raceway.

In the case of transformers it seems logical that the 10-ft tap can be applied to the secondary conductors if the primary overcurrent devices conform to Section **450-3a1** or **b1** and the primary conductors are properly protected by the primary overcurrent devices. In such instances, the previously mentioned general considerations would also apply.

Exception **6** is illustrated in Fig. **240-2**.

Exception **7** is a 25-ft feeder tap rule specifically for transformer applications other than specified in Section **240-5a**, Exception **5**, and Section **240-15**, Exception **5** (as previously described).

Exception **7** would mainly be used where the primary overcurrent devices are rated according to Section **450-3a1** or **450-3b2**, or where more than one secondary 25-ft tap is used. Each such tap must terminate in a single circuit breaker or set of fuses which will limit the load on the conductor to that permitted in Tables **310-12** through **310-15**. See comments following Section **240-5a**, Exception **5**, for explanation of primary-to-secondary and secondary-to-primary ratios.

In all cases the provisions of Sections **450-3** (transformer overcurrent protection) and **384-16a** (panelboard overcurrent protection) must be satisfied. The example in Fig. **240-3** complies with Exception **7** and with Sections **384-16a** and **450-3b2**.

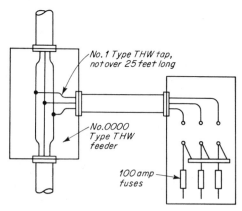

No. 1 Type THW tap, not over 25 feet long

No. 0000 Type THW feeder

100 amp fuses

Fig. 240-2. Feeder taps terminating in a single set of fuses. See Exception 6.

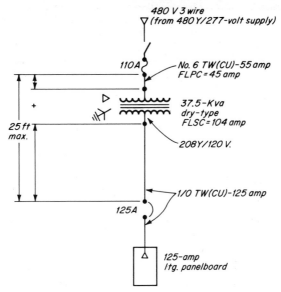

480 V 3 wire
(from 480 Y/277-volt supply)

110 A

No. 6 TW(CU)–55 amp
FLPC = 45 amp

37.5-Kva
dry-type
FLSC = 104 amp

25 ft max.

208 Y/120 V.

1/0 TW(CU)–125 amp

125 A

125-amp
ltg. panelboard

Taps protected from physical damage.
Secondary-to-primary voltage ratio = 208 : 480 = 1 : 2.3

Fig. 240-3. Example of Section 240-15, Exception 7, which also conforms with Sections 384-16a and 450-3b2.

240-16. Location in Premises. Overcurrent devices shall be located where they will be:

(a) Readily accessible, except as provided in Sections 230-91 and 230-92 for service equipment and Section 364-11 for busways.

(b) Not exposed to physical damage.

(c) Not in the vicinity of easily ignitible material.

(d) **Occupant to Have Ready Access.** Each occupant shall have ready access to all overcurrent devices protecting the conductors supplying his occupancy.

Exception: In a multiple-occupancy building where electric service and electrical maintenance are provided by the building management and where these are under continuous building management supervision, the service overcurrent devices and feeder overcurrent devices supplying more than one occupancy may be accessible to authorized management personnel only.

C. Enclosures

240-17. Enclosures for Overcurrent Devices.

(a) **General.** Overcurrent devices shall be enclosed in cutout boxes or cabinets, unless a part of a specially approved assembly which affords equivalent protection, or unless mounted on switchboards, panelboards or controllers located in rooms or enclosures free from easily ignitible material and dampness. The operating handle of a circuit breaker may be accessible without opening a door or cover.

▶ Protective devices are intended to open the circuit in the event of disturbances on the line so that abnormal conditions are limited to a small area. It is in consideration of this fact that every precaution is taken to see that malfunctioning of the protective device or its associated equipment will not create a hazard in that vicinity. This is the basis for the requirements in Sections 240-16 and 240-17. Section 384-4 requires that all switchboards having exposed live parts shall be located where accessible only to qualified persons.

(b) Damp or Wet Locations. Enclosures for overcurrent devices in damp or wet locations shall be of a type approved for such locations and shall be mounted so there is at least one-fourth inch air space between the enclosure and the wall or other supporting surface.

▶ Enclosures approved for outdoor installation are so constructed that they will exclude rain and snow.

(c) Vertical Position. Enclosures for overcurrent devices shall be mounted in a vertical position unless in individual instances this is shown to be impracticable.

▶ The requirement in Section 240-17c is to prevent the mounting of enclosures on ceilings and floors where poor operation of the enclosed equipment may result.

(d) Rosettes. Fuses shall not be mounted in rosettes.

D. Disconnecting and Guarding

240-18. Disconnection of Fuses and Thermal Cutouts Before Handling. Disconnecting means shall be provided on the supply side of all fuses or thermal cutouts in circuits of more than 150 volts to ground and cartridge fuses in circuits of any voltage, where accessible to other than qualified persons, so that each individual circuit containing fuses or thermal cutouts can be independently disconnected from the source of electrical energy, except as provided in Section 230-73 and except that a single disconnecting means may be used to control a group of circuits each protected by fuses or thermal cutouts under the conditions described in Section 430-112.

▶ Whenever cartridge fuses are accessible to other than qualified persons, a disconnect switch must be provided for each circuit.

240-19. Arcing or Suddenly Moving Parts. Arcing or suddenly moving parts shall comply with the following:

(a) Location. Fuses and circuit breakers shall be so located or shielded that persons will not be burned or otherwise injured by their operation.

(b) Suddenly Moving Parts. Handles or levers of circuit breakers, and similar parts which may move suddenly in such a way that persons in the vicinity are liable to be injured by being struck by them, shall be guarded or isolated.

▶ Section **240-19** is intended to apply to switchboards and control panels located in spaces where full enclosure is not required. (See Section **240-17** and comments.) Such equipment should be accessible to qualified operators only, but qualified operators should be protected from unnecessary hazards.

E. Plug Fuses and Fuseholders

240-20. Plug Fuses of the Edison-Base Type. Plug fuses of the Edison-base type shall conform to the following:

(a) Classification. Plug fuses of this type shall be classified at not over 125 volts, 0 to 30 amperes.

(b) Live Parts. Fuses and fuseholders when installed and assembled together shall have no live parts exposed.

(c) Marking. Plug fuses of 15-ampere rating or less shall be distinguished from those of larger rating by an hexagonal opening in the cap through which the mica or similar window shows, or by some other prominent hexagonal feature such as the form of the top or cap itself, or an hexagonal recess or projection in the top or cap.

Plug fuses of the Edison-base type shall be used only for replacements in existing installations where there is no evidence of overfusing or tampering.

240-21. Fuseholders for Plug Fuses. Fuseholders for plug fuses of 30 amperes or less shall not be installed unless they comply with Section 240-22 or are made to comply with Section 240-22 by the insertion of an adapter.

240-22. Plug Fuses and Fuseholders of Type S. Where Type S plug fuses are to be used as the overcurrent device required by this Code, the fuses and fuseholders shall conform to the following requirements:

(a) Classification. Plug fuses and fuseholders of Type S shall be classified at not over 125 volts; 0 to 15 amperes, 16 to 20 amperes, and 21 to 30 amperes.

(b) Use of Fuses in a Fuseholder of a Different Classification. Fuses of the 16 to 20 ampere and the 21 to 30 ampere classification shall not be usable with fuseholders or adapters of a lower ampere classification.

(c) Fuseholders and Adapters. Fuses, fuseholders, and adapters shall be so designed that a fuse other than a Type S fuse cannot be used in a fuseholder or adapter designed for Type S fuses.

(d) Tamperability. Fuses, fuseholders and adapters shall be so designed as to be subject to tampering or bridging only with difficulty.

(e) Adapters to be Nonremovable. Fuse adapters shall be so designed that when once inserted in a fuseholder they cannot be removed.

(f) Interchangeability. Fuses, fuseholders and adapters of various manufacturers shall be interchangeable with each other, and the plugs with adapters shall be suitable for use in the Edison-base type fuseholder.

(g) Plug Type. Fuses and fuseholders shall be of the plug type.

(h) Ampere Rating. Each fuse, fuseholder and adapter shall be marked with its ampere rating.

(i) Marking. Fuses of the 0 to 15 ampere rating shall be distinguished from those of larger rating by an hexagonal opening in the cap through which the mica or similar window shows, or some other prominent hexagonal feature such as the form of the top or cap itself, or an hexagonal recess or projection in the top or cap.

F. Cartridge Fuses and Fuseholders

240-23. Cartridge Fuses and Fuseholders. Cartridge fuses and fuseholders shall conform to the following:

(a) Classification.

(1) 0–600 ampere cartridge fuses and fuseholders shall be classified as regards current and voltage as follows:

Not over 250 volts Amperes	Not over 300 volts Amperes	Not over 600 volts Amperes
0– 30	0–15	0– 30
31– 60	16–20	31– 60
61–100	21–30	61–100
101–200	31–60	101–200
201–400	–	201–400
401–600	–	401–600

(2) 601–6000 ampere cartridge fuses and fuseholders shall be classified at 600 volts as follows:

601– 800	1601–2000	3001–4000
801–1200	2001–2500	4001–5000
1201–1600	2501–3000	5001–6000

There are no 250 volt ratings over 600 amperes, but 600 volt fuses may be used for lower voltages.

(b) Noninterchangeable—0-6000 Ampere Cartridge Fuseholders. Fuseholders shall be so designed that it will be difficult to put a fuse of any given class into a fuseholder which is designed for a current lower, or voltage higher, than that of the class to which it belongs. Fuseholders for current limiting fuses shall not permit insertion of fuses which are not current limiting.

(c) Marking. Fuses shall be plainly marked, either by printing on the fuse barrel or by a label attached to the barrel, showing the following: (1) ampere rating, (2) voltage rating, (3) interrupting rating where other than 10,000 amperes, (4) "current limiting" where applicable, (5) the name or trademark of the manufacturer.

Exception: Interrupting rating marking may be omitted on fuses used for supplementary protection.

G. Circuit Breakers

240-25. Circuit Breakers. Circuit breakers shall conform to the following:

(a) Method of Operation. In general, circuit breakers shall be capable of being closed and opened by hand without employing any other source of power, although normal operation may be by other power such as electrical, pneumatic, and the like. Large circuit breakers which are to be closed and opened by electrical, pneumatic, or other power shall be capable of being closed by hand for maintenance purposes and shall also be capable of being tripped by hand under load without the use of power.

(b) Injury to Operator. Circuit breakers shall be arranged and mounted so that their operation is not likely to injure the operator.

(c) Indication. Circuit breakers shall indicate whether they are in the open or closed position.

(d) Nontamperable. An air circuit breaker, used for the branch circuits described in Article 210, shall be of such design that any alteration of its trip point (calibration), or in the time required for its operation, will be difficult.

▶   With respect to the nontamperable feature mentioned in paragraph *e*, all branch-circuit circuit breakers listed by Underwriters' Laboratories have been checked for this feature.

(e) Marking. Circuit breakers shall be marked with their rating in such a manner that the marking will be durable and visible after installation except that it may be necessary to remove a trim or cover. The ampere rating of circuit breakers rated 100 amperes or less and 600 volts or less shall be molded, stamped, etched, or similarly marked into the handle or the escutcheon area of the circuit breaker. Each circuit breaker rated 240 volts or less and 100 amperes or less and having an interrupting rating other than 5,000 amperes shall have its interrupting rating shown on the circuit breaker or on its label. Each circuit breaker rated more than 240 volts or more than 100 amperes and having an interrupting rating other than 10,000 amperes shall have its interrupting rating shown on the circuit breaker or on its label.

Exception: Interrupting rating marking may be omitted on circuit breakers used for supplementary protection.

▶   Sections **240-23***c* and **240-25***e* concern the marking of fuses and circuit breaker as to interrupting capacity (IC) ratings.

Common cartridge fuses (**250** and **600** volts, **600** amp and less) are designated as Class H types and have IC ratings of **10,000** amp. According to Section **240-23***c* such fuses need not contain an IC rating on the fuse label. Such a marking, however, is required on Class L, K, R, J or G cartridge fuses, which have IC ratings over **10,000** amp. The exception in Section **240-23***c* concerns small fuses where it is impractical to imprint the IC rating on the fuse even though such fuses may have IC rating *less* than **10,000** amp.

Common circuit breakers, rated at **240** volts or less and **100** amp and less, have **5,000** IC ratings and, as indicated in Section **240-25***e*, are not required to have a marked IC rating on the breaker or its label. The same concept applies to circuit breakers rated over 240 volts or 100 amp where no marking is required if the IC ratings are 10,000 amp. All other circuit breakers, rated above or below the 5,000 and 10,000-amp IC classifications previously described, must be marked with appropriate IC ratings (e.g., there are 240-volt breakers, 100 amp or less, with 7,500-amp or higher IC ratings. Accordingly, each such breaker would have to include the IC rating on the breaker or its label. The exception to Section 240-25*e* applies to circuit breakers used for supplemental protection.

H. General

240-27. Current Limiting Overcurrent Protective Device. A current limiting overcurrent protective device is a device which, when interrupting a specified circuit, will consistently limit the short-circuit current in that circuit to a specified magnitude substantially less than that obtainable in the same circuit if the device were replaced with a solid conductor having comparable impedance.

▶   This paragraph is more in the form of a definition than a requirement and has to do with the requirement for marking of current limitation under Section 240-23*c*. It concerns fuses which can open the circuit during the first half cycle before the current reaches its expected short-circuit peak. See comments on Sections 110-9 and 110-10.

240-30. Supplementary Overcurrent Protection. Where supplementary overcurrent protection is utilized in connection with appliances or other utilization equipment to provide individual protection for specific components or internal circuits within the equipment itself, this does not abrogate any of the requirements applicable to branch circuits and is not to be used as a substitute for branch-circuit protection.

It is not the intent of the above requirement that supplementary overcurrent protective devices be subject to the accessibility requirements as given elsewhere in this code for branch circuit overcurrent protective devices.

ARTICLE 250. GROUNDING

A. General

250-1. Scope. This Article covers general requirements for grounding and bonding of electrical installations, and specific requirements for the following:

(a) Systems, circuits, and equipment required, permitted, or not permitted to be grounded.

(b) Circuit conductor to be grounded on grounded systems.

(c) Location of grounding connections.

(d) Types and sizes of grounding and bonding conductors and electrodes.

(e) Methods of grounding and bonding.

(f) Conditions under which guards, isolation, or insulation may be substituted for grounding.

(g) Connections for lightning arresters.

Circuits are grounded to limit excessive voltages from lightning, line surges, or unintentional contact with higher voltage lines and to limit the voltage to ground during normal operation.

Conductive materials enclosing electric conductors or equipment, or forming part of such equipment, are grounded for the purpose of preventing a voltage above ground on these materials.

Circuits and enclosures are grounded to facilitate overcurrent device operation in case of insulation failure or ground faults. See Section 110-10.

▶   The fine print notes accurately describe the purposes of grounding.

250-2. Other Articles. In other Articles, applying to particular cases of installation of conductors and equipment, there are requirements that are in addition to those of this Article or are modifications of them:

B. Circuit and System Grounding

250-3. Direct-Current Systems.

(a) Two-Wire Direct Current—300 Volts or Less.   Two-wire DC systems operating at not more than 300 volts between conductors supplying interior wiring and including wiring installed as overhead conductors outside of buildings shall be grounded.

Exception No. 1: A system equipped with a ground detector and supplying only industrial equipment in limited areas.

Exception No. 2: A system operating at not more than 50 volts between conductors.

(b) Two-Wire Direct Current—Over 300 Volts.   A two-wire DC system operating at more than 300 volts between conductors may be grounded.

It is recommended that 2-wire direct-current systems operating at more than 300 volts between conductors be grounded when a neutral point can be established such that the maximum difference of potential between the neutral point and any other point on the system does not exceed 300 volts.

It is recommended that 2-wire direct-current systems be not grounded when the voltage to ground of either conductor would exceed 300 volts after grounding.

▶   It should be noted that DC systems are not permitted to be grounded at individual services or elsewhere on interior wiring. See Section **250-22**.

250-5. Alternating-Current Circuits and Systems to be Grounded.   AC circuits and systems shall be grounded as provided for in (a), (b), or (c) below. Other circuits and systems may be grounded.

(a) Alternating-Current Circuits of Less than 50 Volts.   AC circuits of less than 50 volts shall be grounded under any of the following conditions:

(1)   Where supplied by transformers if the transformer supply system exceeds 150 volts to ground.

(2)   Where supplied by transformers if the transformer supply system is ungrounded.

(3) Where installed as overhead conductors outside of buildings.

(b) Alternating-Current Systems of 50 Volts and Over. AC systems supplying interior wiring and interior wiring systems shall be grounded under any of the following conditions:

(1) Where the system can be so grounded that the maximum voltage to ground on the ungrounded conductors does not exceed 150 volts.

(2) Where the system is nominally rated 480Y/277-volt, 3-phase, 4-wire in which the neutral is used as a circuit conductor.

(3) Where the system is nominally rated 240/120-volt, 3-phase, 4-wire in which the midpoint of one phase is used as a circuit conductor.

(4) Where a service conductor is uninsulated in accordance with Section 230-4.

Exception: Electric systems used exclusively to supply industrial electric furnaces for melting, refining, tempering, and the like need not be grounded.

The proper use of suitable ground detectors on ungrounded systems can provide additional protection.

(c) Separately Derived Systems. An interior wiring system whose power is derived from generator, transformer, or converter windings that have no direct electrical connection to supply conductors originating in another supply system, if required to be grounded as in (a) or (b) above, shall be grounded as specified in Section 250-26.

250-7. Circuits Not to be Grounded.   The following circuits shall not be grounded.

(1) Circuits for electric cranes operating over combustible fibers in Class III locations, as provided in Section 503-13.

(2) Circuits as provided in Article 517.

▶   See Section 517-63.

C. Location of Grounding Connections

250-21. Current Over Grounding Conductors.   The grounding of wiring systems, circuits, arresters, cable armor, conduit, or other metal raceways as a protective measure shall be so arranged that there will be no objectionable passage of current over the grounding conductors. The temporary currents set up under accidental conditions, while the grounding conductors are performing their intended protective functions, are not to be considered as objectionable. Where an objectionable flow of current occurs over a grounding conductor, due to the use of multiple grounds, (1) one or more of such grounds shall be abandoned, or (2) their location shall be changed, or (3) the continuity of the conductor between the grounding connections shall be suitably interrupted, or (4) other means satisfactory to the authority having jurisdiction shall be taken to limit the current.

▶   If because of an accidental cross, a current flows through the neutral to the ground, the neutral will be raised to a voltage above ground, this voltage being equal to the current times the resistance of the path to ground. Sometimes a relatively poor ground on one installation will result in a continuous flow of current in the grounding conductor of another installation. This would constitute an objectionable flow of current as mentioned in Section 250-21.

250-22. Grounding Connection for Direct-Current Systems. Direct-current systems which are to be grounded shall have the grounding connection made at one or more supply stations but not at individual services nor elsewhere on interior wiring.

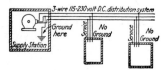

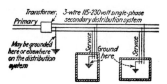

FIG. 250-1. On a three-wire d-c distribution system, the neutral is shown grounded at the supply station only. On a two-wire d-c system, grounding would be accomplished in the same manner.

FIG. 250-2. On a two-wire or three-wire single-phase secondary distribution system, the neutral is grounded at each individual service and at least one other point.

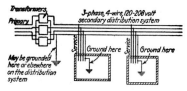

FIG. 250-3. On a four-wire three-phase 208Y/120-volt secondary distribution system, the neutral is grounded at each individual service and at least one other point. When a three-wire three-phase service equipment is installed for power purposes on such a distribution system, the grounded (neutral) conductor must run to the service equipment. See comments following paragraph *b* of Section 250-23.

250-23. Grounding Connections for Alternating-Current Systems.

(a) Secondary AC systems to be grounded shall have a grounding electrode conductor connected to a grounding electrode at each service. Such supply systems that originate outside the building shall have at least one additional grounding connection made to a grounding electrode on the secondary side of the transformer supplying the system, either at the transformer or elsewhere. The grounding electrode conductor shall be connected to the AC system on the supply side of the service disconnecting means, preferably within the enclosure for the service disconnecting means. Grounding connections shall not be made on the load side of the service disconnecting means.

Exception No. 1: A grounding conductor shall be connected to each separately derived system as provided in Section 250-26.

Exception No. 2: A grounding conductor connection shall be made at each separate building where required by Section 250-24.

Exception No. 3: For ranges, counter-mounted cooking units, wall-mounted ovens, and clothes dryers as permitted by Section 250-61.

It is recommended that the grounding electrode conductor of a service of large capacity be connected within the service equipment enclosure.

(b) Ground Conductors Brought to Service Equipment. Where the secondary system is grounded at any point, the grounded conductor shall be run to each service. This conductor shall be not smaller than the required grounding electrode conductor specified in Table 250-94(a) and, in addition, for service phase conductors larger than 1100 MCM the grounded conductor shall be not smaller than 12½ per cent of the area of the largest phase conductor.

Exception: The grounded conductor need not be larger than the largest ungrounded service conductor.

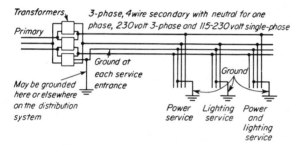

Fig. 250-4. On a four-wire three-phase 230-volt secondary system with a neutral from one transformer to provide for three-wire 115/230-volt service from one phase for lighting, the neutral is grounded at each individual service and at least one other point. When a three-wire three-phase service equipment is installed for power purposes on such a distribution system, the grounded (neutral) conductor must be run to the service equipment. On a three-wire three-phase 220-volt distribution system where there is no neutral, but one of the phase wires is grounded, that phase wire must be grounded at each individual service.

▶   It is the intent of this requirement that line-to-ground fault currents which develop on the premises return to the grounded conductor at the service equipment rather than returning to the transformer or system ground by means of the earth. In other words, a path of low impedance is provided to facilitate the operation of fuses or circuit breakers at buildings in accordance with Section 250-51(3).

It should be noted that paragraph *b* applies only where the secondary is grounded. Some AC systems need not be grounded. See Sections 250-5 and 250-7.

In addition to applying the requirements of paragraph *b*, it is necessary also to apply those of Section 250-53, which requires that a grounding electrode conductor be used to ground both the system (neutral) conductor and the service enclosure (and connecting raceway). This is intended to ensure that the neutral of the system and the service-equipment enclosure are interconnected and that the same grounding conductor is used to connect them both to the grounding electrode. This grounding conductor is to be installed in accordance with the requirements of Section 250-112.

Example: Assume a 115/230-volt single-phase service. Each ungrounded leg consists of three 500,000 cir mil THW (CU) conductors in parallel.

Since the three 500,000 cir mil conductors in parallel provide an area of 1,500,000 cir mil, the *minimum* size of the grounded neutral conductor back to the transformer would be: 1,500,000 cir mil/8 or 187,500 cir mil or 4/0 (CU). However, there will be many instances where the neutral service-entrance conductor will have to be *larger* than 4/0 (CU), depending upon the load conditions. See Section 220-4e.

For "individual service," see Figs. 250-6 and 250-7.

250-24. Two or More Buildings Supplied from Single Service Equipment.   Where two or more buildings are supplied from a single service equipment, a grounding electrode at each building shall be connected to the AC system grounded conductor on the supply side of the building disconnecting means of a grounded system or connected to the metal enclosure of the building disconnecting means of an ungrounded system.

Exception: A grounding electrode at a separate building supplied by a feeder or branch circuit is not required where either of the following conditions are met:

(a) Only one branch circuit is supplied, there is no noncurrent-carrying equipment in the building that requires grounding, and no livestock is housed in the building; or

(b) An equipment grounding conductor is run with the circuit conductors for grounding any noncurrent-carrying equipment, water piping, or building metal frames in the separate building and no livestock is housed in the building. If the separate building has an approved grounding electrode and/or interior metallic piping system, the equipment grounding conductor shall be bonded to the electrode and/or piping system.

▶   When a grounding electrode is required, it shall be located "at such building." This would mean that the water pipe in one building would not be suitable as the grounding electrode for another building unless the water pipe extended to the other building.

Figure 250-5 shows three buildings served by a single service.

On many farm properties the electric service is brought to a centrally located pole. Service drops are run from the pole to a service equipment at each building. See Section 230-23. The neutral conductor and service equipment are grounded at each building. Another method would be to mount a service equipment on the pole, in which case the conductors to the buildings are still treated as service drops and under the conditions described in Section 250-24, for grounding purposes, the disconnecting means in each building are treated as service equipment. See Fig. 250-5 for single service drop to a main building. See also comments following Section 250-54.

Exception *a* indicates an instance when a grounding electrode is not re-

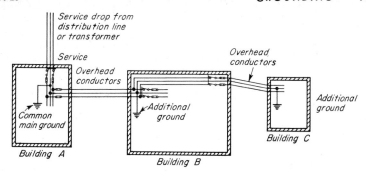

FIG. 250-5. Three buildings served by a single service. The additional grounds are required in most cases under the conditions described in Section 250-24. See Exception *b* for an alternate method.

quired at a separate building. An example would be a small residential garage with a single lighting outlet or switch with no *metal* boxes, faceplates, or lighting fixtures within 8 ft vertically or 5 ft horizontally from a grounded condition.

Exception *b* actually provides an alternate method to achieve grounding in a separate building (other than one housing livestock). If the circuits supplying the separate building contain properly sized equipment grounding conductors, neither a separate grounding electrode nor grounding of the neutral is *required* at that building. However, if the separate building contains an approved grounding electrode, metal frames, or interior metal piping, these components must be bonded to the equipment grounding conductor.

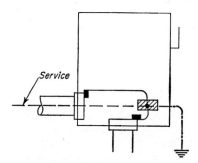

FIG. 250-6. Individual service showing grounding and bonding.

250-25. Conductor to be Grounded. For alternating-current interior wiring systems the conductor to be grounded shall be as follows:

  (a) Single-phase, 2-wire: the identified conductor;
  (b) Single-phase, 3-wire: the identified neutral conductor;

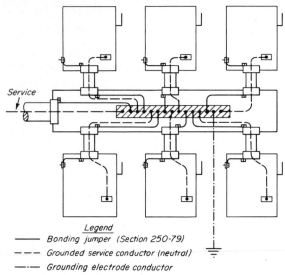

Legend

—— Bonding jumper (Section 250-79)
— — — Grounded service conductor (neutral)
—·— Grounding electrode conductor

FIG. 250-7. Individual service showing grounding and bonding for six service switches.

(c) Multiphase systems having one wire common to all phases: the identified common conductor;

(d) Multiphase systems having one phase grounded: the identified conductor;

(e) Multiphase systems in which one phase is used as in (b): the identified neutral conductor

See Article 200.
The identified conductor is commonly known as "the white wire."

250-26. Grounding Separately Derived Alternating-Current Systems. A separately derived AC system that is required to be grounded by Section 250-5 shall be grounded in the following manner:

(a) A bonding jumper, sized in accordance with Section 250-79(c) for the derived phase conductors, shall be used to connect the system noncurrent-carrying equipment enclosures to the system circuit conductor that is to be grounded. This connection shall be made on the supply side of the separately derived system and ahead of any system disconnecting means or overcurrent device.

(b) A grounding conductor, sized in accordance with Section 250-94(a) for the derived phase conductors, shall be used to connect the circuit conductor of the system that is to be grounded to the grounding electrode as specified in (c) below. This connection shall be made on the supply side of the separately derived system and ahead of any system disconnecting means or overcurrent device.

(c) The grounding electrode shall be as near as practicable to and preferably in the same area as the grounding conductor connection to the system. The grounding electrode shall be: (1) The nearest available effectively grounded structural metal member of the structure; or (2) The nearest available effectively grounded metal water pipe; or (3) Other electrodes as specified in Sections 250-82 and 250-83 where electrodes specified by (1) or (2) above are not available.

(d) In all other respects, grounding methods shall comply with requirements prescribed in other parts of this Code.

▶ A separately derived AC wiring system is a source derived from an on-site generator (emergency or standby), battery-inverter or the secondary supply of a transformer. Any such AC supplies required to be grounded by Section 250-5 must comply with Section 250-26.

The most common applications of Section 250-26 are transformers installed in buildings, such as at load-center unit substations or individual transformers used to transform 480-volt supplies to 120/240-volt single phase or 208Y/120 volts. The purpose of the requirements is to assure proper bonding and grounding so that line-to-ground faults from ungrounded conductors will open overcurrent devices through a *low-impedance* grounding circuit to the grounded conductor of the grounded system.

Figure 250-8 shows a typical arrangement where a 480-volt 3-wire primary supplies a dry-type transformer, and a 208Y/120-volt secondary is provided. The *most important* connection is the bonding jumper between the neutral of the 208Y/120-volt secondary and the metal enclosure of the transformer *or* main secondary circuit breaker. Without such a bonding jumper secondary overcurrent devices would be unable to operate on line-to-ground faults that occur on the load side of such devices. The bonding jumper must be sized according to Section 250-79c. The preferred connection of the bonding jumper is within the transformer between the metal enclosure and the secondary conductor to be grounded. Such an arrangement overcomes the objection of neutral load currents flowing in parallel with conduits if the bonding jumper is located downstream from the transformer at the secondary main shown in Fig. 250-8.

The grounding conductor, extending to the grounding electrode from the secondary grounded conductor, is sized according to Section 250-94a. See Section 250-26b for basic requirements.

Section 250-26c describes the various types of acceptable grounding electrodes. In many instances properly securing a transformer to a grounded, structural, metal-building-member, and installing the bonding jumper according to paragraph *a* will satisfy the requirements of Section 250-26.

D. Enclosure Grounding

250-32. Service Conductor Enclosures. Service raceways, service cable sheaths or armoring, when of metal, shall be grounded.

250-33. Other Conductor Enclosures. Metal enclosures for other than service conductors shall be grounded.

Exception No. 1: Metal enclosures for conductors added to existing installations of open wire, knob and tube work and nonmetallic-sheathed cable in runs of less than 25 feet which are free from probable contact with ground, grounded metal, metal lath or

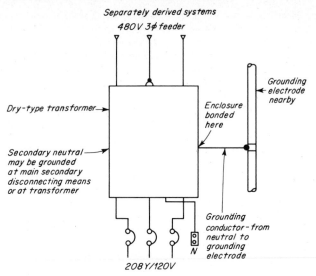

FIG. 250-8. Separately derived system.

other conductive material and which are guarded against contact by persons need not be grounded.

Exception No. 2: Metallic enclosures used to protect approved cable assemblies from physical damage need not be grounded.

▶   **Exception 1** permits the installation of short runs as extensions from existing open wiring, knob and tube work, or nonmetallic-sheathed cable without grounding where there is little likelihood of an accidental connection to ground or of a person touching both the conduit, raceway, or armor and any grounded metal or other grounded surface at the same time.

E. Equipment Grounding

250-42. Fixed Equipment, General.   Exposed noncurrent-carrying metal parts of fixed equipment that are likely to become energized under abnormal conditions shall be grounded under any of the following conditions:

(a)   Where within 8 feet vertically or 5 feet horizontally of ground or grounded metal objects and subject to contact by persons.

(b)   Where located in a wet or damp location and not isolated.

(c)   Where in electrical contact with metal.

(d)   Where in a hazardous location as covered by Articles 500 through 517.

(e)   Where supplied by a metal-clad, metal-sheathed, or metal-raceway wiring method.

Exception: As permitted by Section 250-33 for short sections of raceway.

(f)   Where equipment operates with any terminal in excess of 150 volts to ground.

Exception No. 1: Enclosures for switches or circuit breakers used for other than service equipment and accessible to qualified persons only.

Exception No. 2: Metal frames of electrically heated devices, exempted by special permission, in which case the frames shall be permanently and effectively insulated from ground.

Exception No. 3: Transformer cases mounted on wooden poles at a height exceeding 8 feet above ground or grade level.

250-43. Fixed Equipment—Specific. Exposed, noncurrent-carrying metal parts of the following kinds of equipment, regardless of voltage, shall be grounded:

(a) Frames of motors as specified in Section 430-142;

(b) Controller cases for motors, except lined covers of snap switches;

(c) Electric equipment of elevators and cranes;

(d) Electric equipment in garages, theaters and motion picture studios, except pendant lampholders on circuits of not more than 150 volts to ground;

(e) Motion-picture projection equipment;

(f) Electric signs and associated equipment, unless these are inaccessible to unauthorized persons and are also insulated from ground and from other conductive objects;

(g) Generator and motor frames in an electrically operated organ, unless the generator is effectively insulated both from ground and from the motor driving it;

(h) Switchboard frames and structures supporting switching equipment, except that frames of direct-current, single-polarity switchboards need not be grounded where effectively insulated;

(i) Equipment supplied by Class 1 and Class 2 remote control and signaling circuits where Part B of this Article requires those circuits to be grounded.

250-44. Nonelectrical Equipment. The following metal parts shall be grounded:

(a) Frames and tracks of electrically operated cranes;

(b) The metal frame of a nonelectrically driven elevator car to which electric conductors are attached;

(c) Hand-operated metal shifting ropes or cables of electric elevators;

(d) Metal enclosures such as partitions, grill work, etc., around equipment carrying voltages in excess of 750 volts between conductors, unless in substations or vaults under the sole control of the supply company.

(e) Mobile homes and recreational vehicles as required in Articles 550 and 551.

Where extensive metal in or on buildings may become energized and is subject to personal contact, adequate bonding and grounding will provide additional safety.

250-45. Equipment Connected by Cord and Plug. Under any of the following conditions, exposed noncurrent-carrying metal parts of cord and plug connected equipment, which are liable to become energized, shall be grounded:

(a) In hazardous locations (see Articles 500 through 517);

(b) When operated at more than 150 volts to ground, except:

(1) Motors, where guarded;

(2) Metal frames of electrically heated appliances exempted by Section 422-16.

(c) In residential occupancies, (1) refrigerators, freezers, air conditioners, and (2) clothes-washing, clothes-drying and dish-washing machines, sump pumps and (3) portable, hand held, motor operated tools and appliances of the following types: drills, hedge clippers, lawn mowers, wet scrubbers, sanders and saws.

Exception: Portable tools and appliances protected by an approved system of double insulation, or its equivalent, need not be grounded. Where such an approved system is employed the equipment shall be distinctively marked.

Portable tools or appliances not provided with special insulating or grounding protection are not intended to be used in damp, wet or conductive locations.

(d) In other than residential occupancies, (1) refrigerators, freezers, air conditioners, and (2) clothes-washing, clothes-drying and dish-washing machines, sump pumps and (3) portable, hand held, motor operated tools and appliances of the following types: drills, hedge clippers, lawn mowers, wet scrubbers, sanders and saws, and (4) cord and plug connected appliances used in damp or wet locations, or by persons standing on the ground or on metal floors or working inside of metal tanks or boilers, and (5) portable tools which are likely to be used in wet and conductive locations.

Exception No. 1: Portable tools which are likely to be used in wet and conductive locations need not be grounded where supplied through an insulating transformer with ungrounded secondary of not over 50 volts.

Exception No. 2: Portable tools and appliances protected by an approved system of double insulation, or its equivalent, need not be grounded. Where such an approved system is employed, the equipment shall be distinctively marked. Where conditions of maintenance and supervision assure that proper grounding of tools or appliances will be maintained (as, for example, on some factory production lines) it is recommended that grounded type tools and appliances be used.

It is recommended that the frames of all portable motors which operate at more than 50 volts to ground be grounded.

▶ Except when supplied through an insulating transformer as permitted in paragraph *d* of this section, the frames of portable tools should be grounded by means of an equipment-grounding conductor in the cord or cable through which the motor is supplied.

Portable hand lamps used inside boilers or metal tanks should preferably be supplied through insulating transformers having a secondary voltage of 50 volts or less, with the secondary ungrounded.

Code-recognized double insulated tools and appliances may be used in all types of occupancies other than hazardous locations, in lieu of required grounding.

250-46. Spacing from Lightning Rods. Metal raceways, enclosures, frames, and other noncurrent-carrying metal parts of electric equipment shall be kept at least 6 feet away from lightning rod conductors, or they shall be bonded to the lightning rod conductors.

See Sections 250-86 and 800-31 (b)(5). For further information see the Lightning Protection Code (NFPA No. 78—1968, ANSI C5.1—1969) which contains detailed information on grounding lightning protection systems.

▶ Lightning discharges with their steep wave fronts build up tremendous voltages to metal near the lightning rods, so the 6-ft separation or bonding is to prevent flashover with its attendant hazard.

F. Methods of Grounding

250-50. Equipment Grounding Connections. The grounding connection for metal noncurrent-carrying equipment shall be made on the supply side of the service disconnecting means or as outlined in Section 250-5(c) if for a separately derived system.

(a) For Grounded System. The connection shall be made by bonding the equipment grounding conductor to the grounded circuit conductor and the grounding electrode conductor.

(b) For Ungrounded System. The connection shall be made by bonding the equipment grounding conductor to the grounding electrode conductor.

Exception: For branch-circuit extensions only in existing installations which do not have a grounding conductor in the branch circuit, the grounding conductor of a grounding-type receptacle outlet may be grounded to a grounded cold water pipe near the equipment.

250-51. Effective Grounding. The path to ground from circuits, equipment, and conductor enclosures shall (1) be permanent and continuous and (2) shall have ample carrying capacity to conduct safely any currents liable to be imposed on it, and (3) shall have impedance sufficiently low to limit the potential above ground and to facilitate the operation of the overcurrent devices in the circuit.

▶   *Example:* A single-phase 115/230-volt service is to supply a load of 100 amp. The service-entrance conductors are three No. 3 Type THW conductors. The size of the grounding electrode conductor is based on the size of the largest service-entrance conductor. See Table 250-94a. This table permits a No. 8 copper grounding electrode conductor for a No. 3 service. For connection and installation methods, see Sections 250-81, 250-92, and 250-112. See also comments following Section 250-79.

250-52. Location of System Ground Connection. The grounding electrode conductor may be connected to the grounded conductor of the wiring system at any convenient point on the premises on the supply side of the service disconnecting means.

It is recommended that high capacity services have the grounding conductor connected to the grounded conductor of the system within the service entrance equipment enclosure.

▶   A grounding electrode conductor should be connected to the neutral service conductor as shown in Figs. 250-6 and 250-7 so that it will be accessible for inspection and testing purposes.

250-53. Grounding Path to Grounding Electrode.

(a) Grounding Electrode Conductor. A grounding electrode conductor shall be used to connect the equipment grounding conductors, the service-equipment enclosures and, when the system is grounded, the grounded conductor to the grounding electrode.

(b) Main Bonding Jumper. For a grounded system, an unspliced main bonding jumper shall be used to connect the equipment grounding conductor and the service-equipment enclosure to the grounded conductor of the system.

A main bonding jumper may be a wire, bus, screw, or similar suitable conductor.

▶   On a system having a grounded neutral, the neutral conductor is bonded to the box or cabinet enclosing the service equipment and to the service raceway so that a single grounding electrode conductor serves to ground both the system and the equipment.

250-54. Common Grounding Electrode.   Where the alternating-current system is connected to a grounding electrode in or at a building as specified in Sections 250-23 and 250-24, the same electrode shall be used to ground conductor enclosures and equipment in or on that building.

Two or more electrodes that are effectively bonded together are to be treated as a single electrode in this sense.

▶   In any building housing livestock, all piping systems, metal stanchions, drinking troughs, and other metalwork with which animals might come in contact should be bonded together and to the grounding electrode used to ground the wiring system in the building. See Section 250-81.

250-55. Underground Service Cable.   Where served from a continuous underground metal-sheathed cable system, the sheath or armor of underground service cable metallically connected to the underground system, or underground service conduit containing a metal-sheathed cable bonded to the underground system, need not be grounded at the building and may be insulated from the interior conduit or piping.

250-56. Short Sections of Raceway.   Isolated sections of metal raceway or cable armor, where required to be grounded, shall preferably be grounded by connecting to other grounded raceway or armor, but may be grounded in accordance with Section 250-57.

▶   Where grounding is required, bonding jumpers connected to grounded runs of conduit, raceway, or armor, if available, should be used.

250-57. Fixed Equipment.
(a)   Metal boxes, cabinets and fittings, or noncurrent-carrying metal parts of other fixed equipment may be grounded by the use of any of the conductors specified in Section 250-91(b).
(b)   They may also be grounded in one of the following ways:
(1)   By a grounding conductor run with circuit conductors; this conductor may be uninsulated, but where it is provided with an individual covering, the covering shall be finished a continuous green color or a continuous green color with one or more yellow stripes.
(2)   By a grounding conductor in the supply cord, when cord connected as permitted in Section 400-3;
(3)   By special permission, other means for grounding fixed equipment may be used.

▶   See comments following Section 250-91b.

250-58. Equipment on Structural Metal.

(a) Electric equipment secured to and in contact with the grounded structural metal frame of a building, shall be deemed to be grounded.

(b) Metal car frames supported by metal hoisting cables attached to or running over sheaves or drums of elevator machines shall be deemed to be grounded where the machine is grounded in accordance with this Code.

250-59. Portable and/or Cord and Plug-Connected Equipment.

The noncurrent-carrying metal parts of cord and plug-connected equipment required to be grounded may be grounded in any one of the following ways:

(a) By means of the metal enclosure of the conductors feeding such equipment, provided an approved grounding-type attachment plug is used, one fixed contacting member being for the purpose of grounding the metal enclosure, and provided, further, that the metal enclosure of the conductors is attached to the attachment plug and to the equipment by connectors approved for the purpose;

Exception: The grounding contacting member of grounding type attachment plugs on the power supply cord of portable hand-held, hand-guided or hand-supported tools or appliances may be of the movable self-restoring type.

Attachment plug caps are not intended to be used as terminations for metal-clad cable or flexible metal conduit.

(b) By means of a grounding conductor run with the power supply conductors in a cable assembly or flexible cord that is properly terminated in an approved grounding-type attachment plug having a fixed grounding contacting member. The grounding conductor in a cable assembly may be uninsulated; but where an individual covering is provided for such conductors it shall be finished a continuous green color or a continuous green color with one or more yellow stripes.

Exception: The grounding contacting member of grounding type attachment plugs on the power supply cord of portable hand-held, hand-guided or hand-supported tools or appliances may be of the movable self-restoring type.

▶   See Fig. 250-10.

(c) A separate flexible wire or strap, insulated or bare, protected as well as practicable against physical damage may be used only by special permission except where a part of an approved portable equipment.

▶   The proper method of grounding portable equipment is through an extra conductor in the supply cord. Then if the attachment plug and receptacle comply with the requirements of Section 250-59, the grounding connection will be completed when the plug is inserted in the receptacle.

Figure 250-9 shows a duplex receptacle and an attachment plug intended for use where it is desired to provide for grounding the frames of small portable appliances. These devices are rated 15 amp, 125 volts. The receptacle will receive standard two-pole attachment plugs, so grounding is optional with the user. The grounding contacts in the receptacle are electrically connected to the supporting yoke so that when the box is surface-mounted the connection to ground is provided by a direct metal-to-metal contact between the device yoke and the box. When the box is installed in the wall, a jumper or an approved contact device between the outlet box and the receptacle grounding terminal is required. See Section 250-74.

Fig. 250-9. Grounding-type receptacle and attachment plug. (*Bryant Electric Co.*)

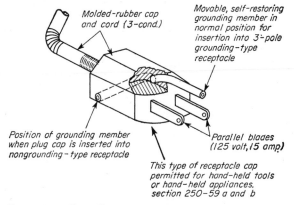

Molded-rubber cap and cord (3-cond.)

Movable, self-restoring grounding member in normal position for insertion into 3-pole grounding-type receptacle

Position of grounding member when plug cap is inserted into nongrounding-type receptacle

Parallel blades (125 volt,15 amp)

This type of receptacle cap permitted for hand-held tools or hand-held appliances. section 250-59 a and b

Fig. 250-10. Grounding-type attachment plug with movable, self-restoring grounding member.

250-60. Frames of Electric Ranges and Electric Clothes Dryers. Frames of electric ranges and electric clothes dryers shall be grounded by any of the means provided for in Sections 250-57 and 250-59; or, where served by a 120/240 volt, single phase, three-wire circuit or a 120/208 volt circuit derived from a three-phase, four-wire supply, they may be grounded by connection to the grounded circuit conductors, provided the grounded circuit conductors are not smaller than No. 10 AWG. Where service-entrance cable having an uninsulated neutral conductor is used, the branch circuit shall originate at the service-entrance equipment. The frames of wall-mounted ovens and counter-mounted cooking units shall be grounded and may be grounded in the same manner as electric ranges. Grounding contacts of receptacles furnished as a part of equipment grounded to the neutral circuit conductor shall be bonded to the equipment which is so grounded.

It is recommended that all branch circuits supplying equipment which is grounded to the grounded circuit conductor originate at the service equipment.

▶ The reason for permitting these appliances to be grounded by connecting them to the circuit neutral is that the circuit is usually short and the grounding conductor is large enough to provide against its being broken. On such equipment, if the neutral were broken the equipment would usually become inoperative and it would be necessary to have repairs made before operation could be resumed.

Where SE cable with an uninsulated neutral supplies these appliances, the circuit must be initiated from the service equipment to avoid multiple neutral grounding which would occur if connected at downstream panelboards.

250-61. Use of Grounded Circuit Conductor for Grounding Equipment.

(a) Supply-Side Equipment. A grounded circuit conductor may be used to ground noncurrent-carrying equipment on the supply side of the service disconnecting means, such as meter enclosures, service raceways, etc., and on the supply side of the main disconnecting means of separate buildings and of separately derived systems as provided in Sections 250-24 and 250-26 respectively.

(b) Load-Side Equipment. A grounded circuit conductor shall not be used for grounding noncurrent-carrying equipment on the load side of the service disconnecting means or on the load side of a separately derived system disconnecting means or the overcurrent devices for a separately derived system not having a main disconnecting means.

Exception No. 1: The frames of ranges, wall-mounted ovens, counter-mounted cooking units, and clothes dryers under the conditions specified by Section 250-60.

Exception No. 2: As permitted in Section 250-24 for separate buildings.

Exception No. 3: By special permission as provided in Section 250-57(b)(3).

▶   The use of a neutral to ground panelboard or other equipment (other than specified in the exceptions) on the load side of service equipment would be extremely hazardous if the neutral became loosened or disconnected. In such cases any line-to-neutral load would energize all metal components connected to the neutral, creating a dangerous potential above ground. Hence, the prohibition of such a practice.

Where a meter housing is mounted outdoors, and the service equipment is mounted separately, with the meter on the supply side of the service equipment, the arrangements shown in Figs. 250-11 and 250-12 are permitted.

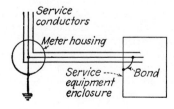

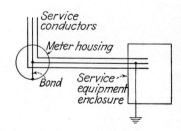

FIG. 250-11. Ground at meter housing, service equipment enclosure grounded to grounded service conductor.

FIG. 250-12. Ground at service equipment, meter housing grounded to grounded service conductor.

In some areas the utilities and inspection departments will not permit the arrangement shown in Fig. 250-11 because the connecting lug in the meter housing is not always accessible for inspection and testing purposes.

250-62. Multiple Circuit Connections.   When an installation of fixed or portable equipment is supplied by separate connection to more than one circuit or grounded interior wiring system, a means for grounding shall be provided for each such connection as described in Sections 250-57 and 250-59.

G. Bonding

250-70. General.   Bonding shall be provided where necessary to assure electrical continuity and the capacity to conduct safely any fault current likely to be imposed.

250-71. Bonding at Service Equipment.   The electrical continuity of the grounding circuit for the following equipment and enclosures shall be assured by one of the means given in Section 250-72.

(a)   The service raceways or service cable armor or sheath;

Exception: Where exempted by Sections 230-63(b) and 250-55.

(b)   All service equipment enclosures containing service entrance conductors,

Fig. 250-13. Grounding bushing for connecting a copper jumper or grounding wire to a conduit. (*Crouse-Hinds Co.*)

Fig. 250-14

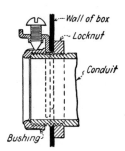

Fig. 250-15

Figs. 250-14 and 250-15. Grounding wedge lug for making suitable electrical connection between a conduit and a box. (*The Thomas & Betts Co.*)

Fig. 250-16. Grounding bushing with openings for set screws to prevent turning. (*General Electric Co.*)

including meter fittings, boxes or the like, interposed in the service raceway or armor;

(c) Any conduit or armor which forms part of the grounding conductor to the service raceway.

250-72. Continuity at Service Equipment. Electrical continuity at service equipment shall be assured by one of the following means:

(a) Bonding equipment to the grounded service conductor in a manner provided in Section 250-113.

(b) Threaded couplings and threaded bosses on enclosures with joints shall be made up wrenchtight where rigid conduit is involved.

(c) Threadless couplings made up tight for rigid metal conduit and electrical metallic tubing.

(d) Bonding jumpers meeting the other requirements of this article. Bonding jumpers shall be used around concentric or eccentric knockouts which are punched or otherwise formed so as to impair the electrical connection to ground.

(e) Other devices (not locknuts and bushings) approved for the purpose.

▶ Bonding jumpers must be used around concentric or eccentric knockouts in service equipment.

250-73. Metal Armor or Tape of Service Cable. With service cable having an uninsulated grounded service conductor in continuous electrical contact with its metallic armor or tape, the metal covering is considered to be adequately grounded.

250-74. Bonding at Grounding-Type Receptacles. Grounding continuity between a grounded outlet box and the grounding circuit of the receptacle shall be established by means of a bonding jumper between the outlet box and the receptacle grounding terminal.

Exception No. 1: When the box is surface-mounted, direct metal-to-metal contact between the device yoke and the box may be used to establish the grounding circuit.

Exception No. 2: Contact devices or yokes designed and approved for the purpose may be used in conjunction with the supporting screws to establish the grounding circuit between the device yoke and flush-type boxes installed in walls.

▶ The first paragraph requires that a jumper be used when the outlet box is installed in the wall. Since boxes installed in walls are very seldom found to be perfectly flush with the wall, direct contact between device yokes and boxes is seldom achieved. Screws and yokes currently in use were designed solely for the support of devices rather than as part of the grounding circuit.

The intent of Exception 2 is to encourage the design of either a modified yoke or a supplemental conducting member to augment the supporting screw in the device-to-box grounding circuit. Figure 250-17 illustrates a grounding device which is intended to provide the electrical grounding continuity between the receptacle yoke and the box on which it is mounted and serves the dual purpose of both a mounting screw and a means of providing electrical grounding continuity in lieu of the required bonding jumper.

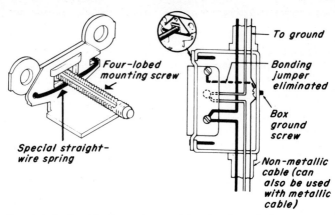

Fig. 250-17. Special wire springs and four-lobed machine screws are part of a receptacle designed for use without a bonding jumper to box. Complies with Section 250-74, Exception 2. (*Slater Electric, Inc.*)

250-75. Bonding Other Enclosures. Metal raceways, cable armor, cable sheath, enclosures, frames, fittings, and other metal noncurrent-carrying parts that are to serve as grounding conductors shall be effectively bonded where necessary to assure electrical continuity and the capacity to conduct safely any fault current likely to be imposed on them. Any nonconductive paint, enamel, or similar coating shall be removed at threads, contact points, and contact surfaces or be connected by means of fittings so designed as to make such removal unnecessary.

250-76. Voltages Exceeding 250 Volts. The electrical continuity of metal raceway or metal sheathed cable which contains any conductor other than service entrance conductors of more than 250 volts to ground shall be assured by one of the methods specified in Sections 250-72(b), (c), (d), and (e), or by one of the following methods:

(a) Threadless fittings, made up tight, with conduit or metal-clad cable;

(b) Two locknuts, one inside and one outside of boxes and cabinets.

▶ Where good electrical continuity is desired on installations of rigid metal conduit, two locknuts are specified so that the metal of the box can be solidly clamped between the locknuts, one being on the outside and one on the inside. The reason for not relying on the bushing in place of the inside locknut is that both conduit and box may be secured in place and if the conduit is placed so that it extends into the box to a greater distance than the thickness of the bushing, the bushing will not make contact with the inside surface of the box.

250-77. Loosely Jointed Metal Raceways. Expansion joints and telescoping sections of raceways shall be made electrically continuous by bonding jumpers or other approved means.

▶ Provision must be made for possible expansion and contraction due to temperature changes by installing expansion joints in long runs of raceways. See Section 300-6*b*.

250-78. Hazardous Locations.   In hazardous locations, regardless of the voltage involved, the electrical continuity of metallic raceway, boxes and the like, shall be assured by one of the methods specified in Sections 250-72(b), (c), (d), and (e).

▶   In a Class I, Division 1 location, the wiring method must be rigid metal conduit with threaded explosion-proof joints and fittings (see Fig. 501-3) or Type MI cable with termination fittings approved for the location (see Fig. 330-4).

In other hazardous locations where threaded hubs or MI termination fittings are not used, bonding jumpers must be used.

250-79. Main and Equipment Bonding Jumpers.

   (a) Material.   Main and equipment bonding jumpers shall be of copper or other corrosion-resistant material.

   (b) Attachment.   Main and equipment bonding jumpers shall be attached in the manner specified by the applicable provisions of Section 250-113 for circuits and equipment and by Section 250-115 for grounding electrodes.

   (c) Size—Equipment Bonding Jumper on Supply Side of Service and Main Bonding Jumper.   The bonding jumper shall not be smaller than the sizes given in Table 250-94(a) for grounding electrode conductors. Where the service-entrance phase conductors are larger than the sizes given in Table 250-94(a), the bonding jumper shall have an area of not less than 12½ per cent of the area of the largest phase conductor. Where the service-entrance conductors are paralleled in two or more raceways, the size of the bonding jumper for each raceway shall be based on the size of service conductors in each raceway.

   (d) Size—Equipment Bonding Jumper on Load Side of Service.   The equipment bonding jumper on the load side of the service overcurrent devices shall not be smaller than the sizes listed by Table 250-95 for equipment grounding conductors.

▶   Bonding-jumper size is based on the size wire that would be required for the corresponding grounding conductor.

Example: In Fig. 250-7, if the No. 1 switch is rated 100 amp and the required supply-conductor ampacity is 85 amp (No. 4 THW), according to Table 250-94*a* the required grounding conductor would be No. 8. The bonding-jumper size would also be No. 8. If switch No. 2 is rated 200 amp and the conductors supplying it are rated 175 amp (No. 2/0 THW), the required grounding conductor and bonding jumper would be No. 4.

In other words, for bonding-jumper purposes each switch should be treated as a separate service equipment and Table 250-94*a* would be applicable to the bonding-jumper size instead of the grounding conductor.

It will be noted that the bonding jumper shown between the incoming service conduit and the neutral terminal block would be the same size as the "grounding electrode conductor" shown between the neutral terminal block and the cold water pipe.

Example: Largest service-entrance conductor 500,000 cir mils would require a No. 0 bonding jumper (see Table 250-94a).

250-80. Bonding of Piping Systems.   All interior metallic water and gas piping which may become energized shall be bonded together and made electrically continuous. A bond having a size in conformance with Table 250-95 shall be made between the bonded piping system(s) and the grounding electrode conductor at the service disconnecting means.

H. Grounding Electrodes

250-81. Water Pipe Electrode.   Where available on the premises, a metal underground water pipe shall always be used as the grounding electrode, regardless of its length and whether supplied by a community or a local underground water piping system or by a well on the premises. Where the buried portion of the water pipe (including any metal well casing effectively bonded to the pipe) is less than 10 feet long or where the water pipe is or is likely to be isolated by insulated sections or joints so that the effectively grounded portion is less than 10 feet long, it shall be supplemented by the use of an additional electrode of a type specified by Section 250-82 or 250-83. The interior metal cold water piping system shall always be bonded to the service-equipment enclosure, the grounded conductor at the service, the grounding electrode conductor where of sufficient size, or to the one or more grounding electrodes used.

Expanding use of nonmetallic piping for water systems and insulating couplings on metal water systems makes it more important that water piping within a building be adequately grounded without depending on connections to an outside piping system. The interior piping system should be electrically continuous. Bonding to sewer piping and metal air ducts within the premises will provide additional safety.

▶   Perhaps the most significant feature of Art. 250 is contained in Section 250-81, where it is specified that a metallic underground water-piping system shall always be used as the grounding electrode where such a piping system is available on the premises. There has been so much misunderstanding over this point between electrical people and water-works people that some years ago a committee consisting of all interested parties was formed to issue an authoritative report on the subject. As a result, there was issued what was called the "Interim Report of the American Research Committee on Grounding," which recorded the unanimous opinion that grounding to water-piping systems has no deleterious effect on either the water or the piping but it does furnish the best available grounding means for the electrical system and thus contributes to the safe use of electricity in buildings. The International Association of Electrical Inspectors published this report in January, 1944, and had reprints made in March, 1949.

It is desirable to avoid the use of dissimilar metals in the soil in close proximity because of the electrolytic action that can be caused by them in wet soil.

On d-c systems, the flow of current through the grounding electrode can cause displacement of metal, depending on the direction of flow. This does not appear to be a problem on a-c systems. The National Bureau of Standards, Washington 25, D.C., has conducted a survey for many years of the corrosion of metals in the soil and has published a number of reports on the results of this work.

Any local water-piping system on the premises, if including 10 ft or more of buried pipe, is considered as an acceptable grounding electrode. If there is buried water piping less than 10 ft long, this piping must still be used as a grounding electrode but must be supplemented by one or more of the electrodes described in Sections 250-82 and 250-83.

250-82. Other Available Electrodes.   Where a water system as described in Section 250-81 is not available, the grounding connection may be made to any of the following:

▶   Although the word "available" is not defined in the Code, its use in Sections 250-81, 250-82, and 250-83 is usually interpreted to mean at or within the building concerned. Unusual conditions should, of course, be subject to individual judgment by the authority having jurisdiction.

(a)   The metal frame of the building, where effectively grounded.

(b)   Where permitted, a continuous metallic underground gas piping system. Underground gas service piping shall not be used as a grounding electrode except when it is electrically continuous uncoated metallic piping and its use as a grounding electrode is acceptable both to the serving gas supplier and to the authority having jurisdiction, since gas piping systems are often constructed with insulating bushings or joints, or are of coated or nonmetallic piping.

(c)   Other local metallic underground systems, such as piping, tanks, and the like.

(d)   The concrete-encased steel reinforcing bar or rod systems of underground footings or foundations, where the total rod length, diameter and depth below earth surface are not less than 50 ft, ⅜ inches and 2½ ft respectively. The required length may be made up of one or more rods.

Connections to the encased rods or bars shall employ metal-fusing methods for any connections to be encased.

▶   Paragraph (d) recognizes concrete-encased steel reinforcing bar or rod systems of underground footings or foundations as an approved grounding electrode where the water piping system, described in Section 250-81, is not available. *If* the grounding electrode conductor connection to a bar or electrode is *embedded in the concrete,* the connection must be by a metal-fusing method (such as a mold-type welding process). The 50-ft length includes one rod or bar or the total of several (none less than ⅜-in. diameter) bonded together.

250-83. Made Electrodes.   Where electrodes described in Sections 250-81 and 250-82 are not available, the grounding electrode shall consist of a driven pipe, driven rod, buried plate or other device approved for the purpose and conforming to the following requirements:

(a) Concrete Encased Electrodes.   Not less than twenty feet of bare copper conductor not smaller than No. 4, encased by at least 2 inches of concrete and located within and near the bottom of a concrete foundation footing that is in direct contact with the earth.

▶   Paragraph (a) recognizes a type of made electrode, which can be used where electrodes specified in Sections 250-81 and 250-82 are not available. This method, known as the "Ufer System" (see Fig. 250-18), has particular merit in new construction where the bare copper conductor can be readily installed in a foundation footing form before concrete is poured. Installations of this type have been installed as far back as 1940, and subsequent tests have proved this system to be highly effective.

The intent of "bottom of the concrete foundation" is to completely encase the copper electrode within the concrete, in the footing near the bottom. The footing shall be in direct contact with the earth which means that dry gravel or polyethylene sheets between the footing and the earth are not permitted.

It may be advisable to provide additional corrosion protection in the form of plastic tubing or sheath at the point where the grounding electrode leaves the concrete foundation.

(b) Plate Electrodes.   Each plate electrode shall present not less than 2 square feet of surface to exterior soil. Electrodes of iron, or steel plates shall be at least ¼ inch in thickness. Electrodes of nonferrous metal shall be at least 0.06 inch in thickness.

(c) Pipe Electrodes.   Electrodes of pipe or conduit shall be not smaller than of the ¾-inch trade size and, where of iron or steel, shall have the outer surface galvanized or otherwise metal-coated for corrosion protection.

(d) Rod Electrodes.   Electrodes of rods of steel or iron shall be at least ⅝ inch

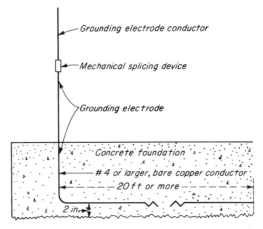

FIG. 250-18. The Ufer grounding system.

in diameter. Approved rods of nonferrous materials or their approved equivalent used for electrodes shall be not less than ½ inch in diameter.

(e) **Installation.** Electrodes should, as far as practicable, be imbedded below permanent moisture level. Except where rock bottom is encountered, pipes or rods shall be driven to a depth of at least 8 feet regardless of size or number of electrodes used. Pipes or rods when less than standard commercial length shall preferably be of one piece. Such pipes or rods shall have clean metal surfaces and shall not be covered with paint, enamel or other poorly conducting materials. Where rock bottom is encountered at a depth of less than 4 feet, electrodes shall be buried in a horizontal trench, and where pipes or rods are used as the electrode they shall comply with Section 250-83(c and d) and shall not be less than 8 feet in length. Each electrode shall be separated at least 6 feet from any other electrode, including those used for signal circuits, radio, lightning rods, or any other purpose.

▶   As a general rule, if a water-piping system or other approved electrode is not available, a driven rod or pipe is used as the electrode. A rod or pipe driven in the ground does not always provide as low a ground resistance as is desirable, particularly where the soil becomes very dry. In some cases where several buildings are supplied, grounding at each building reduces the ground resistance. (See Section 250-24.)

Where it is necessary to bury more than one pipe or rod in order to lower the resistance to ground, they should be placed at least 6 ft apart. If they are placed closer together there would be little improvement.

Where two driven or buried electrodes are used for grounding two different systems that should be kept entirely separate from one another, such as a wiring system for light and power and a lightning rod, care must be taken to guard against the condition of low resistance between the two electrodes and high resistance from each electrode to ground.

If two driven rods or pipes are located 6 ft apart, the resistance between the two is sufficiently high and cannot be greatly increased by increasing the spacing.

250-84. Resistance.   Made electrodes shall, where practicable, have a resistance to ground not to exceed 25 ohms. Where the resistance is not as low as 25 ohms, two or more electrodes connected in parallel shall be used.

Continuous metallic underground water or gas piping systems in general have a resistance to ground of less than 3 ohms. Metal frames of buildings and local metallic underground piping systems, metal well casings, and the like, have, in general, a resistance substantially below 25 ohms. It is recommended that in locations where it is necessary to use made electrodes for grounding interior wiring systems, additional grounds, such as connections to a system ground conductor be placed on the distribution circuit. It is also recommended that single electrode grounds when installed, and periodically afterwards, be tested for resistance.

▶   Insofar as made electrodes are concerned, there is a wide variation of resistance to be expected, and the present requirements of the National Electrical Code concerning the use of such electrodes do not provide for a system that is in any way comparable to that which can be expected where a good underground metallic piping can be utilized.

It is recognized that some types of soil may create a high rate of corrosion and will result in a need for periodic replacement of grounding electrodes.

It will also be noted that the intimate contact of two dissimilar metals, such as iron and copper, when subjected to wet conditions can result in electrolytic corrosion.

Under abnormal conditions, when a cross occurs between a high-tension conductor and one of the conductors of the low-tension secondaries, the electrode may be called upon to conduct a heavy current into the earth. The voltage drop in the ground connection, including the conductor leading to the electrode and the earth immediately around the electrode, will be equal to the current multiplied by the resistance. This results in a difference of potential between the grounded conductor of the wiring system and the ground. It is therefore important that the resistance be as low as practicable.

Where made electrodes are used for grounding interior wiring systems, resistance tests should be conducted on a sufficient number of electrodes to determine the conditions prevailing in each locality. The tests should be repeated several times a year to determine whether the conditions have changed due to corrosion of the electrodes or drying out of the soil.

Figure 250-19 shows how the "Megger" ground tester is used for measuring the ground resistance of a driven electrode. Two auxiliary rod or pipe electrodes are driven to a depth of 1 or 2 ft, the distances A and B in the figure being 50 ft or more. Connections are made as shown between the tester and the electrodes, then the crank is turned to generate the necessary current, and the pointer on the instrument indicates the resistance to earth of the electrode being tested. In place of the two driven electrodes, a water-piping system, if available, may be used as the reference ground, in which case terminals P and C are to be connected to the water pipe.

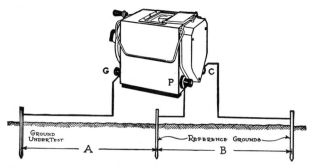

Fig. 250-19. Method of using the Megger ground tester for measuring the resistance to ground of a driven electrode. (*James G. Biddle Co.*)

250-86. Use of Lightning Rods.   Lightning rod conductors and driven pipes, rods or other made electrodes used for grounding lightning rods, shall not be used in lieu of the made grounding electrodes required by this Article for grounding wiring systems and equipment. The foregoing provision shall not be taken to forbid the bonding together of the several made electrodes that are respectively provided for electric wiring systems and equipment, for communication systems, and for lightning protection. See Section 800-31(b-7).

It is recommended that all separate electrodes be bonded together to limit potential differences between them and between their associated wiring systems.

▶   There are cases where fires and shocks have been caused by a potential difference between separate ground electrodes and the neutral of a-c electrical circuits.

J. Grounding Conductors

250-91. Material.   The material for the grounding conductors shall be as follows:

(a) **Grounding Electrode Conductor.**   The grounding electrode conductor shall be of copper, aluminum or other corrosion-resistant material. The material selected shall be resistant to any corrosive condition existing at the installation or shall be suitably protected against corrosion. Where not of copper, its electrical resistance per linear foot shall not exceed that for copper of the size required by Table 250-94(a) or Table 250-94(b). The conductor may be solid or stranded, insulated, covered, or bare and shall be installed in one continuous length without a splice or joint.

Exception No. 1: A bus-bar may be spliced.

Exception No. 2: For a grounding electrode conductor of an ungrounded system only, rigid metal conduit, pipe, and electrical metallic tubing, including such conduit, pipe, and tubing with threaded or threadless joints, may be used and sized in accordance with Table 250-94(b).

(b) **Types of Equipment Grounding Conductors.**   The equipment grounding conductor run with or enclosing the circuit conductors shall be one or more or a combination of the following: (1) A copper or other corrosion-resistant conductor. This conductor may be solid or stranded; insulated, covered, or bare; and in the form of a wire or a bus-bar of any shape; (2) Rigid metal conduit; (3) Electrical metallic tubing; (4) Flexible metal conduit approved for the purpose and installed with fittings approved for the purpose; (5) Armor of Type AC metal-clad cable; (6) The sheath of Type MI cable; (7) The sheath of Type ALS cable; (8) Other raceways specifically approved for grounding purposes.

Exception No. 1: Flexible metal conduit may be used for grounding provided all the following conditions are met:

(a) The length does not exceed 6 feet.

(b) The circuit conductors contained therein are protected by overcurrent devices rated at 20 amperes or less.

(c) The conduit is terminated in fittings approved for the purpose.

Exception No. 2: Liquidtight flexible metal conduit may be used for grounding in the 1¼ inches and smaller trade sizes if the length is 6 feet or less and it is terminated in fittings approved for the purpose.

▶   Section **250-91**b describes the various types of conductors and metallic cables or raceways that are considered suitable for use as equipment grounding conductors.

Exception 1 recognizes a flexible metal conduit with termination fittings "approved for the purpose" as a grounding means (without a separate equipment grounding wire) if the length of the flex is not over 6 ft and the contained circuit conductors are protected by overcurrent devices rated at 20 amp or less.

Exception 2 recognizes a liquidtight flexible metal conduit with termination fittings "approved for the purpose" as a grounding means in sizes not over 1¼ in. and lengths not over 6 ft.

The term "approved for the purpose," as applied to termination fittings, will require the authority having jurisdiction to evaluate the grounding capabilities of fittings used with these short conduit lengths. See also Sections 350-5 and 351-7.

250-92. Installation.   Grounding conductors shall be installed as follows:

(a) **Grounding Electrode Conductor.**   A grounding electrode conductor or its enclosure shall be securely fastened to the surface on which it is carried. A No. 4 or larger conductor shall be protected if exposed to severe physical damage. A No. 6 grounding conductor that is free from exposure to physical damage may be run along the surface of the building construction without metal covering or protection where it is rigidly stapled to the construction; otherwise, it shall be in conduit, electrical metallic tubing or cable armor. Grounding conductors smaller than No. 6 shall be in conduit, electrical metallic tubing or cable armor. Metallic enclosures for grounding conductors shall be electrically continuous from the point of attachment to cabinets or equipment to the grounding electrode, and shall be securely fastened to the ground clamp or fitting. Metallic enclosures that are not physically continuous from cabinet or equipment to the grounding electrode may be made electrically continuous by bonding each end to the grounding conductor. Where rigid metal conduit or steel pipe is used as protection for a grounding conductor, the installation shall comply with the requirements of Article 346; where electrical metallic tubing is used, the installation shall comply with the requirements of Article 348. Aluminum or copper-clad aluminum grounding conductors shall not be used where in direct contact with masonry or the earth or where subject to corrosive conditions. Where used outside, aluminum or copper-clad aluminum grounding conductors shall not be installed within 18 inches of the earth.

It is recommended that magnetic metal enclosures, such as steel pipe or armor, not be used where protection from physical damage can be otherwise obtained, such as by size of the conductor itself or by nonmetallic enclosures.

(b) **Equipment Grounding Conductor.**   An equipment grounding conductor shall be installed as follows:

(1)   Where it consists of a raceway, cable armor, or cable sheath or where it is a wire within a raceway or cable, it shall be installed in accordance with the applicable provisions in this Code using fittings for joints and terminations approved for use with the type raceway or cable used. All connections, joints, and fittings shall be made tight using suitable tools.

(2)   Where it is a separate grounding conductor as provided in Section 210-7 or by special permission as provided by Section 250-57(b) (3), it shall be installed

in accordance with Section 250-92(a) in regard to restrictions for aluminum and also in regard to protection from physical damage.

Exception: Sizes smaller than No. 6 need not be enclosed in a raceway or armor where run in the hollow spaces of a wall or partition or where otherwise installed so as not to be subject to physical damage.

▶   If a steel conduit or tubing is used for mechanical protection of the grounding conductor, it needs to be bonded to the grounding conductor where it enters and where it leaves the protecting steel conduit in order to keep the impedance of the grounding circuit at an acceptable level. See Fig. 250-24.

250-93. Direct Current Systems. The size of the grounding conductor for a direct-current supply system or generator shall be not less than that of the largest conductor supplied by the system, except that where the grounded circuit conductor is a neutral derived from a balancer winding or a balancer set protected in accordance with requirements of Section 445-4(d), the size of the grounding conductor shall not be less than that of the neutral conductor. The grounding conductor shall in no case be smaller than No. 8 copper.

▶   See Fig. 445-2 for balancer set diagram.

250-94. Alternating Current Systems.
   (a) Grounding Electrode Conductor for Grounded Systems. Where the wiring system is grounded, the size of the grounding electrode conductor for an alternating current system shall not be less than is given in Table 250-94(a), except that where connected to made electrodes (as in Section 250-83), that portion of the grounding electrode conductor which is the sole connection between the grounding electrode and the grounded system conductor need not be larger than No. 6 copper wire or its equivalent in ampacity.
   (b) Grounding Electrode Conductor for Ungrounded Systems. Where the wiring system is ungrounded, the size of a grounding electrode conductor for a service raceway, for the metal sheath or armor of a service cable, and for service equipment shall not be less than is given in Table 250-94(b), except that where connected to made electrodes (as in Section 250-83) that portion of the grounding electrode conductor which is the sole connection between the grounding electrode and the service equipment need not be larger than No. 6 copper wire or its equivalent in ampacity.

▶   For copper wire, a minimum size of No. 8 is specified in order to provide sufficient carrying capacity to ensure an effective ground and sufficient mechanical strength to be permanent.
      Where one of the service conductors is a grounded conductor, the same grounding electrode conductor is used for grounding both the system and the equipment. Where the service is from an ungrounded three-phase power system, a grounding electrode conductor of the size given in Table 250-94*b* is required at the service.

Table 250-94(a). Grounding Electrode Conductor
for Grounded Systems

Size of Largest Service-Entrance Conductor or Equivalent for Parallel Conductors		Size of Grounding Electrode Conductor	
Copper	Aluminum or Copper-Clad Aluminum	Copper	*Aluminum or Copper-Clad Aluminum
2 or smaller	0 or smaller	8	6
1 or 0	2/0 or 3/0	6	4
2/0 or 3/0	4/0 or 250 MCM	4	2
Over 3/0 thru 350 MCM	Over 250 MCM thru 500 MCM	2	0
Over 350 MCM thru 600 MCM	Over 500 MCM thru 900 MCM	0	3/0
Over 600 MCM thru 1100 MCM	Over 900 MCM thru 1750 MCM	2/0	4/0
Over 1100 MCM	Over 1750 MCM	3/0	250 MCM

Where there are no service-entrance conductors, the grounding electrode conductor size shall be determined by the equivalent size of the largest service-entrance conductor required for the load to be served.

* See installation restrictions in Section 250-92(a).

See Section 250-23(b).

Table 250-94(b). Grounding Electrode Conductor
for Ungrounded Systems

Size of Largest Service-Entrance Conductor or Equivalent for Parallel Conductors		Size of Grounding Electrode Conductor			
Copper	Aluminum or Copper-Clad Aluminum	Copper	*Aluminum or Copper-Clad Aluminum	Conduit or Pipe	Electrical Metallic Tubing
2 or smaller	0 or smaller	8	6	½	½
1 or 0	2/0 or 3/0	6	4	½	1
2/0 or 3/0	4/0 or 250 MCM	4	2	¾	1¼
Over 3/0 thru 350 MCM	Over 250 MCM thru 500 MCM	2	0	¾	1¼
Over 350 MCM thru 600 MCM	Over 500 MCM thru 900 MCM	0	3/0	1	2
Over 600 MCM thru 1100 MCM	Over 900 MCM thru 1750 MCM	2/0	4/0	1	2
Over 1100 MCM	Over 1750 MCM	3/0	250 MCM	1	2

Where there are no service-entrance conductors the grounding electrode conductor size shall be determined by the equivalent size of the largest service-entrance conductor required for the load to be served.

* See installation restrictions in Section 250-92(a).

▶   Tables 250-94a and 250-94b are based on the largest service-entrance conductor whether made up of a single conductor or paralleled conductors. Thus the total area of the paralleled conductors is to be used in arriving at the size listed in the table. The current rating of the conductors has no bearing on the use of these tables and should not be used.

For example, where two 500 MCM service conductors are used in parallel, the total area is 1000 MCM, and this value should be used in sizing the grounding electrode conductor, and for copper, the grounding conductor would be 2/0.

▶   Section 250-94b and Table 250-94b are not intended for the grounding of the wiring system but are applicable only to installations which do not have a grounded system conductor. The grounding of the service equipment and the service raceway enclosing the ungrounded conductors can be by either a suitably sized conductor or a conduit, pipe, or EMT, in which no conductors are necessary.

250-95. Size of Equipment Grounding Conductors.   The size of copper, aluminum, or copper-clad aluminum equipment grounding conductors shall be not less than given in Table 250-95. For permissible use of the enclosing raceway see Sections 250-57(a) and 250-91(b).

When conductors are run in parallel in multiple raceways, as permitted in Section 310-10, the metallic equipment grounding conductor, when used, also shall be run in parallel. Each parallel equipment grounding conductor shall be sized on the basis of the ampere rating of the overcurrent protective device protecting the circuit conductors in the raceway as per Table 250-95.

Exception No. 1: An equipment grounding conductor not smaller than No. 18 copper and not smaller than the circuit conductors if an integral part of an approved flexible cord assembly, may be used to ground cord-connected equipment where the equipment is protected by overcurrent devices not exceeding 20-ampere rating.

Exception No. 2: The equipment grounding conductor need not be larger than the circuit conductors supplying the equipment.

▶   In general, nonmetallic raceways must contain an equipment grounding conductor. When two or more such raceways contain paralleled conductors (See Section 310-10), each such conduit must contain an equipment grounding conductor, sized in accordance with Table 250-95.

Example: Three 3½-in. nonmetallic conduits each contain four 500,000 cir mil THW copper conductors. The conductors are connected in parallel and are protected by 1200-amp Class L fuses. From Table 250-95 a No. 3/0 copper equipment grounding conductor (bare or insulated) is required. Therefore, *each* 3½-in. conduit must contain such a 3/0 conductor, and the three 3/0 conductors must be connected in parallel.

Enclosing metal raceways, which satisfy the provisions of Section 250-91b, may serve as the equipment grounding conductor.

Exception 2 states that the equipment grounding conductor need not be larger than the circuit conductors. The main application for this exception is for motor circuits where motor starting overcurrent devices are usually considerably larger than the motor branch-circuit-conductor ampacity. Also, a circuit consisting of No. 10 aluminum conductors (with an ampacity of 25) can utilize a *No. 10* aluminum equipment according to Exception 2.

Table 250-95. Size of Equipment Grounding Conductors for Grounding Interior Raceway and Equipment

Rating or Setting of Automatic Overcurrent Device in Circuit Ahead of Equipment, Conduit, etc., Not Exceeding (Amperes)	Size	
	Copper Wire No.	Aluminum or Copper-Clad Aluminum Wire No.*
15	14	12
20	12	10
30	10	8
40	10	8
60	10	8
100	8	6
200	6	4
400	3	1
600	1	2/0
800	0	3/0
1000	2/0	4/0
1200	3/0	250 MCM
1600	4/0	350 "
2000	250 MCM	400 "
2500	350 "	500 "
3000	400 "	600 "
4000	500 "	800 "
5000	700 "	1000 "
6000	800 "	1200 "

* See installation restrictions in Section 250-92(a).

▶   See comments following Section 250-95.

250-97. Outline Lighting.   Isolated noncurrent-carrying metal parts of outline lighting systems may be bonded together by a No. 14 conductor protected from physical damage, where a conductor complying with Section 250-95 is used to ground the group.

250-98. Grounding Conductor in Common Raceway.   A grounding conductor may be installed in the same raceway with other conductors of the system to which it is connected.

250-99. Continuity.   No automatic cutout or switch shall be placed in the grounding conductor of an interior wiring system unless the opening of the cutout or switch disconnects all sources of energy.

K. Grounding Conductor Connections

250-111. To Raceway or Cable Armor.   The point of connection of the grounding conductor to interior metal raceways, cable armor and the like shall be as near as practicable to the source of supply and shall be so chosen that no raceway or cable armor is grounded through a run of smaller size than is called for in Section 250-95.

▶   Figure 250-20 represents a service entrance, service switch, a short main feeder from the switch box to a feeder distribution center, and four feeders running from the distribution center to branch-circuit distribution centers in various parts of the building.

250-112. To Grounding Electrode.   The grounding connection of a grounding conductor to a grounding electrode shall be made at a point and in a manner that will assure a permanent and effective ground. Where necessary to assure this for a metal piping system used as a grounding electrode, effective bonding shall be provided around insulated joints and sections and around any equipment that is likely to be disconnected for repairs or replacement.

▶   As a practical matter, grounding connections at grounding electrodes should be accessible where this can be readily accomplished. Exceptions to this recommendation are where connections are made in concrete (see Section 250-82*d*) or connections in earth to driven electrodes. In most other applications it is no hardship to provide grounding connections at electrodes where they can be conveniently inspected.

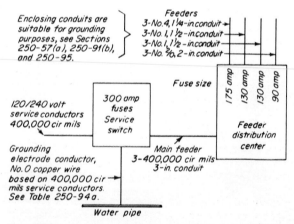

Fig. 250-20. Diagram of a service and feeder system showing application of rules for equipment grounding conductors to ground the various sizes of conduits.

250-113. Attachment to Circuits and Equipment.   The grounding conductor, bond, or bonding jumper shall be attached to circuits, conduits, cabinets, equipment, and the like, which are to be grounded, by means of suitable lugs, pressure connectors, clamps, or other approved means, except that connections which depend upon solder shall not be used.

▶   Figures 250-21 through 250-25 show some of the methods for connecting a conductor to rigid metal conduit, electrical metallic tubing, and outlet boxes.

250-114. Continuity and Attachment of Branch Circuit Equipment Grounding Conductors to Boxes. Where more than one equipment grounding conductor of a branch circuit enters a box, all such conductors shall be in good electrical contact with each other and the arrangement shall be such that the disconnection or removal of a receptacle, fixture, or other device fed from the box will not interfere with or interrupt the grounding continuity.

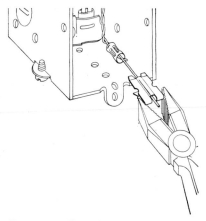

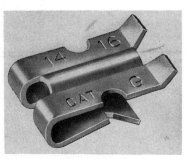

Fig. 250-21. Grounding clip for connecting grounding conductor to box. This clip is intended for use with copper conductors only. (*Steel City Electric Co.*)

Fig. 250-22. Installation of grounding clip (*Steel City Electric Company.*)

Fig. 250-23. Ground clamp for use with No. 8 armored or No. 6 or No. 4 bare grounding conductor. (*Crouse-Hinds Co.*)

(a) **Metallic Boxes.** A connection shall be made between the one or more equipment grounding conductors and a metallic box by means of a grounding screw which shall be used for no other purpose, or an approved grounding device.

(b) **Nonmetallic Boxes.** One or more equipment grounding conductors brought into a nonmetallic outlet box shall be so arranged that a connection can be made to any fitting or device in that box which requires grounding.

250-115. Attachment to Electrodes. The grounding conductor shall be attached to the grounding electrode by means of (1) an approved bolted clamp of cast bronze or brass or of plain or malleable cast iron, or (2) a pipe fitting, plug, or

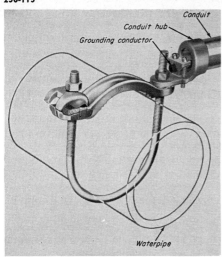

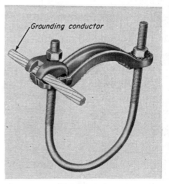

FIG. 250-24   FIG. 250-25

FIGS. 250-24 and 250-25. Heavy-duty ground clamps. Clamps are available for all pipe sizes from 1¼ to 12 in. consisting of steel U-bolt and bronze saddle. One end of the saddle clamps the grounding wire, sizes Nos. 4 through 4/0. The other end is toothed to fit conduit hubs for use when the grounding wire is to be run in conduit. (*The Thomas & Betts Co., Inc.*)

other approved device, screwed into the pipe or into the fitting, or (3) other equally substantial approved means. The grounding conductor shall be attached to the grounding fitting by means of suitable lugs, pressure connectors, clamps, or other approved means, except that connections which depend upon solder shall not be used. Not more than one conductor shall be connected to the grounding electrode by a single clamp or fitting, unless the clamp or fitting is of a type approved for such use.

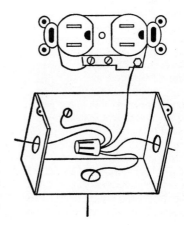

FIG. 250-26. The equipment grounding conductor may be attached to the box by a screw as shown or by other approved means, one of which is shown in Figs. 250-21 and 250-22.

250-116. Ground Clamps. For the grounding conductor of a wiring system the sheet-metal-strap type of ground clamp is not considered adequate unless the strap is attached to a rigid metal base which, when installed, is seated on the water pipe, or other electrode and the strap is of such material and dimensions that it is not liable to stretch during or after installation.

Ground clamps for use on copper water tubing and copper, brass, or lead pipe should preferably be of copper, and those for use on galvanized or iron pipe should preferably be of galvanized iron and so designed as to avoid physical damage to pipe. Ground clamps used with aluminum or copper-clad aluminum grounding conductors should be approved for the purpose.

250-117. Protection of Attachment. Ground clamps or other fittings, unless approved for general use without protection, shall be protected from ordinary physical damage (1) by being placed where they are not liable to be damaged or (2) by being enclosed in metal, wood, or equivalent protective covering.

250-118. Clean Surfaces. Where a nonconductive protective coating, such as paint or enamel, is used on the equipment, conduit, couplings or fittings, such coating shall be removed from threads and other contact surfaces in order to insure a good electrical connection.

L. Instrument Transformers, Relays, etc.

250-121. Instrument Transformer Circuits. The secondary circuits of current and potential instrument transformers shall be grounded where the primary windings are connected to circuits of 300 volts or more to ground, and where on switchboards, shall be grounded irrespective of voltage, except that such circuits need not be grounded where the primary windings are connected to circuits of 750 volts or less and no live parts or wiring are exposed or accessible to other than qualified persons.

250-122. Instrument Transformer Cases. Cases or frames of instrument transformers shall be grounded where accessible to other than qualified persons, except that cases or frames of current transformers, the primaries of which are not over 150 volts to ground and which are used exclusively to supply current to meters, need not be grounded.

250-123. Cases of Instruments, Meters and Relays—Operating Voltage 750 or Less. Instruments, meters and relays which operate with windings or working parts at 750 volts or less shall be grounded as follows:

(a) Not on Switchboards. Instruments, meters, and relays not located on switchboards, which operate with windings or working parts at 300 volts or more to ground, and accessible to other than qualified persons, shall have the cases and other exposed metal parts grounded;

(b) On Dead Front Switchboards. Instruments, meters and relays (whether operated from current and potential transformers, or connected directly in the circuit) on switchboards having no live parts on the front of the panels shall have the cases grounded;

(c) On Live Front Switchboards. Instruments, meters and relays (whether operated from current and potential transformers, or connected directly in the circuit) on switchboards having exposed live parts on the front of panels shall not have their cases grounded. Mats of insulating rubber or other suitable floor insulation, shall be provided for the operator where the voltage to ground exceeds 150.

250-124. Cases of Instruments, Meters and Relays—Operating Voltage Over 750.
Where instruments, meters and relays have current-carrying parts over 750 volts to ground, they shall be isolated by elevation or protected by suitable barriers, grounded metal or insulating covers or guards. Their cases shall not be grounded, except as follows:

(a) In electrostatic ground detectors the internal ground segments of the instrument are connected to the instrument case and grounded; the ground detector shall be isolated by elevation.

250-125. Instrument Grounding Conductor. The grounding conductor for secondary circuits of instrument transformers and for instrument cases shall not be smaller than No. 12, where of copper or where of other metal, shall have equal conductance. Cases of instrument transformers, instruments, meters and relays which are mounted directly on grounded metal surfaces of enclosures or grounded metal switchboard panels shall be considered to be grounded and no additional grounding conductor will be required.

M. Lightning Arresters

250-131. Services of 750 Volts or Less. Where a lightning arrester is installed on a service of 750 volts or less, the connecting conductors shall be as short and straight as practicable and of copper not smaller than No. 14 or of equivalent corrosion-resistant material. Bends, especially sharp bends, shall be avoided where practicable. The arrester grounding conductor shall be connected to one of the following:

(a) The grounded service conductor.

(b) The grounding electrode conductor.

(c) The grounding electrode for the service.

▶   The three methods of grounding the ground terminals of lightning arresters at service entrances are shown in Figs. 250-27, 250-28 and 250-29.

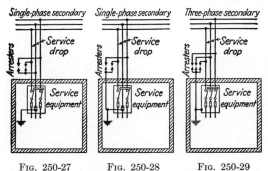

Fig. 250-27   Fig. 250-28   Fig. 250-29

Fig. 250-27. Arrester connected to neutral service conductor. Fig. 250-28. Arrester connected to a grounding electrode conductor. Fig. 250-29. Arrester connected to a grounding electrode conductor of an ungrounded system.

250-132. On Primary Circuits. The grounding conductor of a lightning arrester protecting a transformer which supplies a secondary distribution system may be interconnected as follows:

(a) Metallic Interconnection. A metallic interconnection may be made to the secondary neutral provided that, in addition to the direct grounding connection at the arrester:

(1) The grounded conductor of the secondary has elsewhere a grounding connection to a continuous metallic underground water piping system. However, in urban water pipe areas where there are at least four water pipe connections on the neutral and not less than four such connections in each mile of neutral, the metallic interconnection may be made to the secondary neutral with omission of the direct grounding connection at the arrester.

(2) The grounded conductor of the secondary system is part of a multi-grounded neutral system, of which the primary neutral has at least four ground connections in each mile of line in addition to a ground at each service.

(b) Through Spark Gap. Where the secondary is not grounded as in Section 250-132(a), but is otherwise grounded as in Sections 250-82 and 250-83, such interconnection, where made, shall be through a spark gap having a 60-hertz breakdown voltage of at least twice the primary circuit voltage but not necessarily more than 10 kv, and there shall be at least one other ground on the grounded conductor of the secondary not less than 20 feet distant from the lightning arrester grounding electrode.

(c) By Special Permission. Except as above provided, interconnection of the arrester ground and the secondary neutral may be made only by special permission.

▶   If the grounding conductor of lightning arresters is connected to the secondary neutral it reduces the likelihood of flashover between the transformer primary and secondary.

ARTICLE 280. LIGHTNING ARRESTERS

A. Industrial Stations

280-1. Where Required. Lightning arresters shall be provided in industrial stations in locations where thunderstorms are frequent and adequate protection against lightning is not otherwise provided.

For lightning arresters in hazardous locations, see Articles 500 through 517.

▶   The term *station* means either a generating station or a substation. An industrial station is a generating station or substation serving principally a single industrial plant or factory, as distinguished from a station serving several customers of a public utility corporation.

280-2. Number Required. A lightning arrester shall be connected to each ungrounded overhead conductor entering or leaving the station, except that where there is more than one circuit, a single set of arresters may be installed on the station bus where means are provided to protect circuits that may remain disconnected from the bus.

▶   A double-throw switch which disconnects the outside circuits from the station generator and connects these circuits to ground would satisfy the condition for a single set of arresters for a station bus.

280-3. Where Connected. The arrester shall be connected on the line side of all connected station apparatus.

B. Other Occupancies

280-11. Utilization Equipment. Lightning arresters installed for the protection of utilization equipment may be installed either inside or outside the building or enclosure containing the equipment to be protected. Arresters, unless isolated by elevation or made otherwise inaccessible to unqualified persons, shall be enclosed, and where the operating voltage of the circuit exceeds 750 volts between conductors they shall be inaccessible to unqualified persons.

Secondary lightning protection devices may reduce damage to wiring and equipment caused by lightning disturbances. (See Section 502-3.)

C. General

280-21. Location—Indoors. Arresters installed indoors shall be located well away from other equipment, passageways and combustible parts of buildings, and where containing oil shall be separated from other equipment by walls meeting the requirements of Section 450-42.

280-22. Location—Outdoors. Where arresters containing oil are located outdoors, provision shall be made to drain away any accumulation of oil.

Oil may be drained away by ditches and drains or the oil may be absorbed and danger of spreading removed by paving the yard with cinders or other absorbent material to a depth of several inches.

280-23. Connections—Size and Material. The connections between the arrester and the line wire or bus, and between arrester and ground shall be of copper wire or cable or the equivalent, and, except as provided on secondary services in Section 250-131, shall not be smaller than No. 6, and shall be made as short and as straight as practicable, avoiding as far as possible all bends and turns, especially sharp bends.

▶   Bends and turns enormously increase the impedance to lightning discharges and therefore tend to nullify the effectiveness of a grounding conductor.

280-24. Insulation. Lightning-protection accessories such as gap electrodes, and choke coils where used, shall have an insulation from ground or from other conductors at least equal to the insulation required at other points of the circuit.

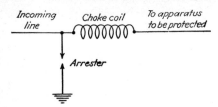

FIG. 280-1. Position of a choke coil
where used with a lightning arrester.

280-25. Switch for Isolating Arrester.   Where isolating switches or disconnecting devices are used, they shall withstand, in full open position, a voltage test between live parts 10 per cent in excess of the maximum voltage test they will withstand to ground.

►   Switches used to disconnect lightning arresters should be so mounted that when they are open a lightning discharge will go to ground rather than jump to another switch or other part of the conductor system.

280-26. Grounding.   Lightning arresters shall be grounded in the manner prescribed in Article 250, except that grounding conductors shall not be run in metallic enclosures unless bonded to both ends of such enclosures.

CHAPTER THREE

Wiring Methods and Materials

ARTICLE 300. WIRING METHODS—GENERAL REQUIREMENTS

300-1. Scope.

(a) The provisions of this Article shall apply to all wiring installations, except for remote-control, including low voltage relay switching, low-energy power and signal systems as provided in Article 725, and communication systems as provided in Article 800.

(b) The provisions of this Article are not intended to apply to the conductors which form an integral part of equipment, such as motors, motor controllers and the like.

300-2. Voltage Limitations.
Wiring methods specified in Chapter 3 may be used for voltages not exceeding 600, unless specifically limited in some Article of Chapter 3. They may be used for voltages over 600 where specifically permitted elsewhere in this code.

300-3. Conductors of Different Systems.

(a) Conductors of light and power systems of 600 volts or less may occupy the same enclosure, without regard to whether the individual circuits are alternating-current or direct-current, only where all conductors are insulated for the maximum voltage of any conductor within the enclosure.

▶ The conductors of a 115/230-volt system may be run in the same enclosure with conductors of any system of not over 600 volts, provided that all the conductors are insulated for 600 volts. For Code purposes conductors of light and power systems of over 600 volts are generally considered medium or high voltage.

(b) Conductors of light and power systems of over 600 volts shall not occupy the same enclosure with conductors of light and power systems of 600 volts or less.

(c) Secondary wiring to electric discharge lamps of 1,000 volts or less, insulated for the secondary voltage involved, may occupy the same fixture enclosure as the branch circuit conductors.

(d) Primary leads of electric discharge lamp ballasts, insulated for the primary voltage of the ballast, when contained within the individual wiring enclosure may occupy the same fixture enclosure as the branch circuit conductors.

(e) Excitation, control, relay and ammeter conductors used in connection with any individual motor or starter may occupy the same enclosure as the motor circuit conductors.

(f) Conductors of signal or radio systems shall not occupy the same enclosure with conductors of light or power systems except as permitted for elevators in Section 620-36; for sound recording in Section 640-6; for remote-control, low-energy power and signal circuits in Sections 725-16 and 725-42; and communication system in Sections 800-3 and 800-21.

▶   Section **300-3c** applies to an installation of fluorescent lamps where a 115- or 230-volt circuit from the panelboard to the ballast is considered as the branch circuit. The ballast, the secondary wiring, and the lamps are considered as being supplied by the branch circuit, *i.e.*, the branch circuit ends at the ballast. The "enclosure" in this case would usually be the housing for the ballast, and it may contain both the branch-circuit wires and the high-voltage secondary wires.

There is always a possibility that the wires in one raceway or box may become crossed with one another. In nearly all cases, a hazardous condition would exist if the conductors of a light and power system should become crossed with radio or signaling conductors.

The conductors of different light and power systems may be installed in the same raceway or other enclosure, provided that the different systems all operate at a voltage of less than 600 between conductors, and provided that all conductors are insulated for the highest voltage at which any conductor in the enclosure operates. Thus, the conductors of a single-phase 115/230-volt system may be run in the same conduit or may be contained in the same box or cabinet with the conductors of a three-phase 220-, 440-, or 550-volt system. Systems of over 600 volts would usually be systems operating at 2,300 volts or more. It is obvious that a hazard would be created by installing conductors of such systems in the same enclosures with conductors of low-voltage (600 volts or less) systems.

300-4. Protection Against Physical Damage.   Where subject to physical damage, conductors shall be adequately protected.

300-5. Protection Against Corrosion.   Metal raceways, cable armor, boxes, cable sheathing, cabinets metallic elbows, couplings, fittings, supports and support hardware shall be of materials suitable for the environment in which they are to be installed.

(a) Ferrous raceways, cable armor, boxes, cable sheathing, cabinets, metallic elbows, couplings, fittings, supports and support hardware shall be suitably protected against corrosion inside and outside (except threads at joints) by a coating of approved corrosion resistant material such as zinc, cadmium, or enamel. Where protected from corrosion solely by enamel, they shall not be used out of doors or in wet locations as described in (c) below. When boxes or cabinets have an approved system of organic coatings and are marked "Raintight" or "Outdoor Type" they may be used out of doors.

(b) Unless made of materials judged suitable for the condition, or unless corrosion protection approved for the condition is provided, ferrous or nonferrous metallic raceways, cable armor, boxes, cable sheathing, cabinets, elbows, couplings, fittings, supports and support hardware shall not be installed in concrete or in direct contact with the earth, or in areas subject to severe corrosive influences.

(c) In portions of dairies, laundries, canneries, and other indoor wet locations, and in locations where walls are frequently washed or where there are surfaces of absorbent materials, such as damp paper or wood, the entire wiring system, including all boxes, fittings, conduits and cable used therewith, shall be mounted so that there is at least one-quarter inch air space between it and the wall or supporting surface.

In general, areas where acids and alkali chemicals are handled and stored may present such corrosive conditions, particularly when wet or damp. Severe corrosive conditions may also be present in portions of meat-packing plants, tanneries, glue houses, some stables; installations immediately adjacent to a seashore, swimming pool areas; areas where chemical de-icers are used; and storage cellars or rooms for hides, casings, fertilizer, salt and bulk chemicals.

▶   Aluminum conduits should not be used in concrete without specific approval of the authority having jurisdiction. All metal raceways used for direct burial in earth should be protected by coatings of asphalt compounds or plastic sheaths to avoid deterioration.

300-6. Raceways Exposed to Different Temperatures.

(a) Sealing. Where portions of an interior raceway system are exposed to widely different temperatures, as in refrigerating or cold-storage plants, provision shall be made to prevent circulation of air from a warmer to a colder section through the raceway.

▶   If the air is allowed to circulate from the warmer to the colder section of the raceway, moisture in the warm air will condense in the cold section of the raceway. This can usually be eliminated by sealing the raceway just outside the cold rooms so as to prevent the circulation of air. Sealing may be accomplished by stuffing a suitable compound in the end of the pipe.

(b) Expansion Joints. Expansion joints for runs of raceway shall be provided where required to compensate for thermal expansion and contraction.

300-7. Underground Runs.
Conductors run underground shall comply with the provisions of Section 230-32 as far as mechanical protection is concerned.

Underground cable run under a building shall be in a raceway that is extended beyond the outside wall of the building.

▶   Damaged underground conductors supplied from interior wiring may overload the conductors inside the building. The preferable means of providing protection from physical damage are to use raceway or cable of a type designed for direct burial in the earth.

300-8. Through Studs, Joists and Rafters.

(a)   Where exposed or concealed wiring conductors in insulating tubes or cables are installed through bored holes in studs, joists or similar wood members, holes shall be bored at the approximate centers of wood members, or at least two inches from the nearest edge where practical.

(b)   Where there is no objection because of weakening the building structure, metal-clad or nonmetallic sheathed cable, aluminum sheathed cable and mineral-insulated metal-sheathed cable may be laid in notches in the studding or joists when the cable at those points is protected against the driving of nails into it by having the notch covered with a steel plate at least ¹⁄₁₆ inch in thickness before building finish is applied.

▶   **Paragraph *a* indicates that the requirements can be met by boring a hole in the approximate center of a stud or not less than 2 in. from the nearest edge. With studs of 4 in. or less in dimension the requirement can be met by locating the bored hole in the approximate center without regard to the distance from the nearest edge. However, on larger lumber greater flexibility is permitted in the requirement in that the hole does not need to be in the center as long as it is at least 2 in. from the nearest edge. The intent here is that the cable shall be so installed as not to reduce below allowable limits the strength of a building or structure, or any part thereof.**

The modern 4-in. stud is approximately 3½ in. and it is not possible to bore a hole through the center and still be "2 inches from the edge."

300-9. Grounding Metal Enclosures.   Metal raceways, boxes, cabinets, cable armor and fittings shall be grounded if and as prescribed in Article 250.

300-10. Electrical Continuity of Metal Raceways and Enclosures.   Metal raceways, cable armor, and other metal enclosures for conductors, shall be metallically joined together into a continuous electrical conductor, and shall be so connected to all boxes, fittings and cabinets as to provide effective electrical continuity. Raceways and cable assemblies shall be mechanically secured to boxes, fittings, cabinets and other enclosures, except as provided for nonmetallic boxes in Section 370-7.

▶   **Metal raceway, cable armor, and outlet boxes and fittings, must form a continuous path to ground of low resistance. In case of an accidental contact between an ungrounded conductor and such metal enclosures, the metal will not be raised to any potential more than a few volts above ground, and sufficient current will flow to ground through the metal enclosure to operate the overcurrent device.**

In Fig. 300-1, outlet boxes *B*, *C*, and *D* depend upon the locknut-bushing connections at box *A* for their electrical connection to the cabinet and through the cabinet to ground.

Figures 300-1 and 300-2 show the locknut-bushing type of connection.

Fɪɢ. 300-1. Locknut-bushing connections between conduit and outlet boxes.

Figure **300-3** shows the double-locknut type of connection. This is considered more reliable than the locknut-bushing type.

The threaded connection shown in Fig. **300-4** makes a very effective electrical connection, and is considered to be mechanically stronger.

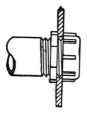
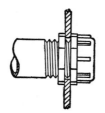
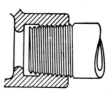

Fig. 300-2. Lock-nut-bushing connection to a box or cabinet.

Fig. 300-3. Double-locknut and bushing type of connection to a box or cabinet.

Fig. 300-4. Threaded connection to a fitting. (*Crouse-Hinds Co.*)

300-11. Secured in Place. Raceways, cable assemblies, boxes, cabinets and fittings shall be securely fastened in place, unless otherwise provided for specific purposes elsewhere in this Code.

See Article 318 for Continuous Rigid Cable Supports.

300-12. Mechanical Continuity—Raceways and Cables. Raceways and cable assemblies shall be continuous from outlet to outlet and from fitting to fitting.
300-13. Mechanical and Electrical Continuity—Conductors. Conductors shall be continuous between outlets, devices, etc., and, except as permitted for auxiliary gutters in Section 374-8, for wireways in Section 362-6, and Section 300-15(a), there shall be no splice or tap within a raceway itself.

In multiwire circuits the continuity of an identified grounded conductor shall not be dependent upon device connections, such as lampholders, receptacles, etc., where the removal of such devices would interrupt the continuity.

▶   The second paragraph in Section **300-13** prohibits splicing of neutral conductors at the terminals of receptacles or other wiring devices where circuits are of the multiwire types (three-wire or four-wire). This is to prevent the establishment of unbalanced voltages if a neutral conductor of such circuits is opened when changing a receptacle or similar device on energized circuits. In such cases, downstream line-to-neutral connections could cause a considerably higher voltage on one part of a multiwire circuit and damage equipment with the neutral "open" if the downstream line-to-neutral loads are appreciably unbalanced. This paragraph does not apply to two-wire circuits or to other circuits that do not contain a grounded neutral conductor.

300-14. Free Length of Conductors at Outlets and Switch Points. At least six inches of free conductor shall be left at each outlet and switch point for the making up of joints or the connection of fixtures or devices, except where conductors are intended to loop without joints through lampholders, receptacles and similar devices.

▶   **Wires looping through the box and intended for connection to outlets at the box need have only sufficient slack so that any connections can be made easily.**

300-15. Boxes or Fittings Where Required.

(a) Box or Fitting.   A box or fitting shall be installed at each conductor splice connection point, outlet, switch point, junction point or pull point for the connection of conduit, electrical metallic tubing, surface raceways or other raceways.

Exception No. 1: A box or fitting is not required for a conductor splice connection in surface raceways, wireways, header ducts, multi-outlet assemblies and auxiliary gutters having a removable cover which is accessible after installation.

Exception No. 2: As permitted in Section 410-26.

(b) Box Only.   A box shall be installed at each conductor splice connection point, outlet, switch point, junction point, or pull point for the connection of metal-clad cable, mineral-insulated metal-sheathed cable, aluminum-sheathed cable, nonmetallic-sheathed cable, or other cables and at each outlet and switch point for concealed knob-and-tube wiring.

Exception No. 1: As permitted by Section 336-11 for insulated outlet devices supplied by nonmetallic-sheathed cable.

Exception No. 2: As permitted by Section 410-60 for rosettes.

Exception No. 3: Where accessible fittings approved for the purpose are used for straight-through splices in mineral-insulated metal-sheathed cable.

▶   **An outlet box provides an enclosure for the circuit wires where they are brought out for connection to a fixture or other device.**

So-called Type T or Type L fittings, shown in Figs. 300-5 and 300-6, actually become a part of the conduit or tubing and should not contain more conductors than permitted for the raceway. Splices should not be made in such fittings unless oversize fittings are used. Where the wiring method requires threaded hub fittings, junction and outlet boxes are available for such use. For conductors No. 6 or larger see Section 370-18a.

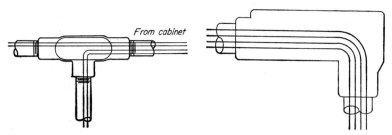

From cabinet

Fɪɢ. 300-5. ½-in. Type T fitting with four No. 14 conductors.

Fɪɢ. 300-6. ½-in. Type L fitting with four No. 14 conductors.

300-16. Raceway or Cable to Open or Concealed Wiring.

(a)   A box or terminal fitting having a separately bushed hole for each conductor shall be used wherever a change is made from conduit, electrical metallic tubing, nonmetallic-sheathed cable, metal-clad cable, aluminum-sheathed cable, or mineral-insulated metal-sheathed cable and surface raceway wiring to open wiring or to concealed knob-and-tube work. A fitting used for this purpose shall contain no taps or splices and shall not be used at fixture outlets.

(b) A bushing may be used in lieu of a box or terminal fitting at the end of a conduit or electrical metallic tubing where the raceway terminates behind an open (unenclosed) switchboard or at an unenclosed control and similar equipment. The bushing shall be of the insulating type for other than lead-sheathed conductors.

▶   Where the wires are run in conduit, tubing, metal raceway, or armored cable, and are brought out for connection to open wiring or concealed knob-and-tube work, a fitting such as is shown in Fig. **300-7** may be used. (See also Fig. **300-8**.)

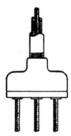

Fig. 300-7. Terminal fitting for use at end of a run of rigid metal conduit. (*Crouse-Hinds Co.*)

Where the terminal fitting is an accessible outlet box, the installation may be made as shown in Fig. 300-9.

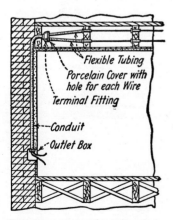

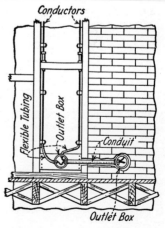

Fig. 300-8. Use of a terminal fitting where a change is made from concealed knob-and-tube work to rigid conduit.

Fig. 300-9. Use of an outlet box where a change is made from concealed knob-and-tube work to rigid conduit.

300-17. Number of Conductors in Raceway. In general the percentage of the total interior cross-sectional area of a raceway occupied by conductors shall not be more than will permit a ready installation or withdrawal of the conductors and dissipation of the heat generated without injury to the insulation of the conductors. See the following Sections of this Code: conduit, Section 346-6; electrical metallic tubing, 348-6; flexible metal conduit, 350-3; surface raceways, 352-4 and 352-25; underfloor raceways, 354-5; cellular metal floor raceways, 356-5; cellular concrete floor raceways, 358-9; wireways, 362-5; auxiliary gutters, 374-5; fixture wire, 402-7; theaters, 520-5; signs, 600-21(d); elevators, 620-33; and sound recording, 640-3 and 640-4; and remote-control, low-energy power, low-voltage power and signal circuits, Article 725.

300-18. Inserting Conductors in Raceways.

(a) Raceways shall first be installed as a complete raceway system without conductors, except those raceways exposed and having a removable cover or capping.

(b) As far as possible, conductors shall not be inserted until the interior of the building has been physically protected from the weather, and all mechanical work on the building which is likely to injure the conductors has been completed.

(c) Pull wires, if to be used, shall not be installed until the raceway system is in place.

(d) Cleaning agents or materials used as lubricants that might have a deleterious effect on conductor coverings shall not be used.

300-19. Supporting Conductors in Vertical Raceways.

(a) Spacing Intervals—Maximum. Conductors in vertical raceways shall be supported. One cable support shall be provided at the top of the vertical raceway or as close to the top as practical, plus a support for each additional interval of spacing as specified in Table 300-19(a).

Exception: If the total vertical riser is less than 25 per cent of the spacing specified in Table 300-19(a), no cable support shall be required.

Table 300-19(a). Spacings for Conductor Supports

	Conductors	
	Aluminum	Copper
No. 18 to No. 8 .... Not Greater Than....	100 feet	100 feet
No. 6 to No. 0 .... " " "	200 feet	100 feet
No. 00 to No. 0000 ...... " " "	180 feet	80 feet
211,601 CM to 350,000 CM.... " " "	135 feet	60 feet
350,001 CM to 500,000 CM.... " " "	120 feet	50 feet
500,001 CM to 750,000 CM.... " " "	95 feet	40 feet
Above 750,000 CM.... " " "	85 feet	35 feet

(b) One of the following methods of support, or a method of equal effectiveness is recommended:

(1) By clamping devices constructed of or employing insulating wedges inserted in the ends of the conduits. With cables having varnished cambric or thermoplastic insulation it may also be necessary to clamp the conductor.

(2) By inserting boxes at the required intervals in which insulating supports are installed and secured in a satisfactory manner to withstand the weight of the conductors attached thereto, the boxes being provided with covers.

(3) In junction boxes, by deflecting the cables not less than 90 degrees and carrying them horizontally to a distance not less than twice the diameter of the cable, the cables being carried on two or more insulating supports, and additionally secured thereto by tie wires if desired.

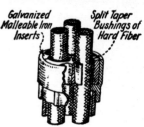

Fig. 300-10. Conductor-support bushing screwed on end of conduit at a cabinet, pull box, or conductor-support box. (*Russell & Stoll.*)

When this method is used cables shall be supported at intervals not greater than 20 per cent of those mentioned in the preceding tabulation.

▶   Long vertical runs of conductors should not be supported by the terminal to which they are connected. Supports as shown in Figs. **300-10** and **300-11** may be used to comply with Section **300-19a**.

Example: A vertical raceway contains 4/0 copper conductors. One cable support—at or near the top of the run—would be required if the vertical run is from 20 to 80 ft. If the vertical run in this example is less than 20 ft, no cable support would be required.

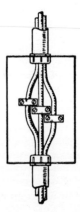

Fig. 300-11. Conductor-support box with single-wire cleats to clamp conductors.

300-20. Induced Currents in Metal Enclosures. When conductors carrying alternating current are installed in metal enclosures they shall be so arranged as to avoid heating the surrounding metal by induction. To accomplish this all phase conductors and, where used, the neutral and all equipment grounding conductors shall be grouped together, except as permitted in Section 250-50(b), Exception.

When a single conductor of a circuit passes through metal with magnetic properties the inductive effect shall be minimized by:

(1) Cutting slots in the metal between the individual holes through which the individual conductors pass, or

(2) Passing all the conductors in the circuit through an insulating wall sufficiently large for all of the conductors of the circuit.

Exception: In the case of circuits supplying vacuum or electric discharge lighting systems or signs, or X-ray apparatus, the currents carried by the conductors are so small that the inductive heating effect may be ignored where these conductors are placed in metal enclosures or pass through metal.

Aluminum being a nonmagnetic metal, there will be no heating due to eddy currents, however, induced currents will be present. These are not considered of sufficient magnitude to require grouping of conductors or special treatment in passing conductors through aluminum wall sections.

300-21. Prevention of Fire Spread.   Electrical installations shall be so made that:

(1) The fire-protective rating of fire walls and fire-resistant or fire-stopped walls, partitions, ceilings, and floors will be substantially equivalent to its original rating.

(2) The possible spread of fire through hollow spaces, vertical shafts, and ventilating or air-handling ducts will be reduced to a minimum.

▶   Electric wiring shall not be installed in such a manner as to interfere with provisions that have been made to prevent fire from being carried from one space to another.

300-22. Wiring in Ducts, Plenums, and Other Air Handling Spaces.

(a) Ducts for Dust, Loose Stock or Vapor Removal.   No wiring systems of any type shall be installed in ducts used to transport dust, loose stock, flammable vapors, nor shall any wiring system of any type be installed in any duct, or shaft containing only such ducts, used for vapor removal or ventilation of commercial type cooking equipment.

(b) Ducts or Plenums Used for Environmental Air.   Wiring systems of mineral-insulated metal-sheathed cable, aluminum-sheathed cable, electrical metallic tubing, or rigid metal conduit may be installed in ducts or plenum chambers used to transport environmental air. Flexible metal conduit may be used, in lengths not to exceed 4 feet, to connect physically adjustable equipment and devices permitted to be in these ducts and plenum chambers. The connectors used with flexible metal conduit shall effectively close any openings in the connection. Equipment and devices may only be installed within such ducts or plenum chambers if necessary for their direct action upon, or sensing of, the contained air. Where equipment or devices are installed and illumination is necessary to facilitate maintenance and repair, enclosed gasketed type fixtures may be installed.

(c) Hollow Spaces Used as Ducts or Plenums for Environmental Air.   Hollow spaces which are used as ducts or plenum chambers for environmental air, other than those described in paragraph (b) above, may contain mineral-insulated metal-sheathed cable, aluminum-sheathed cable, electrical metallic tubing, rigid metal conduit, flexible metal conduit, or metal-clad cables, and other electrical equipment that is permitted within the concealed spaces of such structures, provided that the wiring materials, including fixtures, are suitable for the expected ambient temperature to which they will be subjected.

Exception No. 1: The above provisions shall not apply to integral fan systems specifically approved for the purpose.

Exception No. 2: This section does not include habitable rooms or areas of buildings, the prime purpose of which is not air handling.

NFPA Standard for the Installation of Air Conditioning and Ventilating Systems, No. 90A—1971, sets forth requirements of building used for ducts and plenums.

(d) The wiring systems used for data processing systems and located within air handling areas created by raised floors shall conform to Article 645.

▶ The term "environmental air" is used by the air conditioning industry in talking about the air that people breathe.

Paragraph *b* describes the types of wiring which may be installed in ducts and plenum chambers specifically constructed to transport environmental air.

Paragraph *c* describes the methods to be used as wiring in the hollow spaces of buildings such as the spaces over a hung ceiling which are also used for return or discharge air-handling purposes.

Where a "hung type" ceiling is suspended below the regular ceiling and the space in between is used as a passageway for air (return or discharge) to or from the space below, it is considered as being used for air handling. Whether it is considered as an air-handling duct or a plenum chamber, it would be judged under the requirements of Section 300-22c.

Exception 1 recognizes the installation of motors and control equipment in air-handling ducts where such equipment has been specifically approved for the purpose. Equipment of this type is listed by Underwriters' Laboratories, Inc., and may be found in the "Electrical Appliance and Utilization Equipment List" under the heading "Heating and Ventilating Equipment." This pamphlet may be obtained without cost by writing to Underwriters' Laboratories, Inc.

Exception 2 is intended to exclude from the requirements those areas which may be occupied by people. Hallways and habitable rooms are being used today as portions of air-return systems, and while having air of a heating or cooling system passing through them, the prime purpose of these spaces is obviously not air-handling.

In paragraph *c* the purpose of restricting wiring methods to specific metallic types is to minimize flame spread in such areas. Use of metallic systems reduces the products of combustion and fuel contribution during a fire. See Section **300-21.**

Although Section 300-1a appears to exempt wiring systems in Art. **725** and **800** from the requirements in Art. **300** it would appear that to be consistent with Sections **300-21** and **300-22** that the intent is to include *all* electrical wiring. Note that Section **300-22c** indicates what *wiring methods* may be installed with no respect to the types of systems. Accordingly, many building officials feel that the provisions of Section **300-22** apply to all types of wiring, and this conclusion is consistent with the purpose of fire protection in these areas.

ARTICLE 305. TEMPORARY WIRING

305-1. Scope. The provisions of this Article are applicable to temporary electrical power and lighting wiring methods which may be of a class less than would be required for a permanent installation. Except as specifically modified in this Article, all other requirements of this Code for permanent wiring shall apply to temporary wiring installations.

(a) Temporary electrical power and lighting installations may be used during the period of construction, remodeling, or demolition of buildings, structures, equipment, or similar activities.

(b) Temporary electrical power and lighting installations may be used for a period not to exceed 90 days for Christmas decorative lighting, carnivals, and similar purposes, and for experimental or development work.

305-2. General.

(a) Services. Services shall be installed in conformance with Article 230.

(b) Feeders. Feeders shall be protected as provided in Article 240. They shall originate in an approved distribution center. The conductors may be contained within multi-conductor cord or cable assemblies or where not subject to mechanical injury, they may be run as open conductors on insulators not more than 10 feet apart.

(c) Branch Circuits. All branch circuits shall originate in an approved distribution cabinet or panelboard. Conductors may be contained within multi-conductor cord or cable assemblies or as open wiring. All conductors shall be protected by overcurrent devices at their rated ampacity. When run as open conductors they shall be fastened at ceiling height every 10 feet. No conductor shall be laid on the floor. Each branch circuit which supplies receptacles or fixed equipment shall contain a separate equipment grounding conductor when run as open wiring.

(d) Receptacles. All receptacles shall be of the grounding-type. Unless installed in a complete metallic raceway all branch circuits shall contain a separate equipment grounding conductor and all receptacles shall be electrically connected to the grounding conductor.

See Section 210-7 for receptacles installed on construction sites.

(e) Earth Returns. No bare conductors nor earth returns shall be used for the wiring of any temporary circuit.

(f) Disconnecting Means. Suitable disconnecting switches or plug connectors shall be installed to permit the disconnection of all ungrounded conductors of each temporary circuit.

305-3. Grounding. All grounding shall conform with Article 250.

▶ This Article concerns temporary wiring for limited periods of time. On construction sites the provisions of Section 210-7 require ground-fault protection for 15- and 20-amp receptacle outlets on single-phase circuits.

Other parts of the Article provide rules for services, feeders, branch circuits, receptacles, disconnecting means and grounding.

Section 305-1 defines temporary wiring and where such wiring may be used. Paragraph *b* imposes a 90-day limit for certain types of temporary wiring installations.

ARTICLE 310. CONDUCTORS FOR GENERAL WIRING

310-1. General.

(a) The purpose of this Article is to assure that conductors have mechanical strength, insulation, and ampacity adequate for the particular conditions under which they are to be used.

(b) Conductors shall be insulated, except when covered or bare conductors are specifically permitted in this Code.

(c) The provisions of this Article are not intended to apply to conductors which form an integral part of equipment such as motors, motor controllers, and the like, or which are provided for elsewhere in this Code.

310-2. Application and Construction.

(a) Conductor Application. Conductor insulations as specified in the following Table 310-2(a) may be installed for any of the wiring methods recognized in this Chapter, except as otherwise provided for in the Table or in Section 310-3, or as otherwise specified in this Code. They are suitable for 600 volts unless otherwise specified.

(b) Conductor Construction. Insulated conductors for use at 600 volts or less shall conform to the provisions of Table 310-2(b).

▶ Conductors intended for general wiring under the requirements of the National Electrical Code need to be one of the recognized types listed in the following tables and not smaller than No. 14 AWG. The National Electrical Code does not contain detailed requirements for insulated conductors as these are covered in separate standards such as those of Underwriters' Laboratories, Inc.

"Dry locations" in this case would mean for "general use" in dry locations. It should be noted that "dry locations only" following "Asbestos A" permits such wire to be used in raceways only for leads to or within apparatus.

Table 310-2a permits maximum operating temperatures of 90°C (194°F) in dry locations for Types FEP, FEPB, RHH, XHHW, and THHN wire, but the ampacities for Nos. 14, 12, and 10 copper conductors and Nos. 12, 10, and 8 aluminum conductors are limited to those permitted for 75°C (167°F) insulated conductors. See footnote to Tables 310-12 through 310-15. The reason is that the wiring devices which are commonly connected by these sizes of conductors are not suitable for conditions encountered in the 90°C application. Also, the terminals in most switches, panelboards, etc., have not been tested for maximum insulation temperatures in excess of 75°C.

(c) Identified Conductors. Insulated conductors of No. 6 or smaller, intended for use as identified conductors of circuits shall have an outer identification of a white or natural gray color. Multiple-conductor flat cable No. 4 AWG or larger may employ an external ridge on the identified conductor.

Exception No. 1: Multiple-conductor varnished cloth insulated cables.

Exception No. 2: Fixture wires as outlined below.

(*Exceptions continued on page 174*)

Table 310-2(a). Conductor Application

Trade Name	Type Letter	Max. Operating Temp.	Application Provisions
Rubber-Covered Fixture Wire	*RF-1	60°C 140°F	Fixture wiring. Limited to 300 volts.
Solid or 7-Strand	*RF-2	60°C 140°F	Fixture wiring, and as permitted in Section 725-14.
Rubber-Covered Fixture Wire	*FF-1	60°C 140°F	Fixture wiring. Limited to 300 volts.
Flexible Stranding	*FF-2	60°C 140°F	Fixture wiring, and as permitted in Section 725-14.
Heat-Resistant Rubber-Covered Fixture Wire	*RFH-1	75°C 167°F	Fixture wiring. Limited to 300 volts.
Solid or 7-Strand	*RFH-2	75°C 167°F	Fixture wiring, and as permitted in Section 725-14.
Heat-Resistant Rubber-Covered Fixture Wire	*FFH-1	75°C 167°F	Fixture wiring. Limited to 300 volts.
Flexible Stranding	*FFH-2	75°C 167°F	Fixture wiring, and as permitted in Section 725-14.
Thermoplastic-Covered Fixture Wire—Solid or Stranded	*TF	60°C 140°F	Fixture wiring, and as permitted in Section 725-14.
Thermoplastic-Covered Fixture Wire—Flexible Stranding	*TFF	60°C 140°F	Fixture wiring, and as permitted in Section 725-14.
Heat Resistant, Thermoplastic—Covered Fixture Wire—Solid or Stranded	*TFN	90°C	Fixture wiring, and as permitted in Section 725-14.
Heat Resistant Thermoplastic—Covered Fixture Wire—Flexible Stranding	*TFFN	90°C	Fixture wiring, and as permitted in Section 725-14.
Cotton-Covered, Heat-Resistant, Fixture Wire	*CF	90°C 194°F	Fixture wiring. Limited to 300 volts.

* Fixture wires are not intended for installation as branch circuit conductors except as permitted in Section 725-14.

Table 310-2(a). Conductor Application (*Continued*)

Trade Name	Type Letter	Max. Operating Temp.	Application Provisions
Asbestos-Covered Heat-Resistant, Fixture Wire	*AF	150°C 302°F	Fixture wiring. Limited to 300 volts and Indoor Dry Location.
Fluorinated Ethylene Propylene Fixture Wire Solid or 7 Strand	*PF *PGF	200°C 392°F	Fixture wiring and as permitted in Section 725-14.
Fluorinated Ethylene Propylene Fixture Wire	*PFF *PGFF	150°C 302°F	Fixture wiring and as permitted in Section 725-14.
Extruded Polytetrafluoroethylene (PTFE) Solid or 7-Strand	*PTF	250°C 482°F	Fixture wire, and as permitted in Section 725-14. (Nickel or nickel-coated copper)
Extruded Polytetrafluoroethylene (PTFE) Flexible Stranding (#26-#36 AWG)	*PTFF	150°C 302°F	Fixture wire, and as permitted in Section 725-14. (Silver or nickel-coated copper)
Silicone Rubber Insulated Fixture Wire Solid or 7 Strand	*SF-1	200°C 392°F	Fixture wiring. Limited to 300 volts.
	*SF-2	200°C 392°F	Fixture wiring and as permitted in Section 725-14.
Silicone Rubber Insulated Fixture Wire Flexible Stranding	*SFF-1	150°C 302°F	Fixture wiring. Limited to 300 volts.
	*SFF-2	150°C 302°F	Fixture wiring and as permitted in Section 725-14.
Heat-Resistant Rubber	RH	75°C 167°F	Dry locations.
Heat-Resistant Rubber	RHH	90°C 194°F	Dry locations.
Moisture and Heat Resistant Rubber	RHW	75°C 167°F	Dry and wet locations. For over 2000 volts, insulation shall be ozone-resistant.

* Fixture wires are not intended for installation as branch circuit conductors except as permitted in Section 725-14.

Table 310-2(a). Conductor Application (*Continued*)

Trade Name	Type Letter	Max. Operating Temp.	Application Provisions
Heat Resistant Latex Rubber	RUH	75°C	Dry locations.
Moisture Resistant Latex Rubber	RUW	60°C 140°F	Dry and wet locations.
Thermoplastic	T	60°C 140°F	Dry locations.
Moisture-Resistant Thermoplastic	TW	60°C 140°F	Dry and wet locations.
Heat-Resistant Thermoplastic	THHN	90°C 194°F	Dry locations.
Moisture and Heat-Resistant Thermoplastic	THW	75°C 167°F	Dry and wet locations.
		90°C 194°F	Special applications *within* electric discharge lighting equipment. Limited to 1000 open-circuit volts or less. (Size 14-8 only as permitted in Section 410-26.)
Moisture and Heat-Resistant Thermoplastic	THWN	75°C 167°F	Dry and wet locations.
Moisture and Heat-Resistant Cross-Linked Synthetic Polymer	XHHW	90°C 194°F 75°C 167°F	Dry locations. Wet locations.
Moisture-, Heat- and Oil-Resistant Thermoplastic	MTW	60°C 140°F 90°C 194°F	Machine Tool Wiring in wet locations as permitted in NFPA Standard No. 79 (See Article 670). Machine Tool Wiring in dry locations as permitted in NFPA Standard No. 79 (See Article 670).
Thermoplastic and Asbestos	TA	90°C 194°F	Switchboard wiring only.
Thermoplastic and Fibrous Outer Braid	TBS	90°C 194°F	Switchboard wiring only.
Synthetic Heat-Resistant	SIS	90°C 194°F	Switchboard wiring only.
Mineral Insulation (Metal Sheathed)	MI	85°C 185°F 250°C 482°F	Dry and wet locations. For special application.

Table 310-2(a). Conductor Application *(Continued)*

Trade Name	Type Letter	Max. Operating Temp.	Application Provisions
Extruded Polytetra-fluoroethylene	TFE	250°C 482°F	Dry locations only. Only for leads within apparatus or within raceways connected to apparatus, or as open wiring. (Nickel or nickel-coated copper only.)
Silicone-Asbestos	SA	90°C 194°F 125°C 257°F	Dry locations. For special application.
Fluorinated Ethylene Propylene	FEP or FEPB	90°C 194°F 200°C 392°F	Dry locations. Dry locations—special applications.
Varnished Cambric	V	85°C 185°F	Dry locations only. Smaller than No. 6 by special permission.
Asbestos and Varnished Cambric	AVA	110°C 230°F	Dry locations only.
Asbestos and Varnished Cambric	AVL	110°C 230°F	Dry and wet locations.
Asbestos and Varnished Cambric	AVB	90°C 194°F	Dry locations only.
Asbestos	A	200°C 392°F	Dry locations only. Only for leads within apparatus or within raceways connected to apparatus. Limited to 300 volts.
Asbestos	AA	200°C 392°F	Dry locations only. Only for leads within apparatus or within raceways connected to apparatus or as open wiring. Limited to 300 volts.
Asbestos	AI	125°C 257°F	Dry locations only. Only for leads within apparatus or within raceways connected to apparatus. Limited to 300 volts.
Asbestos	AIA	125°C 257°F	Dry locations only. Only for leads within apparatus or within raceways connected to apparatus or as open wiring.
Paper		85°C 185°F	For underground service conductors, or by special permission.

Table 310-2(b). Conductor Insulations

Trade Name	Type Letter	Insulation	Thickness of Insulation	Outer Covering
Heat-Resistant	RH RHH	Heat-Resistant Rubber	**14-12........30 Mils 10........45 Mils 8-2........60 Mils 1-4/0........80 Mils 213-500........95 Mils 501-1000........110 Mils 1001-2000........125 Mils	*Moisture-resistant, flame-retardant, non-metallic covering
Moisture and Heat-Resistant	RHW	Moisture and Heat Resistant Rubber	14-10........45 Mils 8-2........60 Mils 1-4/0........80 Mils 213-500........95 Mils 501-1000........110 Mils 1001-2000........125 Mils	*Moisture-resistant, flame-retardant, non-metallic covering
Heat-Resistant Latex Rubber	RUH	90% Unmilled, Grainless Rubber	14-10........18 Mils 8-2........25 Mils	Moisture-resistant, flame-retardant, non-metallic covering
Moisture-Resistant Latex Rubber	RUW	90% Unmilled, Grainless Rubber	14-10........18 Mils 8-2........25 Mils	Moisture-resistant, flame-retardant, non-metallic covering
Thermoplastic	T	Flame-Retardant, Thermoplastic Compound	14-10........30 Mils 8........45 Mils 6-2........60 Mils 1-4/0........80 Mils 213-500........95 Mils 501-1000........110 Mils 1001-2000........125 Mils	None

Trade Name	Type Letter	Insulation	AWG or MCM	Thickness of Insulation	Outer Covering
Moisture-Resistant Thermoplastic	TW	Flame-Retardant, Moisture-Resistant Thermoplastic	14–10 8 6–2 1–4/0 213–500 501–1000 1001–2000	30 Mils 45 Mils 60 Mils 80 Mils 95 Mils 110 Mils 125 Mils	None
Heat-Resistant Thermoplastic	THHN	Flame-Retardant Heat-Resistant Thermoplastic	14–12 10 8–6 4–2 1–4/0 250–500 MCM 501–1000 MCM	15 Mils 20 Mils 30 Mils 40 Mils 50 Mils 60 Mils 70 Mils	Nylon Jacket
Moisture and Heat-Resistant Thermoplastic	THW	Flame-Retardant, Moisture and Heat-Resistant Thermoplastic	14–10 8–2 1–4/0 213–500 501–1000 1001–2000	45 Mils 60 Mils 80 Mils 95 Mils 110 Mils 125 Mils	None
Moisture and Heat-Resistant Thermoplastic	THWN	Flame-Retardant, Moisture and Heat-Resistant Thermoplastic	14–12 10 8–6 4–2 1–4/0 250–500 MCM 501–1000 MCM	15 Mils 20 Mils 30 Mils 40 Mils 50 Mils 60 Mils 70 Mils	Nylon Jacket

* Outer covering is not required over rubber insulations which have been specifically approved for the purpose.

** For 14–12 sizes RHH shall be 45 mils thickness insulation.

For insulated aluminum and copper-clad aluminum conductors, the minimum size is No. 12 AWG. See Tables 310-14 and 310-15.

Table 310-2(b). Conductor Insulations (Continued)

Trade Name	Type Letter	Insulation	Thickness of Insulation		Outer Covering
Moisture and Heat-Resistant Cross-Linked Synthetic Polymer	XHHW	Flame-Retardant Cross-Linked Synthetic Polymer	14–10 . . . . 30 Mils 8–2 . . . . 45 Mils 1–4/0 . . . . 55 Mils 213–500 . . . . 65 Mils 501–1000 . . . . 80 Mils 1001–2000 . . . . . . 95 Mils		None
Moisture-, Heat- and Oil-Resistant Thermoplastic	MTW	Flame-Retardant, Moisture-, Heat- and Oil-Resistant Thermoplastic	(A) 22–12 . . . . . 30 Mils 10 . . . . 30 Mils 8 . . . . 45 Mils 6 . . . . 60 Mils 4–2 . . . . 60 Mils 1–4/0 . . . . . . 80 Mils 213–500 MCM . . 95 Mils 501–1000 MCM . . 110 Mils	(B) 15 Mils 20 Mils 30 Mils 30 Mils 40 Mils 50 Mils 60 Mils 70 Mils	(A) None (B) Nylon jacket
Extruded Polytetrafluoroethylene	TFE	Extruded Polytetrafluoroethylene	14–10 . . . . 20 Mils 8–2 . . . . 30 Mils 1–4/0 . . . . 45 Mils		None
Thermoplastic and Asbestos	TA	Thermoplastic and Asbestos	Th'pl'. 14–8 . . . . 20 Mils 6–2 . . . . 30 Mils 1–4/0 . . . . 40 Mils	Asb. 20 Mils 25 Mils 30 Mils	Flame-retardant, non-metallic covering

Trade Name	Type Letter	Insulation	Thickness of Insulation		Outer Covering
Thermoplastic and Fibrous Braid	TBS	Thermoplastic	14–10	30 Mils	Flame-retardant, non-metallic covering
			8	45 Mils	
			6–2	60 Mils	
			1–4/0	80 Mils	
Synthetic Heat-Resistant	SIS	Heat-Resistant Rubber	14–10	30 Mils	None
			8	45 Mils	
			6–2	60 Mils	
			1–4/0	80 Mils	
Mineral-Insulated Metal-Sheathed	MI	Magnesium Oxide	16–4	50 Mils	Copper
			3–250 MCM	55 Mils	
Silicone-Asbestos	SA	Silicone Rubber	14–10	45 Mils	Asbestos or glass
			8–2	60 Mils	
			1–4/0	80 Mils	
			213–500	95 Mils	
			501–1000	110 Mils	
			1001–2000	125 Mils	
Fluorinated Ethylene Propylene	FEP	Fluorinated Ethylene Propylene	14–10	20 Mils	None
			8–2	30 Mils	
Fluorinated Ethylene Propylene	FEPB	Fluorinated Ethylene Propylene	14–8	14 Mils	Glass braid
			6–2	14 Mils	Asbestos braid

For insulated aluminum and copper-clad aluminum conductors, the minimum size is No. 12 AWG. See Tables 310-14 and 310-15.

Table 310-2(b). Conductor Insulations (Continued)

Trade Name	Type Letter	Insulation	Thickness of Insulation	Outer Covering
Varnished Cambric	V	Varnished Cambric	14–8.........45 Mils 6–2.........60 Mils 1–4/0.........80 Mils 213–500.........95 Mils 501–1000.........110 Mils 1001–2000.........125 Mils	Non-metallic covering or lead sheath

Asbestos and Varnished Cambric — Type AVA and AVL — Impregnated Asbestos and Varnished Cambric

(Dimen. in Mils)

	1st Asb.	VC	AVA 2nd Asb.	AVL 2nd Asb.
14–8 (solid only)	—	30	20	25
14–8	10	30	15	25
6–2	15	30	20	25
1–4/0	20	30	30	30
213–500	25	40	40	40
501–1000	30	40	40	40
1001–2000	30	50	50	50

Outer Covering: AVA-asbestos braid or glass; AVL-lead sheath

(Mils)

	VC	Asb.
18–8	30	20
6–2	40	30
1–4/0	40	40

Outer Covering: Flame-retardant, cotton braid (switchboard wiring)

Asbestos and Varnished Cambric — Type AVB — Impregnated Asbestos and Varnished Cambric

(Mils)

	Asb.	VC	2nd Asb.
14–8	10	30	15
6–2	15	30	20
1–4/0	20	40	30
213–500	25	40	40
501–1000	30	40	40
1001–2000	30	50	50

Outer Covering: Flame-retardant, cotton braid

	Type		Size	Sol.	Str.	Outer covering
Asbestos	A	Asbestos	14............		30 Mils	Without asbestos braid
			12–8...........		40 Mils	
Asbestos	AA	Asbestos	14............		30 Mils	With asbestos braid or glass
			12–8...........		30 Mils	
			6–2............		40 Mils	
			1–4/0..........		60 Mils	
Asbestos	AI	Impregnated Asbestos	14............		30 Mils	Without asbestos braid
			12–8...........		40 Mils	
Asbestos	AIA	Impregnated Asbestos	14............	30 Mils	30 Mils	With asbestos braid or glass
			12–8...........	30 Mils	40 Mils	
			6–2............	40 Mils	60 Mils	
			1–4/0..........	60 Mils	75 Mils	
			213–500........		90 Mils	
			501–1000.......		105 Mils	
Paper	Paper	Paper				Lead sheath

The non-metallic covering over individual rubber-covered conductors of aluminum sheathed cable and of lead-sheathed or multiple-conductor cable is not required to be flame retardant. For metal-clad cable, see Section 334-4. For non-metallic-sheathed cable, see Section 336-2. For Type UF cable, see Section 339-1. For aluminum sheathed cable, see Section 331-9.

For insulated aluminum and copper-clad aluminum conductors, the minimum size is No. 12 AWG. See Tables 310-14 and 310-15.

(*Section 310-2(c) continued from page 163*)

Exception No. 3: Mineral insulated-metal sheathed cable.

Exception No. 4: A conductor identified as required by Section 210-5.

For fixture wires the identification shall be as above, or by means of (1) stripes, or (2) by the means described in Section 400-13(a), (b), (c), (d) and (e).

For aerial cable the identification shall be as above, or by means of a ridge so located on the exterior of the cable as to identify it.

Wires having their outer covering finished to show a white or natural gray color but having colored tracer threads in the braid, identifying the source of manufacture, are considered as meeting the provisions of this Section.

(d) Unidentified Conductors. Single conductors, intended for use as unidentified conductors, and conductors other than the identified conductor in multiconductor cables, shall be finished to show a color or combination of colors other than, and contrasting with, white or natural gray. The colors contrasting with white or natural gray, may be provided by means of an approved stripe or stripes on black conductors. For identification requirements for conductors larger than No. 6 see Section 200-6(b).

(e) Insulation Thickness—Over 600 Volts. The thickness of insulation for conductors for use at over 600 volts shall conform to Tables 310-2 (e-1 thru e-4):

310-3. Insulating Materials. The rubber insulations include those made from natural and synthetic rubber, neoprene and other vulcanizable materials.

Thermoplastic insulation may stiffen at temperatures colder than minus 10°C (plus 14°F) requiring care to be exercised during installation at such temperatures. Thermoplastic insulation may also be deformed at normal temperatures where subjected to pressure, requiring care to be exercised during installation and at points of support.

310-4. Temperature Limitations. No conductor shall be used under such conditions that its temperature, even when carrying current, will exceed the temperature specified in Table 310-2(a) for the type of insulation involved.

▶   This requirement is extremely important and is the basis of safe operation of insulated conductors. As shown in Table **310-2a** conductors have various ratings—**60°C, 75°C, 90°C,** etc.

Since Tables **310-12** through **310-15** are based on an assumed ambient (surrounding) temperature of **30°C (86°F)** conductor ampacities are based on the ambient temperature plus the heat (I^2R) produced by the conductor (wire) while carrying current. Therefore, the type of insulation used on the conductor determines the maximum permitted conductor ampacity.

Example: A No. 3/0 THW copper conductor for use in a raceway has an ampacity of **200** according to Table **310-12.** In a **30°C** ambient the conductor is subjected to this temperature when it carries *no* current. Since a THW-insulated conductor is rated at **75°C** this leaves **45°C (75-30)** for increased temperature due to current flow. If the ambient temperature exceeds **30°C,** the conductor ampacity must be reduced proportionally (see Note **13** to Tables **310-12** through **310-15**) so that the *total* temperature (ambient plus conductor temperature-rise due to current flow) will not exceed the temperature rating of the conductor insulation (**60°C, 75°C,** etc.). For the same reason conductor ampacities are derated where more than three conductors are contained in a raceway or cable (See Note 8 to Tables 310-12 through 310-15).

While it can be shown that smaller conductors such as Nos. 14 and 12 60°C-insulated conductors will not reach 60°C at their assigned ampacities (Table 310-12) in a 30°C ambient, ampacities beyond those listed in Tables 310-12 through 310-15 would create excessive voltage drop (IR drop) and would not be compatible with most termination devices.

Although conductor ampacities increase with the rating of conductor insulation, it should be noted that most terminations are designed only for 60°C or 75°C maximum temperatures (ambient plus current). Accordingly, the higher rated ampacities for conductors of 90°C, 110°C, etc., cannot be utilized unless the terminations have comparable ratings.

To find the temperature in degrees Fahrenheit (F) where the temperature is given in degrees Celsius (C), apply the formula:

$$\text{Degrees F} = \text{\%} \times \text{degrees C} + 32$$

Thus, the maximum operating temperature for Type T insulation is 60°C. $\% \times 60° = 108°$. $108° + 32° = 140°$, which is the same temperature on the Fahrenheit scale as 60 degrees on the Celsius scale.

Reversing the process, where the temperature is given in degrees F:

$$\text{Degrees C} = (\text{degrees F} - 32) \times \text{\%}$$

The maximum operating temperature for Type THW insulation is 167°F.

$$167° - 32° = 135°$$

$135° \times \% = 75°$, the corresponding temperature in degrees C.

Table 310-2(e) (1). Thickness of Insulation for Rubber-Covered Wire and Cable, in Mils

Conductor Size AWG-MCM	RHW, RHH, 2000 Volts Unshielded		RHW, RHH, 5000 Volts† Unshielded* or Shielded	
	A	B	A	B
14-10**	80	60	Not Permitted	
8	80	70	155	90
6-2	95	70	155	90
1-2/0	110	90	155	90
3/0-4/0	110	90	155	90
213-500	125	105	170	90
501-1000	140	120	170	90

Column A insulations are limited to natural, SBR and butyl rubbers.
Column B insulations are those specifically approved for the purpose such as cross-linked polyethylene and ethylene-propylene rubber.

* Limited to multi-conductor cables with common overall covering, such as a jacket, sheath, or armor.
** No. 12 AWG is the minimum conductor size for aluminum and copper-clad aluminum.
† Shall be of approved ozone-resistant type for operation at voltages over 2000.

Table 310-2(e) (2). Thickness of Varnished-Cambric Insulation for Single-Conductor Cable, in Mils

Conductor Size AWG or MCM	For Voltages Not Exceeding				
	1000	2000	3000	4000	5000
14	60	..	..	..	..
12	60	80	..	..	..
10	60	80	95	..	..
8-2	60	80	95	110	140
1-4/0	80	95	95	110	140
213-500	95	95	110	125	155
501-1000	110	110	110	125	155
1001-2000	125	125	125	140	155

Table 310-2(e) (3). Thickness of Varnished-Cambric Insulation for Multiple-Conductor Cable, in Mils

Conductor Size AWG or MCM	For Voltages Not Exceeding									
	1000		2000		3000		4000		5000	
	C	B	C	B	C	B	C	B	C	B
14	60	0	..	..	..	..	..	..	..	..
12	60	0	80	0	..	..	..	..	..	..
10	60	0	80	0	80	30	..	..	..	..
8-2	60	0	80	0	80	30	95	45	95	60
1-4/0	80	0	95	0	95	30	95	45	95	60
213-500	95	0	95	0	95	30	95	45	110	60
501-1000	95	30	95	30	95	45	95	60	110	60
1001-2000	110	30	110	30	110	45	110	60	110	80

The thickness given in columns headed "C" are for the insulation on the individual conductors. Those given in the columns headed "B" are for the thickness of the overall belt of insulation.

Table 310-2(e) (4). Thickness of Asbestos and Varnished-Cambric Insulation for Single-Conductor Cable, Types AVA, AVB and AVL, in Mils

Conductor AWG or MCM	1st Wall Asbestos	Varnished Cambric						Asbestos 2nd Wall
		For Voltages Not Exceeding						
	1000-5000	1000	2000	3000	4000	5000		1000-5000
14-2	15	45	60	80	100	120		25
1-4/0	20	45	60	80	100	120		30
213-500	25	45	60	80	100	120		40
501-1000	30	45	60	80	100	120		40
1001-2000	30	55	75	95	115	140		50

310-5. Wet Locations.   Insulated conductors used underground, in concrete slabs or other masonry in direct contact with earth, in wet locations, or where condensation or accumulation of moisture within the raceway is likely to occur, shall be moisture- and heat-resistant, rubber-covered (Type RHW); moisture-resistant latex rubber (Type RUW); moisture-resistant, thermoplastic-covered (Type TW); moisture- and heat-resistant, thermoplastic-covered (Type THW); moisture- and heat-resistant thermoplastic (Type THWN); moisture- and heat-resistant cross-linked synthetic polymer (Type XHHW); lead-covered; aluminum-sheathed cable (Type ALS); mineral-insulated metal-sheathed; or of a type approved for the purpose.

Such conductors are not suitable for direct burial in the earth unless of a type specifically approved for the purpose.

310-6. Buried Conductors.   Cables of one or more conductors for direct burial in the earth shall be of a type approved for the purpose and use, such as Types USE and UF. Where single conductor cables are installed, all conductors of each service, feeder, sub-feeder or branch circuit, including the neutral conductor, shall be run continuously in the same trench or raceway. Supplementary mechanical protection, such as a covering board, concrete pad, raceway, etc., may be required by the authority having jurisdiction. See Section 339-3(c).

310-7. Corrosive Conditions.   Conductors exposed to oils, greases, vapors, gases, fumes, liquids or other substances having a deleterious effect upon the conductor or insulation shall be of a type approved for the purpose.

310-8. Minimum Size of Conductors.   Conductors, whether solid or stranded, shall not be smaller than No. 14, except for printing press control circuits; as provided for flexible cords in Section 400-7; for fixture wire in Section 410-18; for fractional horsepower motors in Section 430-22; for cranes and hoists in Section 610-14; for elevator control and signal circuits in Section 620-12; and for remote-control, low energy power, low-voltage power and signal circuits in Section 725-13.

310-9. Stranded Conductors.   Except when used as bus bars or in mineral-insulated metal-sheathed cable, conductors No. 6 and larger, installed in raceways, shall be stranded. This requirement shall be changed to No. 8 and larger effective January 1, 1973.

▶   The use of solid bars of bare copper or aluminum is permitted in auxiliary gutter and busways. (See Sections **364-1** and **374-1.**)

310-10. Conductors in Parallel.   Aluminum, copper-clad aluminum, or copper conductors of size 1/0 and larger, comprising each phase or neutral, may be connected in parallel (electrically joined at both ends to form a single conductor) only if all of the following conditions are met: All of the parallel conductors shall be of the same length, of the same conductor material, circular-mil area, same insulation type and terminated in the same manner. Where run in separate raceways or cables, the raceways or cables shall have the same physical characteristics.

When metallic equipment grounding conductors are used with conductors in parallel, they shall comply with the requirements of this Section except that they shall be sized as per Section 250-95.

When conductors are used in parallel, space in enclosures should be given consideration.

► This Section recognizes the use of conductors in sizes 1/0 and larger for use in parallel under the conditions which are stated. This provision is intended to allow a practical means of installing large-capacity feeders and services. Paralleling of conductors relies on a number of factors to ensure equal division of current, and thus all these factors must be satisfied in order to ensure that none of the individual conductors will become overloaded. There does not appear to be any practical need to parallel conductors in sizes smaller than 1/0, and such a practice would not be recognized under the requirements of the National Electrical Code.

Where large currents are involved, it is particularly important that the separate phase conductors be located close together to avoid excessive voltage drop and ensure equal division of current. It is also essential that each phase and the neutral, and grounding wires, if any, be run in each conduit even where the conduit is of nonmetallic material.

The reason for the last sentence of the first paragraph is to provide for the same type of raceway or enclosure for conductors in parallel in separate enclosures. The impedance of the circuit in a nonferrous raceway will be different than the same circuit in a ferrous raceway or enclosure. See Section 300-20.

Except where the conductor size is governed by conditions of voltage drop, it is seldom economical to use in raceways conductors of sizes larger than 1,000,000 cir mils, because above this size the increase in ampacity is very small in proportion to the increase in the size of the conductor. Thus, for a 50 per cent increase in the conductor size, *i.e.*, from 1,000,000 to 1,500,000 cir mils, the ampacity of a Type THW conductor increases only 80 amp or less than 15 per cent, and for an increase in size from 1,000,000 to 2,000,000 cir mils, a 100 per cent increase, the ampacity increases only 120 amp or about 20 per cent. In any case where single conductors larger than 500,000 cir mils would be required, it is worth while to compute the total installation cost using single conductors and the cost using two (or more) conductors in parallel.

310-11. Ampacity Reduction Factors.   Where more than three conductors are installed in a raceway or assembled into one or more cables the ampacity of each conductor shall be reduced in accordance with Note 8 to Tables 310-12 through 310-15.

310-12. Marking.

(a) **Required Information.**   All conductors and cables shall be marked to indicate the following information using the applicable method described in Section 310-12(b).

(1)   The maximum working voltage for which the conductor was tested or approved.

(2)   The proper type letter or letters for the type of wire or cable as specified

elsewhere in this Article, in Tables 310-2(a) and 310-2(b) and in Articles **336, 337, 338,** and **339.**

(3) The manufacturer's name, trademark or other distinctive marking by which the organization responsible for the product may be readily identified.

(4) The AWG size or circular-mil area.

(b) Method of Marking

(1) Surface Marking. The following conductors and cables shall be durably marked on the surface at intervals not exceeding 24 inches:

(a)   Single- and multi-conductor rubber- and thermoplastic-insulated wire.

(b)   Nonmetallic-sheathed cable.

(c)   Service-entrance cable.

(d)   Underground feeder and branch-circuit cable.

(e)   Thermoplastic-insulated fixture wire.

(2) Marker Tape. Metallic-covered and multi-conductor cables shall employ a marker tape located within the cable and running for its complete length.

Exception: Mineral-insulated metal-sheathed cable.

Included in the group of metal-covered cables are: aluminum-sheathed cable, Type ALS (Article 331); metal-clad cable (Article 334) and lead-sheathed cable.

(3) Tag Marking. The following conductors and cables shall be marked by means of a printed tag attached to the coil, reel or carton:

(a)   Mineral-insulated, metal-sheathed cable.

(b)   Fixture wire other than thermoplastic.

(c)   Flexible cords.

(d)   Switchboard wires.

(e)   Metallic-covered single-conductor cables.

(f)   Conductors having outer surface of asbestos.

(c) Suffixes to Designate Number of Conductors. A type letter or letters used alone shall indicate a single insulated conductor. The following letter suffixes shall indicate the following:

D—for two insulated conductors laid parallel within an outer nonmetallic covering.

M—for an assembly of two or more insulated conductors twisted spirally within an outer nonmetallic covering.

Notes to Tables 310-12 through 310-15.

Ampacity. The maximum, continuous, ampacities of copper conductors are given in Tables 310-12 and 310-13. The ampacities of aluminum and copper-clad aluminum conductors are given in Tables 310-14 and 310-15.

1. Explanation of Tables. For explanation of Type Letters, and for recognized size of conductors for the various conductor insulations, see Sections 310-2 and 310-3. For installation requirements, see Sections 310-1 through 310-7 and the various Articles of this Code. For flexible cords see Tables 400-9(b) and 400-11.

2. Application of Tables. For open wiring on insulators and for concealed knob-and-tube work, the allowable ampacities of Tables 310-13 and 310-15 shall be used. For all other recognized wiring methods, the allowable ampacities of Tables 310-12 and 310-14 shall be used, unless otherwise provided in this Code.

3. Aluminum and Copper-Clad Aluminum Conductors. For aluminum and copper-clad aluminum conductors, the allowable ampacities shall be in accordance with Tables 310-14 and 310-15.

4. Bare Conductors. Where bare conductors are used with insulated conductors, their allowable ampacities shall be limited to that permitted for the insulated conductors of the same size.

5. Mineral-Insulated Metal-Sheathed Cable. The temperature limitation on which the ampacities of mineral-insulated metal-sheathed cable are based, is determined by the insulating materials used in the end seal. Termination fittings incorporating unimpregnated organic insulating materials are limited to 85°C. operation.

6. Ultimate Insulation Temperature. In no case shall conductors be associated together in such a way with respect to the kind of circuit, the wiring method employed, or the number of conductors, that the limiting temperature of the conductors will be exceeded.

7. Use of Conductors With Higher Operating Temperatures. Where the room temperature is within 10 degrees C of the maximum allowable operating temperature of the insulation, it is desirable to use an insulation with a higher maximum allowable operating temperature; although insulation can be used in a room temperature approaching its maximum allowable operating temperature limit if the current is reduced in accordance with the Correction Factors for different room temperatures as shown in the Correction Factor Table, Note 13.

8. More Than Three Conductors in a Raceway or Cable. Tables 310-12 and 310-14 give the allowable ampacities for not more than three conductors in a raceway or cable. Where the number of conductors in a raceway or cable exceeds three, the allowable ampacity of each conductor shall be reduced as shown in the following Table:

Number of Conductors	Per Cent of Values in Tables 310-12 and 310-14
4 to 6	80
7 to 24	70
25 to 42	60
43 and above	50

Exception No. 1: When conductors of different systems, as provided in Section 300-3, are installed in a common raceway the derating factors shown above apply to the number of Power and Lighting (Articles 210, 215, 220 and 230) conductors only.

Where the number of conductors in a raceway or cable exceeds three, or where single conductors or multi-conductor cables are stacked or bundled without maintaining spacing as required in Article 318 and are not installed in raceways, the individual ampacity of each conductor shall be reduced as shown in the above table.

Exception No. 2: The derating factors of Sections 210-23(b) and 220-2 (second paragraph) do not apply when the above derating factors are also required.

9. Overcurrent Protection. Where the standard ratings and settings of overcurrent devices do not correspond with the ratings and settings allowed for conductors, the next higher standard rating and setting may be used.

Exception—Except as limited in Section 240-5.

10. Neutral Conductor. (a) A neutral conductor which carries only the unbalanced current from other conductors, as in the case of normally balanced circuits of three or more conductors, shall not be counted in determining ampacities as provided for in Note 8.

(b) In a 3-wire circuit consisting of two phase wires and the neutral of a 4-wire, 3-phase WYE connected system, a common conductor carries approximately the same current as the other conductors and shall be counted in determining ampacities as provided in Note 8.

Where the major portion of the load consists of electric discharge lighting there may be harmonic currents present in the neutral conductor which may be equal to the phase currents, thus the neutral could be considered to be a current-carrying conductor.

11. Voltage Drop. The allowable ampacities in Tables 310-12 through 310-15 are based on temperature alone and do not take voltage drop into consideration.

▶   Note 4 provides that, if an uninsulated conductor is used with insulated conductors in a raceway or cable, its size shall be the size that would be required for a conductor having the same insulation as the insulated conductors and having the required ampacity.

Example: Two No. 6 Type THW conductors and one bare No. 6 conductor in a raceway or cable. The ampacity of the bare conductor would be **65** amp.

If the insulated conductors were Type TW, the ampacity of the bare conductor would be **55** amp.

12. Aluminum Sheathed Cable. The ampacities of Type ALS cable are determined by the temperature limitation of the insulated conductors incorporated within the cable. Hence the ampacities of aluminum sheathed cable may be determined from the columns in Tables 310-12 and 310-14 applicable to the type of insulated conductors employed within the cable.

▶ The purpose of Exception 2 in Note 8 is to indicate that while the pyramiding of derating factors is not required, the greatest factor must always be used. Normally the requirements of Note 8 are equal to or greater than that stated in Sections 210-23 and 220-2, but in no case may a continuous load exceed 80 per cent of branch-circuit or feeder overcurrent-device ratings except where the overcurrent devices and associated assemblies are approved for continuous operation at 100 per cent of their ratings.

13. Correction Factors.

Ambient Temps. Over 30°C. 86°F.

C.	F.	60°C (140°F)	75°C (167°F)	85°C (185°F)	90°C (194°F)	110°C (230°F)	125°C (257°F)	200°C (392°F)	250°C (482°F)
40	104	.82	.88	.90	.90	.94	.95	....	....
45	113	.71	.82	.85	.85	.90	.92	....	....
50	122	.58	.75	.80	.80	.87	.89	....	....
55	131	.41	.67	.74	.74	.83	.86	....	....
60	140	....	.58	.67	.67	.79	.83	.91	.95
70	158	....	.35	.52	.52	.71	.76	.87	.91
75	167	....	....	.43	.43	.66	.72	.86	.89
80	176	....	....	.30	.30	.61	.69	.84	.87
90	194	....	....	....	....	.50	.61	.80	.83
100	212	....	....	....	....	....	.51	.77	.80
120	248	....	....	....	....	....	....	.69	.72
140	284	....	....	....	....	....	....	.59	.59
160	320	....	....	....	....	....	....	....	.54
180	356	....	....	....	....	....	....	....	.50
200	392	....	....	....	....	....	....	....	.43
225	437	....	....	....	....	....	....	....	.30

Table 310-12. Allowable Ampacities of Insulated Copper Conductors

Not More than Three Conductors in Raceway or Cable or
Direct Burial (Based on Ambient Temperature of 30°C. 86°F.)

Size	Temperature Rating of Conductor. See Table 310-2(a)							
AWG MCM	60°C (140°F)	75°C (167°F)	85°C (185°F)	90°C (194°F)	110°C (230°F)	125°C (257°F)	200°C (392°F)	250°C (482°F)
	TYPES RUW (14-2), T, TW	TYPES RH, RHW, RUH (14-2), THW, THWN, XHHW	TYPES V, MI	TYPES TA, TBS, SA, AVB, SIS, FEP, FEPB, RHH, THHN, XHHW**	TYPES AVA, AVL	TYPES AI (14-8), AIA	TYPES A (14-8), AA, FEP* FEPB*	TYPES TFE (Nickel or nickel-coated copper only)
14	15	15	25	25†	30	30	30	40
12	20	20	30	30†	35	40	40	55
10	30	30	40	40†	45	50	55	75
8	40	45	50	50	60	65	70	95
6	55	65	70	70	80	85	95	120
***4	70	85	90	90	105	115	120	145
***3	80	100	105	105	120	130	145	170
***2	95	115	120	120	135	145	165	195
***1	110	130	140	140	160	170	190	220
***0	125	150	155	155	190	200	225	250
***00	145	175	185	185	215	230	250	280
000	165	200	210	210	245	265	285	315
0000	195	230	235	235	275	310	340	370
250	215	255	270	270	315	335	....	....
300	240	285	300	300	345	380	....	....
350	260	310	325	325	390	420	....	....
400	280	335	360	360	420	450	....	....
500	320	380	405	405	470	500	....	....
600	355	420	455	455	525	545	....	....
700	385	460	490	490	560	600	....	....
750	400	475	500	500	580	620	....	....
800	410	490	515	515	600	640	....	....
900	435	520	555	555	....	....	....	....
1000	455	545	585	585	680	730		
1250	495	590	645	645	....	....		
1500	520	625	700	700	785	....	....	....
1750	545	650	735	735	....	....	....	....
2000	560	665	775	775	840	....	....	....

* Special use only. See Table 310-2(a).   ** For dry locations only. See Table 310-2(a).
These ampacities relate only to conductors described in Table 310-2(a).

*** For 3-wire, single-phase residential services, the allowable ampacity of RH, RHH, RHW, THW and XHHW copper conductors shall be for sizes No. 4-100 Amp., No. 3-110 Amp., No. 2-125 Amp., No. 1-150 Amp., No. 1/0-175 Amp., and No. 2/0-200 Amp.

† The ampacities for Types FEP, FEPB, RHH, THHN, and XHHW conductors for sizes AWG 14, 12 and 10 shall be the same as designated for 75°C conductors in this Table.

For ambient temperatures over 30°C, see Correction Factors, Note 13.

Table 310-13. Allowable Ampacities of Insulated Copper Conductors

Single Conductor in Free Air
(Based on Ambient Temperature of 30°C. 86°F.)

Size	Temperature Rating of Conductor. See Table 310-2(a)								
AWG MCM	60°C (140°F)	75°C (167°F)	85°C (185°F)	90°C (194°F)	110°C (230°F)	125°C (257°F)	200°C (392°F)	250°C (482°F)	
	TYPES RUW (14-2), T, TW	TYPES RH, RHW, RUH (14-2), THW, THWN, XHHW	TYPES V, MI	TYPES TA, TBS, SA, AVB, SIS, FEP, FEPB, RHH, THHN, XHHW**	TYPES AVA, AVL	TYPES AI (14-8), AIA	TYPES A (14-8), AA, FEP* FEPB*	TYPE TFE (Nickel or nickel-coated copper only)	Bare and Covered Conductors
14	20	20	30	30†	40	40	45	60	30
12	25	25	40	40†	50	50	55	80	40
10	40	40	55	55†	65	70	75	110	55
8	55	65	70	70	85	90	100	145	70
6	80	95	100	100	120	125	135	210	100
4	105	125	135	135	160	170	180	285	130
3	120	145	155	155	180	195	210	335	150
2	140	170	180	180	210	225	240	390	175
1	165	195	210	210	245	265	280	450	205
0	195	230	245	245	285	305	325	545	235
00	225	265	285	285	330	355	370	605	275
000	260	310	330	330	385	410	430	725	320
0000	300	360	385	385	445	475	510	850	370
250	340	405	425	425	495	530	....	....	410
300	375	445	480	480	555	590	....	....	460
350	420	505	530	530	610	655	....	....	510
400	455	545	575	575	665	710	....	....	555
500	515	620	660	660	765	815	....	....	630
600	575	690	740	740	855	910	....	....	710
700	630	755	815	815	940	1005	....	....	780
750	655	785	845	845	980	1045	....	....	810
800	680	815	880	880	1020	1085	....	....	845
900	730	870	940	940	....	....	....	....	905
1000	780	935	1000	1000	1165	1240	....	....	965
1250	890	1065	1130	1130	....	....	....	....	....
1500	980	1175	1260	1260	1450	....	....	....	1215
1750	1070	1280	1370	1370	....	....	....	....	....
2000	1155	1385	1470	1470	1715	....	....	....	1405

* Special use only. See Table 310-2(a).

** For dry locations only. See Table 310-2(a).

These ampacities relate only to conductors described in Table 310-2(a).

† The ampacities for Types FEP, FEPB, RHH, THHN, and XHHW conductors for sizes AWG 14, 12 and 10 shall be the same as designated for 75°C conductors in this Table.

For ambient temperatures over 30°C, see Correction Factors, Note 13.

▶ See Comments following Section **310-4.**

Table 310-14. Allowable Ampacities of Insulated Aluminum and Copper-Clad Aluminum Conductors

Not More than Three Conductors in Raceway or Cable or
Direct Burial (Based on Ambient Temperature of 30°C. 86°F.)

Size	Temperature Rating of Conductor. See Table 310-2(a)						
AWG MCM	60°C (140°F)	75°C (167°F)	85°C (185°F)	90°C (194°F)	110°C (230°F)	125°C (257°F)	200°C (392°F)
	TYPES RUW (12-2), T, TW	TYPES RH, RHW, RUH (12-2), THW, THWN, XHHW	TYPES V, MI	TYPES TA, TBS, SA, AVB, SIS, RHH, THHN, XHHW**	TYPES AVA, AVL	TYPES AI (12-8), AIA	TYPES A (12-8), AA
12	15	15	25	25†	25	30	30
10	25	25	30	30†	35	40	45
8	30	40	40	40	45	50	55
6	40	50	55	55	60	65	75
4	55	65	70	70	80	90	95
3	65	75	80	80	95	100	115
*2	75	90	95	95	105	115	130
*1	85	100	110	110	125	135	150
*0	100	120	125	125	150	160	180
*00	115	135	145	145	170	180	200
*000	130	155	165	165	195	210	225
*0000	155	180	185	185	215	245	270
250	170	205	215	215	250	270	....
300	190	230	240	240	275	305	....
350	210	250	260	260	310	335	....
400	225	270	290	290	335	360	....
500	260	310	330	330	380	405	....
600	285	340	370	370	425	440	....
700	310	375	395	395	455	485	....
750	320	385	405	405	470	500	....
800	330	395	415	415	485	520	....
900	355	425	455	455	....	....	....
1000	375	445	480	480	560	600	....
1250	405	485	530	530	....	....	....
1500	435	520	580	580	650	....	....
1750	455	545	615	615	....	....	....
2000	470	560	650	650	705	....	....

These ampacities relate only to conductors described in Table 310-2(a).

* For three wire, single phase residential services, the allowable ampacity of RH, RHH, RHW, THW, and XHHW conductors shall be for sizes No. 2-100 Amp., No. 1-110 Amp., No. 1/0-125 Amp., No. 2/0-150 Amp., No. 3/0-175 Amp. and No. 4/0-200 Amp.

** For dry locations only. See Table 310-2(a).

† The ampacities for Types RHH, THHN, and XHHW conductors for sizes AWG 12 and 10 shall be the same as designated for 75°C conductors in this Table.

For ambient temperatures over 30°C, see Correction Factors, Note 13.

Table 310-15. Allowable Ampacities of Insulated Aluminum and Copper-Clad Aluminum Conductors

Single Conductor in Free Air
(Based on Ambient Temperature of 30°C. 86°F.)

Size	Temperature Rating of Conductor. See Table 310-2(a)							
AWG MCM	60°C (140°F)	75°C (167°F)	85°C (185°F)	90°C (194°F)	110°C (230°F)	125°C (257°F)	200°C (392°F)	
	TYPES RUW (12-2), T, TW	TYPES RH, RHW, RUH (12-2), THW, THWN, XHHW	TYPES V, MI	TYPES TA, TBS, SA, AVB, SIS, RHH, THHN, XHHW*	TYPES AVA, AVL	TYPES AI (12-8), AIA	TYPES A (12-8), AA	Bare and Covered Conductors
12	20	20	30	30†	40	40	45	30
10	30	30	45	45†	50	55	60	45
8	45	55	55	55	65	70	80	55
6	60	75	80	80	95	100	105	80
4	80	100	105	105	125	135	140	100
3	95	115	120	120	140	150	165	115
2	110	135	140	140	165	175	185	135
1	130	155	165	165	190	205	220	160
0	150	180	190	190	220	240	255	185
00	175	210	220	220	255	275	290	215
000	200	240	255	255	300	320	335	250
0000	230	280	300	300	345	370	400	290
250	265	315	330	330	385	415	....	320
300	290	350	375	375	435	460	....	360
350	330	395	415	415	475	510	....	400
400	355	425	450	450	520	555	....	435
500	405	485	515	515	595	635	....	490
600	455	545	585	585	675	720	....	560
700	500	595	645	645	745	795	....	615
750	515	620	670	670	775	825	....	640
800	535	645	695	695	805	855	....	670
900	580	700	750	750	....	....	....	725
1000	625	750	800	800	930	990	....	770
1250	710	855	905	905	....	....	....	....
1500	795	950	1020	1020	1175	....	....	985
1750	875	1050	1125	1125	....	....	....	....
2000	960	1150	1220	1220	1425	....	....	1165

These ampacities relate only to conductors described in Table 310-2(a).

* For dry locations only. See Table 310-2(a).

† The ampacities for Types RHH, THHN, and XHHW conductors for sizes AWG 12 and 10 shall be the same as designated for 75°C conductors in this Table.

For ambient temperatures over 30°C, see Correction Factors, Note 13.

▶   Newest of the conductor material being used in this country is copper-clad aluminum. This material is made from a metallurgical materials system—using a core of aluminum with a bonded outer skin of copper. There is 10 per cent copper by volume (the outer skin) and **26.8** per cent by weight. Terminations for copper-clad aluminum conductors should be marked "AL-CU" except where listings by Underwriters' Laboratories indicate otherwise. As an example, a recent notice by UL accepted the use of push-in wire-grip terminals, such as used with listed receptacles and snap switches, with copper-clad aluminum conductors provided the terminations are suitable for the wire sizes involved. Such push-in terminations are not suitable for aluminum. See comments following Section 110-14.

The following table compares the characteristics of copper-clad aluminum with copper and aluminum conductors.

Conductor Characteristics

	Copper	Cu/Al	Aluminum
Density LBS/IN³	0.323	0.121	0.098
Density GM/CM³	8.91	3.34	2.71
Resistivity OHMS/CMF	10.37	16.08	16.78
Resistivity Microhm-CM	1.724	2.673	2.790
Conductivity (IACS%)	100	61-63	61
Weight % Copper	100	26.8	....
Tensile K PSI-Hard	65.0	30.0	27.0
Tensile KG/MM²-Hard	45.7	21.1	19.0
Tensile K PSI-Annealed	35.0	17.0	17.0*
Tensile KG/MM²-Annealed	24.6	12.0	12.0
Specific Gravity	8.91	3.34	2.71

* Semi-annealed.

310-20. Simplified Wiring Table. The simplified wiring table, Table 310-21, may be used for the selection of feeder and branch circuit conductor sizes and insulation types only under the conditions stated in this Section. The simplified wiring table shall be used only when a demand factor of 80 per cent or less exists.

Table 310-20(c). Typical Ambient Temperatures

Location	Temperature	Minimum Rating of Required Conductor Insulation
Well ventilated, normally heated buildings	30°C (86°F)	* (See note below)
Buildings with such major heat sources as power stations or industrial processes	40°C (104°F)	75°C (167°F)
Poorly ventilated spaces such as attics	45°C (113°F)	75°C (167°F)
Furnaces and boiler rooms (min.)	40°C (104°F)	75°C (167°F)
(max.)	60°C (140°F)	90°C (194°F)
Outdoors in shade in air	40°C (104°F)	75°C (167°F)
In thermal insulation	45°C (113°F)	75°C (167°F)
Direct solar exposure	45°C (113°F)	75°C (167°F)
Places above 60°C (140°F)		110°C (230°F)

* Note: 60°C for up to and including No. 8 AWG copper and up to and including No. 6 AWG aluminum or copper-clad aluminum. 75°C for over No. 8 AWG copper and No. 6 AWG aluminum or copper-clad aluminum.

(a) Application of Table 310-21.

(1) Determine load amperes, either continuous or noncontinuous. [Section 310-20(b).]

(2) Select conductor sizes from Table 310-21.

(3) Determine ambient temperature. Use 30°C (86°F) except where higher ambients may be expected as covered in Section 310-20(c).

(4) Select wire insulation type from Table 310-20(c) and Section 310-2(a).

Table 310-21. Simplified Wiring Table
(See Section 310-20 for use)
Conductor Size*—6 or Fewer Conductors in Raceway or Cable

Am-peres	Copper Non-Cont.		Continuous		Aluminum and Copper-Clad Aluminum Non-Cont.		Continuous	
	AWG	MCM	AWG	MCM	AWG	MCM	AWG	MCM
15	14		14		12		12	
20	12		12		10		10	
25	10		10		8		8	
30	10		10		8		8	
35	8		8		6		6	
40	8		8		6		6	
45	6		6		4		4	
50	6		6		4		4	
60	4		4		4		4	
70	4		4		3		3	
80	3		3		3		2	
90	3		2		2		1	
100	2		1		1		0	
110	1		0		0		2/0	
125	1		0		2/0		3/0	
150	0		2/0		3/0		4/0	
175	2/0		3/0		4/0			250
200	3/0		4/0			250		300
225	4/0			250		300		350
250		250		300		350		400
300		350		400		400		750
350		400		500		500		1000
400		500		750		750		
450		750		1000		1000		
500		750				1000		
600		1000						

* Neutral conductors shall be treated in accordance with Note 10—Neutral Conductors of Notes to Tables 310-12 through 310-15.

(b) Loads.

(1) **Continuous.** Continuous loads are expected to continue for three hours or longer [see Section 210-23(b).]

(2) Noncontinuous. Loads are noncontinuous where 67 per cent or less of the load is expected to be continuous.

(c) Ambient Temperature. Ambient temperature is the temperature of the medium, such as air, water or earth, into which the heat of the conductor is dissipated. Ambient temperatures vary and values typical of the installation condition shall be used for determining the type of conductor insulation when applying the simplified wiring table. See Table 310-20(c).

(d) Conductors in Air. For ampacities of single conductors in air, use Tables 310-13 and 310-15.

310-21. Conductor Ampacity. In Table 310-21 the values of amperes apply to actual diversified continuous or noncontinuous connected loads. This Table shall not be used to determine conductor ampacity; use Tables 310-12 to 310-15 for this purpose.

ARTICLE 318. CONTINUOUS RIGID CABLE SUPPORTS

318-1. Definition. A continuous rigid cable support is a unit or an assembly of units or sections, and associated fittings, made of metal or other noncombustible materials forming a continuous rigid structure used to support cables. Continuous rigid cable supports include ladders, troughs, channels, and other similar structures.

It is not the intent of this Article to require that cables be supported by continuous rigid cable supports or to recognize the use of conductors described in Article 310 in continuous rigid cable supports for general wiring.

▶   This paragraph warns against the use of cable supports as a wiring method. For example, three No. 4/0 THW conductors could not be placed in the cable support unless they were first installed in an approved raceway or multiple-conductor cable.

Article 318 was put in the National Electrical Code for the purpose of information and guidance because it was found that in many cases these supports had been installed as raceways.

318-2. Use.

(a) Continuous rigid cable supports may be used as the mechanical support for only the following wiring methods under the conditions detailed in the Article for each wiring method: (1) Mineral-insulated metal-sheathed cables, (Article 330), (2) Aluminum sheathed cable, (Article 331), (3) Metal-clad cable, (Article 334), (4) Nonmetallic sheathed cable, (Article 336), (5) Multiple conductor service-entrance cables, (Article 338), (6) Multiple conductor underground feeder and branch circuit cable, (Article 339), (7) Any approved conduit or raceway with its contained conductors, (8) Shielded nonmetallic-sheathed cable (Type SNM) for hazardous locations (Article 337).

(b) Continuous rigid cable supports may be used as the mechanical support for factory-assembled, multiconductor control, signal, and power cables, which are specifically approved for installation in continuous rigid cable supports, in fire-resistive or noncombustible construction, but shall not be used (1) in hoistways, (2) where the cables supported are subject to severe physical damage, (3) in areas having readily combustible contents as determined by the authority enforcing this Code. Continuous rigid cable supports may be used to support cables in hazardous locations when the cables are specifically approved for such use. See Sections 501-4, 502-4, and 503-3.

▶ **There are UL-listed multiple-conductor cables approved for use in continuous rigid cable supports.**

318-3. Construction.   Continuous rigid cable supports shall be approved for the purpose and shall comply with the following:

(1) Shall have suitable strength and rigidity to provide adequate support for all contained wiring.

(2) Shall not present sharp edges, burrs or projections injurious to the insulation or jackets of the wiring.

(3) If made of metal, shall be adequately protected against corrosion or shall be made of corrosion-resistant material.

(4) Shall have side rails or equivalent structural members.

(5) Shall include fittings for changes in direction and elevation of runs.

318-4. Installation.

(a) Continuous rigid cable supports shall be installed as a complete support system.

(b) Each run of continuous rigid cable support shall be complete before the installation of cables.

(c) Continuous rigid cable supports shall be mechanically connected to any enclosure or raceway into which the cables contained in the continuous rigid cable support extend or terminate.

(d) In portions of runs where additional physical protection is required, noncombustible covers or enclosures providing the required protection shall be used.

(e) Installations involving different electrical systems shall comply with Section 300-3 and, where separation is required, the separation shall be a solid noncombustible partition or compartment. Where cables, as permitted by Section 318-2(b), are installed in the same continuous rigid cable support as the cables permitted by Section 318-2(a), the requirements of this section shall apply.

(f) When continuous rigid cable supports are installed in tiers, the minimum vertical clearance between tiers shall be 12 inches.

(g) Continuous rigid cable supports may extend transversely through partitions or walls, other than fire walls, provided the section of the support within the wall is continuous and unventilated. See Section 300-21.

Exception: Where an opening in a partition or wall provides two inches minimum clearance above and on both sides, the continuous rigid cable support may be of a ventilated type.

(h) Continuous rigid cable supports may extend vertically through dry floors and platforms provided the continuous rigid cable support is totally enclosed where it passes through the floor or platform opening and for a distance of six feet above the floor or platform to provide protection from physical injury. See Section 300-21.

(i) Continuous rigid cable supports may extend vertically through floors and platforms in wet locations where: (1) there are curbs or other suitable means to prevent water flow through the floor or platform opening and (2) the continuous rigid cable support is totally enclosed where it passes through the floor or platform opening and for a distance of six feet above the floor or platform to provide protection from physical injury. See Section 300-21.

(j) Cable splices and cable taps shall be made only in junction boxes or fittings approved for the purpose.

(k) In other than horizontal runs, and where side rails do not provide adequate containment of the cables, they shall be fastened securely to transverse members of the continuous rigid cable support.

(l) Where continuous rigid cable supports are located adjacent to one another an adequate working space of 24 inches minimum should be maintained on one side of each continuous rigid cable support, or where grouped in rows adjacent to each other a minimum working space of 32 inches should be maintained over each continuous rigid cable support.

(m) Except as provided in Section 318-4(g), a minimum vertical clearance of 6 inches should be maintained from the top of the continuous rigid cable support to all ceilings, beams, and other obstructions.

318-5. Grounding. All metal sections of continuous rigid cable supports and fittings shall be bonded and effectively grounded to provide a continuous circuit for fault current. A continuous rigid cable support system shall not be used either as a grounded circuit conductor or as an equipment grounding conductor. See Section 250-33.

▶   Even though metal cable supports are required to be bonded and grounded, they are not acceptable for grounding of equipment as is the metal armor of Type AC metal-clad cable, metallic raceway, etc. See comments following Section **318-1**, and see Section **250-91***b*.

318-6. Ampacity. The ampacities of cables installed in continuous rigid cable supports shall be as follows:

(a) Where cables containing not more than three current-carrying conductors are installed in ventilated continuous rigid cable supports and spacing is maintained at from one-quarter to one cable diameter, the factors of Table 318-6(a) shall be applied to the ampacities of the cables used.

Table 318-6(a). Factors for Cables with Maintained Spacing

Number of Cables	Horizontally					
	1	2	3	4	5	6
Vertically						
1	1.00	0.93	0.87	0.84	0.83	0.82
2	0.89	0.83	0.79	0.76	0.75	0.74
3	0.80	0.76	0.72	0.70	0.69	0.68
4	0.77	0.72	0.68	0.67	0.66	0.65
5	0.75	0.70	0.66	0.65	0.64	0.63
6	0.74	0.69	0.64	0.63	0.62	0.61

(b) The ampacities of cables shall be in accordance with the requirements of Note 8 of Notes to Tables 310-12 through 310-15 where (1) cables are not spaced, (2) spacing is maintained between cables of more than three current-carrying conductors, or (3) unventilated continuous rigid cable supports are used.

ARTICLE 320. OPEN WIRING ON INSULATORS

320-1. Definition. Open wiring is a wiring method using cleats, knobs, tubes and flexible tubing for the protection and support of insulated conductors run in or on buildings, and not concealed by the building structure.

▶   Conductors for open wiring may be any of the general-use types listed in Table 310-2a for "dry" locations and "dry and wet" locations such as RH, T, TW, etc.

The conductors are secured to and supported by insulators, of porcelain, glass, or other composition materials. In modern wiring practice open wiring is used for high-tension work in transformer vaults and substations; it is very commonly used for temporary work and is used occasionally for runs of heavy conductors for feeders and power circuits. See Art. 305.

320-2. Use.

(a) Open wiring on insulators may be used for exposed work, either inside or outside building; in dry or wet locations; where subject to corrosive vapors such as covered by Article 480; for services as covered by Article 230, provided the requirements of this Article are satisfied.

(b) Open wiring on insulators shall not be used (1) in commercial garages, (2) in theaters and assembly halls, (3) in motion-picture studios, (4) in hoistways, and (5) in hazardous locations, except in storage compartments of Class III locations as provided in Section 503-3(b).

320-3. Other Articles. In addition to the provisions of this Article, open wiring shall conform to the other applicable provisions of this Code. See especially Articles 300 and 730.

320-4. Conductors. The type of conductors shall conform to Article 310. Only single conductors shall be used.

(a) The allowable ampacities of insulated conductors as shown in Article 310 shall apply to open wiring on insulators.

320-5. Supports.

(a) Conductors shall not be in contact with any object other than their insulating supports. They shall be rigidly supported on noncombustible, non-absorptive insulating material as follows:

(1) Under ordinary circumstances, supports for wiring over flat surfaces shall be not more than 4½ feet apart. Where the conductors are likely to be disturbed, the distance between supports shall be shortened sufficiently to provide adequate support for conductors;

(2) Conductors shall be supported within 6 inches of a tap;

(3) Conductors shall not be dead ended at a rosette, lampholder, or receptacle unless the last support is within 12 inches of the device.

(b) The following exceptions to the provisions of Section 320-5(a) may be permitted:

Exception No. 1: For use of nonmetallic flexible tubing, see Section 320-7.

Exception No. 2: Conductors of No. 8 or larger installed in the open across open spaces where not likely to be disturbed, may be supported at distances not greater than 15 feet provided that approved noncombustible, nonabsorptive insulating separators assuring not less than 2½-inch separation between conductors, are installed at intervals of not over 4½ feet.

Exception No. 3: In buildings of mill construction where not likely to be disturbed, feeders in the open, not smaller than No. 8, may be separated about six inches and installed direct from timber to timber, being supported from each timber only.

(c) When nails are used to mount knobs they shall not be smaller than 10 penny. When screws are used to mount knobs, or when nails or screws are used to mount cleats, they shall be of a length sufficient to penetrate the wood to a depth equal to at least one-half the height of the knob and fully the thickness of the cleat. Cushion washers shall be used with nails.

▶   Mill construction is generally understood to mean the type of building in which the floors are supported on wooden beams spaced about 14 to 16 ft apart. Wires not smaller than No. 8 may safely span such a distance where the ceilings are high and the space is free from obstructions.

Methods of dead-ending open cable runs are shown in Figs. 320-1 and 320-2.

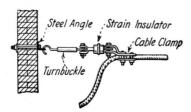

FIG. 320-1. Method of dead-ending heavy conductors used in open wiring.

Where heavy a-c feeders are run as open wiring, the reactance of the circuit is reduced and hence the voltage drop is reduced by using a small spacing between the conductors. Up to a distance of 15 ft between supports the 2½-in. spacing may be used if spacers are clamped to the conductors at intervals not exceeding 4½ ft. A spacer consists of the three porcelain pieces of the same form as used in the support, with a metal clamping ring.

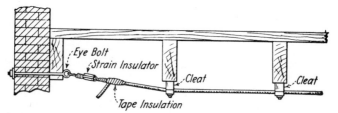

FIG. 320-2. Method of dead-ending heavy conductors used in open wiring.

320-6. Conductor Separation. Open conductors shall be separated as follows:

(a) For voltage not exceeding 300 volts between conductors, 2½ inches from each other and shall be separated from the surface wired over at least ½ inch in dry locations.

(b) For voltages of 301 to 600 volts between conductors, 4 inches from each other and shall be separated from surface wired over at least one inch.

(c) In damp or wet locations, a separation of at least one inch from the surface wired over shall be maintained for all voltages.

▶ Figure 320-3 illustrates a method for the support of No. 14, No. 12, and No. 10 conductors. For conductors of larger size, solid knobs with tie wires or single-wire cleats should be used.

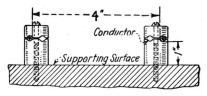

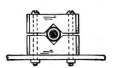

FIG. 320-3. Split knobs for supporting small wires used in open wiring or concealed knob-and-tube work.

FIG. 320-4. Single-wire cleat for supporting large conductors used in open wiring.

320-7. Flexible Nonmetallic Tubing. In dry locations, when not exposed to severe physical damage, conductors may be separately encased in flexible tubing. Tubing shall be in continuous length not exceeding 15 feet, and secured to the surface wired over by straps spaced not exceeding 4½ feet apart.

320-8. Tie Wires. No. 8 or larger conductors supported on solid knobs shall be securely tied thereto. Tie wires shall have a covering equivalent to conductors which they confine.

320-9. Passing Through Walls and Floors. Open conductors shall be separated from contact with walls, floors, timbers or partitions through which they pass by tubes or bushings of noncombustible, nonabsorptive insulating material. Where the bushing is shorter than the hole, a waterproof sleeve of noninductive material shall be inserted in the hole and an insulating bushing slipped into the sleeve at either end in such a manner as to keep the conductors absolutely out of contact with the sleeve. Each conductor must be carried through a separate tube or sleeve.

320-10. Separation from Metal Work. Open conductors shall be separated at least 2 inches from metallic conduit, piping, or other conducting material, and from any exposed lighting, power or signal conductor, or shall be separated therefrom by a continuous and firmly fixed nonconductor additional to the insulation of the conductor. Where any insulating tube is used, it shall be secured at the ends. Deviation from this requirement may, when necessary, be allowed by the authority enforcing this Code.

▶ The additional insulation on the wire is to prevent the wire from coming in contact with the adjacent pipe or other metal.

320-11. Separation from Piping in Damp Locations. Open conductors located close to water pipes or tanks, or in other damp locations, shall be so placed that an air space will be permanently maintained between them and pipes which they cross. Where practicable, conductors shall be installed over, rather than under, pipes upon which moisture is likely to gather or which may leak.

320-12. Protection from Physical Damage. Where open conductors cross ceiling joists and wall studs, and are exposed to physical damage, they shall be protected by one of the following methods. Conductors within 7 feet from the floor shall be considered exposed to physical damage.

(a) By guard strips not less than ⅞ inch in thickness and at least as high as the insulating supports, placed on each side of and close to the wiring.

(b) By a substantial running board at least ½ inch thick back of the conductors with side protections. Running boards shall extend at least 1 inch outside the conductors, but not more than 2 inches and the protecting sides shall be at least 2 inches high and at least ⅞ inch thick.

(c) By boxing made as above and furnished with cover kept at least 1 inch away from the conductors within. Where protecting vertical conductors on side walls the boxing shall be closed at the top and the holes through which the conductors pass shall be bushed.

(d) By rigid metal conduit or electrical metallic tubing, in which case the rules of Articles 346 or 348 shall apply; or by metal piping, in which case the conductors shall be encased in continuous lengths of approved flexible tubing. The conductors passing through metal enclosures shall be so grouped that current in both directions is approximately equal.

320-13. In Accessible Attics. Conductors in unfinished attics or roof spaces shall be installed in accordance with the provisions of Section 324-8.

320-14. Entering Spaces Subject to Dampness, Wetness or Corrosive Vapors. Conductors entering or leaving locations subject to dampness, wetness or corrosive vapors shall have drip loops formed on them and shall then pass upward and inward from the outside of buildings, or from the damp, wet, or corrosive location, through noncombustible, nonabsorptive insulating tubes. See also Sections 230-49 and 730-21.

320-15. Switches.

(a) Surface-type snap switches shall be mounted in accordance with the provisions of Section 380-10. Metal boxes are not required. See Section 380-3.

(b) Other types of switches shall be installed in accordance with the provisions of Section 380-3.

ARTICLE 324. CONCEALED KNOB–AND–TUBE WORK

324-1. Definition. Concealed knob-and-tube wiring is a wiring method using knobs, tubes and flexible nonmetallic tubing for the protection and support of insulated conductors concealed in hollow spaces of walls and ceilings of buildings.

▶   Conductors for concealed knob-and-tube work may be any of the general-use types listed in Table 310-2a for "dry" locations and "dry and wet" locations such as RH, T, TW, etc.

324-2. Use. Concealed knob-and-tube work may be used in the hollow spaces of walls and ceilings. It shall not be used (1) in commercial garages, (2) in theaters and assembly halls, except as provided in Section 520-4, (3) in motion-picture studios, nor (4) in hazardous locations.

324-3. Other Articles. In addition to the provisions of this Article, concealed knob-and-tube wiring shall conform to the other applicable provisions of this Code. See especially Article 300.

324-4. Conductors. Only single conductors shall be used. The ampacity and type of conductor shall conform to Article 310.

324-5. Supports. Conductors shall be supported at intervals not exceeding 4½ feet by knobs or tubes of noncombustible, nonabsorptive, insulating material. There shall be a knob within 6 inches of each side of each tap or splice. Tie wires shall comply with Section 320-8. Where such support is impracticable and the conductors are in a dry location, they may be fished when separately enclosed in flexible nonmetallic tubing extending in continuous lengths from one support to the next or to a box, or from one box to another.

324-6. Conductor Separation.

(a) Conductors shall be separated at least 3 inches and maintained at least one inch from the surface wired over.

(b) At distributing centers, meters, outlets, switches or other places where space is limited and the 3-inch separation cannot be maintained, each conductor shall be encased in a continuous length of flexible tubing.

(c) Where practicable, conductors shall be run singly on separate joists, rafters or studding.

324-7. Separation from Other Objects and Protection. Conductors shall be separated from other conductors and objects as follows:

(a) The provisions as to rigid supporting and clearance from foreign wires and other objects, as specified for open wiring in Sections 320-9, 320-10, 320-11, and 320-15, shall be complied with.

(b) Conductors passing through wood cross members in plastered partitions shall be protected by an additional noncombustible, nonabsorptive insulating tube extending at least 3 inches above the member.

▶   The additional tube is to protect the wire from contact with the plaster that is likely to accumulate on any horizontal cross timber in a plastered wall.

324-8. In Unfinished Attics and Roof Spaces. Conductors in unfinished attics or roof spaces shall comply with the following:

(a) Conductors in unfinished attics and roof spaces shall be run through or on the sides of joists, studs and rafters, except in attics and roof spaces having head room at all points of less than 3 feet in buildings completed before the wiring is installed.

(b) Where conductors in accessible unfinished attics or roof spaces reached by stairway or permanent ladder are run through bored holes in floor joists or through bored holes in studs or rafters within 7 feet of the floor or floor joists, such conductors shall be protected by substantial running boards extending at least one inch on each side of the conductors and securely fastened in place.

(c) Where carried along the sides of rafters, studs or floor joists, neither running boards nor guard strips will be required.

▶   Where wires are run on knobs or through tubes in a closed-in and inaccessible attic or roof space, the wiring is concealed knob-and-tube work, but if the attic or roof space is accessible the wiring is open wiring on insulators. Both cases are covered by the foregoing rules.

Where the wiring is installed at any time after the building is completed, in a roof space having less than **3** ft headroom at any point, the wires may be run on knobs across the faces of the joists, studs, or rafters or through or on the sides of the joists, studs, or rafters. Such a space would not be used for storage purposes and the wiring may be considered as concealed knob-and-tube work.

If a new building is being wired, the wires in any attic or roof space must not be run across the face of joists, studs, or rafters but must always be run through tubes in holes bored through the timbers or on the knobs on the sides of the timbers.

An attic or roof space is considered accessible if it can be reached by means of a stairway or a permanent ladder. In any such attic or roof space wires run through the floor joists where there is no floor must be protected by a running board and wires run through the studs or rafters must be

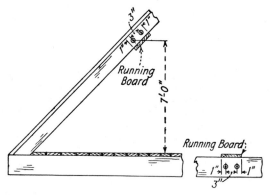

Fig. 324-1. Open wiring in an accessible attic. Wires run through rafters, and wires run through joists where there is no floor.

protected by a running board if within **7** ft from the floor or floor joists. These two cases are shown in Fig. **324-1**.

324-9. Boxes of Insulating Material.   Nonmetallic outlet boxes may be used as provided in Sections 370-3 and 370-7.

324-10. Switches.   See Sections 380-3 and 380-10.

324-11. Splices.   Splices shall be made only where close to knobs or tubes using solder or specially approved splicing devices. In-line or strain splices shall not be used.

ARTICLE 330. MINERAL-INSULATED METAL-SHEATHED CABLE

Type MI

A. General

330-1. Definition and Construction. For the purpose of this Article, mineral-insulated metal-sheathed Type MI cable is a cable in which one or more electrical conductors are insulated with a highly compressed refractory mineral insulation and enclosed in a liquidtight and gastight metallic tube sheathing. It shall be used with approved fittings for terminating and connecting to boxes, outlets and other equipment.

330-2. Use. Mineral insulated-metal sheathed cable may be used for services, feeders and branch circuits in both exposed and concealed work, in dry or wet locations; in Class I, Class II, and Class III hazardous locations as noted in the appropriate Articles; for underplaster extensions as provided in Article 344; and embedded in plaster finish on brick or other masonry. It may be used where exposed to weather or continuous moisture, for underground runs and embedded in masonry, concrete or fill, in buildings in course of construction or where exposed to oil, gasoline, or other conditions not having a deteriorating effect on the metal sheath. The sheath of mineral insulated-metal sheathed cable exposed to destructive corrosive conditions, such as some types of cinder fill, shall be protected by materials suitable for those conditions.

▶   Section **330-2** describes the general usage of mineral-insulated-metal-sheathed cable, designated Type **MI**. Briefly, it includes, basically, general use as services, feeders, and branch circuits in exposed and concealed work, in dry and wet locations, for underplaster extensions and embedded in plaster, masonry, concrete, or fill, for underground runs, or where exposed to weather, continuous moisture, oil, or other conditions not having a deteriorating effect on the metallic sheath. It may be installed where exposed to gasoline when used with termination fittings approved for Class 1 locations. See Fig. **330-4**. The maximum permissible operating temperature for general use is **85°C** (determined by present standard terminations). The cable itself, however, is recognized for **250°C** in special applications. Permissible current ratings will be those given in Table **310-12**. Type **MI** cable in its many sizes and constructions is suitable for all power and control circuits up to 600 volts.

330-3. Other Articles. In addition to the provisions of this Article, the installation of mineral insulated-metal sheathed cable shall comply with the other applicable provisions of this Code. See especially Article 300.

▶   Mineral insulated 600-volt power and control wiring is a system in which the conductors are spaced and insulated by a densely compressed mineral insulation encased in a seamless metallic tube.

The original intent was to provide a wiring material which would be completely noncombustible, thus eliminating the fire hazards resulting from faults or excessive overloads on electrical circuits. To accomplish this, it is constructed entirely of inorganic materials. The conductors, sheath, and protective armor are of metal. The insulation is highly compressed magnesium oxide, which is extremely stable at high temperatures (fusion temperature of 2800 C).

Mineral insulated-metal sheathed cable is manufactured in a single-conductor construction from No. 16 AWG through No. 4/0 AWG, two- and three-conductor from No. 16 AWG through No. 4 AWG, four-conductor from No. 16 AWG through No. 6 AWG, and seven-conductor Nos. 16, 14, 12, and 10 AWG. The standard length in which any size is furnished depends on the final diameter of the cable. The smallest cable, 1/C No. 16 AWG,

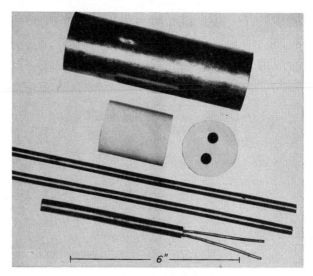

FIG. 330-1. Component parts and finished cable, No. 14 AWG, two-conductor.

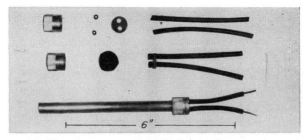

FIG. 330-2. Cable seal termination. Component parts of assembly (top); neoprene tubing mounted in insulating cap and sealing compound; and (bottom) completed cable seal termination.

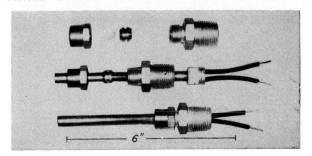

Fig. 330-3. Cable seal termination and gland. Component parts of gland (top); gland in place before tightening; and (bottom) gland locked in finished position.

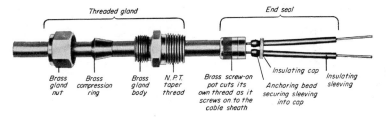

Fig. 330-4. Mineral insulated cable fittings for use in hazardous locations. (*General Cable Corp.*)

has a diameter of 0.216 in. and can be furnished in lengths of approximately 1,900 ft. Cables of larger diameter have proportionally shorter lengths. The cable is shipped in paper-wrapped coils ranging in diameter from 3 to 5 ft.

The terminating of this cable incorporates both the sealing and the insulating of the cable ends. (See Figs. **330-1** through **330-3**. See also Mineral Insulated Cable Fittings for Use in Hazardous Locations, Fig. **330-4**.)

B. Installation

330-4. Supports. Mineral insulated-metal sheathed cable shall be securely supported by approved staples, straps, hangers or similar fittings, so designed and installed as not to injure the cable. Cable shall be secured at intervals not exceeding 6 feet except where cable is fished.

330-5. Through Studs, Joists and Rafters. See Section 300-8.

330-6. Wet Locations. See Section 300-5.

330-7. Bends. All bends shall be so made that the cable will not be damaged and the radius of the curve of the inner edge of any bend shall be not less than 5 times the diameter of the cable.

330-8. Terminating Seal. At all points where mineral insulated-metal sheathed cable terminates an approved seal shall be provided immediately after stripping to prevent entrance of moisture into the mineral insulation. The conductors extending beyond the sheath shall be insulated with an approved insulating material.

330-9. Fittings. When Type MI cable is connected to boxes or equipment, the fittings shall be approved for the conditions of service. When single conductor Type MI cables enter metal boxes through separate openings, refer to Section 300-20.

330-10. Insulation Resistance. The completed wiring system shall be tested for insulation resistance in accordance with Section 110-20.

C. Construction Specifications

330-11. General. Type MI Cable for 600 volts shall conform to the following:

(a) Conductors. The conductors are solid copper and have cross sectional areas corresponding to the standard American Wire Gage sizes.

(b) Insulation. The insulation is a highly compressed refractory mineral which provides proper spacing for the conductors.

(c) Outer Sheath. The outer sheath shall be of a continuous copper construction to provide mechanical protection and a moisture seal, and an adequate path for grounding purposes.

ARTICLE 331. ALUMINUM-SHEATHED CABLE

Type ALS

A. General

331-1. Definition and Construction. Aluminum-sheathed Type ALS cable is a factory assembled cable consisting of one or more insulated conductors enclosed in an impervious, continuous, closely fitting tube of aluminum. It shall be used with approved fittings for terminating and connecting to boxes, outlets and other equipment.

▶   This is a self-contained wiring system in which one or more insulated conductors are enclosed in an impervious, continuous, closely fitting seamless tube of aluminum.

It may be used in both exposed and concealed work, in dry or wet locations. The insulated conductors are protected by the sheath which also provides a means of grounding outlet boxes, fixtures, and other equipment.

331-2. Use. Aluminum-sheathed cable may be used in both exposed and concealed work, in dry or wet locations. The sheath of aluminum sheathed cable exposed to destructive corrosive conditions such as environments containing strong chlorides or caustic alkalis, or where vapors of chlorine or hydrochloric acid are present or where the cable is installed underground, shall be protected by materials suitable for those conditions. See Section 300-5.

Aluminum-sheathed cable and fittings shall not be embedded or buried directly in concrete or used in areas subject to severe corrosive influences unless suitable supplemental corrosion protection is provided.

See Section 310-6.

▶   **See comments following Section 346-1.**

331-3. Other Articles. In addition to the provisions of this Article, the installation of aluminum-sheathed cable shall comply with the other applicable provisions of this Code. See especially Article 300.

B. Installations

331-4. Supports. Aluminum-sheathed cable shall be securely supported by staples, straps, hangers, or similar fittings so designed and installed as not to injure the cable. Cable shall be secured at intervals not exceeding 6 feet except where the cable is fished.

331-5. Through Studs, Joists and Rafters. See Section 300-8.

331-6. Wet Locations. See Section 300-5.

331-7. Bends. All bends shall be so made that the cable will not be damaged and the radius of the curve on the inner edge of any bend shall be not less than:

    (a) Ten times the external diameter of the sheath for cable not more than ¾ inch in external diameter.

    (b) Twelve times the external diameter of the sheath for cable more than ¾ inch but not more than 1½ inches in external diameter; and

    (c) Fifteen times the external diameter of the sheath for cable more than 1½ inches in external diameter.

331-8. Fittings. When aluminum sheathed cable is connected to boxes or equipment, the fittings shall be approved for the conditions of service. When single conductor aluminum sheathed cables enter metal boxes through separate openings refer to Section 300-20.

C. Construction

331-9. General. Type ALS cable shall conform to the following:

    (a) Conductors. The conductors shall be copper, copper-clad aluminum, or electrical conductor grade aluminum, solid or stranded.

    (b) Insulation. The insulation shall be a type listed in Table 310-2(b).

    (c) Insulation Covering. The covering over the insulation shall be the same as permitted for lead sheathed cable or multiple conductor cable.

    (d) Outer Sheath. The outer sheath shall be of a continuous, closely fitting tube of aluminum to provide mechanical protection, a moisture seal and an adequate path for equipment grounding purposes and shall conform with provisions of Section 331-2. The sheath shall not be used as a current-carrying conductor.

ARTICLE 334. METAL–CLAD CABLE

Type MC and AC Series

334-1. Definition. A metal-clad cable is a fabricated assembly of insulated conductors in a flexible metallic enclosure. See Section 334-4.

334-2. Voltage. See Section 300-2. For systems in excess of 600 volts see Article 710.

334-3. Marking. The provisions of Section 310-12 shall apply, except that Type AC cable shall have ready identification of the maker by distinctive external markers in the cable sheath throughout its entire length.

334-4. Construction. Metal-clad cable shall be an approved cable of Type MC or AC Series, with acceptable metal covering. The insulated conductors shall conform with Section 334-5.

(a) Type MC. Type MC cables are power cables limited in size, for the voltages of this article, to conductors of No. 4 AWG and larger for copper and No. 2 AWG and larger for aluminum and copper-clad aluminum. The metal enclosures shall be either a covering of interlocking metal tape, or an impervious, close fitting, corrugated tube. Supplemental protection of an outer covering of corrosion-resistant material shall be required where such protection is needed. See Section 300-5. The cables shall provide adequate path for grounding purposes.

FIG. 334-1. Type MC cable.

▶   Type MC series employs rubber, varnished cloth, or composite varnished-cloth–thermoplastic-insulated conductors. A marker tape reading "Type MC cable" and indicating the type designation of the insulated conductor is included in the cable under the armor.

An uninsulated grounding conductor is included in the cable assembly under the metal armor. This grounding conductor is required to be at least 45 per cent of the nominal cross-sectional area of one of the circuit conductors.

See Tentative Interim Amendment No. 170 in back of book.

(b) Type AC. Type AC cables are branch circuit and feeder cables with armor of flexible metal tape. Cables of the AC type, except ACL, shall have an internal bonding strip of copper or aluminum, in intimate contact with the armor for its entire length.

334-5. Conductors. Conductors for metal-clad cable shall conform with the following:

(a) Type MC. For cables of Type MC, insulated conductors shall be of a type listed in Table 310-2(b) for rubber, thermoplastic, varnished cloth, asbestos-varnished cloth, or of a type especially approved for the purpose.

(b) Type AC. For cables of Type AC, insulated conductors shall be of a type listed in Table 310-2(b). In addition, the conductors shall have an over-all

Fig. 334-2. Metal-clad cable, Type AC. (*General Electric Co.*)

moisture-resistant and fire-retardant fibrous covering; for Type ACT, a moisture-resistant fibrous covering is required only on the individual conductors.

334-6. Use. Except where otherwise specified elsewhere in this Code, and where not subject to physical damage, metal-clad cable may be installed for branch circuits and feeders in both exposed and concealed work as follows:

(a) Type MC. This type of power cable may be used in partially protected areas, such as in continuous rigid cable supports and the like, in dry locations and when any of the following conditions are met it may be used in wet locations:

(1) The metallic covering is impervious to moisture.

(2) A lead sheath or moisture impervious jacket is provided under the metal covering.

(3) The insulated conductors under the metallic covering are approved for use in wet locations.

See Section 300-5.

(b) Type AC. Metal-clad cable of the AC type may be used in dry locations; for underplaster extensions as provided in Article 344; and embedded in plaster finish on brick or other masonry, except in damp or wet locations. This cable may be run or fished in the air voids of masonry block or tile walls; where such walls are exposed or subject to excessive moisture or dampness or are below grade line, Type ACL cable shall be used. This cable shall contain lead-covered conductors (Type ACL), if used where exposed to the weather or to continuous moisture, for underground runs in duct or raceway and embedded in masonry, concrete or fill in buildings in course of construction, or where exposed to oil, or other conditions having a deteriorating effect on the insulation. Type AC metal-clad cable shall not be used where prohibited elsewhere in this Code, including (1) in theaters and assembly halls, except as provided in Section 520-4; (2) in motion-picture studios; (3) in any hazardous locations; (4) where exposed to corrosive fumes or vapors; (5) on cranes or hoists, except as provided in Section 610-11 Exception No. 3; (6) in storage battery rooms; (7) in hoistways or on elevators, except as provided in Section 620-21; or (8) commercial garages where prohibited in Article 511. Type ACL cable shall not be used for direct burial in the earth.

Fig. 334-3. Metal-clad cable with lead sheath, Type ACL. (*General Electric Co.*)

▶   Type AC cable is approved in all buildings except in the locations noted above. The flexibility of the cable is a valuable point in its favor for concealed wiring but limits its usefulness for exposed work to locations where a finished appearance is not essential. The insulated conductors in Type AC cable are well protected, and the bonding strip in addition to the metal armor provides a means of grounding outlet boxes, fixtures, and other such equipment.

334-7. Other Articles.   In addition to the provisions of this Article, metal-clad cable shall conform to other applicable provisions of this Code. See especially Article 300.

334-8. Supports.   Metal-clad cable shall be secured by approved staples, straps, hangers or similar fittings so designed and installed as not to injure the cable.

Fig. 334-4   Fig. 334-5

Fig. 334-4. Strap for securing cable in place.

Fig. 334-5. Staple for securing cable in place.

(a)   Type MC cable shall be secured at intervals not exceeding six feet, and within two feet from every box or fitting, except where cable is fished. Cable may be installed on metal racks, trays, troughs, or continuous rigid cable supports grounded as required by Article 250. The cables shall be separated from each other by a distance of not less than one-quarter of a cable diameter. There shall be no more than one layer of cables on a rack or other support member; each cable so installed shall be supported at intervals not exceeding six feet and within two feet from every box or fitting, and each cable shall be attached to the support at intervals of not more than ten feet horizontally and two feet vertically.

(b)   Type AC cable shall be secured at intervals of not exceeding 4½ feet and within 12 inches from every outlet box or fitting, except where cable is fished and except lengths of not over 24 inches at terminals where flexibility is necessary.

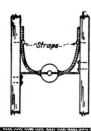

Fig. 334-6. Method of securing cable at outlets.

▶   In exposed work, both as a precaution against physical damage and to ensure a workmanlike appearance, fastenings should be spaced not more than 24 to 30 in. apart. In concealed work in new buildings the cable should be supported at intervals of not over 4½ ft for Type AC and 6 ft for Type MC, so as to keep it out of the way of possible injury by mechanics of other trades. In either exposed work or concealed work, the cable should be securely fastened in place within 1 ft of each outlet box or fitting for Type AC and 2 ft for Type MC, so that there will be no tendency for the cable to pull away from the box connector. The method of securing the cable at outlets in concealed work is shown in Fig. **334-6**.

334-9. Bends. All bends shall be so made that the cable will not be injured, and the radius of the curve of the inner edge of any bend shall not be less than 7 times the diameter of Type MC cable nor 5 times the diameter of Type AC cable.

334-10. Boxes and Fittings.

(a) At all points where Type MC metal-clad cable terminates, suitable fittings designed for use with the particular wiring cable and the conditions of service, shall be used.

(b) At all points where the armor of AC cable terminates, a fitting shall be provided to protect wires from abrasion, unless the design of the outlet boxes or fittings is such as to afford equivalent protection, and in addition, an approved insulating bushing or its equivalent approved protection shall be provided between the conductors and the armor. The connector or clamp by which the metal-clad cable is fastened to boxes or cabinets shall be of such design that the insulating bushing or its equivalent will be visible for inspection. This bushing is not required with lead-covered cables which shall be so installed that the lead sheath will be visible for inspection. Where change is made from metal-clad cable to other cable or raceway wiring methods, a box shall be installed at junction point as required in Section 300-15.

▶   A standard type of box connector for securing the cable to outlet boxes and cabinets is shown in Fig. 334-7.

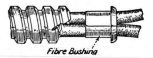

Fibre Bushing

Fig. 334-7. Box connector for Type AC cable. (*General Electric Co.*)

Fig. 334-8. Fiber bushing to protect the conductors in Type AC cable from the sharp edges of the armor.

A fiber bushing as shown in Fig. 334-8 can be inserted between the armor and the conductors. The fiber bushing, which can be seen through slots in the connector after installation, prevents the sharp edges of the armor from cutting into the insulation on the conductors and so grounding the copper wire.

The box shown in Fig. 334-9 is equipped with clamps to secure Type AC cables, making it unnecessary to use separate cable connectors such as shown in Fig. 334-7.

The box shown in Fig. 334-10 is similar to the other but has the cable clamps outside, thus permitting one more conductor in the box. See Section 370-6*a*.

334-11. Through Studs, Joists and Rafters. See Section 300-8.

334-12. Exposed Work. Exposed runs of cable shall closely follow the surface of the building finish or of running boards, except:

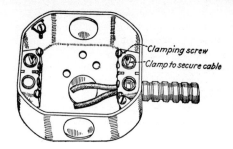

Fig. 334-9. Outlet box with clamps for Type AC cable. (*National Electric Div., H. K. Porter Co., Inc.*)

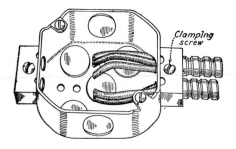

Fig. 334-10. Outlet box with clamps for Type AC cable. (*Allsteel Equipment Co.*)

(a) Lengths of not more than 24 inches at terminals where flexibility is necessary.

(b) Where suitably supported in accordance with Section 334-8(a).

(c) On the underside of floor joists in basements where supported at each joist and so located as not to be subject to physical damage.

▶   Paragraph *a* refers to a length not over **24 in.** to a motor or a range where some flexibility is necessary.

334-13. In Accessible Attics.   Type AC cables in accessible attics or roof spaces shall be installed as follows:

(a) Where run across the top of floor joists, or within 7 feet of floor or floor joists across the face of rafters or studding, in attics and roof spaces which are accessible, the cable shall be protected by substantial guard strips which are at least as high as the cable. Where this space is not accessible by permanent stairs or ladders, protection will only be required within 6 feet of the nearest edge of scuttle hole or attic entrance.

(b) Where cable is carried along the sides of rafters, studs or floor joists, neither guard strips nor running boards shall be required.

▶   In many cases an accessible attic is used for storage, and care should be taken to protect the wiring properly.

ARTICLE 336. NONMETALLIC-SHEATHED CABLE

Types NM and NMC

336-1. Definition. A nonmetallic-sheathed cable is an assembly of two or more insulated conductors having an outer sheath of moisture-resistant, flame-retardant, nonmetallic material.

▶   This type of wiring may be used either for exposed or for concealed wiring. It may be regarded as a substitute for concealed knob-and-tube work and open wiring on insulators, and has the advantages that continuous protection is provided over the entire length of the conductor in addition to the insulation applied to ordinary rubber-covered or thermoplastic wire, and, as in the case of armored cable, no insulating supports are required and only one hole need be bored where the cable passes through a timber. Insulating bushings or inserts should be used where the cable passes through holes in metal studs or similar members.

336-2. Construction.   Nonmetallic sheathed cable shall be an approved Type NM or NMC in sizes No. 14 through 2 AWG with copper conductors and in sizes No. 12 through 2 with aluminum and copper-clad aluminum conductors. In addition to the insulated conductors, the cable may have an approved size of uninsulated or bare conductor for grounding purposes only.

(a) Type NM.   The conductors shall comply with the requirements for the type of conductor used. Over-all fibrous coverings shall have a flame-retardant and moisture-resistant finish.

(b) Type NMC.   The cable shall be of a type approved for the purpose. The over-all covering shall be flame-retardant, moisture-resistant, fungus-resistant and corrosion-resistant.

(c) Marking.   In addition to the provisions of Section 310-12, the cable shall have a distinctive marking on the exterior for its entire length specifying cable type.

336-3. Use.   Nonmetallic-sheathed cable may be installed for both exposed and concealed work as follows:

(a) Type NM.   This type of nonmetallic-sheathed cable may be installed for both exposed and concealed work in normally dry locations. It may be installed or fished in air voids in masonry block or tile walls where such walls are not exposed or subject to excessive moisture or dampness. Type NM cable shall not be installed where exposed to corrosive fumes or vapors; nor shall it be embedded in masonry, concrete, fill or plaster; nor run in shallow chase in masonry or concrete and covered with plaster or similar finish.

(b) Moisture and Corrosion-Resistant Type NMC.   This type of nonmetallic-sheathed cable may be installed for both exposed and concealed work in dry, moist, damp or corrosive locations, and in outside and inside walls of masonry block or tile. Where embedded in plaster or run in a shallow chase in masonry walls and covered with plaster within 2 inches of the finished surface, it shall be protected against damage from nails by a cover of corrosion-resistant coated steel at least $\frac{1}{16}$ inch in thickness and $\frac{3}{4}$ inch wide in the chase or under the final surface finish.

(c) Uses Not Permissible for Either Type NM or NMC Nonmetallic Sheathed Cable. These types shall not be used as: (1) service-entrance cable, (2) in commercial garages, (3) in theaters and assembly halls, except as provided in Section 520-4, (4) in motion picture studios, (5) in storage battery rooms, (6) in hoistways, (7) in any hazardous location, (8) embedded in poured cement, concrete or aggregate.

▶   Where temperatures of 0°F or below are frequently experienced during the winter, the ordinary types of nonmetallic-sheathed cable, where installed in dairy barns and similar farm buildings, have in some cases deteriorated rapidly, due to the growth of fungus or mold. Type NMC cable has proved very helpful in these locations.

The cable may be made with an equipment grounding wire as a part of the assembly. (See Section 250-57 and Table 250-95.)

336-4. Other Articles.   In addition to the provisions of this Article, installations of nonmetallic-sheathed cable shall conform to the other applicable provisions of this Code. See especially Article 300.

336-5. Supports.   Nonmetallic-sheathed cable shall be secured by approved staples, straps, or similar fittings, so designed and installed as not to injure the cable. Cable shall be secured in place at intervals not exceeding $4\frac{1}{2}$ feet and within 12 inches from every cabinet, box or fitting, except that in concealed work in finished buildings or finished panels for prefabricated buildings where such supporting is impracticable, the cable may be fished between points of access.

▶   In concealed work the cable should if possible be so installed that it will be out of reach of nails. Care should be taken to avoid wherever possible the parts of a wall where the trim will be nailed in place, *e.g.*, door and window casings, baseboards, and picture moldings.

336-6. Exposed Work—General.   In exposed work, except as provided in Sections 336-8 and 336-9, the cable shall be installed as follows:

(a) The cable shall closely follow the surface of the building finish or of running boards.

(b) It shall be protected from physical damage where necessary, by conduit, pipe, guard strips or other means. Where passing through a floor the cable shall be enclosed in rigid metal conduit or metal pipe extending at least 6 inches above the floor.

336-7. Through Studs, Joists and Rafters.   See Section 300-8.

336-8. In Unfinished Basements.   Where the cable is run at angles with joists in unfinished basements, assemblies not smaller than two No. 6 or three No. 8 conductors may be secured directly to the lower edges of the joists; smaller assemblies shall either be run through bored holes in the joists or on running boards. Where run parallel to joists, cable of any size shall be secured to the sides or face of the joists.

336-9. In Accessible Attics.   Cable in accessible attics or roof spaces shall also conform with Section 334-13.

336-10. Bends.   Bends in cable shall be so made, and other handling shall be such, that the protective coverings of the cable will not be injured, and no bend shall have a radius less than 5 times the diameter of the cable.

336-11. Devices of Insulating Material.   Switch, outlet, and tap devices of insulating material may be used without boxes in exposed cable wiring, and for concealed work for rewiring in existing buildings where the cable is concealed and fished. Openings in such devices shall form a close fit around the outer covering of the cable and the device shall fully enclose that part of the cable from which any part of the covering has been removed.

Where connections to conductors are by binding screw terminals, there shall be available as many terminals as conductors, unless cables are clamped within the structure and terminals are of a type approved for multiple conductors.

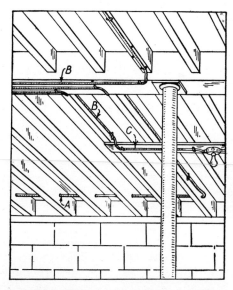

Fig. 336-1. Methods of installing nonmetallic-sheathed cable in an unfinished basement. *A*, through joists; *B*, on side or face of joist or beam; *C*, on running board.

336-12. Boxes of Insulating Material.   Nonmetallic outlet boxes approved for the purpose may be used as provided in Section 370-3.

▶   By using nonmetallic outlet and switch boxes a completely "nonmetallic" wiring system is provided. Such a system has certain advantages in locations where corrosive vapors are present. See Section **370-5**.

ARTICLE 337. SHIELDED NONMETALLIC-SHEATHED CABLE

Type SNM

337-1. Scope. This Article covers a wiring method of shielded nonmetallic-sheathed cable and fittings and defines installation and construction specifications.

337-2. Definitions Type SNM, shielded nonmetallic-sheathed cable, is a factory assembly of two or more insulated conductors in an extruded core of moisture-resistant, flame-resistant nonmetallic material, covered with an overlapping spiral metal tape and wire shield and jacketed with an extruded moisture, flame, oil, corrosion, fungus and sunlight-resistant nonmetallic material.

337-3. Other Articles. In addition to the provisions of this Article, installation of Type SNM cable shall conform to other applicable provisions, such as Articles 300 and 318 of the Code.

337-4. Uses Permitted. Type SNM cable may be used only as follows:

(1) Where operating temperatures do not exceed the rating marked on the cable.

(2) In continuous rigid cable supports or in raceways.

(3) In hazardous locations where permitted in Articles 500 through 516.

337-5. Bends. Bends in Type SNM cable shall be so made as not to damage the cable or its covering. The radius of the inner edge shall not be less than 5 times the cable diameter.

337-6. Handling. Type SNM cable shall be handled in such a manner as not to damage the cable or its covering.

337-7. Fittings. Fittings for connecting Type SNM cable to enclosures or equipment shall be approved for the purpose and for the conditions of use.

337-8. Construction. The conductors of Type SNM cable shall be Type THHN or THWN in sizes No. 14 through No. 2 copper and No. 12 through No. 2 in aluminum and copper-clad aluminum. Conductor sizes may be mixed in individual cables. The flat overlapping metal tapes shall be spiraled with a long lay. The shield wires shall have a total cross-sectional area as required by Article 250 and not less than the largest circuit conductor in the cable.

The outer jacket shall be water, oil, flame, corrosion, fungus, and sunlight resistant suitable for installation in continuous rigid cable supports.

337-9. Marking. Type SNM cable shall have a distinctive marking on its exterior surface for its entire length indicating its type and maximum operating temperature. It shall comply with the general marking requirements of Section 310-12.

The conductors shall each be numbered for identification from each other by durable marking on two sides 180° apart every 6 inches of length, with alternate legends inverted to facilitate reading from both sides.

▶   Type SNM cable is primarily designed for use in continuous rigid cable supports or raceways in Class I, Division 2 and Class II, Division 2 hazardous locations. The cable features an overlapping spiral metal tape and wire shield with an outer jacket. Figure 337-1 shows a cutaway view of a typical cable, and Fig. 337-2 shows fittings for connecting the cable to a rigid metal conduit.

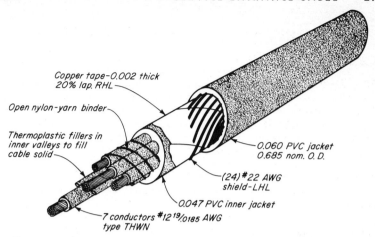

Copper tape-0.002 thick
20% lap. RHL

Open nylon-yarn binder

Thermoplastic fillers in
inner valleys to fill
cable solid

0.060 PVC jacket
0.685 nom. O.D.

(24) #22 AWG
shield-LHL

0.047 PVC inner jacket

7 conductors #12 19/0185 AWG
type THWN

FIG. 337-1. Cutaway view of a seven-conductor No. 12 Type SNM cable.

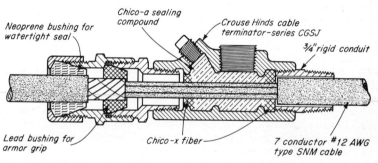

Chico-a sealing
compound

Neoprene bushing for
watertight seal

Crouse Hinds cable
terminator-series CGSJ

¾" rigid conduit

Lead bushing for
armor grip

Chico-x fiber

7 conductor #12 AWG
type SNM cable

FIG. 337-2. Drawing shows fittings used where Type SNM cable enters ¾-in.
rigid metal conduit in Class I and II, Div. 2 hazardous locations.

ARTICLE 338. SERVICE–ENTRANCE CABLE

Types SE and USE

338-1. Definition.   Service-entrance cable is a conductor assembly provided with
a suitable over-all covering, primarily used for services and of the following types.
When consisting of two or more conductors, one may be without individual
insulation.

(a)   Type SE, having a flame-retardant, moisture-resistant covering, but not
required to have inherent protection against mechanical abuse.

(b)   Type USE, recognized for underground use, having a moisture-resistant covering, but not required to have a flame-retardant covering or inherent protection against mechanical abuse. Single conductor cables having rubber insulation specifically approved for the purpose do not require an outer covering.

▶   The Code contains no specifications for the construction of this cable; it is left to Underwriters' Laboratories, Inc. to determine what types of cable should be approved for this purpose. The types listed by the Laboratories at the present time are multiple-conductor cables, with all conductors insulated or having an uninsulated neutral conductor, usually with a steel tape armor and a saturated braid over the armor to protect it from the corrosive action of the atmosphere.

Service-entrance cable is labeled in sizes No. 12 AWG and larger. The temperature rating or the conductor-type designation may be marked on the outside surface of the cable. If no such markings appear, the rating shall be considered to be 60°C.

Type USE cable is listed for underground installation including burial directly in the earth. Many single-conductor cables are dual-rated (Type USE or RHW or RHH) and may be used in raceways.

338-2. Use as Service-Entrance Conductors.   Service-entrance cable used as service-entrance conductors shall be installed as required by Article 230.

338-3. Use as Branch Circuit or Feeders.

(a)   Type SE, service-entrance cables may be used in interior wiring systems where all of the *circuit* conductors of the cable are of the rubber-covered or thermoplastic type.

(b)   Type SE, service-entrance cables without individual insulation on the grounded circuit conductor shall not be used as a branch circuit or as a feeder within a building, except a cable which has a final nonmetallic outer covering and when supplied by alternating current at not exceeding 150 volts to ground, may be used: (1) As a branch circuit to supply only a range, wall-mounted oven, counter-mounted cooking unit, or clothes dryer as covered in Section 250-60, or (2) as a feeder to supply only other buildings on the same premises. It shall not be used as a feeder terminating within the same building in which it originates.

The above provisions do not intend to deny the use of service entrance cable for interior use when the fully insulated conductors are used for circuit wiring and the uninsulated conductor is used for equipment grounding purposes.

▶   Where a group of buildings is supplied by a single service, such as in farm wiring, where a distribution center is installed inside one building, this type of cable may be used from the distribution center to the outside of the building for feeders or branch circuits supplying other buildings, and may also be used for such feeders or branch circuits from the outsides of the other buildings to the main cutoff switches.

Paragraph *b* permits the use of service-entrance cable with an uninsulated grounded conductor for the neutral to supply a range, wall-mounted oven, counter-mounted cooking unit, or a clothes dryer. Section **250-60** permits the use of this conductor for grounding these appliances if the circuit originates from the service equipment.

(c) Type SE service-entrance cable used to supply appliances shall not be subject to conductor temperatures in excess of the temperature specified for the type of insulation involved.

338-4. Installation Methods.

(a) In addition to the provisions of this Article, Type SE service-entrance cable used for interior wiring shall comply with the applicable provisions of Article 300.

(b) Unarmored cable shall be installed in accordance with the applicable provisions of Article 336.

(c) Cables through studs, joists and rafters shall be installed as required in Section 300-8.

338-5. Marking.   Service-entrance cable shall conform with the marking required in Section 310-12. Cable with the neutral conductor smaller than the ungrounded conductors shall be so marked.

ARTICLE 339. UNDERGROUND FEEDER AND BRANCH-CIRCUIT CABLE

Type UF

339-1. Description and Marking.

(a) Description.   Underground feeder and branch circuit cable shall be an approved Type UF cable in sizes No. 14 to No. 4/0 AWG, inclusive. The conductors shall be Types TW, RHW, or other conductors approved for the purpose. In addition to the insulated conductors, the cable may have an approved size of uninsulated or bare conductor for grounding purposes only. The over-all covering shall be flame-retardant, moisture-resistant, fungus-resistant and corrosive-resistant, and suitable for direct burial in the earth.

(b) Marking.   In addition to the provisions of Section 310-12, the cable shall have a distinctive marking on the exterior for its entire length specifying cable type.

339-2. Other Articles.   In addition to the provisions of this Article, installations of underground feeder and branch circuit cable (Type UF) shall comply with other applicable provisions of this Code. See especially Article 300, and Section 310-2(b).

▶   This type of cable may be used underground, including direct burial in the earth, as feeder or branch-circuit cable when provided with overcurrent protection not in excess of the rated ampacity of the individual conductors. If single-conductor cables are installed, all cables of the feeder circuit, subfeeder or branch circuit, including the neutral circuit, must be run together in close proximity in the same trench or raceway. It may be necessary in some installations to provide additional mechanical protection, such as a covering board, concrete pad, raceway, etc., when required by the authority enforcing the Code. Multiple-conductor Type UF cable may also be used for interior wiring when complying with the provisions of Art. 336 of the Code, and may be used in wet locations.

Single-conductor Type UF cable embedded in poured cement, concrete, or aggregate may be used for nonheating leads of fixed electric space heating cables; see paragraph *d* of Section **339-3.**

339-3. Use.

(a)   Underground feeder and branch circuit cable may be used underground, including direct burial in the earth, as feeder or branch circuit cable when provided with overcurrent protection of the rated ampacity as required in Section 339-4.

(b)   Where single conductor cables are installed, all cables of the feeder circuit, sub-feeder circuit, or branch circuit, including the neutral conductor, if any, shall be run together in the same trench or raceway.

(c)   A minimum depth of 18 inches shall be maintained for conductors and cables buried directly in the earth. This depth may be reduced to 12 inches provided supplemental protective covering such as a 2 inch concrete pad, metal raceway, pipe or other suitable protection is used.

▶   See Fig. **339-1.**

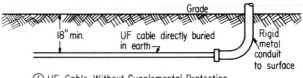

① UF Cable Without Supplemental Protection.

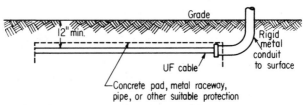

② UF Cable With Supplemental Protective Coverings

Fig. 339-1. Underground or direct burial of Type UF cable that complies with Section 339-3*c.*

(d)   Type UF cable may be used for interior wiring in wet, dry, or corrosive locations under the recognized wiring methods of this Code, and when installed as nonmetallic sheathed cable it shall conform with the installation provisions of Article 336 and shall be of the multiple conductor type, except where recognized under the provisions of Section 424-43. Type UF cable supported by continuous rigid cable supports shall be of the multiple conductor type.

(e)   This type of cable shall not be used: (1) as service-entrance cables; (2) in commercial garages; (3) in theaters or assembly halls, except as provided in Section 520-4; (4) in motion picture studios; (5) in storage battery rooms; (6) in hoistways; (7) in any hazardous location; (8) embedded in poured cement, concrete or aggregate, except where recognized in Article 424; (9) when exposed to direct rays of the sun, unless approved for the purpose.

▶   **Cables suitable for exposure to direct rays of the sun are indicated by tag marking and marking on the surface of the cable with the designation "sunlight resistant."**

339-4. Overcurrent Protection. Overcurrent protection shall be provided in accordance with provisions of Section 240-5.

339-5. Rated Ampacity. The ampacities of conductors in Type UF cable shall be according to Tables 310-12 and 310-14.

ARTICLE 342. NONMETALLIC EXTENSIONS

342-1. Description. Nonmetallic extensions are an assembly of two insulated conductors within a nonmetallic jacket or an extruded thermoplastic covering. The classification includes both surface extensions, intended for mounting directly on the surface of walls or ceilings, and aerial cable, containing a supporting messenger cable as an integral part of the cable assembly.

342-2. Other Articles. In addition to the provisions of this Article, nonmetallic extensions shall conform to other applicable provisions of this Code.

342-3. Use Permitted. Nonmetallic extensions may be used only where all of the following conditions are met:

(a) The extension is from an existing outlet on a 15 or 20 ampere branch circuit in conformity with the requirements of Article 210.

(b) The extension is run exposed and in a dry location.

(c) For nonmetallic surface extensions, the building is occupied for residential or office purposes.

(d) For aerial cable, the building is occupied for industrial purposes, and the nature of the occupancy requires a highly flexible means for connecting equipment.

▶   **A nonmetallic extension is an assembly of two conductors without a metallic envelope, designed specially for a 15- or 20-amp branch circuit as an extension from an existing outlet. Surface extensions are limited to residences and offices. Aerial extensions are limited to industrial purposes where it has been determined that the nature of the occupancy would require such wiring for connecting equipment.**

342-4. Use Prohibited. Nonmetallic extensions shall not be installed:

(a) As aerial cable to substitute for one of the general wiring methods specified by this Code.

(b) In unfinished basements, attics, or roof spaces.

(c) Where voltage between conductors exceeds 150 volts for nonmetallic surface extension and 300 volts for aerial cable.

(d) Where subject to corrosive vapors.

(e) Where run through a floor or partition, or outside the room in which it originates.

342-5. Splices and Taps. Extensions shall consist of a continuous unbroken length of the assembly, without splices, and without exposed conductors between fittings. Taps may be made where approved fittings completely covering the tap connections are used. Aerial cable and its tap connectors shall be provided with an approved means for polarization. Receptacle type tap connectors shall be of the locking type.

342-6. Fittings. Each run shall terminate in a fitting which covers the end of the assembly. All fittings and devices shall be of a type approved for the purpose.

342-7. Installation.   Nonmetallic extensions shall be installed in conformity with the following requirements:

(a) Nonmetallic Surface Extensions.

(1) One or more extensions may be run in any direction from an existing outlet, but not on the floor or within 2 inches from the floor.

(2) Nonmetallic surface extensions shall be secured in place by approved means at intervals not exceeding 8 inches, except that where connection to the supplying outlet is made by means of an attachment plug the first fastening may be placed 12 inches or less from the plug. There shall be at least one fastening between each two adjacent outlets supplied. An extension shall be attached only to woodwork or plaster finish, and shall not be in contact with any metal work or other conductive material except with metal plates on receptacles.

(3) A bend which reduces the normal spacing between the conductors shall be covered with a cap to protect the assembly from physical damage.

(b) Aerial Cable.

(1) Aerial cable shall be supported by its messenger cable, securely attached at each end with approved clamps and turnbuckles. Intermediate supports shall be provided at not more than 20 foot intervals. Cable tension shall be adjusted to eliminate excessive sag. The cable shall have a clearance of not less than 2 inches from steel structural members or other conductive material.

(2) Aerial cable shall have a clearance of not less than 10 feet above floor areas accessible to pedestrian traffic, and not less than 14 feet above floor areas accessible to vehicular traffic.

(3) Cable suspended over work benches, not accessible to pedestrian traffic, shall have a clearance of not less than 8 feet above the floor.

(4) Aerial cable may serve to support lighting fixtures when the total load on the supporting messenger cable does not exceed that for which the assembly is intended.

(5) The supporting messenger cable, when conforming to the applicable provisions of Article 250 and when properly identified as a grounding conductor, may be used for the grounding of equipment. The messenger cable shall not be used as a branch circuit conductor.

ARTICLE 344. UNDERPLASTER EXTENSIONS

344-1. Use. An underplaster extension installed as permitted by this Article, may be used only for extending an existing branch circuit in a building of fire-resistive construction.

▶   Such extensions are permitted in order to provide a suitable means of extending from existing outlets to new outlets without excessive expense, where there are no open spaces in walls or floors that will permit fishing from one outlet to another. In installing this work, the plaster is channeled and the conduit, cable, raceway, or tubing is secured to the concrete or tile and then plastered over.

344-2. Materials.   Such extensions shall be run in rigid or flexible conduit, Type AC metal-clad cable, electrical metallic tubing, Type MI cable or metal raceways approved for the purpose. Standard sizes of conduit, cable, tubing and raceways shall be used except that for a single conductor only conduit or tubing having not less than $\frac{5}{16}$ inch inside diameter, single-conductor Type AC metal-clad cable or single conductor Type MI cable may be used.

344-3. Box and Fittings.   See Article 370.

344-4. Installation.   An underplaster extension shall be laid on the face of masonry or other material and buried in the plaster finish of ceilings or walls. The methods of installation of the raceway or cable for such extension shall be as specified elsewhere in this Code for the particular type of material used.

344-5. Extension to Another Floor.   No such extension shall extend beyond the floor on which it originates unless installed in a standard size of rigid metal conduit, electrical metallic tubing, Type AC metal-clad cable, or MI cable.

▶   Such wiring is an expedient permitted for the purpose of avoiding an excessive amount of channeling and drilling of walls and floors. It is an expensive method, and from the standpoint of permanence, safety, and reliability the standard types of wiring are much to be preferred. For these reasons, underplaster extensions are limited to the floor within which they originate. In practice, the use of this method generally is, and should be, limited to short runs feeding not more than two or three additional outlets from one existing outlet.

ARTICLE 346. RIGID METAL CONDUIT

Note: Where conduit is threaded in the field, it is assumed that a standard conduit cutting die providing $\frac{3}{4}$ inch taper per foot will be employed.

346-1. Use.   Rigid metal conduit may be used under all atmospheric conditions and occupancies, except that ferrous raceways and fittings protected from corrosion solely by enamel may be used only indoors and in occupancies not subject to severe corrosive influences. Where practicable dissimilar metals in contact anywhere in the system shall be avoided to eliminate the possibility of galvanic action.

Unless made of a material judged suitable for the condition, or unless corrosion protection approved for the condition is provided, ferrous or nonferrous metallic conduit, elbows, couplings, and fittings shall not be installed in concrete or in direct contact with the earth, or in areas subject to severe corrosive influences.

▶   The above requirement was inserted into the Code on the basis of unsatisfactory performance of aluminum conduit in concrete which presumably had chloride additives that contributed to the high rate of corrosion. See comments following Section **300-5c.**

346-2. Other Articles.   Installations of rigid metal conduit shall comply with the provisions of the applicable Sections of Article 300.

A. Installation

346-3. Cinder Fill.   Conduit, unless of corrosion-resistant material suitable for the purpose shall not be used in or under cinder fill where subject to permanent moisture unless protected on all sides by a layer of noncinder concrete at least 2 inches thick or unless the conduit is at least 18 inches under the fill.

▶   Cinders usually contain sulfur, and if there is much moisture sulfuric acid is formed, which attacks steel conduit. A cinder fill outdoors should be considered as "subject to permanent moisture." In such a place conduit runs should be buried in the ground at least **18 in.** below the fill. This would not apply if cinders were not present.

346-4. Wet Locations.   All supports, bolts, straps, screws, etc., shall be of corrosion-resistant materials or protected against corrosion by approved corrosion-resistant materials.

See Section 300-5.

346-5. Minimum Size.   No conduit smaller than ½ inch, electrical trade size, shall be used, except as provided for underplaster extensions in Article 344, and for enclosing the leads of motors as permitted in Section 430-145(b).

346-6. Number of Conductors in Conduit.   The number of conductors permitted in a single conduit shall be in accordance with the percentage fill specified in Table 1, Chapter 9.

▶   Conduit fill is based on the percentages specified in Table 1, Chapter 9, and applies equally to new and old work and concealed or exposed work.

346-7. Reaming.   All cut ends of conduits shall be reamed to remove rough edges.

346-8. Bushings.   Where a conduit enters a box or other fitting, a bushing shall be provided to protect the wire from abrasion unless the design of the box or fitting is such as to afford equivalent protection. See Section 373-6(b) for the protection of conductors at bushings.

346-9. Couplings and Connectors.

(a)   Threadless couplings and connectors used with conduit shall be made tight. Where buried in masonry or concrete, they shall be of the concrete-tight type, or where installed in wet locations, shall be of the raintight type.

(b)   Running threads shall not be used on conduit for connection at couplings.

▶ Figure **346-1** is effective both mechanically and electrically if any non-conducting coating is removed from the conduit.

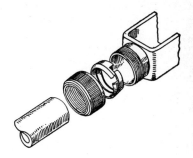

FIG. 346-1. Threadless connection to a fitting. (*Appleton Electric Co.*)

A running thread is considered mechanically weak and has poor electrical conductivity.

Where two lengths of conduit must be coupled together but it is impossible to screw both lengths into an ordinary coupling, the Erickson coupling shown in Fig. **346-2** may be used. This makes a rigid joint which is both mechanically and electrically effective. Also, bolted split couplings are available.

FIG. 346-2. Erickson couplings. (*The Thomas & Betts Co., Inc.*)

It is not intended that conduit threads be treated with paint or other materials in order to assure water tightness. It is assumed that the conductors are approved for the location and that the prime purpose of the conduit is for protection from physical damage and easy withdrawal of conductors for replacement.

346-10. Bends—How Made.   Bends of rigid conduit shall be so made that the conduit will not be injured, and that the internal diameter of the conduit will not be effectively reduced. The radius of the curve of the inner edge of any field bend shall not be less than shown in Table 346-10(a).

▶ *Field bend* means any bend made by workmen during the installation of the conduit.

Exception: For field bends for conductors without lead sheath and made with a single operation (one shot) bending machine designed for the purpose, the minimum radius may be in accordance with Table 346-10(b).

Table 346-10(a). Radius of Conduit Bends (Inches)

Size of Conduit (In.)	Conductors Without Lead Sheath (In.)	Conductors With Lead Sheath (In.)
½	4	6
¾	5	8
1	6	11
1¼	8	14
1½	10	16
2	12	21
2½	15	25
3	18	31
3½	21	36
4	24	40
4½	27	45
5	30	50
6	36	61

Table 346-10(b). Radius of Conduit Bends (Inches)

Size of Conduit (In.)	Radius to Center of Conduit (In.)
½	4
¾	4½
1	5¾
1¼	7¼
1½	8¼
2	9½
2½	10½
3	13
3½	15
4	16
4½	20
5	24
6	30

346-11. Bends—Number in One Run. A run of conduit between outlet and outlet, between fitting and fitting, or between outlet and fitting shall not contain more than the equivalent of 4 quarter bends (360 degrees, total), including those bends located immediately at the outlet or fitting.

▶ Conduit runs should be so installed that the conductors can be pulled in without injuring the insulation or stretching small wires, and so that the conductors can be withdrawn easily.

346-12. Supports. Rigid metal conduit shall be installed as a complete system as provided in Article 300 and shall be securely fastened in place. Conduit shall be firmly fastened within 3 feet of each outlet box, junction box, cabinet, or fitting. Conduit shall be supported at least every ten feet except that straight runs of rigid conduit made up with approved threaded couplings may be secured in accordance with Table 346-12, provided such fastening prevents transmission of stresses to terminus when conduit is deflected between supports.

Table 346-12. Supports for Rigid Metal Conduit

Conduit Size (Inches)	Maximum distance between rigid metal conduit supports (Feet)
½–¾	10
1	12
1¼–1½	14
2–2½	16
3 and larger	20

346-13. Boxes and Fittings. See Article 370.

B. Construction Specifications

346-14. General. Rigid metal conduit shall conform to the following:

(a) Rigid conduit as shipped shall be in standard lengths of 10 feet including coupling, one coupling to be furnished with each length. Each length shall be reamed and threaded on each end. For specific applications or uses, lengths shorter or longer than 10 feet, with or without couplings, may be shipped.

(b) Nonferrous conduit of corrosion-resistant material shall have suitable markings.

(c) Each length shall be clearly and durably identified in every 10 feet as required in the first sentence of Section 110-21.

ARTICLE 347. RIGID NONMETALLIC CONDUIT

347-1. Description. The provisions of this Article shall apply to a type of conduit and fittings of suitable nonmetallic material which is resistant to moisture and chemical atmospheres. For use aboveground, it shall also be flame retardant, resistant to impact and crushing, shall resist distortion due to heat under conditions likely to be encountered in service and shall be resistant to low temperature and sunlight effects. For use underground, the material shall be acceptably resistant to moisture and corrosive agents and shall be of sufficient strength to withstand abuse, such as by impact and crushing, in handling and during installation. Where intended for direct burial, without encasement in concrete, the material shall also be capable of withstanding continued loading which is likely to be encountered after installation.

Materials which have been recognized as having suitable physical characteristics when properly formed and treated include fiber, asbestos cement, soapstone, rigid polyvinyl chloride and high density polyethylene for underground use and rigid polyvinyl chloride for use aboveground.

▶ All approved rigid nonmetallic conduits are suitable for underground installations. Some types are approved for direct burial in the earth while other types must be encased in concrete for underground applications. Listings by Underwriters' Laboratories, Inc. include such information.

The only nonmetallic conduit approved for use aboveground at the present time is rigid polyvinyl chloride (PVC) of the heavy-wall type. Since not all PVC conduits are suitable for use aboveground the UL label in each conduit length will indicate if the conduit is suitable for such use.

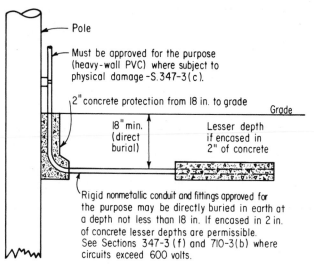

Fig. 347-1. Typical application of PVC rigid nonmetallic conduit that complies with Section 347-2a.

347-2. Use Permitted. Rigid nonmetallic conduit and fittings approved for the purpose may be used under the following conditions and where the potential is 600 volts or less except as noted in Section 347-3.

(a) Direct earth burial not less than 18 inches below the surface. If less than 18 inches it shall be encased in not less than 2 inches of concrete.

▶ See Fig. 347-1.

(b) In walls, floors and ceilings.

(c) In locations subject to severe corrosive influences as set forth in Section 300-5 and where subject to chemicals for which the materials are specifically approved.

(d) Cinder fill.

(e) Wet Locations. In portions of dairies, laundries, canneries or other wet locations and in locations where walls are frequently washed, the entire conduit system including boxes and fittings used therewith shall be so installed and equipped as to prevent water from entering the conduit. All supports, bolts, straps, screws, etc., shall be of corrosion-resistant materials or protected against corrosion by approved corrosion-resistant materials.

(f) In dry and damp locations not prohibited by Section 347-3.

347-3. Use Prohibited. Rigid nonmetallic conduit shall not be used:

(a) In hazardous locations except as covered in Sections 514-8 and 515-5.

(b) For the support of fixtures or other equipment.

(c) Where subject to physical damage unless approved for the purpose.

(d) Where subject to ambient temperatures exceeding those for which the conduit had been approved.

(e) For conductors whose insulation temperature limitations would exceed those for which the conduit had been approved.

(f) For potentials exceeding 600 volts unless encased in not less than 2 inches of concrete.

▶   **It should be noted that nonmetallic conduit is not permitted in ducts, plenums and other air-handling spaces. See Section 300-22. Also, such conduits or other nonmetallic materials should not be used in hollow spaces in buildings of fire-resistant construction because PVC conduits are combustible and add products of combustion and fuel contribution in the event of fire. See Section 300-21 and the comments following Section 300-22.**

347-4. Other Articles. Installation of rigid nonmetallic conduit shall comply with provisions of the applicable Sections of Article 300. When equipment grounding is required by Article 250, a separate grounding conductor shall be installed in the conduit.

A. Installations

347-5. Trimming. All cut ends shall be trimmed inside and outside to remove rough edges.

347-6. Joints. All joints between lengths of conduit, and between conduit and couplings, fittings and boxes shall be made by a method specifically approved for the purpose.

Table 347-8. Support of Rigid Nonmetallic Conduit

Conduit Size (Inches)	Maximum Spacing between Supports (Feet)	
	Conductors Rated 60°C and Below	Conductors Rated More Than 60°C
½–¾	4	2
1–2	5	2½
2½–3	6	3
3½–5	7	3½
6	8	4

▶   **In regard to the spacing requirements in Table 347-8, where conductors are rated more than 60°C, the maximum spacing between supports is sub-**

stantially reduced to compensate for slight sags that occur in PVC conduits at elevated temperatures.

It seems logical, however, that the phrase, "Conductors Rated More Than 60°C," would not apply when such conductors (75°C or 90°C) are protected by overcurrent devices rated or set not greater than the ampacities listed in the 60°C column in Tables 310-12 and 310-14. For example, Type THW conductors are rated at 75°C and THHN conductors are rated at 90°C. For sizes 14 to 10 in Table 310-12, and sizes 12 and 10 in Table 310-14, Types THW and THHN have the same ampacities as 60°C conductors such as Type TW. Accordingly, there would be no reason why such conductors should not be considered as 60°C conductors in determining the spacing requirements in Table **347-8**.

347-8. Supports.   Rigid nonmetallic conduit shall be adequately supported as required in Table 347-8. In addition, there shall be a support within 4 feet of each box, cabinet or other conduit termination.

347-9. Expansion Joints.   Expansion joints for rigid nonmetallic conduit shall be provided where required to compensate for thermal expansion and contraction.

▶   Where conduits are subject to constantly changing temperatures and the runs are long, expansion and contraction of PVC conduit must be considered. In such instances an expansion coupling should be installed near the fixed end of the run to take up any expansion or contraction that may occur. Available expansion couplings have a normal expansion range of 6 in. The coefficient of linear expansion of PVC conduit can be obtained from manufacturers' data.

Expansion couplings are normally used where conduits are exposed. In underground or slab applications such couplings are seldom used because expansion and contraction can be controlled by *bowing* the conduit slightly or by immediate burial. After the conduit is buried, expansion and contraction are not a problem. Conduits left exposed for an extended period of time during widely variable temperature conditions should be examined to see if contraction has occurred.

347-10. Minimum Size.   No conduit smaller than ½ inch electrical trade size shall be used.

347-11. Number of Conductors.   The number of conductors permitted in a single conduit shall be in accordance with the percentage fill specified in Table 1, Chapter 9.

▶   See comments following Section **346-6**.

347-12. Bushings.   Where a conduit enters a box or other fitting, a bushing or adapter shall be provided to protect the wire from abrasion unless the design of the box or fitting is such as to provide equivalent protection. See Section 373-6(b) for the protection of conductors at bushings.

347-13. Bends, How Made.   Bends of rigid nonmetallic conduit shall be so made that the conduit will not be injured and that the internal diameter of the conduit will not be effectively reduced. Field bends shall be made only with bending equipment specifically intended for the purpose, and the radius of the curve of the inner edge of such bends shall be not less than shown in Table 346-10(a).

347-14. Bends, Number in One Run. A run of conduit between outlet and outlet, between fitting and fitting or between outlet and fitting shall not contain more than the equivalent of four quarter bends (360°) total including those bends located immediately at the outlet or fitting.

347-15. Boxes and Fittings. See Article 370.

B. Construction Specifications

347-16. General. Rigid nonmetallic conduit shall conform to the following:

(a) Rigid nonmetallic polyvinyl chloride conduit as shipped shall be in standard lengths of 10 feet including couplings, one coupling to be furnished with each length. For specific applications or uses, lengths shorter or longer than 10 feet with or without couplings may be shipped.

(b) High density polyethylene conduit as shipped shall be in standard lengths of 10 feet. One threaded coupling shall be furnished with each threaded length of high density polyethylene conduit. For specific applications or uses, lengths shorter or longer than 10 feet with or without couplings may be shipped.

(c) Each length of nonmetallic conduit shall be clearly and durably marked at least every ten feet as required in the first sentence of Section 110-21. The type of material shall also be included in the marking unless it is visually identifiable.

For conduit recognized for use aboveground these markings shall be permanent. For conduit limited to underground use only, these markings shall be sufficiently durable to remain legible until the material is installed.

ARTICLE 348. ELECTRICAL METALLIC TUBING

348-1. Use. Electrical metallic tubing may be used for both exposed and concealed work. Electrical metallic tubing protected from corrosion solely by enamel shall not be used. Electrical metallic tubing shall not be used (1) where during installation or afterward, it will be subject to severe physical damage; (2) in cinder concrete or fill where subject to permanent moisture unless protected on all sides by a layer of noncinder concrete at least 2 inches thick or unless the tubing is at least 18 inches under the fill. Where practicable, the use of dissimilar metals throughout the system shall be avoided to eliminate the possibility of galvanic action.

Unless made of a material judged suitable for the condition, or unless corrosion protection approved for the condition is provided, ferrous or nonferrous electrical metallic tubing, elbows, couplings and fittings shall not be installed in concrete or in direct contact with the earth, or in areas subject to severe corrosive influences.

348-2. Other Articles. Installations of electrical metallic tubing shall comply with the provisions of the applicable sections of Article 300.

A. Installation

348-4. Wet Locations. All supports, bolts, straps, screws, etc. shall be of corrosion-resistant materials or protected against corrosion by approved corrosion-resistant materials. See Section 300-5.

▶   Silicon-bronze tubing and fittings having corrosion-resisting characteristics are available and are particularly suitable in the presence of corrosive atmospheres.

348-5. Minimum and Maximum Sizes. No tubing smaller than ½ inch, electrical trade size, shall be used except as provided for underplaster extensions in Article 344 and for enclosing the leads of motors as permitted in Section 430-145(b). The maximum size of tubing shall be the 4-inch electrical trade size.

348-6. Number of Conductors in Tubing. One tubing shall not contain more conductors than as provided in Section 346-6.

348-7. Threads. Tubing shall not be coupled together nor connected to boxes, fittings, or cabinets by means of threads in the wall of the tubing, except by fittings approved for the purpose. Threads shall not be of the standard pipe thread dimensions.

348-8. Couplings and Connectors. Threadless couplings and connectors used with tubing shall be made up tight. Where buried in masonry or concrete, they shall be concrete-tight type, or where installed in wet locations, shall be of the raintight type.

▶   Couplings of the raintight type are required wherever electrical metallic tubing is used on the exteriors of buildings. (See Sections **230-52** and **730-23**.)

Section **370-7** requires that conductors entering a box, cabinet, or fitting be protected from abrasion. The end of a connector projecting inside a box, cabinet, or fitting must have smooth, well-rounded edges so that the covering of the wire will not be abraded while the wire is being pulled in. Where ungrounded conductors of size No. 4 or larger enter a raceway in a cabinet, etc., see Section **373-6b**.

348-9. Bends—How Made. Bends in the tubing shall be so made that the tubing will not be injured and that the internal diameter of the tubing will not be effectively reduced. The radius of the curve of the inner edge of any field bend shall not be less than shown in Table 346-10(a).

Exception: For field bends made with a bending machine designed for the purpose, the minimum radius may be in accordance with the dimensions of Table 346-10(b).

348-10. Bends—Number in One Run. A run of electrical metallic tubing between outlet and outlet, between fitting and fitting, or between outlet and fitting, shall not contain more than the equivalent of four quarter bends (360 degrees, total), including those bends located immediately at the outlet or fitting.

▶   See comment following Section **346-11**.

348-11. Reaming. All cut ends of electrical metallic tubing shall be reamed to remove rough edges.

348-12. Supports. Electrical metallic tubing shall be installed as a complete system as provided in Article 300 and shall be securely fastened in place at least every 10 feet and within 3 feet of each outlet box, junction box, cabinet, or fitting.

348-13. Boxes and Fittings. See Article 370.

B. Construction Specifications

348-14. General. Electrical metallic tubing shall conform to the following:

  (a) Cross Section. The tubing, and elbows and bends for use with the tubing, shall have a circular cross section.

  (b) Finish. Tubing shall have such a finish or treatment of outer surfaces as will provide an approved durable means of readily distinguishing, after installation, from rigid conduit.

  (c) Connectors. Where the tubing is coupled together by threads, the connector shall be so designed as to prevent bending of the tubing at any part of the thread.

ARTICLE 350. FLEXIBLE METAL CONDUIT

350-1. Other Articles. Installations of flexible metal conduit shall comply with the appropriate (or applicable) provisions of Articles 300, 334, and 346.

350-2. Use. Flexible metal conduit shall not be used (1) in wet locations, unless conductors are of the lead-covered type or of other type specially approved for the conditions; (2) in hoistways, except as provided in Section 620-21; (3) in storage-battery rooms; (4) in any hazardous location except as permitted in Sections 501-4(b), 502-4 and 503-3; nor (5) where rubber-covered conductors are exposed to oil, gasoline, or other materials having a deteriorating effect on rubber.

350-3. Minimum Size. No flexible metal conduit less than one-half inch electrical trade size shall be used except (1) as permitted for underplaster extensions by Section 344-2; (2) as permitted for motors by Section 430-145(b); and (3) flexible metal conduit of ⅜-inch nominal trade size may be used in lengths not in excess of 72 inches as a part of an approved assembly or for lighting fixtures.

Table 350-3. Maximum Number of Insulated Conductors in ⅜ In.
Flexible Metal Conduit.*
Col. A = With fitting inside conduit.
Col. B = With fitting outside conduit.

Size AWG	Types RF-2, RFH-2, SF-2		Types TF, T, XHHW, AF, TW, RUH, RUW		Types TFN, THHN, THWN		Types FEP, FEPB, PF, PGF	
	A	B	A	B	A	B	A	B
18	..	3	3	7	4	8	5	8
16	..	2	2	4	3	7	4	8
14	..	..	..	4	3	7	3	7
12	..	..	..	3	..	4	..	4
10	..	..	..	..	..	2	..	3

* In addition one uninsulated grounding conductor of the same AWG size may be installed.

350-4. Supports.   When flexible metal conduit is installed it shall be secured by approved means at intervals not exceeding 4½ feet and within 12 inches on each side of every outlet box or fitting.

Exception No. 1: Where flexible metal conduit is fished.

Exception No. 2: Lengths of not more than 3 feet at terminals where flexibility is necessary.

Exception No. 3: Lengths of not more than 6 feet from a fixture terminal connection for tap connections to lighting fixtures as required in Section 410-65(b)(2).

▶   Straps or other means of securing the conduit in place should be spaced much closer together for flexible conduit than is necessary for rigid conduit. Every bend should be rigidly secured so that it will not be deformed when the wires are being pulled in, thus causing the wires to bind.

350-5. Grounding.   Flexible metal conduit may be used as a grounding means where both the conduit and the fittings are approved for the purpose.

Exception: Flexible metal conduit may be used for grounding if the length is 6 feet or less, it is terminated in fittings approved for the purpose, and the circuit conductors contained therein are protected by overcurrent devices rated at 20 amperes or less.

▶   This means that where flexible metal conduit and fittings have not been specifically approved as a grounding means, a separate grounding conductor (insulated or bare) shall be run inside the conduit and bonded at each box or similar equipment to which the conduit is connected.

In regard to the Exception, see comments following Section 250-91*b*.

ARTICLE 351. LIQUIDTIGHT FLEXIBLE METAL CONDUIT

351-1. Scope.   The provisions of this Article shall apply to a type of flexible metal conduit having an outer liquidtight nonmetallic sunlight-resistant jacket.

▶   Liquidtight flexible metal conduit is approved for use in wet locations and where exposed to mineral oil, both at a maximum temperature of 60°C. It is not for use where exposed to gasoline or similar light-petroleum solvents. It is being widely used in the wiring of machine tools. It is similar in construction to the common type of flexible metal conduit, but is covered with an outer sheath of thermoplastic material. Figure 351-1 shows a grounding bushing designed to be slipped inside each end of a length of conduit to ensure an adequate grounding connection, and Fig. 351-2 shows the construction of the conduit. The use of the bushing makes it unnecessary to remove any burrs or sharp edges where the conduit has been cut. This conduit can be terminated at any connector or other fitting of suitable size that is designed to receive unthreaded rigid conduit.

FIG. 351-1. Grounding bushing for use where liquidtight flexible conduit is terminated. (*American Brass Co.*)

Fig. 351-2. Liquidtight flexible conduit. (*American Brass Co.*)

351-2. Use.

(a) Liquidtight flexible metal conduit may be used in exposed or concealed locations:

(1) Where conditions of installation, operation or maintenance require flexibility or protection from liquids, vapors or solids.

(2) As permitted by Sections 501-4(b), 502-4 and 503-3, and in other hazardous locations where specifically approved.

(b) Liquidtight flexible metal conduit shall not be used:

(1) Where subject to physical damage.

(2) Where any combination of ambient and/or conductor temperature will produce an operating temperature in excess of that for which the material is approved.

351-3. Size. The sizes of liquidtight flexible metal conduit shall be electrical trade sizes ½ to 4 inch inclusive.

Exception: ⅜-inch size may be used as permitted in Section 350-3.

351-4. Number of Conductors.

(a) The number of conductors permitted in a single conduit shall be in accordance with the percentage of fill specified in Table 1, Chapter 9.

(b) See Table 350-3 for maximum number of conductors in ⅜-inch liquidtight flexible metal conduit.

351-5. Fittings. Liquidtight flexible metal conduit shall be used only with terminal fittings approved for the purpose.

351-6. Supports. Where liquidtight flexible metal conduit is installed as a fixed raceway, it shall be secured by approved means at intervals not exceeding 4½ feet and within 12 inches on each side of every outlet box or fitting except where the conduit is fished.

351-7. Grounding.

(a) Liquidtight flexible metal conduit may be used for grounding in the 1¼ inch and smaller trade sizes if the length is 6 feet or less and it is terminated in fittings approved for the purpose.

(b) Liquidtight flexible metal conduit may be used as a grounding means where both the conduit and fittings are approved for the purpose.

▶   In regard to paragraph *a*, see comments following Section 250-91*b*.

ARTICLE 352. SURFACE RACEWAYS

Metal Raceways

352-1. Use. Surface metal raceways may be installed in dry locations. They shall not be used (1) where subject to severe physical damage unless approved for the purpose; (2) where the voltage is 300 volts or more between conductors unless the metal has a thickness of not less than .040 inch; (3) where subject to corrosive vapors; (4) in hoistways; (5) in any hazardous location; nor (6) concealed except as follows:

Exception No. 1: Surface metal raceways approved for the purpose may be used for underplaster extensions.

Exception No. 2: Where accessible, surface metal raceways may be used in nonair-handling plenum chamber areas.

See definition of "Exposed—(As applied to wiring methods)" in Article 100.

352-2. Other Articles.   Installations of surface metal raceways shall comply with the applicable provisions of Article 300.

▶   In every type of wiring having a metal enclosure around the conductors, it is important that the metal shall be mechanically continuous in order to provide protection for the conductors and that the metal shall form a continuous electrical conductor of low impedance from the last outlet on the run to the cabinet or cutout box. A path to ground is thus provided through the box or cabinet, in case any conductor comes in contact with the metal enclosure, an outlet box, or any other fitting. See Section 250-91*b*.

A. Installation

352-3. Size of Conductors.   No conductor larger than that for which the raceway is designed shall be installed in surface metal raceway.

▶   The manufacturers of surface metal raceways have provided the following illustrations and details (Figs. 352-1 through 352-4) on their products.

352-4. Number of Conductors in Raceways.   The number of conductors installed in any raceway shall be no greater than the number for which the raceway is designed.

352-5. Extension Through Walls and Floors.   Except in multioutlet assemblies, raceways may be extended through dry walls, dry partitions and dry floors, if in unbroken lengths where passing through.

352-6. Combination Raceways.   Where combination metal raceways are used both for signal and for lighting and power circuits, the different systems shall be run in separate compartments, identified by sharply contrasting colors of the interior finish, and the same relative position of compartments shall be maintained throughout the premises.

352-7. Splices and Taps.   Splices and taps shall be made only in junction boxes except that they may be made in surface metal raceway having a removable cover which is accessible after installation. The conductors, including splices and taps, shall not fill the raceway to more than 75 per cent of its area at that point. All splices and taps shall be made by approved methods.

B. Construction Specifications

352-8. General. Surface metal raceways shall be of such construction as will distinguish them from other raceways. Surface metal raceways and their elbows,

Type of raceway	Wire size gage No.	Type RH	Types T, TW	Types THWN
No. 200 (11/32″, 1/2″)	14	3	3	3
	12	2	3	3
No. 500 (17/32″, 3/4″)	14	5	6	8
	12	4	6	7
	10	2	4	4
	8		2	2
No. 700 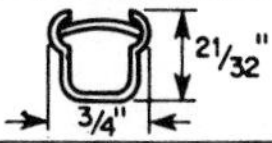 (21/32″, 3/4″)	14	7	8	11
	12	6	8	10
	10	3	6	6
	8	2	3	3
No. 1000 (15/16″, 15/16″)	14	10	10	21
	12	10	10	18
	10	6	8	10
	8	5	8	10
	6	4	5	6
No. 1500 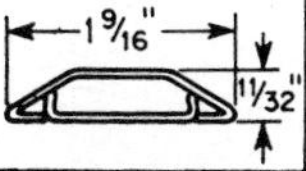 (1 9/16″, 11/32″)	14	4	8	10
	12	4	6	8
	10		4	5
	8		4	3
	6			2

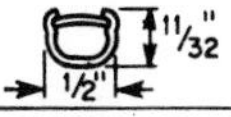

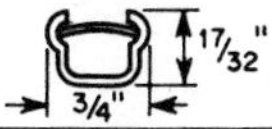

† Typical number of wires in one raceway. Number of wires columns: Type RH, Types T, TW, Types THWN.

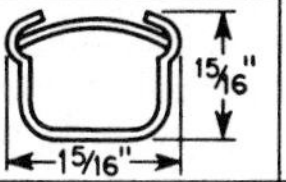

Type of raceway	Wire size gage No.	Type RH — With receptacles	Type RH — Without receptacles	Types T, TW — With receptacles	Types T, TW — Without receptacles	Types THWN — Without receptacles
No. 1900 (9/16″, 13/16″)	14	3	3	3	3	3
	12	3	3	3	3	3
No. 2000 (1 9/32″, 3/4″)	14	3	3	3	3	3
	12	3	3	3	3	3
No. 2100 (1 1/4″, 7/8″)	14	*	17	*	17	23
	12	*	14	*	14	18
	10		10	*	10	12
	8		6		8	10
	6		4		5	7

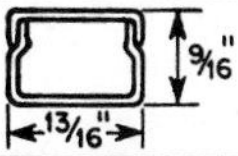

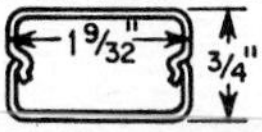

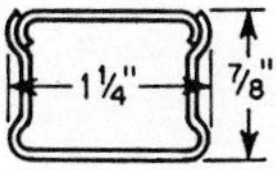

* See wiremold catalog

Type of raceway	Wire size gage No.	With receptacles	Without receptacles	With receptacles	Without receptacles	Without receptacles
No. 2200 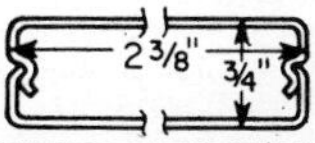 (2 3/8″, 3/4″)	14		10		10	14
	12		10		10	13
	10		6		10	12
	8		4		7	10
	6				3	7
No. 3000 (2 3/4″, 1 7/16″)				Types RU, T, TW		
	14	*	44	*	56	75
	12	*	40	*	42	55
	10	*	20	*	20	24
	8	*	14	*	16	18
	6	*	10	*	14	13

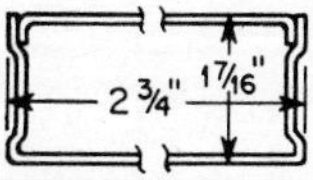

* Type RH, T, TW with devices in place with standard flush-mounted snap switches and attachment-plug receptacles of a type not having pilot lights. 10 No.6; 10 No. 8; 10 No.10; 10 No.12; 10 No.14.

† Recommended only for straight runs with no bends nor elbows.

FIG. 352-1. Wiremold surface metal raceway. (*The Wiremold Co.*)

▶ See Wiremold catalog No. 23 for additional information.

Type of raceway		Wire size gage No.	Number of wires	
			Type RH	Type T
No. 111	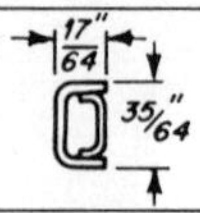	14 12	3 2	3 3
No. 333	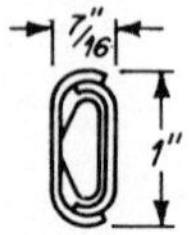	14 12 10 8 6	7 6 3 2	9 8 6 3 2
No. 888	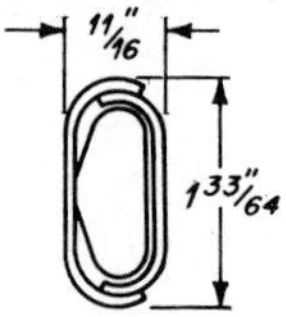	14 12 10 8 6	10 10 9 7 4	10 10 10 10 5
No. 711-A	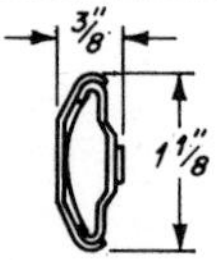	14 12 10 8	7 4 2 2	9 5 4 3
No. 733-A	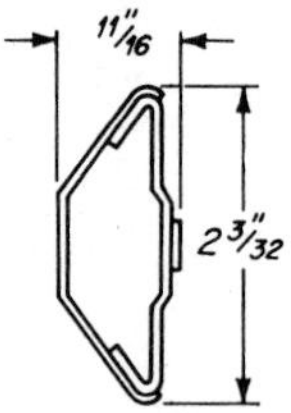	14 12 10 8 6	10 10 10 7 4	10 10 10 10 6

Number of wires in one raceway

Type of raceway	Wire size gage No.	With devices	Without devices	With devices	Without devices
No. 1700	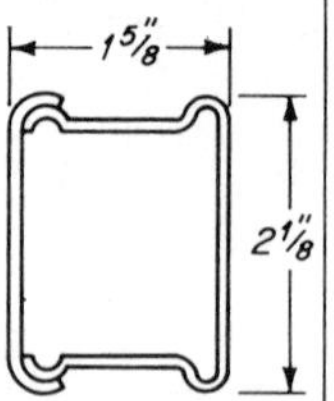 14 12 10 8 6	10 10 10 10 8	38 34 18 12 8	10 10 10 10 10	54 34 18 16 12
No. 3400	Catalog No. 3400 is a raceway consisting of two No. 1700 housings in a common cover. Each channel has the same wire fill as 1700.				

Fig. 352-2. Types of surface metal raceways. (*National Electric Division, H. K. Porter Company, Inc.*)

Fig. 352-3. Typical use of small surface metal raceway for extensions from existing receptacle outlets. (*National Electric Division, H. K. Porter Company, Inc.*)

Fig. 352-4. Shallow switch and receptacle box with 500 Wiremold raceway. (*The Wiremold Co.*)

couplings, and similar fittings shall be so designed that the sections can be electrically and mechanically coupled together, while protecting the wires from abrasion. Holes for screws or bolts inside the raceway shall be so designed that when screws or bolts are in place their heads will be flush with the metal surface.

Nonmetallic Raceways

352-21. Description. The provisions of the following Sections of this Article shall apply to a type of surface nonmetallic raceway and fittings of suitable nonmetallic material which is resistant to moisture and chemical atmospheres. It shall also be flame retardant, resistant to impact and crushing, shall resist distortion due to heat under conditions likely to be encountered in service and shall be resistant to low temperature effects.

352-22. Use. Surface nonmetallic raceways may be installed in dry locations. They shall not be used (1) where concealed; (2) where subject to severe physical damage unless approved for the purpose; (3) where the voltage is 300 volts or more between conductors; (4) in hoistways; (5) in any hazardous location; (6) where subject to ambient temperatures exceeding 50°C; nor (7) for conductors whose insulation temperature exceeds 75°C.

352-23. Other Articles. Installations of surface nonmetallic raceways shall comply with the applicable provisions of Article 300.

A. Installation

352-24. Size of Conductors. No conductor larger than that for which the raceway is designed shall be installed in surface nonmetallic raceway.

352-25. Number of Conductors in Raceways. The number of conductors installed in any raceway shall be no greater than the number for which the raceway is designed.

352-26. Combination Raceways. Where combination nonmetallic raceways are used both for signal and for lighting and power circuits, the different systems shall be run in separate compartments, identified by printed legend or by sharply contrasting colors of the interior finish, and the same relative position of compartments shall be maintained throughout the premises.

B. Construction Specifications

352-27. General. Surface nonmetallic raceways shall be of such construction as will distinguish them from other raceways. Surface nonmetallic raceways and their elbows, couplings, and similar fittings shall be so designed that the sections can be mechanically coupled together, while protecting the wires from abrasion. Holes for screws or bolts inside the raceway shall be so designed that when screws or bolts are in place their heads will be flush with the nonmetallic surface.

ARTICLE 353. MULTIOUTLET ASSEMBLY

353-1. Other Articles. Installations of multioutlet assembly shall comply with applicable provisions of Article 300. See definition in Article 100.

▶   **These assemblies are intended for surface mounting except that the metal type may be surrounded by the building finish or recessed so long as the front is not covered. The nonmetallic type may be recessed in baseboards. In calculating the load for branch circuits supplying multioutlet assembly, see Section 220-2c, Exception 3.**

353-2. Use. Multioutlet assembly may be installed in dry locations. It shall not be installed (1) where concealed, except that the back and sides of metal multioutlet assembly may be surrounded by the building finish and nonmetallic multioutlet assembly may be recessed in the baseboard; (2) where subject to severe physical damage unless approved for the purpose; (3) where the voltage is 300 volts or more between conductors unless assembly is of metal having a thickness of not less than .040 inch; (4) where subject to corrosive vapors; (5) in hoistways; nor (6) in any hazardous locations.

353-3. Metal Multioutlet Assembly Through Dry Partitions. Metal multioutlet assembly may be extended through (not run within) dry partitions, providing arrangements are made for removing the cap or cover on all exposed portions and no outlet is located within the partitions.

ARTICLE 354. UNDERFLOOR RACEWAYS

354-1. Other Articles. Installations of underfloor raceways shall comply with the applicable provisions of Article 300.

▶   Underfloor raceway was developed to provide a practical means of bringing conductors for lighting, power, and signaling systems to office desks and tables. It is also used in large retail stores, making it possible to secure connections for display-case lighting at any desired location.

This wiring method makes it possible to place a desk or table in any location where it will always be over, or very near to, a duct line. The wiring method for lighting and power between cabinets and the raceway junction boxes may be conduit, underfloor raceway, wall elbows and cabinet connectors.

354-2. Use. Underfloor raceways may be installed beneath the surface of concrete or other flooring material, or in office occupancies, where laid flush with the concrete floor and covered with linoleum or equivalent floor covering. Underfloor raceways shall not be installed (1) where subject to corrosive vapors nor (2) in any hazardous location. Unless made of a material judged suitable for the condition, or unless corrosion protection approved for the condition is provided, ferrous or nonferrous metallic underfloor raceways, junction boxes, and fittings shall not be installed in concrete; or in areas subject to severe corrosive influences.

354-3. Covering. Raceway coverings shall conform to the following:

(a) Raceways Not Over 4 Inches Wide. Half-round raceways not over 4 inches in width, and, except as permitted in (c) flat top raceways not over 4 inches in width, shall have not less than ¾ inch of concrete or wood above the raceway

(b) Raceways Over 4 Inches Wide but Not Over 8 Inches Wide. Flat top raceways over 4 but not over 8 inches wide with a minimum of 1 inch spacing between raceways shall be covered with concrete to a depth of not less than 1 inch. Raceways spaced less than 1 inch apart shall be covered with concrete to a depth of 1½ inches.

(c) Raceways Flush With Concrete. Approved flush raceways with removable covers may be laid flush with the floor surface. Such approved raceways shall be

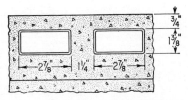

Fig. 354-1. Nepcoduct metal raceway. A ¾-in. wood or concrete covering is required. See Section 354-3a. (*National Electric Division, H. K. Porter Company, Inc.*)

Fig. 354-2. Any flat top raceway over 4 in. wide and spaced less than 1 in. from another raceway must be covered with concrete at least 1½ in. in thickness. See Section 354-3b. (*National Electric Division, H. K. Porter Company, Inc.*)

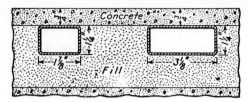

Fig. 354-3. Walker All-Steel metal raceway. A ¾-in. wood or concrete covering is required except for flush raceways covered in Section 354-3c. (*Walker Bros.*)

so designed that the cover plates will provide adequate mechanical protection and rigidity equivalent to junction box covers.

▶ **The intent in paragraphs (a) and (b) is to provide a sufficient amount of concrete over the ducts to prevent cracks in a cement, tile, or similar floor finish.**

354-4. Size of Conductors. No conductor larger than that for which the raceway is designed shall be installed in underfloor raceways.

354-5. Number of Conductors in Raceway. The combined cross-sectional area of all conductors shall not exceed 40 per cent of the interior area of the raceway; except that where the raceway contains only Type AC metal-clad cable or nonmetallic sheathed cable, these requirements shall not apply.

354-6. Splices and Taps. Splices and taps shall be made only in junction boxes.

For the purposes of this Section, so-called loop wiring (continuous, unbroken conductor connecting the individual outlets) is not considered to be a splice or tap.

▶ **The fine-print note recognizes "loop wiring" where "unbroken" wires extend from underfloor raceways to terminals of attached receptacles, and then back into the raceway to other outlets. See Fig. 354-4.**

354-7. Discontinued Outlets. When an outlet is abandoned, discontinued, or removed, the sections of circuit conductors supplying the outlet shall be removed

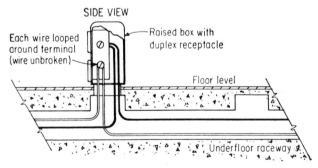

Fig. 354-4. "Loop" method permitted at outlets supplied from underfloor raceways.

from the raceway. No splices or reinsulated conductors such as would be the case with abandoned outlets on loop wiring, shall be allowed in raceways.

354-8. Laid in Straight Lines.   Underfloor raceways shall be laid so that a straight line from the center of one junction box to the center of the next junction box will coincide with the center line of the raceway system. Raceways shall be firmly held in place to prevent disturbing this alignment during construction.

354-9. Markers at Ends.   At every end of line of raceway, and at other locations where the location of the raceway is not apparent, a suitable number of markers shall be installed extending through the floor for future location of inserts and for system identification.

354-10. Dead Ends.   Dead ends of raceways shall be closed.

354-11. Low Points.   Where practicable, raceways and their fittings shall be so arranged as to avoid low points that may form traps for water.

354-12. Fittings at Angles.   Where raceways are run at other than right angles, special fittings shall be provided.

354-13. Junction Boxes.   Junction boxes shall be leveled to the floor grade and sealed against the entrance of water. Junction boxes used with metal raceways shall be metal and shall be electrically continuous with the raceways.

354-14. Inserts.   Inserts shall be leveled to the floor grade and sealed against the entrance of water. Inserts used with metal raceways shall be metal and shall be electrically continuous with the raceway. Inserts set in or on fiber raceways before the floor is laid shall be mechanically secured to the raceway. Inserts set in fiber raceways after the floor is laid shall be screwed into the raceway. In cutting through the raceway wall and setting inserts, chips and other dirt shall not be allowed to fall into the raceway, and tools shall be used which are so designed as to prevent the tool from entering the raceway and injuring conductors that may be in place.

354-15. Connections to Cabinets and Wall Outlets.   Connections between raceways and distribution centers and wall outlets shall be made by means of rigid or flexible metal conduit or by means of fittings approved for the purpose.

ARTICLE 356. CELLULAR METAL FLOOR RACEWAYS

356-1. Definitions.   For the purposes of this Article, a "cellular metal floor raceway" shall be defined as the hollow spaces of cellular metal floors, together with suitable fittings, which may be approved as enclosures for electrical conductors; a "cell" shall be defined as a single, enclosed tubular space in a cellular metal floor member, the axis of the cell being parallel to the axis of the metal floor member; a "header" shall be defined as a transverse raceway for electrical conductors, providing access to predetermined cells of a cellular metal floor, thereby permitting the installation of electrical conductors from a distribution center to the cells.

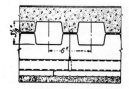

Fig. 356-1. Cross section of floor showing one type of cellular metal floor construction. (*H. H. Robertson Co.*)

▶   This is a type of floor construction designed for use in steel-frame buildings in which the members supporting the floor between the beams consist of sheet steel rolled into shapes which are so combined as to form cells, or closed passage-ways, extending across the building. The cells are of various shapes and sizes, depending upon the structural strength required.

The cellular members in this type of floor construction form raceways. A cross-sectional view of one type of cellular metal floor is shown in Fig. 356-1. Figure 356-2 shows a part of a building under construction, with the cellular metal floor in place and before the concrete covering over the steel members has been applied. See Fig. 356-5 for a typical installation of trench header duct.

Fig. 356-2. Cellular metal floor in place in a building under construction. (*H. H. Robertson Co.*)

356-2. Use. Conductors shall not be installed in cellular metal floor raceways (1) where subject to corrosive vapor; (2) in any hazardous location; nor (3) in commercial garages, except for supplying ceiling outlets or extensions to the area below the floor but not above. No electric conductors shall be installed in any cell or header which contains a pipe for steam, water, air, gas, drainage, or other service than electrical.

356-3. Other Articles. Installations of conductors in the raceways of cellular metal floor shall comply with the applicable provisions of Article 300.

A. Installation

356-4. Size of Conductors. No conductor larger than No. 0 shall be installed, except by special permission.

356-5. Number of Conductors in Raceway. The total cross-sectional area of all conductors in a header or in an individual cell shall not exceed 40% of the cross-sectional area of the header or cell in which they are located; except that where the raceway contains only Type AC metal-clad cable or nonmetallic sheathed cable, these requirements shall not apply.

▶ Connections to the ducts are made by means of *headers* extending across the cells. A header connects only to those cells which are to be used as raceways for conductors. Two or three separate headers, connecting to different sets of cells, may be used for different systems; for example, for light and power, signaling systems, and public telephones.

Figure 356-3 shows the cells, or ducts, with a header in place. By means of a special elbow fitting the header is extended up to a cabinet or distribution center on a wall or column. A junction box or access fitting is provided at each point where the header crosses a cell to which it connects.

Fig. 356-3. Header connecting to cells, junction boxes, and special fitting for connecting the header to a cabinet. (*H. H. Robertson Co.*)

356-6. Splices and Taps. Splices and taps shall be made only in header access units or junction boxes.

For the purposes of this Section so-called loop wiring (continuous, unbroken conductor connecting the individual outlets) is not considered to be a splice or tap.

▶ See Fig. 354-4.

356-7. Discontinued Outlets. When an outlet is abandoned, discontinued, or removed, the sections of circuit conductors supplying the outlet shall be removed from the raceway. No splices or reinsulated conductors, such as would be the case with abandoned outlets on loop wiring, shall be allowed in raceways.

356-8. Markers. A suitable number of markers shall be installed extending through the floor for the future locating of cells and for system identification.

▶   The markers used with this system consist of special flat-head brass screws, screwed into the upper side of the cells and with their heads flush with the floor finish.

356-9. Junction Boxes.   Junction boxes shall be levelled to the floor grade and sealed against the entrance of water. Junction boxes used with these raceways shall be of metal and shall be electrically continuous with the raceway.

▶   The fittings with round covers shown in Figs. **356-2** and **356-3** are termed "access fittings" by the manufacturer but actually serve as junction boxes. Where additional junction boxes are needed, a similar fitting but of larger size is provided which may be attached to a cell at any point.

356-10. Inserts.   Inserts shall be levelled to the floor grade and sealed against the entrance of water. Inserts shall be of metal and shall be electrically continuous with the raceway. In cutting through the cell wall and setting inserts, chips and other dirt shall not be allowed to fall into the raceway, and tools shall be used which are designed to prevent the tool from entering the cell and injuring the conductors.

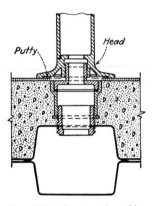

Fig. 356-4. Construction of insert used with cellular metal floor raceway. (*H. H. Robertson Co.*)

▶   The construction of an insert is shown in Fig. **356-4**. A 1⅝-in.-diameter hole is cut in the top of the cell with a special tool. The lower end of the insert is provided with coarse threads of such form that the insert can be screwed into the hole in the cell, thus forming a substantial mechanical and electrical connection.

The fitting used for connecting a header to a cabinet is shown in Fig. **356-3**. Junction boxes can be obtained with integral hubs to receive rigid conduit so that, if desired, the connections to cabinets can be made with conduit, or conduit may be run from junction boxes to wall outlets.

356-11. Connection to Cabinets and Extensions from Cells.   Connections to cabinets and extensions from cells to outlets shall be made by means of rigid or flexible conduit or by means of fittings approved for the purpose.

B. Construction Specifications

356-12. General.   Cellular metal floor raceways shall be so constructed that adequate electrical and mechanical continuity of the complete system will be secured. They shall provide a complete enclosure for the conductors. The interior surfaces shall be free from burrs and sharp edges, and surfaces over which conductors are drawn shall be smooth. Suitable bushings or fittings having smooth rounded edges shall be provided where conductors pass.

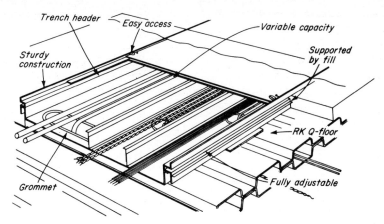

FIG. 356-5. Trench header duct used for cellular-metal-floor raceway. (*American Electricians' Handbook*)

ARTICLE 357. STRUCTURAL RACEWAYS

357-1. Definitions. Structural raceways are formed steel members approved for the installation of electrical wires or cables within them.

  (a) Vertical members used for studs or columns shall be tubes or channels.

  (b) Horizontal headers used as beams or top plates shall be provided with suitable covers, end closers, and fittings.

357-2. Use. Structural raceways used to enclose electrical conductors shall be used only in single-family dwellings.

▶   **This wiring method has been recognized only for limited application.**

357-3. Other Articles. Installation of conductors in structural raceways shall comply with the applicable provisions of Article 300.

A. Installation

357-4. Openings in Vertical Members. Vertical members may have openings provided in them for the purpose of installing wiring devices. Vertical members may be concealed. Openings in vertical members shall provide access to wiring. The size of such openings shall comply with the provisions of Section 300-15 and Article 370. Wiring devices may be installed in openings in vertical members without the use of individual boxes, provided that the back and sides of each device are surrounded by terminal barriers.

357-5. Horizontal Headers. Horizontal headers shall be securely fastened to vertical members.

357-6. Number of Conductors in Raceway. Structural raceways shall not contain more than 20 current-carrying conductors at any cross-section, and the total cross-sectional areas of all contained conductors shall not exceed 20 per cent of the interior cross-section.

357-7. Splices and Taps. Splices and taps shall be made only in horizontal headers, or junction boxes. The conductors including splices and taps shall not fill the structural raceway to more than 75 per cent of its area at that point. All splices and taps shall be made and insulated by approved methods.

357-8. Size of Conductors. No conductor larger than Number 6 AWG shall be installed in vertical or horizontal members.

357-9. Accessibility. The covers of the horizontal members shall be accessible after installation and shall not be obstructed by the wall finish.

357-10. Fittings. Fittings shall be designed and installed to prevent physical damage to electrical conductors. Fittings shall be free from burrs and sharp edges.

357-11. Extensions from Vertical Structural Members. Extensions from vertical structural members shall be made with rigid or flexible metal conduit, electrical metallic tubing, surface metal raceway or metal-clad cable.

357-12. Dead Ends. Dead ends of structural raceways shall be closed.

357-13. Installation of Electrical Devices. The installation of switches, receptacles, and outlets shall be in accordance with the requirements of Articles 380 and 410, except as otherwise permitted in this Article.

357-14. Grounding. All elements of structural raceway systems shall be bonded and effectively grounded.

B. Construction Specifications

357-15. Marking. Structural raceways and fittings shall be marked with the manufacturer's name, trademark, or identification symbol.

357-16. General. All metal components shall be properly coated to prevent corrosion. The interior shall be free from sharp edges and burrs. The structural raceway systems shall be constructed to provide electrical and mechanical continuity of the complete system. They shall provide a complete enclosure for the conductors. Enclosures shall be approved for the purpose.

ARTICLE 358. CELLULAR CONCRETE FLOOR RACEWAYS

358-1. Scope. Approved precast cellular concrete floor raceways shall comply with the applicable requirements of Article 300, and shall also comply with the provisions of Sections 358-2 to 358-11 inclusive. For the purpose of this Article, "precast cellular concrete floor raceways" shall be defined as the hollow spaces in floors constructed of precast cellular concrete slabs, together with suitable metal fittings designed to provide access to the floor cells in an approved manner. A "cell" shall be defined as a single, enclosed tubular space in a floor made of precast cellular concrete slabs, the direction of the cell being parallel to the direction of the floor member. "Header ducts" shall be defined as transverse metal raceways for electrical conductors, furnishing access to predetermined cells of a precast cellular concrete floor, thus providing for the installation of electrical conductors from a distribution center to the floor cells.

▶   The term *precast cellular concrete floor* refers to a type of floor construction designed for use in steel frame, concrete frame, and wall bearing construction, in which the monolithically precast reinforced concrete floor members form the structural floor and are supported by beams or bearing walls. The floor members are precast with hollow voids which form smooth round cells. The cells are of various sizes depending on the size of floor member used.

Fig. 358-1. Precast cellular concrete floor erected on steel frame. (*The Flexicore Co., Inc.*)

The cells form raceways which by means of suitable fittings can be adapted for use as underfloor raceways. Figure 358-1 shows a building under construction with precast cellular concrete floor in place. This floor is fire-resistant and requires no additional fireproofing.

The trench header duct shown in Fig. 356-5 is similar to those used with cellular concrete floor raceways.

358-2. Use. Conductors shall not be installed in precast cellular concrete floor raceways (1) where subject to corrosive vapor; (2) in hazardous locations; nor (3) in commercial garages, except for supplying ceiling outlets or extensions to the area below the floor but not above. No electrical conductors shall be installed in any cell or header which contains a pipe for steam, water, air, gas, drainage, or any service other than electrical.

358-3. Header Duct. The header duct shall be installed in a straight line, at right angles to the cells. The header duct shall be mechanically secured to the top of the precast cellular concrete floor. The end joints shall be closed by metallic closure fittings and sealed against the penetration of water. The header duct shall be electrically continuous throughout its entire length and shall be electrically bonded to the enclosure of the distribution center.

358-4. Connection to Cabinets and Other Enclosures. Connection from header duct to cabinets and other enclosures shall be made by means of metallic duct and fittings approved for the purpose.

358-5. Junction Boxes. Junction boxes shall be levelled to the floor grade and sealed against the entrance of water. Junction boxes shall be of metal and shall be mechanically and electrically continuous with the header ducts.

▶   Connections to the cells are made by means of *headers* extending from cabinets and across the cells. A header connects only those cells which are used as raceways for conductors. Two or three separate headers, connected to different sets of cells, may be used for different systems; for example, for light and power, signaling, and telephones.

Figure **358-2** shows three headers installed, each header connecting a cabinet with separate groups of cells. Special elbows extend the header to the cabinet.

Figure **358-3** shows a junction box where a header connects to a cell.

358-6. Markers. Each hidden access point between a header and a cell intended for future use shall be provided with a marker extending through the floor covering. A suitable number of markers shall be installed, extending through the floor covering, to locate the cells and to provide system identification.

▶   Markers used with this system are special flat head brass screws which are installed level with the finished floor. One type of marker marks the location of an access point between a header and a spare cell reserved for, but not connected to, the header. A junction box can be installed at the point located by the marker if the spare cell is needed in the future. The screw for this type marker is installed in the center of a special knockout provided in the top of the header at the access point. The second type of marker is installed over the center of cells at various points on the floor to locate and identify the cells below. Screws with specially designed heads identify the type of service in the cell.

358-7. Inserts. Inserts shall be levelled to the floor grade and sealed against the entrance of water. Inserts shall be of metal and shall be fitted with receptacles of the grounded type. A ground conductor shall connect the insert receptacles to a positive ground connection provided on the header duct. In cutting through the cell wall for setting inserts or other purposes (such as providing access openings between header duct and cells) chips and other dirt shall not be allowed to fall into the raceway, and the tool used shall be so designed as to prevent the tool from entering the cell and injuring the conductors.

▶   A $1\frac{7}{8}$-in.-diameter hole is cut through the floor and into the center of a cell with a concrete drill bit. A plug is driven into the hole and a nipple is screwed into the plug. The nipple is designed to receive an outlet with duplex electrical receptacle or an outlet designed for telephone or signal system.

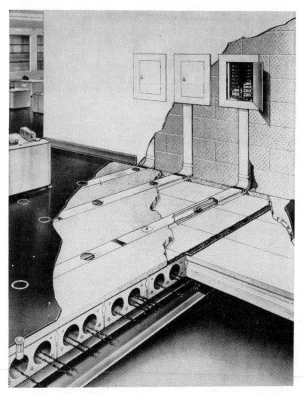

Fig. 358-2. Headers connecting wall cabinets to cells in floor. (*The Conduflor Corporation.*)

Fig. 358-3. Junction box connecting header and cell. (*The Conduflor Corporation.*)

358-8. Size of Conductors. No conductor larger than No. 0 shall be installed, except by special permission.

358-9. Number of Conductors. The total cross-sectional area of all conductors in a header or in an individual cell shall not exceed 40% of the cross-sectional area of the header or cell in which they are located; except that where the raceway contains only Type AC metal-clad cable or nonmetallic sheathed cable, these requirements shall not apply.

358-10. Splices and Taps. Splices and taps shall be made only in header duct access units or junction boxes.

358-11. Discontinued Outlets. When an outlet is discontinued, the conductors supplying the outlet shall be removed from the header and cell.

ARTICLE 362. WIREWAYS

362-1. Definition. Wireways are sheet-metal troughs with hinged or removable covers for housing and protecting electrical wires and cable and in which conductors are laid in place after the wireway has been installed as a complete system.

▶ Wireways are sheet-metal troughs in which conductors are laid in place after the wireway has been installed as a complete system. Figure 362-1 shows a length of wireway, as made by one manufacturer, furnished in lengths of 5 feet. Sections 1 and 2 ft long may also be obtained, so that runs of any exact number of feet can be made up without cutting the duct. The cover may be a hinged or removable type. Unlike auxiliary gutters, wireways represent a type of wiring, because they are used to carry conductors between points located considerable distances apart.

The purpose of a wireway is to provide a flexible system of wiring in which the circuits can be changed to meet changing conditions, and one of its principal uses is for exposed work in industrial plants. Wireways are also used to carry control wires from the control board to remotely con-

FIG. 362-1. A length of wireway with hinged cover. (*Square D Co.*)

trolled stage switchboard equipment. A wireway is approved for any voltage not exceeding 600 volts between conductors or 600 volts to ground. See comments following Section 374-1. An installation of wireway is shown in Fig. 362-2.

362-2. Use. Wireways may be installed only for exposed work. Wireways intended for outdoor use shall be of approved raintight construction. Wireways shall not be installed: (1) where subject to severe physical damage or corrosive vapor; nor (2) in any hazardous location except Class II, Division 2. See Section 502-4(b).

Fig. 362-2. An installation of wireway.

362-3. Other Articles. Installations of wireways shall comply with the applicable provisions of Article 300.

362-4. Size of Conductors. No conductor larger than that for which the wireway is designed shall be installed in any wireway.

362-5. Number of Conductors. Wireways shall not contain more than 30 current carrying conductors at any cross section. The sum of the cross-sectional areas of all contained conductors at any cross-section of a wireway shall not exceed 20 per cent of the interior cross-sectional area of the wireway.

Exception No. 1: See Section 620-32.

The correction factors specified in Note 8 to Tables 310-12 through 310-15 are not applicable to the foregoing.

Exception No. 2: Conductors for signal circuits or controller conductors between a motor and its starter and used only for starting duty shall not be considered as current carrying conductors.

Exception No. 3: When the correction factors specified in Note 8 of Tables 310-12 through 310-15 are applied, no limit on the number of current-carrying conductors is needed, but the sum of the cross sectional areas of all contained conductors at any cross section of the wireway shall not exceed 20 per cent of the interior cross-sectional area of the wireway.

Exception No. 4: See Section 520-5.

362-6. Splices and Taps.   Splices and taps, made and insulated by approved methods, may be located within the wireway provided they are accessible. The conductors, including splices and taps, shall not fill the wireway to more than 75 per cent of its area at that point.

▶   The conductors should be reasonably accessible so that any circuit can be replaced with conductors of a different size if necessary and so that taps can readily be made to supply motors or other equipment. Accessibility is ensured by limiting the number of conductors and the space they occupy as provided in Sections 362-5 and 362-6.

The cross-sectional areas of rubber- and thermoplastic-insulated conductors of all common sizes are given in Table 5, Chap. 9.

362-7. Supports.   Wireways shall be securely supported at intervals not exceeding 5 feet, unless specially approved for supports at greater intervals, but in no case shall the distance between supports exceed 10 feet.

Exception: Vertical runs of wireways shall be securely supported at intervals not exceeding 15 feet and shall have not more than one joint between supports. Adjoining wireway sections shall be securely fastened together to provide a rigid joint.

362-8. Extension Through Walls.   Wireways may extend transversely through walls if in unbroken lengths where passing through.

362-9. Dead Ends.   Dead ends of wireways shall be closed.

362-10. Extensions From Wireways.   Extensions from wireways shall be made with rigid or flexible metal conduit, electrical metallic tubing, surface metal raceway or metal-clad cable.

▶   Knockouts are provided so that circuits can be run to motors or other apparatus at any point.

Sections of wireways are joined to one another by means of flanges which are bolted together, thus providing rigid mechanical connection and electrical continuity. Fittings with bolted flanges are provided for elbows, tees, and crosses, and for connections to cabinets. See Section 250-91*b*.

362-11. Marking.   Wireways shall be marked so that their manufacturer's name or trademark will be visible after installation.

ARTICLE 363. FLAT CABLE ASSEMBLIES

Type FC

363-1. Scope.   This Article covers a field-installed wiring method using Type FC, flat cable assembly, in an approved surface metal raceway.

363-2. Definition. Type FC, a flat cable assembly, is an assembly of parallel conductors formed integrally with an insulating material web specifically designed for field installation in surface metal raceway approved for the purpose.

▶   Type FC cable is a flat assembly with three or four parallel No. 10 special stranded copper conductors. The assembly is installed in an approved U-channel surface metal raceway with one side open. Then tap devices can be inserted anywhere along the run. Connections from tap devices to the flat cable assembly are made by "pin-type" contacts when the tap devices are fastened in place. The pin-type contacts penetrate the insulation of the cable assembly and contact the multistranded conductors in a matched-phase sequence (Phase 1 to neutral, Phase 2 to neutral, and Phase 3 to neutral).

Covers are required when the installation is less than 8 ft from the floor. The maximum branch-circuit rating is 30 amp.

Figures 363-1 and 363-2 show the basic components of this wiring method.

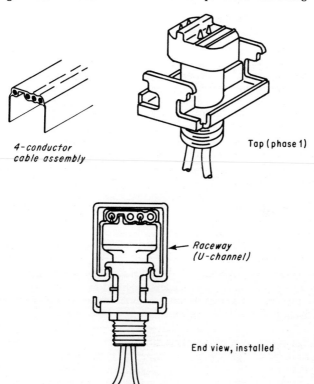

4-conductor cable assembly

Tap (phase 1)

Raceway (U-channel)

End view, installed

Fig. 363-1. Basic components of flat cable assembly system. (*Insul-8-Corp.*)

Insulating end cap

Fixture hanger

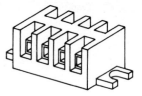

Terminal block for channel box

Fig. 363-2. Miscellaneous fittings for use with flat cable assemblies. (*Insul-8-Corp.*)

363-3. Other Articles. In addition to the provisions of this Article, installation of Type FC cable shall conform with the applicable provisions of Articles 210, 220, 250, 300, 310 and 352.

363-4. Uses Permitted. Flat cable assemblies may be used only as branch circuits to supply suitable tap devices for lighting, small appliances or small power loads. Flat cable assemblies shall be installed for exposed work only. Flat cable assemblies shall be installed in locations where they will not be subjected to severe physical damage.

363-5. Uses Not Permitted. Flat cable assemblies shall not be installed: (1) where subject to corrosive vapors unless specifically approved for the purpose; (2) in hoistways; (3) in any hazardous location; or (4) outdoors or in wet or damp locations unless specifically approved for the purpose.

363-6. Installation. Flat cable assemblies shall be installed in the field only in surface metal raceways approved for the purpose. The surface metal raceway systems shall be installed as complete systems before the flat cable assemblies are pulled into the raceways.

363-7. Number of Conductors. The flat cable assemblies may consist of either 3 or 4 conductors.

363-8. Size of Conductors. Flat cable assemblies shall have conductors of No. 10 AWG special stranded copper wires.

363-9. Conductor Insulation. The entire flat cable assembly shall be formed to provide a suitable insulation covering all of the conductors and using one of the materials recognized in Table 310-2(a) for general branch-circuit wiring.

363-10. Splices. Splices shall be made in approved junction boxes using approved terminal blocks.

363-11. Taps. Taps shall be made only between any phase conductor and the neutral by means of devices and fittings approved for the purpose. Tap devices shall be rated at not less than 15 amperes or more than 300 volts, and they shall be color-coded in accordance with the requirements of Section 363-21.

363-12. Dead Ends. Each flat cable assembly dead end shall be terminated in an end-cap device approved for the purpose.

The dead-end fitting for the enclosing surface metal raceway shall be approved for the purpose.

363-13. Fixture Hangers. Fixture hangers installed with the flat cable assemblies shall be approved for the purpose.

363-14. Fittings. Fittings to be installed with flat cable assemblies shall be designed and installed to prevent physical damage to the cable assemblies.

363-15. Extensions. All extensions from flat cable assemblies shall be made from the terminal blocks enclosed within the junction boxes, installed at either end of the flat cable assembly runs.

All extensions shall be made with wiring methods approved for the purpose.

363-16. Supports. The flat cable assemblies shall be supported by means of their special design features, within the surface metal raceways with which they are specifically approved to be used.

The surface metal raceways shall be supported as required for the specific raceway to be installed.

363-17. Rating. The rating of the branch circuit shall not exceed 30 amperes.

363-18. Marking. In addition to the provisions of Section 310-12, Type FC cable shall have the temperature rating durably marked on the surface at intervals not exceeding 24 inches.

363-19. Protective Covers. When a flat cable assembly is installed less than 8 feet from the floor it shall be protected by a metal cover approved for the purpose.

363-20. Identification. The neutral conductor shall be identified throughout its length by means of a distinctive and durable white or natural gray marking.

363-21. Terminal Block Identification. Terminal blocks approved for the purpose shall have distinctive and durable markings for color or word coding. The neutral section shall have a white marking or other suitable designation. The next adjacent section of the terminal block shall have a black marking or other suitable designation. The next section shall have a red marking or other suitable designation. The final or outer section, opposite the neutral section of the terminal block, shall have a blue marking or other suitable designation.

ARTICLE 364. BUSWAYS

364-1. Other Articles. Installations of busways shall comply with the applicable provisions of Article 300.

▶   A busway consists of a sheet-metal trough containing busbars of copper or aluminum insulated from each other and the enclosure. With some busways provision is made for plug-in units for taking current from the busbars.

Figure 364-2 is a cross-sectional view of a small busway known as "Trol-E-Duct," with a trolley in place. The duct is formed from a single piece of sheet steel. This type of busway has an ampacity of 50 amp and is used for the supply of portable motor-driven tools or portable lamps through a cord connected to the busway by means of the trolley. Connection may also be made by means of the stationary plug-in device shown in Fig. 364-3 where lamps or motor need not be portable but flexibility in location is desirable.

Busways are necessarily made up in the shop or factory as a complete assembly in sections ready to be bolted together. The sections are commonly 10 ft or longer. Special sections are made to exact dimensions for terminals at switchboards and cabinets and where changes in direction are necessary.

364-2. Use. Busways may be installed only for exposed work. Busways shall not be installed (1) where subject to severe physical damage or corrosive vapors; (2) in hoistways; (3) in any hazardous location; nor (4) outdoors or in wet or damp locations unless specially approved for the purpose.

Busways may be used for service-entrance conductors. See Section 230-44.

It is recommended that where secondary systems are operated ungrounded, a combination ground detector and potentializer plug be used as an auxiliary fitting for busway systems to establish a definite potential difference between the bus-bars and the grounded casing of the busways. This will serve to drain off any static or other charge from the entire busway system including its connected apparatus, supply and branch circuit conductors.

▶ Busways are to be installed only for exposed work. This requirement is not only to ensure that the busway is accessible but also that the heat developed by the busway can be properly dissipated. Because busway ampacity is based on the allowable temperature rise of the conductors, it is necessary to ascertain whether the space in which the busway is to be installed is suitable for the intended application. The temperature rise for plated busbars permitted by the Standards of the Underwriters' Laboratories is 55°C (99°F). The maximum rating of listed busway is 600 volts. Busway is marked for its intended use, for example: Lighting Busway, Continuous Plug-in Busway, Trolley Busway, etc.

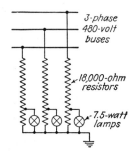

The principal use for busways is in industrial plants, but they are also used in lieu of conduit and insulated conductors for feeders in high rise and commercial buildings.

On ungrounded power systems it has been found that in some cases an abnormal potential is built up on one of the conductors, which may be high enough to cause a flashover at some point on the system. To overcome this difficulty, a device has been developed known as a *potentializer plug,* which is designed as a complete assembly in a sheet-metal enclosure with suitable contacts so that it can be plugged into a busway. The assembly contains three 18,000-ohm resistors connected as shown in Fig. 364-1. This serves to maintain each of the conductors at a normal potential to ground.

FIG. 364-1. Potentializer plug—diagram of connections. (*I-T-E Imperial Corp.*)

Each resistor is tapped at the proper point to provide 120 volts between the tap and the ground, and three 7.5-watt incandescent lamps, connected as shown in the diagram, serve as ground detectors.

364-3. Support. Busways shall be securely supported at intervals not exceeding 5 feet, unless specially approved for supports at greater intervals, but in no case shall the distance between supports exceed 10 feet. Where a busway is installed in a vertical position, the supports for the bus-bars shall be designed for vertical installation.

▶ Busways are installed vertically or horizontally. For a vertical run of more than a few feet the copper bars must be so supported that they cannot move vertically within the enclosure.

364-4. Through Walls and Floors. Busways may extend transversely through
dry walls if in unbroken lengths where passing through. Busways may extend
vertically through dry floors when totally enclosed (unventilated) where passing
through and for a minimum distance of six feet above the floor to provide adequate protection from physical damage.

364-5. Dead Ends. A dead end of a busway shall be closed.

364-7. Branches from Busways. Branches from busways shall be made with busways or with rigid or flexible metal conduit, electrical metallic tubing, surface
metal raceway, metal-clad cable or with suitable cord assemblies approved for
hard usage for portable equipment or for the connection of stationary equipment
to facilitate their interchange.

364-8. Overcurrent Protection. Overcurrent protection shall be provided in accordance with Sections 364-9 through 364-13.

364-9. Rating of Overcurrent Protection—Feeders and Sub-Feeders. Where the
allowable current rating of the busway does not correspond to a standard rating
of the overcurrent device, the next higher rating may be used.

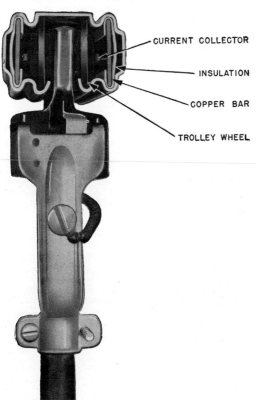

CURRENT COLLECTOR

INSULATION

COPPER BAR

TROLLEY WHEEL

Fig. 364-2. Cross-sectional view of Trol-E-Duct 50-amp
busway with trolley in place. (*I-T-E Imperial Corp.*)

▶ The rated ampacity of a busway is fixed by the allowable temperature rise of the conductors. The ampacity can be determined in the field only by reference to the nameplate.

364-10. Reduction in Size of Busway. Overcurrent protection may be omitted at points where busways are reduced in size, provided that the smaller busway does not extend more than 50 feet and has a current rating at least equal to one-third the rating or setting of the overcurrent device next back on the line, and provided further that such busway is free from contact with combustible material.

▶ Where the smaller busway is kept within the limits specified, the hazards involved are very slight and the additional cost of providing overcurrent protection at the point where the size is changed is not considered as being warranted.

364-11. Branch Circuits. Where a busway is used as a feeder, devices or plug-in connections for tapping off branch-circuits from the busway shall contain the overcurrent devices required for the protection of the branch circuits.

Exception No. 1: For overcurrent protection of taps, see Section 240-15.

Exception No. 2: For fixed or semi-fixed lighting fixtures, the branch circuit overcurrent device may be part of the fixture cord plug on cord-connected fixtures.

Exception No. 3: Where fixtures without cords are plugged directly into the busway, the overcurrent device may be mounted on the fixture.

▶ The busway shown in Fig. 364-2 has an ampacity of 50 and can therefore be used as a 15-, 20-, 30-, 40-, or 50-amp branch circuit, depending upon the rating or setting of the overcurrent device protecting the conductors of the busway. Appliances may be connected directly to the busway without individual overcurrent protection where permitted by Section 210-24, provided that, in the case of motor-driven appliances, all applicable rules of Art. 430 are complied with.

364-12. Rating of Overcurrent Protection—Branch Circuits. A busway may be used as a branch circuit of any one of the types described in Article 210. When so used, the rating or setting of the overcurrent device protecting the busway shall determine the ampere rating of the branch circuit, and the circuit shall in all respects conform with the requirements of Article 210 that apply to branch circuits of that rating.

364-13. Length of Busways Used as Branch Circuits. Busways which are used as branch circuits and which are so designed that loads can be connected at any point shall be limited to such lengths as will provide that in normal use the circuits will not be overloaded.

In general, the length of such run in feet should not exceed three times the ampere rating of the branch circuit.

▶ A busway used as a branch circuit is usually installed for a specific purpose, and the probable maximum load to be supplied by the circuit can be estimated without difficulty.

SUPPORT BRACKET

CURRENT COLLECTOR

INSULATION

COPPER BAR

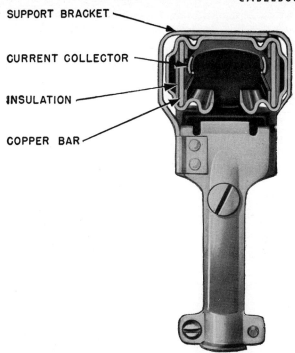

Fig. 364-3. Stationary plug-in device for use in place of trolley shown in Fig. 364-2. (*I-T-E Imperial Corp.*)

364-14. Marking. Busways shall be marked with the voltage and current rating for which they are designed, and with the manufacturer's name or trademark in such manner as to be visible after installation.

ARTICLE 365. CABLEBUS

365-1. Definition. Cablebus is an approved assembly of insulated conductors mounted in spaced relationship in a ventilated metal protective supporting structure including fittings and conductor terminations. Cablebus may be used at any voltage or current for which the spaced conductors are rated.

Cablebus is ordinarily assembled at the point of installation, from components furnished or specified by the manufacturer.

▶   Cablebus framework is installed in a manner similar to continuous rigid cable support systems. Insulated conductors are supported on special insulating blocks at specified intervals in the framework. Finally, a removable (ventilated) top is attached to the framework. See Fig. 365-1.

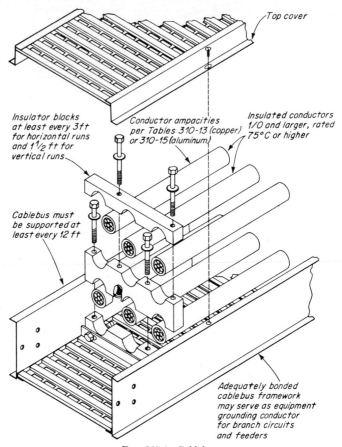

Top cover

Insulator blocks at least every 3 ft for horizontal runs and 1½ ft for vertical runs

Conductor ampacities per Tables 310-13 (copper) or 310-15 (aluminum)

Insulated conductors 1/0 and larger, rated 75°C or higher

Cablebus must be supported at least every 12 ft

Adequately bonded cablebus framework may serve as equipment grounding conductor for branch circuits and feeders

Fig. 365-1. Cablebus.

365-2. Use. Cablebus shall be installed only for exposed work. Cablebus installed outdoors or in corrosive, wet or damp locations shall be approved for the purpose. Cablebus shall not be installed in hoistways or in hazardous locations unless specifically approved for such use. Cablebus may be used for branch circuits, feeders and services.

Approved cablebus framework where adequately bonded may be used as the equipment grounding conductor for branch circuits and feeders.

365-3. Conductors.

(a) Types of Conductor. The current carrying conductors in cablebus shall have an insulation rating of 75°C or better of an approved type and suitable for the application in accordance with Articles 310 and 710.

(b) Ampacity of Conductors. The ampacity of conductors in cablebus shall be in accordance with Tables 310-13 and 310-15.

(c) Size and Number of Conductors. The size and number of conductors shall be that for which the cablebus is designed, and in no case smaller than 1/0 AWG.

(d) Conductor Supports. The insulated conductors shall be supported on blocks or other mounting means designed for the purpose.

The individual conductors in a cablebus shall be supported at intervals not greater than 3 feet for horizontal runs and 1½ feet for vertical runs. Vertical and horizontal spacing between supported conductors shall be not less than one conductor diameter at the points of support.

365-5. Overcurrent Protection. When the allowable current rating of the cablebus conductors does not correspond to a standard rating of the overcurrent device, the next higher rated overcurrent device may be used.

365-6. Support.

(a) Cablebus shall be securely supported at intervals not exceeding 12 feet.

(b) Cablebus may extend transversely through partitions or walls, other than fire walls, provided the section within the wall is continuous, protected against physical damage and unventilated.

(c) Except where fire stops are required, cablebus may extend vertically through dry floors and platforms, provided the cablebus is totally enclosed at the point where it passes through the floor or platform and for a distance of six feet above the floor or platform.

(d) Except where fire stops are required, cablebus may extend vertically through floors and platforms in wet locations where (1) there are curbs or other suitable means to prevent waterflow through the floor or platform opening and (2) where the cablebus is totally enclosed at the point where it passes through the floor or platform and for a distance of six feet above the floor or platform.

365-7. Fittings.

(a) Cablebus system shall provide approved fittings for:

(1) Changes in horizontal or vertical direction of the run.

(2) Dead ends.

(3) Terminations in or on connected apparatus or equipment or the enclosures for such equipment.

(4) Additional physical protection where required such as guards for severe mechanical exposure.

365-8. Conductor Terminations. Approved terminating means shall be used for connections to cablebus conductors.

365-9. Grounding. Sections of cablebus shall be electrically bonded either by inherent design of the mechanical joints or by applied bonding means. See Section 250-75.

A cablebus installation shall be grounded in accordance with the requirements of Sections 250-32 and 250-33.

365-10. Marking. Each section of cablebus shall be marked with the manufacturer's name or trade designation and the maximum diameter, number, voltage rating and ampacity of the conductors to be installed. Markings shall be so located as to be visible after installation.

ARTICLE 370. OUTLET, SWITCH AND JUNCTION BOXES, AND FITTINGS

A. Scope and General

370-1. Scope.   The provisions of this Article shall apply to the installation of outlet, switch and junction boxes, and fittings as required by Section 300-15. Installations in hazardous locations shall conform to Articles 500 through 517.

The provisions contained in this Article for boxes shall also apply to those conduit fittings with covers which serve to enclose the conductors in that conduit system.

370-2. Round Boxes.   Round boxes shall not be used where conduits or connectors requiring the use of locknuts or bushings are to be connected to the side of the box.

▶ The purpose of this rule is to require the use of rectangular or octagonal boxes having at each knockout or opening a flat bearing surface for the locknut or bushing.

370-3. Nonmetallic Boxes.   Nonmetallic boxes approved for the purpose may be used only with open wiring on insulators, concealed knob-and-tube work, nonmetallic sheathed cable, and with approved nonmetallic conduit.

370-4. Metallic Boxes.   Where used with knob-and-tube work or nonmetallic sheathed cable, and mounted on metal or metal lath ceilings or walls, such boxes shall be insulated from their supports and from the metal or metal lath, or shall be grounded.

▶ With a metal box in contact with metal walls or ceilings covered with metal, or with metal lath or with conductive thermal insulation, a stray current may flow to ground through an unknown path if a "hot" wire should accidentally become grounded on the box. To prevent this, the box should be effectively grounded by means of a separate grounding conductor. It would usually be difficult to insulate the box thoroughly.

B. Installation

370-5. Damp or Wet Locations.   In damp or wet locations, boxes and fittings shall be so placed or equipped as to prevent moisture or water from entering and accumulating within the box or fitting. Boxes and fittings installed in wet locations shall be weatherproof. For boxes in floors, see Section 370-17.

It is recommended that approved boxes of nonconductive material be used with nonmetallic sheathed cable or approved nonmetallic conduit when such cable or conduit is used in locations where there is likely to be occasional moisture present such as in dairy barns.

▶ *Weatherproof* is defined as meaning "so constructed or protected that exposure to the weather will not interfere with its successful operation."

A box or fitting may be considered weatherproof when so made and installed that it will exclude rain and snow. Such a box or fitting need not necessarily be sealed against the entrance of moisture.

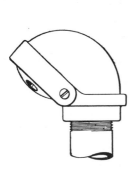

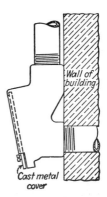

Fig. 370-1. Fitting for use at the outer end of a service conduit.

Fig. 370-2. Type LB conduit fitting used where a service conduit passes through a building wall.

Figure 370-1 shows a fitting which is considered as weatherproof because the openings for the conductors are so placed that rain or snow cannot enter the fitting.

Figure 370-2 shows a fitting made weatherproof by means of a metal cover that slides under flanges on the face of the fitting, and, as required by Section 230-52, an opening is provided through which any moisture condensing in the conduit can drain out.

370-6. Number of Conductors in a Box. Boxes shall be of sufficient size to provide free space for all conductors enclosed in the box.

The provisions of this Section shall not apply to terminal housings supplied with motors. See Section 430-12.

Sections 370-6(a) and (b) do not apply to conductors used for rewiring existing raceways as referred to in Table 1, Chapter 9.

(a) The maximum number of conductors, not counting fixture wires, permitted in outlet and junction boxes shall be as in Tables 370-6(a)(1) and (a)(2) with the exceptions noted.

▶   In paragraph *a*, one or more grounding conductors are counted as one conductor in determining the number of conductors permitted in a box.

Figure 370-3 illustrates a nonmetallic sheathed cable with three No. 14 copper conductors supplying a 15-ampere duplex receptacle (one ungrounded conductor, one grounded conductor and one "bare" grounding conductor).

After supplying the receptacle, these conductors are extended to other outlets and the conductor count would be as follows:

Circuit conductors	4
Grounding conductors	1
For internal cable clamps	1
For receptacle	1
Total	7

The No. 14 conductor column of the table indicates that a device box not less than $3 \times 2 \times 2\frac{3}{4}$ in. is required. Where a square box with plaster ring is used, a $4 \times 1\frac{1}{2}$ in. size is required.

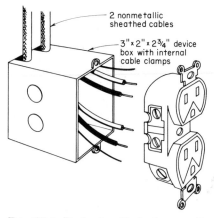

Fig. 370-3. Device box illustrating compliance with Section 370-6a by including *one* equipment grounding conductor in determining box size.

Table **370-6(a-1)** includes the most popular types of metal "trade-size" boxes used with wires No. 14 to No. 8. Cubic-inch capacities are listed for each box shown in the table. According to paragraph *c*, boxes other than those shown in Tables **370-6(a-1)** and **370-6(a-2)** are required to be marked with the cubic inch content so wire combinations can be readily computed.

Tables 370-6(a)(1) and (a)(2) apply where no fittings or devices, such as fixture studs, cable clamps, hickeys, switches or receptacles, are contained in the box and where no grounding conductors are part of the wiring within the box. Where one or more fixture studs, cable clamps, or hickeys are contained in the box, the number of conductors shall be one less than shown in the Tables; an additional deduction of one conductor shall be made for each strap containing one or more devices; and a further deduction of one conductor shall be made for one or more grounding conductors entering the box. A conductor running through the box is counted as one conductor, and each conductor originating outside the box and terminating inside the box is counted as one conductor. Conductors, no part of which leaves the box, are not to be counted. The volume of a wiring enclosure (box) shall be the total volume of the assembled sections.

Table 370-6(a-1). Deep Boxes

Box Dimensions, Inches Trade Size	Cubic Inch Cap.	Maximum Number of Conductors			
		No. 14	No. 12	No. 10	No. 8
3¼ × 1½ octagonal	10.9	5	4	4	3
3½ × 1½ octagonal	11.9	5	5	4	3
4 × 1½ octagonal	17.1	8	7	6	5
4 × 2⅛ octagonal	23.6	11	10	9	7
4 × 1½ square	22.6	11	10	9	7
4 × 2⅛ square	31.9	15	14	12	10
4¹¹⁄₁₆ × 1½ square	32.2	16	14	12	10
4¹¹⁄₁₆ × 2⅛ square	46.4	23	20	18	15
3 × 2 × 1½ device	7.9	3	3	3	2
3 × 2 × 2 device	10.7	5	4	4	3
3 × 2 × 2¼ device	11.3	5	5	4	3
3 × 2 × 2½ device	13	6	5	5	4
3 × 2 × 2¾ device	14.6	7	6	5	4
3 × 2 × 3½ device	18.3	9	8	7	6
4 × 2⅛ × 1½ device	11.1	5	4	4	3
4 × 2⅛ × 1⅞ device	13.9	6	6	5	4
4 × 2⅛ × 2⅛ device	15.6	7	6	6	5

See Section 370-18 where boxes are used as pull and junction boxes.

▶ The purpose of these provisions is to prevent the excessive crowding of wires and splices in outlet and junction boxes. A wire passing through the box without a splice or tap is counted as one wire, and each wire that is tapped or spliced to another wire is considered as one wire. Fixture wires are not counted.

Table 370-6(a-2). Shallow Boxes

Box Dimensions, Inches Trade Size	Maximum Number of Conductors		
	No. 14	No. 12	No. 10
3¼	4	4	3
4	6	6	4
1¼ x 4 Square	9	7	6
4¹¹⁄₁₆	8	6	6

Any box less than 1½ inch deep is considered to be a shallow box.

(b) For combinations or conductor sizes not shown in Tables 370-6(a)(1) and 370-6(a)(2), Table 370-6(b) shall apply.

Table 370-6(b). Volume Required Per Conductor

Size of Conductor	Free Space Within Box for Each Conductor
No. 14	2. cubic inches
No. 12	2.25 cubic inches
No. 10	2.5 cubic inches
No. 8	3. cubic inches
No. 6	5. cubic inches

(c) Boxes, other than those described in Tables 370-6(a) (1) and 370-6(a) (2), shall be durably and legibly marked by the manufacturer with their cubic inch content. All boxes shall be durably and legibly marked with the manufacturer's name or trademark.

370-7. Conductors Entering Boxes or Fittings. Conductors entering boxes or fittings shall be protected from abrasion, and shall conform to the following:

(a) **Openings to Be Closed.** Openings through which conductors enter shall be adequately closed.

(b) **Metal Boxes and Fittings.** Where metal outlet boxes or fittings are installed with open wiring or concealed knob-and-tube work, conductors shall enter through insulating bushings or, in dry places, through flexible tubing extending from the last insulating support and firmly secured to the box or fitting. Where raceway or cable is installed with metal outlet boxes or fittings, the raceway or cable shall be secured to such boxes and fittings.

(c) **Nonmetallic Boxes.** Where nonmetallic boxes are used with open wiring or concealed knob-and-tube work, the conductors shall enter through individual holes. Where flexible tubing is used to encase the conductor, the tubing shall extend from the last insulating support and may be run into the box or terminate at the wall of the box. If nonmetallic sheathed cable is used, the cable assembly shall enter the box through a knockout opening. Clamping of individual conductors or cables to the box is not required where supported within 8 inches of the box. Where nonmetallic conduit is installed with nonmetallic boxes or fittings, the conduit shall be secured to such boxes and fittings in an approved manner.

▶   When used with open wiring on insulators, knob-and-tube work, or nonmetallic sheathed cable, nonmetallic boxes have the advantage that an accidental contact between a "hot" wire and the box will not ordinarily create a hazard.

370-8. Unused Openings. Unused openings in boxes and fittings shall be effectively closed to afford protection substantially equivalent to that of the wall of the box or fitting. Metal plugs or plates used with nonmetallic boxes or fittings shall be recessed at least $\frac{1}{4}$ inch from the outer surface.

370-9. Boxes Enclosing Flush Devices. Boxes used to enclose flush devices shall be of such design that the devices will be completely enclosed on back and sides, and that substantial support for the devices will be provided. Screws for supporting the box shall not be used in attachment of the device contained therein.

▶   If the screws used for attaching the receptacles and switches to boxes were used also for the mounting of the boxes, a poor mechanical job would result, since the boxes would be insecurely held whenever the devices were not installed and the screws loosened for adjustment of the device position. Hence the prohibition.

370-10. In Wall or Ceiling.   In walls or ceilings of concrete, tile or other non-combustible material, boxes and fittings shall be so installed that the front edge of the box or fitting will not set back of the finished surface more than ¼ inch. In walls and ceilings constructed of wood or other combustible material, outlet boxes and fittings shall be flush with the finished surface or project therefrom.

370-11. Repairing Plaster.   Except on walls or ceilings of concrete, tile or other noncombustible material, a plaster surface which is broken or incomplete shall be repaired so that there will be no gaps or open spaces at the edge of the box or fitting.

▶   The purpose of Sections **370-10** and **370-11** is to prevent openings around the edge of the box through which fire could be readily communicated to combustible material in the wall or ceiling.

370-12. Exposed Extensions.   In making an exposed extension from an existing outlet of concealed wiring, a box, extension ring or blank cover shall be mounted over the original box and electrically and mechanically secured to it. The extension shall then be connected to this box in the manner prescribed for the method of wiring employed in making the extension.

▶   The extension should be made as illustrated in Fig. **370-4**. The extension ring is secured to the original box by two screws passing through ears attached to the box. Extensions may also be made from a blank cover attached to the original box.

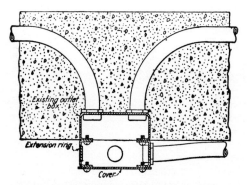

Fig. 370-4. Method of making a surface extension from concealed wiring.

370-13. Supports.   Boxes shall be securely and rigidly fastened to the surface upon which they are mounted, or securely and rigidly embedded in concrete or masonry. Except as otherwise provided in this Section, boxes shall be supported from a structural member of the building either directly or by using a substantial and approved metallic or wooden brace. If of wood the brace shall not be less than nominal 1 inch thickness. If of metal it shall be corrosion resistant and shall be not less than No. 24 MSG.

Where mounted in new walls in which no structural members are provided or in existing walls in previously occupied buildings, boxes not over 100 cubic inches in size, specifically approved for the purpose, shall be affixed with approved anchors or clamps so as to provide a rigid and secure installation.

Threaded boxes or fittings, not over 100 cubic inches in size, which do not contain devices or support fixtures may be considered adequately supported if two or more conduits are threaded into the box wrench-tight and are supported within three feet of the box on two or more sides as is required by this Section.

Threaded boxes or fittings, not over 100 cubic inches in size, may be considered to be adequately supported if two or more conduits are threaded into the box wrenchtight and are supported as required by this Section within 18 inches of the box.

▶   Where locknut and bushing connections are used, the box must be independently fastened in place.

The requirement of metal or wood supports for boxes applies to concealed work in walls and floors of wood-frame construction and other types of construction having open spaces in which the wiring is installed. In walls or floors of concrete, brick, or tile where conduit and boxes are solidly built into the wall or floor material, special box supports are not usually necessary.

An outlet box built into a concrete floor as shown in Fig. 370-5 seldom needs any special support. At such an outlet, if it is intended for a fixture

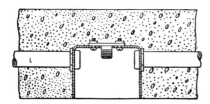

Fig. 370-5. Outlet box built into a concrete floor.

of too great weight to be safely hung on an ordinary ⅜-in. fixture stud, a special fixture support consisting of a threaded pipe or rod is required, such as is shown in Fig. 370-6.

In a tile arch floor (Fig. 370-6) a large opening must be cut through the tile to receive the conduit and outlet box.

In an existing building, where any type of wiring is installed either exposed or concealed, the boxes may be mounted on plaster or any other ceiling or wall finish, the only requirement being that they must be securely fastened in place. Where no structural members are provided for, boxes not over 100

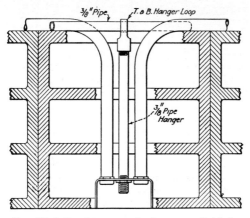

Fig. 370-6. Box hanger used where an outlet is installed in a tile arch floor.

cubic inches in size, specifically approved for the purpose, shall be affixed with approved anchors or clamps. Figures **370-7** and **370-8** illustrate the intent of "specifically approved for the purpose."

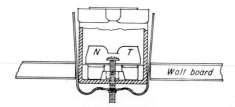

Fig. 370-7. Inserting box and bracket through wall board. (*Union Insulating Co., Inc.*)

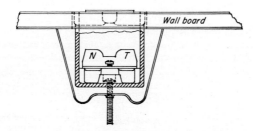

Fig. 370-8. Box anchored to wall. (*Union Insulating Co., Inc.*)

► Figures **370-7** and **370-8** illustrate the use of approved mounting brackets as required in the second paragraph of Section **370-13**.

The last paragraph of Section **370-13** permits two or more conduits to be threaded into threaded boxes or fittings (not over **100 cu in.** in size) where such conduits are properly supported within **18 in.** of the box. This recognizes the support of elevated threaded-hub junction boxes by conduits emerging from the earth, such as those used near swimming pools, patios, or shrubbery. Support by a single conduit is not recognized.

370-14. Depth of Outlet Boxes for Concealed Work.   Outlet boxes for concealed work shall have an internal depth of at least 1½ inches, except that where the installation of such a box will result in injury to the building structure or is impracticable, a box not less than ½ inch internal depth may be installed.

▶   Sufficient space should be provided inside the box so that the wires do not have to be jammed together or against the box, and the box should provide enough of an enclosure so that in case of trouble, burning insulation cannot readily ignite flammable material outside the box. A box ½ in. deep is permitted to be used only where a deeper box would require cutting a supporting member, such as a floor joist, to such a depth as would seriously weaken the member, or where for some other reason it is impracticable to install the deeper box.

370-15. Covers and Canopies.   In completed installations each outlet box shall be provided with a cover unless a fixture canopy is used.

(a)   Nonmetallic covers and plates or metallic covers and plates may be used with nonmetallic outlet boxes. When metallic covers or plates are used, they shall comply with the grounding requirements of Section 250-42.

See Section 410-95.

(b)   Where a fixture canopy or pan is used, any combustible wall or ceiling finish exposed between the edge of the canopy or pan and the outlet box shall be covered with noncombustible material.

▶   If the ceiling or wall finish is of combustible material, the canopy and box must form a complete enclosure. The chief purpose of this rule is to require that no open space be left between the canopy and the edge of the box where the finish is wood or other combustible material. Where the wall or ceiling finish is plaster the requirement does not apply, since plaster is not classed as a combustible material; however, the plaster must be continuous up to the box, leaving no openings around the box.

(c)   Covers of outlet boxes having holes through which flexible cord pendants pass, shall be provided with bushings designed for the purpose or shall have smooth, well-rounded surfaces on which the cords may bear. So-called hard-rubber or composition bushings shall not be used.

▶   See Figs. **370-9** and **370-10.**

Fig. 370-9. Steel box cover with bushed hole for cord.

Fig. 370-10. Porcelain box cover with hole for cord.

370-16. Fastened to Gas Pipes. Outlet boxes used where gas outlets are present shall be so fastened to the gas pipes as to be mechanically secure.

370-17. Outlet Boxes.

(a) Boxes at Lighting Fixture Outlets. Boxes used at lighting fixture outlets shall be designed for the purpose. At every outlet used exclusively for lighting, the box shall be so designed or installed that a lighting fixture may be attached.

(b) Floor Boxes. Floor boxes especially approved for the purpose shall be used for receptacles located in the floor.

Exception: The standard approved type of flush receptacle box may be used where receptacles are located in elevated floors of show windows or other locations when the authority enforcing this Code judges them to be free from physical damage, moisture and dirt.

370-18. Pull and Junction Boxes. Pull and junction boxes shall conform to the following:

(a) Minimum Size. For raceways of 1 inch trade size and larger, containing conductors of No. 6 or larger, and for cables* containing conductors of No. 6 or larger, the minimum dimensions of a pull or junction box installed in a raceway or cable run shall conform to the following:

(1) Straight Pulls. In straight pulls the length of the box shall be not less than 8 times the trade diameter of the largest raceway.

(2) Angle or U Pulls. Where angle or U pulls are made, the distance between each raceway entry inside the box and the opposite wall of the box shall not be less than 6 times the trade diameter of the largest raceway. This distance shall be increased for additional entries by the amount of the sum of the diameters of all other raceway entries on the same wall of the box. The distance between raceway entries enclosing the same conductor shall not be less than 6 times the trade diameter of the larger raceway.

* When transposing cable size into raceway size in (1) and (2) above, the minimum trade size raceway required for the number and size of conductors in the cable shall be used.

(3) Boxes of lesser dimensions than those required in sub-sections (1) and (2) of this Section may be used for installations of combinations of conductors which are less than the maximum conduit fill (of conduits being used) permitted by Table 1, Chapter 9, provided the box has been approved for and is permanently marked with the maximum number of conductors and the maximum AWG size permitted.

Exception: Terminal housings supplied with motors which shall comply with the provisions of Section 430-12.

(b) Conductors in Pull or Junction Boxes.   In pull boxes or junction boxes having any dimension over 6 feet, all conductors shall be cabled or racked up in an approved manner.

See Section 373-6(b) for insulation of conductors at bushings.

(c) Covers.   All pull boxes, junction boxes and fittings shall be provided with covers approved for the purpose. Where metallic covers are used, they shall comply with the grounding requirements of Section 250-42.

▶   In computing pull-box sizes, all raceways smaller than 1 in. and cables containing conductors smaller than size No. 6 may be neglected.

Example 1. Straight Pull

A pull box is to be installed in a group of straight runs of conduit in which the largest size is **3** in. **8** × **3** in. = **24** in., which is the minimum length of the pull box.

A **3**-in. conduit could contain three **500,000**-cir mil conductors, and practical considerations dictate a minimum length of about **30** in.

Example 2. Right-angle Pull

A pull box is to be installed to make a right-angle turn in a group of conduits consisting of two **3**-in., two **2½**-in., and four **2**-in. conduits.

Subparagraph **2** gives two methods for computing the box dimensions. First method:

$$
\begin{aligned}
6 \times 3 \text{ in.} &= 18 \text{ in.} \\
1 \times 3 \text{ in.} &= 3 \\
2 \times 2\tfrac{1}{2} \text{ in.} &= 5 \\
4 \times 2 \text{ in.} &= \underline{\hspace{0.3em}8} \\
\text{Total} &= 34 \text{ in.}
\end{aligned}
$$

Second method:

Assuming that the conduits are to leave the box in the same order in which they enter, the arrangement is shown in Fig. 370-11 and the distance *A* between the ends of the two conduits must be not less than **6** × **2** in. = **12** in. It can be assumed that this measurement is to be made between the centers of the two conduits. By calculation, or by laying out the corner of the box, it is found that the distance *C* should be about **8½** in.

The distance *B* should be not less than **30½** in., approximately, as determined by applying practical data for the spacing between centers of conduits,

$$30\tfrac{1}{2} \text{ in.} + 8\tfrac{1}{2} \text{ in.} = 39 \text{ in.}$$

which is the minimum allowable dimension

In this case the box dimensions are governed by the second method. The largest dimension computed by either of the two methods is of course the one to be used.

The most practical method of determining the proper size of a pull box is to sketch the box layout with its contained conductors on a paper.

Section **370-18** applies particularly to the pull boxes commonly placed above distribution switchboards and which are often, and with good reason,

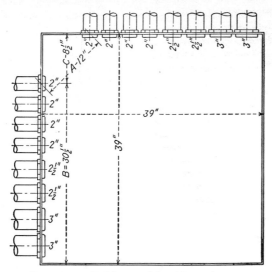

Fig. 370-11. Pull box used for right-angle turn.

termed *tangle boxes*. In such boxes, all conductors of each circuit should be cabled together by serving them with twine so as to form a self-supporting assembly that can be formed into shape, or the conductors should be supported in an orderly manner on racks. The conductors should not rest directly on any metalwork inside the box, and insulating bushings should be provided wherever required by Section **373-6b**.

For example, the box illustrated in Fig. **370-11** could be approximately 5 in. deep and accommodate one horizontal row of conduits.

By making it twice as deep, two horizontal rows or twice the number of conduits could be installed.

Insulating racks are usually placed between conductor layers, and space must be allowed for them.

Paragraph *a* provides the necessary guidance for determining the minimum dimensions of boxes based on the size and number of conduit and cable entries and the bending space to the opposite wall.

370-19. Junction, Pull and Outlet Boxes to Be Accessible.   Junction, pull and outlet boxes shall be so installed that the wiring contained in them may be rendered accessible without removing any part of the building, sidewalks or paving.

▶   The term *box* may be considered as a covered box used at any point where it is necessary to tap a run of conduit, tubing, or cable and where the box is used for this purpose. See also comments under Section **300-15**.

C. Construction Specifications

370-20. Metallic Outlet, Switch and Junction Boxes and Fittings.   Outlet, switch and junction boxes and fittings, when of metal, shall conform to the following:

(a) Corrosion-Resistant. Metallic boxes and fittings, unless of corrosion-resistant metal, shall be well galvanized, enameled, or otherwise properly coated, inside and out, to prevent corrosion.

See Section 300-5 for limitation in the use of boxes and fittings protected from corrosion solely by enamel.

It is recommended that the protective coating be of conductive material, such as cadmium, tin or zinc, in order to secure better electrical contact.

(b) Thickness of Metal. Sheet metal boxes and fittings not over 100 cubic inches in size shall be made from metal not less than No. 14 MSG. Cast metal boxes shall have a wall thickness not less than $\frac{1}{8}$ inch, except that boxes of malleable iron shall have a wall thickness of not less than $\frac{3}{32}$ inch.

(c) Boxes Over 100 Cubic Inches. Boxes of over 100 cubic inches in size shall be composed of metal and shall conform to the requirements for cabinets and cutout boxes, except that the covers may consist of single flat sheets secured to the box proper by screws, or bolts instead of hinges. Boxes having covers of this form are for use only for enclosing joints in conductors or to facilitate the drawing in of wires and cables. They are not intended to enclose switches, cutouts or other control devices.

370-21. Covers. Metal covers shall be of a thickness not less than that specified for the walls of the box or fitting of the same material and with which they are designed to be used, or shall be lined with firmly attached insulating material not less than $\frac{1}{32}$ inch in thickness. Covers of porcelain or other approved insulating material may be used when of such form and thickness as to afford the requisite protection and strength.

370-22. Bushings. Covers of outlet boxes and outlet fittings having holes through which flexible cord pendants may pass, shall be provided with approved bushings or shall have smooth, well-rounded surfaces, upon which the cord may bear. Where conductors other than flexible cord may pass through a metal cover, there shall be provided a separate hole for each wire, said hole being equipped with a bushing of suitable insulating material.

370-23. Nonmetallic Boxes. Provisions for supports, or other mounting means, for nonmetallic boxes, shall be outside of the box, or the box shall be so constructed as to prevent contact between the conductors in the box and the supporting screws.

ARTICLE 373. CABINETS AND CUTOUT BOXES

373-1. Scope. The provisions of this Article shall apply to the installation of cabinets and cutout boxes. Installations in hazardous locations shall conform to the provisions of Articles 500 through 517.

▶ Cabinets and cutout boxes, according to the definitions, must have doors and are thus distinguished from large boxes with covers consisting of plates attached with screws or bolts.

Article **373** applies to all boxes used to enclose operating apparatus, *i.e.*, apparatus having moving parts or requiring inspection or attention, such as panelboards, cutouts, switches, circuit breakers, or control apparatus.

A. Installation

373-2. Damp or Wet Locations.   In damp or wet locations, cabinets and cutout boxes of the surface type shall be so placed or equipped as to prevent moisture or water from entering and accumulating within the cabinet or cutout box, and shall be mounted so there is at least ¼ inch air space between the enclosure and the wall or other supporting surface. Cabinets or cutout boxes installed in wet locations shall be weatherproof.

It is recommended that boxes of nonconductive material be used with nonmetallic sheathed cable when such cable is used in locations where there is likely to be moisture present.

373-3. Position in Wall.   In walls of concrete, tile, or other noncombustible material, cabinets shall be so installed that the front edge of the cabinet will not set back of the finished surface more than ¼ inch. In walls constructed of wood or other combustible material, cabinets shall be flush with the finished surface or project therefrom.

373-4. Unused Openings.   Unused openings in cabinet or cutout boxes shall be effectively closed to afford protection substantially equivalent to that of the wall of the cabinet or cutout box. Where metal plugs or plates are used with nonmetallic cabinets or cutout boxes, they shall be recessed at least ¼ inch from the outer surface.

373-5. Conductors Entering Cabinets or Cutout Boxes.   Conductors entering cabinets or cutout boxes shall be protected from abrasion and shall conform to the following:

   (a) Openings to Be Closed.   Openings through which conductors enter shall be adequately closed.

   (b) Metal Cabinets and Cutout Boxes.   Where metal cabinets or cutout boxes are installed with open wiring or concealed knob-and-tube work, conductors shall enter through insulating bushings or, in dry places, through flexible tubing extending from the last insulating support and firmly secured to the cabinet or cutout box.

373-6. Deflection of Conductors.   Conductors at terminals or conductors entering or leaving cabinets or cutout boxes and the like shall conform to the following:

   (a) Width of Wiring Gutters.   Conductors shall not be deflected within a cabinet or cutout box unless a gutter having a width in accordance with Table 373-6(a) is provided. Conductors in parallel in accordance with Section 310-10 are judged on the basis of the number of conductors in parallel.

   (1) Wire Bending Space at Terminals.   Conductors shall not be deflected at a terminal unless bending space in accordance with Table 373-6(a) is provided.

   (b) Insulation at Bushings.   Where ungrounded conductors of No. 4 or larger enter a raceway in a cabinet, pull box, junction box, or auxiliary gutter, the conductors shall be protected by a substantial bushing providing a smoothly rounded insulating surface, unless the conductors are separated from the raceway fitting by substantial insulating material securely fastened in place. Where conduit bushings are constructed wholly of insulating material, a locknut shall be installed both inside and outside the enclosure to which the conduit is attached.

▶ Paragraph *b* applies to all conductors of size No. **4** or larger entering a cabinet or box from rigid metal conduit, flexible metal conduit, electrical metallic tubing, etc.

To protect the conductors a smoothly rounded insulating surface is required. While many fittings are provided with insulated sleeves or linings, it is also possible to use a separate insulating lining or sleeve to meet the requirements of the Code. Figure 373-1 shows an approved sleeve which may be used to separate the conductors from the raceway fitting.

Table 373-6(a). Minimum Wire Bending Space at Terminals and Minimum Width of Wiring Gutters in Inches

AWG or Circular-Mil Size of Wire	Wires per Terminal				
	1	2	3	4	5
14–8	Not Specified	—	—	—	—
6	1½	—	—	—	—
4–3	2	—	—	—	—
2	2½	—	—	—	—
1	3	—	—	—	—
0–00	3½	5	7	—	—
000–0000	4	6	8	—	—
250 MCM	4½	6	8	10	—
300–350 MCM	5	8	10	12	—
400–500 MCM	6	8	10	12	14
600–700 MCM	8	10	12	14	16
750–900 MCM	8	12	14	16	18
1,000–1,250 MCM	10	—	—	—	—
1,500–2,000 MCM	12	—	—	—	—

Bending space at terminals shall be measured in a straight line from the end of the lug or wire connector (in the direction that the wire leaves the terminal) to the wall or barrier.

373-7. Space in Enclosures. Cabinets and cutout boxes shall conform to the following:

(a) To Accommodate Conductors. Cabinets and cutout boxes shall be selected which have sufficient space to accommodate all conductors installed in them without crowding.

373-8. Enclosures for Switches or Overcurrent Devices. Enclosures for switches or overcurrent devices shall not be used as junction boxes, auxiliary gutters or raceways for conductors feeding through or tapping off to other switches or overcurrent devices, unless adequate space is provided so that the conductors do not fill the wiring space at any cross section to more than 40 per cent of the cross-sectional area of the space, and so that the conductors, splices and taps do not fill the wiring space at any cross section to more than 75 per cent of the cross-sectional area of the space.

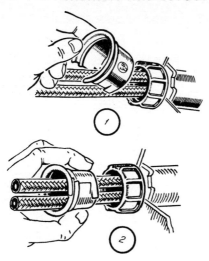

Fig. 373-1. Insulating sleeve. (*The Thomas & Betts Co., Inc.*)

▶   Most enclosures for switches and/or overcurrent devices have been designed to accommodate only those conductors intended to be connected to terminals within such enclosures. And in designing such equipment it would be virtually impossible for manufacturers to anticipate various types of "foreign" circuits, feed-through circuits or numerous splices or taps.

In general, the most satisfactory way to connect various enclosures together is through the use of properly sized auxiliary gutters (Sections **374-5** and **374-8**) or junction boxes (Sections **370-6** and **370-18**). Following this concept enclosures for switches and/or overcurrent devices will not be overcrowded.

There are cases where large enclosures for switches and/or overcurrent devices will accommodate additional small conductors (No. 10 and less) and this is generally where the 40 per cent (conductor space) and 75 per cent (splices or taps) at one cross section would apply. An example would be control circuits tapped off or extending through 200-amp or larger fusible switches or circuit breaker enclosures.

The cross-sectional area within such enclosures is the *free gutter wiring space* intended for conductors.

Example: If an enclosure has a gutter space of 3 in. × 3 in. the cross-sectional area would be 9 sq in. Thus, the total conductor fill (use Table **5**, Chapter 9) at any cross section could not exceed 3.6 sq in. (9 × .4), and the maximum space for splices at any cross section (including conductors) could not exceed 6.75 sq in. (9 × .75).

In the case of large conductors, a splice other than a wire-to-wire "C" or "tube" splice would not be acceptable if the conductors at the cross section are near a 40 per cent fill because this would leave only a **35** per cent space for the splice. Most splices for larger conductors with split-bolt connectors or similar types are usually twice the size of the conductors being spliced. Accordingly, where larger conductors are to be spliced within enclosures, the total conductor fill should not exceed *20 per cent* to allow for any bulky splice at a cross section.

373-9. Side or Back Wiring Spaces or Gutters.   Cabinets and cutout boxes shall be provided with back wiring spaces, gutters, or wiring compartments as required by Section 373-11(c and d).

B. Construction Specifications

373-10. Material.   Cabinets and cutout boxes shall conform to the following:

(a) **Metal Cabinets and Boxes.**   Metal cabinets and cutout boxes shall be well galvanized, plated with cadmium or other approved metallic finish, enameled, or otherwise properly coated, inside and out, to prevent corrosion.

It is recommended that the protective coating be of conductive material, such as cadmium, tin or zinc, in order to secure better electrical contact.

(b) **Strength.**   The design and construction of cabinets and cutout boxes shall be such as to secure ample strength and rigidity. If constructed of sheet steel, the metal shall be of not less than No. 16 MSG.

(c) **Composition Cabinets.**   Composition cabinets shall be submitted for approval prior to installation.

373-11. Spacing.   The spacing within cabinets and cutout boxes shall conform to the following:

(a) **General.**   The spacing within cabinets and cutout boxes shall be sufficient to provide ample room for the distribution of wires and cables placed in them, and for a separation between metal parts of devices and apparatus mounted within them as follows:

(1) **Base.**   There shall be an air space of at least $\frac{1}{16}$ inch, except at points of support, between the base of the device and the wall of any metal cabinet or cutout box in which the device is mounted.

(2) **Doors.**   There shall be an air space of at least 1 inch between any live metal part (including live metal parts of enclosed fuses) and the door, unless the door is lined with an approved insulating material or is of a thickness of metal not less than No. 12 MSG when the air space shall be not less than $\frac{1}{2}$ inch.

(3) **Doors and Walls—Link Fuses.**   There shall be a space of at least 2 inches between open link fuses and metal-lined walls or metal, metal-lined or glass-paneled doors.

(4) **Live Parts.**   Except as noted above, there shall be an air space of at least $\frac{1}{2}$ inch between the walls, back, gutter partition, if of metal, or door of any cabinet or cutout box and the nearest exposed current-carrying part of devices mounted within the cabinet where the potentials do not exceed 250 volts. This spacing shall be increased to at least one inch where the potentials exceed 250 volts.

(b) **Switch Clearance.**   Cabinets and cutout boxes shall be deep enough to allow the closing of the doors when 30-ampere branch-circuit panelboard switches are in any position, or when combination cutout switches are in any position, or when other single-throw switches are opened as far as their construction will permit.

(c) **Wiring Space.** Cabinets and cutout boxes which contain devices or apparatus connected within the cabinet or box to more than 8 conductors, including those of branch circuits, meter loops, sub-feeder circuits, power circuits and similar circuits, but not including the supply circuit or a continuation thereof, shall have back wiring spaces or one or more side wiring spaces, side gutters or wiring compartments.

(d) **Wiring Space—Enclosure.** Side wiring spaces, side gutters or side wiring compartments of cabinets and cutout boxes shall be rendered tight enclosures by means of covers, barriers or partitions extending from the bases of the devices, contained in the cabinet, to the door, frame, or sides of the cabinet; provided, however, that where the enclosure contains only those conductors which are led from the cabinet at points directly opposite their terminal connections to devices within the cabinet, such covers, barriers or partitions may be omitted. Partially enclosed back wiring spaces shall be provided with covers to complete enclosure. Wiring spaces that are required by Section 373-11(c) and which are exposed when doors are open, shall be provided with covers to complete the enclosure. Where adequate space is provided for feed-through conductors and for splices as is required in Section 373-8, additional barriers are not required.

▶   See comments following Section **373-8.**

ARTICLE 374. AUXILIARY GUTTERS

374-1. Purpose. Auxiliary gutters, used to supplement wiring spaces at meter centers, distribution centers, switchboards and similar points of wiring systems, may enclose conductors or bus-bars, but shall not be used to enclose switches, overcurrent devices, appliances, or other similar equipment.

▶   Auxiliary gutters are sheet-metal troughs in which conductors are laid in place after the gutter has been installed. Auxiliary gutters are used as parts of complete assemblies of apparatus such as switchboards, distribution centers, and control equipment, and are not permitted to extend more than 30 ft beyond the equipment which they supplement, except in elevator work. Where an extension beyond 30 ft is necessary, Art. 362 for Wireways must be complied with. The label of Underwriters' Laboratories, Inc., on each length of trough bears the legend "Wireways or Auxiliary Gutters," which indicates that they may be identical troughs but are distinguished one from the other only by their use. See comments following Section 362-1.

374-2. Extension Beyond Equipment. An auxiliary gutter shall not extend a greater distance than 30 feet beyond the equipment which it supplements except in elevator work. Any extension beyond this distance shall comply with the provisions for wireways in Article 362 or with the provisions for busways in Article 364.

374-3. Supports. Gutters shall be supported throughout their entire length at intervals not exceeding 5 feet.

374-4. Covers. Covers shall be securely fastened to the gutter.

374-5. Number of Conductors. Auxiliary gutters shall not contain more than 30 current-carrying conductors at any cross section. The sum of the cross-sectional areas of all contained conductors at any cross section of an auxiliary gutter shall not exceed 20 per cent of the interior cross-sectional area of the auxiliary gutter.

Exception No. 1: See Section 620-35 for elevators.

Exception No. 2: Conductors for signal circuits or controller conductors between a motor and its starter and used only for starting duty shall not be considered as current-carrying conductors.

Exception No. 3: When the correction factors specified in Note 8 to Tables 310-12 through 310-15 are applied, no limit on the number of current-carrying conductors is needed, but the sum of the cross-sectional area of all contained conductors at any cross section of the auxiliary gutter shall not exceed 20 per cent of the interior cross-sectional area of the auxiliary gutter.

▶ No limit is placed on the size of conductors that may be installed in an auxiliary gutter.

The cross-sectional area of rubber-covered and thermoplastic-covered conductors given in Table 5, Chap. 9, may be used in computing the size of gutters required to contain a given combination of such conductors.

374-6. Ampacity of Conductors. The ampacities of insulated copper and aluminum conductors are given in Tables 310-12 and 310-14 respectively. When the number of current-carrying conductors contained in the auxiliary gutter is 30 or less, the correction factors specified in Note 8 of these Tables shall not apply. The current carried continuously in bare copper bars in auxiliary gutters shall not exceed 1000 amperes per square inch of cross section of the conductor. For aluminum bars the current carried continuously shall not exceed 700 amperes per square inch of cross section of the conductor.

▶ The air cannot circulate freely inside a gutter, and where enclosed in such a dead-air space 1,000 amp per sq in. is considered a safe rating for copper bars of sizes up to about 4 by ¼ in., and 6 by ¼ in. for aluminum.

374-7. Clearance of Bare Live Parts. Bare conductors shall be securely and rigidly supported so that the minimum clearance between bare current-carrying metal parts of opposite polarities mounted on the same surface shall be not less than 2 inches, nor less than 1 inch for parts that are held free in the air. A clearance not less than 1 inch shall be secured between bare current-carrying metal parts and any metal surface. Adequate provisions shall be made for the expansion and contraction of bus-bars.

374-8. Splices and Taps. Splices and taps shall conform to the following:

(a) Splices or taps, made and insulated by approved methods, may be located within gutters when they are accessible by means of removable covers or doors.

The conductors, including splices and taps, shall not fill the gutter to more than 75 per cent of its area.

(b) Taps from bare conductors shall leave the gutter opposite their terminal connections and conductors shall not be brought in contact with uninsulated current-carrying parts of opposite polarity.

(c) All taps shall be suitably identified at the gutter as to the circuit or equipment which they supply.

(d) Tap connections from conductors in auxiliary gutters shall be provided with overcurrent protection in conformity with the provisions of Section 240-15.

▶   **The insulation might be cut by resting on the sharp edge of the bar or the bar might become hot enough to injure the insulation. When taps are made to bare conductors in a gutter, care should be taken so to place and form the wires that they will remain permanently separated from the bare bars.**

All taps shall be suitably identified at the gutter as to the circuit or equipment which they supply.

Identification shall be provided wherever it is not clearly evident what apparatus is supplied by the tap. Thus if a single set of tap conductors are carried through a short length of conduit from a gutter to a switch and the conduit is in plain view, the tap is fully identified and needs no special marking; but if two or more sets of taps are carried in a single conduit to two or more different pieces of apparatus, each tap should be identified by some marking such as a small tag secured to each wire.

Tap connections from conductors in auxiliary gutters shall be provided with overcurrent protection in conformity with the provisions of Section 240-15.

374-9. Construction and Installation. Auxiliary gutters shall be constructed in accordance with the following:

(a) Gutters shall be so constructed and installed that adequate electrical and mechanical continuity of the complete system will be secured.

(b) Gutters shall be of substantial construction and shall provide a complete enclosure for the contained conductors. All surfaces, both interior and exterior, shall be suitably protected from corrosion. Corner joints shall be made tight and where the assembly is held together by rivets or bolts, these shall be spaced not more than 12 inches apart.

(c) Suitable bushings, shields or fittings having smooth rounded edges shall be provided where conductors pass between gutters, through partitions, around bends, between gutters and cabinets or junction boxes and at other locations where necessary to prevent abrasion of the insulation of the conductors.

(d) Gutters shall be constructed of sheet metal of thicknesses not less than in the following table:

Table 374-9(d). Maximum Width of the Widest Surface of Gutters
Thickness (Manufacturers Standard Gage)

Up to and including 6 inches	No. 16
Over 6 in. and not over 18 in.	No. 14
Over 18 in. and not over 30 in.	No. 12
Over 30 inches	No. 10

(e) Where insulated conductors are deflected within the auxiliary gutter, either at the ends or where conduits, fittings or other raceways enter or leave the gutter, or where the direction of the gutter is deflected greater than 30 degrees, dimensions corresponding to Section 373-6 shall apply.

(f) Auxiliary gutters intended for outdoor use shall be of approved raintight construction.

ARTICLE 380. SWITCHES

A. Installation

380-1. Grounded Conductors. No switch or circuit breaker shall disconnect the grounded conductor of a circuit unless the switch or circuit breaker simultaneously disconnects the ungrounded conductor or conductors, or unless the switch or circuit breaker is so arranged that the grounded conductor cannot be disconnected until the ungrounded conductor or conductors have first been disconnected.

▶   Switches having a suitable number of poles for controlling three of the more common types of circuits are shown in Figs. **380-1, 380-2,** and **380-3.**

Opening only the grounded wire of a two-wire circuit would leave all devices that are connected to the circuit alive and at a voltage to ground equal to the voltage between wires on the mains, and in case of an accidental ground on the grounded wire, the circuit would not be controlled by the single-pole switch.

In either of the circuits shown in Figs. **380-2** and **380-3,** if the load consists of lamps connected between the neutral and the two or three outer wires and is not balanced, opening the neutral while the other wires are connected would cause the voltages to become unbalanced and might burn out all lamps on the more lightly loaded side.

In any case a switch may be arranged to open the grounded conductor if it simultaneously opens all the other conductors of the circuit. Thus a two-pole switch may be used to control the circuit of Fig. **380-1,** a three-pole switch for the circuit of Fig. **380-2,** and a four-pole switch for the circuit of Fig. **380-3.**

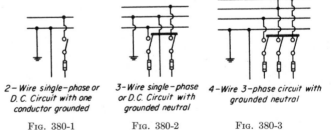

2 – Wire single-phase or D. C. Circuit with one conductor grounded	3 – Wire single-phase or D.C. Circuit with grounded neutral	4 – Wire 3-phase circuit with grounded neutral
Fig. 380-1	Fig. 380-2	Fig. 380-3

Figs. 380-1, 380-2, and 380-3. Number of poles required for switches to control three common types of circuits.

380-2. Three-Way and Four-Way Switches. Three-way and four-way switches shall be so wired that all switching is done only in the ungrounded circuit conductor. Wiring between switches and outlets shall, where in metal enclosures, be run with both polarities in the same enclosure.

▶   Three-way and four-way switches are actually single-pole switches and must not be used to disconnect the grounded circuit wire, because this would be a violation of Section **380-1**.

380-3. Enclosures. Switches and circuit breakers shall be of the externally operable type enclosed in metal boxes or cabinets, except pendant and surface type snap switches and knife switches mounted on an open face switchboard or panelboard.

380-4. Wet Locations. A switch or circuit breaker in a wet location or outside of a building shall be enclosed in a weatherproof enclosure or cabinet installed to conform to Section 373-2.

380-5. Time Switches, Flashers, and Similar Devices. Time switches, flashers, and similar devices need not be of the externally operable type. They shall be enclosed in metal boxes or cabinets except:

Exception No. 1: Where mounted on switchboards or control panels.

Exception No. 2: Where enclosed in approved individual housings.

▶   Any automatic switching device should be enclosed in a metal box unless it is a part of a switchboard or control panel which is located as required for live-front switchboards.

380-6. Position of Knife Switches. Single-throw knife switches shall be so placed that gravity will not tend to close them. Double-throw knife switches may be mounted so that the throw will be either vertical or horizontal as preferred, but where the throw be vertical a locking device shall be provided which will insure the blades remaining in the open position when so set.

380-7. Connection of Knife Switches. Knife switches, unless of the double-throw type, shall be so connected that the blades are dead when the switch is in the open position.

380-8. Accessibility and Grouping. Switches and circuit breakers, so far as practicable, shall be readily accessible and shall be grouped.

Snap switches shall not be grouped or ganged in outlet boxes unless they can be so arranged that the voltage between adjacent switches does not exceed 300, or unless they are installed in boxes equipped with permanently installed barriers between adjacent switches.

380-9. Faceplates for Flush-Mounted Snap Switches. Flush snap switches, that are mounted in ungrounded metal boxes and located within reach of conducting floors or other conducting surfaces, shall be provided with faceplates of non-

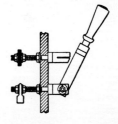

Fig. 380-4. A single-throw switch, if mounted vertically, must be mounted as here shown so that gravity will not tend to close it. A single-throw switch may also be mounted horizontally.

conducting, noncombustible material. Metallic faceplates shall be of ferrous metal not less than 0.030 inch in thickness or of nonferrous metal not less than 0.040 inch in thickness. Faceplates of insulating material shall be noncombustible and not less than 0.10 inch in thickness but may be less than 0.10 inch in thickness if formed or reinforced to provide adequate mechanical strength.

▶ A metal switch plate, if not grounded, may become "alive" by reason of contact of the ungrounded circuit wire with the plate or switch box, and a hazard is thus created if the plate is within reach from any conductive object. The hazard still exists, however, if a plate of insulating material is attached by means of metal screws with exposed metal heads. Insulated screws and metal screws with insulated heads are available.

380-10. Mounting of Snap Switches.

(a) **Surface-Type.** Snap switches used with open wiring on insulators shall be mounted on sub-bases of insulating material which will separate the conductors at least ½ inch from the surface wired over.

(b) **Box Mounted.** Flush-type snap switches mounted in boxes which are set back of the wall surface as permitted in Section 370-10 shall be installed so that the extension plaster ears are seated against the surface of the wall. Flush-type snap switches mounted in boxes which are flush with the wall surface or project therefrom shall be so installed that the mounting yoke or strap of the switch is seated against the box.

▶ The purpose of paragraph *b* is to prevent "loose switches" where openings around *recessed* boxes provide no means of seating the switch "ears" properly. It also permits the maximum projection of switch handles through the installed switch plate. The cooperation of other crafts, such as dry-wall installers, will be required to satisfy this rule.

380-11. Circuit Breakers as Switches. A circuit breaker operable directly by applying the hand to a lever or handle may serve as a switch provided it has the number of poles required for such switch.

▶ Molded-case circuit breakers are intended to be mounted on a vertical surface in an upright position or on their side. Their use in any other position requires their evaluation for such use.

"On" and "Off" legends on circuit breakers and switches are not intended to be mounted upside down.

380-12. Grounding of Enclosures. Enclosures for switches or circuit breakers on circuits of over 150 volts to ground shall be grounded in the manner specified in Article 250, except where accessible to qualified operators only.

380-13. Knife Switches.

(a) Knife switches rated for more than 1200 amperes at 250 volts or less, and for more than 600 amperes at 251 to 600 volts, shall be used only as isolating switches and shall not be opened under load.

(b) To interrupt currents greater than 1200 amperes at 250 volts or less, or 600 amperes at 251 to 600 volts, a circuit breaker or a switch of special design approved for such purpose shall be used.

(c) Knife switches of lower rating may be used as general-use switches and may be opened under load.

(d) Motor-circuit switches (see Definition in Article 100) may be of the knife-switch type.

380-14. Rating and Use of Snap Switches. Snap switches shall be used within their ratings and as follows:

(a) **AC General-Use Snap Switch.** A form of general-use snap switch suitable only for use on alternating-current circuits for controlling the following:

(1) Resistive and inductive loads, including electric-discharge lamps, not exceeding the ampere rating of the switch at the voltage applied.

(2) Tungsten-filament lamp loads not exceeding the ampere rating of the switch at 120 volts.

(3) Motor loads not exceeding 80 per cent of the ampere rating of the switch at its rated voltage.

(b) **AC-DC General-Use Snap Switch.** A form of general-use snap switch suitable for use on either AC or DC circuits for controlling the following:

(1) Resistive loads not exceeding the ampere rating of the switch at the voltage applied.

(2) Inductive loads not exceeding 50 per cent of the ampere rating of the switch at the applied voltage. Switches rated in horsepower are suitable for controlling motor loads within their rating at voltage applied.

(3) Tungsten-filament lamp loads not exceeding the ampere rating of the switch at the applied voltage, when "T" rated.

For switches on signs and outline lighting, see Section 600-2.
For switches controlling motors, see Sections 430-83, 430-109 and 430-110.

▶   For a noninductive load not including any tungsten-filament lamps, a snap switch is merely required to have an ampere rating at least equal to the ampere rating of the load it controls. Electrically heated appliances are about the only common examples of such loads.

For the control of loads consisting of tungsten lamps alone, or tungsten lamps combined with any other noninductive load, snap switches should be "T" rated or for alternating current circuits, a general-use a-c snap switch should be used.

The term *snap switch* as used here and elsewhere in the Code is intended to include, in general, the common types of flush and surface-mounted switches used for the control of lighting equipment and small appliances and the switches used to control branch circuits on lighting panelboards. These switches are now usually of the tumbler or toggle type but can be the rotary-snap or pushbutton type. The term is not applied to circuit breakers or to switches of the type that are commonly known as *knife switches*. See definition of "Switches" in Art. 100.

B. Construction Specifications

380-15. Marking. Switches shall be marked with the current and voltage and, if horsepower rated, the maximum rating for which they are designed.

380-16. 600-Volt Knife Switches.   Auxiliary contacts of a renewable or quick-break type or the equivalent, shall be provided on all 600-volt knife switches designed for use in breaking currents over 200 amperes.

It is recommended that such auxiliary contacts be provided on all direct-current switches rated at over 250 volts.

380-17. Fused Switches.   A fused switch shall not have fuses in parallel.

ARTICLE 384. SWITCHBOARDS AND PANELBOARDS

384-1. Scope.   The requirements of this Article shall apply to all switchboards, panelboards, and distribution boards installed for the control of light and power circuits.

Exception No. 1: Switchboards in utility company operated central stations or substations, which directly control energy derived from generators or transforming devices.

Exception No. 2: Switchboards or portions thereof used exclusively to control signal circuits operated by batteries.

The requirements of this Article shall apply to battery-charging panels where current is taken from light or power circuits.

384-2. Application of Other Articles.   Switches, circuit breakers and overcurrent devices used on switchboards, panelboards and distribution boards, the boards and their enclosures, shall conform to the requirements of Articles 240, 250, 370, 380 and other Articles which apply. Switchboards and panelboards in hazardous locations shall conform to the requirements of Articles 500 through 517.

384-3. Support and Arrangement of Bus-bars and Conductors.

   (a)   Conductors and bus-bars on a switchboard, panelboard or control board shall be so located as to be free from physical damage and shall be held firmly in place.

   (b)   The arrangement of bus-bars and conductors shall be such as to avoid overheating due to inductive effects.

   (c)   Each switchboard, switchboard section or panelboard, if used as service equipment, shall be provided with an equipment grounding means placed within the service disconnect section for connecting the grounded circuit conductor on its supply side to the switchboard or panelboard frame. The equipment grounding means shall not be smaller than called for in Table 250-95 nor smaller than No. 8 AWG copper conductor or approved equivalent.

   (d)   Load terminals in switchboards and panelboards shall be so located that it will be unnecessary to reach across or beyond a line bus in order to make load connections.

A. Switchboards

384-4. Location of Switchboards.   Switchboards which have any exposed live parts shall be located in permanently dry locations and then only where under competent supervision and accessible only to qualified persons.

384-5. Wet Locations.   Where a switchboard is in a wet location or outside of a building, it shall be enclosed in a weatherproof enclosure or cabinet installed to conform to Section 373-2.

384-6. Location Relative to Easily Ignitible Material.   Switchboards shall be so placed as to reduce to a minimum the probability of communicating fire to adjacent easily ignitible material.

384-7. Clearance from Ceiling.   Switchboards shall not be built up to a non-fireproof ceiling, a space of 3 feet being left between the ceiling and the board, unless an adequate fireproof shield is provided between the board and the ceiling.

▶   This restriction does not apply to metal-enclosed dead-front switchboards which are commonly used today. At the time this rule was put in the Code as a recommendation in 1897, it was the practice to fabricate the switchboard on the job. These were mostly open-top live-front switchboards with open-type switches, etc.

384-8. Clearance Around Switchboards.   Clearances around switchboards shall conform to the provisions for working space about electrical equipment as specified in Section 110-16 of this Code.

▶   Accessibility and working space are very necessary to avoid possible shock hazards and to provide easy access for maintenance, repair, operation, and housekeeping. It is preferable to increase the minimum space behind a switchboard where space will permit.

384-9. Conductor Covering.   Insulated conductors where closely grouped, as on the rear of switchboards, shall each have a flame-retardant outer covering. The conductor covering shall be stripped back a sufficient distance from the terminals so as to not make contact with them. Insulated conductors used for instrument and control wiring on the back of switchboards shall be flame-retardant, either inherently or by means of an outer covering, such as one of the following types: RH, RHH, RHW, V, ALS, AVA, AVB, SIS, T, TA, TBS, TW, THHN, THWN, THW, MI, XHHW, or other types specifically approved for the purpose.

384-11. Grounding Switchboard Frames.   Switchboard frames and structures supporting switching equipment shall be grounded, except that frames of direct-current single-polarity switchboards need not be grounded if effectively insulated.

384-12. Grounding of Instruments, Relays, Meters and Instrument Transformers on Switchboards.   Instruments, relays, meters and instrument transformers located on switchboards shall be grounded as specified in Sections 250-121 through 250-125.

B. Panelboards

384-13. General.   All panelboards shall have a rating not less than the minimum feeder capacity required for the load as computed from Article 220. Panelboards shall be durably marked by the manufacturer with the voltage and the current rating and the number of phases for which they are designed and with the manufacturer's name or trademark in such a manner as to be visible after installation, without disturbing the interior parts or wiring.

▶   The rating of a panelboard indicates the ampacity of the busbars which supply the overcurrent devices connected to them. The first sentence requires that after the load has been computed in accordance with Article 220, the feeder and panelboard ratings must be not less than the computed load. Panelboards which are suitable for use with aluminum conductors need to be marked to indicate such use. This marking can appear on the individual terminals and on the wiring diagram. Any terminal that is not identified for use with aluminum should be assumed suitable for use only with copper.

384-14. Lighting and Appliance Branch Circuit Panelboard.   For the purposes of this Article, a lighting and appliance branch circuit panelboard is one having more than 10 per cent of its overcurrent devices rated 30 amperes or less, for which neutral connections are provided.

▶   This definition is intended to describe the types of panelboards to which the overcurrent protection requirements in Section **384-16**(a) are applied.

Even though a panelboard may be used largely for other than lighting purposes, it is to be judged under the requirements for lighting and appliance branch-circuit panelboards if it conforms to the specific conditions stated in the definition. On the other hand, a panelboard which feeds only lighting but has no provision for neutrals is not so classified.

According to the Underwriters' Laboratories, Inc., Standard for Panelboards the rating of a general application lighting and appliance branch-circuit panelboard is based on an assumed average load current of 10 amperes for each overcurrent protective device connected to the main bus.

Such panelboards should be used on ordinary residential and similarly diversified loads. For example, a 115/230-volt 10-circuit panelboard rated at 50 amperes used for lighting and small appliances in a dwelling would normally not be overloaded because of diversity of loading. The same panelboard in a commercial or industrial occupancy used for 15- and 20-ampere lighting would normally be overloaded because the lighting load is considered continuous and would most likely be more than 10 amperes per pole.

384-15. Number of Overcurrent Devices on One Panelboard.   Not more than 42 overcurrent devices (other than those provided for in the mains) of a lighting and appliance branch circuit panelboard shall be installed in any one cabinet or cutout box.

A lighting and appliance branch circuit panelboard shall be provided with physical means to prevent the installation of more overcurrent devices than that number for which the panelboard was designed, rated and approved.

For the purposes of this Article a two-pole circuit breaker shall be considered two overcurrent devices; a three-pole breaker shall be considered three overcurrent devices.

▶   Figure 384-1 illustrates a panel base assembly with a 200-amp main which provides for the insertion of class CTL* overcurrent devices. The top three stab receivers are of an F slot configuration. Each F slot will receive only one breaker pole. The remainder of the slots are of an E configuration which will

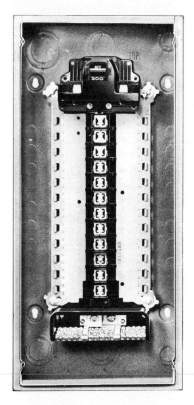

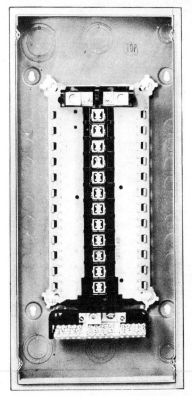

Fig. 384-1. Main circuit breaker service equipment panel. (*Federal Pacific Electric Company.*)

Fig. 384-2. Panelboard without main breaker. (*Federal Pacific Electric Company.*)

receive two breaker poles per slot. Thus there is provision for installing not more than 42 overcurrent devices, which does not include the main circuit breaker. This panelboard may also be supplied without main overcurrent protection and used as a load center (see Fig. 384-2) where such overcurrent protection is supplied elsewhere as shown in Fig. 384-3.

*Class CTL is the Underwriters' Laboratories, Inc., designation for the code requirement for circuit limitation within a lighting and appliance branch circuit panelboard. It means "circuit-limiting."

384-16. Overcurrent Protection.

(a) Each lighting and appliance branch circuit panelboard shall be individually protected on the supply side by not more than two main circuit breakers or two sets of fuses having a combined rating not greater than that of the panelboard.

Exception No. 1: Individual protection for a lighting and appliance panelboard is not required when the panelboard feeder has overcurrent protection not greater than that of the panelboard.

▶   The main fuses or main circuit breakers may be mounted either in the panelboard or ahead of the panelboard. In Fig. **384-3** the 200-amp overcurrent device ahead of panelboard A protects the panelboard because it is rated 200 amp. The 200-amp overcurrent device ahead of panelboards B and C protects both panelboards because each is rated 200 amp. Exception 1 is complied with in both cases.

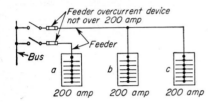

Fig. 384-3. Lighting and appliance branch-circuit panelboards.

Exception No. 2: Individual protection for lighting and appliance branch circuit panelboards is not required where such panelboards are used as service equipment in supplying an individual residential occupancy and where any bus supplying 15 or 20 ampere circuits is protected on the supply side by an overcurrent device.

▶   Individual residential occupancy means a single-family dwelling or an individual apartment in a multi-family occupancy.

Exception **2** must be taken in conjunction with paragraph *g* of Section **230-70** in order to have a complete picture. In effect the intent is to permit the use of a lighting and appliance branch-circuit panelboard as the service equipment in an individual residential occupancy provided that no switch or circuit breaker rated at 20 amp or less may serve as one of the six permissible disconnecting means. Such 20-amp or smaller devices must have an overcurrent device of larger rating on the supply side as shown in Fig. **384-4**.

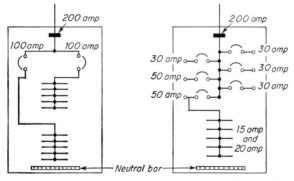

Fig. 384-4. 200-amp lighting and appliance branch-circuit panelboards.

(b) Panelboards equipped with snap switches rated at 30 amperes or less, shall have overcurrent protection not in excess of 200 amperes.

▶   **In this case the limitation on snap switches does not apply to circuit breakers.**

(c) The total load on any overcurrent device located in a panelboard shall not exceed 80% of its rating where in normal operation the load will continue for 3 hours or more.

Exception: Except where the assembly including the overcurrent device is approved for continuous duty at 100% of its rating.

384-17. Panelboards in Damp or Wet Locations. Panelboards in damp or wet locations shall be installed in conformity to Section 373-2.

384-18. Enclosure. Panelboards shall be mounted in cabinets or cutout boxes.

384-19. Relative Arrangement of Switches and Fuses. Panelboards having switches on the load side of any type of fuses shall not be installed except for use as service equipment as provided in Section 230-94.

▶   **For service equipment, switches are permitted on either the supply side or the load side of the fuses. In all other cases if the panelboards are accessible to other than qualified persons, Section 240-18 requires that the switches shall be on the supply side so that when replacing fuses all danger of shock or short circuit can be eliminated by opening the switch.**

C. Construction Specifications

384-20. Panels. The panels of switchboards shall be made of moisture-resistant, noncombustible material.

384-21. Bus-bars. Bus-bars may be of bare metal provided they are rigidly mounted.

384-22. Protection of Instrument Circuits. Instruments, pilot lights, potential transformers, and other switchboard devices with potential coils, except where the operation of the overcurrent device might introduce a hazard in the operation of devices, shall be supplied by a circuit that is protected by standard overcurrent devices of a rating not greater than 15 amperes, except that for ratings of 2 amperes or less special types of enclosed fuses may be used.

384-23. Component Parts. Switches, fuses, and fuseholders used on panelboards shall conform to the requirements of Articles 240 and 380 so far as they apply.

384-24. Knife Switches. Knife switches shall be so arranged that the blades, when exposed during operation, will be dead when the switches are open.

384-25. Color Coding. On switchboards or panelboards that are provided with color markings to indicate the main bus-bars to which branch circuit bus-bars are connected, the colors shall conform to the color coding of Section 210-5.

384-26. Spacings. Except at switches and circuit breakers, the distance between bare metal parts, bus-bars, etc., shall be not less than specified in the following Table:

Table 384-26. Spacings Between Bare Metal Parts

	Opposite Polarity When Mounted on the Same Surface	Opposite Polarity When Held Free in Air	*Live Parts to Ground
Not over 125 volts..........	¾ inch	½ inch	½ inch
Not over 250 volts..........	1¼ inch	¾ inch	½ inch
Not over 600 volts..........	2 inches	1 inch	1 inch

* For spacing between live parts and doors of cabinets, see Section 373-11(a)(1), (2), (3) and (4).
It should be noted that the above distances are the minimum allowable, and it is recommended that greater distances be provided wherever the conditions will permit.

At switches, enclosed fuses, etc., parts of the same polarity may be placed as close together as convenience in handling will allow, unless close proximity causes excessive heating.

384-27. Grounding of Panelboards.   Panelboard cabinets shall be grounded in the manner specified in Article 250 or Section 384-3(c). An approved terminal bar for equipment grounding conductors shall be provided and secured inside of the cabinet for the attachment of all the feeder and branch-circuit equipment grounding conductors, when the panelboard is used with nonmetallic raceway, cable wiring or where separate grounding conductors are provided. The terminal bar shall be bonded to the cabinet or panelboard frame and shall not be connected to the neutral bar except at service equipment as permitted in Section 250-52.

▶   A terminal bar for connecting equipment grounding conductors may be an inherent part of a panelboard, or terminal bar kits may be obtained for simple installation in any panelboard.

ARTICLE 390. PREFABRICATED BUILDINGS

390-1. Scope.   The intent and purpose of the following sections is to define approved methods for the wiring of prefabricated building sections, panels, or units designed for later erection or assembly as integral parts of buildings whether wired in the process of manufacture or at the site of erection or assembly.

390-2. Wiring Methods.   Only wiring methods recognized in this Code shall be used.

390-3. Code Provisions to Apply.   The provisions of this Code shall apply for the type of wiring method used and the type of construction employed.

▶   The intent of this Article is to require that prefabricated buildings comply with the requirements of the Code that would be applicable to other "on the site" constructed buildings.

Where such buildings are permitted by the local building codes, the electrical inspection authority has, in some cases, gone to the factory where such sections are assembled to ascertain that the materials and construction used were in conformance with the National Electrical Code requirements. Since many metropolitan areas require inspection prior to concealment, electrical approval on such buildings, in some cases, is withheld. Underwriters' Laboratories, Inc., has listed a number of prefabricated assemblies on the basis of compliance not only with the National Electrical Code but with several other building-construction features which are related to safety from fire.

CHAPTER FOUR _____

Equipment for General Use

ARTICLE 400. FLEXIBLE CORDS AND CABLES

A. General and Types

400-1. General. Flexible cords and cables and their associated fittings shall be suitable for the conditions of use and location.

400-2. Types. Cords of the several types shall conform to the descriptions of Table 400-11. Types of flexible cords other than those listed in Table 400-11 and other uses for types listed in the Table, shall be the subject of special investigations and shall not be used before being approved.

B. Use and Installation

400-3. Use.

(a) Flexible cord may be used only for (1) pendants; (2) wiring of fixtures; (3) connection of portable lamps or appliances; (4) elevator cables; (5) wiring of cranes and hoists; (6) connection of stationary equipment to facilitate their frequent interchange; or (7) prevention of the transmission of noise or vibration; or (8) facilitating the removal or disconnection of fixed or stationary appliances for maintenance or repair.

(b) Where used as permitted in sub-sections (a) (3), (a) (6), and (a) (8) of this Section, each flexible cord shall be equipped with an attachment plug and shall be energized from an approved receptacle outlet.

▶ It should be noted that the cords referred to are the cords attached to the appliance and not extension cords supplementing or extending the regular supply cords. The use of an extension cord would represent a conflict with the requirements of the Code in that it would serve as a substitute for a receptacle to be located near the appliance.

Extension cords are intended for temporary use with portable appliances, tools, and similar equipment which are not normally used at one specific location.

400-4. Prohibited Uses. Except where installed in accordance with Article 645, flexible cord shall not be used (1) as a substitute for the fixed wiring of a structure; (2) where run through holes in walls, ceilings, or floors; (3) where run through doorways, windows, or similar openings; (4) where attached to building surfaces; or (5) where concealed behind building walls, ceilings, or floors.

400-5. Splices. Flexible cord shall be used only in continuous lengths without splice or tap.

400-6. Cords in Show Windows and Show Cases. Flexible cord used in show windows and show cases shall be of Types S, SO, SJ, SJO, ST, STO, SJT, SJTO and AFS, except for the wiring of chain-supported fixtures, and for supplying current to portable lamps and other merchandise for exhibition purposes.

▶ On account of the inflammable material nearly always present in show windows, great care should be taken to ensure that only approved types of cords are used and that they are maintained in good condition.

400-7. Minimum Size. The individual conductors of a flexible cord or cable shall be not smaller than the sizes shown in Table 400-11.

400-8. Insulation—Over 300 Volts. Where the voltage between any two conductors exceeds 300, but does not exceed 600, flexible cord of No. 10 and smaller shall have rubber or thermoplastic insulation on the individual conductors at least 45 mils in thickness, unless Type S, SO, ST or STO cord is used.

400-9. Overcurrent Protection and Ampacities of Flexible Cords.

Flexible cords not smaller than No. 18, and tinsel cords, or cords having equivalent characteristics, of smaller size approved for use with specific appliances, shall be considered as protected against overcurrent by the overcurrent devices described in Section 240-5. Cords shall be not smaller than required in Table 400-9(b) for the rated current of the connected equipment.

Table 400-9(b). Ampacity of Flexible Cord

Table 400-9(b) gives the allowable ampacity for not more than three current-carrying conductors in a cord. If the number of current-carrying conductors in a cord is from four to six, the allowable ampacity of each conductor shall be reduced to 80 per cent of the values for not more than three current-carrying conductors in the Table. A conductor used for equipment grounding and a neutral conductor which carries only the unbalanced current from other conductors, as in the case of normally balanced circuits of three or more conductors, are not considered to be current-carrying conductors. Where a single conductor is used for both equipment grounding and to carry unbalanced current from other conductors, it shall not be considered to be a current-carrying conductor. (See Section 250-60.)

(Based on Ambient Temperature of 30°C (86°F). See Section 400-9 and Table 400-11)

Size AWG	Rubber Types TP, TS / Thermoplastic Types TPT, TST	Rubber Types PO, C, PD, E, EO, EN, S, SO, SRD, SJ, SJO, SV, SVO, SP / Thermoplastic Types ET, ETT, ETLB, ETP, ST, STO, SRDT, SJT, SJTO, SVT, SVTO, SPT		Types AFS, AFSJ, HC, HPD, HSJ, HSJO, HS, HSO, HPN, SVHT	Types AVPO, AVPD	Cotton Types CFPD* / Asbestos Types AFC*, AFPD*
		A†	B†			
27**	0.5	..	..	..	..	..
18	..	7	10	10	17	6
17	..	..	..	12	..	..
16	..	10	13	15	22	8
15	..	..	..	17	..	..
14	..	15	18	20	28	17
12	..	20	25	30	36	23
10	..	25	30	35	47	28
8	..	35	40	..	..	..
6	..	45	55	..	..	..
4	..	60	70	..	..	..
2	..	80	95	..	..	..

* These types are used almost exclusively in fixtures where they are exposed to high temperatures and ampere ratings are assigned accordingly.

** Tinsel Cord.

† The ampacities under sub-heading A are applicable to three conductor cords and other multi-conductor cords connected to utilization equipment so that only three conductors are current carrying. The ampacities under sub-heading B are applicable to two conductor cords and other multi-conductor cords connected to utilization equipment so that only two conductors are current carrying.

NOTE 1. Ultimate Insulation Temperature. In no case shall conductors be associated together in such a way with respect to the kind of circuit, the wiring method employed, or the number of conductors, that the limiting temperature of the conductors will be exceeded.

NOTE 2. SVHT made only in No. 18 and 17 AWG sizes.

400-10. Pull at Joints and Terminals. Flexible cords shall be so connected to devices and to fittings that tension will not be transmitted to joints or terminal screws. This shall be accomplished by a knot in the cord, winding with tape, by a special fitting designed for that purpose, or by other approved means which will prevent a pull on the cord from being directly transmitted to joints or terminal screws.

▶   The "Underwriters' knot" (Fig. 400-1) has been used for many years and is a good method for taking the strain from the socket terminals where lamp cord is used for the pendant. For reinforced cords and junior hard-service cords, sockets with cord grips such as shown in Fig. 400-2 provide an effective means of relieving the terminals of all strain.

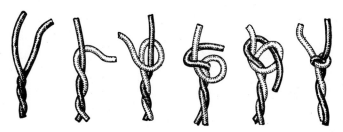

Fig. 400-1. Underwriters' knot.

Fig. 400-2. Lampholder with cord grip.

Table 400-11. Flexible Cord
(See Section 400-2)

Trade Name	Type Letter	Size AWG	No. of Conductors	Insulation	Braid on Each Conductor	Outer Covering	Use		
Parallel Tinsel Cord	TP See Note 3	27	2	Rubber	None	Rubber	Attached to an Appliance	Damp Places	Not Hard Usage
	TPT See Note 3	27	2	Thermoplastic	None	Thermoplastic	Attached to an Appliance	Damp Places	Not Hard Usage
Jacketed Tinsel Cord	TS See Note 3	27	2 or 3	Rubber	None	Rubber	Attached to an Appliance	Damp Places	Not Hard Usage
	TST See Note 3	27	2 or 3	Thermoplastic	None	Thermoplastic	Attached to an Appliance	Damp Places	Not Hard Usage
Asbestos-Covered Heat-Resistant Cord	AFC	18-10	2 or 3	Impregnated Asbestos	Cotton or Rayon	None	Pendant	Dry Places	Not Hard Usage
	AFPD		2		None	Cotton, Rayon or Saturated Asbestos			
Cotton-Covered Heat-Resistant Cord		18-10	2 or 3	Impregnated Cotton	Cotton or Rayon	None	Pendant	Dry Places	Not Hard Usage
			2						
	CFPD		2 or 3		None	Cotton or Rayon			

Trade Name	Type	Size (AWG)	No.	Insulation	Braid	Outer Covering	Use (See Note 2)		
Parallel Cord	PO-1	18		Rubber	Cotton	Cotton or Rayon	Pendant or Portable	Dry Places	Not Hard Usage
	PO-2	18-16	2						
	PO	18-10							
All Rubber Parallel Cord	SP-1	18	2	Rubber	None	Rubber	Pendant or Portable	Damp Places	Not Hard Usage
	SP-2 See Note 7	18-16	2 or 3						
	SP-3 See Note 7	18-12		Rubber	None	Rubber	Refrigerators or Room Air Conditioners	Damp Places	Not Hard Usage
All Plastic Parallel Cord	SPT-1	18	2	Thermoplastic	None	Thermoplastic	Pendant or Portable	Damp Places	Not Hard Usage
	SPT-2 See Note 7	18-16	2 or 3						
All Plastic Parallel Cord	SPT-3 See Note 7	18-10		Thermoplastic	None	Thermoplastic	Refrigerators or Room Air Conditioners	Damp Places	Not Hard Usage
Lamp Cord	C	18-10	2 or more	Rubber	Cotton	None	Pendant or Port.	Dry Places	Not Hard Usage
Twisted Portable Cord	PD	18-10	2 or more	Rubber	Cotton	Cotton or Rayon	Pendant or Port.	Dry Places	Not Hard Usage

See Notes 1 through 8.

Table 400-11. Flexible Cord (Continued)

Trade Name	Type Letter	Size AWG	No. of Conductors	Insulation	Braid on Each Conductor	Outer Covering	Use		
Vacuum Cleaner Cord	SV, SVO	18		Rubber	None	Rubber	Pendant or Portable	Damp Places	Not Hard Usage
	SVT	18-17	2	Thermopl'		Thermoplastic			
	SVTO See Note 7	18	2 or 3						
Heat Resistant V.C. Cord	SVHT	18-17	2	Thermopl'	None	Thermoplastic	Pendant or Portable	Damp Places	Not Hard Usage
Junior Hard Service Cord	SJ	18-16	2, 3, or 4	Rubber	None	Rubber	Pendant or Portable	Damp Places	Hard Usage
	SJO					Oil Resistant Compound			
	SJT SJTO			Thermopl' or Rubber		Thermoplastic			
Hard Service Cord	S See Note 5	18-2	2 or more	Rubber	None	Rubber	Pendant or Portable	Damp Places	Extra Hard Usage
	SO					Oil Resist. Compound			
	ST			Thermopl' or Rubber		Thermoplastic			
	STO					Oil Resistant Thermoplastic			
Rubber-Jacketed Heat-Resistant Cord	AFSJ	18-16	2 or 3	Impregnated Asbestos	None	Rubber	Portable	Damp Places	Portable Heaters
	AFS	18-16-14							

Name	Type	Size AWG	No. of Conductors	Insulation	Braid	Outer Covering	Use		
Heater Cord	HC	18–12	2, 3 or 4	Rubber or thermoplastic & Asbestos	Cotton	None	Portable	Dry Places	Portable Heaters
	HPD	18–12	2, 3 or 4	Rubber or thermoplastic with Asbestos or All Neoprene	None	Cotton or Rayon			
Rubber Jacketed Heater Cord	HSJ	18–16	2, 3 or 4	Rubber or thermoplastic with Asbestos or All Neoprene	None	Cotton and Rubber	Portable	Damp Places	Portable Heaters
Jacketed Heater Cord	HSJO	18–16	2, 3 or 4	Rubber with Asbestos or All Neoprene	None	Cotton and Oil Resistant Compound	Portable	Damp Places	Portable Heaters
	HS	14–12				Cotton and Rubber or Neoprene			
	HSO	14–12				Cotton and Oil Resistant Compound			
Parallel Heater Cord	HPN See Note 7	18–12	2 or 3	Thermosetting	None.	Thermosetting	Portable	Damp Places	Not Hard Usage
Heat & Moisture-Resistant Cord	AVPO	18–10	2	Asbestos & Var. Cam.	None	Asbestos, Flame-Ret. Moisture Resistant	Pendant or Portable	Damp Places	Not Hard Usage
	AVPD	18–10	2 or 3						
Range, Dryer Cable	SRD	10–4	3 or 4	Rubber	None	Rubber or Neoprene	Portable	Damp Places	Ranges, Dryers
	SRDT	10–4	3 or 4	Thermoplastic	None	Thermoplastic	Portable	Damp Places	Ranges, Dryers

See Notes 1 through 8.

Table 400-11. Flexible Cord (Continued)

Trade Name	Type Letter	Size AWG	No. of Conductors	Insulation	Braid on Each Conductor	Outer Covering	Use — Dry Places	Use — Power and Signal Circuits
Data Processing Cable	DP	30-Min.	2 or more	Thermopl' Rubber or Cross-linked Synthetic Polymer	None	Thermoplastic, Rubber or Cross-linked Synthetic Polymer	Data Processing Systems	Non-Hazardous Locations
Elevator Cable	E See Note 6	18-14	2 or more	Rubber	Cotton	Three Cotton, Outer one Flame-Retardant & Moisture-Resist. See Note 4	Elevator Lighting & Control	Non-Hazardous Locations
	EO See Note 6		2 or more	Rubber	Cotton	One Cotton and a Neoprene Jacket See Note 4	Elevator Lighting & Control	Hazardous Locations
	EN See Note 6	18-14	2 or more	Rubber	Flexible Nylon Jacket	Three Cotton, Outer one Flame-Retardant & Moisture-Resist. See Note 4		Non-Hazardous Locations
	ET See Note 6			Thermoplastic	Rayon	One Cotton and a Neoprene or Thermoplastic Jacket See Note 4	Elevator Lighting & Control	Hazardous Locations
	ETLB See Note 6				None	Three Cotton, Outer one Flame-Retardant & Moisture-Resist. See Note 4		Non-Hazardous Locations
	ETP See Note 6			Thermoplastic	Rayon	Thermoplastic		
	ETT See Note 6				None	One Cotton and a Thermopl' Jacket		Hazardous Locations

See Notes 1 through 8.

Notes to Table 400-11

1. Except for Types PO-1, PO-2, PO, SP-1, SP-2, SPT-1, SPT-2, TP, TPT, and AVPO, individual conductors are twisted together.

2. Type PO-1 is for use only with portable lamps, portable radio receiving appliances, portable clocks and similar appliances which are not liable to be moved frequently and where appearance is a consideration.

3. Types TP, TPT, TS, and TST are suitable for use in lengths not exceeding eight feet when attached directly, or by means of a special type of plug, to a portable appliance rated at 50 watts or less and of such nature that extreme flexibility of the cord is essential.

4. Rubber-filled or varnished cambric tapes may be substituted for the inner braids.

5. Types S, SO, ST, and STO are suitable for use on theater stages, in garages and elsewhere, where flexible cords are permitted by this Code.

6. Traveling cables for operating, control and signal circuits may have one or more non-metallic fillers or may have a supporting filler of stranded steel wires having its own protective braid or cover. Cables exceeding 100 feet between supports shall have steel supporting fillers, except in locations subject to excessive moisture or corrosive vapors or gases. Where steel supporting fillers are used, they shall run straight through the center of the cable assembly and shall not be cabled with the copper strands of any conductor.

Types E, EO, EN, ET, ETP, ETLB, and ETT cables may incorporate in the construction No. 20 gauge conductors formed as a pair, and covered with suitable shielding for telephone and other audio or higher frequency communication circuits. The insulation of the conductors may be rubber or thermoplastic of thickness specified for the other conductors of the particular type of cable. The shield shall have its own protective covering. This component may be incorporated in any layer of the cable assembly, and shall not run straight through the center.

7. A third conductor in these cables is for grounding purposes only.

8. The individual conductors of all cords except those of heat-resistant cords (Types AFC, AFPD, AFS, AFSJ, AVPO, AVPD and CFPD) shall have a rubber or thermoplastic insulation, except that the grounding conductor, where used, shall be in accordance with Section 400-14(b). A rubber compound shall be vulcanized for heater cords (Types HC, HPD and HSJ).

C. Construction Specifications

400-12. Labels. Flexible cords shall be examined and tested at the factory and shall be labeled before shipment.

400-13. Grounded Conductor Identification. One conductor of flexible cords which is intended to be used as a grounded circuit conductor shall have a continuous marker readily distinguishing it from the other conductor or conductors. The identification shall consist of one of the following:

(a) Colored Braid. A braid finished to show a white or natural gray color and the braid on the other conductor or conductors finished to show a readily distinguishable solid color or colors.

(b) Tracer in Braid. A tracer in a braid of any color contrasting with that of the braid and no tracer in the braid of the other conductor or conductors. No tracer shall be used in the braid of any conductor of a flexible cord which contains a conductor having a braid finished to show white or natural gray, except, in the case of Types C, PD and PO cords having the braids on the individual conductors finished to show white or natural gray. In such Types C, PD and PO cords the identifying marker may consist of the solid white or natural gray finish on one conductor provided there is a colored tracer in the braid of each other conductor.

(c) Colored Insulation. A white or natural gray insulation on one conductor and insulation of a readily distinguishable color or colors on the other conductor or conductors for cords having no braids on the individual conductors (except cords which have insulation on the individual conductors integral with the jacket). The insulation may be covered with an outer finish to provide the desired color.

(d) **Colored Separator.**   A white or natural gray separator on one conductor and a separator of a readily distinguishable solid color on the other conductor or conductors of cords having insulation on the individual conductors integral with the jacket.

(e) **Tinned Conductors.**   One conductor having the individual strands tinned and the other conductor or conductors having the individual strands untinned for cords having insulation on the individual conductors integral with the jacket.

(f) **Surface Marking.**   One or more stripes, ridges or grooves so located on the exterior of the cord as to identify one conductor for cords having insulation on the individual conductors integral with the jacket.

400-14. Grounding Conductor Identification.   A conductor intended to be used as a grounding conductor shall have a continuous identifying marker readily distinguishing it from the other conductor or conductors. Conductors having a continuous green color or a continuous green color with one or more yellow stripes shall not be used for other than grounding purposes. The identifying marker shall consist of one of the following:

(a) **Colored Braid.**   A braid finished to show a continuous green color or a continuous green color with one or more yellow stripes.

(b) **Colored Insulation or Covering.**   For cords having no braids on the individual conductors, an insulation of a continuous green color or a continuous green color with one or more yellow stripes.

400-15. Insulation Thickness.   The nominal thickness of rubber or thermoplastic conductor insulation in Types TS, TST, PO-1, SV, SVT, and SVHT shall be not less than 15 mils. The nominal thickness of rubber insulation in Types HC, HPD, HSJ, and HS shall not be less than 15 mils for the Nos. 18-16 AWG sizes, and not less than 30 mils for the Nos. 14-12 AWG sizes. For heater cord other than Types HC and HPN, the all neoprene insulation shall be 30 mils for No. 18 and No. 16 AWG sizes and 45 mils for No. 14 and No. 12 AWG sizes. The nominal thickness of the thermoplastic insulation in Type ET and ETP elevator cable shall be not less than 20 mils for the No. 18 and No. 16 AWG sizes and not less than 30 mils for the No. 14 AWG size. The nominal thickness of the rubber insulation in Types E, EO, and EN elevator cables shall be not less than 20 mils for the No. 18 and 16 AWG sizes and not less than 30 mils for the No. 14 AWG size for ratings not exceeding 300 volts. The nominal thickness of latex-rubber insulation, when employed, in Types SJ, SJO, S and SO shall be not less than 15 mils for the Nos. 18-16 AWG sizes and not less than 18 mils for the No. 14 AWG and larger sizes. The nominal thickness of conductor insulation in Types PO, SP-2, SPT-2, HPN, SRD, and SRDT shall be not less than 45 mils. The nominal thickness of thermoplastic insulation in Type SPT-3 shall be not less than 60 mils for sizes 18-16 and 80 mils for No. 14, 95 mils for No. 12 and 110 mils for No. 10 AWG. The nominal thickness of the thermoplastic insulation on the individual conductors in Type DP cable shall be not less than 8 mils for sizes Nos. 30-27 AWG, not less than 12 mils for sizes Nos. 26-23 AWG, not less than 16 mils for sizes Nos. 22-20 AWG, when the voltage impressed is less than 50; when the voltage is more than 50 but less than 300, the nominal thickness of the thermoplastic insulation on the individual conductors shall be not less than 20 mils for sizes 30-16 AWG, not less than 30 mils for sizes Nos. 14-10 AWG and not less than 60 mils for sizes Nos.

8-2 AWG. For other types, the minimum nominal thickness of rubber or thermoplastic conductor insulation shall be as follows: size AWG 27, and 18 to 16—30
mils; 14 to 10—45 mils; 8 to 2—60 mils.

400-16. Attached to Receptacle Plugs. Where a flexible cord is provided with
a grounding conductor and equipped with an attachment plug, the plug shall
comply with Sections 250-59(a and b).

ARTICLE 402. FIXTURE WIRES

402-1. Use. Fixture wires are designed for installation in lighting fixtures and
in similar equipment where enclosed or protected and not subject to bending
or twisting in use. Also, they are used for connecting lighting fixtures to the
conductors of the circuit that supplies the fixtures.

For application in lighting fixtures, see Article 410.

Fixture wires are not intended for installation as branch circuit conductors, except as permitted
in Section 725-14.

402-2. Minimum Size. Fixture wires shall not be smaller than No. 18.

402-3. Insulation.

(a) The rubber insulations include those made from natural and synthetic
rubber, neoprene and other vulcanized materials.

Thermoplastic insulation may stiffen at temperatures below minus 10°C. (14°F.) and care
should be used in its installation at such temperatures. It may be deformed when subject to
pressure; care should be taken in its installation, as for example, at bushings, or points of support.
See Section 373-6(b).

(b) No conductor shall be used under such conditions that its temperature,
even when carrying current, will exceed the temperature specified in Table 310-2(a) for the type of insulation involved.

Table 402-4. Allowable Ampacity of Fixture Wire
(Based on Ambient Temperature of 30°C., 86°F.)

Size AWG	Fixture Wire	
	Rubber Types RF-1, RF-2, FF-1, FF-2, RFH-1, RFH-2, FFH-1, FFH-2	Thermoplastic Types TF, TFF, TFN, TFFN
		Cotton Type CF*
		Asbestos Type AF*
		Silicone Rubber Types SF-1*, SF-2*, SFF-1*, SFF-2*
		Fluorinated Ethylene Propylene Types PF*, PGF*, PFF*, PGFF* Extruded Polytetrafluoro-ethylene Types PTF*, PTFF*
18	5	6
16	7	8
14	..	17

* These types are used almost exclusively in fixtures where they are exposed to high temperatures and ampere ratings are assigned accordingly.

Table 402-6. Fixture Wire

Trade Name	Type Letter	Insulation	Thickness of Insulation	Outer Covering
Rubber-Covered Fixture Wire Solid or 7-Strand	RF-1	Code Rubber	18................. 15 Mils	Non-metallic covering
	RF-2	Code Rubber	18–16................. 30 Mils	Non-metallic covering
		Latex Rubber	18–16................. 18 Mils	
Rubber-Covered Fixture Wire Flexible Stranding	FF-1	Code Rubber	18................. 15 Mils	Non-metallic covering
	FF-2	Code Rubber	18–16................. 30 Mils	Non-metallic covering
		Latex Rubber	18–16................. 18 Mils	
Heat Resistant Rubber-Covered Fixture Wire Solid or 7-Strand	RFH-1	Heat-Resistant Rubber	18................. 15 Mils	Non-metallic covering
	RFH-2	Heat-Resistant Rubber	18–16................. 30 Mils	Non-metallic covering
		Heat-Resistant Latex Rubber	18–16................. 18 Mils	
Heat Resistant Rubber-Covered Fixture Wire Flexible Stranding	FFH-1	Heat-Resistant Rubber	18................. 15 Mils	Non-metallic covering
	FFH-2	Heat-Resistant Rubber	18–16................. 30 Mils	Non-metallic covering
		Heat-Resistant Latex Rubber	18–16................. 18 Mils	
Thermoplastic-Covered Fixture Wire—Solid or Stranded	TF	Thermoplastic	18–16................. 30 Mils	None
Thermoplastic-Covered Fixture Wire—Flexible Stranding	TFF	Thermoplastic	18–16................. 30 Mils	None
Heat-Resistant Thermoplastic-Covered Fixture Wire—Solid or Stranded	TFN	Thermoplastic	18–16................. 15 Mils	Nylon Jacketed

	TFFN	Thermoplastic	AWG	Mils	Nylon Jacketed
Heat Resistant Thermoplastic-Covered Fixture Wire—Flexible Stranded	TFFN	Thermoplastic	18–16	15 Mils	Nylon Jacketed
Cotton-Covered, Heat-Resistant, Fixture Wire	CF	Impregnated Cotton	18–14	30 Mils	None
Asbestos-Covered, Heat-Resistant, Fixture Wire	AF	Impregnated Asbestos	18–14	30 Mils	None
Silicone Insulated Fixture Wire	SF-1	Silicone Rubber	18	15 Mils	Non-metallic covering
Solid or 7-Strand	SF-2	Silicone Rubber	18–14	30 Mils	Non-metallic covering
Silicone Insulated Fixture Wire	SFF-1	Silicone Rubber	18	15 Mils	Non-metallic covering
Flexible Stranding	SFF-2	Silicone Rubber	18–14	30 Mils	Non-metallic covering
Fluorinated Ethylene Propylene Fixture Wire Solid or 7 Strand	PF	Fluorinated Ethylene Propylene	18–14	20 Mils	None
	PGF		18–14	14 Mils	Glass Braid
Fluorinated Ethylene Propylene Fixture Wire Flexible Stranding	PFF	Fluorinated Ethylene Propylene	18–14	20 Mils	None
	PGFF		18–14	14 Mils	Glass Braid
Extruded Polytetrafluoroethylene Solid or 7-Strand (Nickel or Nickel Coated Copper)	PTF	Extruded Polytetrafluoroethylene	18–14	20 Mils	None
Extruded Polytetrafluoroethylene Flexible Stranding (No. 26–36 AWG Silver or Nickel Coated Copper)	PTFF	Extruded Polytetrafluoroethylene	18–14	20 Mils	None

Ultimate Insulation Temperature. In no case shall conductors be associated together in such a way with respect to the kind of circuit, the wiring method employed, or the number of conductors, that the limiting temperature of the conductors will be exceeded.

402-5. Overcurrent Protection.   See Section 240-5(a), Exception No. 2.

402-7. Number of Conductors in Conduit.   The number of fixture wires permitted in a single conduit shall be as given in Table 2 of Chapter 9.

ARTICLE 410. LIGHTING FIXTURES, LAMPHOLDERS, LAMPS, RECEPTACLES AND ROSETTES

A. General

410-1. Scope.   Lighting fixtures, lampholders, pendants, receptacles, and rosettes, incandescent filament lamps, arc lamps, electric discharge lamps, the wiring and equipment forming part of such lamps, fixtures and lighting installations shall conform to the provisions of this Article, except as otherwise provided in this Code.

410-2. Application to Other Articles.   Equipment for use in hazardous locations shall conform to Articles 500 through 517.

410-3. Live Parts.   Fixtures, lampholders, lamps, rosettes and receptacles shall have no live parts normally exposed to contact, except in the case of cleat-type lampholders, receptacles and rosettes which are located at least 8 feet above the floor. Lampholders, receptacles and switches which have exposed accessible terminals shall not be installed in metal fixture canopies or in open bases of portable table or floor lamps.

B. Provisions for Fixture Locations

410-4. Fixtures in Specific Locations.

(a)   Fixtures installed in damp or wet locations shall be approved for such locations and shall be so constructed or installed that water cannot enter or accumulate in wireways, lampholders or other electrical parts. All fixtures installed in wet locations shall be marked, "Suitable for Wet Locations." All fixtures installed in damp locations shall be marked, "Suitable for Wet Locations" or "Suitable for Damp Locations."

Installations underground or in concrete slabs or masonry in direct contact with the earth, and locations subject to saturation with water or other liquids, such as locations exposed to weather and unprotected, vehicle washing areas, and like locations, are considered to be wet locations with respect to the above requirement.

Interior locations protected from weather but subject to moderate degrees of moisture, such as some basements, some barns, some cold storage warehouses and the like, and partially protected locations under canopies, marquees, roofed open porches, and the like, are considered to be damp locations with respect to the above requirement.

(b)   Fixtures installed in corrosive locations shall be of a type approved for such locations.

See Section 210-21(b) for receptacles in fixtures.

▶   An enclosed and gasketed fixture would fulfill the requirement that water shall be prevented from entering the fixture, though under some conditions water vapor might enter and a small amount of water might accumulate in the bottom of the globe.

Fixtures in the form of post lanterns, fixtures for use on service-station islands, and fixtures which are marked to indicate that they are intended for outdoor use have been investigated for outdoor installation.

An example of fixtures in "damp" locations would be those installed under canopies of stores in shopping centers where they would be protected against exposure to rain but would be subject to outside temperature variation and corresponding high humidity and condensation. Thus the internal parts of the fixture need to be of nonhygroscopic materials which will not absorb moisture and which will function under conditions of high humidity.

(c)   Fixtures in nonresidential occupancies shall not be installed in ducts or hoods used for removal of cooking smoke or grease-laden vapors or located in the path of travel of such exhaust products unless specifically approved for such use.

Fixtures in nonresidential occupancies having approved metallic enclosures mounted on the outer surface of the hood and separated from exhaust products by tight fitting glass may be used. Fixtures on hoods in nonresidential occupancies shall not be located in concealed spaces unless part of an approved grease extractor.

▶   This requirement has been taken from NFPA No. 96—Vapor Removal from Commercial Equipment. It is extremely important that lighting fixtures on hoods be located out of the path of travel of exhaust products (smoke or grease-laden vapors), unless the entire hood assembly including fixtures have been tested and approved for such applications.

The use of enclosed-and-gasketed fixtures, unless located out of the path of travel of exhaust products, is not acceptable because a fire could result from high temperatures of lamps within an enclosed glass bowl coated with grease on the outer surface. In addition, grease can cause shorts or grounds in wiring within such areas.

410-5. Fixtures near Combustible Material.   Fixtures shall be so constructed, or installed, or equipped with shades or guards that combustible material will not be subjected to temperatures in excess of 90° C (194° F).

410-6. Fixtures over Combustible Material.   Lampholders installed over highly combustible material shall be of the unswitched type and unless an individual switch is provided for each fixture, shall be located at least 8 feet above the floor, or shall be otherwise so located or guarded that the lamps cannot be readily removed or damaged.

▶   This refers to pendants and fixed lighting equipment, not to portable lamps. Where the lamp cannot be located out of reach, the requirement can be met by equipping the lamp with a guard.

410-7. Fixtures in Show Windows.   Externally wired fixtures shall not be used in a show window.

Exception: Fixtures of the chain-supported type may be externally wired.

410-8. Fixtures in Clothes Closets.

(a)   A fixture in a clothes closet shall be installed:

(1)   On the wall above the closet door, provided the clearance between the fixture and a storage area where combustible material may be stored within the closet is not less than 18 inches, or

(2)   On the ceiling over an area which is unobstructed to the floor, maintaining an 18-inch clearance horizontally between the fixture and a storage area where combustible material may be stored within the closet.

NOTE: A flush recessed fixture equipped with a solid lens is considered to be outside the closet area.

(b)   Pendants shall not be installed in clothes closets.

▶   The intent is to prevent lamps from coming in contact with cartons or boxes stored on shelves and clothing hung in the closet, which would, of course, constitute a fire hazard.

It is quite obvious from the drawing in Fig. 410-1 that fixtures other than flush recessed types with solid lens cannot be located in *small* clothes closets that seem to prevail in building construction these days.

These requirements apply to incandescent and fluorescent lighting and all types of occupancies.

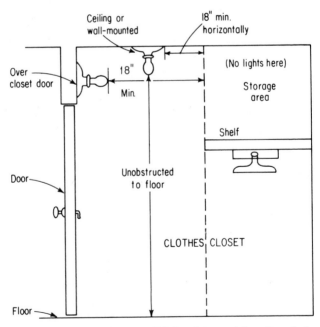

FIG. 410-1. Requirements for lighting fixtures (other than flush recessed types with a solid lens) in clothes closets.

For small clothes closets proper lighting may be achieved by locating fixtures on the outside ceiling in front of the closet door—especially in hallways where such fixtures can serve a dual function. Flush recessed fixtures with a solid lens are considered outside of the closet because the lamp is recessed behind the wall or ceiling line.

410-9. Space for Cove Lighting. Coves shall have adequate space and shall be so located that lamps and equipment can be properly installed and maintained.

▶   Adequate space also improves ventilation, which is equally important for such equipment.

C. Provisions at Fixture Outlet Boxes, Canopies and Pans

410-10. Space for Conductors. Canopies and outlet boxes taken together shall provide adequate space so that fixture conductors and their connecting devices may be properly installed.

410-11. Temperature Limit of Conductors in Outlet Boxes. Fixtures shall be of such construction or so installed that the conductors in outlet boxes shall not be subjected to temperatures greater than that for which the conductors are approved.

Branch circuit wiring shall not be passed through an outlet box that is an integral part of an incandescent fixture unless the fixture is approved for the purpose.

▶   Fixtures equipped with incandescent lamps may cause the temperature in the outlet boxes to become excessively high. The remedy is to use fixtures of improved design, or in some special cases to use circuit conductors having insulation that will withstand the high temperature.

The second paragraph applies mainly to "prewired" recessed incandescent fixtures which have been designed to permit 60°C supply conductors in a junction box equipped with the fixture. Some of these fixtures have been listed by Underwriters' Laboratories, Inc., only on the basis of the heat contribution by the supply conductors at not more than the maximum permitted lamp load of the fixture (see Fig. 410-2).

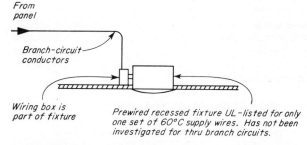

Fig. 410-2. Fixture with attached junction box suitable for terminating branch-circuit conductors only.

Other fixtures have been investigated and listed for "feed through" circuit wiring (see Fig. 410-3).

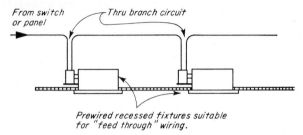

Fig. 410-3. Fixtures with attached junction boxes suitable for "feeding through."

The following paragraph is an excerpt from the Underwriters' Laboratories, Inc., Electrical Construction Materials List (1971).

"With the exception of fluorescent lamp fixtures, recessed fixtures are marked with the required minimum temperature rating of wiring supplying the fixture. This marking does not allow for any heat contributed by a single branch circuit supplying and passing through the fixture enclosure or through a splice compartment (outlet box or otherwise) that is part of the fixture construction. A higher-temperature-rated insulation than that indicated on the fixture may be required for such branch-circuit conductors. Recessed incandescent fixture constructions which have been investigated for use with through branch circuits other than that supplying the fixture are marked to indicate the maximum number and size, and minimum temperature rating of the branch-circuit conductors with which they have been tested."

410-12. Outlet Boxes to be Covered.   In a completed installation, each outlet box shall be provided with a cover unless covered by means of a fixture canopy, lampholder, receptacle, rosette, or similar device.

▶   The canopy may serve as the box cover, but if the ceiling or wall finish is of combustible material, the canopy and box must form a complete enclosure. The chief purpose of this is to require that no open space be left between the canopy and the edge of the box where the finish is wood or fibrous or any similar material. Where the wall or ceiling finish is plaster the requirement does not apply, since plaster is not classed as a combustible material; however, the plaster must be continuous up to the box, leaving no openings around the box.

410-13. Covering of Combustible Material at Outlet Boxes.   Any combustible wall or ceiling finish exposed between the edge of a fixture canopy or pan and an outlet box shall be covered with noncombustible material.

▶   See comment following Section 410-12.

410-14. Connection of Electric Discharge Lighting Fixtures. Electric discharge lighting fixtures when supported independently of the outlet box shall be connected through metal raceways, metal-clad cable or nonmetallic sheathed cable. Cord-equipped fixtures may be suspended directly below the outlet box, provided that the cord is continuously visible for its entire length outside the fixture and is not subject to strain or physical damage. Such cord-equipped fixtures shall terminate at the outer end of the cord in a grounding-type attachment plug (cap) or busway plug.

Electric-discharge lighting fixtures provided with mogul-base screw-shell lampholders may be connected to branch circuits of 50 amperes or less by cords complying with Exception No. 2 of Section 240-5(a). Receptacles and caps may be of lower ampere rating but not less than 125 per cent of the fixture full-load current.

Fixtures may be connected in accordance with Section 364-11.

▶ This permits the fixtures to be connected by means of cords only when such cords are not used as the supporting means, and when the fixture is suspended directly below the outlet boxes supplying such fixtures. Cord-connected fixtures are not permitted in lift-out-type ceilings. The second paragraph recognizes smaller receptacle ratings for certain types of mercury vapor or metal halide fixtures.

D. Fixture Supports

410-15. Supports—General. Fixtures, lampholders, rosettes and receptacles shall be securely supported. A fixture which weighs more than 6 pounds or exceeds 16 inches in any dimension shall not be supported by the screw shell of a lampholder.

410-16. Means of Support. Where the outlet box or fitting will provide adequate support, a fixture shall be attached thereto; otherwise a fixture shall be supported as required by Section 370-13. A fixture which weighs more than 50 pounds shall be supported independently of the outlet box.

▶ The most common method of supporting fixtures is by means of fixture bars or straps bolted to the outlet boxes, as shown in Fig. 410-4. A fixture weighing over 50 lb can be supported on a hanger such as is shown in Fig. 370-6. Care should be taken to see that the pipe used in the construction of the hanger is of such size that the threads will have ample strength to support the weight.

E. Wiring of Fixtures

410-17. Fixture Wiring—General. Wiring on or within fixtures shall be neatly arranged and shall not be exposed to physical damage. Excess wiring shall be avoided. Conductors shall be so arranged that they shall not be subjected to temperatures above those for which they are approved.

410-18. Conductor Size. Fixture conductors shall not be smaller than No. 18 AWG.

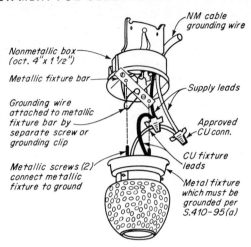

NM cable grounding wire

Nonmetallic box (oct. 4"x 1½")

Metallic fixture bar

Grounding wire attached to metallic fixture bar by separate screw or grounding clip

Supply leads

Approved CU conn.

CU fixture leads

Metallic screws (2) connect metallic fixture to ground

Metal fixture which must be grounded per S.410-95(a)

Fig. 410-4. Fixture and outlet box.

410-19. Conductor Insulation.

(a) Fixtures shall be wired with conductors having insulation suitable for the current, voltage, and temperature to which the conductors will be subjected.

(b) Where fixtures are installed in damp, wet, or corrosive locations, conductors shall be of a type approved for such locations.

(c) For ampacity of fixture wire, see Table 402-4.

(d) For maximum operating temperature and voltage limitation of fixture wires, see Section 310-2.

410-20. Conductors for Certain Conditions.

(a) Fixtures provided with mogul-base screw-shell lampholders and operating at not more than 300 volts between conductors shall be wired with Type AF, SF-1, SF-2, SFF-1, SFF-2, PF, PGF, PFF, PGFF, PTF or PTFF fixture wire.

(b) Fixtures provided with other than mogul-base screw-shell lampholders and operating at not more than 300 volts between conductors shall be wired with Type AF, SF-1, SF-2, PF, PGF, PFF, PGFF, PTF or PTFF fixture wire or Type AFC or AFPD flexible cord.

Exception No. 1: Where temperatures do not exceed 90°C (194°F), Type CF, TFN and TFFN fixture wire or Type CFPD, flexible cord may be used.

Exception No. 2: Where temperatures exceed 60°C (140°F) but are not higher than 75°C (167°F) Type RH and RHW rubber-covered wire, Type RFH-1, RFH-2, FFH-1, and FFH-2 fixture wires may be used.

Exception No. 3: Where temperatures do not exceed 60°C (140°F), Type T thermoplastic wire, Types TF and TFF fixture wire, and Types RF-1, RF-2, FF-1, FF-2 fixture wires may be used, including use in fixtures of decorative type on which lamps of not over 60-watt rating are used in connection with imitation candles.

See Table 402-6 and Section 310-2 for fixture wires and conductors; also, Table 400-9(b) for flexible cords.

410-21. Conductors for Movable Parts.

(a) Stranded conductors shall be used for wiring on fixture chains and on other movable or flexible parts.

(b) Conductors shall be so arranged that the weight of the fixture or movable parts will not put a tension on the conductors.

410-22. Pendant Conductors for Incandescent Filament Lamps.

(a) Pendant lampholders with permanently attached leads, where used in other than festoon wiring, shall be hung from separate stranded rubber-covered conductors which are soldered directly to the circuit conductors but supported independently thereof.

(b) Such pendant conductors shall be not smaller than No. 14 AWG for heavy-duty or medium-base screw-shell lampholders, nor, except for approved Christmas tree and decorative lighting outfits, smaller than No. 18 AWG for intermediate or candelabra-base lampholders.

(c) Pendant conductors longer than 3 feet shall be twisted together where not cabled in an approved assembly.

410-23. Protection of Conductors and Insulation.

(a) Conductors shall be secured in a manner that will not tend to cut or abrade the insulation.

(b) Conductor insulation shall be protected from abrasion where it passes through metal.

(c) Individual showcases, other than fixed, may be connected by flexible cord to permanently installed receptacles, and groups of not more than six such showcases may be coupled together by flexible cord and separable locking-type connectors with one of the group connected by flexible cord to a permanently installed receptacle.

The installation shall comply with the following requirements:

(1) Flexible cord shall be hard-service type, having conductors not smaller than the branch circuit conductors, having ampacity at least equal to the branch circuit overcurrent device, and having an equipment grounding conductor. See Table 250-95.

(2) Receptacles, connectors and plugs (caps) shall be of an approved grounding type rated 15 or 20 amperes.

(3) Flexible cords shall be secured to the undersides of showcases so that:

(a) Wiring will not be exposed to mechanical damage.

(b) Will allow a separation between cases not in excess of two inches, nor more than 12 inches between the first case and the supply receptacle.

(c) The free lead at the end of a group of showcases will have a female fitting not extending beyond the case.

(4) Equipment other than showcases shall not be electrically connected to showcases.

(5) Standpipes of floor receptacles shall allow floor cleaning equipment to be operated without damage to receptacles.

410-24. Conductor Protection at Lampholders. Where a metal lampholder is attached to a flexible cord, the inlet shall be equipped with an insulating bushing which, if threaded, shall not be smaller than nominal ⅜ inch pipe size. The cord hole shall be of a size appropriate for the cord and all burrs and fins removed in order to provide a smooth bearing surface for the cord.

Bushings having holes $\frac{9}{32}$ inch in diameter are suitable for use with plain pendant cord and holes $\frac{13}{32}$ inch in diameter with reinforced cord.

▶   Lampholders for cord pendants, if of the brass-shell type, should preferably have caps with insulating bushings permanently secured in place, or they may be of the nonmetallic type requiring no bushings.

410-25. Connections, Splices and Taps.

(a) Fixtures shall be so installed that the connections between the fixture conductors and the circuit conductors may be inspected without requiring the disconnection of any part of the wiring, unless the fixture is connected by means of a plug and receptacle.

(b) Splices and taps shall not be located within fixture arms or stems.

(c) No unnecessary splices or taps shall be made within or on a fixture.

(d) For approved means of making connections, see Section 110-14.

410-26. Fixture Raceways.
Fixtures shall not be used as a raceway for circuit conductors unless the fixtures meet the requirements for approved raceways, except that the conductors of the single branch circuit supplying the fixtures may be carried through as follows:

▶   Fixtures meeting the requirements for "approved raceways" are labeled by Underwriters' Laboratories as "Fixtures Suitable for Use as Raceways." A multiwire branch circuit (see definition in Art. 100) is considered as a "single-branch circuit" for the purposes of this Section.

Exception No. 1: An installation of fixtures approved for end-to-end assembly to form a continuous raceway, or

Exception No. 2: Fixtures which are connected together by approved wiring methods.

Branch circuit conductors within 3 inches of a ballast within the ballast compartment shall be recognized for use at temperatures not lower than 90°C (194°F), such as Types RHH, THHN, FEP, FEPB, SA, XHHW and AVA. See Table 310-2(a) for Type THW.

410-27. Polarization of Fixtures.
Fixtures shall be so wired that the screw shells of lampholders will be connected to the same fixture or circuit conductor or terminal. For polarity identification of conductors to screw shells of lampholders, see Section 200-8.

▶   This method of wiring fixtures is required in order to ensure that the screw shells of sockets will be connected to the grounded circuit wire. See Section 200-8.

F. Construction of Fixtures

410-28. Combustible Shades and Enclosures.
Adequate air space shall be provided between lamps and shades or other enclosures of combustible material.

410-29. Fixture Rating.

(a) All fixtures requiring ballasts or transformers shall be plainly marked with their electrical rating and the manufacturer's name, trademark or other suitable means of identification.

(b) The electrical rating shall include the voltage and frequency, and shall indicate the current rating of the unit including the ballast, transformer or auto-transformer.

410-30. Design and Material. Fixtures shall be constructed of metal, wood, or other approved material and shall be so designed and assembled as to secure requisite mechanical strength and rigidity. Wireways, including the entrances thereto, shall be such that conductors may be drawn in and withdrawn without injury.

410-31. Nonmetallic Fixtures. In all fixtures not made entirely of metal, wireways shall be lined with metal or approved noncombustible materials unless approved armored or lead-covered conductors with suitable fittings are used.

410-32. Mechanical Strength.

(a) Tubing used for arms and stems where provided with cut threads shall be not less than 0.040 inch in thickness and when provided with rolled (pressed) threads shall be not less than 0.025 inch in thickness. Arms and other parts shall be fastened to prevent turning.

(b) Metal canopies supporting lampholders, shades, etc., exceeding 8 lbs., or incorporating attachment plug receptacles, shall be not less than 0.020 inch in thickness. Other canopies shall be not less than 0.016 inch when made of steel and not less than 0.020 inch when of other metals.

(c) Pull type canopy switches shall not be inserted in the rims of metal canopies which are less than 0.025 inch in thickness unless the rims are reinforced by the turning of a bead or the equivalent. Pull type canopy switches, whether mounted in the rims or elsewhere in sheet metal canopies, shall be located not more than 3½ inches from the center of the canopy. Double set screws, double canopy rings, a screw ring, or equal method shall be used where the canopy supports a pull type switch or pendant receptacle.

The above thickness requirements apply to measurements made on finished (formed) canopies.

410-33. Wiring Space. Bodies of fixtures, including portable lamps, shall provide ample space for splices and taps and for the installation of devices, if any. Splice compartments shall be of nonabsorptive, noncombustible material.

410-34. Fixture Studs. Fixture studs which are not parts of outlet boxes, hickeys, tripods, and crowfeet shall be made of steel, malleable iron, or other approved material.

410-35. Insulating Joints. Insulating joints shall be composed of materials especially approved for the purpose. Those which are not designed to be mounted with screws or bolts shall have a substantial exterior metal casing, insulated from both screw connections.

410-36. Portable Lamps. Portable table and floor lamps and fan motors on ceiling fixtures may be wired with approved rubber-covered conductors, provided the wiring is not located so as to be subject to undue heating from lamps.

410-37. Portable Handlamps. Handlamps of the portable type supplied through flexible cords shall be of the molded composition or other type approved for the purpose. Metal-shell paper-lined lampholders shall not be used. Handlamps shall be equipped with a handle. Where subject to physical damage or where lamps may come in contact with combustible material, handlamps shall be equipped with a substantial guard attached to the lampholder or the handle.

For garages, see Section 511-6.

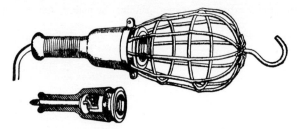

Fɪɢ. 410-5. Guard with handle and socket for portable lamp. (*McGill Manufacturing Co.*)

410-38. Cord Bushings.   A bushing or the equivalent shall be provided where flexible cord enters the base or stem of a portable lamp. The bushing shall be of insulating material unless a jacketed type of cord is used.

410-39. Tests.   All wiring shall be free from short-circuits and grounds, and shall be tested for these defects prior to being connected to the circuit.

410-40. Live Parts.   Exposed live parts within porcelain fixtures shall be suitably recessed and so located as to make it improbable that wires will come in contact with them. There shall be a spacing of at least ½ inch between live parts and the mounting plane of the fixture.

G. Installation of Lampholders

410-41. Screw-Shell Type.   Lampholders of the screw-shell type shall be installed for use as lampholders only.

▶   This warns against the previously common practice of installing screw-shell lampholders with screw-plug adapters in baseboards and walls for the connecting of cord-connected appliances and lighting equipment and thereby exposing live parts to contact by persons when the adapters were moved from place to place. See Section **410-52a.**

410-42. Double-Pole Switched Lampholders.   Where used on unidentified 2-wire circuits tapped from the ungrounded conductors of multiwire circuits, the switching device of lampholders of the switched type shall simultaneously disconnect both conductors of the circuit. See Section 200-5.

▶   On a circuit having one wire grounded, the grounded wire must always be connected to the screw shell of the socket, and sockets having a single-pole switching mechanism may be used. (See Section **410-46.**) On a two-wire circuit tapped from the outside (ungrounded) wires of a three-wire or four-wire system, if sockets having switching mechanisms are used, these must be double-pole so that they will disconnect both of the ungrounded wires.

410-43. Lampholders in Damp or Wet Locations.   Lampholders installed in damp or wet locations shall be of the weatherproof type.

H. Construction of Lampholders

410-44. Insulation. The outer metal shell and the cap shall be lined with insulating material which shall prevent the shell and cap from becoming a part of the circuit. The lining shall not extend beyond the metal shell more than ⅛ inch, but shall prevent any current-carrying part of the lamp base from being exposed when a lamp is in the lampholding device.

410-45. Lead Wires. Lead wires, furnished as a part of weatherproof lampholders and intended to be exposed after installation, shall be of approved, stranded, rubber-covered conductors, not less than No. 14 AWG (No. 18 AWG for candelabra sockets), and shall be sealed in place or otherwise made raintight.

410-46. Switched Lampholders. Switched lampholders shall be of such construction that the switching mechanism interrupts the electrical connection to the center contact. The switching mechanism may also interrupt the electrical connection to the screw shell when connection to the center contact is simultaneously interrupted.

J. Lamps

410-49. Bases, Incandescent Lamps. An incandescent lamp for general use on lighting branch circuits shall not be equipped with a medium base when rated over 300 watts, nor with a mogul base when rated over 1,500 watts. Above 1,500 watts, special approved bases or other devices shall be used.

410-50. Enclosures, Mercury-Vapor Lamp Auxiliary Equipment. Resistors or regulators for mercury-vapor lamps shall be enclosed in noncombustible cases and treated as sources of heat.

410-51. Arc Lamps. Arc lamps used in theaters shall conform to Section 520-61, and arc lamps used in projection machines shall conform to Section 540-20. Arc lamps used on constant-current systems shall conform to the general requirements of Article 710.

K. Receptacles, Cord Connectors and Attachment Plugs (Caps)

410-52. Rating and Type.

(a) Receptacles installed for the attachment of portable cords shall be rated at not less than 15 amperes, 125 volts, or 10 amperes, 250 volts, and shall be of a type not suitable for use as lampholders.

(b) Metallic faceplates shall be of ferrous metal not less than 0.030 inch in thickness or of nonferrous metal not less than 0.040 inch in thickness. Faceplates of insulating material shall be noncombustible and not less than 0.10 inch in thickness but may be less than 0.10 inch in thickness if formed or reinforced to provide adequate mechanical strength.

(c) After installation, receptacle faces shall be flush with or project from faceplates of insulating material. Receptacle faces shall project a minimum of 0.015 inches from metal faceplates after installation. Faceplates shall be installed so as to seat against mounting surfaces. Boxes shall be installed in accordance with Section 370-10.

(d) All 15- and 20-ampere attachment plugs and connectors shall be so constructed that there are no exposed current-carrying parts except the prongs, blades or pins. The cover for wire terminations shall be mechanically secured, or an integral part of the attachment plug or connector.

▶   Section **410-52c**, concerning receptacle faces, is necessary to assure a solid backing for receptacles so that attachment plugs can be inserted without difficulty. The requirement for receptacle faces to project at least 0.015 inch from installed metal faceplates is to prevent faults caused by countless existing attachment plugs with exposed bare terminal screws. The new design requirements for attachment plugs and connectors in Section **410-52d** should prevent such faults at metal plates, but the problem of existing attachment plugs in this regard will be around for many years.

With receptacle faces and faceplates installed according to Section **410-52c**, attachment plugs can be fully inserted into receptacles and will provide a better contact. The cooperation of other crafts, such as plasterers or dry-wall applicators, will be required to satisfy the requirements of Section **410-52c**.

410-54. Receptacles in Damp or Wet Locations.

(a) **Damp Locations.**   A receptacle outlet installed outdoors in a location protected from the weather or in other damp locations shall have an enclosure for the receptacle which is weatherproof when the receptacle is covered (attachment plug cap not inserted and receptacle covers closed).

An installation suitable where exposed to wet locations is also suitable for damp locations.

A receptacle outlet may be considered to be in a location protected from the weather when located under roofed open porches, canopies, marquees, and the like, so as not to be subjected to a beating rain or water run-off.

(b) **Wet Locations.**   A receptacle installed outdoors where exposed to weather or in other wet locations shall be in a weatherproof enclosure, the integrity of which is not affected when the receptacle is in use (attachment plug cap inserted).

Exception: An enclosure which is weatherproof only when a self-closing receptacle cover is closed may be used for a receptacle installed outdoors where the receptacle is not likely to be used with other than portable tools or other portable equipment not usually left connected to the outlet indefinitely.

(c) **Flush Mounting with Faceplate.**   The enclosure for a receptacle installed in an outlet box flush-mounted on a wall surface may be weatherproof when a faceplate assembly for use in weatherproof installation is used and the connection between the plate and wall surface has been made watertight.

(d) **Installation Height.**   A receptacle outlet installed outdoors shall be located above the ground or floor such that water accumulation is not likely to touch the outlet cover or plate.

▶   In *damp* locations (Section **410-54a**) most existing receptacle covers with hinged covers or screw caps (see Fig. 410-6) for receptacle faces will suffice.

In *wet* locations (Section **410-54b**) receptacles with attachment plugs inserted must form a weatherproof connection. The exception permits outdoor receptacles to have *self-closing* receptacle covers to accommodate temporary uses of attachment plugs with portable tools and similar equip-

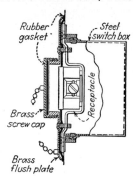

Fig. 410-6. Weatherproof receptacle suitable for installation in damp locations. (*Bryant Electric Co.*)

ment which are not intended or designed to be connected to the receptacle for other than short periods of time.

Section **410-54c** pertains to flush-mounted boxes in which receptacles are installed in wet locations, and Section **410-54d** requires an elevation of outdoor receptacles to prevent accumulation of water.

410-55. Grounding Type Receptacles, Adapters, Cord Connectors and Attachment Plugs.

(a) Receptacles, cord connectors and attachment plugs of the grounding type shall be provided with one fixed grounding member in addition to the circuit members.

Exception: The grounding contacting member of grounding type attachment plugs on the power supply cords of portable hand-held, hand-guided or hand-supported tools or appliances may be of the movable self-restoring type on circuits operating at not to exceed 150 volts between any two conductors nor 150 volts between any conductor and ground.

(b) Grounding type receptacles, adapters, cord connectors and attachment plugs shall have a means for connection of a grounding conductor to the grounding member. A terminal for connection to the grounding member shall be designated by:

(1) A hexagonal headed or shaped terminal screw or nut, not readily removable, and green colored; or

(2) A pressure wire connector which has a green colored body (a wire barrel); or

(3) A similar green-colored connection device in the case of adapters. The grounding terminal of a grounding adapter shall be a green-colored rigid ear, lug, or similar device. The grounding connection shall be so designed that it cannot make contact with current-carrying parts of the receptacle, adapter, or attachment plug. The adapter shall be polarized.

(4) If the terminal for the equipment grounding conductor is not visible, the conductor entrance hole shall be marked with the word "Green" or otherwise identified a distinctive green color.

▶   **Subparagraph 3 removes the recognition of adapters with pigtail grounding leads.**

(c)   In no case shall a grounding terminal or grounding type device be used for purposes other than grounding.

(d)   Grounding type attachment plugs and mating cord connectors and receptacles shall be so designed that the grounding connection is made before the current-carrying connections. Grounding type devices shall be designed so grounding members of attachment plugs cannot be brought into contact with current-carrying parts of receptacles or cord connectors.

▶   See Fig. 250-9.

L. Rosettes

410-57. Approved Types.
(a)   Fusible rosettes shall not be installed.

(b)   Separable rosettes which make possible a change in polarity shall not be used.

410-58. Rosettes in Damp or Wet Locations.   Rosettes installed in damp or wet locations shall be of the weatherproof type.

410-59. Rating.   Rosettes shall be rated at 660 watts, 250 volts, with a maximum current rating of 6 amperes.

410-60. Rosettes for Exposed Wiring.   When designed for use with exposed wiring, rosettes shall be provided with bases which shall have at least two holes for supporting screws, shall be high enough to keep the wires and terminals at least $\frac{1}{2}$ inch from the surface wired over, and shall have a porcelain lug under each terminal to prevent the rosette being placed over projections which would reduce the separation to less than $\frac{1}{2}$ inch.

410-61. Rosettes for Use with Boxes or Raceways.   When designed for use with conduit boxes or wire raceways, rosette bases shall be high enough to keep wires and terminals at least $\frac{3}{8}$ inch from the surface wired over.

M. Special Provisions for Flush and Recessed Fixtures

410-62. Approved Type.   Fixtures which are installed in recessed cavities in walls or ceilings shall be of an approved type and shall conform to Sections 410-63 through 410-70.

410-63. Temperature.
(a)   Fixtures shall be so constructed or installed that adjacent combustible material will not be subjected to temperatures in excess of 90°C (194°F).

(b)   Where a fixture is recessed in fire-resistant material in a building of fire-resistant construction, a temperature higher than 90°C (194°F), but not higher than 150°C (302°F) is acceptable if the fixture is plainly marked that it is approved for that service.

410-64. Clearance.   Recessed portions of enclosures, other than at points of support, shall be spaced at least $\frac{1}{2}$ inch from combustible material and thermal insulation.

410-65. Wiring.
(a)   Conductors having insulation suitable for the temperature encountered shall be used.

(b) Fixtures having branch circuit terminal connections which operate at temperatures higher than 60°C (140°F) shall have circuit conductors as described in Sections 410-65(b-1 and b-2):

(1) Branch circuit conductors having an insulation suitable for the temperature encountered may be run directly to the fixture.

(2) Tap connection conductors having an insulation suitable for the temperature encountered shall be run from the fixture terminal connection to an outlet box placed at least one foot from the fixture. Such a tap shall be in a suitable metal raceway which shall extend for at least four feet but not more than six feet.

▶ Recessed fixtures are, in all cases, marked with the required minimum-temperature rating of wiring supplying the fixture. This marking does not allow for any heat contributed by a branch circuit passing through the fixture enclosure or through a splice compartment (outlet box or otherwise) that is part of the fixture construction. An insulation with a temperature rating higher than that indicated on the fixture may be required for such branch-circuit conductors. See Section **410-11**.

The requirements given in Section **410-65**b **(2)** are special provisions that apply to recessed fixtures and take precedence over the general requirements. This means that the tap conductors (usually in flexible conduit) connecting an unwired recessed fixture to the outlet box must be in metal raceway of at least 4 ft in length and not over 6 ft. The box is required to be at least 1 ft away from the fixture and the flexible conduit may be looped to use up the excess length (see Section **350-4**, Exception **3**). This rule does not apply to "prewired" fixtures designed for connection to 60°C supply wires.

The purpose of this requirement is to allow the heat to dissipate so that heat from the fixture will not cause an excessive temperature in the outlet box and thus overheat the branch-circuit conductors which could be of the general-use type limited to 60°C or 75°C temperatures.

N. Construction, Flush and Recessed Fixtures

410-66. Temperature. Fixtures shall be so constructed that adjacent combustible material will not be subject to temperatures in excess of 90°C (194°F).

410-67. Enclosure. Sheet metal enclosures shall be protected against corrosion and shall not be less than No. 22 MSG.

Exception: Where a wireway cover is within the No. 22 MSG enclosure, it may be of No. 24 MSG metal.

410-68. Lamp Wattage Marking. Incandescent lamp fixtures shall be marked to indicate the maximum allowable wattage of lamps. The markings shall be permanently installed, in letters at least ¼ inch high, and located where visible during relamping.

410-69. Solder Prohibited. No solder shall be used in the construction of the fixture box.

410-70. Lampholders. Lampholders of the screw-shell type shall be of porcelain unless specially approved for the purpose. Cements, where used, shall be of the high-heat type.

P. Special Provisions for Electric Discharge Lighting Systems of 1,000 Volts or Less

410-71. General.

(a) Equipment for use with electric discharge lighting systems and designed for an open-circuit voltage of 1,000 volts or less shall be of a type approved for such service.

(b) The terminals of an electric discharge lamp shall be considered as alive where any lamp terminal is connected to a potential of more than 300 volts.

(c) Transformers of the oil-filled type shall not be used.

(d) In addition to complying with the general requirements for lighting fixtures, such equipment shall conform to Part P of this Article.

(e) Integral ballast protection shall be provided for fluorescent fixtures installed indoors.

Exception: Fluorescent fixtures when they employ simple reactance ballasts.

▶ Paragraph *e* pertains only to fluorescent lamp ballasts used indoors. The protection called for must be a part of the ballast. Underwriters' Laboratories, Inc., has made an extensive investigation of various types of protective devices for use within such ballasts, and ballasts found to meet U/L requirements for these applications are listed and marked as "Class P." The protective devices are thermal trip devices or thermal fuses, which are responsive to abnormal heat developed within the ballast because of a fault in components such as autotransformers, capacitors, reactors, etc.

Simple reactance-type ballasts are equipped with two leads only, and are connected as shown in Fig. 410-7. These series reactors are used with preheat-type fluorescent lamp circuits for lamps rated less than 30 watts. Also, a manual (momentary-contact) or automatic-type starter is used to start the lamp. The simple reactor-type ballast supplies one lamp only, has no autotransformer or capacitor, and can be readily identified by the presence of only two external leads.

Preheat lamps of 30 watts and larger use an autotransformer in series with one or more reactors in typical preheat circuits with auxiliary starting devices.

410-72. Direct-Current Equipment. Fixtures installed on direct-current circuits shall be equipped with auxiliary equipment and resistors especially designed and approved for direct-current operation and the fixtures shall be so marked.

410-73. Voltages—Dwelling Occupancies.

(a) Equipment having an open-circuit voltage of more than 1000 volts shall not be installed in dwelling occupancies.

(b) Equipment having an open-circuit voltage of more than 300 volts shall not be installed in dwelling occupancies unless such equipment is so designed that there shall be no exposed live parts when lamps are being inserted, are in place, or are being removed.

▶ Fixtures which are intended for use in other than dwelling occupancies are so marked. This usually indicates that the fixture has maintenance

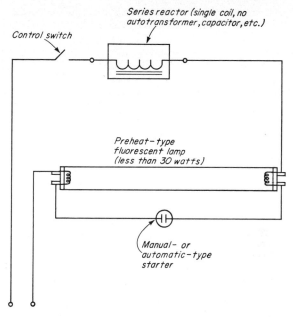

Fɪɢ. 410-7. A simple reactance-type ballast circuit.

features which are considered to be beyond the capabilities of the ordinary householder, or involves voltages in excess of those permitted by the National Electrical Code for dwelling occupancies.

410-74. Fixture Mounting.

(a) Exposed Ballasts. Fixtures having exposed ballasts or transformers shall be so installed that such ballasts or transformers shall not be in contact with combustible material.

(b) Combustible Low-Density Cellulose Fiberboard. Where a fixture containing a ballast is to be installed on combustible low-density cellulose fiberboard it shall, where surface mounted:

(1) Be approved for this condition, or

(2) Be spaced not less than 1½ inches from the surface of the fiberboard.

(3) Where such fixtures are partially or wholly recessed, the provisions of Sections 410-62 through 410-70 shall apply.

Combustible low-density cellulose fiberboard is considered to include sheets, panels and tiles which have a density of 20 pounds per cubic foot or less, and which are formed of bonded plant fiber material; but does not include solid or laminated wood, nor fiberboard which has a density in excess of 20 pounds per cubic foot or is an approved material which has been integrally treated with fire retarding chemicals to the degree that the flame spread in any plane of the material will not exceed twenty-five as determined by the method of NFPA No. 255-1969, ASTM Designation-1961 E-84 or U.L. No. 723-1968.

▶ Material meeting these requirements is listed in Underwriters' Laboratories, Inc., Building Materials List and in addition to other pertinent information includes the following: "This material has been found to comply with the flame spread requirements stipulated in Section 410-74 of the National Electrical Code as described therein."

Electric-discharge lamp fixtures which have been investigated for mounting directly on combustible low-density cellulose fiberboard ceilings are marked "Suitable for Surface Mounting on Combustible Low-Density Cellulose Fiberboard."

It should be noted that these fixtures have been investigated and found to operate within applicable temperature limits only with the ballast or ballasts specified by the marking in the fixture.

410-75. Auxiliary Equipment Not Integral with Fixture.

(a) Auxiliary equipment, including reactors, capacitors, resistors, and similar equipment, where not installed as part of a lighting fixture assembly shall be enclosed in accessible, permanently installed metal cabinets.

(b) Where display cases are not permanently installed, no portion of a secondary circuit may be included in more than a single case.

(c) Ballasts approved for separate mounting and for direct connection to an approved wiring system need not be separately enclosed.

410-76. Autotransformers. An autotransformer which is used as part of a ballast for supplying lighting units and which raises the voltage to more than 300 volts shall be supplied only by a grounded system.

410-77. Switches. Snap switches shall conform to Section 380-14.

Q. Special Provisions for Electric Discharge Lighting Systems of More Than 1,000 Volts

410-78. General.

(a) Equipment for use with electric discharge lighting systems and designed for an open-circuit voltage of more than 1,000 volts shall be of a type approved for such service.

(b) The terminal of an electric discharge lamp shall be considered as alive when any lamp terminal is connected to a potential of more than 300 volts.

(c) In addition to complying with the general requirements for lighting fixtures, such equipment shall conform to Sections 410-78 through 410-90.

For signs and outline lighting, see Article 600.

▶ These sections apply to interior neon-tube lighting, lighting with long fluorescent tubes requiring more than 1,000 volts, and cold-cathode fluorescent-lamp installations arranged to operate with several tubes in series.

410-79. Control.

(a) Fixtures or lamp installations shall be controlled either singly or in groups by an externally operable switch or circuit breaker which shall open all ungrounded primary conductors.

(b) The switch or circuit breaker shall be located within sight of the fixtures or lamps, or it may be located elsewhere if it is provided with means for locking in the open position.

▶   When any part of the equipment is being serviced, the primary circuit should be opened and the serviceman should have assurance that the disconnecting means will not be closed without his knowledge.

410-80. Lamp Terminals and Lampholders. Parts which must be removed for lamp replacement shall be hinged or fastened by an approved means. Lamps or lampholders or both shall be so designed that there shall be no exposed live parts when lamps are being inserted or are being removed.

410-81. Transformer Ratings. Transformers and ballasts shall have a secondary open-circuit voltage of not more than 15,000 volts with an allowance on test of 1,000 volts additional. The secondary current rating shall be not more than 120 milliamperes when the open circuit voltage is more than 7500 volts, and not more than 240 milliamperes when the open circuit voltage is 7500 volts or less.

410-82. Transformer Type. Transformers shall be of an approved enclosed type. Transformers of other than the askarel insulated or dry type shall not be used.

410-83. Transformer Secondary Connections.

  (a) The high-voltage windings of transformers shall not be connected in series or in parallel, except that for two transformers, each having one end of its high-voltage winding grounded and connected to the enclosure, the high-voltage windings may be connected in series to form the equivalent of a mid-point grounded transformer.

  (b) The grounded ends shall be connected by an insulated conductor not smaller than No. 14 AWG.

410-84. Transformer Locations.

  (a) Transformers shall be accessible after installation.

  (b) The transformers should be installed as near to the lamps as practicable to keep the secondary conductors as short as possible.

  (c) Transformers shall be so located that adjacent combustible materials will not be subjected to temperatures in excess of 90° C (194° F).

410-85. Transformer Loading. The lamps connected to any transformer shall be of such length and characteristics as not to cause a condition of continuous over-voltage on the transformer.

▶   See comments following Section 600-32.

410-86. Wiring Method. Secondary Conductors. Approved gas-tube sign cable suitable for the voltage of the circuit shall be used. For installation of conductors, see Section 600-31.

▶   This type of cable is not included in the table in Chap. 3 listing various types of insulated conductors, but Underwriters' Laboratories, Inc., have standards for such cables. The following information is an excerpt from the Underwriters' Laboratories, Inc., Electrical Construction Materials List:

    "Gas tube sign and ignition cable is classified as Type GTO-5 (5,000 volts), GTO-10 (10,000 volts), or GTO-15 (15,000 volts), and is labeled in sizes

Nos. 14, 12, and 10 Awg. This material is intended for use with gas tube signs, oil burners, and inside lighting.

"L-used as a suffix in combination with any of the preceding type letter designations indicates that an outer covering of lead has been applied.

Underwriters' Laboratories, Inc.
®
L I S T E D
GAS TUBE SIGN
AND IGNITION CABLE

"The label of Underwriters' Laboratories, Inc., (illustrated above) on the product is the only method provided by Underwriters' Laboratories, Inc., to identify Gas Tube Sign and Ignition Cable which has been produced under the Label Service."

410-87. Lamp Supports. Lamps shall be adequately supported as required in Section 600-33.

410-88. Exposure to Damage. Lamps shall not be located where normally exposed to physical damage.

410-89. Marking. Each fixture or each secondary circuit of tubing having an open-circuit voltage of more than 1,000 volts shall have a clearly legible marking in letters not less than ¼ inch high reading "Caution . . . . volts." The voltage indicated shall be the rated open-circuit voltage.

410-90. Switches. Snap switches shall conform to Section 380-14.

R. Grounding

410-91. General. Fixtures and lighting equipment shall be grounded as provided in Sections 410-92 through 410-96.

410-92. Metallic Wiring Systems. Metal fixtures directly wired, or attached to outlets wired with grounded metal raceways or grounded Type MI, AC, or ALS cable shall be grounded.

410-93. Nonmetallic Wiring Systems. Metal fixtures installed on outlets wired with knob-and-tube work, nonmetallic raceways, or nonmetallic sheathed cable, on circuits operating at 150 volts or less to ground, shall be grounded.

Exception: Fixtures and their outlet boxes mounted on electrically nonconducting ceilings or walls need not be grounded where located not less than 8 feet vertically or 5 feet horizontally from grounded surfaces. (See Section 410-95).

Fixtures made of insulating materials, and lampholders with shells of insulating material, are recommended for use with wiring systems that do not afford a ready means for grounding the exposed noncurrent-carrying parts of fixtures and lampholders.

410-94. Equipment of More Than 150 Volts to Ground.

(a) Metal fixtures, transformers and transformer enclosures on circuits operating at more than 150 volts to ground shall be grounded.

(b) Other exposed metal parts shall be grounded unless they are insulated from ground and other conducting surfaces and are inaccessible to unqualified persons, except that lamp tie wires, mounting screws, clips and decorative bands on glass lamps spaced not less than 1½ inches from lamp terminals need not be grounded.

410-95. Equipment Near Grounded Surfaces.

(a)　Ungrounded metal lighting fixtures, lampholders and faceplates shall not be installed in contact with conducting surfaces nor within 8 feet vertically or 5 feet horizontally of laundry tubs, bath tubs, shower baths, plumbing fixtures, steam pipes or other grounded metal work or grounded surfaces.

(b)　Metal pull chains used at these locations shall be provided with insulating links.

410-96. Methods of Grounding.　Equipment shall be considered as grounded where mechanically connected in a permanent and effective manner to metal raceway, the armor of Types AC, MI and ALS metal-clad cable, the grounding conductor in nonmetallic sheathed cable, or to a separate grounding conductor sized in accordance with Table 250-95, provided that the raceway, armor, or grounding conductor is grounded in a manner specified in Article 250.

ARTICLE 422. APPLIANCES

A. General

422-1. Scope.　This Article shall apply to electric appliances used in any occupancy. Equipment shall be of a type approved for the purpose and location where installed.

▶　　See definition for "Appliance," Art. 100.

　　For purposes of the Code, the definition for an appliance indicates that it is utilization equipment other than industrial and generally means small equipment such as may be used in a dwelling or office (clothes washer, clothes dryer, air conditioner, food mixer, coffee maker, etc.). See also definition for "Utilization Equipment" in Art. 100.

422-2. Live Parts.　Appliances shall have no live parts normally exposed to contact, except for toasters, grills or other appliances in which the current-carrying parts at high temperatures are necessarily exposed.

422-3. Other Articles.　All requirements of this Code shall apply when applicable. Appliances for use in hazardous locations shall be installed to conform to Articles 500 through 517.

　　The requirements of Article 430 apply to the installation of motor-operated appliances except as specifically amended in this Article.

B. Branch-Circuit Requirements

422-5. Branch-Circuit Sizing.　The provisions of this Section specify sizes of conductors capable of carrying appliance current without overheating under the conditions specified (see Article 210). They are not intended to apply to conductors which form an integral part of the appliance.

(a) The rating of an individual branch circuit shall not be less than the marked rating of the appliance or the marked rating of an appliance having combined loads (see Section 422-32).

Exception No. 1: For household cooking appliances, see Table 220-5.

Exception No. 2: For motor-operated appliances not having a marked rating the branch-circuit size shall be in accordance with Part B of Article 430.

Exception No. 3: Except as noted in Section 210-23(b), Exception No. 1, an appliance, other than a motor-operated appliance, which is continuously loaded, the branch-circuit rating shall not be less than 125 per cent of the marked rating.

(b) For branch circuits supplying appliance and other loads, the rating shall be determined in accordance with Section 210-24.

422-6. Branch-Circuit Overcurrent Protection. Branch circuits shall be protected in accordance with Section 240-5.

When there is a protective device rating marked on an appliance, the branch-circuit overcurrent device rating shall not exceed the protective device rating marked on the appliance.

C. Installation of Appliances

422-7. General. All appliances shall be installed in an approved manner.

422-8. Flexible Cords. Flexible cords used to connect appliances shall comply with the following:

(a) **Heater Cords Required.** All smoothing irons and portable electrically heated appliances rated at more than 50 watts and which produce temperatures in excess of 121°C (250°F) on surfaces with which the cord is liable to be in contact shall be provided with one of the types of approved heater cords listed in Table 400-11.

(b) **Other Heating Appliances.** All other portable electrically heated appliances shall be connected with one of the approved types of cord listed in Table 400-11, selected in accordance with the usage specified in that Table.

▶ Experience shows that more injury to the cord insulation is caused by heat conducted through the cord itself from the appliance or from poor contacts than by the cord coming in contact with the hot surface of the appliance. Where the cord is not subjected to excessive heat from either cause, the important consideration is to select a type of cord that will withstand the mechanical wear and tear.

(c) **Other Appliances.** Flexible cord may be used for: (1) connection of portable appliances; (2) connection of stationary appliances to facilitate their frequent interchange or prevention of the transmission of noise or vibration; or (3) facilitating the removal or disconnection of fixed appliances for maintenance or repair.

422-9. Portable Immersion Heaters. Electric heaters of the portable immersion type shall be so constructed and installed that current-carrying parts are effectively insulated from electrical contact with the substance in which immersed. The authority having jurisdiction may make exception of special applications of apparatus where suitable precautionary measures are followed.

422-10. Protection of Combustible Material. Each electrically heated appliance that is obviously intended by size, weight and service to be located in a fixed position shall be so placed as to provide ample protection between the appliance and adjacent combustible material.

422-11. Stands for Portable Appliances. Each smoothing iron and other portable electrically heated appliance which is intended to be applied to combustible material shall be equipped with an approved stand, which may be a separate piece of equipment or may be a part of the appliance.

422-12. Signals for Heated Appliances. In other than residence occupancies, each electrically heated appliance, or group of electrically heated appliances, intended to be applied to combustible material, shall be installed in connection with a signal unless the appliance is provided with an integral temperature-limiting device.

▶   The standard form of signal is a red light so connected that the lamp remains lighted as long as the appliance is connected to the circuit. No signal lamp is required if the appliance is equipped with a thermostatic switch which automatically opens the circuit after the appliance has been heated to a certain temperature.

422-13. Flatirons. Electrically heated smoothing irons intended for use in residences shall be equipped with approved temperature-limiting means.

422-14. Water Heaters—Storage and Instantaneous Types. Each storage- or instantaneous-type water heater shall be equipped with temperature-limiting means in addition to the control thermostat to disconnect all ungrounded conductors, and such means shall be: (1) installed to sense maximum water temperature; (2) trip-free, manually reset, or it shall use a replacement element. Such water heaters shall be marked to require the installation of a temperature and pressure relief valve. See ANSI Standard Z-21.22-1971.

Exception: Each water heater with supply water temperature of 180°F or above and capacity of 60 kw or above, and water heaters with a capacity of one gallon or less, approved for the purpose.

422-15. Infrared Lamp Industrial Heating Appliances.

(a) Infrared heating lamps rated at 300 watts or less may be used with lampholders of the medium-base unswitched porcelain type, or other types approved for the purpose.

(b) Screw-shell lampholders shall not be used with infrared lamps over 300 watts rating unless the lampholders are especially approved for the purpose.

(c) Lampholders may be connected to any of the branch circuits of Article 210 and, in industrial occupancies, may be operated in series on circuits of more than 150 volts to ground provided the voltage rating of the lampholders is not less than the circuit voltage.

Each section, panel or strip carrying a number of infrared lampholders (including the internal wiring of such section, panel or strip) is considered an appliance. The terminal connection block of each such assembly is deemed an individual outlet.

▶   So-called "infrared" lamps are tungsten-filament incandescent lamps, similar to lamps used for lighting, except that they are designed for operation with the filaments at a lower temperature, resulting, for a given wattage, in more heat radiation and less light output, also in a much longer lamp life.

Figure 422-1 is a view of an oven of medium size. The lampholders are

Fig. 422-1. Oven heated by infrared lamps.

mounted on panels which are hinged so that they can be swung out for inspection and relamping. The lampholders are so placed that the axis of each lamp is at an angle of about 45 deg from the surface of the panel, the object of this being to ensure that all sides of an object passing through the oven will receive a uniform amount of heat radiation.

422-16. Grounding.   Metal frames of portable, stationary and fixed electrically heated appliances, operating on circuits above 150 volts to ground, shall be grounded in the manner specified in Article 250; provided, however, that where this is impracticable, grounding may be omitted by special permission, in which case the frames shall be permanently and effectively insulated from the ground.

Refrigerators, freezers and air conditioners shall comply with the requirements of Sections 250-42, 250-43 and 250-45.

It is recommended that the frames be grounded in all cases. For methods of grounding frames of electric ranges and clothes dryers, see Sections 250-57 and 250-60.

422-17. Wall-Mounted Ovens and Counter-Mounted Cooking Units.

(a) Wall-mounted ovens and counter-mounted cooking units complete with provisions for mounting and for making electrical connections shall be considered as fixed appliances.

(b) A separable connector or a plug and receptacle combination in the supply line to an oven or cooking unit used only for ease in servicing or for installation shall:

(1) Not be installed as the disconnecting means required by Section 422-20;

(2) Be approved for the temperature of the space in which it is located.

422-18. Other Installation Methods. Appliances employing methods of installation other than covered by this Article may be used only by special permission.

D. Control and Protection of Appliances

422-20. Disconnecting Means. Means shall be provided to disconnect each appliance from all ungrounded conductors as required by the following Sections of Part D. Where an appliance is supplied by more than one source the disconnecting means shall be grouped and identified.

422-21. Disconnection of Fixed Appliances.

(a) For fixed appliances rated at not over 300 volt amperes or ⅛ hp. the branch circuit overcurrent device may serve as the disconnecting means.

(b) For fixed appliances of greater rating the branch-circuit switch or circuit breaker may, where readily accessible to the user of the appliance, serve as the disconnecting means.

422-22. Disconnection of Portable Appliances.

(a) For portable appliances a separable connector or an attachment plug and receptacle may serve as the disconnecting means.

(b) The rating of a receptacle or of a separable connector shall not be less than the rating of any appliance connected thereto, except that demand factors authorized elsewhere in this Code may be applied.

(c) Attachment plugs and connectors shall conform to the following:

(1) Live Parts. They shall be so constructed and installed as to guard against inadvertent contact with live parts.

(2) Interrupting Capacity. They shall be capable of interrupting their rated current without hazard to the operator.

(3) Interchangeability. They shall be so designed that they will not fit into receptacles of lesser rating.

422-23. Disconnection of Stationary Appliances.

(a) For stationary appliances rated at not over 300 volt amperes or ⅛ horsepower, the branch-circuit overcurrent device may serve as the disconnecting means.

(b) For stationary appliances of greater rating the branch-circuit switch or circuit breaker may, where readily accessible to the user of the appliance, serve as the disconnecting means.

(c) For cord-connected appliances such as free-standing household-type ranges and clothes dryers, a separable connector or an attachment plug and receptacle may serve as the disconnecting means. Attachment plugs and connectors shall conform to Section 422-22(c).

For household electric ranges, a plug and receptacle connection at the rear base of a range, if it is accessible from the front by removal of a drawer, is considered as meeting the intent of this rule.

▶   Examples of the application of this section for disconnecting means for appliances are found in the installation of household electric ranges and clothes dryers. The purpose of these requirements is to provide that for every such appliance there will be some means for opening the circuit to the appliance when it is to be serviced or repaired or when it is to be removed.

422-24. Unit Switches as Disconnecting Means.   Unit switches which are a part of an appliance shall not be considered as taking the place of the disconnecting means required by Part D (Control and Protection of Appliances) of this Article, unless there are other means for disconnection as follows:

(a) Multi-Family Dwellings.   In multi-family (more than two) dwellings, the disconnecting means shall be within the apartment, or on the same floor as the apartment in which the appliance is installed, and may control lamps and other appliances.

(b) Two-Family Dwellings.   In two-family dwellings, the disconnecting means may be outside the apartment in which the appliance is installed. This will permit an individual switch for the apartment to be used.

(c) Single-Family Dwellings.   In single-family dwellings, the service disconnecting means may be used.

(d) Other Occupancies.   In other occupancies, the branch-circuit switch or circuit breaker, where readily accessible to the user of the appliance, may be used for this purpose.

422-25. Switch and Circuit Breaker to Be Indicating.   Switches and circuit breakers used as disconnecting means shall be of the indicating type.

422-26. Disconnecting Means for Motor-Driven Appliances.   When a switch or circuit breaker serves as the disconnecting means for a stationary or fixed motor-driven appliance of more than $\frac{1}{8}$ horsepower, it shall be located within sight of the motor controller and shall comply with Part H of Article 430.

422-27. Overcurrent Protection.

(a)   Appliances shall be considered as protected against overcurrent when supplied by branch circuits as specified in Sections 422-5, 422-6 and (e) below.

Exception: Motors of motor-operated appliances shall be provided with overload protection in accordance with Part C of Article 430. Sealed (hermetic-type) motor-compressors in air conditioning or refrigerating equipment shall be provided with overload protection in accordance with Part F of Article 440. When appliance overcurrent protective devices separate from the appliance are required, data for selection of these devices shall be marked on the appliance. The minimum marking shall be that specified in Sections 430-7 and 440-3.

(b)   A household type appliance with surface heating elements and which has a maximum demand of more than 60 amperes as calculated in accordance with Table 220-5 shall have its power supply subdivided into two or more circuits each of which is provided with overcurrent protection rated at not more than 50 amperes.

(c)   Infrared lamp heating appliances shall have overcurrent protection not exceeding 50 amperes.

(d) Open-coil or exposed sheathed-coil types of surface heating elements in commercial-type heating appliances shall be protected by overcurrent protective devices which are rated at not more than 50 amperes.

(e) When the branch circuit supplies a single nonmotor-operated appliance, rated at 10 amperes or more, the overcurrent device rating shall not exceed 150 per cent of the appliance rating.

E. Marking of Appliances

422-30. Nameplate.

(a) Each electric appliance shall be provided with a nameplate, giving the identifying name and the rating in volts and amperes, or in volts and watts. When the appliance is to be used on a specific frequency or frequencies, it shall be so marked.

Where motor overload protection external to the appliance is required, the appliance shall be so marked. See Section 422-27(a) Exception.

(b) This marking shall be located so as to be visible or easily accessible after installation.

422-31. Marking of Heating Elements.
All heating elements rated more than one ampere which are replaceable in the field and which are a part of an appliance shall be legibly marked with the ratings in volts and amperes, or in volts and watts, or the manufacturer's part number.

422-32. Appliances Consisting of Motors and Other Loads.
Appliances shall be marked in accordance with Section 422-32(a) or (b).

(a) In addition to the marking required in Section 422-30, the marking on an appliance consisting of a motor with other load(s) or motors with or without other load(s) shall specify the minimum circuit size and the maximum rating of the circuit overcurrent protective device.

Exception No. 1: Portable appliances and other appliances, factory-equipped with cords and caps, complying with Section 422-30.

Exception No. 2: An appliance where both the minimum circuit size and maximum rating of the circuit overcurrent protective device are not more than 15 amperes and complies with Section 422-30.

(b) An alternate marking method may specify the rating of the largest motor in volts and amperes, and the additional load(s) in volts and amperes, or volts and watts in addition to the marking required in Section 422-30.

Exception No. 1: Portable appliances and other appliances, factory-equipped with cords and caps, complying with Section 422-30.

Exception No. 2: The current value of a motor ⅛ hp or less, or a nonmotor load one ampere or less may be omitted unless such loads constitute the principal load.

F. Provisions for Room Air-conditioning Units

422-40. General.
The provisions of Sections 422-41 through 44 shall apply to electrically energized room air-conditioning units which control temperature and humidity. For the purpose of these Sections a room air conditioner is an alternating-current, hermetic-type, air-cooled, window console or in-wall air-conditioner which is installed in the conditioned room. These Sections cover equip-

ment rated not greater than 250 volts, single phase, and such equipment may be cord- and plug-connected. These Sections also apply to such an air conditioner if it has provisions for heating.

Room air conditioners rated at 3-phase or above 250 volts shall be directly connected to a wiring method recognized in Chapter 3. See Part H of Article 430 for disconnecting means.

422-41. Grounding. See Sections 250-42, 43, and 45.

422-42. Branch Circuit Requirements.

(a) The total marked rating of motor-operated air-conditioning equipment shall not exceed 80 per cent of the rating of a branch circuit which supplies no other load.

(b) The total marked rating of air-conditioning equipment shall not exceed 50 per cent of the rating of a branch circuit where lighting units or other appliances are also supplied.

(c) The nameplate marking of a room air conditioner shall be used in determining the branch-circuit requirements, and each unit shall be considered as a single motor unit unless the nameplate is otherwise marked. When marked to indicate two or more motors, see Article 440.

422-43. Disconnecting Means. An attachment plug and receptacle may serve as the disconnecting means for a single-phase room air-conditioning unit, rated 250 volts or less when:

(1)   The manual controls on the air-conditioning units are readily accessible and located within 6 feet of the floor; or

(2)   An approved manually operable switch is installed in a readily accessible location within sight of the air-conditioning unit.

▶   This section indicates the conditions under which an attachment plug and receptacle may serve as a disconnecting means for air-conditioning units.

422-44. Supply Cords. Where flexible cords are used to supply air-conditioning equipment the length of such cords shall not exceed: (1) 10 feet for nominal 125 volt rating, and (2) 6 feet for nominal 250 volt rating.

ARTICLE 424. FIXED ELECTRIC SPACE HEATING EQUIPMENT

A. General

424-1. Scope. The requirements of this Article shall apply to fixed electrical equipment used for space heating. Equipment shall be of a type approved for the purpose and location where installed. For the purpose of this Article, heating equipment may be heating cable, unit heaters, boilers, central systems, or other approved fixed electric space heating equipment. This Article does not cover process heating and room air conditioning.

424-2. Other Articles. All requirements of this Code shall apply where applicable. Fixed electric space heating equipment for use in hazardous locations shall be installed to conform with Articles 500 through 517. Fixed electric space heating equipment incorporating a sealed (hermetic-type) motor-compressor shall also comply with Article 440.

424-3. (a) Branch-Circuit Requirements.   Individual branch circuits may supply any size fixed electric space heating equipment.

Branch circuits supplying two or more outlets for fixed electric space heating equipment shall be rated 15, 20, or 30 amperes.

Exception: In other than residential occupancies fixed infrared heating equipment may be supplied from branch circuits rated not more than 50 amperes as provided in Section 424-22.

(b) Branch-Circuit Sizing.   The size of branch-circuit conductors and overcurrent protective devices supplying fixed electric space heating equipment consisting of resistance elements with or without a motor shall be calculated on the basis of 125 per cent of the total load of the motors and the heaters. A contactor, thermostat, relay or similar device, approved for continuous operation at 100 per cent of its rating, may supply its full rated load. See Section 210-23(b), Exception Nos. 1 and 2.

The size of the branch-circuit conductors and overcurrent protective devices supplying fixed electric space heating equipment consisting of mechanical refrigeration with or without resistance units shall be calculated as provided for in Sections 440-34 and 440-35.

The provisions of this Section are not intended to apply to conductors, which form an integral part of approved fixed electric space heating equipment.

▶   The 125 per cent requirement in paragraph *b* means that branch circuits for electric space heating equipment cannot be loaded to more than 80 per cent of the branch-circuit *rating* unless the branch-circuit overcurrent devices and their assemblies are approved for 100 per cent load.

Many line thermostats and contactors are approved for 100 per cent load, and derating of such devices is not required.

B. Installation

424-9. General.   All fixed electric space heating equipment shall be installed in an approved manner.

424-10. Special-Type Heaters.   Fixed electric space heating systems employing methods of installation other than covered by this Article may be used only by special permission.

424-11. Supply Conductors.   Fixed electric space heating equipment requiring supply conductors with over 60°C insulation shall be clearly and permanently marked. This marking shall be plainly visible after installation and may be adjacent to the field-connection box.

424-12. Locations.

(a)   Fixed electric space heating equipment shall not be used where exposed to severe physical damage unless adequately protected.

(b)   Heaters and related equipment installed in damp or wet locations shall be approved for such locations and shall be constructed and installed so that water cannot enter or accumulate in wireways, electrical components or duct work. See Section 110-11.

424-13. Spacing from Combustible Materials.   Fixed electric space heating equipment shall be installed to provide the required spacing between the equipment and adjacent combustible material, unless it has been found to be acceptable when installed in direct contact with combustible material.

424-14. Grounding.   All exposed metal parts of fixed electric space heating equipment liable to become energized shall be grounded as required in Article 250.

C. Control and Protection of Fixed Electric Space Heating Equipment

424-19. Disconnecting Means.   Means shall be provided to disconnect all fixed electric space heating equipment from all ungrounded conductors. Where heating equipment is supplied by more than one source, the disconnecting means shall be grouped and identified.

(a)   For fixed electric space heating equipment rated at not over 300 volt-amperes or ⅛ horsepower, the branch-circuit overcurrent device may serve as the disconnecting means.

(b)   For fixed electric space heating equipment of greater rating, the branch-circuit switch or circuit breaker may, where readily accessible to the user of the equipment, serve as the disconnecting means.

(c) **Motor-Driven Heating Equipment.**   A switch or circuit breaker that serves as the disconnecting means for a motor-driven heater having a motor more than ⅛ horsepower shall be located within sight of the motor controller.

(d) **Unit Switches as Disconnecting Means.**   Unit switches with a marked "off" position, which are part of a fixed heater, that disconnect all ungrounded conductors may be used as the disconnecting means required by this Article when other means for disconnection are provided in the following types of occupancies:

(1) **Multi-Family Dwellings.**   In multi-family (more than two) dwellings, the other disconnecting means shall be within the apartment, or on the same floor as the apartment in which the fixed heater is installed, and may also control lamps and appliances.

(2) **Two-Family Dwellings.**   In two-family dwellings, the other disconnecting means may be located either inside or outside of the apartment in which the fixed heater is installed.

(3) **Single-Family Dwellings.**   In single-family dwellings, the service disconnecting means may be the other disconnecting means.

(4) **Other Occupancies.**   In other occupancies, the branch-circuit switch or circuit breaker, where readily accessible to the user of the fixed heater, may be used for the other disconnecting means.

424-20. Controllers and Disconnecting Means.

(a)   Thermostats and thermostatically controlled switching devices which indicate an off position and which interrupt line current shall open all ungrounded conductors when the control device is in this off position.

(b)   Thermostats and thermostatically controlled switching devices which do not have an off position are not required to open all ungrounded conductors.

(c)   Remote-control thermostats do not need to meet the requirements of paragraphs (a) and (b) above. These devices shall not serve as the disconnecting means.

(d) Switching devices consisting of combined thermostats and manually controlled switches which serve both as controllers and disconnecting means shall:

(1) Open all ungrounded conductors when manually placed in the off position.

(2) Be so designed that the circuit cannot be energized automatically after the device has been manually placed in the off position.

424-21. Switch and Circuit Breaker to be Indicating. Switches and circuit breakers used as disconnecting means shall be of the indicating type.

424-22. Overcurrent Protection.

(a) Electric space heating equipment, other than such motor-operated equipment as required by Article 430 to have additional overcurrent protection, shall be considered as protected against overcurrent when supplied by one of the circuits of Article 210 and in accordance with the requirements therein specified.

(b) Infrared electric space heating equipment shall have overcurrent protection not exceeding 50 amperes.

(c) Electric space heating equipment employing resistance-type heating elements rated more than 48 amperes shall have the heating elements subdivided. Each subdivided load shall not exceed 48 amperes and shall be protected at not more than 60 amperes.

Exception: Water heating boilers, steam boilers and heat transfer fluid heating boilers employing resistance-type immersion electric heating elements contained in an ASME rated and stamped vessel may be subdivided into circuits not exceeding 120 amperes and protected at not more than 150 amperes.

These overcurrent protective devices shall be: (1) factory-installed within or on the heater enclosure or provided as a separate assembly by the heater manufacturer, and (2) accessible, but need not be readily accessible, and (3) suitable for branch-circuit protection.

The main conductors supplying these overcurrent protective devices shall be considered branch-circuit conductors.

▶ The purpose of the paragraph following the exception in paragraph *c* is to require the heating manufacturer to furnish the necessary overcurrent protective devices where subdivided loads are required.

Main conductors supplying overcurrent protective devices for subdivided loads are considered as branch circuits to avoid controversies about applying the 125 per cent requirement in Section **424-3***b* to branch circuits *only*. It is not the intent, however, to deny the use of the *feeder tap* rules in Section **240-15** for these *main* conductors.

D. Marking of Heating Equipment

424-28. Nameplate.

(a) Each unit of fixed electric space heating equipment shall be provided with a nameplate giving the identifying name and the normal rating in volts and amperes, or in volts and watts.

Electric space heating equipment intended for use on alternating current only or direct current only shall be marked to so indicate. The marking of equipment consisting of motors over ⅛ horsepower and other loads shall specify the rating of the motor in volts, amperes, and frequency, and the heating load in volts and watts or amperes.

(b) This nameplate shall be located so as to be visible or easily accessible after installation.

424-29. Marking of Heating Elements. All heating elements which are replaceable in the field, and are a part of an electric heater shall be legibly marked with the ratings in volts and amperes, or in volts and watts.

E. Electric Space Heating Cables and Panels

424-34. Heating Cable Construction. Heating cable shall be furnished complete with factory-assembled nonheating leads at least 7 feet in length.

424-35. Marking of Heating Cables and Panels. Each unit shall be marked with the identifying name or identification symbol, catalog number, ratings in volts and watts or amperes.

(a) Heating Cables. Each unit length of heating cable shall have a permanent legible marking on each nonheating lead located within 3 inches of the terminal end. The lead wire shall have the following color identification: 120 volt nominal, yellow; 208 volt nominal, blue; 240 volt nominal, red; and 277 volt nominal, brown.

(b) Heating Panels. Permanent marking in a location that is readily visible prior to building finishing shall be provided.

424-36. Clearances of Wiring in Ceilings.

(a) Wiring located above heated ceilings shall be spaced not less than 2 inches above the heated ceiling and shall be considered as operating at an ambient of 50°C. The ampacities of conductors shall be computed on the basis of the correction factors given in Note 13 to Tables 310-12 through 310-15.

Exception: Wiring located above heated ceilings and over thermal insulation having a minimum thickness of 2 inches requires no correction for temperature.

424-37. Clearances of Branch-Circuit Wiring in Walls.

(a) Where located in exterior walls, wiring shall be located outside the thermal insulation.

(b) Where located in interior walls or partitions, wiring shall be considered as operating at an ambient of 40°C (104°F); and the ampacities of conductors shall be computed on the basis of the correction factors given in Note 13 to Tables 310-12 through 310-15.

424-38. Area Restrictions.

(a) Heating cables and panels shall not extend beyond the room or area in which they originate.

(b) Cables and panels shall not be installed in closets, over walls or partitions that extend to the ceiling, or over cabinets whose clearance from the ceiling is less than the minimum horizontal dimension of the cabinet to the nearest cabinet edge that is open to the room or area.

Exception: Isolated single runs of cable may pass over partitions where they are embedded.

(c) This provision shall not prevent the use of cable or panels in closet ceilings as low temperature heat sources to control relative humidity, provided they are used only in those portions of the ceiling which are unobstructed to the floor by shelves, or other permanent fixtures.

424-39. Clearance from Other Objects and Openings. Panels and cables shall be separated at least 8 inches from the edge of outlet boxes and junction boxes that are to be used for mounting surface lighting fixtures. Two inches shall be provided from recessed fixtures and their trims, ventilating openings and other such openings in room surfaces. Sufficient area shall be provided to assure that no heating cable or panel will be covered by other surface mounted lighting units.

424-40. Splices. Embedded cables may be spliced only where necessary and only by approved means, and in no case shall the length of the heating cable be altered.

424-41. Installation of Heating Cables on Dry Board, in Plaster and on Concrete Ceilings.

(a) Cables shall not be installed in walls.

Exception: Isolated single runs of cable may run down a vertical surface to reach a dropped ceiling.

(b) Adjacent runs of cable not exceeding 2¾ watts per foot shall be installed not less than 1½ inches on centers.

(c) Heating cables may be applied only to gypsum board, plaster lath or other fire-resistant material. With metal lath or other electrical conducting surface, a coat of plaster shall be applied to completely separate the metal lath or conducting surface from the cable. (See also Section 424-41(f).)

(d) All the heating cables, the splice between the heating cable and non-heating leads, and 3 inch minimum of the nonheating lead at the splice shall be embedded in plaster or dry board in the same manner as the heating cable.

(e) The entire ceiling surface shall have a finish of thermally noninsulating sand plaster having a nominal thickness of ½ inch, or other specially approved noninsulating material applied according to specified thickness and directions.

(f) Cables shall be secured at intervals not exceeding 16 inches by means of approved stapling, tape, plaster, nonmetallic spreaders or other approved means. Staples or metal fasteners which straddle the cable shall not be used with metal lath or other electrical conducting surfaces.

(g) In dry board installations, the entire ceiling below the heating cable shall be covered with gypsum board not exceeding ½ inch thickness. The void between the upper layer of gypsum board, plaster lath or other fire resistant material and the surface layer of gypsum board shall be completely filled with thermally conducting nonshrinking plaster or other approved material of equivalent thermal conductivity.

(h) Cables shall be kept free from contact with metal or other electrical conducting surfaces.

(i) In dry board applications, cable shall be installed parallel to the joist, leaving a clear space centered under the joist of 2½ inches (width) between centers of adjacent runs of cable. Crossing of joist by cable shall be kept to a minimum and should be at the ends of the room. Surface layer of gypsum board shall be mounted so that the nails or other fastenings do not pierce the heating cable.

424-42. Finished Ceilings. Finished ceilings may be covered with paint, wall-paper or other approved surface finishes.

424-43. Installation of Nonheating Leads of Cables and Panels.

(a) Nonheating leads of cables and panels shall be installed in accordance with approved wiring methods from the junction box to a location within the ceiling. Such installations may be single conductors in approved raceways, single or multi-conductor Type UF, Type NMC, Type MI, or other approved conductors.

(b) Not less than 6 inches of nonheating leads shall be free within the junction box. The marking of the leads shall be visible in the junction box.

(c) Excess leads shall not be cut but shall be secured to the underside of the ceiling and embedded in plaster or other approved material, leaving only a length sufficient to reach the junction box with not less than 6 inches of free lead within the box.

424-44. Installation of Panels or Cables in Concrete or Poured Masonry Floors.

(a) Panels or heating units shall not exceed 33 watts per square foot of heated area or 16½ watts per linear foot of cable.

(b) The spacing between adjacent runs of cable shall be not less than 1 inch on centers.

(c) Cables shall be secured in place by nonmetallic frames or spreaders or other approved means while the concrete or other finish is applied.

Cables, units, and panels shall not be installed where they bridge expansion joints unless protected from expansion and contraction.

(d) Spacings shall be maintained between the heating cable and metal embedded in the floor.

Exception: Grounded metal-clad cable may be in contact with metal embedded in the floor.

(e) Leads shall be protected where they leave the floor by rigid metal conduit, electrical metallic tubing, or by other approved means.

(f) Bushings or approved fittings shall be used where the leads emerge within the floor slab.

424-45. Tests During and After Installation.

(a) Embedded cable installations shall be made with due care to prevent damage to the cable assembly and shall be inspected and approved before cables are covered or concealed.

(b) Cables should be tested for insulation resistance after plastering the ceiling or the pouring of floors.

424-46. Panels—General. Sections 424-46 through 424-48 cover only heating panels of less than 25 watts per square foot assembled together in the field to form a heating installation in one room or area using approved methods of interconnection. Such an installation shall be connected by a recognized wiring method.

424-47. Panels to be Complete Units. Panels shall be installed as complete units unless approved for field cutting in a recognized manner.

424-48. Installation. Panels shall be installed in an approved manner. Nails, staples, or other electrically conducting fasteners shall not be used where they penetrate current-carrying parts.

Exception: Insulated fasteners may be used with systems for which they are recognized.

F. Duct Heaters

424-57. General.　The provisions in Part F shall apply to any heater mounted in the air stream of a forced air system where the air moving unit is not provided as an integral part of the equipment.

424-58. Approval.　Heaters installed in an air duct shall be approved for the purpose and installed in the approved manner.

424-59. Air Flow.　Means shall be provided to assure uniform and adequate air flow over the face of the heater.

Heaters installed near (within 4 feet) a fan outlet, elbows, baffle plates or other obstruction in duct work may require turning vanes, pressure plates or other devices on the inlet side of the duct heater to assure an even distribution of air over the face of the heater.

424-60. Elevated Inlet Temperature.　Duct heaters intended for use with elevated inlet air temperature (such as heat pumps) shall be approved for the purpose and so marked.

424-61. Installation of Duct Heaters with Heat Pumps and Air Conditioners.　Heat pumps and air conditioners having duct heaters closer than 4 feet to the heat pump or air conditioner shall be approved for such installation and so marked.

424-62. Condensation.　Duct heaters used with air conditioners or other air cooling equipment which may result in condensation of moisture shall be approved for use with air conditioners.

424-63. Fan Circuit Interlock.　Means shall be provided to insure that the fan circuit is energized when the first heater circuit is energized.

This does not prohibit time- or temperature-controlled delay in energizing the fan motor.

424-64. Limit Controls.　Each duct heater shall be provided with an integral approved automatic reset temperature limiting control or controllers to de-energize the circuit or circuits.

In addition, an integral independent supplementary control or controllers shall be provided in each duct heater which will disconnect a sufficient number of conductors to interrupt current flow. This device shall be manually resettable or replaceable.

424-65. Location of Disconnecting Means.　Duct heater controller equipment shall be accessible with the disconnecting means installed at or within sight of the controller.

424-66. Installation.　See NFPA Pamphlets Nos. 90A-1971 and 90B-1971.

ARTICLE 426. FIXED OUTDOOR ELECTRIC DE-ICING AND SNOW MELTING EQUIPMENT

A. General

426-1. Scope.　The requirements of this Article shall apply to electrically energized heating units, panels, and cables where embedded in driveways, walks, steps, and other areas.

426-2. Application of Other Articles. All requirements of this Code shall apply where applicable.

426-3. Branch-Circuit Requirements. Fixed outdoor electric de-icing and snow melting equipment shall be: (1) considered as a continuous load for sizing branch circuits, and (2) installed according to Section 210-24.

▶　　Being classified as a continuous load, branch circuits for fixed outdoor electric de-icing and snow-melting systems must be sized so that the load will not exceed 80 per cent of the branch-circuit rating.

　　A fine print note in Section 210-24 permits snow-melting and de-icing systems to be connected to branch circuits of 50 amp or less if only these systems are supplied.

B. Installation

426-9. General. Equipment for use with fixed outdoor electric de-icing and snow melting systems shall be of a type approved for such service and for the location where installed.

426-10. Use.

(a) De-icing and snow melting equipment shall be installed only in the specific materials for which they are approved.

(b) De-icing and snow melting units shall be protected from physical damage.

426-11. Complete Units.

(a) Units, panels, and cables shall be installed in their complete sizes or lengths as supplied by the manufacturer, except that the nonheating leads may be shortened if the marking specified in Section 426-26 is retained. Units without nameplates shall not be installed.

(b) Units shall be suitable for use with approved wiring systems.

426-12. Special-Type Equipment. Fixed outdoor electric de-icing and snow melting equipment employing methods of construction or installation other than that covered by this Article may be used only by special permission.

C. Control and Protection

426-20. Disconnecting Means. All fixed outdoor electric de-icing and snow melting equipment shall be provided with a means for disconnection from all ungrounded conductors. The branch-circuit switch or circuit breaker may, where readily accessible to the user of the equipment, serve as the disconnecting means. Switches used as disconnecting means shall be of the indicating type.

426-21. Controllers.

(a) Thermostats and thermostatically controlled switching devices which indicate an off position and which interrupt line current shall open all ungrounded conductors when the control device is in the off position, and may be used as the disconnecting means.

(b) Thermostats and thermostatically controlled switching devices shall be so designed that the circuit cannot be energized automatically after the device has been manually placed in the off position.

(c) Thermostats and thermostatically controlled switching devices which do not have an off position are not required to open all ungrounded conductors, but shall not be used as the disconnecting means required in Section 426-20.

426-22. Overcurrent Protection. Fixed outdoor electric de-icing and snow melting equipment shall be considered as protected against overcurrent when supplied by one of the circuits of Article 210 and in accordance with the requirements therein specified.

426-23. Nonheating Leads. Nonheating leads on the cables, panels, or units shall be furnished as part of the factory assembly. The leads shall consist of conductors and wiring approved for general use, or other wiring approved for the purpose.

426-24. Installation of Heating Cables, Units, or Panels.

(a) The operating characteristics of embedded assemblies of fixed outdoor electric de-icing and snow melting equipment depend upon the specific materials involved, and, therefore, embedded equipment shall be installed as designed for use in such materials.

(b) Panels or units shall not exceed 120 watts per square foot of heated area.

(c) The spacings between adjacent cable runs is dependent upon the rating of the cable, and shall be not less than one inch on centers.

(d) Units, panels, and cables shall be installed:

(1) On a substantial asphalt or masonry base at least 2 inches thick and have at least 1½ inches of asphalt or masonry applied over the units, panels, or cables, or

(2) They may be installed over other approved bases and embedded within 3½ inches of masonry or asphalt but not less than 1½ inches from the top surface, or

(3) Equipment which has been specially investigated for other forms of installation shall be installed only in the manner for which it has been investigated.

(e) Cables shall be secured in place by frames or spreaders, or other approved means, while the masonry or asphalt finish is applied.

(f) Cables, units, and panels shall not be installed where they bridge expansion joints unless adequately protected from expansion and contraction.

426-25. Installation of Nonheating Leads.

(a) Nonheating leads having a grounding sheath or braid may be embedded in masonry or asphalt in the same manner as the heating cable without additional protection.

(b) All but one to 6 inches of nonheating leads of Type TW and other approved types not having a grounding sheath shall be enclosed in conduit, electrical metallic tubing or other raceways within the asphalt or masonry, and the distance from the factory splice to the raceway shall be not less than one inch nor more than 6 inches.

(c) Insulating bushings shall be used in the asphalt or masonry where leads enter conduit, tubing, or raceway.

(d) Leads shall be protected in expansion joints and where they emerge from masonry or asphalt by conduit, electrical metallic tubing, other raceways, or other approved means.

(e) Not less than 6 inches of nonheating leads shall be within the junction box.

426-26. Marking. Each heating unit, panel, and cable shall be legibly marked within 3 inches of each end of the nonheating leads with the identification symbol, catalog number, and ratings in volts and watts or amperes.

426-27. Junction Boxes.   All splices other than factory splices shall be made in properly installed boxes approved for the location.

426-28. Grounding.

(a)   All exposed metal parts of fixed outdoor electric de-icing and snow melting equipment, raceways, boxes, etc., liable to become energized shall be grounded as required in Article 250.

(b)   Grounding means such as copper braid, lead or copper sheath, or other approved means, shall be provided as part of the heating section of the approved cable, panel, or unit.

(c)   All noncurrent-carrying parts which are liable to become energized shall be bonded together and positively connected to a continuous (unbroken) No. 14 AWG or larger covered copper wire sized in accordance with Table 250-95 extending to the distribution panelboard. Where the bonding conductor is subject to physical damage, it shall be at least No. 10 AWG copper.

426-29. Tests.   Embedded heating installations shall be inspected and approved before being covered.

ARTICLE 430. MOTORS, MOTOR CIRCUITS AND CONTROLLERS

A. General

430-1. (a) Motor Feeder and Branch Circuits.   See Diagram 430-1(a).

(b) General.   The following general requirements cover provisions for motors, motor circuits, and controllers which do not properly fall into the other parts of this Article. See Article 440 for air-conditioning and refrigerating equipment.

430-3. Part-Winding Motors.   A part-winding-start induction or synchronous motor is one arranged for starting by first energizing part of its primary (armature) winding and, subsequently, energizing the remainder of this winding in one or more steps. The purpose is to reduce the initial values of the starting current drawn or the starting torque developed by the motor A standard part-winding-start induction motor is arranged so that one-half of its primary winding can be energized initially and, subsequently, the remaining half can be energized, both halves then carrying the same current. A sealed "hermetic type" refrigeration compressor motor is not to be considered a standard part-winding-start induction motor.

When separate overcurrent devices are used with a standard part-winding-start induction motor, each half of the motor winding shall be individually protected in accordance with Sections 430-32 and 430-37, except that the trip current shall be one-half that specified.

Each motor winding connection shall have short circuit and ground fault protection rated at not more than one-half that specified by Section 430-52 except that a single device having this half rating may be used for both windings if this will allow the motor to start.

430-4. In Sight From.   Where in this Article it is specified that some equipment shall be "in sight from" another equipment, it means that the equipment must be visible and not more than 50 feet distant.

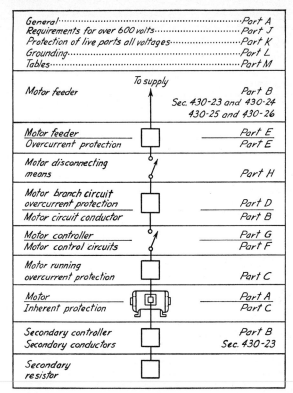

Diagram 430-1(a).

430-5. Other Articles.
Motors and controllers shall also comply with the applicable provisions of the following:

430-6. Ampacity Determination.
Ampacities shall be determined as follows:
  (a) General Motor Applications. Except as noted in Section 430-6(b) when-

ever the current rating of a motor is used to determine the ampacity of conductors, switches, branch-circuit overcurrent devices, etc., the values given in Tables 430-147, 430-148, 430-149, and 430-150, including notes, shall be used instead of actual current rating marked on the motor nameplate. Separate motor running overcurrent protection shall be based on the motor nameplate current rating. When a motor is marked in amperes, but not horsepower, the horsepower rating shall be assumed to be that corresponding to the value given in Tables 430-147, 430-148, 430-149, and 430-150 interpolated if necessary.

Exception: For multispeed motors, see Sections 430-22(a) and 430-52.

(b) Torque Motors. For torque motors the rated current shall be locked-rotor current and this nameplate current shall be used to determine the ampacity of the branch-circuit conductors (see Sections 430-22 and 430-24) and motor operating overcurrent protection. For motor controllers and disconnecting means, see Section 430-83, Exception No. 3 and Section 430-110.

430-7. Marking on Motors and Multimotor Equipment.

(a) Usual Motor Applications. A motor shall be marked with the following information:

(1) Maker's name.

(2) Rated volts and full-load amperes.

(3) Rated frequency and number of phases, if an alternating-current motor.

(4) Rated full-load speed.

(5) Rated temperature rise or the insulation system class and rated ambient temperature.

(6) Time rating.

(7) Rated horsepower if ⅛ horsepower or more.

(8) Code letter if an alternating-current motor rated ½ horsepower or more (see Section 430-7(b)).

(9) Secondary volts and full-load amperes if a wound-rotor induction motor.

(10) Winding: straight shunt, stabilized shunt, compound or series, if a direct-current motor.

A multispeed motor, except a shaded-pole or permanent-split capacitor motor, shall be marked with the amperes and horsepower at each speed. A motor provided with a thermal protector complying with Section 430-32 (a-2) or 430-32(c-2) shall be marked "Thermally Protected." A motor complying with Section 430-32(c-4) shall be marked "Impedance Protected." The time rating shall be 5, 15, 30, or 60 minutes, or continuous.

Exception No. 1: On motors of arc welders, the horsepower rating may be omitted.
Exception No. 2: On polyphase wound-rotor motors the code letter shall be omitted.

(b) Locked-Rotor Indicating Code Letters. Code letters marked on motor nameplates to show motor input with locked rotor shall be in accordance with Table 430-7(b).

The code letter indicating motor input with locked rotor must be in an individual block on the nameplate, properly designated. This code letter is to be used for determining branch-circuit overcurrent protection by reference to Table 430-152, as provided in Section 430-52.

(1) Multispeed motors shall be marked with the code letter designating the locked-rotor KVA per horsepower for the highest speed at which the motor can

Table 430-7(b). Locked Rotor Indicating Code Letters

Code Letter	Kilovolt-Amperes per Horsepower with Locked Rotor		
A	0	—	3.14
B	3.15	—	3.54
C	3.55	—	3.99
D	4.0	—	4.49
E	4.5	—	4.99
F	5.0	—	5.59
G	5.6	—	6.29
H	6.3	—	7.09
J	7.1	—	7.99
K	8.0	—	8.99
L	9.0	—	9.99
M	10.0	—	11.19
N	11.2	—	12.49
P	12.5	—	13.99
R	14.0	—	15.99
S	16.0	—	17.99
T	18.0	—	19.99
U	20.0	—	22.39
V	22.4	—	and up

The above table is an adopted standard of the National Electrical Manufacturers Association.

be started, except constant horsepower motors which shall be marked with the code letter giving the highest locked-rotor KVA per horsepower.

(2) Single-speed motors starting on Y connection and running on delta connections shall be marked with a code letter corresponding to the locked-rotor KVA per horsepower for the Y connection.

(3) Dual-voltage motors which have a different locked-rotor KVA per horsepower on the two voltages shall be marked with the code letter for the voltage giving the highest locked-rotor KVA per horsepower.

(4) Motors with 60- and 50-hertz ratings shall be marked with a code letter designating the locked rotor KVA per horsepower on 60 hertz.

(5) Part-winding-start motors shall be marked with a code letter designating the locked-rotor KVA per horsepower that is based upon the locked-rotor current for the full winding of the motor.

(c) Torque Motors. Torque motors are rated for operation at standstill and shall be marked in accordance with paragraph (a) except that locked rotor torque shall replace horsepower.

(d) Multimotor and Combination-Load Equipment. Multimotor and combination-load equipment shall be provided with a visible nameplate marked with the maker's name, the rating in volts, frequency and number of phases, minimum circuit ampacity, and the maximum rating of the circuit protective device. The ampacity shall be calculated by using Section 430-25 and counting all of the motors and other loads which will be operated at the same time. The protective device rating shall not exceed the value calculated by using Section 430-53.

Multimotor equipment for use on two or more circuits shall be marked with the above information for each circuit.

When the equipment is not factory wired and the individual nameplates of motors and other loads are visible after assembly of the equipment, these nameplates may serve as the required marking.

430-8. Marking on Controllers. A controller shall be marked with the maker's name or identification, the voltage, the current or horsepower rating, and such other data as may be needed to properly indicate the motors for which it is suitable. A controller which includes motor running overcurrent protection, when suitable for group motor application shall be marked with the motor running overcurrent protection and the maximum branch circuit overcurrent protection for such applications.

Combination controllers employing adjustable instantaneous circuit breakers (without time delay) shall be clearly marked to indicate the ampere settings of the adjustable trip element.

Where a controller is built in as an integral part of a motor or of a motor-generator set, the controller need not be individually marked when the necessary data is on the motor nameplate. For controllers which are an integral part of equipment approved as a unit, the above marking may be on the equipment nameplate.

430-9. Marking at Terminals. Terminals of motors and controllers shall be suitably marked or colored where necessary to indicate the proper connections.

430-10. Wiring Space in Enclosures. Enclosures for controllers and disconnecting means for motors shall not be used as junction boxes, auxiliary gutters, or raceways for conductors feeding through or tapping off to the other apparatus unless designs are employed which provide adequate space for this purpose. See Section 373-8.

▶ The standard types of enclosures for motor controllers provide space that is sufficient only for the branch-circuit conductors entering and leaving the enclosure and any control-circuit conductors that may be required. No additional conductors should be brought into the enclosure. For switches, see comments following Section **373-8.**

430-11. Protection Against Liquids. Suitable guards or enclosures shall be provided to protect exposed current-carrying parts of motors and the insulation of motor leads where installed directly under equipment, or in other locations where dripping or spraying oil, water, or other injurious liquid may occur, unless the motor is designed for the existing conditions.

▶ Excessive moisture, steam, dripping oil, etc., on the exposed current-carrying parts of a motor may cause an insulation breakdown which in turn may be the cause of a fire.

430-12. Motor Terminal Housings.

(a) When motors are provided with terminal housings, the housings shall be of metal and of substantial construction.

Exception: In other than hazardous locations, substantial nonmetallic, nonburning housings may be used on motors larger than 34 inches in diameter provided internal grounding means between the machine frame and the conduit connection is incorporated within the housing.

See ANSI Standard Method of Test for Flammability of Rigid Plastics over 0.127CM (0.050 inch) in thickness, K65.21-1969 for nonburning test.

(b) When these terminal housings enclose wire-to-wire connections, they shall have minimum dimensions and usable volumes in accordance with the following:

Table 430-12(b). Terminal Housing—Wire-to-Wire Connections

Hp	Cover Opening, Minimum Dimension, Inches	Usable Volume, Minimum, Cubic Inches
1 and smaller*	1⅝	7½
1½, 2 and 3†	1¾	12
5 and 7½	2	16
10 and 15	2¼	22½
20 and 25	2⅞	33
30 and 40	3	44
50 and 60	3½	72½
75 and 100	3½	100
125 and 150	6	216

* For motors rated 1 horsepower and smaller and with the terminal housing partially or wholly integral with the frame or end shield, the volume of the terminal housing shall be not less than 0.8 cubic inch per wire-to-wire connection. The minimum cover opening dimension is not specified.

† For motors rated 1½, 2 and 3 horsepower and with the terminal housing partially or wholly integral with the frame or end shield, the volume of the terminal housing shall be not less than 1.0 cubic inch per wire-to-wire connection. The minimum cover opening dimension is not specified.

(c) When these terminal housings enclose rigidly mounted motor terminals, the terminal housing shall be of sufficient size to provide minimum terminal spacings and usable volumes in accordance with the following:

Table 430-12(c)(1). Terminal Spacings—Fixed Terminals

Volts	Minimum Spacing, Inches	
	Between Line Terminals	Between Line Terminals and Other Uninsulated Metal Parts
250 or less	¼	¼
251 to 600, incl.	⅜	⅜

Table 430-12(c)(2). Usable Volumes—Fixed Terminals

Power Supply Conductor Size, AWG	Minimum Usable Volume per Power Supply Conductor, Cubic Inches
14	1.0
12 and 10	1¼
8 and 6	2¼

(d)   For larger wire sizes or when motors are installed as a part of factory-wired equipment, without additional connection being required at the motor terminal housing during equipment installation, the terminal housing shall be of ample size to make connections, but the foregoing provisions for the volumes of terminal housings need not apply.

430-13. Bushing.   Where wires pass through an opening in an enclosure, conduit box or barrier, a bushing shall be used to protect the conductors from the edges of the openings having sharp edges. The bushing shall have smooth, well-rounded surfaces where it may be in contact with the conductors. If used where there may be a presence of oils, greases, or other contaminants, the bushing shall be made of material not deleteriously affected.

For conductors, see Section 310-7.

430-14. Location of Motors.

(a) Ventilation and Maintenance.   Motors shall be located so that adequate ventilation is provided and so that maintenance such as lubrication of bearings and replacing of brushes can be readily accomplished.

(b) Open Motors.   Open motors having commutators or collector rings shall be located or protected so that sparks cannot reach adjacent combustible material. This does not prohibit the installation of these motors on wooden floors or supports.

430-16. Overheating from Dust Accumulations.   In locations where dust or flying material will collect on or in motors in such quantities as to seriously interfere with the ventilation or cooling of motors, and thereby cause dangerous temperatures, suitable types of enclosed motors which will not overheat under the prevailing conditions, shall be used. Especially severe conditions may require the use of enclosed pipe ventilated motors, or enclosure in separate dust-tight rooms, properly ventilated from a source of clean air.

▶   The conditions described in this section could make the location a Class II, Division 2 location; the types of motors required are specified in Art. 502.

430-17. Highest Rated (Largest) Motor.   In determining compliance with Sections 430-24, 430-53(b), 430-53(c), and 430-62(a), the highest rated (largest) motor shall be considered to be that motor which has the highest rated full-load current. The full-load current used to determine the highest rated motor shall be the equivalent value corresponding to the motor horsepower rating selected from Tables 430-147, 430-148, 430-149, and 430-150.

B. Motor Circuit Conductors

430-21. General.   The provisions of Part B specify sizes of conductors capable of carrying the motor current without overheating under the conditions specified.

(a)   The provisions of Articles 250, 300, and 310 are not intended to apply to conductors which form an integral part of approved equipment, or to integral conductors of motors, motor controllers, and the like. See Sections 300-1(b) and 310-1(c).

Table 430-22 (a-Exception). Duty Cycle Service

Classification of Service	Percentages of Nameplate Current Rating			
	5-Minute Rated Motor	15-Minute Rated Motor	30 & 60 Minute Rated Motor	Continuous Rated Motor
Short-Time Duty				
Operating valves, raising or lowering rolls, etc.	110	120	150	. . .
Intermittent Duty				
Freight and passenger elevators, tool heads, pumps, drawbridges, turntables, etc. For arc welders, see Section 630-21.................	85	85	90	140
Periodic Duty				
Rolls, ore and coal-handling machines, etc.....	85	90	95	140
Varying Duty...............................	110	120	150	200

Any motor application is considered to be for continuous duty unless the nature of the apparatus which it drives is such that the motor will not operate continuously with load under any condition of use.

For long runs, it may be necessary, in order to avoid excessive voltage drop, to use conductors of sizes larger than the minimum sizes selected from Tables 310-12 through 310-15.

See Example No. 8, Ch. 9, and Diagram 430-1(a).

► **Types of Layouts**

Figures **430-1** through **430-4** indicate the use of cartridge-type fuses, and Section **240-18** requires a switch ahead of each set of fuses.

Type 1

An individual branch circuit leads to each motor from a distribution center. This type of layout can be used under any conditions and is the one most commonly used.

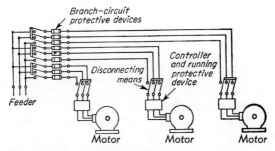

Fɪɢ. 430-1. Type 1 layout. Individual branch circuit to each motor from a distribution center.

Type 2

A feeder or subfeeder with branch circuits tapped on at convenient points. This is the same as Type 1 except that the branch-circuit overcurrent

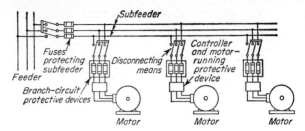

FIG. 430-2. Type 2 layout. Individual branch circuit to each motor from a subfeeder, no distribution center.

protective devices are mounted individually at the points where taps are made to the subfeeder, instead of being assembled at one location in the form of a branch-circuit distribution center. Under certain conditions, the branch-circuit protective devices may be located at any point not more than **25** ft distance from the point where the branch circuit is tapped to the feeder.

Type 3

Small motors, lamps, and appliances may be supplied by a **15**- or **20**-amp circuit as described in Art. **210**. Motors connected to these circuits must be provided with running overcurrent protective devices in most cases.

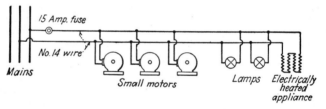

FIG. 430-3. Type 3 layout. 15-amp branch circuit supplying small motors and other loads.

Motor Branch Circuits

Data are provided in this article governing three essential parts of a typical motor branch circuit, as employed in a Type 1 or Type 2 layout: (1) branch-circuit conductors, (2) branch-circuit overcurrent protective devices, and (3) motor-running protective devices. These three parts of a motor circuit are shown in Fig. **430-4**.

The branch-circuit overcurrent protective device may be fuses or a circuit breaker.

A motor-running protective device is always required, except for some small motors. This device is frequently combined with the motor controller.

430-22. Single Motor.

(a) Branch-circuit conductors supplying a single motor shall have an ampacity not less than 125 per cent of the motor full-load current rating.

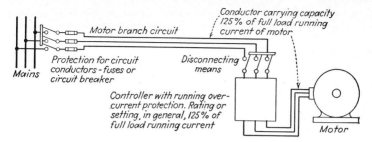

Fig. 430-4. The essential parts of a typical motor branch circuit.

In case of a multispeed motor, the selection of branch circuit conductors on the line side of the controller shall be based on the highest of the full load current ratings shown on the motor nameplate; selection of branch circuit conductors between the controller and the motor, which are energized for that particular speed, shall be based on the current rating for that speed.

Exception: Conductors for a motor used for short-time, intermittent, periodic, or varying duty shall have an ampacity not less than the percentage of the motor nameplate current rating as shown in Table 430-22 (a-Exception) unless the authority having jurisdiction grants special permission for conductors of smaller size.

(b) The conductors between a stationary motor rated one horsepower or less, and the separate terminal enclosures permitted in Section 430-145(b) may be smaller than No. 14 but not smaller than No. 18, provided they have an ampacity as specified above.

▶   In general, it is required that every motor shall be provided with a running protective device that will open the circuit on any current exceeding prescribed percentages of the full-load motor current, the percentage depending upon the type of motor. The running protective device is intended primarily to protect the windings of the motor, but by providing that the circuit conductors shall have an ampacity not less than 125 per cent of the full-load motor current, it is obvious that these conductors are reasonably protected by the running protective device against any overcurrent caused by an overload on the motor.

When a motor is used for one of the classes of service listed in Table 430-22 (a-Exception), the necessary ampacity of the branch-circuit conductors depends upon the class of service and upon the rating of the motor. A motor having a 5-min rating is designed to deliver its rated horsepower during periods of approximately 5 min each, with cooling intervals between the operating periods. The branch-circuit conductors have the advantage of the same cooling intervals and hence can safely be smaller than for a motor of the same horsepower but having a 60-min rating.

In the case of elevator motors, the many considerations involved in determining the smallest permissible size of the branch-circuit conductors make this a complex problem, and it is always the safest plan to be guided by the recommendations of the manufacturer of the equipment. This applies also to feeders supplying two or more elevator motors and to circuits supplying non-continuous-duty motors used for driving some other machines.

430-23. Wound-Rotor Secondary.

(a)   For continuous duty the conductors connecting the secondary of a wound-rotor alternating-current motor to its controller shall have an ampacity which is not less than 125 per cent of the full-load secondary current of the motor.

(b)   For other than continuous duty, these conductors shall have an ampacity, in per cent of full load secondary current, not less than that specified in Table 430-22 (a-Exception).

(c)   Where the secondary resistor is separate from the controller, the ampacity of the conductors between controller and resistor shall be not less than that given in Table 430-23(c).

Table 430-23(c). Secondary Conductor

Resistor Duty Classification	Ampacity of Wire in Per Cent of Full-Load Secondary Current
Light starting duty...............................	35
Heavy starting duty..............................	45
Extra heavy starting duty.......................	55
Light intermittent duty..........................	65
Medium intermittent duty.......................	75
Heavy intermittent duty.........................	85
Continuous duty.................................	110

▶   The full-load secondary current of a wound-rotor or slip-ring motor must be obtained from the motor nameplate or from the manufacturer.

The starting, or starting and speed-regulating, portion of the controller for a wound-rotor motor usually consists of two parts—a dial-type or drum controller and a resistor bank. These two parts must, in many cases, be assembled and connected by the installer. (See Fig. 430-5.)

The conductors from the slip rings on the motor to the controller are in circuit continuously while the motor is running and hence, for a continuous-duty motor, must be large enough to carry the secondary current of the motor continuously.

If the controller is used for starting only and is not used for regulating the speed of the motor, the conductors between the dial or drum and the resistors are in use only during the starting period and are cut out of the circuit as soon as the motor has come up to full speed. These conductors may therefore be of a smaller size than would be needed for continuous duty.

If the controller is to be used for speed regulation of the motor, some part of the resistance may be left in circuit continuously and the conductors between the dial or drum and the resistors must be large enough to carry the continuous load without overheating. In Table **430-23**c the term *continuous duty* applies to this condition.

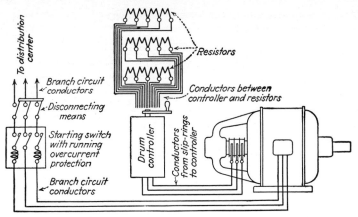

Fig. 430-5. Wound-rotor induction motor with drum-type controller and separately mounted resistors.

430-24. Conductors Supplying Several Motors.

Conductors supplying two or more motors shall have an ampacity equal to the sum of the full load current rating of all the motors plus 25 per cent of the highest rated motor in the group.

Where one or more motors of the group are used on short time intermittent, periodic, or varying duty, the ampacity of the conductors shall be calculated as follows:

(a) Determine the needed ampacity for each motor used for other than continuous duty from Table 430-22(a-Exception).

(b) Determine the needed ampacity for each continuous duty motor based on 100 per cent motor full load current rating.

(c) Multiply the largest single motor ampacity determined from (a) or (b) above by 1.25. Add all other motor ampacities from (a) and (b) above and select the conductor for this total ampacity.

Exception: When the circuitry is so interlocked as to prevent the starting and running of a second motor or group of motors, the conductor size shall be determined from the larger motor or group of motors that is to be operated at a given time.

See Example No. 8, Chapter 9.

▶   For the overcurrent protection of feeder conductors of the minimum size permitted by this Section, the highest permissible rating or setting of the protective device is specified in Section **430-62**. Where a feeder protective device of higher rating or setting is used because two or more motors must be started simultaneously, the size of the feeder conductors shall be increased correspondingly.

These requirements and those of Section **430-62** for the overcurrent protection of power feeders are based upon the principle that a power feeder should be of such size that it will have an ampacity equal to that required for the starting current of the largest motor supplied by the feeder, plus the full-load running currents of all other motors supplied by the feeder. Except under the unusual condition where two or more motors may be started simultaneously, the heaviest load that a power feeder will ever be required to carry is the load under the condition where the largest motor is started at a time when all the other motors supplied by the feeder are running and delivering their full-rated horsepower.

430-25. Supply Conductors.

(a) **Combination Load.**   Conductors supplying a motor load, and in addition a lighting or appliance load as computed from Article 220 and other applicable Sections, shall have an ampacity sufficient for the lighting or appliance load plus the required capacity for the motor load determined in accordance with Section 430-24, or, for a single motor, in accordance with Section 430-22.

▶   For computing the minimum allowable conductor size for a combination lighting and power feeder, the required ampacity for the lighting load is to be determined according to the rules for feeders carrying lighting (or lighting and appliance) loads only. Where the motor load consists of one motor only, the required ampacity for this load is the capacity for the motor branch circuit, or 125 per cent of the full-load motor current, as specified in Section 430-22. Where the motor load consists of two or more motors, the required ampacity for the motor load is the capacity computed according to Section 430-24.

(b) **Multimotor and Combination Load Equipment.**   The ampacity of the conductors supplying multimotor and combination load equipment shall not be less than the minimum circuit ampacity marked on the equipment in accordance with Section 430-7(d).

430-26. Feeder Demand Factor.   Where a reduced heating of the conductors results from motors operating on duty-cycle, intermittently, or from all motors not operating at one time the authority having jurisdiction may grant permission for feeder conductors to be of a capacity less than specified in the Sections 430-24 and 430-25, provided the conductor is of sufficient ampacity for the maximum load determined by the sizes and number of motors supplied and the character of their loads and duties.

▶   A demand factor of less than 100 per cent may be applied in the case of some industrial plants where the nature of the work is such that there is never a time when all the motors are operating at one time.

430-27. Capacitors with Motors.   For provisions covering conductors where capacitors are installed on motor circuits, see Sections 460-7, 460-8, 460-9.

C. Motor and Branch Circuit Running Overcurrent (Overload) Protection

430-31. General.   The provisions of Part C specify overcurrent devices intended to protect the motors, the motor-control apparatus, and the branch-circuit conductors against excessive heating due to motor overloads or failure to start.

(a)   Overload in electrical apparatus is an operating overcurrent which, when it persists for a sufficient length of time, would cause damage or dangerous overheating of the apparatus. It does not include short circuits or ground faults.

(b) These provisions shall not be interpreted as requiring overcurrent protection where it might introduce additional or increased hazards as in the case of fire pumps. See NFPA Standard for Centrifugal Fire Pumps (No. 20-1971).

▶ Detailed requirements for the installation of fire pumps is not included in the National Electrical Code, but this is covered in NFPA Pamphlet No. 20.

As intended by Section **430-52**, the motor branch-circuit protective device provides short-circuit protection for the circuit conductors. In order to carry the starting current of the motor, this device must have a rating or setting so high that it cannot protect the motor against overload.

For a squirrel-cage induction motor it shall be of the time-delay type with a setting of not over 20 sec at 600 per cent of the motor full-load current. It is the intent that the fire-pump motor attempt to run under any condition of loading and not be automatically disconnected by an overcurrent protection device. It will be noted that modern installations generally employ straight induction motors.

Pamphlet No. 20 requires a circuit breaker instead of a fuse as the short-circuit protection for the branch circuit and also requires an unfused isolating switch ahead of the circuit breaker.

Except where the special types of fuses described in Section **430-54** are used, in practically all cases where motor-running overcurrent protection is provided the motor controller consists of two parts: (1) a switch or contactor to control the circuit to the motor and (2) the motor-running protective device. Most of the protective devices make use of a heater coil, usually consisting of a few turns of high-resistance metal, though the heater may be of other form.

Figure **430-6** shows a typical starter of the full-voltage or "across-the-line" type. The illustration shows the starter with one insulating cover removed so that one of the main contacts is exposed to view.

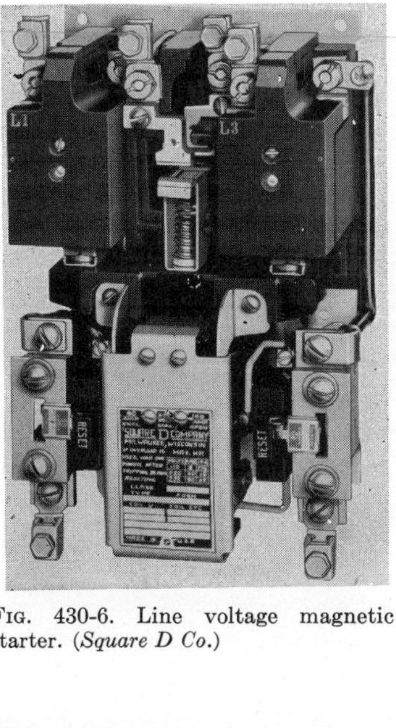

FIG. 430-6. Line voltage magnetic starter. (*Square D Co.*)

FIG. 430-7. Fustat fuse. (*Bussmann Mfg. Co.*)

430-32. Continuous Duty Motors.

(a) More Than One Horsepower. Each continuous duty motor rated more than one horsepower shall be protected against overcurrent by one of the following means:

(1) A separate overcurrent device which is responsive to motor current. This device shall be rated or selected to trip at no more than the following per cent of the motor full-load current rating:

Motors with a marked service factor not less than 1.15	125%
Motors with a marked temperature rise not over 40°C	125%
All other motors	115%

For a multispeed motor, each winding connection shall be considered separately. This value may be modified as permitted by Section 430-34.

When a separate motor running-overcurrent device is so connected that it does not carry the total current designated on the motor nameplate, such as for wye-delta starting, the proper percentage of nameplate current applying to the selection or setting of the overcurrent device shall be clearly designated on the equipment or the manufacturer's selection table shall take this into account.

(2) A thermal protector integral with the motor, approved for use with the motor which it protects on the basis that it will prevent dangerous overheating of the motor due to overload and failure to start. The ultimate trip current of a thermally protected motor shall not exceed the following percentage of motor full-load current given in Tables 430-148, 430-149 and 430-150:

Motor full-load current not exceeding 9 amperes	170%
Motor full-load current 9.1 to and including 20 amperes	156%
Motor full-load current greater than 20 amperes	140%

If the motor current-interrupting device is separate from the motor and its control circuit is operated by a protective device integral with the motor, it shall be so arranged that the opening of the control circuit will result in interruption of current to the motor.

(3) The motor shall be considered as being properly protected where it is a part of an approved assembly which does not normally subject the motor to overloads and if there is a protective device integral with the motor which will protect the motor against damage due to failure to start.

(4) For motors larger than 1500 horsepower, a protective device employing embedded temperature detectors which cause current to the motor to be interrupted when the motor attains a temperature rise greater than marked on the nameplate in an ambient of 40° C.

Standards for the application of embedded temperature detectors are given in Standards for Rotating Electrical Machinery, ANSI C50.2-1955 and C50.4-1965.

(b) One Horsepower or Less, Manually Started.

(1) Each continuous duty motor rated at one horsepower or less which is not permanently installed, is manually started and is within sight from the controller location, shall be considered as protected against overcurrent by the overcurrent device protecting the conductors of the branch circuit. This branch circuit overcurrent device shall not be larger than that specified in Part D of Article 430, except that any such motor may be used at 125 volts or less on a branch circuit protected at 20 amperes.

(2) Any such motor which is not in sight from the controller location shall be protected as specified in Section 430-32(c). Any motor rated at one horsepower or less which is permanently installed, shall be protected in accordance with Section 430-32(c).

(c) One Horsepower or Less, Automatically Started. Any motor of one horsepower or less which is started automatically shall be protected against overcurrent by the use of one of the following means:

(1) A separate overcurrent device which is responsive to motor current. This device shall be rated or selected to trip at no more than the following per cent of the motor full-load current rating:

Motors with a marked service factor not less than 1.15	125%
Motors with a marked temperature rise not over 40°C	125%
All other motors	115%

For a multispeed motor, each winding connection shall be considered separately. This value may be modified as permitted by Section 430-34.

(2) A thermal protector integral with the motor, approved for use with the motor which it protects on the basis that it will prevent dangerous overheating of the motor due to overload and failure to start. Where the motor current interrupting device is separate from the motor and its control circuit is operated by a protective device integral with the motor, it shall be so arranged that the opening of the control circuit will result in interruption of current to the motor.

(3) The motor shall be considered as being properly protected where it is part of an approved assembly which does not normally subject the motor to overloads and if there is a protective device integral with the motor which will protect the motor against damage due to failure to start, or if the assembly is also equipped with other safety controls (such as the safety combustion controls of a domestic oil burner) which protect the motor against damage due to failure to start. Where the assembly has safety controls which protect the motor it shall be so indicated on the nameplate of the assembly where it will be visible after installation.

(4) In case the impedance of the motor windings is sufficient to prevent overheating due to failure to start, the motor may be protected as specified in Section 430-32(b) (1) for manually started motors provided that the motor is part of an approved assembly in which the motor will limit itself so that it will not be dangerously overheated.

Many alternating-current motors of less than $\frac{1}{20}$ horsepower, such as clock motors, series motors, etc., and also some larger motors such as torque motors, come within this classification. It does not include split-phase motors having automatic switches to disconnect the starting windings.

(d) Wound-Rotor Secondaries. The secondary circuits of wound-rotor alternating-current motors, including conductors, controllers, resistors, etc., shall be considered as protected against overcurrent by the motor-running overcurrent device.

▶ The term *rating or setting* as here used means the current at which the device will open the circuit if this current continues for a considerable length of time.

A motor having a temperature rise of 40°C when operated continuously at full load can carry a **25** per cent overload for some time without injury to the motor. Other types of motors, such as enclosed types, do not have so high an overload capacity and the running protective device should therefore open the circuit on a prolonged overload which causes the motor to draw **115** per cent of its rated full-load current.

A protective device integral with the motor as used for the protection of motors is shown in Figs. **430-8** and **430-9**. This device is placed inside the motor frame and is connected in series with the motor winding. It contains a bimetallic disk carrying two contacts, through which the circuit is normally closed. If the motor is overloaded and its temperature is raised to a certain limiting value, the disk snaps to the "open" position and opens the circuit. The device also includes a heating coil in series with the motor

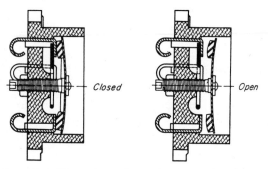

Fig. 430-8. Klixon integral running protective device. (*Spencer Thermostat Co.*)

windings which causes the disk to become heated more rapidly in case of a sudden heavy overload.

Single-phase motors equipped with integral protective devices of the general type shown in Figs. **430-8** and **430-9** are obtainable in ratings of 1 hp and less and in a few larger ratings. For motors of larger size a similar device is used which serves as a relay to actuate a separate contactor through a control circuit.

After opening the circuit on an overload, the integral device shown here will automatically reclose and start the motor after the motor has cooled. For some applications this may not be desirable and for such cases the device is so designed that after it has opened, it must be manually returned to the closed position by means of a reset button. (See Section **430-43**.)

The motor and the integral device should be tested together as a complete assembly and the protective device should open the circuit on an overcurrent as specified in Section **430-32a(2)**.

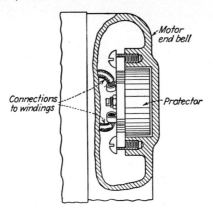

FIG. 430-9. Mounting of integral protective device shown in Fig. 430-8. (*Spencer Thermostat Co.*)

Where the circuit-interrupting device is separate from the motor and is actuated by a device integral with the motor, the two devices must be so designed and connected that any accidental opening of the control circuit will stop the motor, otherwise the motor would be left operating without any overcurrent protection.

There is special need for running protection on an automatically started motor because, if the motor is stalled when the starter operates, the motor will probably burn out if it has no running protection.

430-33. Intermittent and Similar Duty. A motor used for a condition of service which is inherently short time, intermittent, periodic, or varying duty, as illustrated by Table 430-22 (a-Exception), shall be considered as protected against overcurrent by the branch-circuit overcurrent device, provided the overcurrent protection does not exceed that specified in Table 430-152.

Any motor application shall be considered to be for continuous duty unless the nature of the apparatus which it drives shall be such that the motor cannot operate continuously with load under any condition of use.

▶ Where a motor is used for one of the "conditions of service" on account of the character of the machine or other apparatus which the motor drives, long-continued overloads are not likely to occur, except that some trouble in the driven machine or apparatus might stall the motor, and in this case the branch-circuit protective device would open the circuit. Running overcurrent protection for such motors is therefore not considered necessary. It should be noted that omission of the running protection is based upon the type of "duty" and is not in any way dependent upon the time rating of the motor.

430-34. Selection or Setting of Protective Device.   Where the values specified for motor-running overcurrent protection in Sections 430-32 (a-1) and 430-32 (c-1) do not correspond to the standard sizes or ratings of fuses, nonadjustable circuit breakers, thermal cutouts, thermal relays, the heating elements of thermal trip motor switches, or the possible settings of adjustable circuit breakers adequate to carry the load, the next higher size, rating, or setting may be used, but not higher than the following per cent of motor full-load current rating:

Motors with a marked service factor not less than 1.15	140%
Motors with a marked temperature rise not over 40°C	140%
All other motors	130%

In case it is not shunted during the starting period of the motor (see Section 430-35), the protective device shall have sufficient time delay to permit the motor to start and accelerate its load.

430-35. Shunting During Starting Period.

(a)   In the case of a motor that is manually started (including starting with a magnetic starter having pushbutton control), the running overcurrent protection may be shunted or cut out of circuit during the starting period of the motor, provided the device by which the overcurrent protection is shunted or cut out cannot be left in the starting position, and fuses or time-delay circuit breakers rated or set at not over 400 per cent of the full-load current of the motor, are so located in the circuit as to be operative during the starting period of the motor.

(b)   The motor-running overcurrent protection shall not be shunted or cut out during the starting period if the motor is automatically started.

▶   Where fuses are used as the motor-running protection, they may be cut out of the circuit during the starting period. (See Fig. **430-10.**) This leaves

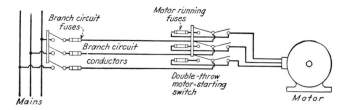

Fig. 430-10. Double-throw switch arranged for across-the-line starting. The switch is thrown to the right to start the motor, thus cutting the running fuses out of the circuit. The switch must be so made that it cannot be left in the starting position.

the motor protected only by the branch-circuit fuses, but the rating of these fuses will always be well within the limits specified in the above rule. If the branch-circuit fuses are omitted, as allowed by the rules in Section **430-53**, it is not permitted to use a starter that cuts out the motor fuses during the starting period unless the protection of the feeder is within the limits set by this rule.

430-36. Fuses—In Which Conductor.   Where fuses are used for motor-running protection, a fuse shall be inserted in each ungrounded conductor.

Exception: A fuse shall also be inserted in the grounded conductor when the supply system is 3-wire, 3-phase AC, one conductor grounded.

430-37. Devices Other Than Fuses—In Which Conductor.   Where devices other than fuses are used for motor-running overload protection, Table 430-37 shall govern the minimum allowable number and location of overcurrent units such as trip coils, relays, or thermal cutouts.

Table 430-37. Running Overcurrent Units

Kind of Motor	Supply System	Number and location of overcurrent units, such as trip coils, relays or thermal cutouts
1-phase A.C. or D.C.	2-wire, 1-phase A.C. or D.C. ungrounded	1 in either conductor
1-phase A.C. or D.C.	2-wire, 1-phase A.C. or D.C., one conductor grounded	1 in ungrounded conductor
1-phase A.C. or D.C.	3-wire, 1-phase A.C. or D.C., grounded-neutral	1 in either ungrounded conductor
2-phase A.C.	3-wire, 2-phase A.C., ungrounded	2, one in each phase
2-phase A.C.	3-wire, 2-phase A.C., one conductor grounded	2 in ungrounded conductors
2-phase A.C.	4-wire, 2-phase A.C. grounded or ungrounded	2, one per phase in ungrounded conductors
2-phase A.C.	5-wire, 2-phase, A.C., grounded neutral or ungrounded	2, one per phase in any ungrounded phase wire
3-phase A.C.	Any 3-phase	*3, one in each phase

Exception: Unless protected by other approved means.

▶ Three-element protection must be provided for all three-phase motors unless protected by other approved means (such as specially designed embedded detectors with or without supplementary external protective devices).

430-38. Number of Conductors Opened by Overcurrent Device.   Motor-running protective devices, other than fuses, thermal cutouts, or thermal protectors, shall simultaneously open a sufficient number of ungrounded conductors to interrupt current flow to the motor.

430-39. Motor Controller as Running Overcurrent Protection.   A motor controller may also serve as the running overcurrent device where the number of overcurrent units complies with Section 430-37 and where these overcurrent units are operative in both the starting and running position in the case of a direct-current motor, and in the running position in the case of an alternating-current motor. When a nonautomatic motor controller serves as the running overcurrent device, it is recommended that all ungrounded conductors be opened.

▶ If fuses are used as the running protective device, Section **430-36** requires a fuse in each ungrounded conductor. If the protective device consists of an automatically operated contactor or circuit breaker, the device must open a sufficient number of conductors to stop the current flow to the motor and must be equipped with the number of overcurrent units specified in Table 430-37.

430-40. Thermal Cutouts and Overload Relays. Thermal cutouts, overload relays, and other devices for motor-running protection which are not capable of opening short circuits, shall be protected by fuses or circuit breakers with ratings or settings or by a motor short-circuit protector in accordance with Section 430-52, unless approved for group installation and marked to indicate the maximum size of fuse or time limit circuit breaker by which they must be protected.

Exception: The fuse or circuit breaker ampere rating may be marked on the nameplate of approved equipment in which the thermal cutout or relay is used.

For instantaneous circuit breakers or motor short-circuit protectors see Section 430-52.

430-42. Motors on General Purpose Branch Circuits. Overcurrent protection for motors used on general purpose branch circuits as permitted in Article 210, shall be provided as follows:

(a) One or more motors without individual running overcurrent protection may be connected to general purpose branch circuits only where the limiting conditions specified for each of two or more motors in Section 430-53(a) are complied with.

(b) Motors of larger ratings than specified in Section 430-53(a) may be connected to general purpose branch circuits only in case each motor is protected by running overcurrent protection selected to protect the motor as specified in Section 430-32. Both the controller and the motor-running overcurrent device shall be approved for group installation with the protective device of the branch circuit to which the motor is connected. See Section 430-53.

(c) Where a motor is connected to a branch circuit by means of a plug and receptacle, and individual running overcurrent protection is omitted as provided in Section 430-42(a), a rating of the plug and receptacle shall not exceed 15 amperes at 125 volts or 10 amperes at 250 volts. Where individual overcurrent protection is required as provided in Section 430-42(b) for a motor or motor-operated appliance provided with an attachment plug for attaching to the branch circuit through a receptacle, the running overcurrent device shall be an integral part of the motor or of the appliance. The rating of the plug and receptacle shall be assumed to determine the rating of the circuit to which the motor may be connected, as provided in Article 210.

(d) The overcurrent device protecting a branch circuit to which a motor or motor-operated appliance is connected shall have sufficient time delay to permit the motor to start and accelerate its load.

▶ Branch circuits supplying lamps are usually 115-volt single-phase circuits, and on such a circuit the effect of subparagraph (a) is that any motor larger than 6 amp must be provided with a starter that is approved for group operation.

It is provided in Section 210-25 that receptacles on a 20-amp branch circuit may have a rating of 20 amp, and in such case subparagraph (b) requires that any motor or motor-driven appliance connected through a plug and receptacle must have running overcurrent protection. If the motor rating exceeds 1 hp or 6 amp, the protective device must be permanently attached to the motor and subparagraph (a) must be complied with.

The requirements of Section **430-32** for the running overcurrent protection of motors must be complied with in all cases, regardless of the type of branch circuit by which the motor is supplied and regardless of the number of motors connected to the circuit.

430-43. Automatic Restarting.   A motor-running protective device which can restart a motor automatically after overcurrent tripping shall not be installed unless approved for use with the motor which it protects. A motor which can restart automatically after shutdown shall not be installed so that its automatic restarting can result in injury to persons.

▶   As noted in the comments to Section **430-32**, an integral motor-running protective device may be of the type which will automatically restart, or it may be so constructed that after tripping out it must be closed by means of a reset button.

D. Motor-Branch-Circuit Short Circuit and Ground Fault Protection

430-51. General.   The provisions of Part D specify overcurrent devices intended to protect the motor-branch-circuit conductors, the motor control apparatus, and the motors against overcurrent due to short circuits or grounds. They are in addition to or amendatory of the provisions of Article 240.

430-52. Rating or Setting for Individual Motor Circuit.   The motor branch-circuit overcurrent device shall be capable of carrying the starting current of the motor. Short-circuit and ground-fault overcurrent protection shall be considered as being obtained when the overcurrent device has a rating or setting not exceeding the values given in Table 430-152. An instantaneous-trip circuit breaker (without time delay) shall be used only if adjustable and if part of a combination controller having motor-running overcurrent and short-circuit protection in each conductor and the combination is especially approved for the purpose. A motor short-circuit protector may be used in lieu of devices listed in Table 430-152, provided the motor short-circuit protector is part of a combination controller having motor-running overcurrent and short-circuit protection in each conductor, will operate at not more than 1300 per cent of full-load motor current, and provided the combination is especially approved for the purpose.

In case the values for branch-circuit protective devices determined by Table 430-152 do not correspond to the standard sizes or ratings of fuses, nonadjustable circuit breakers, or thermal devices, or possible settings of adjustable circuit breakers adequate to carry the load, the next higher size, rating or setting may be used. See Section 240-5(b) for standard ratings.

Exception: Where the overcurrent protection specified in Table 430-152 is not sufficient for the starting current of the motor:

(a) The rating or setting of a nontime-delay fuse or time limit circuit breaker may be increased but shall in no case exceed 400 per cent of the full-load current.

(b) *The rating of a time-delay (dual-element) fuse may be increased but shall in no case exceed 225 per cent of the full-load current.*

(c) *The setting of an instantaneous-trip circuit breaker (without time delay) may be increased over 700 per cent but shall in no case exceed 1300 per cent of the motor full-load current.*

(d) *Torque motor branch circuits shall be protected at the motor nameplate current rating. See Section 240-5(a), Exception No. 1.*

For a multispeed motor, a single short-circuit and ground-fault protective device may be used for two or more windings of the motor provided the rating of the protective device does not exceed the above applicable percentage of the nameplate rating of the smallest winding protected.

Where maximum protective device ratings are shown in the manufacturer's heater table for use with a marked controller or are otherwise marked with the equipment, they shall not be exceeded even if higher values are allowed as shown above.

See Example No. 8, Chapter 9, and Diagram 430-1(a).

▶   Where a motor is supplied by an individual branch circuit, having branch-circuit protection, the circuit protective devices may be either fuses or a circuit breaker and the rating or setting of these devices must not exceed the values specified in Table 430-152 (exceptions noted). (See Fig. 430-1.)

Section 430-6 permits the rating or setting of these overcurrent devices to be based on the values of full-load motor current given in Tables 430-147 to 430-150.

In Fig. 430-4, the fuses or circuit breaker at the panelboard must carry the starting current of the motor, and in order to carry this current the fuse rating or circuit-breaker setting may be 150 to 300 per cent of the running current of the motor, depending on the size and type of motor. It is evident that to install motor-circuit conductors having an ampacity of 150 to 300 per cent of the motor full-load current would be unnecessary. See Section 430-52 for instantaneous-trip circuit breakers or motor short-circuit protectors.

There are three possible causes of excess current in the conductors between the panelboard and the motor controller, viz., a short circuit between two of these conductors, a ground on one conductor that forms a short circuit, and an overload on the motor. A short circuit would draw so heavy a current that the fuses or breaker at the panelboard would immediately open the circuit, even though the rating or setting is in excess of the conductor ampacity. Any excess current due to an overload on the motor must pass through the protective device at the motor controller, causing this device to open the circuit. Therefore with circuit conductors having an ampacity equal to 125 per cent of the motor-running current and with the motor-protective device set to operate at near the same current, the conductors are reasonably protected.

Section 430-7 provides for marking the nameplates of a-c motors, ½ hp and larger, to show the kilovolt-ampere input per horsepower with locked rotor. The use of the Code letters provides a more accurate and satisfactory means of determining the correct rating or setting of the protective devices than is otherwise possible. Motors without the Code letters will, however, be in use for a number of years, and the data in Table **430-152** apply to such motors and also to motors smaller than ½ hp.

Certain types of motor controllers provide protection for the motors they control against all ordinary overloads but are not intended to open short circuits. Fuses, circuit breakers, or motor short-circuit protectors used as the branch-circuit protective device will open short circuits and therefore provide short-circuit protection for both the motor and the running protective device.

Under exceptionally severe starting conditions where the nature of the load is such that an unusually long time is required for the motor to accelerate to full speed, the fuse or circuit-breaker rating or setting recommended in Table **430-152** may not be high enough to allow the motor to start. It is desirable to keep the branch-circuit protection at as low a rating as possible, but in unusual cases, it is permissible to use a higher rating or setting, up to the maximum values stated in the exception to Section **430-52**.

It should be noted that for No. **14** branch-circuit conductors the branch-circuit fuse ratings given in Part D of Article **430** are in no case less than **15** amp. The ampacity of the wire is **15** amp, and the wire is therefore protected by overcurrent devices of this rating.

The supply of two or more small motors by one branch circuit is mentioned in Section **430-42**. In such cases the rating or setting of the overcurrent protection should not be less than the rating or setting for the protection of power feeders as given in Section **430-62**, *i.e.*, the highest rating or setting of the branch-circuit overcurrent protection for any one of the motors as given in Part D of Article **430**, plus the sum of the full-load current ratings for all the other motors.

430-53. Several Motors on One Branch Circuit. Two or more motors or a motor(s) and other loads may be connected to the same branch circuit under any of the following conditions:

(a)   Several motors each not exceeding 1 hp in rating may be used on a branch circuit protected at not more than 20 amperes at 125 volts or less, or 15 amperes at 600 volts or less, provided that all of the following conditions are met:

(1)   The full-load rating of each motor shall not exceed six amperes.

(2)   The rating of the branch-circuit protective device marked on any of the controllers shall not be exceeded.

(3)   Individual running overcurrent protection shall conform to Section 430-32.

(b)   If the branch-circuit protective device is selected not to exceed that allowed by Section 430-52 for the motor of the smallest rating, two or more motors or a motor(s) and other load(s), with each motor having individual running overcurrent protection, may be connected to a branch circuit when it can be determined that branch-circuit protective device will not open under the most severe normal conditions of service which might be encountered.

▶   The reference to Section **430-52** pertains to overcurrent protection not exceeding the values given in Table **430-152.**

(c) Two or more motors of any rating or a motor(s) and other loads, with each motor having individual running overcurrent protection, may be connected to one branch circuit provided all of the following conditions are complied with:

(1) Each motor-running overcurrent device must be approved for group installation with a specified maximum rating of fuse and/or circuit breaker.

(2) Each motor controller must be approved for group installation with a specified maximum rating of fuse and/or circuit breaker.

(3) Each circuit breaker must be of the time-limit type and approved for group installation.

(4) The branch circuit shall be protected by fuses or time-limit circuit breakers having a rating not exceeding that specified in Section 430-52 for the largest motor connected to the branch circuit plus an amount equal to the sum of the full-load current ratings of all other motors and the ratings of other loads connected to the circuit. Where this calculation results in a rating less than the ampacity of the supply conductors, the rating of the fuses or circuit breakers may be increased to a value not exceeding the ampacity of the supply conductors.

(5) The branch-circuit fuses or time-limit circuit breakers must not be larger than allowed by Section 430-40 for the thermal cutout or relay protecting the smallest motor of the group.

(6) The conductors of any tap supplying a single motor need not have individual branch-circuit protection, provided they comply with either of the following: (1) no conductor to the motor shall have an ampacity less than that of the branch-circuit conductors, or (2) no conductor to the motor shall have an ampacity less than one-third that of the branch-circuit conductors, with a minimum in accordance with Section 430-22; the conductors to the motor-running protective device being not more than 25 feet long and being protected from physical damage.

Omission of Branch-Circuit Protective Device

Case A

Motor branch-circuit protective devices may be omitted at each motor if the taps to each motor-running protective device have the same ampacity as the main branch-circuit conductors, as illustrated by Fig. 430-11. Such con-

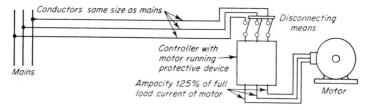

Fɪɢ. 430-11. Omission of branch-circuit protective devices. Case A—conductors to motor controller same size as feeder conductors.

ductors are in fact a part of the circuit and it is evident that there is no need for any fuses or circuit breaker at the point where the conductors are connected together to the feeder. In this case the conductors between the motor-running protective device and the motor are branch-circuit conductors, and their size is governed by Section **430-22**. The motor starter must be of the type approved for group installation.

Case B

Motor branch-circuit protective devices may be omitted provided that the tap conductors from the mains to the motor-running protective device have at least one-third the ampacity of the feeder, are not more than **25** ft long, are suitably protected from physical damage, and have at least the ampacity required by Section **430-22**.

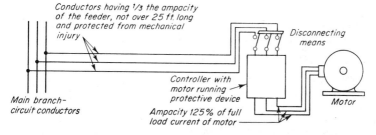

Conductors having 1/3 the ampacity of the feeder, not over 25 ft. long and protected from mechanical injury

Disconnecting means

Main branch-circuit conductors

Controller with motor running protective device

Ampacity 125% of full load current of motor

Motor

Fig. 430-12. Omission of branch-circuit protective devices. Case B—conductors to motor controller having one-third the ampacity of the mains.

The conditions of Case B are illustrated by Fig. **430-12**. As in Case A, the size of the conductors from the motor protective device to the motor is determined by the rule for the conductors of motor branch circuits in Section **430-22**, and the starter or controller must be of the type approved for group installation.

The principle applied here is that, since the conductors are short and protected from physical damage, it is unlikely that trouble will occur in the run between the mains and the motor protection which will cause the conductors to be overloaded, except some accident resulting in an actual short circuit. A short circuit will blow the fuses or trip the circuit breaker protecting the mains. An overload on the conductors caused by overloading the motor or trouble in the motor itself will cause the motor protective device to operate and so protect the conductors.

It should be noted that the tap conductors should never be of smaller size than the branch-circuit conductors required by Section **430-22**. Thus if a 20-hp 230-volt three-phase squirrel-cage motor is to be supplied from a No. 000 circuit, assuming the use of Type T conductors, the branch-circuit tap conductors must not be smaller than No. 4 and conductors tapped solidly to the mains as permitted in the above rule must be not smaller than this size.

430-54. Multimotor and Combination Load Equipment. The rating of the branch circuit protective device for multimotor and combination load equipment shall not exceed the rating marked on the equipment in accordance with Section 430-7(d).

430-55. Combined Overcurrent Protection. Motor-branch-circuit overcurrent protection and motor-running overcurrent protection may be combined in a single overcurrent device when the rating or setting of the device provides the running overcurrent protection specified in Section 430-32.

▶ Circuit breakers can be made having time-delay characteristics such that a single breaker can serve as both the branch-circuit protective device and the motor-running protective device, but this use of circuit breakers is not common.

The special time-delay fuses shown in Figs. **430-7, 430-13,** and **430-14**

Fig. 430-13. Fusetron cartridge-type fuse. (*Bussmann Mfg. Co.*)

are examples of devices which combine in a single unit the functions of a motor branch-circuit protective device and a motor-running protective device.

Fig. 430-14. Trion time-delay cartridge-type fuse. (*Chase-Shawmut Co.*)

The "Fustat" (Fig. **430-7**) consists of two elements, (1) a fuse link which operates the same as any standard types of fuse, opening the circuit almost instantaneously on a short circuit or heavy overload, and (2) a heater element which, under a continued overload which would injure the motor, melts the solder retaining one end of the fuse link, thus permitting the spring to open the circuit by withdrawing the link from the melted solder.

These fuses may be used on circuits where the use of plug fuses is permitted. (See Section **240-6a.**) They are obtainable in ratings up to **30** amp. To provide running protection for a motor, for ordinary service, the rating should be selected which is about **110** per cent of the full-load current rating of the motor.

The cartridge-type fuses shown in Figs. **430-13** and **430-14** are available in all standard fuse ratings up to **600** amp at **250** and **600** volts. These fuses have sufficient time delay so that if used for the protection of a motor branch circuit, and if fuses are selected having a rating close to the full-load current of the motor, in most cases the fuses will not blow on the starting current of the motor but will blow on a continued overload.

430-56. Overcurrent Devices—In Which Conductor. Overcurrent devices shall comply with the provisions of Section 240-11.

▶   Motor branch circuits are to be protected in the same way as other circuits with regard to the number of fuses and the number of poles and overcurrent units of circuit breakers. If fuses are used, a fuse is required in each ungrounded conductor. If a circuit breaker is used, there must be an overcurrent unit in each ungrounded conductor.

430-57. Size of Fuseholder.   Where fuses are used for motor-branch-circuit protection, the fuseholders shall not be of a smaller size than required to accommodate the fuses specified by Table 430-152.

Exception: Where fuses having time delay appropriate for the starting characteristics of the motor are used, fuseholders of smaller size than specified in Table 430-152 may be used.

▶   Special time-delay fuses can be of lower ratings than the maximum ratings specified in Part D of Article 430, and better protection is secured by the use of fuses having the lower ratings. Where such fuses are used, it is possible to use smaller cutout bases, or smaller fusible switches, than would be required for fuses of the standard type. (See Table 430-152.)

430-58. Rating of Circuit Breaker.   A circuit breaker for motor-branch-circuit protection shall have a current rating in accordance with Sections 430-52 and 430-110.

▶   In the case of a circuit breaker having an adjustable trip point, this rule refers to the capacity of the circuit breaker to carry current without overheating and has nothing to do with the setting of the breaker. The breaker most commonly used as a motor branch-circuit protective device is the nonadjustable circuit breaker (see Section 240-5b), and any breaker of this type having a rating in conformity with the requirements of Section 430-52 will have an ampacity considerably in excess of 115 per cent of the full-load motor current.

430-59. Feeder Taps in Inaccessible Location.   If the location of the connection of a tap to the feeder conductors is not accessible, the motor-branch-circuit overcurrent device may be placed where it will be accessible, provided the conductors between the tap and the overcurrent device have the same ampacity as the feeder; or provided they have an ampacity of at least ⅓ that of the feeder and are not more than 25 feet long and are protected from physical damage.

▶   If conductors equal in size to the conductors of a feeder are connected to the feeder, no fuses or other overcurrent protection are needed at the point where the tap is made, since the tap conductors will be protected by the fuses or circuit breaker protecting the feeder.

The more important circuit arrangement permitted by the above rule is shown in Fig. 430-15. This is another example of the Type 2 layout shown in Fig. 430-2.

Instead of placing the fuses or other branch-circuit protective device at the point where the connections are made to the feeder, conductors having at least one-third the ampacity of the feeder are tapped solidly to the feeder and may be run any distance not exceeding **25 ft** to the branch-circuit protective device. From this point on to the motor-running protective device and thence to the motor, conductors are run having the standard ampacity, *i.e.*, **125** per cent of the full-load motor current, as specified in Section **430-22.**

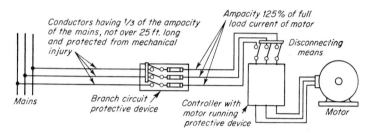

Fig. 430-15. Branch-circuit protective devices located at a distance not exceeding 25 ft from the point where the connection is made to the feeder.

Example

A **15**-hp **230**-volt three-phase motor with autotransformer starter is to be supplied by a tap made to a **250,000**-cir mil feeder. All conductors are to be Type THW.

The feeder has an ampacity of **255** amp; one-third of **255** amp equals **85** amp. Therefore the tap cannot be smaller than No. **4**, which has an ampacity of **85** amp for 75°C ratings.

The full-load current of the motor is **40** amp and, according to Part D of Article 430, assuming that the motor is not marked with a Code letter, the branch-circuit fuses should be rated at **125** amp or less. With the motor-running protection set at **50** amp the tap conductors are well protected from overload.

The conductors tapped solidly to the feeder must never be smaller than the size of branch-circuit conductors required by Section **430-22.**

E. Motor-Feeder Short-Circuit and Ground-Fault Protection

430-61. General.   The provisions of Part E specify overcurrent devices intended to protect feeder conductors supplying motors against overcurrents due to short circuits or grounds.

430-62. Rating or Setting—Motor Load.

(a) A feeder which supplies a specific fixed motor load and consisting of conductor sizes based on Section 430-24 shall be provided with overcurrent protection which shall not be greater than the largest rating or setting of the branch-circuit protective device, for any motor of the group (based on Table 430-152), plus the sum of the full-load currents of the other motors of the group.

Where two or more motors of equal horsepower rating are the largest in the group, one of these motors shall be considered as the largest for the above calculations.

Where two or more motors of a group must be started simultaneously, it may be necessary to install larger feeder conductors and correspondingly larger ratings or settings of feeder overcurrent protection.

See Example No. 8, Chapter 9.

(b) For large-capacity installations, where heavy-capacity feeders are installed to provide for future additions or changes, the feeder overcurrent protection may be based on the rated ampacity of the feeder conductors.

430-63. Rating or Setting—Power and Light Loads. Where a feeder supplies a motor load, and in addition a lighting or a lighting and appliance load, the feeder overcurrent protective device may have a rating or setting sufficient to carry the lighting or the lighting and appliance load as determined in accordance with Articles 210 and 220, plus, for a single motor, the rating permitted by Section 430-52, and for two or more motors, the rating permitted by Section 430-62.

F. Motor Control Circuits

430-71. General. Part F contains modifications of the general requirements and applies to the particular conditions of motor control circuits.

CONTROL CIRCUIT (Definition): The control circuit of a control apparatus or system is the circuit which carries the electric signals directing the performance of the controller, but does not carry the main power circuit.

430-72. Overcurrent Protection. Conductors of control circuits shall be protected against overcurrent in accordance with Section 240-5(a), Exception No. 3.

Exception. Such conductors shall be considered as being properly protected by the branch-circuit overcurrent devices under any one of the following conditions:

(1) Where the rating or setting of the branch-circuit overcurrent device is not more than 500 per cent of the ampacity of the control-circuit conductors.

(2) Where the opening of the control circuit would create a hazard; as for example, the control circuit of fire-pump motors, and the like.

430-73. Mechanical Protection of Conductor. Where damage to a control circuit would constitute a hazard, all conductors of such remote-control circuit shall be installed in a raceway or be otherwise suitably protected from physical damage outside the control device itself.

When one side of the control circuit is grounded, the control circuit shall be so arranged that an accidental ground in the remote-control devices will not start the motor.

▶ There are two different conditions under which protection of the control-circuit conductors from physical damage becomes necessary: (1) where the conductors do not have overcurrent protection in accordance with the general rules for such protection given in Art. 725 and (2) where damage to the conductors would constitute either a fire or an accident hazard. Damage to the control-circuit conductors resulting in short-circuiting two or more of the conductors or breaking one of the conductors would result either in causing the device to operate or in rendering it inoperative, and in some cases either condition would constitute a hazard either to persons or to property; hence, in such cases the conductors should be installed in rigid or other metal conduit. On the other hand, damage to the conductors of the low-voltage control circuit of a domestic oil burner or automatic stoker does not constitute a hazard, because the boiler or furnace is equipped with an automatic safety control.

430-74. Disconnection.

(a) Control circuits shall be so arranged that they will be disconnected from all sources of supply when the disconnecting means is in the open position. The disconnecting means may consist of two separate devices, one of which disconnects the motor and the controller from the source of power supply for the motor, and the other, the control circuit from its power supply. Where the two separate devices are used, they shall be located immediately adjacent one to the other.

(b) Where a transformer or other device is used to obtain a reduced voltage for the control circuit and is located in the controller, such transformer or other device shall be connected to the load side of the disconnecting means for the control circuit.

▶ The control circuit of a remote-control motor controller shall always be so connected that it will be cut off when the disconnecting means is opened, unless a separate disconnecting means is provided for the control circuit. (For overcurrent protection of remote-control circuits, see Art. 725.)

G. Motor Controllers

430-81. General. The provisions of Part G are intended to require suitable controllers for all motors.

(a) Definition. For definition of "Controller," see Article 100. For the purpose of this Article, the term "Controller" includes any switch or device normally used to start and stop the motor.

(b) Stationary Motor of ⅛ Horsepower or Less. For a stationary motor rated at ⅛ horsepower or less, that is normally left running and is so constructed that it cannot be damaged by overload or failure to start, such as clock motors and the like, the branch-circuit overcurrent device may serve as the controller.

(c) Portable Motor of ⅓ Horsepower or Less. For a portable motor rated at ⅓ horsepower or less, the controller may be an attachment plug and receptacle.

430-82. Controller Design.

(a) Each controller shall be capable of starting and stopping the motor which it controls, and for an alternating-current motor shall be capable of interrupting the stalled-rotor current of the motor.

(b) Autotransformer. An autotransformer starter shall provide an off position, a running position, and at least one starting position. It shall be so designed that it cannot rest in the starting position, or in any position which will render inoperative the overcurrent protective device in the circuit.

(c) Rheostats.   Rheostats shall conform to the following:

(1) Internal Connections.   Motor-starting rheostats shall be so designed that the contact arm cannot be left on intermediate segments. The point or plate on which the arm rests when in the starting position shall have no electrical connection with the resistor.

(2) Undervoltage Release, Direct-Current Motors.   Motor-starting rheostats for direct-current motors operated from a constant voltage supply shall be equipped with automatic devices which will interrupt the supply before the speed of the motor has fallen to less than one-third its normal value.

430-83. Rating.   The controller shall have a horsepower rating, which shall not be lower than the horsepower rating of the motor, except as follows:

Exception No. 1: Stationary Motor of 2 Horsepower or Less. For a stationary motor rated at 2 horsepower or less, and 300 volts or less, the controller may be a general-use switch having an ampere rating at least twice the full-load current rating of the motor.

On AC circuits, general use snap switches suitable only for use on AC (not general use AC-DC snap switches) may be used to control a motor rated at 2 horsepower or less and 300 volts or less having a full-load current rating not exceeding 80 per cent of the ampere rating of the switch.

Exception No. 2: Circuit Breaker as Controller. A branch-circuit circuit breaker, rated in amperes only, may be used as a controller. Where this circuit breaker is also used for overcurrent protection, it shall conform to the appropriate provisions of this Article governing overcurrent protection.

Exception No. 3: Torque Motors. The motor controller shall have a continuous duty full-load current rating not less than the nameplate current of the motor. In case the motor controller is rated in horsepower, but is without the foregoing current rating, the equivalent current rating shall be determined from the horsepower rating by using Table 430-147, 430-148, 430-149, or 430-150.

▶   If used only as a controller, *i.e.*, as a device for starting and stopping the motor, a circuit breaker is entirely suitable. In general, however, circuit breakers of the branch-circuit type are not well adapted for use as running protective devices for motors.

430-84. Need Not Open All Conductors.   Except when it serves also as a disconnecting means (see Section 430-111), the controller need not open all conductors to the motor.

▶   A motor controller need open only as many of the conductors of the motor circuit as may be necessary to stop the motor. Thus for a d-c or single-phase motor the controller need open only one conductor; for a three-phase motor, two conductors; and for a two-phase motor, three conductors.

430-85. In Grounded Conductors.   One pole of the controller may be placed in a permanently grounded conductor provided the controller is so designed that the pole in the grounded conductor cannot be opened without simultaneously opening all conductors of the circuit.

▶   Generally, one conductor of a 115-volt circuit is grounded, and on such a circuit a single-pole controller may be used if connected in the ungrounded conductor, or a two-pole controller is permitted if both poles are opened together. In a 230-volt circuit there is usually no grounded conductor, but if one conductor is grounded the rule applies.

430-86. Motor Not in Sight from Controller.   Where a motor and the driven machinery are not in sight from the controller location, the installation shall comply with one of the following conditions:

(a)   The controller disconnecting means is capable of being locked in the open position.

(b)   A manually operable switch which will disconnect the motor from its source of supply is placed within sight from the motor location.

▶   The intent in paragraph *a* is to permit a workman to lock the disconnecting means in the open position and keep the key in his possession so that the circuit cannot be energized while he is working on it. This does not mean that a cabinet enclosing several switches could be locked to accomplish this purpose, because the other switches would be rendered inaccessible. Also it does not mean that removing a "pull out"-type switch serves the purpose, because a "spare" could be inserted in the opening.

Figures 430-16 through 430-18 illustrate arrangements that may be used

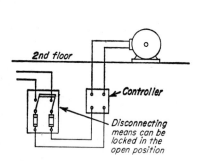

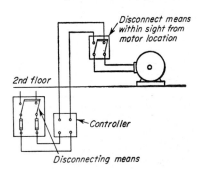

Fig. 430-16. Controller disconnecting means capable of being locked in the open position. See paragraph *a*.

Fig. 430-17. A manually operable switch which will disconnect the motor from its source of supply is placed within sight from the motor location. See paragraph *b*.

where the motor is installed at a point that is not within sight from the controller location. See also Section 430-102.

The pushbutton station in Figure 430-18 operates only the holding coil in the magnetic starter. The magnetic starter "controls" the current to the motor; for example, the control wires to a pushbutton station could become shorted after the motor is in operation and pushing the "stop" button would not release the holding coil in the magnetic starter and the motor would continue to run. This is the reason that a disconnecting means is required to be within sight from the controller. In this case operating the dis-

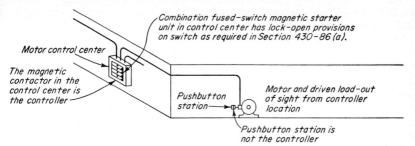

Fɪɢ. 430-18. Control center with lock-open provisions and pushbutton station at motor.

connecting means will open the supply to the controller and shut off the motor.

430-87. Number of Motors Served by Each Controller.   Each motor shall be provided with an individual controller.

Exception: For motors of 600 volts or less a single controller rated at not less than the sum of the horsepower ratings of all of the motors of the group may serve the group of motors under any one of the following conditions:

(a) Where a number of motors drive several parts of a single machine or piece of apparatus such as metal and woodworking machines, cranes, hoists, and similar apparatus.

(b) Where a group of motors is under the protection of one overcurrent device as permitted in Section 430-53(a).

(c) Where a group of motors is located in a single room within sight from the controller location.

▶   These conditions are the same as those under which a single disconnecting means can be used for a group of motors. (See Section **430-112**.)

430-88. Adjustable-Speed Motors.   Adjustable-speed motors that are controlled by means of field regulation shall be so equipped and connected that they cannot be started under weakened field, unless the motor is designed for such starting.

▶   Field weakening is quite commonly used as a method of controlling the speed of d-c motors. If such a motor were started under a weakened field, the starting current would be excessive unless the motor is specially designed for starting in this manner.

430-89. Speed Limitation.   Machines of the following types shall be provided with speed limiting devices.

(a)   Separately excited direct-current motors.

(b)   Series motors.

(c)   Motor-generators and converters which can be driven at excessive speed from the direct-current end, as by a reversal of current or decrease in load.

Exception No. 1: Unless the inherent characteristics of the machines, the system, or the load and the mechanical connection thereto, are such as to safely limit the speed.

Exception No. 2: Unless the machine is always under the manual control of a qualified operator.

▶ A common example of a separately excited d-c motor is found in the Ward Leonard speed control system, which is widely used for electric elevators, hoists, and other applications where smooth control of speed from standstill to full speed is necessary. In the diagram, Fig. 430-19, G_1 and G_2

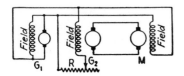

Fig. 430-19. Ward Leonard speed control system.

are two generators having their armatures mounted on a shaft which is driven by a motor, not shown in the diagram. *M* is a motor driving the elevator drum or other machine. The fields of generator G_1 and motor *M* are excited by G_1. By adjusting the rheostat R, the voltage generated by G_2 is varied, and this in turn varies the speed of motor *M*. It is evident that if the field circuit of motor *M* should be accidentally opened while the motor is lightly loaded, the motor would reach an excessive speed. In many applications of this system the motor is always loaded and no speed-limiting device is required.

The speed of a series motor depends upon its load and will become excessive at no load or very light loads. Traction motors are commonly series motors, but such a motor is geared to the drive wheels of the car or locomotive and hence is always loaded.

Where a motor generator, consisting of a motor driving a compound-wound d-c generator, is operated in parallel with a similar machine or is used to charge a storage battery, if the motor circuit is accidentally opened while the generator is still connected to the d-c buses or battery, the generator will be driven as a motor and its speed may become dangerously high. A synchronous converter operating under similar conditions may also reach an excessive speed if the a-c supply is accidentally cut off.

A safeguard against overspeed is provided by a centrifugal device on the shaft of the machine, arranged to close (or open) a contact at a predetermined speed, thus tripping a circuit breaker which cuts the machine off from the current supply.

430-90. Combination Fuseholder and Switch as Controller. The rating of a combination fuseholder and switch used as a motor controller shall be such that the fuseholder will accommodate the size of fuse specified in Part C of Article 430 for motor-running overcurrent protection.

Exception: Where fuses having time delay appropriate for the starting characteristics of the motor are used, fuseholders of smaller size than specified in Part C of Article 430 may be used.

▶   The use of a fusible switch as a motor controller with fuses as motor-running protective devices is seldom practicable unless special types of fuses are used. The rating of the fuses must not exceed 125 per cent, or in some cases 115 per cent, of the full-load motor current, and fuses of this rating would, in most cases, be blown by the starting current drawn by the motor, particularly where the motor turns on and off frequently. (See Section 430-35.)

H. Disconnecting Means

430-101. General.   The provisions of Part H are intended to require disconnecting means capable of disconnecting motors and controllers from the circuit.

    See Diagram 430-1(a). |

430-102. In Sight from Controller Location.   A disconnecting means shall be located in sight from the controller location. |

▶   See comment following Section 430-86.

430-103. To Disconnect Both Motor and Controller.   The disconnecting means shall disconnect the motor and the controller from all ungrounded supply conductors and shall be so designed that no pole can be operated independently. The disconnecting means may be in the same enclosure with the controller. See Section 430-113.

▶   The foregoing rule defines the meaning of the term *disconnecting means*.
    In order that the necessary periodical inspection and servicing of motors and their controllers may be done with safety, the Code requires that a switch, circuit breaker or other device shall be provided for this purpose. Since the disconnecting means must disconnect the controller as well as the motor, it must be a separate device and cannot be a part of the controller, though it could be mounted on the same panel or enclosed in the same box with the controller.
    The disconnecting means may be a motor-circuit switch, a general-use switch, an isolating switch, a circuit breaker, an attachment plug and receptacle, or the branch-circuit overcurrent protective device, the type depending upon the size of the motor and other conditions.
    In case the motor controller fails to open the circuit if the motor is stalled, or under other conditions of heavy overload, the disconnecting means can be used to open the circuit. It is therefore required that a switch used as the disconnecting means shall be capable of interrupting a very heavy current. An exception is made in the case of motors larger than 100 hp. Switches rated up to 100 hp are readily available.

430-104. To Be Indicating.   The disconnecting means shall plainly indicate whether it is in the open or closed position.
430-105. Grounded Conductors.   One pole of the disconnecting means may dis-

connect a permanently grounded conductor, provided the disconnecting means is so designed that the pole in the grounded conductor cannot be opened without simultaneously disconnecting all conductors of the circuit.

430-106. Service Switch as Disconnecting Means. Where an installation consists of a single motor, the service switch may serve as the disconnecting means, provided it conforms to the requirements of this Article, and is within sight from the controller location.

430-107. Readily Accessible. One of the disconnecting means shall be readily accessible.

430-108. Every Switch. Every switch in the motor branch circuit within sight from the controller location shall comply with the requirements of Part H.

430-109. Type. The disconnecting means shall be a motor-circuit switch, rated in horsepower, or a circuit breaker, except as follows:

Exception No. 1: One-Eighth Horsepower or Less. For stationary motors of ⅛ horsepower or less, the branch-circuit overcurrent device may serve as the disconnecting means.

Exception No. 2: Two Horsepower or Less. For stationary motors rated at 2 horsepower or less and 300 volts or less, the disconnecting means may be a general-use switch having an ampere rating not less than twice the full-load current rating of the motor.

On AC circuits, general use snap switches suitable only for use on AC (not general use AC-DC snap switches) may be used to disconnect a motor having a full-load current rating not exceeding 80 per cent of the ampere rating of the switch.

Exception No. 3: Over Two Horsepower to and Including 100 Horsepower. The separate disconnecting means required for a motor with an autotransformer-type controller may be a general-use switch where all of the following provisions are complied with:

(a) The motor drives a generator which is provided with overcurrent protection.

(b) The controller (1) is capable of interrupting the stalled-rotor current of the motor, (2) is provided with a no-voltage release, and (3) is provided with running-overcurrent protection not exceeding 125 per cent of the motor full-load current rating.

(c) Separate fuses or a circuit breaker, rated or set at not more than 150 per cent of the motor full-load current, are provided in the motor branch circuit.

Exception No. 4: Exceeding 100 Horsepower. For stationary motors rated at more than 100 horsepower, the disconnecting means may be a motor-circuit switch also rated in amperes, a general-use switch, or an isolating switch.

Isolating switches for motors exceeding 100 horsepower, not capable of interrupting stalled-rotor currents, shall be plainly marked "Do not open under load."

Exception No. 5: Portable Motors. For portable motors an attachment plug and receptacle may serve as the disconnecting means.

▶ If in addition to the disconnecting means there is any other switch in the motor circuit and it is at all likely that this switch might be opened in case of trouble, this switch must have the interrupting capacity required for a switch intended for use as the disconnecting means.

For a motor larger than 2 hp, not larger than 100 hp, and not portable, a motor-circuit switch or a circuit breaker must be used as the disconnecting means, if a disconnecting means is required. A motor-circuit switch is a horsepower-rated switch. (See definition, Art. 100) The exceptions to the general rule are shown in Figs. **430-20** through **430-23.**

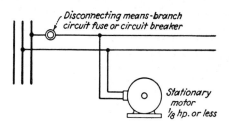

Fig. 430-20. Exception 1—for a stationary motor of ⅛ hp or less, the branch-circuit overcurrent device may serve as the disconnecting means.

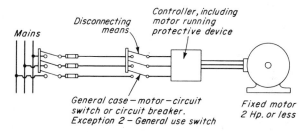

Fig. 430-21. Exception 2—for a 2-hp or smaller motor operating at 300 volts or less, the disconnecting means may be a general-use switch rated at twice the full-load current rating of the motor.

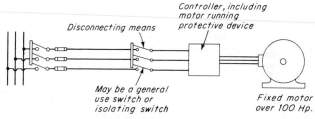

Fig. 430-22. Exception 4—for a fixed motor of over 100 hp the disconnecting means may be either a general-use switch or an isolating switch.

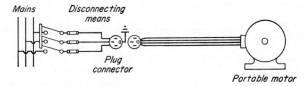

Fig. 430-23. Exception 5—for any portable motor a plug and receptacle may serve as the disconnecting means.

It may be found that a switch having the required horsepower rating is not provided with fuse terminals of the size required to accommodate the branch-circuit fuses. For example, assume a 7½-hp 230-volt three-phase motor started at full-line voltage. A switch used as the disconnecting means for this motor must be rated at not less than 7½ hp, but this would probably be a 60-amp switch and therefore, if fusible, would be equipped with terminals to receive 35- to 60-amp fuses. Section 430-90 provides that fuse terminals must be installed that will receive fuses of 70-amp rating. In any such case a switch of the next higher rating must be provided.

Exception: Where fuses having time delay appropriate for the starting characteristics of the motor are used, fuseholders of smaller size than specified in Part C of Article 430 may be used. (See Section 430-57.)

Horsepower-rated enclosed fusible switches usually have a marking within the switch which permits a dual horsepower rating. A larger horsepower rating for such switches is generally permitted where time-delay fuses are used as the branch-circuit overcurrent protection.

430-110. Ampacity and Interrupting Capacity.

(a) The disconnecting means shall have an ampacity of at least 115 per cent of the full-load current rating of the motor.

(b) The disconnecting means for a torque motor shall be selected on the basis of the nameplate current as follows:

(1) The ampacity shall be at least 115 per cent of the nameplate current.

(2) To determine the equivalent horsepower in complying with the requirements of Section 430-109, select the horsepower rating from Table 430-147, 430-148, 430-149, or 430-150 corresponding to the motor current. In case the nameplate current does not correspond to a current shown in the Table, the horsepower rating corresponding to the next higher value shall be selected.

(c) Where one or more motors are used together or are used in combination with other loads, such as resistance heaters, and where the combined load may be simultaneous on a single disconnecting means, the rating and ampacity of the combined load is to be determined as follows:

(1) The rating of the disconnecting means shall be determined from the summation of all currents, including resistance loads, at the full-load condition and also at the locked-rotor condition. The combined full-load current and the combined locked-rotor current so obtained shall be considered as a single motor for the purpose of this requirement as follows:

The full-load current equivalent to the horsepower rating of each motor shall be selected from Table 430-148, 430-149, or 430-150. These full-load currents shall be added to the rating in amperes of other loads to obtain an equivalent full-load current for the combined load.

The locked-rotor current equivalent to the horsepower rating of each motor shall be selected from Table 430-151. The locked-rotor currents shall be added to the rating in amperes of other loads to obtain an equivalent locked-rotor current for the combined load. Where two or more motors and/or other loads cannot be started simultaneously, appropriate combinations of locked-rotor and full-load current may be employed to determine the equivalent locked-rotor current for the simultaneous combined loads.

(2) The ampacity of the disconnecting means shall be at least 115 per cent of the summation of all currents at the full-load condition determined in accordance with Section 430-110(c) (1).

(3) For small motors not covered by Table 430-147, 430-148, 430-149, or 430-150, the locked-rotor current shall be assumed to be six times the full-load current.

(4) Where part of the concurrent load is resistance load and the disconnecting means is a switch rated in horsepower and amperes, the horsepower rating of the switch shall not be less than the combined load of the motor at the locked-rotor condition and the ampere rating shall not be less than the locked-rotor load plus the resistance load.

▶ A general-use switch, circuit breaker, plug and receptacle, or fuse, used as a disconnecting means, must have an ampacity of not less than 115 per cent of the full-load current of the motor.

430-111. Switch or Circuit Breaker as Both Controller and Disconnecting Means.
A switch or circuit breaker complying with the provisions of Section 430-83 may serve as both controller and disconnecting means provided it opens all ungrounded conductors to the motor, is protected by an overcurrent device (which may be the branch circuit fuses) which opens all ungrounded conductors to the switch or circuit breaker, and is of one of the following types:

(a) An air-break switch, operable directly by applying the hand to a lever or handle.

(b) A circuit breaker operable directly by applying the hand to a lever or handle.

(c) An oil switch used on a circuit whose rating does not exceed 600 volts or 100 amperes, or by special permission on a circuit exceeding this capacity where under expert supervision.

The oil switch or circuit breaker specified above may be both power and manually operable. If power operable, provision should be made to lock it in the open position.

The overcurrent device protecting the controller may be part of the controller assembly or may be separate.

An autotransformer-type controller is not included above and will require a separate disconnecting means.

▶ *Paragraph a. Manually Operable Air-break Switch.*

The intention in this case is to permit omission of the disconnecting means only where all other specified conditions are met and where the controller consists of, or includes, a manually operable switch, except that a separate disconnecting means must always be provided if the controller is of the autotransformer or "compensator" type. The switch may be combined with a motor-running protective device.

Where the controller consists of a manually operable air-break switch, a manually operable circuit breaker, or, for a motor operating at 600 volts or less, an oil switch of 100 amp rating (or of higher rating by special permission), the controller itself is considered as a satisfactory disconnecting means and no additional device to serve as a disconnecting means is required. The switch or circuit breaker used as the controller must meet all requirements for controllers and must be protected by an overcurrent device that opens all ungrounded conductors.

The condition that the switch or circuit breaker shall be protected by an overcurrent device which opens all ungrounded conductors will always be fulfilled if branch-circuit overcurrent protective devices (fuses or a circuit breaker) are installed. The only cases where this condition will not be fulfilled are those where the branch-circuit protection is omitted, as permitted by Section 430-53.

The conditions under which the controller may serve also as the disconnecting means, or, in other words, where no disconnecting means is required, are shown in Fig. 430-24.

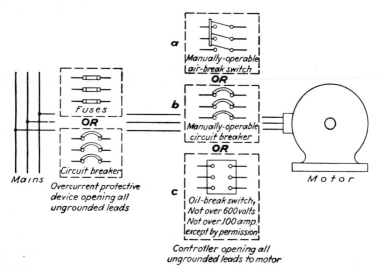

FIG. 430-24. Conditions where no disconnecting means in addition to the controller are required.

430-112. Motors Served by a Single Disconnecting Means.
Each motor shall be provided with individual disconnecting means.

Exception: For motors of 600 volts or less a single disconnecting means may serve a group of motors under any one of the following conditions:

(a) Where a number of motors drive several parts of a single machine or piece of apparatus such as metal and woodworking machines, cranes, and hoists.

(b) Where a group of motors is under the protection of one set of overcurrent devices as permitted by Section 430-53(a).

(c) Where a group of motors is in a single room within sight from the location of the disconnecting means.

The disconnecting means shall have a rating not less than is required by Section 430-109 for a single motor the rating of which equals the sum of the horsepowers or currents of all the motors of the group.

▶ *Exception a*

In Section **610-31** it is required that the main collector wires of a traveling crane shall be controlled by a switch located within sight of the wires and readily operable from the floor or ground. This switch would serve as the disconnecting means for the motors on the crane. When repair or maintenance work is to be done on the electrical equipment of the crane, it is safer to cut off the current from all this equipment by opening one switch, rather than to use a separate switch for each motor. Also, in the case of a machine tool driven by two or more motors, a single disconnecting means for the group of motors is more serviceable than an individual switch for each motor, because repair and maintenance work can be done with greater safety when the entire electrical equipment is "dead."

Exception b

Such groups may consist of motors having full-load currents not exceeding 6 amp each, with circuit fuses not exceeding **20** amp at **125** volts or less, or **15** amp at **600** volts or less. Because the expense of providing an individual disconnecting means for each motor is not always warranted for motors of such small size, and also because the entire group of small motors could probably be shut down for servicing without causing inconvenience, a single disconnecting means for the entire group is permitted.

Exception c

"Within sight" should be interpreted as meaning so located that there will always be an unobstructed view of the disconnecting switch from the motor and Section **430-4** limits the distance in this case between the disconnecting means and any motor to a maximum of **50** ft.

These conditions are the same as those under which the use of a single controller is permitted for a group of motors. (See Section **430-87**.) The use of a single disconnecting means for two or more motors is quite common, but in the majority of cases the most practicable arrangement is to provide an individual controller for each motor.

If a switch is used as the disconnecting means, it must be of the type and rating required by Section **430-109** for a single motor having a horsepower rating equal to the sum of the horsepower ratings of all the motors it controls. Thus, for six 5-hp motors the disconnecting means should be a motor-circuit switch rated at not less than **30** hp. If the total of the horsepower ratings is over 2 hp, a horsepower-rated switch must be used.

430-113. Energy From More Than One Source. Equipment receiving electrical energy from more than one source shall be provided with disconnecting means from each source of electrical energy immediately adjacent to the equipment served. Each source may have a separate disconnecting means.

J. Requirements for Over 600 Volts

430-121. General. The provisions of Part J recognize the additional hazard due to the use of high voltage. They are in addition to or amendatory of the other provisions of this Article. Other requirements for circuits and equipment operating at more than 600 volts are in Article 710.

430-123. Motor Running Overcurrent (Overload) Protection. Running overcurrent protection for a motor of over 600 volts shall consist either of a circuit breaker, or of overcurrent units integral with the controller which shall simultaneously open all ungrounded conductors to the motor. The overcurrent device shall have a setting as specified elsewhere in this Article for motor-running overcurrent (overload) protection.

430-124. Short Circuit and Ground-Fault Protection. Each motor branch circuit and feeder of more than 600 volts shall be protected against overcurrent by one of the following means:

(a) A circuit breaker of suitable rating so arranged that it can be serviced without hazard.

(b) Fuses of the oil-filled or other suitable type. Fuses shall be used with suitable disconnecting means or they shall be of a type which can also serve as the disconnecting means. They shall be so arranged that they cannot be re-fused or replaced while they are energized.

(c) Differential protection may be employed to protect an alternating-current motor, the motor control apparatus, and the branch-circuit conductors against overcurrent due to short circuits or grounds. When all these elements are included within the protected zone of a differential protective system, the ratings or settings specified in Section 430-52 do not apply.

DIFFERENTIAL PROTECTIVE SYSTEM (Definition): A differential protective system is a combination of two or more sets of current transformers and a relay or relays energized from their interconnected secondaries.

The primaries of the current transformers are connected on both sides of the equipment to be protected, both ends of the motor phase windings being brought out for this purpose. All of the apparatus and circuits included between the sets of current transformer primaries constitute the protected zone. The current transformer secondaries and the relay elements are so interconnected that the relay elements respond only to a predetermined difference between the currents entering and leaving the protected zone. When actuated, the relay or relays serve to trip the branch-circuit circuit breaker, thus disconnecting the motor, control apparatus in the motor circuit and the branch-circuit conductors from the source of power and, in the case of a synchronous motor, de-energizing its field circuit.

430-126. Disconnecting Means. The circuit breaker or the fuses specified in Section 430-124 may constitute the disconnecting means if they conform to the other applicable requirements of this Article.

K. Protection of Live Parts—All Voltages

430-131. General. The provisions of Part K specify that live parts shall be protected in a manner judged adequate to the hazard involved.

430-132. Where Required. Exposed live parts of motors and controllers operating at 50 volts or more between terminals, shall be guarded against accidental contact by enclosure, or by location as follows:

(a) By installation in a room or enclosure which is accessible only to qualified persons;

(b) By installation on a suitable balcony, gallery or platform, so elevated and arranged as to exclude unqualified persons;

(c) By elevation 8 feet or more above the floor;

(d) So that it will be protected by a guard rail when the motor operates at 600 volts or less.

Exception: Stationary motors having commutators, collectors and brush rigging located inside of motor end brackets and not conductively connected to supply circuits operating at more than 150 volts to ground.

430-133. Guards for Attendants. Where the live parts of motors or controllers operating at more than 150 volts to ground are guarded against accidental contact only by location as specified in Section 430-132, and where adjustment or other attendance may be necessary during the operation of the apparatus, suitable insulating mats or platforms shall be provided so that the attendant cannot readily touch live parts unless standing on the mats or platforms. Where necessary, steps and hand-rails should be installed on or about large machines to afford safe access to parts which must be examined or adjusted during operation.

L. Grounding

430-141. General. The provisions of Part L specify the grounding of motor and controller frames to prevent a potential above ground in the event of accidental contact between live parts and frames. Insulation, isolation, or guarding are suitable alternatives to grounding of motors under certain conditions.

430-142. Stationary Motors. The frames of stationary motors shall be grounded where any of the following conditions exist:

(a) supplied by means of metal-enclosed wiring.

(b) located in a wet place and not isolated nor guarded.

(c) in a hazardous location. (See Articles 500 through 517.)

(d) the motor operates with any terminal at more than 150 volts to ground.

Grounding of the motor frame is preferable, but where the frame of the motor is not grounded, it shall be permanently and effectively insulated from the ground.

▶ Usually stationary motors are supplied by wiring in metal raceway or metal-clad cable. The motor frames of such motors must be grounded, the raceway or cable armor being attached to the frame and serving as the grounding conductor. (See Section 250-91*b*.)

Any motor in a wet location constitutes a serious hazard to persons and should be grounded unless it is so located or guarded that it is out of reach.

430-143. Portable Motors. The frames of portable motors which operate at more than 150 volts to ground shall be guarded or grounded. See Section 250-45(d) on grounding of portable appliances in other than residential occupancies.

It is recommended that the frames of motors which operate at less than 150 volts to ground be grounded where this can be readily accomplished.

See Section 250-59(b) for color of grounding conductor.

430-144. Controllers. Controller cases, except those attached to ungrounded portable equipment and except the lined covers of snap switches, shall be grounded regardless of voltage.

430-145. Method of Grounding. Grounding where required shall be done in the manner specified in Article 250.

(a) Grounding Through Terminal Housings. Where the wiring to fixed motors is in Type AC metal-clad cable or metal raceways, junction boxes to house motor terminals shall be provided, and the armor of the cable or the metal raceways shall be connected to them in the manner specified in Article 250.

(b) Separation of Junction Box from Motor. The junction box required by Section 430-145(a) may be separated from the motor not more than 6 feet provided the leads to the motor are Type AC metal-clad cable or armored cord or are stranded leads enclosed in flexible or rigid conduit or electrical metallic tubing not smaller than ⅜ inch electrical trade size, the armor or raceway being connected both to the motor and to the box. Where stranded leads are used, protected as specified above, they shall not be larger than No. 10, and shall comply with other requirements of this Code for conductors to be used in raceways.

(c) Grounding of Controller Mounted Devices. Instrument transformer secondaries, and exposed noncurrent-carrying metal or other conductive parts or cases of instrument transformers, meters, instruments, and relays shall be grounded as specified in Sections 250-121 through 250-125.

▶   Good practice requires in nearly all cases that the wiring to motors which are not portable shall, at the motor, be installed in rigid or flexible metal conduit, electrical metallic tubing, or metal-clad cable and that such motors should be equipped with terminal housings. The method of connecting the conduit to the motor where some flexibility is necessary is shown in Fig. 430-25. The motor shown drives a compressor by means of a V belt and the

Fig. 430-25. Use of flexible conduit for connection to a motor.

motor must be movable on its base so that the belt tension can be adjusted. The motor circuit is installed in rigid conduit extending about 12 in. above a concrete foundation and a short length of flexible conduit is provided between the end of the rigid conduit and the terminal housing on the motor.

This section permits the use of fixed motors without terminal housings. If a motor has no terminal housing, the branch-circuit conductors must be brought to a junction box not over 6 ft from the motor. Between the junction box and the motor, the following provisions apply:

1. The conductors must either be in the form of metal-clad cable or armored cord, or be installed in rigid or flexible metal conduit or electrical metallic tubing. See Section **350-5** for flexible metal conduit.

2. The conductors may be as small as No. **18**, provided that they must always have the ampacity required by Section **430-22**.

3. If installed in ⅜-in. rigid or flexible conduit or tubing, conductors must not be larger than No. 10 and must be stranded. See Table **350-3**.

According to Section **300-16**, the conduit, tubing, or metal-clad cable must terminate close to the motor in a fitting having a separable bushed hole for each wire. The method of making the connection to the motor is not specified; presumably, it is the intention that the wires brought out from the terminal fitting shall be connected to binding posts on the motor or spliced to the motor leads. The conduit, tubing, or cable must be rigidly secured to the frame of the motor.

Table 430-147. Full-Load Currents in Amperes
Direct-Current Motors

The following values of full-load currents are for motors running at base speed.

HP	120 V	240 V
¼	2.9	1.5
⅓	3.6	1.8
½	5.2	2.6
¾	7.4	3.7
1	9.4	4.7
1½	13.2	6.6
2	17	8.5
3	25	12.2
5	40	20
7½	58	29
10	76	38
15		55
20		72
25		89
30		106
40		140
50		173
60		206
75		255
100		341
125		425
150		506
200		675

Table 430-148. Full-Load Currents in Amperes
Single-Phase Alternating-Current Motors

The following values of full-load currents are for motors running at usual speeds and motors with normal torque characteristics. Motors built for especially low speeds or high torques may have higher full-load currents, and multispeed motors will have full load current varying with speed, in which case the nameplate current ratings shall be used.

To obtain full-load currents of 208- and 200-volt motors, increase corresponding 230-volt motor full-load currents by 10 and 15 per cent, respectively.

The voltages listed are rated motor voltages. Corresponding nominal system voltages are 110 to 120 and 220 to 240.

HP	115 V	230 V
⅙	4.4	2.2
¼	5.8	2.9
⅓	7.2	3.6
½	9.8	4.9
¾	13.8	6.9
1	16	8
1½	20	10
2	24	12
3	34	17
5	56	28
7½	80	40
10	100	50

Table 430-149. Full-Load Current
Two-Phase A.C. Motors (4-wire)

The following values of full-load current are for motors running at speeds usual for belted motors and motors with normal torque characteristics. Motors built for especially low speeds or high torques may require more running current, and multispeed motors will have full load current varying with speed, in which case the nameplate current rating shall be used. Current in common conductor of 2-phase, 3-wire system will be 1.41 times value given.

The voltages listed are rated motor voltages. Corresponding nominal system voltages are 110 to 120, 220 to 240, 440 to 480 and 550 to 600 volts.

HP	Induction Type Squirrel-Cage and Wound Rotor Amperes					Synchronous Type †Unity Power Factor Amperes			
	115 V	230 V	460 V	575 V	2300 V	220 V	440 V	550 V	2300 V
½	4	2	1	.8					
¾	4.8	2.4	1.2	1.0					
1	6.4	3.2	1.6	1.3					
1½	9	4.5	2.3	1.8					
2	11.8	5.9	3	2.4					
3		8.3	4.2	3.3					
5		13.2	6.6	5.3					
7½		19	9	8					
10		24	12	10					
15		36	18	14					
20		47	23	19					
25		59	29	24		47	24	19	
30		69	35	28		56	29	23	
40		90	45	36		75	37	31	
50		113	56	45		94	47	38	
60		133	67	53	14	111	56	44	11
75		166	83	66	18	140	70	57	13
100		218	109	87	23	182	93	74	17
125		270	135	108	28	228	114	93	22
150		312	156	125	32		137	110	26
200		416	208	167	43		182	145	35

† For 90 and 80 per cent power factor the above figures should be multiplied by 1.1 and 1.25 respectively.

Table 430-150. Full-Load Current*
Three-Phase A.C. Motors

HP	Induction Type Squirrel-Cage and Wound Rotor Amperes					Synchronous Type †Unity Power Factor Amperes			
	115 V	230 V	460 V	575 V	2300 V	220 V	440 V	550 V	2300 V
½	4	2	1	.8					
¾	5.6	2.8	1.4	1.1					
1	7.2	3.6	1.8	1.4					
1½	10.4	5.2	2.6	2.1					
2	13.6	6.8	3.4	2.7					
3		9.6	4.8	3.9					
5		15.2	7.6	6.1					
7½		22	11	9					
10		28	14	11					
15		42	21	17					
20		54	27	22					
25		68	34	27		54	27	22	
30		80	40	32		65	33	26	
40		104	52	41		86	43	35	
50		130	65	52		108	54	44	
60		154	77	62	16	128	64	51	12
75		192	96	77	20	161	81	65	15
100		248	124	99	26	211	106	85	20
125		312	156	125	31	264	132	106	25
150		360	180	144	37		158	127	30
200		480	240	192	49		210	168	40

For full-load currents of 208- and 200-volt motors, increase the corresponding 230-volt motor full-load current by 10 and 15 per cent, respectively.

* These values of full-load current are for motors running at speeds usual for belted motors and motors with normal torque characteristics. Motors built for especially low speeds or high torques may require more running current, and multispeed motors will have full load current varying with speed, in which case the nameplate current rating shall be used.

† For 90 and 80 per cent power factor the above figures shall be multiplied by 1.1 and 1.25 respectively.

The voltages listed are rated motor voltages. Corresponding nominal system voltages are 110 to 120, 220 to 240, 440 to 480 and 550 to 600 volts.

Table 430-151. Locked-Rotor Current Conversion Table

As Determined from Horsepower and Voltage Rating
For Use Only With Sections 430-110, 440-12 and 440-41.

Conversion Table

| Max HP Rating | Motor Locked-Rotor Current Amperes | | | | | |
| | Single Phase | | Two or Three Phase | | | |
	115 V	230 V	115 V	230 V	460 V	575 V
½	58.8	29.4	24	12	6	4.8
¾	82.8	41.4	33.6	16.8	8.4	6.6
1	96	48	42	21	10.8	8.4
1½	120	60	60	30	15	12
2	144	72	78	39	19.8	15.6
3	204	102	—	54	27	24
5	336	168	—	90	45	36
7½	480	240	—	132	66	54
10	600	300	—	162	84	66
15	—	—	—	240	120	96
20	—	—	—	312	156	126
25	—	—	—	384	192	156
30	—	—	—	468	234	186
40	—	—	—	624	312	246
50	—	—	—	750	378	300
60	—	—	—	900	450	360
75	—	—	—	1110	558	444
100	—	—	—	1476	738	588
125	—	—	—	1860	930	744
150	—	—	—	2160	1080	864
200	—	—	—	2880	1440	1152

Table 430-152. Maximum Rating or Setting of
Motor Branch-Circuit Protective Devices

Type of Motor	Percent of Full-Load Current			
	Nontime Delay Fuse	Dual-Element (Time-Delay) Fuse	Instantaneous Type Breaker	Time-Limit Breaker
Single-phase, all types				
No code letter............	300	175	700	250
All AC single-phase and polyphase squirrel-cage and synchronous motors with full-voltage, resistor or reactor starting:				
No code letter..............	300	175	700	250
Code letter F to V...........	300	175	700	250
Code letter B to E..........	250	175	700	200
Code letter A..............	150	150	700	150
All AC squirrel-cage and synchronous motors with autotransformer starting:				
Not more than 30 amps				
No code letter............	250	175	700	200
More than 30 amps				
No code letter............	200	175	700	200
Code letter F to V........	250	175	700	200
Code letter B to E........	200	175	700	200
Code letter A.............	150	150	700	150
High-reactance squirrel-cage				
Not more than 30 amps				
No code letter............	250	175	700	250
More than 30 amps				
No code letter............	200	175	700	200
Wound-rotor—No code letter...	150	150	700	150
Direct-current				
No more than 50 hp				
No code letter............	150	150	250	150
More than 50 hp				
No code letter............	150	150	175	150

For explanation of Code Letter Marking, see Table 430-7 (b).

For certain exceptions to the values specified see Sections 430-52, -54. The values given in the last column also cover the ratings of nonadjustable time-limit types of circuit breakers which may be modified as in Section 430-52.

Synchronous motors of the low-torque, low-speed type (usually 450 RPM or lower), such as are used to drive reciprocating compressors, pumps, etc., which start unloaded, do not require a fuse rating or circuit-breaker setting in excess of 200 per cent of full-load current.

ARTICLE 440. AIR-CONDITIONING AND REFRIGERATING EQUIPMENT

A. General

440-1. Scope.

The provisions of this Article apply to electric motor-driven air-conditioning and refrigerating equipment, and to the branch circuits and controllers for such equipment. It provides for the special considerations necessary for circuits supplying sealed (hermetic-type) motor-compressors and for any air-conditioning and/or refrigerating equipment which is supplied from an individual branch circuit which supplies a sealed (hermetic-type) motor-compressor.

440-2. Other Articles.

(a) These provisions are in addition to, or amendatory of, the provisions of Article 430 and other Articles in this Code, which apply except as modified in this Article.

(b) The rules of Articles 422, 424, or 430, as applicable, shall apply to air-conditioning and refrigerating equipment which does not incorporate a sealed (hermetic-type) motor-compressor. Examples of such equipment are devices which employ refrigeration compressors driven by conventional motors, furnaces with air-conditioning evaporator coils installed, fan-coil units, remote forced air-cooled condensers, remote commercial refrigerators, etc.

(c) Devices such as room air conditioners, household refrigerators and freezers, drinking-water coolers, and beverage dispensers are to be considered appliances and the provisions of Article 422 shall also apply.

(d) Hermetic motor-compressors, circuits, controllers, and equipment shall also comply with the applicable provisions of the following:

Capacitors . . . . Section 460-9
Garages, Aircraft Hangars, Gasoline Dispensing and Service
  Stations, Bulk Storage Plants, Finishing Processes and
  Flammable Anesthetics . . . . Articles 511, 513, 514, 515, 516, and 517-E
Hazardous Locations . . . . Articles 500 thru 503
Motion-Picture Studios . . . . Article 530
Resistors and Reactors . . . . Article 470

▶   Many of the requirements in new Art. **440** formerly appeared in various parts of Art. **430**. Because of the need for some special rules for sealed (hermetic-type) motor-compressors it was found desirable to establish a new article for such equipment.

Article **440** is patterned after Art. **430** and many rules, such as disconnecting means, controllers, conductor sizes and group installation, are identical or quite similar in both articles.

Rules for room air-conditioning units are found in Part F of Art. **422**. (Sections **422-40** through **422-44**.)

New concepts for sealed (hermetic-type) motor-compressors are the terms "rated-load current" and "branch-circuit selection current." Definitions of these terms are in notes following Sections **440-3a** and **c**.

When the equipment is marked with the branch-circuit selection current this greatly simplifies the sizing of motor-branch-circuit conductors, disconnecting means, controllers and overcurrent devices for circuit conductors and motors.

440-3. Marking on Sealed (Hermetic-Type) Motor-Compressors and Equipment.

(a) A sealed (hermetic-type) motor-compressor shall be provided with a nameplate which shall give the manufacturer's name, trademark or symbol; identifying designation; the phase; voltage; and frequency. The rated-load current in amperes of the motor-compressor shall be marked on either or both the motor-compressor nameplate and the nameplate of the equipment in which the motor-compressor is used. The locked-rotor current of each single-phase motor-compressor having a rated-load current of more than 9 amperes at 115 volts or more than 4.5 amperes at 230 volts and each polyphase motor-compressor shall be marked on the motor-compressor nameplate. Where a thermal protector complying with Sections 440-52(a)(2) and (b)(2) is used, the motor compressor nameplate or the equipment nameplate shall be marked with the words "Thermally Protected." Where a protective system, complying with Sections 440-52(a)(4) and 440-52(b)(4), is used and is furnished with the equipment, the equipment nameplate shall be appropriately marked. Where a protective system complying with Sections 440-52(a)(4) and 440-52(b)(4) is specified, the equipment nameplate shall be appropriately marked.

Note: The rated-load current for a sealed (hermetic-type) motor-compressor is the current resulting when the motor-compressor is operated at the rated load, rated voltage and rated frequency of the equipment it serves.

(b) Multimotor and combination-load equipment shall be provided with a visible nameplate marked with the maker's name, the rating in volts, frequency and number of phases, minimum circuit ampacity, and the maximum rating of the branch-circuit short-circuit and ground-fault protective device. The ampacity shall be calculated by using Part D and counting all the motors and other loads which will be operated at the same time. The branch-circuit short-circuit and ground-fault protective device rating shall not exceed the value calculated by using Part C. Multimotor or combination-load equipment for use on two or more circuits shall be marked with the above information for each circuit. For multimotor compressor equipment where the motor-compressor markings are shown on the equipment nameplate in lieu of the motor-compressor nameplate(s), as permitted in Section 440-3(a), these markings shall indicate the specific motor-compressor(s) with which the markings are associated.

Exception: Multimotor and combination-load equipment which is suitable under the provisions of this Article for connection to a single 15- or 20-ampere, 120-volt, or a 15-ampere, 208- or 240-volt single-phase branch circuit may be marked as a single load.

(c) Sealed (hermetic-type) motor-compressors or equipment containing such compressor(s) in which the protection system, approved for use with the motor-compressor which it protects, permits continuous current in excess of the specified percentage of nameplate rated-load current given in Section 440-52(b)(2) or (b)(4) shall also be marked with a branch-circuit selection current that complies with Section 440-52(b)(2) or (b)(4). This marking shall be on the nameplate(s) where the rated-load current(s) appears.

Note: Branch-circuit selection current is the value in amperes to be used instead of the rated-load current in determining the ratings of motor branch-circuit conductors, disconnecting means, controllers and branch-circuit short-circuit and ground-fault protective devices wherever the running overload protective device permits a sustained current greater than the specified percentage of the rated-load current.

440-4. Marking on Controllers. A controller shall be marked with the maker's name, trademark, or symbol; identifying designation; the voltage; phase; full-load and locked-rotor current (or horsepower) rating; and such other data as may be needed to properly indicate the motor-compressor for which it is suitable.

440-5. Ampacity and Rating. Ampacity of conductors and rating of equipment shall be determined as follows:

(a) For a sealed (hermetic-type) motor-compressor, the rated-load current marked on the nameplate of the equipment in which the motor-compressor is employed shall be used in determining the rating or ampacity of the disconnecting means, the branch-circuit conductors, the controller, the branch-circuit short-circuit and ground-fault protection, and the separate motor overload protection. Where no rated-load current is shown on the equipment nameplate, the rated-load current shown on the compressor nameplate shall be used. For disconnecting means and controllers, see also Sections 440-12 and 440-41.

Exception No. 1: When so marked, the branch-circuit selection current shall be used instead of the rated-load current to determine the rating or ampacity of the disconnecting means, the branch-circuit conductors, the controller, and the branch-circuit short-circuit and ground-fault protection.

Exception No. 2: See Section 440-22(b) for branch-circuit short-circuit and ground-fault protection of cord- and plug-connected equipment.

(b) For multimotor equipment employing a shaded-pole or permanent split-capacitor-type fan or blower motor, the full-load current for such motor marked on the nameplate of the equipment in which the fan or blower motor is employed shall be used instead of the horsepower rating to determine the ampacity or rating of the disconnecting means, the branch-circuit conductors, the controller, the branch-circuit short-circuit and ground-fault protection, and the separate overload protection. This marking on the equipment nameplate shall not be less than the current marked on the fan or blower motor nameplate.

440-6. Highest Rated (Largest) Motor. In determining compliance with this Article and with Sections 430-24, 430-53(b), 430-53(c), and 430-62(a), the highest rated (largest) motor shall be considered to be that motor which has the highest rated-load current. Where two or more motors have the same rated-load current, only one of them shall be considered as the highest rated (largest) motor. For other than sealed (hermetic-type) motor-compressors, and fan or blower motors as covered in Section 440-5(b), the full-load current used to determine the highest rated motor shall be the equivalent value corresponding to the motor horsepower rating selected from Table 430-148, 430-149, or 430-150.

Exception: When so marked, the branch-circuit selection current shall be used instead of the rated-load current in determining the highest rated (largest) motor-compressor.

440-7. Single Machine. An air-conditioning or refrigerating system shall be considered to be a single machine under the provisions of Section 430-87 Exception and Section 430-112 Exception. The motors may be located remotely from each other.

B. Disconnecting Means

440-11. General. The provisions of Part B are intended to require disconnecting means capable of disconnecting air-conditioning and refrigerating equipment including motor-compressors, and controllers, from the circuit feeder. See Diagram 430-1(a).

440-12. Rating and Interrupting Capacity.

(a) A disconnecting means serving a sealed (hermetic-type) motor-compressor shall be selected on the basis of the nameplate rated-load current or branch-circuit selection current, whichever is greater, and locked-rotor current, respectively, of the motor-compressor as follows:

(1) The ampacity shall be at least 115 per cent of the nameplate rated-load current or branch-circuit selection current, whichever is greater.

(2) To determine the equivalent horsepower in complying with the requirements of Section 430-109, select the horsepower rating from Table 430-148, 430-149, or 430-150 corresponding to the rated-load current or branch-circuit selection current, whichever is greater, and also the horsepower rating from Table 430-151 corresponding to the locked-rotor current. In case the nameplate rated-load current or branch-circuit selection current and locked-rotor current do not correspond to the currents shown in Table 430-148, 430-149, 430-150, or 430-151, the horsepower rating corresponding to the next higher value shall be selected. In case different horsepower ratings are obtained when applying these Tables, a horsepower rating at least equal to the larger of the values obtained shall be selected.

(b) Where one or more sealed (hermetic-type) motor-compressors are used together or are used in combination with other motors and/or loads such as resistance heaters and where the combined load may be simultaneous on a single disconnecting means, the rating for the combined load is to be determined as follows:

(1) The horsepower rating of the disconnecting means shall be determined from the summation of all currents, including resistance loads, at the rated-load condition and also at the locked-rotor condition. The combined rated-load current and the combined locked-rotor current so obtained shall be considered as a single motor for the purpose of this requirement as follows:

a. The full-load current equivalent to the horsepower rating of each motor, other than a sealed (hermetic-type) motor-compressor, and fan or blower motors as covered in Section 440-5(b) shall be selected from Table 430-148, 430-149, or 430-150. These full-load currents shall be added to the motor-compressor rated-load current(s) or branch-circuit selection current(s), whichever is greater, and to the rating in amperes of other loads to obtain an equivalent full-load current for the combined load.

b. The locked-rotor current equivalent to the horsepower rating of each motor, other than a sealed (hermetic-type) motor-compressor, shall be selected from Table 430-151, and for fan and blower motors of the shaded-pole or permanent split-capacitor type marked with the locked-rotor current, the marked value shall be used. The locked-rotor currents shall be added to the motor-compressor locked-rotor current(s) and to the rating in amperes of other loads to obtain an equivalent locked-rotor current for the combined load. Where two or more motors and/or other loads cannot be started simultaneously appropriate combinations of locked-rotor and rated-load current or branch-circuit selection current, whichever is greater, may be employed to determine the equivalent locked-rotor current for the simultaneous combined load.

Exception: Where part of the concurrent load is a resistance load and the disconnecting means is a switch rated in horsepower and amperes, the horsepower rating of the switch shall be not less than the combined load of the motor-compressor(s) and other motor(s) at the locked-rotor condition and the ampere rating shall be not less than this locked-rotor load plus the resistance load.

(2) The ampacity of the disconnecting means shall be at least 115 per cent of the summation of all currents at the rated-load condition determined in accordance with Section 440-12(b)(1).

(c) For small motor-compressors not having the locked-rotor current marked on the nameplate, or for small motors not covered by Table 430-147, 430-148, 430-149, or 430-150, the locked-rotor current shall be assumed to be 6 times the rated-load current. See Section 440-3(a).

(d) Where the rated-load or locked-rotor current as determined above would indicate a disconnecting means rated in excess of 100 horsepower, the provisions of Section 430-109, Exception No. 4, shall apply.

440-13. Cord-Connected Equipment. For cord-connected equipment such as room air conditioners, household refrigerators and freezers, drinking water coolers and beverage dispensers, a separable connector or an attachment plug and receptacle may serve as the disconnecting means. See also Section 422-43.

C. Branch-Circuit Short-Circuit and Ground-Fault Protection

440-21. General. The provisions of Part C specify overcurrent devices intended to protect the branch-circuit conductors, control apparatus and motors in circuits supplying sealed (hermetic-type) motor-compressors against overcurrent due to short circuits and grounds. They are in addition to or amendatory of the provisions of Article 240.

440-22. Application and Selection.

(a) Rating or Setting for Individual Motor-Compressor. The motor-compressor branch-circuit short-circuit and ground-fault protective device shall be capable of carrying the starting current of the motor. The required protection shall be considered as being obtained when this device has a rating or setting not exceeding 175 per cent of the motor-compressor rated-load current or branch-circuit selection current, whichever is greater (15 amperes size minimum); provided that where the protection specified is not sufficient for the starting current of the motor, it may be increased, but shall not exceed 225 per cent of the motor rated-load current or branch-circuit selection current, whichever is greater.

(b) Rating or Setting for Equipment. The equipment branch-circuit short-circuit and ground-fault protective device shall be capable of carrying the starting current of the equipment. Where the sealed (hermetic-type) motor-compressor is the only load on the circuit, the protection shall conform with Section 440-22(a). Where the equipment incorporates more than one sealed (hermetic-type) motor-compressor or a sealed (hermetic-type) motor-compressor and other motors or other loads, the equipment protection shall conform with Section 430-53 and the following:

(1) Where a sealed (hermetic-type) motor-compressor is the largest load connected to the circuit, the rating or setting of the protective device shall not exceed the value specified in Section 440-22(a) for the largest motor-compressor plus the sum of the rated-load current or branch-circuit selection current, whichever is greater, of the other motor-compressor(s) and the ratings of the other loads supplied.

(2) Where a sealed (hermetic-type) motor-compressor is not the largest load connected to the circuit, the rating or setting of the protective device shall not exceed a value equal to the sum of the rated-load current or branch-circuit selection current, whichever is greater, rating(s) for the motor-compressor(s) plus the value specified in Section 430-53(c)(4) where other motor loads are supplied, or the value specified in Section 240-5 where only nonmotor loads are supplied in addition to the motor-compressor(s).

Exception No. 1: A room air conditioner shall be treated as a single motor unit in determining its branch-circuit requirements when all the following conditions are met: a. The unit is cord- and plug-connected. b. Its rating is not more than 40 amperes and 250 volts, single phase. c. Total rated-load current is shown on the unit nameplate rather than individual motor currents. d. The rating of the branch-circuit short-circuit and ground-fault protective device does not exceed the ampacity of the branch-circuit conductors or the rating of the receptacle, whichever is less. See Section 422-40.

Note: For the purpose of this paragraph, a room air conditioner is an alternating-current sealed (hermetic-type) air-cooled window, console, or in-wall room air conditioner which is installed in the conditioned room. It also applies to a room air conditioner having provisions for heating.

Exception No. 2: Equipment which will start and operate on a 15- or 20-ampere, 120-volt or 15-ampere, 208- or 240-volt, single-phase branch circuit shall be considered as protected by the 15- or 20-ampere overcurrent device protecting the branch circuit except that where the maximum circuit protective device rating marked on the equipment is less than these values, the circuit protective device shall not exceed the value marked on the equipment nameplate.

Exception No. 3: The nameplate marking of cord- and plug-connected equipment rated not greater than 250 volts, single-phase, such as household refrigerators and freezers, drinking-water coolers, and beverage dispensers shall be used in determining the branch-circuit requirements, and each unit shall be considered as a single motor unless the nameplate is marked otherwise.

(c) Where maximum protective device ratings shown on a manufacturer's heater table for use with a motor controller are less than the rating or setting selected in accordance with Sections 440-22(a) and (b), the protective device rating shall not exceed the manufacturer's values marked on the equipment.

D. Branch-Circuit Conductors

440-31. General. The provisions of Part D and Articles 300 and 310 specify sizes of conductors required to carry the motor current without overheating under the conditions specified, except as modified in Section 440-5(a), Exception

No. 1. The provisions of these Articles are not intended to apply to integral conductors of motors, motor controllers and the like, or to conductors which form an integral part of approved equipment. See Sections 300-1(b) and 310-1(c).

440-32. Single Motor-Compressor. Branch-circuit conductors supplying a single motor-compressor shall have an ampacity not less than 125 per cent of either the motor-compressor rated-load current or the branch-circuit selection current, whichever is greater.

440-33. Several Motor-Compressors. Conductors supplying two or more motor-compressors shall have an ampacity not less than the sum of the rated-load current or branch-circuit selection current ratings, whichever is greater, of all the motor-compressors plus 25 per cent of the highest rated motor-compressor in the group.

Exception: When the circuitry is so interlocked as to prevent the starting and running of a second motor-compressor or group of motor-compressors, the conductor size shall be determined from the largest motor-compressor or group of motor-compressors that is to be operated at a given time.

440-34. Combination Load. Conductors supplying a motor-compressor load in addition to a lighting or appliance load as computed from Article 220 and other applicable Articles, shall have an ampacity sufficient for the lighting or appliance load plus the required ampacity for the motor-compressor load determined in accordance with Section 440-33, or, for a single motor-compressor, in accordance with Section 440-32.

Exception: When the circuitry is so interlocked as to prevent simultaneous operation of the motor-compressor(s) and all other loads connected, the conductor size shall be determined from the largest size required for the motor-compressor(s) and other loads to be operated at a given time.

440-35. Multimotor and Combination-Load Equipment. The ampacity of the conductors supplying multimotor and combination-load equipment shall not be less than the minimum circuit ampacity marked on the equipment in accordance with Section 440-3(b).

E. Controllers for Motor-Compressors

440-41. Rating.

(a) A motor-compressor controller shall have both a continuous-duty full-load current rating, and a locked-rotor current rating, not less than the nameplate rated-load current or branch-circuit selection current, whichever is greater, and locked-rotor current, respectively (see Sections 440-5 and 440-6) of the compressor. In case the motor controller is rated in horsepower, but is without one or both of the foregoing current ratings, equivalent currents shall be determined from the ratings as follows: Use Table 430-148, 430-149, or 430-150 to determine the equivalent full-load current rating. Use Table 430-151 to determine the equivalent locked-rotor current rating.

(b) A controller, serving more than one motor-compressor or a motor-compressor and other loads, shall have a continuous-duty full-load current rating, and a locked-rotor current rating not less than the combined load as determined in accordance with Section 440-12(b).

F. Motor-Compressor and Branch-Circuit Overload Protection

440-51. General. The provisions of Part F specify devices intended to protect the motor-compressor, the motor-control apparatus, and the branch-circuit conductors against excessive heating due to motor overload and failure to start. (See Section 240-5(a), Exception No. 3.)

Note: Overload in electrically driven apparatus is an operating overcurrent which, when it persists for a sufficient length of time, would cause damage or dangerous overheating. It does not include short circuits or ground faults.

440-52. Application and Selection.

(a) Protection of Motor-Compressor. Each motor-compressor shall be protected against overload and failure to start by one of the following means:

(1) A separate overload relay which is responsive to motor-compressor current. This device shall be selected to trip at not more than 140 per cent of the motor-compressor rated-load current.

(2) A thermal protector integral with the motor-compressor, approved for use with the motor-compressor which it protects, on the basis that it will prevent dangerous overheating of the motor-compressor due to overload and failure to start. If the current-interrupting device is separate from the motor-compressor and its control circuit is operated by a protective device integral with the motor-compressor, it shall be so arranged that the opening of the control circuit will result in interruption of current to the motor-compressor.

(3) A fuse or time-limit circuit breaker responsive to motor current, which may also serve as the branch-circuit short-circuit and ground-fault protective device. This device shall be rated at not more than 125 per cent of the motor-compressor rated-load current. It shall have sufficient time delay to permit the motor-compressor to start and accelerate its load. The equipment or the motor-compressor shall be marked with this maximum branch-circuit fuse or time-limit circuit-breaker rating.

Exception: Where the standard sizes of fuses or time-limit circuit breakers are not adequate to carry the load, the next higher size or rating may be used but not higher than 140 per cent of the motor-compressor rated-load current rating.

(4) A protective system, furnished or specified and approved for use with the motor-compressor which it protects on the basis that it will prevent dangerous overheating of the motor-compressor due to overload and failure to start. If the current interrupting device is separate from the motor-compressor and its control circuit is operated by a protective device which is not integral with the current-interrupting device, it shall be so arranged that the opening of the control circuit will result in interruption of current to the motor-compressor.

(b) Protection of Motor-Compressor Control Apparatus and Branch-Circuit Conductors. The motor-compressor controller(s), the disconnecting means and branch-circuit conductors shall be protected against overcurrent due to motor overload and failure to start by one of the following means which may be the same device or system protecting the motor-compressor in accordance with Section 440-52(a):

(1) An overload relay selected in accordance with Section 440-52(a)(1).

(2) A thermal protector applied in accordance with Section 440-52(a)(2) and

which will not permit a continuous current in excess of 156 per cent of the marked rated-load current or branch-circuit selection current.

(3) A fuse or time-limit circuit breaker selected in accordance with Section 440-52(a)(3).

(4) A protective system in accordance with Section 440-52(a)(4) and which will not permit a continuous current in excess of 156 per cent of the marked rated-load current or branch-circuit selection current.

440-53. Overload Relays. Overload relays and other devices for motor overload protection, which are not capable of opening short circuits, shall be protected by fuses or time-limit circuit breakers with ratings or settings in accordance with Part C unless approved for group installation or for part-winding motors and marked to indicate the maximum size of fuse or time-limit circuit breaker by which they must be protected.

Exception: The fuse or time-limit circuit-breaker-size marking may be located on the nameplate of approved equipment in which the overload relay or other overload device is used.

440-54. Motor-Compressors and Equipment on General-Purpose Branch Circuits. Overload protection for motor-compressors and equipment used on general-purpose branch circuits as permitted in Article 210, shall be provided in (a), (b) and (c) below.

(a) Motor-compressors and equipment may be connected to general-purpose branch circuits only if the motor-compressor is provided with overload protection selected as specified in Section 440-52(a). Both the controller and the motor-overload protective device shall be approved for installation with a short-circuit and ground-fault protective device of the branch circuit to which the equipment is connected.

(b) Where a motor-compressor or equipment is connected to a general-purpose branch circuit by means of a cap and receptacle, the rating of the cap and receptacle shall not exceed 20 amperes at 125 volts or 15 amperes at 250 volts. See Article 210.

(c) The short-circuit and ground-fault protective device protecting a branch circuit to which a motor-compressor or equipment is connected shall have sufficient time delay to permit the motor-compressor and other motors to start and accelerate their load(s).

ARTICLE 445. GENERATORS

445-1. Location. Generators shall be located in dry places, and also so as to meet the requirements for motors in Section 430-14. Generators installed in hazardous locations as described in Articles 500 through 503, or in other locations as described in Articles 510 through 517, 520, 530, and 665, shall also comply with the provisions of those Articles.

It is recommended that waterproof covers be provided for use in emergency.

445-2. Marking. Each generator shall be provided with a nameplate giving the maker's name, the rating in kilowatts or kilovolt-amperes, the normal volts and amperes corresponding to the rating, and the revolutions per minute.

445-3. Drip Pans. Generators shall be provided with suitable drip pans if required by the authority having jurisdiction.

445-4. Overcurrent Protection.

(a) Constant-Potential Generators. Constant-potential generators, except alternating-current generators and their exciters, shall be protected from excessive current by circuit breakers or fuses.

(b) Two-Wire Generators. Two-wire, direct-current generators may have overcurrent protection in one conductor only if the overcurrent device is actuated by the entire current generated, except that in the shunt field. The overcurrent device shall not open the shunt field.

(c) 65 Volts or Less. Generators operating at 65 volts or less and driven by individual motors shall be considered as protected by the overcurrent device protecting the motor if these devices will operate when the generators are delivering not more than 150 per cent of their full-load rated current.

(d) Balancer Sets. Two-wire, direct-current generators used in conjunction with balancer sets to obtain neutrals for 3-wire systems shall be equipped with overcurrent devices which will disconnect the 3-wire system in the case of excessive unbalancing of voltages or currents.

(e) 3-Wire, Direct-Current Generators. Three-wire, direct-current generators, whether compound or shunt wound, shall be equipped with overcurrent devices, one in each armature lead, and so connected as to be actuated by the entire current from the armature. Such overcurrent devices shall consist either of a double-pole, double-coil circuit breaker, or of a 4-pole circuit breaker connected in the main and equalizer leads and tripped by two overcurrent devices, one in each armature lead. Such protective devices shall be so interlocked that no one pole can be opened without simultaneously disconnecting both leads of the armature from the system.

▶   Alternating-current generators can be so designed that on excessive overload the voltage falls off sufficiently to limit the current and power output to values that will not injure the generator during a short period of time. Whether or not automatic overcurrent protection of a generator should be omitted in any particular case is a question that can best be answered by the manufacturer of the generator. It is common practice to operate an exciter without overcurrent protection, rather than to risk the shutdown of the main generator due to accidental opening of the exciter fuse or circuit breaker.

Figure 445-1 shows the connections of a two-wire d-c generator with a single-pole protective device. If the machine is operated in multiple with one or more other generators and so has an equalizer lead connected to the positive terminal, the current may divide at the positive terminal, part passing through the series field and positive lead and part passing through the equalizer lead. The entire current generated passes through the negative lead, therefore the fuse or circuit breaker, or at least the operating coil of a circuit breaker, must be placed in the negative lead.

The protective device should not open the shunt-field circuit, because if this circuit were opened with the field at full strength, a very high voltage

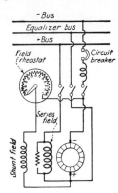

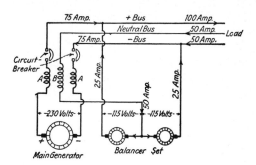

FIG. 445-1. Connections of a two-wire direct-current generator protected by a single-pole circuit breaker.

FIG. 445-2. Connection diagram of a balancer set used with a two-wire 230-volt generator to supply a three-wire system, showing (approximately) the currents flowing when the system supplies an unbalanced load of 100 amp on one side and 50 amp on the other side.

would be induced which might break down the insulation of the field winding.

Paragraph *c* is intended to apply particularly to generators used in electrolytic work. Where such a generator forms part of a motor-generator set, no fuse or circuit breaker is necessary in the generator leads if the motor-running protective device will open when the generator delivers 150 per cent of its rated full-load current.

Each of the two generators used as a balancer set carries approximately one-half the unbalanced load; hence these two machines are always much smaller than the main generator. In case of an excessive unbalance of the load, the balancer set might be overloaded while there is no overload on the main generator. This condition may be guarded against by installing a double-pole circuit breaker with one pole connected in each lead of the main generator and with the operating coil properly designed to be connected in the neutral of the three-wire system. (See Fig. 445-2. In this diagram, the circuit breaker is arranged so as to be operated by either one of the coils *A* in the leads from the main generator or by coil *B* in the neutral lead from the balancer set.)

445-5. Size of Conductors. The conductors from the generator terminals to supplied equipment shall have an ampacity not less than 115 per cent of the nameplate current rating of the generator. Neutral conductors shall be the same size as the conductors of the outside legs.

445-6. Protection of Live Parts. Live parts of generators of more than 150 volts to ground shall not be exposed to accidental contact where accessible to unqualified persons.

▶   As a general rule, no generator should be "accessible to unqualified persons." If necessary to place a generator operating at over 150 volts to ground in a location where it is so exposed, the commutator or collector rings, brushes, and any exposed terminals should be provided with guards which will prevent any accidental contact with these live parts.

445-7. Guards for Attendants.   Where necessary for the safety of attendants the provisions of Section 430-133 shall be complied with.

445-8. Grounding.   If a generator operates at a terminal voltage in excess of 150 volts to ground, the frame shall be grounded in the manner specified in Article 250. If the frame is not grounded, it shall be permanently and effectively insulated from the ground.

445-9. Bushings.   Where wires pass through an opening in an enclosure, conduit box, or barrier, a bushing shall be used to protect the conductors from the edges of the opening having sharp edges. The bushing shall have smooth, well rounded surfaces where it may be in contact with the conductors. If used where there may be a presence of oils, grease, or other contaminants, the bushing shall be made of a material not deleteriously affected.

ARTICLE 450. TRANSFORMERS AND TRANSFORMER VAULTS

(Including Secondary Ties)

450-1. Application.   This Article applies to the installation of all transformers except:

Exception No. 1: Current transformers.

Exception No. 2: Dry-type transformers which constitute a component part of other apparatus and which conform to the requirements for such apparatus.

Exception No. 3: Transformers which are an integral part of an X-ray or high frequency apparatus.

Exception No. 4: Transformers used with Class 1 low-voltage power circuits or Class 2 remote control low energy power and signal circuits which shall conform to Article 725.

Exception No. 5: Transformers for sign and outline lighting which shall conform to Article 600.

Exception No. 6: Transformers for electric discharge lighting which shall conform to Article 410.

This Article applies to the installation of transformers in hazardous locations except as modified by Article 500.

A. General Provisions

450-2. Location.   Transformers and transformer vaults shall be readily accessible to qualified personnel for inspection and maintenance.

Exception No. 1: Dry-type transformers 600 volts or less, located in the open on walls, columns or structures, need not be readily accessible.

Exception No. 2: Dry-type transformers not exceeding 600 volts and 50 kva may be installed in fire-resistant hollow spaces of buildings not permanently closed in by structure and provided they meet the ventilation requirements of Section 450-8.

The location of oil-insulated transformers and transformer vaults is covered in Sections 450-24, 450-25, and 450-41; dry-type transformers in Section 450-21 and askarel-insulated in Section 450-23.

450-3. Overcurrent Protection. Overcurrent protection shall conform to the following. As used in this Section, the word "transformer" means a transformer or polyphase bank of two or three single phase transformers operating as a unit.

(a) Askarel- and Oil-Insulated Transformers.

(1) Primary Side. Each askarel- or oil-insulated transformer shall be protected by an individual overcurrent device in the primary connection, rated or set at not more than 250 per cent of the rated primary current of the transformer, except that an individual overcurrent device is not required when the primary circuit overcurrent device provides the protection specified in this Section, and except as provided in Section 450-3(a)(2).

(2) Primary and Secondary Side. An askarel- or oil-insulated transformer having an overcurrent device in the secondary connection, rated or set at not more than 250 per cent of the rated secondary current of the transformer, or a transformer equipped with a coordinated thermal overload protection by the manufacturer, is not required to have an individual overcurrent device in the primary connection provided the primary feeder overcurrent device is rated or set to open at a current value not more than 6 times the rated current of the transformer for transformers having not more than 6 per cent impedance, and not more than 4 times rated current of the transformer for transformers having more than 6 but not more than 10 per cent impedance.

(b) Dry-Type Transformers.

(1) Primary Side. Each dry-type transformer shall be protected by an individual overcurrent device in the primary connection, rated or set at not more than 125 per cent of the rated primary current of the transformer, except that an individual overcurrent device is not required when the primary circuit overcurrent device provides the protection specified in this Section, and except as provided in Section 450-3(b)(2).

(2) Primary and Secondary Side. A dry-type transformer having an overcurrent device in the secondary connection, rated or set at not more than 125 per cent of the rated secondary current of the transformer, is not required to have an individual overcurrent device in the primary connection provided the primary feeder overcurrent device is rated or set to open at a current value not more than 250 per cent of the rated primary current of the transformer.

A dry-type transformer, equipped with a coordinated thermal overload protection by the manufacturer and arranged to interrupt the primary current, is not required to have an individual overcurrent device in the primary connection provided the primary feeder overcurrent device is rated or set to open at a current value not more than 6 times the rated current of the transformer for transformers having not more than 6 per cent impedance, and not more than 4 times rated current of the transformer for transformers having more than 6 but not more than 10 per cent impedance.

▶   Paragraph *a* applies to askarel- or oil-insulated transformers while paragraph *b* applies to dry-type transformers.

In either case it should be understood that the overcurrent protection stated in Section **450-3** is for the transformers *only*. Such overcurrent protection will not necessarily protect the primary or secondary conductors or equipment connected on the secondary side of the transformer. Using overcurrent protection to the maximum values shown in Figures **450-1** and **450-2**

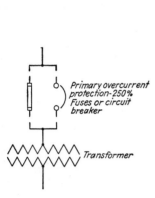

FIG. 450-1. Overcurrent protection of an askarel- or oil-insulated transformer. See Section 450-3*b*(1) and *b*(2) for dry-type transformers.

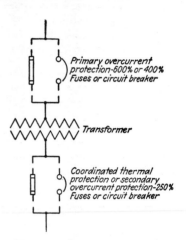

FIG. 450-2. Overcurrent protection of an askarel- or oil-insulated transformer.

would require much larger conductors than the full-load current rating of the transformer (other than permitted in the 25-ft tap rule in Section **240-15**, Exception **7**). Accordingly, to avoid using oversized conductors, overcurrent devices should be selected at about 110 to 125 per cent of the transformer full-load current rating. And when using such smaller overcurrent protection, devices should be of the time-delay type (on the primary side) to compensate for in-rush currents which reach eight to ten times the full-load primary current of the transformer for about 1/10 sec. when energized initially.

In approaching a transformer installation it is best to use a one-line diagram, such as shown in Fig. **240-3**. Then by applying the tap rules in Section **240-15** proper protection of the conductors and equipment, which are part of the system, will be achieved. See comments following Section **240-15**.

Sections **230-105** and **240-5***a*, Exception **5** are the only code rules that consider properly sized primary overcurrent devices to protect the secondary conductors without secondary protection and no limit to the length of secondary conductors. The strict requirements in Section **230-105** apply where the transformers are in a *vault,* the primary load-interrupter switch is manually operable from outside the vault, and large secondary conductors are provided to achieve reflected protection through the transformer to the primary overcurrent protection.

Exception **5** to Section **240-5***a* applies where the primary and secondary each have a two-wire winding. (See comments following this exception and Section 240-15.)

In spite of the larger overcurrent protection permitted in Section **450-3a** for askarel- or oil-insulated transformers, it is less costly to use the lower ratings specified for dry-type transformers in Section **450-3b**, and better overall protection will be achieved.

(c) Potential (Voltage) Transformers.   Potential transformers installed indoors or enclosed shall be protected with primary fuses.

450-5. Secondary Ties.   As used in this Section, the word "transformer" means a transformer or a bank of transformers operating as a unit. A secondary tie is a circuit operating at 600 volts or less between phases which connects two power sources or power supply points, such as the secondaries of two transformers. The tie may consist of one or more conductors per phase.

(a) Tie Circuits.   Tie circuits shall be provided at each end with overcurrent protection as required in Article 240 of this Code, except under the conditions described in Sections 450-5 (a-1 and a-2), in which cases the overcurrent protection may be in accordance with Section 450-5 (a-3).

(1) Loads at Transformer Supply Points Only.   Where all loads are connected at the transformer supply points at each end of the tie and overcurrent protection is not provided in accordance with Article 240, the rated ampacity of the tie shall be not less than 67 per cent of the rated secondary current of the largest transformer connected to the secondary tie system.

(2) Loads Connected Between Transformer Supply Points.   Where load is connected to the tie at any point between transformer supply points and overcurrent protection is not provided in accordance with Article 240, the rated ampacity of the tie shall be not less than 100 per cent of the rated secondary current of the largest transformer connected to the secondary tie system except as otherwise provided in Section 450-5 (a-4).

(3) Tie Circuit Protection.   Under the conditions described in Sections 450-5 (a-1 and 2), both ends of each tie conductor shall be equipped with a protective device which will open at a predetermined temperature of the tie conductor under short circuit conditions. This protection shall consist of one of the following: (1) a fusible link cable connector, terminal or lug, commonly known as a limiter, each being of a size corresponding with that of the conductor and of approved construction and characteristics according to the operating voltage and the type of insulation on the tie conductors, or (2) automatic circuit breakers actuated by devices having comparable current-time characteristics.

(4) Interconnection of Phase Conductors Between Transformer Supply Points. Where the tie consists of more than one conductor per phase, the conductors of each phase shall be interconnected in order to establish a load supply point, and the protection specified in Section 450-5(a-3) shall be provided in each tie conductor at this point, except as follows:

Exception: Loads may be connected to the individual conductors of a multiple-conductor tie without interconnecting the conductors of each phase and without the protection specified in Section 450-5(a-3) at load connection points provided; the tie conductors of each phase have a combined capacity not less than 133 per cent of the rated secondary current of the largest transformer connected to the secondary tie system; the total load of such taps does not exceed the rated secondary current of the largest transformer; the loads are equally divided on each phase and on the individual conductors of each phase as far as practicable.

(5) Tie Circuit Control. Where the operating voltage exceeds 150 volts to ground, secondary ties provided with limiters shall have a switch at each end which when open will de-energize the associated tie conductors and limiters. The current rating of the switch shall be not less than the rated current of the conductors connected to the switch. It shall be capable of opening its rated current, and it shall be constructed so that it will not open under the magnetic forces resulting from short-circuit current.

(b) Overcurrent Protection for Secondary Connections. When secondary ties are used an overcurrent device rated or set at not more than 250 per cent of the rated secondary current of the transformers shall be provided in the secondary connections of each transformer, and in addition an automatic circuit breaker actuated by a reverse-current relay set to open the circuit at not more than the rated secondary current of the transformer shall be provided in the secondary connection of each transformer.

▶ In industrial plants having very heavy power loads it is usually economical to install a number of large transformers at various locations within each building, the transformers being supplied by primary feeders operating at voltages up to 13,800 volts. One of the secondary systems that may be used in such cases is the network system.

The term *network system* as commonly used is applied to any secondary distribution system in which the secondaries of two or more transformers at different locations are connected together by secondary ties. The purpose of the system is to equalize the loading of the transformers, to reduce voltage drop, and to ensure continuity of service. The use of this system introduces certain complications and, to ensure successful operation, the system must be designed by an experienced electrical engineer.

The protection required at each transformer is shown in Fig. 450-3. The provisions of Section 450-3 govern the protection in the primary.

The network protector consists of a circuit breaker and a reverse-power relay. The protector is necessary because without this device, if a fault develops in the transformer, or, in some cases, in the primary feeder, power will be fed back to the fault from the other transformers through the secondary ties. The relay is set to trip the breaker on a reverse-power current not greater than the rated secondary current of the transformer. This breaker is not arranged to be tripped by an overload on the secondary of the transformer.

Section 450-5a-3 provides that:

1. Where two or more conductors are installed in parallel, an individual protective device is provided at each end of each conductor.

2. The protective device (fusible link or circuit breaker) does not provide overload protection, but provides short-circuit protection only.

In case of a short circuit, the protective device must open the circuit before the conductor reaches a temperature that would injure its insulation. The principles involved are that the entire system is so designed that

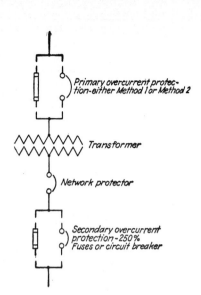

FIG. 450-3. Overcurrent protection of a transformer—network system.

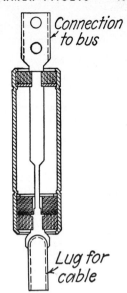

FIG. 450-4. Limiter for protection of secondary ties in a network system. (*Westinghouse Electric Corp.*)

the tie conductors will never be continuously overloaded in normal operation, hence protection against overloads of less severity than short circuits is not necessary, and that the protective devices should not open the circuit and thus cause an interruption of service on load peaks of such short duration that the conductors do not become overheated.

A limiter is a special type of fuse having a very high interrupting capacity. Figure 450-4 is a cross-sectional view of one type of limiter. The cable lug, the fusible section, and the extension for connection to the bus are all made in one piece from a length of copper tubing, and the enclosing case is also copper. It is stated that this device will interrupt a current of 50,000 amperes without perceptible noise and without the escape of flame or gases from the case.

Figure 450-5 is a single-line diagram of a simple three-phase industrial-plant network system. The primary feeders may operate at any standard voltage up to 13,800 volts, and the secondary voltage would commonly be 480 volts. The rating of the transformers used in such a system would usually be within the range of 300 to 1,000 kva. The diagram shows two primary feeders, both of which are carried to each transformer so that by means of a double-throw switch each transformer can be connected to either feeder. Each feeder would be large enough to carry the entire load. It is assumed that the feeders are protected in accordance with Section

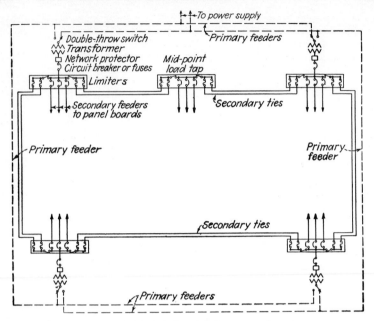

Fig. 450-5. A simple industrial-plant network system.

450-3b(2) so that no primary overcurrent devices are required at the transformers. The secondary ties consist of two conductors in multiple per phase and it will be noted that these conductors form a closed loop. Switches are provided so that any section of the loop, including the limiters protecting that section, can be isolated in case repairs or replacements should be necessary.

450-6. Parallel Operation. Transformers may be operated in parallel and switched as a unit provided that the overcurrent protection for each transformer meets the requirements of 450-3.

To obtain balanced division of load current, both transformers should have the same rated per cent impedance and be operated on the same voltage-ratio tap.

▶   To operate satisfactorily in parallel, transformers should have the same percentage impedance and the same ratio of reactance to resistance. Information on these characteristics should be obtained from the manufacturer of the transformers.

450-7. Guarding. Transformers shall be guarded as follows:
(a) **Mechanical Protection.** Appropriate provisions shall be made to minimize the possibility of damage to transformers from external causes where the transformers are located where they are exposed to physical damage.

(b) Case or Enclosure. Dry-type transformers shall be provided with a non-combustible moisture-resistant case or enclosure which will provide reasonable protection against the accidental insertion of foreign objects.

(c) Exposed Live Parts. The transformer installation shall conform with the provisions for guarding of live parts in Section 110-17.

(d) Voltage Warning. The operating voltage of exposed live parts of transformer installations shall be indicated by signs or visible markings on the equipment or structures.

450-8. Ventilation. The ventilation shall be adequate to prevent a transformer temperature in excess of the values prescribed in ANSI C57.12.00-1968.

450-9. Grounding. Exposed noncurrent carrying metal parts of transformer installations including fences, guards, etc., shall be grounded where required under the conditions and in the manner prescribed for electrical equipment and other exposed metal parts in Article 250.

450-10. Marking. Each transformer shall be provided with a nameplate giving the name of the manufacturer; rated kilovolt-amperes, frequency, primary and secondary voltage; and the amount and kind of insulating liquid where used and the transformer rating exceeds 25 kva. Where Class B insulation is used in the construction of dry-type transformers rated more than 100 kva, the nameplate shall indicate the temperature rise for this insulation system.

▶   Article 220 provides a means of establishing the loads in buildings, and where the supply is derived from a transformer it must be assumed that the transformer would need to be of sufficient capacity to carry this connected load.

B. Specific Provisions Applicable to Different Types of Transformers

450-21. Dry-Type Transformers Installed Indoors. Transformers rated 112½ kva or less shall have a separation of at least 12 inches from combustible material unless separated therefrom by a fire-resistant heat-insulating barrier, or unless of a rating not exceeding 600 volts and completely enclosed except for ventilating openings.

Transformers of more than 112½ kva rating shall be installed in a transformer room of fire-resistant construction unless they are constructed with 80° C rise (Class B) or 150° C rise (Class H) insulation, and are separated from combustible material not less than 6 feet horizontally and 12 feet vertically or are separated therefrom by a fire-resistant heat-insulating barrier.

Transformers rated more than 35,000 volts shall be installed in a vault. See Part C of this Article.

▶   Dry-type transformers are those in which the windings are not immersed in any liquid. Transformers of this type of less than 112½ kva rating are quite commonly used in large industrial plants to supply lighting at 115 volts, the primaries being connected to a power system operating at 480 volts.

Where transformers of larger sizes are installed indoors and the primary voltage is not over 35,000 volts, either the dry type or the askarel-filled type (see Section 450-23) is often preferred because no transformer vault is required.

Figure 450-6 shows the core and coil assembly of a 500-kva three-phase dry-type transformer having a primary voltage rating of 13,800 volts with

FIG. 450-6. Core and coil assembly of a 500-kva dry-type transformer. (*Westinghouse Electric Corp.*)

a secondary voltage of **480** volts. Figure **450-7** is a view of the transformer with the outside casing in place. The coils are cooled by circulation of air through the open spaces at the bottom of the casing and the louvers near the top. The lever shown in Fig. **450-7** operates a primary feeder-selector switch, i.e., a three-pole double-throw switch by means of which the primary of the transformer can be connected to either one of two feeders.

Dry-type transformers of over $112\frac{1}{2}$ kva rating are usually constructed with Class B insulation, which consists of mica, asbestos, fibre glass and similar inorganic materials in built-up form, with organic building substances. Although mica, asbestos, and fibre glass are practically noncombustible, in using these materials as transformer insulation it is necessary to use some binder material, such as varnish, which may be combustible. If a fault should develop in the transformer, it is possible that some flame might escape from the enclosure for a short time. It is therefore necessary that the transformers be kept well away from any combustible part of the building structure or that a barrier of noncombustible material be provided.

450-22. Dry-Type Transformers Installed Outdoors.   Dry-type   transformers   installed outdoors shall have an approved weatherproof enclosure.

450-23. Askarel-Insulated Transformers Installed Indoors.   Askarel-insulated trans-

Fig. 450-7. Dry-type transformer shown in Fig. 450-6 with outside casing in place. (*Westinghouse Electric Corp.*)

formers rated in excess of 25 kva shall be furnished with a pressure-relief vent. Where installed in a poorly ventilated place they shall be furnished with a means for absorbing any gases generated by arcing inside the case, or the pressure relief vent shall be connected to a chimney or flue which will carry such gases outside the building. Askarel-insulated transformers rated more than 35,000 volts shall be installed in a vault.

▶   See definition of "askarel" in Art. 100.

The use of oil-filled transformers involves some fire hazard, which can be avoided by using a noninflammable liquid in place of oil. As in the case of dry-type transformers, no vault is required for an askarel-filled transformer if the primary voltage is not over 35,000 volts. Considerable economy can often be effected by locating a transformer of one or the other of these two types close to a heavy load, thus avoiding the use of long secondary feeders of large size.

450-24. Oil-Insulated Transformers Installed Indoors.   Oil-insulated transformers shall be installed in a vault constructed as specified in this Article except as follows:

(a) Not Over 112½ kva Total Capacity.   The provisions for transformer vaults specified in Part C of this Article apply except that the vault may be constructed of reinforced concrete not less than 4 inches thick.

(b) Not Over 600 Volts.   A vault is not required provided suitable arrangements are made where necessary to prevent a transformer oil fire igniting other materials, and the total transformer capacity in one location does not exceed 10 kva in a section of the building classified as combustible, or 75 kva where the surrounding structure is classified as fire-resistant construction.

(c) Furnace Transformers.   Electric furnace transformers of a total rating not exceeding 75 kva may be installed without a vault in a building or room of fire-resistant construction provided suitable arrangements are made to prevent a transformer oil fire spreading to other combustible material.

(d) Detached Buildings.   Transformers may be installed in a building which does not conform with the provisions specified in this Code for transformer vaults, provided neither the building nor its contents present a fire hazard to any other building or property, and provided the building is used only in supplying electric service and the interior is accessible only to qualified persons.

450-25. Oil-Insulated Transformers Installed Outdoors.   Combustible material, combustible buildings and parts of buildings, fire escapes, door and window openings shall be safeguarded from fires originating in oil-insulated transformers installed on, attached to, or adjacent to a building or combustible material. Space separations, fire-resistant barriers, automatic water spray systems and enclosures which confine the oil of a ruptured transformer tank are recognized safeguards. One or more of these safeguards shall be applied according to the degree of hazard involved in cases where the transformer installation presents a fire hazard. Oil enclosures may consist of fire-resistant dikes, curbed areas or basins, or trenches filled with coarse crushed stone. Oil enclosures shall be provided with trapped drains in cases where the exposure and the quantity of oil involved are such that removal of oil is important.

C. Provisions for Transformer Vaults

450-41. Location.   Vaults shall be located where they can be ventilated to the outside air without using flues or ducts wherever such an arrangement is practicable.

450-42. Walls, Roof, and Floor.   The walls and roofs of vaults shall be constructed of reinforced concrete, brick, load bearing tile, concrete block, or other fire resistive constructions which have adequate structural strength for the conditions, and a minimum fire resistance of 3 hours according to ASTM Standard E119-67; Fire Tests of Building Construction and Materials; (NFPA No. 251-1969). The floors of vaults in contact with the earth shall be of concrete not less than 4 inches thick but when the vault is constructed with a vacant space or other stories below it, the floor shall have adequate structural strength for the load imposed thereon and a minimum fire resistance of 3 hours.

450-43. Doorways.   Vault doorways shall be protected as follows:

(a) Type of Door.   Each doorway leading into a building shall be provided with a tight-fitting door of a type approved for openings in Class A situations as defined in the NFPA Standard for the Installation of Fire Doors and Windows, No. 80-1970. The authority enforcing this Code may require such a door for an exterior wall opening or on each side of an interior wall opening where conditions warrant.

(b) Sills. A door sill or curb of sufficient height to confine within the vault the oil from the largest transformer shall be provided and in no case shall the height be less than 4 inches.

(c) Locks. Entrance doors shall be equipped with locks, and doors shall be kept locked, access being allowed only to qualified persons. Locks and latches shall be so arranged that the door may be readily and quickly opened from the inside.

▶ The purpose of a transformer vault is to isolate the transformers and other apparatus and to confine any fire that might be caused by the failure of any of the apparatus. It is important that the door as well as the remainder of the enclosure be of proper construction and that a substantial lock be provided.

450-45. Ventilation Openings. When required by Section 450-8, openings for ventilation shall be provided in accordance with the following:

(a) Location. Ventilation openings shall be located as far away as possible from doors, windows, fire escapes, and combustible material.

(b) Arrangement. Vaults ventilated by natural circulation of air may have roughly half of the total area of openings required for ventilation in one or more openings near the floor and the remainder in one or more openings in the roof or in the sidewalls near the roof; or all of the area required for ventilation may be provided in one or more openings in or near the roof.

(c) Size. In the case of vaults ventilated to an outdoor area without using ducts or flues the combined net area of all ventilating openings after deducting the area occupied by screens, gratings, or louvers, shall be not less than 3 square inches per kva of transformer capacity in service, except that the net area shall be not less than 1 square foot for any capacity under 50 kva.

(d) Covering. Ventilation openings shall be covered with durable gratings, screens, or louvers, according to the treatment required in order to avoid unsafe conditions.

(e) Dampers. All ventilation openings to the indoors shall be provided with automatic closing dampers of not less than No. 10 MSG steel which operate in response to a vault fire.

(f) Ducts. Ventilating ducts shall be constructed of fire-resistant material.

450-46. Drainage. Where practicable, vaults containing more than 100 kva transformer capacity shall be provided with a drain or other means which will carry off any accumulation of oil or water in the vault unless local conditions make this impracticable. The floor shall be pitched to the drain when provided.

450-47. Water Pipes and Accessories. Any pipe or duct systems foreign to the electrical installation should not enter or pass through a transformer vault. Where the presence of such foreign systems cannot be avoided, appurtenances thereto which require maintenance at regular intervals shall not be located inside the vault. Arrangements shall be made where necessary to avoid possible trouble from condensation, leaks and breaks in such foreign systems. Piping or other facilities provided for fire protection or for water-cooled transformers are not deemed to be foreign to the electrical installation.

450-48. Storage in Vaults. Materials shall not be stored in transformer vaults.

ARTICLE 460. CAPACITORS

460-1. Application.   This Article applies to installation of capacitors on electric circuits in or on buildings.

Exception No. 1: Capacitors that are components of other apparatus shall conform to the requirements for such apparatus.

Exception No. 2: Capacitors in hazardous locations shall comply with additional requirements in Articles 500 through 517.

▶   The following Sections apply chiefly to capacitors used for the power-factor correction of electric-power installations in industrial plants and for correcting the power factors of individual motors. These provisions apply only to capacitors used for surge protection, as such capacitors are not component parts of other apparatus.

In an industrial plant using induction motors, the power factor may be considerably less than 100 per cent, particularly when all or part of the motors operate most of the time at much less than their full load. The lagging current can be counteracted and the power factor improved by installing capacitors across the line. By raising the power factor, for the same actual power delivered the current is decreased in the generator, transformers, and lines, up to the point where the capacitor is connected.

Figure 460-1 shows a capacitor assembly designed for connection to the main power circuit of a small industrial plant. Figure 460-2 is a diagram of the connections. An externally operable switch mounted on the wall is used

Fig. 460-1. Three-phase capacitor assembly rated at 45 kva, 230 volts, or 90 kva, 460 volts, with front cover plate removed. (*General Electric Co.*)

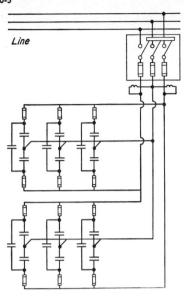

Fig. 460-2. Diagram of connections of capacitor assembly shown in Fig. 460-1.

Fig. 460-3. One unit of the capacitor assembly shown in Fig. 460-1. Each unit is internally delta-connected three-phase.

as the disconnecting means and the discharge device required by Section 460-6 consists of two high-impedance coils inside the switch enclosure which consume only a small amount of power, but, having a comparatively low d-c resistance, permit the charge to drain off rapidly after the capacitor assembly has been disconnected from the line.

460-2. Location. An installation of capacitors in which any single unit contains more than three gallons of combustible liquid shall be in a vault conforming to Part C of Article 450.

460-3. Mechanical Protection. Capacitors shall be protected from physical damage by location or by suitable fences, barriers or other enclosures.

460-4. Cases and Supports. Capacitors shall be provided with noncombustible cases and supports.

460-5. Transformers Used with Capacitors. Transformers that are components of capacitor installations and are used for the purpose of connecting the capacitor to a power circuit shall be installed in accordance with Article 450. The kva rating shall not be less than 135 per cent of the capacitor rating in kvar.

▶   For reasons that have to do with the design and manufacture of the apparatus, it is desirable in some cases to use transformers with capacitors in order that the voltage applied to the capacitors may be different from the operating voltage of the wiring system.

For the same reasons as outlined in the comment of Section 460-8, a transformer used with a capacitor should have a kilovolt-ampere rating not less than 135 per cent of the capacitor rating.

460-6. Drainage of Stored Charge.　Capacitors shall be provided with a means of draining the stored charge.

(a) Time of Discharge.　The residual voltage of a capacitor shall be reduced to 50 volts or less within one minute after the capacitor is disconnected from the source of supply in the case of capacitors rated 600 volts or less and in five minutes in the case of capacitors rated more than 600 volts.

(b) Means of Discharge.　The discharge circuit shall be either permanently connected to the terminals of the capacitor or capacitor bank, or provided with automatic means of connecting it to the terminals of the capacitor bank on removal of voltage from the line. Manual means of switching or connecting the discharge circuit shall not be used. The windings of motors, of transformers, or of other equipment directly connected to capacitors without a switch or over-current device interposed, constitutes a suitable discharge means.

▶　　If no means were provided for draining off the charge stored in a capacitor after it is disconnected from the line, a severe shock might be received by a person servicing the equipment or the equipment might be damaged by a short circuit.

If a capacitor is permanently connected to the windings of a motor, as in Fig. 460-4, the stored charge will drain off rapidly through the windings when the circuit is opened. Reactors or resistors used as discharge devices must either be permanently connected across the terminals of the capacitor or a device must be provided that will automatically connect the discharge devices when the capacitor is disconnected from the source of supply.

460-7. Power Factor Correction—Motor Circuit.　The total kvar rating of capacitors which are connected on the load side of a motor controller shall not exceed the value required to raise the no-load power factor of the motor to unity.

460-8. Conductor Rating.

(a)　The ampacity of capacitor circuit conductors shall be not less than 135 per cent of the rated current of the capacitor. The ampacity of conductors which connect a capacitor to the terminals of a motor or to motor circuit conductors shall be not less than one-third the ampacity of the motor circuit conductors but not less than 135 per cent of the rated current of the capacitor.

(b) Overcurrent Protection.

(1)　An overcurrent device shall be provided in each ungrounded conductor for each capacitor bank.

Exception: A separate overcurrent device is not required on the load-side of a motor running overcurrent device.

(2)　The rating or setting of the overcurrent device shall be as low as practicable.

(c) Disconnecting Means.

(1)　A disconnecting means shall be provided in each ungrounded conductor for each capacitor bank.

Exception: A separate disconnecting means is not required for a capacitor connected on the load side of a motor-running overcurrent device.

(2) The disconnecting device need not open all ungrounded conductors simultaneously.

(3) The disconnecting device may be used for disconnecting the capacitor from the line as a regular operating procedure.

(4) The continuous ampacity of the disconnecting device shall be not less than 135 per cent of the rated current of the capacitor.

▶   Figure 460-4 shows a capacitor used to correct the power factor of a single motor. The capacitor may be connected to the motor circuit between the starter and the motor or may be connected between the disconnecting means and the starter, as indicated by the dotted lines in the diagram, and in either case no switch is required in the capacitor leads; however, if connected as shown by the dotted lines, an overcurrent device must be provided in these leads. The capacitor is shown as having discharge devices consisting in this case of resistors, though when connected as shown by the solid lines in the diagram, no discharge coils or resistors are required because the capacitor discharges through the motor windings.

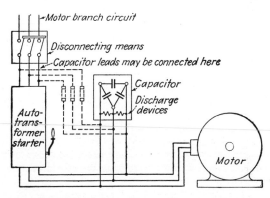

Fig. 460-4. Individual capacitor used to correct the power factor of a motor.

Capacitors of the type to which Section 460-8 applies are commonly rated in kilovolt-amperes, or the rating may be in "kilovars," meaning "reactive kilovolt-amperes," abbreviated kvar. The capacitors are usually designed for connection to a three-phase system and constructed as a unit with three leads brought out.

The current corresponding to the kilovolt-ampere rating of a capacitor is computed in the same manner as for a motor or other load having the same rating in kilovolt-amperes. Thus, the capacitor assembly shown in Fig. 460-1, used at 460 volts, has a rating of 90 kva and the current rating is $90,000/(460 \times 1.73) = 113$ amp. The minimum required ampacity of the conductors would be 1.35×113 amp, or 153 amp.

The manufacturing standards for capacitors for power-factor correction call for a rating tolerance of "−0, +15 per cent," meaning that the actual rating in kilovolt-amperes is never below the nominal rating and may be as much as 15 per cent higher. Thus, a capacitor having a nameplate rating of 100 kva might actually draw a current corresponding to 115 kva. The current drawn by a capacitor varies directly with the line voltage, so that, if the line voltage is higher than the rated voltage, the current will be correspondingly increased. Also, any variation of the line voltage from a pure sine wave form will cause a capacitor to draw an increased current. It is for these reasons that the conductors leading to a capacitor are required to have an ampacity not less than 135 per cent of the rated current of the capacitor.

When a capacitor is thrown on the line, it may momentarily draw an excess current. A rating or setting of 250 per cent of the capacitor current rating will provide short-circuit protection. Being a fixed load, a capacitor does not need overload protection such as is necessary for a motor.

A capacitor is a good example of a "continuous" load, *i.e.*, it will draw at least its full rated current all the time it is connected to the line. If the rated current of a capacitor is 74 amp, to comply with the rule, a switch used as the disconnecting means would have to be capable of carrying a load of 100 amp continuously without overheating.

460-9. Rating or Setting of the Motor-Running Overcurrent Device.   Where a motor installation includes a capacitor connected on the load side of the motor-running overcurrent device, and the overcurrent device used can be adjusted, the rating or setting of the motor overcurrent device shall be determined as provided in Section 430-32, except that instead of using the full-load rated current of the motor as provided in that Section a lower value corresponding with the improved power factor of the motor circuit shall be used. Section 430-22 applies with respect to the rating of the motor circuit conductors.

▶   If a capacitor is connected to a motor circuit as shown by the full lines in Fig. 460-4, the current passing through the overcurrent units, or relays, in the autotransformer starter is the reduced current corresponding with the improved power factor, and if the relays are rated at 125 per cent of the full-load motor current (see Section 430-32), the motor will not be properly protected.

460-10. Grounding.   Capacitor cases shall be grounded in accordance with Article 250.

460-11. Guarding.   All live parts of capacitors which are connected to circuits of more than 600 volts between conductors and are accessible to unqualified persons, shall be enclosed or isolated. For isolation by elevation, see Section 710-34(f).

460-12. Marking.   Each capacitor shall be provided with a nameplate giving the maker's name, rated voltage, frequency, kvar, or amperes, number of phases, and if filled with a combustible liquid, the amount of liquid in gallons. When filled with a nonflammable liquid, the nameplate shall so state. The nameplate shall also indicate if a capacitor has a discharge device inside the case.

ARTICLE 470. RESISTORS AND REACTORS

For Rheostats see Section 430-82.

470-1. Location. Resistors and reactors shall not be placed where exposed to physical damage. Where in the immediate vicinity of easily ignitible material they shall be of the oil-immersed type or shall be enclosed in metal boxes or cabinets. See Article 500 for Hazardous Locations.

470-2. Space Separation. Unless attached to a switchboard or other noncombustible material, or unless mounted as provided in Section 470-3, resistors and reactors shall be separated from combustible material by a distance of not less than 1 foot.

470-3. On or In a Proximity to Combustible Material. Where placed within a distance of 1 foot from combustible material, resistors and reactors shall be installed as follows:

(a) Slab or Panel. They shall be attached to a slab or panel of noncombustible, nonabsorptive material such as slate, soapstone, or marble.

(b) Size of Slab. The slab shall extend beyond the edges of the device and shall have a thickness proportioned to the size and weight of the device but shall not be less than ½ inch thick.

(c) Supports. The slab shall be secured in position by supports independent of those fastening the device to the slab. Bolts which support the device shall be countersunk at least ⅛ inch below the rear surface of the slab and shall be covered with insulating material.

▶ Except when installed in connection with switchboards or control panels that are so located that they are suitably guarded from physical damage and accidental contact with live parts, resistors should always be completely enclosed in properly ventilated metal boxes. A resistor is always a source of heat, and when mounted on a wooden wall or partition, the slab of slate or marble called for by the above rule is needed for heat insulation. The enclosing box should be grounded when located in any of the areas specified in Section 250-42, and when grounded there is no object in insulating the heads or nuts of the bolts on the back of the slab.

Large reactors are commonly connected in series with the main leads of large generators or the supply conductors from high-capacity network systems to assist in limiting the current delivered on short circuit. Small reactors are used with lightning arresters, the object here being to offer a high impedance to the passage of a high-frequency lightning discharge and so to aid in directing the discharge to ground. Another type of reactor, having an iron core and closely resembling a transformer, is used as a remote-control dimmer for stage lighting. Reactors as well as resistors are sources of heat and should therefore be mounted in the same manner as resistors.

470-4. Contacts. Fixed and movable contacts shall be so designed that arcing will be kept at a minimum.

470-5. Reactor Materials. Reactors shall be composed of noncombustible materials, and shall be mounted on noncombustible bases.

470-6. Mounting.   Enclosures when mounted on plain surfaces shall make contact with such surfaces only at the point of support, an air space of at least ¼ inch being maintained between the enclosures and surfaces.

470-7. Conductor Insulation.   Insulated conductors used for connection between resistance elements and controllers shall be suitable for an operating temperature of not less than 90°C (194°F). For elevator motor starting service, see Section 620-11(a).

Exception: For motor starting service other conductor insulations may be used.

470-8. Incandescent Lamps as Resistors.   Incandescent lamps may be used as protective resistors for automatic controllers, or may by special permission be used as resistors in series with other devices and shall conform to the following:

(a) Mounting.   They shall be mounted in porcelain receptacles on noncombustible supports.

(b) Voltage.   They shall be so arranged that they cannot have impressed upon them a voltage greater than that for which they are rated.

(c) Nameplate.   They shall be provided with a nameplate, permanently attached, giving the wattage and voltage of the lamp to be used in each receptacle.

(d) Not Carry Main Current.   They shall not carry or control the main current nor constitute the regulating resistance of the device.

ARTICLE 480. STORAGE BATTERIES

480-1. Scope.   The provisions of this Article shall apply to all stationary installations of storage batteries using acid or alkali as the electrolyte and consisting of a number of cells connected in series with a nominal voltage in excess of 16 volts.

▶   Storage cells are of two general types: the so-called lead-acid type, in which the positive plates consist of lead grids having openings filled with a semisolid compound, commonly lead peroxide, and the negative plates are covered with sponge lead, the plates being immersed in dilute sulphuric acid; and the alkali type, in which the active materials are nickel peroxide for the positive plate and iron oxide for the negative plate, and the electrolyte is chiefly potassium hydroxide.

480-2. Definition of Nominal Battery Voltage.   The nominal battery voltage shall be calculated on the basis of 2.0 volts per cell for the lead-acid type, and 1.2 volts per cell for the alkali type.

▶   The voltage of each cell of a storage battery varies according to its condition of charge or discharge. It is therefore necessary to base the rules on a nominal voltage per cell for each type of battery.

480-3. Wiring and Apparatus Supplied from Batteries.   Wiring, appliances, and apparatus supplied from storage batteries shall be subject to the requirements of this Code applying to wiring, appliances, and apparatus operating at the same voltage, except as otherwise provided for communication systems in Article 800.

480-4. Insulation of Batteries of Not Over 250 Volts. The provisions of this Section shall apply to storage batteries having the cells so connected as to operate at a nominal battery voltage not exceeding 250 volts.

(a) Lead-Acid Batteries. Cells in lead-lined wood tanks, where the number of cells in series does not exceed 25, shall be supported individually on glass or glazed porcelain insulators. Where the number of the cells in series exceeds 25, the cells shall be supported individually on oil insulators.

(b) Alkali-Type Batteries. Cells of the alkali type in jars made of conducting material shall be installed in trays of nonconducting material, with not over 20 cells in a series circuit in any one such tray, or the cells may be supported singly or in groups on porcelain or other suitable insulators.

(c) Unsealed Jars. Cells in unsealed jars made of nonconductive material shall be assembled in trays of glass or supported on glass or glazed porcelain insulators; or, where installed on a rack, shall be supported singly or in groups on glass or other suitable insulators.

(d) Sealed Rubber Jars. Cells in sealed rubber or composition containers shall require no additional insulating support where the total nominal voltage of all cells in series does not exceed 150 volts. Where the total voltage exceeds 150 volts, batteries shall be sectionalized into groups of 150 volts or less and each group shall have the individual cells installed in trays or on racks. Where trays or racks are required for this type of cell, such trays or racks shall be supported on glass or glazed porcelain insulators or oil-type insulators.

(e) Sealed Glass or Plastic Jars. Cells in sealed glass jars or in sealed jars of approved heat resistant plastic, with or without wood trays, require no additional insulation.

480-5. Insulation of Batteries of Over 250 Volts. The provisions of Section 480-4 shall apply to storage batteries having the cells so connected as to operate at a nominal voltage exceeding 250 volts and, in addition, the provisions of this section shall also apply to such batteries. Cells shall be installed in groups having a total nominal voltage of not over 250 volts, in trays or on racks supported on oil insulators.

Exception No. 1: Where each individual cell, or sub-group in the tray or rack, is supported on oil insulators, no additional insulation for the group need be provided.

Exception No. 2: Cells of not over 10 ampere-hour capacity in sealed glass jars may be grouped in trays, the total nominal voltage of all cells in such group not to exceed 250 volts, and each such tray to be supported on glass or glazed porcelain insulators, the trays being mounted on racks supported on oil insulators with a total nominal voltage of not over 500 volts for all cells in series on each such insulated rack.

Maximum protection is secured by sectionalizing high-voltage batteries into cell groups insulated from each other.

480-6. Racks and Trays. Racks and trays shall conform to the following:

(a) Racks. Racks, as required in this Article, refer to frames designed to support cells or trays. They shall be substantial, and made of:

(1) Wood, so treated as to be resistant to deteriorating action by the electrolyte; or

(2) Metal, so treated as to be resistant to deteriorating action by the electrolyte, and provided with nonconducting members directly supporting the cells or with suitable insulating material on conducting members; or

(3) Other similar suitable construction.

(b) Trays. Trays refer to frames such as crates or shallow boxes usually of wood or other nonconducting material, so constructed or treated as to be resistant to deteriorating action by the electrolyte.

480-7. Battery Rooms. Battery rooms shall conform to the following:

(a) Use. Separate battery rooms or enclosures shall be required only for batteries in unsealed jars and tanks where the aggregate capacity at the 8-hour discharge rate exceeds 5 kilowatt hours.

(b) Ventilation. Provision shall be made for sufficient diffusion and ventilation of the gases from the battery to prevent the accumulation of an explosive mixture in the battery room.

▶ Because the fumes given off by a storage battery are very corrosive, the type of wiring must be such that it will withstand the corrosive action and special precautions are necessary as to the type of insulation used as well as protection of all metalwork.

It is stated by the respective manufacturers that conduit made of aluminum or Everdur (silicon-bronze) is well suited to withstand the corrosive effects of the fumes in battery rooms. If steel conduit is used, it is recommended that the conduit be zinc-coated and that it be kept well painted with asphaltum paint.

Batteries of the lead-acid type sometimes throw off a fine spray of the dilute acid which fills the air around the cells; hence steel conduit or tubing should not be brought close to any cell. On overcharge hydrogen and oxygen are given off, and the mixture of these two gases may be explosive.

There are no special requirements on the type of fixtures or other electrical equipment used in the battery room. Proper ventilation of the room will prevent explosions. See Sections 300-5 and 410-4b.

(c) Wiring Method. In storage battery rooms, bare conductors, open wiring, Type MI cable, Type ALS cable, or conductors in rigid conduit or electrical metallic tubing shall be used as the wiring method. Rigid metal conduit, or electrical metallic tubing, where used, shall be of corrosion-resistant material or shall be suitably protected from corrosion.

(d) Varnished-Cambric Conductors. Varnished-cambric-covered conductors, Type V, shall not be used.

(e) Bare Conductors. Bare conductors shall not be taped.

(f) Terminals. Where metal raceway or other metallic covering is used in the battery room, at least 12 inches of the conductor at the end connected to a cell terminal shall be free from the raceway or metallic covering and shall be bushed by a substantial glazed insulating bushing. The end of the raceway shall be sealed tightly to resist the entrance of electrolyte by spray or by creepage. Sealing compound, rubber insulating tape or other suitable material shall be used for this purpose.

CHAPTER FIVE

Special Occupancies

ARTICLE 500. HAZARDOUS LOCATIONS

500-1. Scope. The provisions of Articles 500 through 503 apply to locations in which the authority having jurisdiction judges the apparatus and wiring to be subject to the conditions indicated by the following classifications. It is intended that each room, section or area (including motor and generator rooms, and rooms for the enclosure of control equipment) shall be considered individually in determining its classification. Except as modified in Articles 500 through 503, all other applicable rules contained in this Code shall apply to electrical apparatus and wiring installed in hazardous locations. For definitions of "approved" and "explosion-proof" as used in these Articles, refer to Article 100; "dust-ignition-proof" is defined in Section 502-1.

Equipment and associated wiring approved as intrinsically safe may be installed in any hazardous location for which it is approved, and the provisions of Articles 500 through 517 need not apply to such installation. Intrinsically safe equipment and wiring are incapable of releasing sufficient electrical energy under normal or abnormal conditions to cause ignition of a specific hazardous atmospheric mixture. Abnormal conditions will include accidental damage to any part of the equipment or wiring, insulation or other failure of electrical components, application of overvoltage, adjustment and maintenance operations, and other similar conditions.

For further information see NFPA No. 493-1969 Standard for Intrinsically Safe Process Control Equipment for use in Class I Hazardous Locations.

Through the exercise of ingenuity in the layout of electrical installations for hazardous locations, it is frequently possible to locate much of the equipment in less hazardous or in nonhazardous areas and thus to reduce the amount of special equipment required. In some cases, hazards may be reduced or hazardous areas limited or eliminated by adequate positive-pressure ventilation from a source of clean air in conjunction with effective safeguards against ventilation failure. For further information see NFPA No. 496-1967 Standard for Purged Enclosures for Electrical Equipment in

Hazardous Locations. It is recommended also that the authority having jurisdiction be familiar with such recorded industrial experience as well as with such standards of the National Fire Protection Association as may be of use in the classification of various areas with respect to hazard. For further information see NFPA No. 30, Flammable and Combustible Liquids Code-1969; NFPA No. 32, Dry Cleaning Plants-1970; NFPA No. 35, Manufacture of Organic Coatings-1970; NFPA No. 36, Solvent Extraction Plants-1967; NFPA No. 58 (ANSI Z106.1) Storage and Handling of Liquefied Petroleum Gases-1969; and NFPA No. 59, Storage and Handling of Liquefied Petroleum Gases at Utility Gas Plants-1968.

For recommendations for protection against static electricity hazards, refer to the standards of the National Fire Protection Association on this subject.

Where rigid conduit is used in hazardous locations, it is necessary to have all threaded joints made up wrench tight to minimize sparking when fault current flows through the conduit system. Where it is impractical to make a threaded joint tight, a bonding jumper should be utilized.

All conduit referred to herein shall be threaded with standard conduit cutting die which provides ¾ in. taper per foot. Such conduit shall be made up wrench tight to minimize sparking when fault current flows through the conduit system. Where it is impractical to make a threaded joint tight, a bonding jumper shall be utilized.

500-2. Special Precaution.   The intent of Articles 500 through 503 is to require a form of construction of equipment, and of installation that will insure safe performance under conditions of proper use and maintenance. It, therefore, is assumed that inspection authorities and users will exercise more than ordinary care with regard to installation and maintenance.

The explosion characteristics of air mixtures of hazardous gases, vapors, or dusts vary with the specific material involved. Classification of a hazardous mixture into a Class I hazardous location, Group A, B, C or D, involves determinations of maximum explosion pressure, maximum safe clearance between parts of a clamped joint in an enclosure, and the minimum ignition temperature of the atmospheric mixture. For Class II location, Groups E, F, and G, the classification involves the tightness of the joints of assembly and shaft openings to prevent entrance of dust in the dust-ignition-proof enclosure, the blanketing effect of layers of dust on the equipment that may cause overheating, electrical conductivity of the dust, and the ignition temperature of the dust. It is necessary, therefore, that equipment be approved not only for the class of location but also for the specific group of the gas, vapor or dust that will be present.

For purposes of testing and approval, various atmospheric mixtures (not oxygen enriched) have been grouped on the basis of their hazardous characteristics, and facilities have been made available for testing and approval of equipment for use in the following atmospheric groups:

For Groups A, B, C and D see Table 500-2(c).

Group E, Atmospheres containing metal dust, including aluminum, magnesium, and their commercial alloys, and other metals of similarly hazardous characteristics.

Group F, Atmospheres containing carbon black, coal or coke dust.

Group G, Atmospheres containing flour, starch, or grain dusts.

Certain chemical atmospheres may have characteristics which would require safeguards beyond those required for any of the above groups. Carbon disulfide is one of these chemicals because of its low ignition temperature (100°C) and the small joint clearance required to arrest its flame. For a complete list noting properties of flammable liquids, gases and solids refer to NFPA No. 325M-1969.

▶   While the Code rules for Class I locations do not differ for different kinds of gas or vapor contained in the atmosphere, it is to be noted that it is necessary to select equipment designed for use in the particular atmospheric group to be encountered. This is necessary for the reason that explosive mixtures of the different groups have different flash points and explosion pressures; also, because the ignition temperatures vary with the groups.

Underwriters' Laboratories, Inc., lists fittings and equipment as suitable for use in all groups of Class I, although the listings for Groups A and B are not as complete as those for Groups C and D.

In Class II locations the Code, in a few cases, differentiates between the different kinds of dust, particularly dusts which are electrically conductive and those which are not conductive. Here again, as in Class I locations, care must be used to determine that the equipment selected is suitable for use where a particular kind of dust is present.

In addition to the use of more than ordinary care in selecting equipment for use in hazardous locations, special attention should be given to installation and maintenance details in order that the installations will be permanently free from electrical hazards. In making subsequent additions or changes, the high standards of the original installation must be maintained.

For a more thorough knowledge of specific hazardous areas and equipment selection and location it is essential to obtain copies of the various NFPA and ANSI standards referenced in Articles 500 through 517.

(a) Approval for Class and Properties.   Equipment shall be approved not only for the class of location but also for the explosion properties of the specific gas, vapor, or dust that will be present. In addition, equipment shall not have exposed any surface that operates at a temperature in excess of the ignition temperature of the specific gas vapor or dust.

The characteristics of various atmospheric mixtures of hazardous gases, vapors, and dusts depend on the specific hazardous material involved.

(b) Marking.   Approved equipment shall be marked to show the Class, Group and operating temperature, or temperature range, based on operation in a 40°C ambient for which it is approved.

The temperature range, if provided, shall be indicated in identification numbers, as shown in Table 500-2(b).

Table 500-2(b). Identification Numbers

Maximum temperature Degrees C	Degrees F	Identification number
450	842	T1
300	572	T2
280	536	T2A
260	500	T2B
230	446	T2C
215	419	T2D
200	392	T3
180	356	T3A
165	329	T3B
160	320	T3C
135	275	T4
120	248	T4A
100	212	T5
85	185	T6

Identification numbers marked on equipment nameplates shall be in accordance with Table 500-2(b).

Exception: Equipment of the nonheat-producing type, such as junction boxes, conduit and fittings, are not required to have a marked operating temperature.

For purposes of testing and approval, various atmospheric mixtures (not oxygen enriched) have been grouped on the basis of their hazardous characteristics, and facilities have been made available

Table 500-2(c). Chemicals by Groups

Group A atmospheres	Group D atmospheres
Chemical	Chemical
acetylene	acetone
	acrylonitrile
Group B atmospheres	ammonia[3]
	benzene
butadiene[1]	butane
ethylene oxide[2]	1-butanol (butyl alcohol)
hydrogen	2-butanol (secondary butyl alcohol)
manufactured gases containing more	n-butyl acetate
than 30% hydrogen (by volume)	isobutyl acetate
propylene oxide[2]	ethane
	ethanol (ethyl alcohol)
Group C atmospheres	ethyl acetate
	ethylene dichloride
acetaldehyde	gasoline
cyclopropane	heptanes
diethyl ether	hexanes
ethylene	methane (natural gas)
isoprene	methanol (methyl alcohol)
unsymmetrical dimethyl hydrazine	3-methyl-1-butanol (isoamyl alcohol)
(UDMH 1, 1-dimethyl hydrazine)	methyl ethyl ketone
	methyl isobutyl ketone
	2-methyl-1-propanol (isobutyl alcohol)
	2-methyl-2-propanol
	(tertiary butyl alcohol)
	petroleum naphtha[4]
	octanes
	pentanes
	1-pentanol (amyl alcohol)
	propane
	1-propanol (propyl alcohol)
	2-propanol (isopropyl alcohol)
	propylene
	styrene
	toluene
	vinyl acetate
	vinyl chloride
	xylenes

[1] Group D equipment may be used for this atmosphere if such equipment is isolated in accordance with Section 501-5(a) by sealing all conduit ½-inch size or larger.

[2] Group C equipment may be used for this atmosphere if such equipment is isolated in accordance with Section 501-5(a) by sealing all conduit ½-inch size or larger.

[3] For Classification of areas involving ammonia atmosphere refer to ANSI B9.1 Safety Code for Mechanical Refrigeration-1971 and ANSI K61.1 Storage and Handling of Anhydrous Ammonia-1971.

[4] A saturated hydrocarbon mixture boiling in the range 20–135°C (68–275°F). Also known by the synonyms benzine, ligroin, petroleum ether or naphtha.

for testing and approval of equipment for use in the atmospheric groups listed in Table 500-2(c). Since there is no consistent relationship between explosion properties and ignition temperature, the two must be regarded as independent requirements.

▶   The requirements of Section 500-2 and Tables 500-2*b* and *c* provide the means of properly identifying and classifying equipment for use in hazardous locations. The identification numbers in Table 500-2*b* pertain to temperature range classifications as used by Underwriters' Laboratories, Inc. in U/L Hazardous Location Standards.

(c) Temperature.   The temperature marking specified in (b) above shall not exceed the ignition temperature of the specific gas or vapor to be encountered. For information regarding ignition temperatures see NFPA 325M, Fire Hazard Properties of Flammable Liquids, Gases, Volatile Solids—1969.

Formerly the temperature limit of each Group was assumed to be the lowest ignition temperature of any material in the Group, i.e., 280°C for Group D, 180°C for Group C. To avoid revising this limit as new gases are added (see hexane in Group D and acetaldehyde in Group C) temperature will be specified in future markings.

The ignition temperature for which equipment was approved prior to this requirement may be assumed to be as follows:

Group A 280°C (536°F)
Group B 280°C (536°F)
Group C 180°C (356°F)
Group D 280°C (536°F)

500-3. Specific Occupancies.   See Articles 510 through 517 for rules applying to garages, aircraft hangars, gasoline dispensing and service stations, bulk storage plants, finishing processes, and flammable anesthetics.

500-4. Class I Locations.   Class I locations are those in which flammable gases or vapors are or may be present in the air in quantities sufficient to produce explosive or ignitible mixtures. Class I locations shall include the following:

(a) Class I, Division 1.   Locations (1) in which hazardous concentrations of flammable gases or vapors exist continuously, intermittently, or periodically under normal operating conditions, (2) in which hazardous concentrations of such gases or vapors may exist frequently because of repair or maintenance operations or because of leakage, or (3) in which breakdown or faulty operation of equipment or processes which might release hazardous concentrations of flammable gases or vapors, might also cause simultaneous failure of electrical equipment.

This classification usually includes locations where volatile flammable liquids or liquefied flammable gases are transferred from one container to another; interiors of spray booths and areas in the vicinity of spraying and painting operations where volatile flammable solvents are used; locations containing open tanks or vats of volatile flammable liquids; drying rooms or compartments for the evaporation of flammable solvents; locations containing fat and oil extraction apparatus using volatile flammable solvents; portions of cleaning and dyeing plants where hazardous liquids are used; gas generator rooms and other portions of gas manufacturing plants where flammable gas may escape; inadequately ventilated pump rooms for flammable gas or for volatile flammable liquids; the interiors of refrigerators and freezers in which volatile, flammable materials are stored in open, lightly stoppered, or easily ruptured containers, and all other locations where hazardous concentrations of flammable vapors or gases are likely to occur in the course of normal operations.

(b) Class I, Division 2.   Locations (1) in which volatile flammable liquids or flammable gases are handled, processed or used, but in which the hazardous liquids, vapors or gases will normally be confined within closed containers or closed systems from which they can escape only in case of accidental rupture or breakdown of such containers or systems, or in case of abnormal operation of equipment, (2) in which hazardous concentrations of gases or vapors are normally prevented by positive mechanical ventilation, but which might become hazardous through failure or abnormal operation of the ventilating equipment, or (3) which are adjacent to Class I, Division 1 locations, and to which hazardous concentrations of gases or vapors might occasionally be communicated unless such communication is prevented by adequate positive-pressure ventilation from a source of clean air, and effective safeguards against ventilation failure are provided.

This classification usually includes locations where volatile flammable liquids or flammable gases or vapors are used, but which, in the judgment of the authority having jurisdiction, would become hazardous only in case of an accident or of some unusual operating condition. The quantity of hazardous material that might escape in case of accident, the adequacy of ventilating equipment, the total area involved, and the record of the industry or business with respect to explosions or fires are all factors that should receive consideration in determining the classification and extent of each hazardous area.

Piping without valves, checks, meters and similar devices would not ordinarily be deemed to introduce a hazardous condition even though used for hazardous liquids or gases. Locations used for the storage of hazardous liquids or of liquefied or compressed gases in sealed containers would not normally be considered hazardous unless subject to other hazardous conditions also.

Electrical conduits and their associated enclosures separated from process fluids by a single seal or barrier shall be classed as Division 2 locations if the outside of conduit and enclosures is a nonhazardous area.

500-5. Class II Locations.   Class II locations are those which are hazardous because of the presence of combustible dust. Class II locations shall include the following:

(a) Class II, Division 1.   Locations (1) in which combustible dust is or may be in suspension in the air continuously, intermittently, or periodically under normal operating conditions, in quantities sufficient to produce explosive or ignitible mixtures, (2) where mechanical failure or abnormal operation of machinery or equipment might cause such mixtures to be produced, and might also provide a source of ignition through simultaneous failure of electrical equipment, operation of protection devices, or from other causes, or (3) in which dusts of an electrically conducting nature may be present.

This classification usually includes the working areas of grain handling and storage plants; rooms containing grinders or pulverizers, cleaners, graders, scalpers, open conveyors or spouts, open bins or hoppers, mixers or blenders, automatic or hopper scales, packing machinery, elevator heads and boots, stock distributors, dust and stock collectors (except all-metal collectors vented to the outside), and all similar dust producing machinery and equipment in grain processing plants, starch plants, sugar pulverizing plants, malting plants, hay grinding plants, and other occupancies of similar nature; coal pulverizing plants (except where the pulverizing equipment is essentially dust-tight); all working areas where metal dusts and powders are produced, processed, handled, packed or stored (except in tight containers); and all other similar locations where combustible dust may, under normal operating conditions, be present in the air in quantities sufficient to produce explosive or ignitible mixtures.

Combustible dusts which are electrically nonconducting include dusts produced in the handling and processing of grain and grain products, pulverized sugar and cocoa, dried egg and milk powders, pulverized spices, starch and pastes, potato and woodflour, oil meal from beans and seed, dried hay, and other organic materials which may produce combustible dusts when processed or handled. Electrically conducting nonmetallic dusts include dusts from pulverized coal, coke and charcoal. Dusts containing magnesium or aluminum are particularly hazardous and every precaution must be taken to avoid ignition and explosion.

(b) Class II, Division 2. Locations in which combustible dust will not normally be in suspension in the air, or will not be likely to be thrown into suspension by the normal operation of equipment or apparatus, in quantities sufficient to produce explosive or ignitible mixtures, but (1) where deposits or accumulations of such dust may be sufficient to interfere with the safe dissipation of heat from electrical equipment or apparatus, or (2) where such deposits or accumulations of dust on, in, or in the vicinity of electrical equipment might be ignited by arcs, sparks or burning material from such equipment.

Locations where dangerous concentrations of suspended dust would not be likely, but where dust accumulations might form on, or in the vicinity of electrical equipment, would include rooms and areas containing only closed spouting and conveyors, closed bins or hoppers, or machines and equipment from which appreciable quantities of dust would escape only under abnormal operating conditions; rooms or areas adjacent to locations described in Section 500-5(a), and into which explosive or ignitible concentrations of suspended dust might be communicated only under abnormal operating conditions; rooms or areas where the formation of explosive or ignitible concentrations of suspended dust is prevented by the operation of effective dust control equipment; warehouses and shipping rooms where dust producing materials are stored or handled only in bags or containers; and other similar locations.

500-6. Class III Locations. Class III locations are those which are hazardous because of the presence of easily ignitible fibers or flyings, but in which such fibers or flyings are not likely to be in suspension in air in quantities sufficient to produce ignitible mixtures. Class III locations shall include the following:

(a) Class III, Division 1. Locations in which easily ignitible fibers or materials producing combustible flyings are handled, manufactured or used.

Such locations usually include some parts of rayon, cotton and other textile mills; combustible fiber manufacturing and processing plants; cotton gins and cotton-seed mills; flax processing plants; clothing manufacturing plants; woodworking plants; and establishments and industries involving similar hazardous processes or conditions.

Easily ignitible fibers and flyings include rayon, cotton (including cotton linters and cotton waste), sisal or henequen, istle, jute, hemp, tow, cocoa fiber, oakum, baled waste kapok, Spanish moss, excelsior and other materials of similar nature.

(b) Class III, Division 2. Locations in which easily ignitible fibers are stored or handled (except in process of manufacture).

▶ In each of the three classes of hazardous locations discussed in Sections 500-4, 500-5, and 500-6, the Code recognizes varying degrees of hazard, hence under each class two divisions are defined. In the installation rules that follow, the requirements for Division 1 of each class are more rigid than the requirements for Division 2.

Briefly, the hazards in the three classes of locations are due to the following causes:

Class I, Highly inflammable gases or vapors
Class II, Combustible dust

Class III, Combustible fibers or flyings

The classifications are easily understood and, if a given location is to be classed as hazardous, it should not be difficult to determine in which of the three classes it belongs. However, it is obviously impossible to make rules that will in every case determine positively whether the location is or is not hazardous; considerable common sense and good judgment must be exercised in determining whether the location under consideration should be considered as hazardous or likely to become hazardous because of a change in the processes carried on, and if so, what portion of the premises should be classed as coming under Division 1 and what part may safely be considered as being in Division 2.

ARTICLE 501. CLASS I INSTALLATIONS—HAZARDOUS LOCATIONS

501-1. General.   The general rules of this Code shall apply to the installation of electrical wiring and equipment in locations classified as Class I under Section 500-4 except as modified by this Article.

▶ *Installations in Class I Locations*

The more common Class I locations are those where some process is carried on involving the use of a highly volatile and inflammable liquid, such as gasoline, petroleum naphtha, benzene, diethyl ether, or acetone, or inflammable gases.

In any Class I location an explosive mixture of air and inflammable gas or vapor may be present which can be caused to explode by an arc or spark. To avoid the danger of explosions all electrical apparatus which may create arcs or sparks should if possible be kept out of the rooms where the hazardous locations exist, or, if this is not possible, such apparatus must be "of types approved for use in explosive atmospheres."

All equipment such as switches, circuit breakers, or motors must have some movable operating part projecting through the enclosing case, and any such part, as for example the operating lever of a switch or the shaft of a motor, must have sufficient clearance so that it will work freely; hence the equipment cannot be hermetically sealed. Also, the necessity for subsequent opening of the enclosures for servicing makes hermetically sealing impracticable. Furthermore, the enclosure of the equipment must be entered by a run of conduit and it is practically impossible to make conduit joints absolutely air- and gastight. Due to slight changes in temperature, the conduit system and the apparatus enclosures "breathe"; that is, any inflammable gas in the room may gradually find its way inside the conduit and enclosures and form an explosive mixture with air. Under this condition, when an arc occurs inside the enclosure an explosion may take place.

When the gas and air mixture explodes inside the enclosing case, the burning mixture must be confined entirely within the enclosure, so as to prevent the ignition of inflammable gases in the room. In the first place it is necessary that the enclosing case be so constructed that it will have sufficient strength to withstand the high pressure generated by an internal explosion. The pressure in pounds per square inch produced by the explosion of a given gas and air mixture has been quite definitely determined and the enclosure can be designed accordingly.

Since the enclosures for apparatus cannot be made absolutely tight, when an internal explosion occurs some of the burning gas will be forced out through any openings that exist. It has been found that the flame will not be carried out through an opening that is quite long in proportion to its width. This principle is applied in the design of so-called explosion-proof enclosures for apparatus by providing a wide flange at the joint between the body of the enclosure and grinding these flanges to a definitely determined fit. In this case the flanges are so ground that when the cover is in

Fig. 501-1. Explosion-proof junction box and cover. (*Crouse-Hinds Co.*)

place the clearance between the two surfaces will at no point exceed 0.0015 in. Thus, if an explosion occurs within the enclosure, in order to escape from the enclosure the burning gas must travel a considerable distance through an opening not more than 0.0015 in. wide. The same result may be accomplished by the use of a screwed-on cover having five full threads engaged as shown in Figs. 501-1 and 501-2. The fundamental principle of this construction is the same as has been used for many years in miners' safety lamps.

Fig. 501-2. Explosion-proof junction box and cover. (*Appleton Electric Co.*)

501-2. Transformers and Capacitors. The installation of transformers and capacitors shall conform to the following:

(a) Class I, Division 1. In Class I, Division 1 locations, transformers and capacitors shall conform to the following:

(1) Containing a Liquid That Will Burn. Transformers and capacitors containing a liquid that will burn shall be installed only in approved vaults, which shall conform to Sections 450-41 through 450-48, and in addition, (1) there shall be no door or other communicating opening between the vault and the hazardous area, (2) ample ventilation shall be provided for the continuous removal of hazardous gases or vapor, (3) vent openings or ducts shall lead to a safe location outside of buildings, and (4) vent ducts and openings shall be of sufficient area to relieve explosion pressures within the vault, and all portions of vent ducts within the buildings shall be of reinforced concrete construction.

(2) Not Containing a Liquid That Will Burn. Transformers and capacitors which do not contain a liquid that will burn shall (1) be installed in vaults conforming to the requirements of Section 501-2(a-1), or (2) be approved for Class I locations (explosion-proof).

(b) Class I, Division 2. In Class I, Division 2 locations, transformers and capacitors shall conform to Sections 450-21 through 450-25.

501-3. Meters, Instruments and Relays. The installation of meters, instruments and relays shall conform to the following:

(a) Class I, Division 1. In Class I, Division 1 locations, meters, instruments and relays, including kilowatt-hour meters, instrument transformers and resistors, rectifiers and thermionic tubes, shall be provided with enclosures approved for Class I locations.

(b) Class I, Division 2. In Class I, Division 2 locations, meters, instruments and relays shall conform to the following:

(1) Contacts. Switches and circuit breakers, and make-and-break contacts of pushbuttons, relays, and alarm bells or horns, shall have enclosures approved for Class I locations, unless general purpose enclosures are provided, and current interrupting contacts are (1) immersed in oil, (2) enclosed within a chamber hermetically sealed against the entrance of gases or vapors, or (3) in circuits which under normal conditions do not release sufficient energy to ignite a specific hazardous atmospheric mixture.

(2) Resistors and Similar Equipment. Resistors, resistance devices, thermionic tubes, and rectifiers, which are used in or in connection with meters, instruments and relays, shall conform to Section 501-3(a), except that enclosures may be of general purpose type when such equipment is without make-and-break or sliding contacts (other than as provided in Section 501-3(b) (1)) and when the maximum operating temperature of any exposed surface will not exceed 80 per cent of the ignition temperature in degrees Celsius of the gas or vapor involved as determined by ASTM test procedure (Designation D2155-66).

(3) Without Make-or-Break Contacts. Transformer windings, impedance coils, solenoids and other windings which do not incorporate sliding or make-and-break contacts shall be provided with enclosures which may be of the general purpose type.

(4) General Purpose Assemblies. Where an assembly is made up of components for which general purpose enclosures are acceptable under Sections 501-3 (b-1, b-2 and b-3), a single general purpose enclosure is acceptable for the assembly. Where such an assembly includes any of the equipment described in Section 501-3(b-2) the maximum obtainable surface temperature of any component of the assembly shall be clearly and permanently indicated on the outside of the enclosure.

(5) Fuses. Where general purpose enclosures are permitted under Sections 501-3(b-1, b-2, b-3 and b-4), fuses for overcurrent protection of the instrument circuits may be mounted in general purpose enclosures provided such fuses do not exceed 3 ampere rating at 120 volts and provided each such fuse is preceded by a switch conforming to Section 501-3(b) (1).

(6) Connections. To facilitate replacements, process control instruments may be connected through flexible cord, attachment plug and receptacle, provided:

1. a switch conforming to Section 501-3(b) (1) is provided so that the plug is not depended on to interrupt current, and
2. the current does not exceed 3 amperes at 120 volts, and
3. the power supply cord does not exceed 3 feet, is of a type approved for extra hard usage or for hard usage if protected by location and is supplied through a plug-cap and receptacle of the locking and grounding type, and
4. only necessary receptacles are provided, and
5. the receptacle carries a label warning against unplugging under load.

501-4. Wiring Methods. Wiring methods shall conform to the following:

(a) Class I, Division 1. In Class I, Division 1 locations, threaded rigid metal conduit or Type MI cable with termination fittings approved for the location shall be the wiring method employed. All boxes, fittings, and joints shall be threaded for connection to conduit or cable terminations, and shall be explosion-proof. Threaded joints shall be made up with at least five threads fully engaged. Type MI cable shall be installed and supported in a manner to avoid tensile stress at the termination fittings. Where necessary to employ flexible connections, as at motor terminals, flexible fittings approved for Class I locations (explosion-proof) shall be used.

▶ The term "approved for the location" in paragraph *a* means that approval is to be based on the performance of a fitting or equipment when subjected to a specific atmosphere.

As applied to rigid metal conduit, to be explosion-proof, threaded joints must be used at couplings and for connection to fittings, the threads must be cleanly cut, five full threads must be engaged, and each joint must be made up tight.

All fittings, such as outlet boxes, junction boxes, and switch boxes, also all enclosures for apparatus, should have threaded hubs to receive the conduit and must be provided with suitable covers. The box and cover must be of sufficient strength to withstand an internal explosion, the method of securing the cover to the box must likewise provide sufficient strength, and the joint between the cover and the box must be explosion-proof.

Explosion-proof junction boxes are available in a wide variety of types. Figure 501-1 shows one of a series of boxes designed for general use in hazardous locations. The opening to receive the cover is threaded internally and the cover is made of the same material as the box. Figure 501-2 shows a larger type of box having 10 threaded hubs, making it adaptable to a variety of conditions. Unused openings are closed with threaded plugs. The body of this box is malleable iron and the cover is brass, the cover being threaded internally in this design.

Box covers may have threaded connections with the boxes as shown in Figs. 501-1 and 501-2 or the cover may be attached with machine screws, in which case a carefully ground flanged joint is required.

A flexible fitting suitable for use in Class I hazardous locations is shown in Fig. 501-3. The flexible portion consists of a tube of bronze having deeply

Fig. 501-3. Pyle-o-flex flexible explosion-proof fitting. (*The Pyle-National Co.*)

corrugated walls and reinforced by a braid of fine bronze wires. A heavy threaded fitting is securely joined to each end of the flexible tube and a fibrous tubular lining, similar to "circular loom," is provided in order to prevent abrasion of the enclosed conductors that might result from long-continued vibration. The complete assembly is obtainable in various lengths up to a maximum of 3 ft.

In Class I, Division 2 locations explosion-proof outlet boxes are not required at lighting outlets nor at junction boxes containing no arcing device; however, where conduit is used, it should enter the box through threaded openings as shown in Fig. 501-1, or if locknut-bushing attachment is used, a bonding jumper and/or fittings must be provided between the boxes and conduits.

(b) Class I, Division 2.   In Class I, Division 2 locations, threaded rigid metal conduit or Type MI, MC, ALS or SNM cable with approved termination fittings shall be the wiring method employed. Type MI, MC, ALS or SNM cable shall be installed in a manner to avoid tensile stress at the termination fittings. Boxes, fittings and joints need not be explosion proof except as required by Sections 501-5(b)(1) and (b)(2). Where provision must be made for limited flexibility, as at motor terminals, flexible metal fittings, flexible metal conduit with approved fittings, liquidtight flexible metal conduit with approved fittings, or flexible cord approved for extra-hard usage and provided with approved bushed fittings shall be used. An additional conductor for grounding shall be included in the flexible cord unless other acceptable means of grounding are provided.

▶   Flexible connections permitted in Class I, Division 2 locations may consist of flexible conduit with approved fittings, and such fittings are not required to be specifically approved for Class I locations. It should be noted that a separate grounding conductor is necessary to bond across such flexible connections as required in Section 501-16b.

Ordinary knockout-type boxes may be installed in such locations, but Section 501-16b rules out the use of locknuts and bushings for bonding purposes, and the requirement specifies either bonding jumpers or other approved means to assure adequate grounding from the hazardous area to the point of grounding at the service.

501-5. Sealing and Drainage.　Seals are provided in conduit and cable systems to prevent the passage of gases, vapors or flames from one portion of the electrical installation to another through the conduit. Such communication through Type MI cable is inherently prevented by construction of the cable, but sealing compound is used in cable termination fittings to exclude moisture and other fluids from the cable insulation, and shall be of a type approved for the conditions of use. Seals in conduit and cable systems shall conform to the following:

(a) Class I, Division 1.　In Class I, Division 1 locations, seals shall be located as follows:

(1)　In each conduit run entering an enclosure for switches, circuit breakers, fuses, relays, resistors or other apparatus which may produce arcs, sparks or high temperatures. Seals shall be placed as close as practicable and in no case more than 18 inches from such enclosures. There shall be no junction box or similar enclosure in the conduit run between the sealing fitting and the apparatus enclosure.

(2)　In each conduit run of 2-inch size or larger entering the enclosure or fitting housing terminals, splices or taps, and within 18 inches of such enclosure or fitting.

See notes under Group B in Section 500-2.

Where two or more enclosures for which seals are required under Sections 501-5(a-1, 2) are connected by nipples or by runs of conduit not more than 36 inches long, a single seal in each such nipple connection or run of conduit would be sufficient if located not more than 18 inches from either enclosure. Conduit fittings approved for Class I locations (explosion-proof) and similar to the "L," "T" or "Cross" type would not usually be classed as enclosures when not larger than the trade size of the conduit.

(3)　In each conduit run leaving the Class I, Division 1 hazardous area. The sealing fitting may be located on either side of the boundary of such hazardous area, but shall be so designed and installed that any gases or vapors which may enter the conduit system, within the Division 1 hazardous area, will not enter or be communicated to the conduit beyond the seal. There shall be no union, coupling, box or fitting in the conduit between the sealing fitting and the point at which the conduit leaves the Division 1 hazardous area.

Exception: Rigid unbroken conduit which passes completely through a Class I, Division 1 area with no fittings 12 inches beyond each boundary, providing that the termination points of the unbroken conduit are in nonhazardous areas, need not be sealed.

(b) Class I, Division 2.　In Class I, Division 2 locations, seals shall be located as follows:

(1)　For connections to enclosures which are required to be approved for Class I locations, seals shall be provided in conformance to Sections 501-5(a-1 and a-2). All portions of the conduit run or nipple between the seal and such enclosure shall conform to Section 501-4(a).

(2) In each conduit run passing from the Class I, Division 2 hazardous area into a nonhazardous area. The sealing fitting may be located on either side of the boundary of such hazardous area, but shall be so designed and installed that any gases or vapors which may enter the conduit system, within the Division 2 hazardous area, will not enter or be communicated to the conduit beyond the seal. Rigid conduit shall be used between the sealing fitting and the point at which the conduit leaves the hazardous area, and a threaded connection shall be used at the sealing fitting. There shall be no union, coupling, box or fitting in the conduit between the sealing fitting and the point at which the conduit leaves the hazardous area.

Exception: Rigid unbroken conduit which passes completely through a Class I, Division 2 area with no fittings 12 inches beyond each boundary, providing that the termination points of the unbroken conduit are in nonhazardous areas, need not be sealed.

(c) Class I, Divisions 1 and 2. Where seals are required, they shall conform to the following:

(1) Fittings. Enclosures for connections or for equipment shall be provided with approved integral means for sealing, or sealing fittings approved for Class I locations shall be used. Sealing fittings shall be accessible.

(2) Compound. Sealing compound shall be approved for the purpose, shall not be affected by the surrounding atmosphere or liquids, and shall not have a melting point of less than 93°C. (200°F.).

(3) Thickness of Compound. In the completed seal, the minimum thickness of the sealing compound shall be not less than the trade size of the conduit, and in no case less than ⅝ inch.

(4) Splices and Taps. Splices and taps shall not be made in fittings intended only for sealing with compound, nor shall other fittings in which splices or taps are made be filled with compound.

(5) Assemblies. In an assembly where equipment which may produce arcs, sparks or high temperatures is located in a compartment separate from the compartment containing splices or taps, and an integral seal is provided where conductors pass from one compartment to the other, the entire assembly shall be approved for Class I locations. Seals in conduit connections to the compartment containing splices or taps shall be provided in Class I, Division 1 locations where required by Section 501-5(a-2).

(d) Drainage.

(1) Control Equipment. Where there is probability that liquid or other condensed vapor may be trapped within enclosures for control equipment or at any point in the raceway system, approved means shall be provided to prevent accumulation or to permit periodic draining of such liquid or condensed vapor.

(2) Motors and Generators. Where the authority having jurisdiction judges that there is probability that liquid or condensed vapor may accumulate within motors or generators, joints and conduit systems shall be arranged to minimize entrance of liquid. If means to prevent accumulation or to permit periodic draining are judged necessary, such means shall be provided at the time of manufacture, and shall be deemed an integral part of the machine.

(3) Canned Pumps, Etc. Canned pumps, process connections for flow, pressure, or analysis measurement, etc., frequently depend upon a single seal diaphragm or tube to prevent process fluids from entering the electrical conduit system. An additional approved seal or barrier shall be provided with an adequate drain between the seals in such a manner that leaks would be obvious.

See also the last paragraph of footnote in Section 500-4(b).

▶   The proper sealing of conduits in Class I locations is an important matter. In Class I, Division 1 and Division 2 locations, each piece of apparatus such as a motor controller, switch, or receptacle, should be isolated from all other apparatus by sealing so that an explosion in one enclosure cannot be communicated through the conduit to any other enclosure. Where two such pieces of apparatus are connected by a run of conduit not over 3 ft long, a single seal in this run is considered satisfactory if located at the center of the run. For runs of 2 in. or larger size it is required that a seal be provided within 18 in. of each enclosure that is required to be explosion-proof if the enclosure contains terminals, splices, or taps.

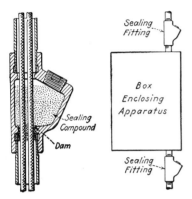

FIG. 501-4. A fitting providing means for sealing off a run of conduit to prevent the passage of gases. (*Crouse-Hinds Co.*)

Each run of conduit from a hazardous location to a nonhazardous location should also be sealed, preferably just outside the hazardous area. The purpose of this sealing is twofold: (1) The conduit usually terminates in some enclosure in the nonhazardous area containing an arc-producing device, such as a switch or fuse. If not sealed, the conduit and apparatus enclosure are likely to become filled with an explosive mixture and the ignition of this mixture may cause local damage in the nonhazardous location. (2) An explosion or ignition of the mixture in the conduit in the nonhazardous area would probably travel back through the conduit to the hazardous area and might cause an explosion there if due to some defective fitting or poor workmanship the installation is not completely explosion-proof.

In Class I, Division 2 locations a seal is required in each run of conduit entering an enclosure that is required to be explosion-proof, also in each conduit run leaving the hazardous area.

FIG. 501-5. Sealing fitting for horizontal conduit runs. (*Crouse-Hinds Co.*)

The necessary sealing may be accomplished by inserting in the conduit runs special sealing fittings such as that shown in Figs. 501-4 through 501-6, or provision may be made for sealing in the enclosure for the apparatus. Thus an explosion-proof motor is made with the leads sealed where they pass from the terminal housing to the interior of the motor and no other seal is needed where a conduit terminates at the motor, except that if the conduit is 2 in. or larger in size, a seal must be provided not more than 18 in. from the motor terminal housing.

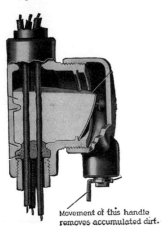

Movement of this handle removes accumulated dirt.

FIG. 501-6. Sealing fitting with provision for drainage. (*Crouse-Hinds Co.*)

The sealing compound used must be one which has a melting point of not less than 200°F and is not affected by the liquid or gas which causes the location to be hazardous. Most of the insulating compounds commonly used in cable splices and potheads are soluble in gasoline and lacquer solvents and hence are unsuitable for sealing conduits in locations where these liquids are used. A mixture of litharge and glycerin is insoluble in nearly all liquids and gases found in Class I locations and meets all other requirements, though this mixture is open to the objection that it becomes very hard and is difficult to remove if the wires must be pulled out. No sealing compounds are listed by Underwriters' Laboratories, Inc., as suitable for this use except in connection with the explosion-proof fittings of specific manufacturers.

Where conduit is run overhead and is brought down vertically to an enclosure for apparatus, any condensation of moisture in the vertical run would be trapped by the seal above the apparatus enclosure.

Figure 501-6 shows a sealing fitting designed to provide drainage for a vertical conduit run. Any water coming down from above runs over the surface of the sealing compound and down to an explosion-proof drain, through which the water is automatically drained off. The construction of the drain is shown in Fig. 501-7, which illustrates a separate fitting that may be screwed into a tapped opening to drain any explosion-proof enclosure.

Figure 501-8 shows an explosion-proof "breather valve," designed to be screwed into a tapped opening in the top of an explosion-proof enclosure; its purpose is to permit the escape of hot, moisture-laden air, which might otherwise cause the formation of mildew on the insulation of conductors within the enclosure.

Where either of the fittings shown in Fig. 501-7 or Fig. 501-8 is used, the

FIG. 501-7. Drainage fitting. (*Crouse-Hinds Co.*)

FIG. 501-8. Breather valve. (*Crouse-Hinds Co.*)

metal into which the fitting is inserted must be of sufficient thickness so that five full threads will be engaged, in order to fulfill the requirements for an explosion-proof joint.

Figure 501-9 is a wiring layout for a Class I, Division 1 location. The wiring is all rigid metal conduit with threaded joints. All fittings and equipment are explosion-proof; this includes the motors, the motor controller for motor No. 1 (lower part of drawing), the pushbutton control station for

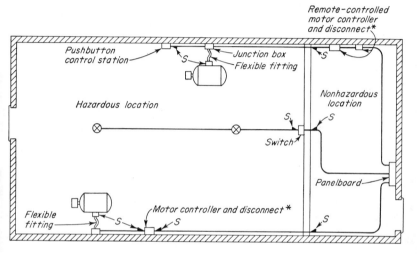

Fig. 501-9. Wiring layout for power and light in a Class I, Division 1 location. *S* indicates a point where conduit or equipment is sealed.
* Disconnecting means may be in same enclosure. See Section 430-103.

motor No. 2 (upper part of drawing), and all outlet and junction boxes. The cabinet and a remote controller for motor No. 2 are placed outside the hazardous area and hence need not be explosion-proof.

Each of the three runs of conduit from the cabinet is sealed just outside the hazardous area. A sealing fitting is provided in the conduit each side of the controller for motor No. 1 (lower part of drawing.) The leads are sealed where they pass through the frame of the motor into the terminal housing and no other seal is needed at this point provided that the conduit and flexible fitting enclosing the leads to the motor are smaller than 2 in. The pushbutton control station for motor No. 2 (upper part of drawing) is considered an arc-producing device, even though the contacts may be oil-immersed, and hence the conduit is sealed where it terminates at this device.

A seal is provided on each side of the switch controlling the lighting fixtures; one of these seals is in the nonhazardous room. The lighting fixtures are hung on rigid conduit stems threaded to the covers of explosion-proof boxes on the ceiling.

501-6. Switches, Circuit Breakers, Motor Controllers and Fuses. Switches, circuit breakers, motor controllers and fuses shall conform to the following:

(a) Class I, Division 1. In Class I, Division 1 locations, switches, circuit breakers, motor controllers and fuses, including pushbuttons, relays and similar devices, shall be provided with enclosures, and the enclosure in each case together with the enclosed apparatus shall be approved as a complete assembly for use in Class I locations.

(b) Class I, Division 2. Switches, circuit breakers, motor controllers and fuses in Class I, Division 2 locations shall conform to the following:

(1) Type Required. Circuit breakers, motor controllers and switches intended to interrupt current in the normal performance of the function for which they are installed shall be provided with enclosures approved for Class I locations, unless general purpose enclosures are provided and (1) the interruption of current occurs within a chamber hermetically sealed against the entrance of gases and vapors, or (2) the current interrupting contacts are oil-immersed and the device is approved for locations of this class and division.

This includes service and branch circuit switches and circuit breakers; motor controllers, including pushbuttons, pilot switches, relays and motor-overload protective devices; and switches and circuit breakers for the control of lighting and appliance circuits. Oil-immersed circuit breakers and controllers of ordinary general use type may not confine completely the arc produced in the interruption of heavy overloads, and specific approval for locations of this class and division is therefore necessary.

(2) Isolating Switches. Enclosures for disconnecting and isolating switches without fuses and which are not intended to interrupt current may be of general purpose type.

(3) Fuses. For the protection of motors, appliances and lamps, except as provided in Section 501-6(b-4): (1) standard plug or cartridge fus ɛ may be used provided they are placed within enclosures approved for the purpose and for the location, or (2) fuses of a type in which the operating element is immersed in oil or other approved liquid, or is enclosed within a chamber hermetically sealed against the entrance of gases and vapors may be used provided they are approved for the purpose and are placed within general purpose enclosures.

(4) Fuses or Circuit Breakers for Overcurrent Protection. When not more than 10 sets of approved enclosed fuses, or not more than 10 circuit breakers which are not intended to be used as switches for the interruption of current, are installed for branch or feeder circuit protection in any one room, area or section of this class and division, the enclosures for such fuses or circuit breakers may be of general purpose type, provided the fuses or circuit breakers are for the protection of circuits or feeders supplying lamps in fixed positions only.

A set of fuses is construed to mean a group containing as many fuses as are required to perform a single protective function in a circuit. For example, a group of 3 fuses protecting an ungrounded three-phase circuit, and a single fuse protecting the ungrounded conductor of an identified two-wire single-phase circuit, would each be considered as a set of fuses. Fuses conforming to Section 501-6(b-3) need not be included in counting the 10 sets of fuses permitted in general purpose enclosures.

▶   Figure 501-10 shows a 12-circuit explosion-proof panelboard. This device consists of an assembly of branch-circuit circuit breakers, each pair of cir-

Fig. 501-10. Twelve-circuit explosion-proof panelboard. (*Crouse-Hinds Co.*)

cuit breakers being enclosed in a cast-metal explosion-proof housing. Access to the circuit breakers and to the wiring compartment is through handholes with threaded covers, and threaded hubs are provided for the conduits.

An individually mounted branch-circuit circuit breaker is shown in Fig. 501-11. Motor controllers mounted in similar enclosures are available.

Figure 501-12 shows a magnetically operated motor starter control switch enclosed in a cast-iron box, so as to be suitable for use in Class I, Group D,

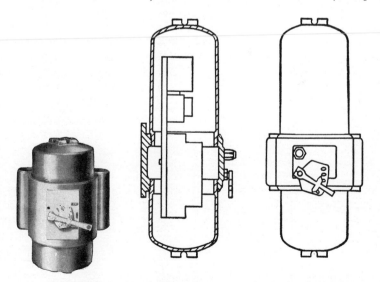

Fig. 501-11. A circuit breaker in an explosion-proof housing. (*Crouse-Hinds Co.*)

Fig. 501-12. Magnetic motor starter for use in a Class I, Group D location. (*General Electric Co.*)

locations. The wide flanges on the box form a metal-to-metal joint with the cover plate. The cover is secured in place with **24** bolts in order to ensure a flame-tight joint between the box and cover. The illustration shows a starter that is designed for use with a separate pushbutton station; however, similar starters are available with "start" and "stop" pushbuttons mounted in the cover.

Housings similar to that shown in Fig. **501-11** can be obtained which are designed to contain any one of quite a wide variety of across-the-line type motor starters, either manually or magnetically operable and in ratings up to **25** hp at **220** volts three-phase, or **50** hp at **440** volts three-phase.

A snap switch in an explosion-proof enclosure is shown in Fig. **501-13**.

With reference to subparagraph *b.*2. it is assumed that fuses will very seldom blow, or circuit breakers will very seldom open, if used to protect feeders or branch circuits that supply only lamps in fixed positions. In Division 2 locations the conditions are not normally hazardous but may

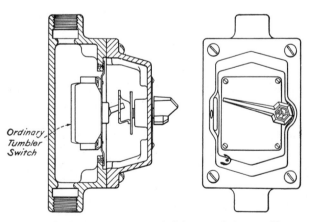

Fig. 501-13. Tumbler-type snap switch in an explosion-proof housing. (*Crouse-Hinds Co.*)

sometimes become so. There is very little probability that one of the over-current devices will operate at the same time that the hazardous conditions exist, hence it is not considered necessary to require that these overcurrent devices be in explosion-proof enclosures.

501-7. Control Transformers and Resistors.   Transformers, impedance coils and resistors used as or in conjunction with control equipment for motors, generators and appliances shall conform to the following:

(a) Class I, Division 1.   In Class I, Division 1 locations, transformers, impedance coils and resistors, together with any switching mechanism associated with them, shall be provided with enclosures approved for Class I locations (explosion-proof).

(b) Class I, Division 2.   In Class I, Division 2 locations, control transformers and resistors shall conform to the following:

(1) Switching Mechanisms.   Switching mechanisms used in conjunction with transformers, impedance coils and resistors shall conform to Section 501-6(b).

(2) Coils and Windings.   Enclosures for windings of transformers, solenoids or impedance coils may be of the general purpose types.

(3) Resistors.   Resistors shall be provided with enclosures and the assembly shall be approved for Class I locations, unless resistance is nonvariable and maximum operating temperature, in degrees Celsius, will not exceed 80 per cent of the ignition temperature of the gas or vapor involved as determined by ASTM test procedure (Designation D 2155-66).

▶   The term *control transformer* is commonly applied to a small dry-type transformer used to supply the control circuits of one or more motors, stepping down the voltage of a 480 volt power circuit to 120 volts.

501-8. Motors and Generators.   Motors and generators shall conform to the following:

(a) Class I, Division 1.   In Class I, Division 1 locations, motors, generators and other rotating electrical machinery shall be: (1) approved for Class I locations (explosion-proof), or (2) of the totally enclosed type supplied with positive-pressure ventilation from a source of clean air with discharge to a safe area, so arranged to prevent energizing of the machine until ventilation has been established and the enclosure has been purged with at least ten volumes of air, and also arranged to automatically de-energize the equipment when the air supply fails, or (3) of the totally enclosed inert-gas-filled type supplied with a suitable reliable source of inert gas for pressuring the enclosure, with devices provided to insure a positive pressure in the enclosure and arranged to automatically de-energize the equipment when the gas supply fails. Totally enclosed motors of types (2) or (3) shall have no external surface with an operating temperature in degrees Celsius in excess of 80 per cent of the ignition temperature of the gas or vapor involved, as determined by ASTM test procedure (Designation: D-2155-66). Appropriate devices shall also be provided to detect any increase in temperature of the motor beyond design limits and automatically de-energize the equipment. Auxiliary equipment shall be of a type approved for the location in which it is installed.

Fig. 501-14. Totally enclosed fan-cooled motor of special type approved for use in explosive atmospheres. (*General Electric Co.*)

▶   See Tentative Interim Amendment No. 166 in back of book.

(b) Class I, Division 2. In Class I, Division 2 locations, motors, generators and other rotating electrical machinery in which are employed sliding contacts, centrifugal or other types of switching mechanism (including motor overcurrent devices), or integral resistance devices, either while starting or while running, shall be approved for Class I locations (explosion-proof), unless such sliding contacts, switching mechanisms and resistance devices are provided with enclosures approved for such locations.

This rule does not prohibit installation of open or nonexplosion-proof enclosed motors, such as squirrel cage induction motors, without brushes, switching mechanism, etc., in Class I, Division 2 locations.

Fig. 501-15. View showing internal construction of motor shown in Fig. 501-14. (*General Electric Co.*)

▶　　A motor of a type approved for use in explosive atmospheres is shown in Figs. 501-14 and 501-15. This motor is of the totally enclosed, fan-cooled type. The main frame and end housings are made with sufficient strength to withstand internal pressures due to ignition of a combustible mixture inside the motor. Wide metal-to-metal joints are provided between the frame and housings. Circulation of the air is maintained inside the inner enclosure by fan blades on each end of the rotor. At the left side of the sectional view (Fig. 501-15) a fan is shown in the space between the inner and outer housings. This fan draws in air through a screen and drives it across the surface of the stator punchings and out through openings at the drive end of the motor.

Standard open-type squirrel-cage induction motors may be used in Division 2 locations. Motors having commutators or integral switching or control equipment must be explosion-proof.

501-9. Lighting Fixtures.　Lamps shall be installed in fixtures which shall conform to the following:

(a) Class I, Division 1.　In Class I, Division 1 locations, lighting fixtures shall conform to the following:

Fig. 501-16. Lighting fixture suitable for Class I, Group C and D locations. (*Crouse-Hinds Co.*)

(1) Approved Fixtures.　Each fixture shall be approved as a complete assembly for locations of this class, and shall be clearly marked to indicate the maximum wattage of lamps for which it is approved. Fixtures intended for portable use shall be specifically approved as a complete assembly for that use.

(2) Physical Damage.　Each fixture shall be protected against physical damage by a suitable guard or by location.

(3) Pendant Fixtures.　Pendant fixtures shall be suspended by and supplied through threaded rigid conduit stems and threaded joints shall be provided with set-screws or other effective means to prevent loosening. For stems longer than 12 inches, permanent and effective bracing against lateral displacement shall be provided at a level not more than 12 inches above the lower end of the stem, or flexibility in the form of a fitting or flexible connector approved for the purpose and for the location shall be provided not more than 12 inches from the point of attachment to the supporting box or fitting.

(4) Supports.   Boxes, box assemblies or fittings used for the support of lighting fixtures shall be approved for the purpose and for Class I locations.

(b) Class I, Division 2.   In Class I, Division 2 locations, lighting fixtures shall conform to the following:

(1) Portable Lamps.   Portable lamps shall conform to Section 501-9(a-1).

(2) Fixed Lighting.   Lighting fixtures for fixed lighting shall be protected from physical damage by suitable guards or by location. Where there is danger that falling sparks or hot metal from lamps or fixtures might ignite localized concentrations of flammable vapors or gases, suitable enclosures or other effective protective means shall be provided. Where lamps are of a size or type which may, under normal operating conditions, reach surface temperatures exceeding 80 per cent of the ignition temperature in degrees Celsius of the gas or vapor involved, as determined by ASTM test procedure (Designation D-2155-66), fixtures shall conform to Section 501-9(a-1).

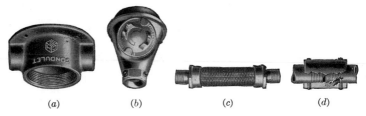

(a)   (b)   (c)   (d)

Fig. 501-17. Parts for a lighting fixture installation. (a) Outlet box. (b) Canopy. (c) Flexible support. (d) Coupling. (*Crouse-Hinds Co.*)

(3) Pendant Fixtures.   Pendant fixtures shall be suspended by threaded rigid conduit stems or by other approved means. For rigid stems longer than 12 inches, permanent and effective bracing against lateral displacement shall be provided at a level not more than 12 inches above the lower end of the stem, or flexibility in the form of a fitting or flexible connector approved for the purpose shall be provided not more than 12 inches from the point of attachment to the supporting box or fitting.

(4) Supports.   Boxes, box assemblies, or fittings used for the support of lighting fixtures shall be approved for the purpose.

(5) Switches.   Switches which are a part of an assembled fixture or of an individual lampholder shall conform to the requirements of Section 501-6(b-1).

(6) Starting Equipment.   Starting and control equipment for electric-discharge lamps shall conform to the requirements of Section 501-7(b).

▶   Typical parts for a complete lighting-fixture assembly for a Class I, Division 1, location are shown in Figs. 501-16 and 501-17.

Figure 501-17a shows an outlet box having an internally threaded opening designed to receive the canopy cover shown in Fig. 501-17b. A flexible fixture support (c) makes a threaded connection with the canopy and by means of a coupling (d) is connected to the desired length of ¾-in. rigid conduit

FIG. 501-18. Hand lamp suitable for use in Class I locations. (*Crouse-Hinds Co.*)

extending to the lighting fixture shown in Fig. 501-16. The flexible support is required if the total length of the fixture stem exceeds 12 in. All threaded connections are provided with set-screws to prevent any possible loosening when the fixture is being cleaned or relamped.

The body of the fixture, Fig. 501-16, is provided with a threaded hub to receive the ¾-in. rigid conduit stem. A globeholder is threaded to the outside of the body and supports a heavy glass globe, guard, and reflector. This fixture can be obtained in sizes suitable for lamps of any size from 40 to 500 watt.

Any desired type of lighting fixture may be installed in a Division 2 location if provided with a guard as specified. A stem, if used, must comply with subparagraph 3.

An explosion-proof hand lamp is shown in Fig. 501-18. The construction of this device is in general similar to that of the lighting fixture shown in Fig. 501-16. Section 501-11 requires that a three-conductor cord shall be used and the device is provided with a terminal for the third, or grounding conductor, which serves to ground the exposed metal parts.

501-10. Utilization Equipment, Fixed and Portable. Utilization equipment, fixed and portable, shall conform to the following:

(a) Class I, Division 1. In Class I, Division 1 locations, utilization equipment, including electrically-heated and motor-driven equipment shall be approved for Class I locations.

(b) Class I, Division 2. In Class I, Division 2 locations, utilization equipment, fixed and portable, shall conform to the following:

(1) Heaters. Electrically-heated utilization equipment shall be approved for Class I locations.

(2) Motors. Motors of motor-driven utilization equipment shall conform to Section 501-8(b).

(3) Switches, Circuit Breakers, and Fuses. Switches, circuit breakers and fuses shall conform to Section 501-6(b).

▶   It is seldom necessary to use an appliance in a Class I location. The requirements are practically the same for Division 1 and Division 2 locations.

501-11. Flexible Cords, Class I, Divisions 1 and 2. A flexible cord may be used only for connection between a portable lamp or other portable utilization equipment and the fixed portion of its supply circuit and where used shall: (1) be of a type approved for extra hard usage, (2) contain, in addition to the conductors of the circuit, a grounding conductor conforming to Section 400-14, (3) be connected to terminals or to supply conductors in an approved manner, (4) be supported by clamps or by other suitable means in such a manner that there will be no tension on the terminal connections, and (5) suitable seals shall be provided where the flexible cord enters boxes, fittings or enclosures of explosion-proof type.

Refer to Section 501-13 when flexible cords are exposed to liquids having a deleterious effect on the conductor insulation.

501-12. Receptacles and Attachment Plugs, Class I, Divisions 1 and 2.   Receptacles and attachment plugs shall be of the type providing for connection to the grounding conductor of the flexible cord, and shall be approved for Class I locations, except as provided in Section 501-3(b) (6).

▶   A unit device consisting of a receptacle and plug interlocked with an explosion-proof switch is shown in Fig. 501-19. The plug cannot be inserted or withdrawn unless the switch is open and the switch cannot be closed until the plug has been inserted. An additional pole is provided in the plug and receptacle for connection to a grounding conductor in the cord.

Figure 501-20 shows a three-pole 30-amp receptacle and attachment plug which is so designed as to seal the arc when the circuit is broken, and therefore is suitable for use without a switch.

Fig. 501-19. Explosion-proof receptacle and attachment plug with interlocking switch. (*Appleton Electric Co.*)

Fig. 501-20. Explosion-proof receptacle and attachment plug. (*Crouse-Hinds Co.*)

The circuit conductors are brought into the base or body through rigid conduit screwed into a tapped opening and are spliced to pigtail leads from the receptacle. The receptacle housing is then attached to the base, the joint being made at wide flanges ground to a suitable fit. All necessary sealing is provided in the device itself and no additional sealing is required when it is installed.

The parts are so constructed that the plug must first be partially withdrawn, which breaks each pole of the circuit in a closed chamber, and the resulting arcs are quickly smothered. A sleeve on the receptacle must then be rotated through a small angle before the plug can be fully withdrawn;

thus the action is delayed so that the arcs are always extinguished before the contacts are withdrawn from the closed chamber.

The plug is designed to receive a three-conductor cord for a two-wire circuit or a four-conductor cord for a three-wire three-phase circuit, and is provided with a clamping device to relieve the terminals from any strain. The extra conductor is used to ground the equipment supplied.

501-13. Conductor Insulation Class I, Divisions 1 and 2.   Where condensed vapors or liquids may collect on or come in contact with the insulation on conductors, such insulation shall be of a type approved for use under such conditions or the insulation shall be protected by a sheath of lead or by other approved means.

▶   Because of economics and greater ease in handling, nylon-jacketed types TW and THWN wires suitable for use where exposed to gasoline have in most cases replaced lead-covered conductors.

An excerpt from Underwriters' Laboratories, Inc. "Electrical Construction Materials List" states as follows:

Wires, Thermoplastic.
Gasoline Resistant TW—Indicates a TW conductor with a jacket of extruded nylon suitable for use in wet locations, and for exposure to mineral oil, and to liquid gasoline and gasoline vapors at ordinary ambient temperature. It is identified by tag marking and by printing on the insulation or nylon jacket with the designation "Type TW Gasoline and Oil Resistant."

Also listed for the above use is "Gasoline Resistant THWN" with the designation "Type THWN Gasoline and Oil Resistant."

It should be noted that other thermoplastic wires may be suitable for exposure to mineral oil but with the exception of those marked "Gasoline and Oil Resistant," reference to mineral oil does not include gasoline or similar light-petroleum solvents.

The conductor itself must bear the marking legend designating its use as suitable for gasoline exposure and not rely on the tag alone.

501-14. Signal, Alarm, Remote-Control and Communication Systems.   Signal, alarm, remote-control and communication systems shall conform to the following:

   (a) Class I, Division 1.   In Class I, Division 1 locations, all apparatus and equipment of signaling, alarm, remote-control and communication systems, irrespective of voltage, shall be approved for Class I locations, and all wiring shall conform to Sections 501-4(a) and 501-5(a and c).

   (b) Class I, Division 2.   In Class I, Division 2 locations, signal, alarm, remote-control and communication systems shall conform to the following:

   (1) Contacts.   Switches and circuit breakers, and make-and-break contacts of pushbuttons, relays, and alarm bells or horns, shall have enclosures approved for Class I locations, unless general purpose enclosures are provided and current interrupting contacts are (1) immersed in oil, or (2) enclosed within a chamber hermetically sealed against the entrance of gases or vapors, or (3) in circuits which under normal conditions do not release sufficient energy to ignite a specific hazardous atmospheric mixture.

(2) Resistors and Similar Equipment. Resistors, resistance devices, thermionic tubes and rectifiers shall conform to Section 501-3(b-2).

(3) Protectors. Enclosures which may be of general purpose type shall be provided for lightning protective devices and for fuses.

(4) All wiring shall conform to Section 501-4(b) and 501-5(b) and (c).

▶   Nearly all signaling, remote-control, and communication equipment involves make-or-break contacts; hence in Division 1 locations all devices

Fig. 501-21. Telephone signal bell for use in Class I hazardous locations. (*Crouse-Hinds Co.*)

must be explosion-proof and the wiring must comply with the requirements for light and power wiring in such locations, including seals.

Figure 501-21 shows a telephone signal bell having the operating mechanism mounted in an explosion-proof housing. Similar equipment may be obtained for operating horns or sirens.

Referring to subparagraph 1, it would usually be the more simple method to use explosion-proof devices, rather than devices having contacts immersed in oil or devices in hermetically sealed enclosures, though mercury switches, which are hermetically sealed, may be used for some purposes.

501-15. Live Parts, Class I, Divisions 1 and 2. There shall be no exposed live parts.

501-16. Grounding, Class I, Divisions 1 and 2. Wiring and equipment shall be grounded in conformity with the following:

(a) Exposed Parts. The exposed noncurrent-carrying metal parts of equipment such as the frames or metal exteriors of motors, fixed or portable lamps or other utilization equipment, lighting fixtures, cabinets, cases, and conduit, shall be grounded as specified in Article 250.

(b) Bonding. The locknut-bushing and double-locknut types of contacts shall not be depended upon for bonding purposes, but bonding jumpers with proper fittings or other approved means shall be used. Such means of bonding shall apply to all intervening raceways, fittings, boxes, enclosures, etc. between hazardous areas and the point of grounding for service equipment. Where flexible conduit is used as permitted in Section 501-4(b), bonding jumpers with proper fittings shall be provided around such conduit.

(c) Lightning Protection. Each ungrounded service conductor of a wiring system in a Class I location, when supplied from an overhead line in an area where lightning disturbances are prevalent, shall be protected by a lightning protective device of proper type. Lightning protective devices shall be connected to the service conductors on the supply side of the service disconnecting means, and shall be bonded to the raceway system at the service entrance.

Also refer to Section 502-3.

(d) Grounded Service Conductor Bonded to Raceway. Wiring in a Class I location, when supplied from a grounded alternating current supply system in which a grounded conductor is a part of the service, shall have the grounded service conductor bonded to the raceway system and to the grounding conductor for the raceway system. The bonding connection to the grounded service conductor shall be made on the supply side of the service disconnecting means.

(e) Transformer Ground Bonded to Raceway. Wiring in a Class I location, when supplied from a grounded alternating current supply system in which no grounded conductor is a part of the service, shall be provided with a metallic connection between the supply system ground and the raceway system at the service entrance. The metallic connection shall have an ampacity not less than $\frac{1}{3}$ that of the service conductors, and shall in no case be smaller than No. 10 when of soft copper, or No. 12 when of medium or hard-drawn copper.

(f) Multiple Grounds. Where, in the application of Section 250-21, it is necessary to abandon one or more grounding connections to avoid objectionable passage of current over the grounding conductors, the connection required in Section 501-16(d and e) shall not be abandoned while any other grounding connection remains connected to the supply system.

▶ Special care in the grounding of all equipment is necessary in order to prevent the possibility of arcs or sparks when any grounded metal comes in contact with the frame or case of the equipment. All connections of conduit to boxes, cabinets, enclosures for apparatus, and motor frames must be so made as to secure permanent and effective electrical connections. To be effective, this form of construction is not only necessary in the spaces that are classed as hazardous but should also be carried out back to the point where the connection for grounding the conduit is made to the water-piping system. Outside the space where the hazardous conditions exist, threaded connections should be used for conduit.

Lightning arresters are spark-producing devices and should be installed outside the building. The arresters must have grounding connections as provided in Section 250-131, and in addition, the grounding connection must be bonded to the service entrance conduit.

If the service voltage is not over 600 volts, the supply system is a secondary system and the provisions of Art. 250 apply; hence the grounded service conductor will always be bonded to the equipment grounding conductor. It might be possible to install a system operating at over 600 volts in a Class I, Division 2 location, but this would be an unusual case.

The conditions described in paragraph *e* would seldom be met in practice. The conductor used for making the connection would usually be an outdoor overhead conductor, in which case, according to Section 730-6, the conductor should not be smaller than No. 10. If the supply system has a grounded conductor, connection of this conductor to the equipment ground will help to provide proper operation to overcurrent protective devices.

ARTICLE 502. CLASS II INSTALLATIONS—HAZARDOUS LOCATIONS

502-1. General. The general rules of this Code shall apply to the installation of electrical wiring and apparatus in locations classified as Class II under Section 500-5 except as modified by this Article.

"Dust-ignition-proof," as used in this Article, shall mean enclosed in a manner which will exclude ignitible amounts of dusts or amounts which might affect performance or rating and which, when installation and protection are in conformance with this Code, will not permit arcs, sparks or heat otherwise generated or liberated inside of the enclosure, to cause ignition of exterior accumulations or atmospheric suspensions of a specified dust on or in the vicinity of the enclosure.

Equipment installed in Class II locations shall be able to function at full rating without developing surface temperatures high enough to cause excessive dehydration or gradual carbonization of any organic dust deposits that may occur. Dust which is carbonized or is excessively dry is highly susceptible to spontaneous ignition. In general, maximum surface temperatures under actual operating conditions shall not exceed 165°C (329°F) for equipment which is not subject to overloading, and 120°C (248°F) for equipment such as motors, power transformers, etc., which may be overloaded.

Equipment and wiring of the type defined in Article 100 as explosion-proof is not required in Class II locations, and may not be acceptable unless approved for such locations.

▶ Referring to Section 500-5, the hazards in Class II locations are due to the presence of combustible dust. These locations are subdivided into three groups, as follows:

Group E, Atmospheres containing metal dust;
Group F, Atmospheres containing carbon black, coal dust, or coke dust;
Group G, Atmospheres containing grain dust.

It is important to note that some equipment that is suitable for Class II, Group G, is not suitable for Class II, Groups E and F.

Any one of four hazards, or a combination of two or more, may exist in a Class II location; (1) an explosive mixture of air and dust, (2) the collection of conductive dust on and around live parts, (3) overheating of equipment because deposits of dust interfere with the normal radiation of heat, and (4) the possible ignition of deposits of dust by arcs or sparks. A large number of processes which may produce combustible dusts are listed in Section 500-5. Most of the equipment listed as suitable for Class I locations is also dust-tight, but it should not be taken for granted that all explosion-proof equipment is suitable for use in Class II locations. Some explosion-proof equipment may reach too high a temperature if blanketed by a heavy deposit of dust. Grain dust will ignite at a temperature of **329°F.**

Location of service equipment, switchboards, and panelboards in a separate room away from the dusty atmosphere is always preferable.

502-2. Transformers and Capacitors. The installation of transformers and capacitors shall conform to the following:

(a) Class II, Division 1. In Class II, Division 1 locations, transformers and capacitors shall conform to the following:

(1) Containing a Liquid That Will Burn. Transformers and capacitors containing a liquid that will burn shall be installed only in approved vaults conforming to Sections 450-41 through 450-48, and in addition (1) door or other openings communicating with the hazardous area shall have self-closing fire doors on both sides of the wall, and the doors shall be carefully fitted and provided with suitable seals (such as weather stripping) to minimize the entrance of dust into the vault, (2) vent openings and ducts shall communicate only with the outside air, and (3) suitable pressure-relief openings communicating with the outside air shall be provided.

(2) Not Containing a Liquid That Will Burn. Transformers and capacitors which do not contain a liquid that will burn shall: (1) be installed in vaults conforming to Sections 450-41 through 450-48, or (2) be approved as a complete assembly including terminal connections for Class II locations.

(3) Metal Dusts. No transformer or capacitor shall be installed in a location where dust from magnesium, aluminum, aluminum bronze powders, or other metals of similarly hazardous characteristics may be present.

(b) Class II, Division 2. In Class II, Division 2 locations, transformers and capacitors shall conform to the following:

(1) Containing a Liquid That Will Burn. Transformers and capacitors containing a liquid that will burn shall be installed in vaults conforming to Sections 450-41 through 450-48.

(2) Containing Askarel. Transformers containing askarel and rated in excess of 25 kva shall: (1) be provided with pressure-relief vents, (2) be provided with means for absorbing any gases generated by arcing inside the case, or the pressure-relief vents shall be connected to a chimney or flue which will carry such gases outside the building and (3) have an air space of not less than 6 inches between the transformer cases and any adjacent combustible material.

(3) Dry-Type Transformers. Dry-type transformers shall be installed in vaults or shall: (1) have their windings and terminal connections enclosed in tight metal housings without ventilating or other openings, and (2) operate at voltages not exceeding 600 volts.

▶　　So far as can be learned, no askarel-insulated or dry-type transformers can be obtained which are dust-tight.

Capacitors of the type used for the correction of the power factor of individual motors are of sealed construction, but must be provided with dust-tight terminal enclosures if installed in these locations.

It would no doubt be possible to construct a small, low-voltage dry-type transformer without ventilating openings, but transformers having a primary voltage rating of over 600 volts must either be askarel-filled or must be installed in vaults. It would seldom be necessary to install any transformer in a Class II, Division 2 location.

There are no special requirements for capacitors in Division 2 locations except that they must not contain oil or any other "liquid that will burn."

502-3. Surge Protection, Class II, Divisions 1 and 2.   In geographical locations where lightning disturbances are prevalent, wiring systems in Class II locations shall, when supplied from overhead lines, be suitably protected against high-voltage surges. This protection shall include suitable lightning protective devices, interconnection of all grounds, and surge-protective capacitors.

Interconnection of all grounds shall include grounds for primary and secondary lightning protective devices, secondary system grounds if any, and grounds of conduit and equipment of the interior wiring system. For ungrounded secondary systems, secondary lightning protective devices may be provided both at the service and at the point where the secondary system receives its supply, and the intervening secondary conductors may be accepted as the metallic connection between the secondary protective devices, provided grounds for the primary and secondary devices are metallically interconnected at the supply end of the secondary system and the secondary devices are grounded to the raceway system at the load end of the secondary system.

Surge protective capacitors shall be of a type especially designed for the duty, shall be connected to each ungrounded service conductor, and shall be grounded to the interior conduit system. Capacitors shall be protected by 30-ampere fuses of suitable type and voltage rating, or by automatic circuit breakers of suitable type and rating and shall be connected to the supply conductors on the supply side of the service disconnecting means.

▶   A common application of this requirement is found in grain-handling properties in localities where severe lightning storms are prevalent. Assuming a building supplied through a bank of transformers located a short distance from the building, the recommendations are, in general, as shown in the single-line diagram in Fig. 502-1.

The surge-protective equipment consists of primary lightning arresters at the transformers and surge-protective capacitors connected to the supply side of the service equipment. The lightning-arrester ground and the secondary system ground should be solidly connected together. All grounds should be bonded together and to the service conduit and to all boxes enclosing the service equipment, metering equipment, and capacitors.

Complete information on methods of providing surge protection may be obtained from the Mill Mutual Fire Prevention Bureau, 2 North Riverside Plaza, Chicago, Ill., 60606.

502-4. Wiring Methods.   Wiring methods shall conform to the following:

(a) Class II, Division 1.   In Class II, Division 1 locations, threaded rigid metal conduit or Type MI cable with termination fittings approved for the location

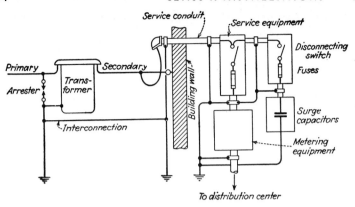

Fɪɢ. 502-1. Method of providing surge protection.

shall be the wiring method employed. Type MI cable shall be installed and supported in a manner to avoid tensile stress at the termination fittings.

(1) Fittings and Boxes. Fittings and boxes shall be provided with threaded bosses for connection to conduit or cable terminations, shall have close fitting covers, and shall have no openings (such as holes for attachment screws) through which dust might enter, or through which sparks or burning material might escape. Fittings and boxes in which taps, joints or terminal connections are made, or which are used in locations where dusts are of an electrically conducting nature shall be dust-ignition-proof and approved for Class II locations.

(2) Flexible Connections. Where necessary to employ flexible connections, dust-tight flexible connectors, flexible metal conduit with approved fittings, liquidtight flexible metal conduit with approved fittings, or flexible cord approved for extra-hard usage and provided with bushed fittings shall be used, except that where dusts are of an electrically conducting nature, flexible metal conduit shall not be used, and flexible cords shall be provided with dust-tight seals at both ends. An additional conductor for grounding shall be provided in the flexible cord unless other acceptable means of grounding is provided. Where flexible connections are subject to oil or other corrosive conditions, the insulation of the conductors shall be of a type approved for the condition or shall be protected by means of a suitable sheath.

(b) Class II, Division 2. In Class II, Division 2 locations, rigid metal conduit, electrical metallic tubing, or Type MI, MC, ALS or SNM cable with approved termination fittings or dust-tight wireways shall be the wiring method employed.

(1) Wireways, and Fittings and Boxes. Wireways, and fittings and boxes in which taps, joints or terminal connections are made, shall be designed to minimize the entrance of dust, and: (1) shall be provided with telescoping or close fitting covers, or other effective means to prevent the escape of sparks or burning material, and (2) shall have no openings (such as holes for attachment screws) through which, after installation, sparks or burning material might escape, or through which adjacent combustible material might be ignited.

(2) Flexible Connections.   Where flexible connections are necessary the provisions of Section 502-4(a-2) shall apply.

▶   Where a flexible connection is necessary, it would usually be preferable to use a flexible fitting as shown in Fig. 501-17c. Standard flexible conduit may be used except where conductive dust is present, but in such case Section 502-4 requires that a bonding jumper must be provided around the conduit. The use of a hard-service cord having one conductor serving as a grounding conductor is permitted.

In Division 1 locations, threaded connections must be used for connecting rigid conduit to boxes and fittings. If any conducting dust is present or if tape or joints are contained, boxes and fittings must be dust-tight, such as the type shown in Fig. 502-2.

In Division 2 locations, in order to provide adequate bonding, threaded fittings such as those shown in Figs. 502-2 and 502-3 should be used with rigid conduit. The requirement for close-fitting covers could best be taken care of by using the dust-tight fitting shown in Fig. 502-2. The standard types of pressed steel boxes cannot be used in any case where the box contains taps or splices, and even if no taps or splices are contained, a bonding jumper must be provided around any such box. In runs of conduit, seals can be provided by using any of the sealing fittings designed for use in Class I locations.

Fig. 502-2. Fitting for use in Class II locations where conducting dust is present. (*Appleton Electric Co.*)

Fig. 502-3. An explosion-proof and dust-tight switch. (*Appleton Electric Co.*)

502-5. Sealing, Class II, Divisions 1 and 2.   Where a raceway provides communication between an enclosure which is required to be dust-ignition-proof and one which is not, suitable means shall be provided to prevent the entrance of dust into the dust-ignition-proof enclosure through the raceway. This means may be: (1) a permanent and effective seal, (2) a horizontal section not less than 10 feet long in the raceway, or (3) a vertical section of raceway not less than 5 feet long and extending downward from the dust-ignition-proof enclosure. Sealing fittings shall be accessible.

▶   Dust-tight enclosures are required in many cases in Division 1 locations and under some conditions in Division 2 locations. Where a raceway connects two enclosures, only one of which is required to be dust-tight, three alternative methods are provided for preventing the travel of dust through the raceway into the dust-tight enclosure.

502-6. Switches, Circuit Breakers, Motor Controllers, and Fuses.   Switches, circuit breakers, motor controllers and fuses shall conform to the following:

   (a) Class II, Division 1.   In Class II, Division 1 locations, switches, circuit breakers, motor controllers and fuses shall conform to the following:

   (1) Type Required.   Switches, circuit breakers, motor controllers and fuses, including pushbuttons, relays and similar devices, which are intended to interrupt current in the normal performance of the function for which they are installed, or which are installed where dusts of an electrically conducting nature may be present, shall be provided with dust-ignition-proof enclosures which, together with the enclosed apparatus in each case, shall be approved as a complete assembly for Class II locations.

   This includes service and branch circuit fuses, switches and circuit breakers, motor controllers (including pushbuttons, pilot switches, relays, and motor overload protective devices), and switches, fuses and circuit breakers for the control and protection of lighting and appliance circuits.

   (2) Isolating Switches.   Disconnecting and isolating switches containing no fuses and not intended to interrupt current, and which are not installed where dusts may be of an electrically conducting nature, shall be provided with tight metal enclosures which shall be designed to minimize the entrance of dust, and which shall: (1) be equipped with telescoping or close fitting covers, or with other effective means to prevent the escape of sparks or burning material, and (2) have no openings (such as holes for attachment screws) through which, after installation, sparks or burning material might escape, or through which exterior accumulations of dust or adjacent combustible material might be ignited.

   (3) Metal Dusts.   In locations where dust from magnesium, aluminum, aluminum bronze powders, or other metals of similarly hazardous characteristics may be present, fuses, switches, motor controllers and circuit breakers shall have enclosures specifically approved for such locations.

   (b) Class II, Division 2.   In Class II, Division 2 locations, enclosures for fuses, switches, circuit breakers and motor controllers including pushbuttons, relays and similar devices, shall conform to the requirements of Section 502-6(a-2).

▶   Figure 502-4 shows a panelboard in a dust-tight cabinet which is approved for use in Class II locations.

Fig. 502-4. Panelboard in a dust-tight cabinet, suitable for use in Class II, Group E, F, and G locations. (*Crouse-Hinds Co.*)

Most of the switches and circuit breakers approved for Class I, Division 1, locations are also approved for use in Class II locations.

Switches conforming with the definition of the term *isolating switch* would seldom be used in any hazardous location. Such switches are permitted for use as the disconnecting means for motors larger than 100 hp.

502-7. Control Transformers and Resistors. Transformers, solenoids, impedance coils and resistors used as or in conjunction with control equipment for motors, generators and appliances shall conform to the following:

(a) Class II, Division 1. In Class II, Division 1 locations, control transformers, solenoids, impedance coils and resistors, and any overcurrent devices or switching mechanisms associated with them shall have dust-ignition-proof enclosures approved for Class II locations. No control transformer, impedance coil or resistor shall be installed in a location where dust from magnesium, aluminum, aluminum bronze powders, or other metals of similarly hazardous characteristics may be present unless provided with an enclosure specifically approved for such locations.

(b) Class II, Division 2. In Class II, Division 2 locations, transformers and resistors shall conform to the following:

(1) Switching Mechanisms. Switching mechanisms (including overcurrent devices) associated with control transformers, solenoids, impedance coils and resistors, shall be provided with enclosures conforming to Section 502-6(a-2).

(2) Coils and Windings. Where not located in the same enclosure with switching mechanisms, control transformers, solenoids and impedance coils shall be provided with tight metal housings without ventilating openings.

(3) Resistors. Resistors and resistance devices shall have dust-ignition-proof enclosures approved for Class II locations, except that where the maximum normal operating temperature of the resistor will not exceed 120°C (248°F) nonadjustable resistors and resistors which are part of an automatically timed starting sequence may have enclosures conforming to Section 502-7(b-2).

502-8. Motors and Generators. Motors and generators shall conform to the following:

(a) Class II, Division 1. In Class II, Division 1 locations, motors, generators and other rotating electrical machinery should be dust-ignition-proof or totally enclosed pipe ventilated and shall be approved for Class II locations.

(b) Class II, Division 2. In Class II, Division 2 locations, motors, generators and other rotating electrical machinery shall be dust-ignition-proof or totally enclosed pipe ventilated, for which maximum surface temperatures shall not exceed 120°C (248°F).

Exception: If the authority having jurisdiction believes accumulations of nonconducting, nonabrasive dust will be moderate, and if machines can be easily reached for routine cleaning and maintenance, the following may be installed:

Standard open-type machines without sliding contacts, centrifugal or other types of switching mechanism (including motor overcurrent devices) or integral resistance devices.

Standard open-type machines with such contacts, switching mechanisms or resistance devices enclosed within tight metal housings without ventilating or other openings.

Self-cleaning textile motors of the squirrel-cage type.

Fɪɢ. 502-5. Totally enclosed pipe-ventilated motor. (*Westinghouse Electric Corp.*)

▶ Figure 502-5 is a totally enclosed pipe-ventilated motor. A motor of this type is cooled by clean air forced through a pipe by a fan or blower. The cut shows the intake opening where air is delivered to the motor through the pipe from the blower. The exhaust opening is on the opposite side; this should be connected to a pipe terminating outside the building, so that dust will not collect inside the motor while it is not running.

Motors of the common totally enclosed type without special provision for cooling may be used in Class II locations, but to deliver the same horsepower, a plain totally enclosed motor must be considerably larger and heavier than a motor of the open type or an enclosed fan-cooled or pipe-ventilated motor.

502-9. Ventilating Piping. Vent pipes for motors, generators or other rotating electrical machinery, or for enclosures for electrical apparatus or equipment, shall be of metal not lighter than No. 24 MSG, or of equally substantial noncombustible material, and shall: (1) lead directly to a source of clean air outside of buildings, (2) be screened at the outer ends to prevent the entrance of small animals or birds, (3) be protected against physical damage and against rusting or other corrosive influences. In addition, vent pipes shall conform to the following:

(a) Class II, Division 1. In Class II, Division 1 locations, vent pipes, including their connections to motors or to the dust-ignition-proof enclosures for other equipment or apparatus, shall be dust-tight throughout their length. For metal pipes, seams and joints shall be: (1) riveted (or bolted) and soldered, (2) welded, or (3) rendered dust-tight by some other equally effective means.

(b) Class II, Division 2. In Class II, Division 2 locations, vent pipes and their connections shall be sufficiently tight to prevent the entrance of appreciable quantities of dust into the ventilated equipment or enclosure, and to prevent the escape of sparks, flame or burning material which might ignite dust accumulations or combustible material in the vicinity. For metal pipes, lock seams and riveted or welded joints may be used, and tight-fitting slip joints may be used where some flexibility is necessary as at connections to motors.

502-10. Utilization Equipment, Fixed and Portable.   Utilization equipment, fixed and portable, shall conform to the following:

(a) Class II, Division 1.   In Class II, Division 1 locations, utilization equipment, including electrically heated and motor-driven equipment, shall be dust-ignition-proof approved for Class II locations. Where dust from magnesium, aluminum, aluminum bronze powders, or other metals of similarly hazardous characteristics may be present, such equipment shall be specifically approved for such locations.

(b) Class II, Division 2.   In Class II, Division 2 locations, utilization equipment, fixed and portable, shall conform to the following:

(1) Heaters.   Electrically heated utilization equipment shall be dust-ignition-proof approved for Class II locations.

(2) Motors.   Motors of motor-driven utilization equipment shall conform to Section 502-8(b).

(3) Switches, Circuit Breakers and Fuses.   Enclosures for switches, circuit breakers, and fuses shall conform to Section 502-6(a-2).

(4) Transformers, Impedance Coils and Resistors.   Transformers, solenoids, impedance coils and resistors shall conform to Section 502-7(b).

502-11. Lighting Fixtures.   Lamps shall be installed in fixtures which shall conform to the following:

(a) Class II, Division 1.   In Class II, Division 1 locations, lighting fixtures for fixed and portable lighting shall conform to the following:

(1) Approved Fixtures.   Each fixture shall be dust-ignition-proof and approved for Class II locations, and shall be clearly marked to indicate the maximum wattage of the lamp for which it is approved. In locations where dust from magnesium, aluminum, aluminum bronze powders, or other metals of similarly hazardous characteristics may be present, fixtures for fixed or portable lighting, and all auxiliary equipment, shall be specifically approved for such locations.

(2) Physical Damage.   Each fixture shall be protected against physical damage by a suitable guard or by location.

(3) Pendant Fixtures.   Pendant fixtures shall be suspended by threaded rigid conduit stems or chains with approved fittings, or by other approved means. For rigid stems longer than 12 inches permanent and effective bracing against lateral displacement shall be provided at a level not more than 12 inches above the lower end of the stem, or flexibility in the form of a fitting or a flexible connector approved for the purpose and for the location shall be provided not more than 12 inches from the point of attachment to the supporting box or fitting. Threaded joints shall be provided with set-screws or other effective means to prevent loosening. Where wiring between an outlet box or fitting and a pendant fixture is not enclosed in conduit, flexible cord approved for hard usage shall be used, and suitable seals shall be provided where the cord enters the fixture and the outlet box or fitting. Flexible cord shall not serve as the supporting means for a fixture.

(4) Supports. Boxes, box assemblies or fittings used for the support of lighting fixtures shall be approved for the purpose and for Class II locations.

(b) Class II, Division 2. In Class II, Division 2 locations, lighting fixtures shall conform to the following:

(1) Portable Lamps. Portable lamps shall be dust-ignition-proof and approved for Class II locations. They shall be clearly marked to indicate the maximum wattage of lamps for which they are approved.

(2) Fixed Lighting. Lighting fixtures for fixed lighting, when not of a type approved for Class II locations, shall provide enclosures for lamps and lamp-holders which shall be designed to minimize the deposit of dust on lamps and to prevent the escape of sparks, burning material or hot metal. Each fixture shall be clearly marked to indicate the maximum wattage of lamp which may be used without exceeding a maximum exposed surface temperature of 165°C (329°F) under normal conditions of use.

(3) Physical Damage. Lighting fixtures for fixed lighting shall be protected from physical damage by suitable guards or by location.

(4) Pendant Fixtures. Pendant fixtures shall be suspended by threaded rigid conduit stems or chains with approved fittings, or by other approved means. For rigid stems longer than 12 inches permanent and effective bracing against lateral displacement shall be provided at a level not more than 12 inches above the lower end of the stem, or flexibility in the form of a fitting or a flexible connector approved for the purpose shall be provided not more than 12 inches from the point of attachment to the supporting box or fitting. When wiring between an outlet box or fitting and a pendant fixture is not enclosed in conduit, flexible cord approved for hard usage shall be used. Flexible cord shall not serve as the supporting means for a fixture.

(5) Supports. Boxes, box assemblies and fittings used for the support of lighting fixtures shall be approved for that purpose.

(6) Electric-Discharge Lamps. Starting and control equipment for electric-discharge lamps shall conform to the requirement of Section 502-7(b).

▶ Where metal dusts are present, lighting fixtures must be approved for use in Group E atmospheres. The fixture shown in Fig. 502-6 is listed by

Fɪɢ. 502-6. Lighting fixture for use in Class II, Division 1 locations. (*Crouse-Hinds Co.*)

Underwriters' Laboratories, Inc., as suitable for use in all three of the locations classed as Groups E, F, and G.

The purpose of the latter part of subparagraph (a)(3) is to specify the type of cord to be used for wiring a chain-suspended fixture. It is not the intention to permit a fixture to be suspended by means of a cord pendant or drop cord.

The only special requirements for lighting fixtures in Class II, Division 2 locations are that the lamp must be enclosed in a suitable glass globe and that a guard must be provided unless the fixture is so located that it will not be exposed to physical damage. The enclosing globe should be tight enough so that it will practically exclude dust, though dust-tight construction is not called for.

The portable handlamp shown in Fig. 501-18 is approved for use in any Class II, Group G location, *i.e.*, where the hazards are due to grain dust.

502-12. Flexible Cords, Class II, Divisions 1 and 2. Flexible cords used in Class II locations shall: (1) be of a type approved for extra hard usage, (2) contain, in addition to the conductors of the circuit, a grounding conductor conforming to Section 400-14, (3) be connected to terminals or to supply conductors in an approved manner, (4) be supported by clamps or by other suitable means in such a manner that there will be no tension on the terminal connections, and (5) be provided with suitable seals to prevent the entrance of dust where the flexible cord enters boxes or fittings which are required to be dust-ignition-proof.

502-13. Receptacles and Attachment Plugs.

(a) Class II, Division 1. In Class II, Division 1 locations, receptacles and attachment plugs shall be of the type providing for connection to the grounding conductor of the flexible cord, and shall be dust-ignition-proof approved for Class II locations.

(b) Class II, Division 2. In Class II, Division 2 locations, receptacles and attachment plugs shall be of the type providing for connection to the grounding conductor of the flexible cord and shall be so designed that connection to the supply circuit cannot be made or broken while live parts are exposed.

502-14. Signal, Alarm, Remote-Control, and Local Loud-Speaker Intercommunication Systems. Signal, alarm, remote-control and local loud-speaker intercommunication systems shall conform to the following:

Refer to Article 800 for rules governing the installation of communication circuits as defined in Article 100.

(a) Class II, Division 1. In Class II, Division 1 locations, signal, alarm, remote-control and local loud-speaker intercommunication systems shall conform to the following:

(1) Wiring Method. Where accidental damage or breakdown of insulation might cause arcs, sparks or high temperatures, rigid metal conduit, electrical metallic tubing, or Type MI cable with approved termination fittings shall be the wiring method employed. For conduit or electrical metallic tubing, the number of conductors shall be limited only by the requirement that the cross-sectional area of all conductors shall not exceed 40 per cent of the area of the raceway. Where limited flexibility is desirable or where exposure to physical damage is not severe, flexible cord approved for extra-hard usage may be used.

(2) Contacts. Switches, circuit breakers, relays, contactors and fuses which may interrupt other than voice currents, and current-breaking contacts for bells, horns, howlers, sirens and other devices in which sparks or arcs may be produced, shall be provided with enclosures approved for the location, unless current-breaking contacts are immersed in oil, or unless the interruption of current occurs within a chamber sealed against the entrance of dust, in which case enclosures may be of general purpose type.

(3) Resistors and Similar Equipment. Resistors, transformers and choke coils which may carry other than voice currents, and rectifiers, thermionic tubes, and other heat generating equipment or apparatus shall be provided with dust-ignition-proof enclosures approved for Class II locations.

(4) Rotating Machinery. Motors, generators and other rotating electrical machinery shall conform to Section 502-8(a).

(5) Electrical Conducting Dusts. Where dusts are of an electrically conducting nature, all wiring and equipment shall be approved for Class II locations.

(6) Metal Dusts. Where dust from magnesium, aluminum, aluminum bronze powders, or other metals of similarly hazardous characteristics may be present, all apparatus and equipment shall be specifically approved for such conditions.

(b) Class II, Division 2. In Class II, Division 2 locations, signal, alarm, remote-control and local loudspeaker intercommunication systems shall conform to the following:

(1) Contacts. Enclosures shall conform to Section 502-14(a-2) or contacts shall have tight metal enclosures designed to minimize the entrance of dust, and shall have telescoping or tight fitting covers and no openings through which, after installation, sparks or burning material might escape.

(2) Transformers and Similar Equipment. The windings and terminal connections of transformers and choke coils shall be provided with tight metal enclosures without ventilating openings.

(3) Resistors and Similar Equipment. Resistors, resistance devices, thermionic tubes, and rectifiers shall conform to Section 502-14(a-3), except that enclosures for thermionic tubes, nonadjustable resistors or rectifiers for which maximum operating temperature will not exceed 120°C (248°F) may be of general purpose type.

(4) Rotating Machinery. Motors, generators and other rotating electrical machinery shall conform to Section 502-8(b).

502-15. Live Parts, Class II, Divisions 1 and 2. There shall be no exposed live parts.

502-16. Grounding, Class II, Divisions 1 and 2. Wiring and equipment shall be grounded in conformity with the following:

(a) Exposed Parts. The exposed noncurrent-carrying metal parts of equipment such as the frames or metal exteriors of motors, fixed or portable lamps or other utilization equipment, lighting fixtures, cabinets, cases, and conduit, shall be grounded as specified in Article 250.

(b) Bonding. The locknut-bushing and double-locknut types of contact shall not be depended upon for bonding purposes, but bonding jumpers with proper fittings, or other approved means shall be used. Such means of bonding shall apply to all intervening raceways, fittings, boxes, enclosures, etc., between hazardous areas and the point of grounding for service equipment. Where flexible conduit is used as permitted in Section 502-4, bonding jumpers with proper fittings shall be provided around such conduit.

▶   Paragraph *b* prohibits the use of locknuts and bushings and double locknuts and bushings for any of the raceways, boxes, fittings, enclosures, etc.,
between the hazardous area and the grounding electrode conductor connection at the service equipment. Bonding jumpers, with approved bonding
fittings, are required for such intervening raceway and enclosures all the
way to the grounding electrode conductor. See Section **250-79**.

(c) **Lightning Protection.**   Each ungrounded service conductor of a wiring system in a Class II location, when supplied from an ungrounded overhead electrical
supply system in an area where lightning disturbances are prevalent, shall be
protected by a lightning protective device of proper type. Lightning protective
devices shall be connected to the service conductors on the supply side of the
service disconnecting means, and shall be bonded to the raceway system at the
service entrance.

(d) **Grounded Service Conductor Bonded to Raceway.**   Wiring in a Class II location, when supplied from a grounded alternating-current supply system in
which a grounded conductor is a part of the service, shall have the grounded
service conductor bonded to the raceway system and to the grounding conductor
for the raceway system. The bonding connection to the grounded service conductor shall be made on the supply side of the service disconnecting means.

(e) **Transformer Ground Bonded to Raceway.**   Wiring in a Class II location,
where supplied from a grounded alternating-current supply system in which no
grounded conductor is a part of the service, shall be provided with a metallic
connection between the supply system ground and the raceway system at the
service entrance. The metallic connection shall have an ampacity not less than
⅛ that of the service conductors, and shall in no case be smaller than No. 10 when
of soft copper, or No. 12 when of medium or hard-drawn copper.

(f) **Multiple Grounds.**   Where, in the application of Section 250-21, it is necessary to abandon one or more grounding connections to avoid objectionable
passage of current over the grounding conductors, the connection required in
Section 502-16(d or e) shall not be abandoned while any other grounding connection remains connected to the supply system.

ARTICLE 503. CLASS III INSTALLATIONS—HAZARDOUS LOCATIONS

503-1. General.   The general rules of this Code shall apply to the installation
of electrical wiring and apparatus in locations classified as Class III under Section 500-6 except as modified by this Article.

Equipment installed in Class III locations shall be able to function at full rating
without developing surface temperatures high enough to cause excessive dehydration or gradual carbonization of accumulated fibers or flyings. Organic material
which is carbonized or is excessively dry is highly susceptible to spontaneous
ignition. In general, maximum surface temperatures under operating conditions
shall not exceed 165°C (329°F) for equipment which is not subject to overloading,
and 120°C (248°F) for equipment such as motors, power transformers, etc., which
may be overloaded.

▶   The small fibers of cotton that are carried everywhere by air currents in some parts of cotton mills and the wood shavings that collect around planers in woodworking plants are common examples of the combustible flyings or fibers that cause the hazards in Class III, Division 1 locations. A cotton warehouse is a common example of a Class III, Division 2 location.

503-2. Transformers and Capacitors, Class III, Divisions 1 and 2.   Transformers and capacitors shall conform to Section 502-2(b).

503-3. Wiring Methods.   Wiring methods shall conform to the following:

(a) Class III, Division 1.   In Class III, Division 1 locations, rigid metal conduit, or approved Type MI, MC or ALS cables shall be the wiring method employed.

(1) Boxes and Fittings.   Fittings and boxes in which taps, joints or terminal connections are made shall (1) be provided with telescoping or close fitting covers, or other effective means to prevent the escape of sparks or burning material, and (2) shall have no openings (such as holes for attachment screws) through which, after installation, sparks or burning material might escape, or through which adjacent combustible material might be ignited.

(2) Flexible Connections.   Where flexible connections are necessary the provisions of Section 502-4(a-2) shall apply.

(b) Class III, Division 2.   In Class III, Division 2 locations, the wiring method shall conform to Section 503-3(a), except that in sections, compartments or areas used solely for storage and containing no machinery, open wiring on insulators may be employed when installed to conform to Article 320, but only on condition that protection as required by Section 320-12 be provided where conductors are not run in roof spaces, and well out of reach of sources of physical damage.

503-4. Switches, Circuit Breakers, Motor Controllers and Fuses, Class III, Divisions 1 and 2.   Switches, circuit breakers, motor controllers and fuses, including push buttons, relays and similar devices, shall be provided with tight metal enclosures designed to minimize entrance of fibers and flyings, and which shall: (1) be equipped with telescoping or close fitting covers, or with other effective means to prevent escape of sparks or burning material, and (2) have no openings (such as holes for attachment screws) through which, after installation, sparks or burning material might escape, or through which exterior accumulations of fibers or flyings or adjacent combustible material might be ignited.

503-5. Control Transformers and Resistors, Class III, Divisions 1 and 2.   Transformers, impedance coils and resistors used as or in conjunction with control equipment for motors, generators and appliances, shall conform to Section 502-7(b), with the exception that, in Class III, Division 1 locations, when these devices are in the same enclosure with switching devices of such control equipment, and are used only for starting or short time duty, the enclosure shall conform to the requirements of Section 503-4.

503-6. Motors and Generators.   Motors and Generators shall conform to the following:

(a) Class III, Division 1.   In Class III, Division 1 locations, motors, generators, and other rotating electrical machinery shall be totally enclosed not ventilated, totally enclosed pipe ventilated, or totally enclosed fan-cooled, except that in locations where, in the judgment of the authority having jurisdiction, only moderate accumulations of lint and flyings will be likely to collect on, in, or in the vicinity of a rotating electrical machine, and where such machine is readily accessible for routine cleaning and maintenance, self-cleaning textile motors of the squirrel-cage type, standard open type machines without sliding contacts, centrifugal or other types of switching mechanism (including motor overload devices), or standard open type machines having such contacts, switching mechanisms or resistance devices enclosed within tight metal housings without ventilating or other openings, may be installed.

(b) Class III, Division 2. In Class III, Division 2 locations, motors, generators, and other rotating electrical machinery shall be totally enclosed not ventilated, totally enclosed pipe ventilated, or totally enclosed fan-cooled.

(c) Partially Enclosed Type, Class III, Divisions 1 and 2. Motors, generators or other rotating electrical machinery of the partially enclosed or splash-proof type shall not be installed in Class III locations.

503-7. Ventilating Piping, Class III, Divisions 1 and 2. Vent pipes for motors, generators or other rotating electrical machinery, or for enclosures for electrical apparatus or equipment, shall be of metal not lighter than No. 24 MSG, or of equally substantial noncombustible material, and shall: (1) lead directly to a source of clean air outside of buildings, (2) be screened at the outer ends to prevent the entrance of small animals or birds, (3) be protected against physical damage and against rusting or other corrosive influences, and (4) vent pipes and their connections shall be sufficiently tight to prevent the entrance of appreciable quantities of fibers or flyings into the ventilated equipment or enclosure, and to prevent the escape of sparks, flame or burning material which might ignite accumulations of fibers or flyings or combustible material in the vicinity. For metal pipes, lock seams and riveted or welded joints may be used, and tight fitting slip joints may be used where some flexibility is necessary as at connections to motors.

503-8. Utilization Equipment, Fixed and Portable, Class III, Divisions 1 and 2. Utilization equipment shall conform to the following:

(a) Heaters. Electrically heated utilization equipment shall be approved for Class III locations.

(b) Motors. Motors of motor-driven utilization equipment shall conform to Section 503-6(b). Utilization equipment which may be readily moved from one location to another should conform to requirements for the most hazardous location.

(c) Switches, Circuit Breakers, Motor Controllers and Fuses. Switches, circuit breakers, motor controllers and fuses shall conform to Section 503-4.

503-9. Lighting Fixtures, Class III, Divisions 1 and 2. Lamps shall be installed in fixtures which shall conform to the following:

(a) Fixed Lighting. Lighting fixtures for fixed lighting shall provide enclosures for lamps and lampholders which shall be designed to minimize entrance of fibers and flyings, and to prevent the escape of sparks, burning material or hot metal. Each fixture shall be clearly marked to show wattage of lamp which may be used without exceeding a maximum exposed surface temperature of 165°C (329°F) under operating conditions of use.

(b) Physical Damage. A fixture which may be exposed to physical damage shall be protected by a suitable guard.

(c) Pendant Fixtures. Pendant fixtures shall be suspended by stems of threaded rigid conduit or threaded metal tubing of equivalent thickness. For stems longer than 12 inches, permanent and effective bracing against lateral displacement shall be provided at a level not more than 12 inches above the lower end of the stem, or flexibility in the form of a fitting or a flexible connector approved for the purpose shall be provided not more than 12 inches from the point of attachment to the supporting box or fitting.

(d) Supports. Boxes, box assemblies or fittings used for the support of lighting fixtures shall be of a type approved for the purpose.

(e) Portable Lamps. Portable lamps shall be equipped with handles and protected with substantial guards, and lampholders shall be of unswitched type with no exposed metal parts and without provision for receiving attachment plugs. In all other respects, portable lamps shall conform to Section 503-9(a).

503-10. Flexible Cords, Class III, Divisions 1 and 2. Flexible cords shall conform to Section 502-12.

503-11. Receptacles and Attachment Plugs, Class III, Divisions 1 and 2. Receptacles and attachment plugs shall conform to Section 502-13(b).

503-12. Signal, Alarm, Remote-Control and Local Loud-Speaker Intercommunication Systems, Class III, Divisions 1 and 2. Signal, alarm, remote-control and local loud-speaker intercommunication systems shall conform to Section 502-14(a).

503-13. Electric Cranes and Hoists, and Similar Equipment, Class III, Divisions 1 and 2. Where installed for operation over combustible fibers or accumulations of flyings, traveling cranes and hoists for material handling, traveling cleaners for textile machinery, and similar equipment shall conform to the following:

(a) Power supply to contact conductors shall be isolated from all other systems and shall be ungrounded, and shall be equipped with an acceptable recording ground detector which will give an alarm and will automatically de-energize the contact conductors in case of a fault to ground, or with an acceptable ground fault indicator which will give a visual and audible alarm, and maintain the alarm as long as power is supplied to the system and the ground fault remains.

(b) Contact conductors shall be so located or guarded as to be inaccessible to other than authorized persons, and shall be protected against accidental contact with foreign objects.

(c) Current collectors shall be arranged or guarded to confine normal sparking and to prevent escape of sparks or hot particles. To reduce sparking, two or more separate surfaces of contact shall be provided for each contact conductor. Reliable means shall be provided to keep contact conductors and current collectors free of accumulations of lint or flyings.

(d) Control equipment shall conform to Sections 503-4 and 503-5.

It is recommended that where the distance of travel permits, current to the crane be supplied through flexible cord approved for extra hard usage and equipped with approved type of reel or takeup device.

►   A crane operating in a Class III location and having rolling or sliding collectors making contact with bare conductors introduces two hazards:

1. Any arcing between a collector and a conductor rail or wire may ignite flyings of combustible fibers that have collected on or near to the bare conductor. This danger may be guarded against by proper alignment of the bare conductor and by using a collector of such form that contact is always

maintained, and by the use of guards or barriers which will confine the hot particles of metal that may be thrown off when an arc is formed.

2. Dust and flyings collecting on the insulating supports of the bare conductors may form a conducting path between the conductors or from one conductor to ground and permit enough current to flow to ignite the fibers. This condition is much more likely to exist if moisture is present. Operation on a system having no grounded conductor makes it somewhat less likely that a fire will be started by a current flowing to ground. A recording ground detector will show when the insulation resistance is being lowered by an accumulation of dust and flyings on the insulators, and a relay actuated by excessively low insulation resistance and arranged to trip a circuit breaker provides automatic disconnection of the bare conductors when the conditions become dangerous.

Both classes of hazards may be avoided, where the crane travels only a short distance, by providing current supply to the crane motor through a suitable flexible cable. This method is recommended in preference to the use of sliding contacts; however, the cable introduces a hazard of its own in that the stranded conductors may break and cause arcing if not properly taken care of.

503-14. Electric Trucks.   Electric trucks shall conform to NFPA Standard for the Use, Maintenance and Operation of Industrial Trucks (No. 505-1971).

503-15. Storage-Battery Charging Equipment, Class III, Divisions 1 and 2.   Storage-battery charging equipment shall be located in separate rooms built or lined with substantial noncombustible materials so constructed as to adequately exclude flyings or lint, and shall be well ventilated.

503-16. Live Parts, Class III, Divisions 1 and 2.   There shall be no exposed live parts except as provided in Section 503-13.

503-17. Grounding, Class III, Divisions 1 and 2.   Wiring and equipment shall be grounded in conformity with Section 502-16.

ARTICLE 510. HAZARDOUS LOCATIONS—SPECIFIC

510-1. Scope.   The provisions of Articles 511 through 517 shall apply to occupancies or parts of occupancies which are or may be hazardous because of atmospheric concentrations of hazardous gases or vapors, or because of deposits or accumulations of materials which may be readily ignitible. It is the intent to assist the authority having jurisdiction in the classification of areas with respect to hazardous conditions which may or may not require construction and equipment conforming to Articles 501 through 503, and to set forth such additional special requirements as are applicable to the specific occupancy.

510-2. General.   The general rules of this Code shall apply to the installation of electrical wiring and equipment in occupancies within the scope of Articles 511 through 517, except as such rules are modified in those Articles. Where unusual conditions exist in a specific occupancy, the authority having jurisdiction shall judge with respect to the application of specific rules.

It is recommended that the authority having jurisdiction be familiar with National Fire Protection Association standards applying to occupancies included within the scope of Articles 511 through 517 inclusive.

▶   Copies and price lists of the National Fire Protection Association Standards may be obtained from the NFPA offices at 60 Batterymarch St., Boston, Mass. 02110.

ARTICLE 511. COMMERCIAL GARAGES, REPAIR AND STORAGE

511-1. Scope. These occupancies shall include locations used for service and repair operations in connection with self-propelled vehicles (including passenger automobiles, buses, trucks, tractors, etc.) in which volatile flammable liquids or flammable gases are used for fuel or power, and locations in which more than three such vehicles are or may be stored at one time.

For further information regarding classification of garages, refer to the NFPA Standard for Garages (No. 88-1968).

▶   The National Electrical Code does not include in its scope nonelectrical hazards and attention is called to other NFPA Standards such as the Standard for Garages, No. 88. The following information is taken in part from NFPA Standard No. 88

Prologue

Private residential garages of three car capacity or less when not used for commercial repair or servicing operations are excluded from the application of this Standard although many of the principles therein continue to apply. This exclusion is based upon the belief that the parking or storage of modern passenger cars does not involve any hazards substantially greater than various other fire hazards normally present in residential occupancies, such as heating and cooking equipment and the hazard of possible ignition of combustible furnishings through careless smoking.

2111. No heater employing an open flame or glowing element shall be installed in garage storage parking or repair areas or sections communicating therewith, except as hereinafter specifically provided.

2122. Garage heating plants, fired with gas, liquid or solid fuels which are not located in a detached building except suspended unit heaters covered elsewhere in this Standard, should be located in a room separated from other parts of the garage by construction having at least a one hour fire-resistance rating. This separated room shall not be used for any other hazardous purpose or for combustible storage and should have no direct access from the garage storage or repair areas.

2251. Enclosed parking or storage garages accommodating 20 or more motor vehicles shall have mechanical ventilation capable of discharging ¾ cubic foot of air per minute for each square foot of floor area.

2263. Location of Air Inlets. Mechanical systems introducing outside air and combination systems delivering heated recirculated and outside air shall deliver air horizontally in sufficient volume and with sufficient velocity to secure distribution to all parts of the building. All air inlet openings shall be above the tops of the cars in repair and storage areas.

511-2. Hazardous Areas. Classification under Article 500.

(a) For each floor at or above grade, the entire area up to a level 18 inches above the floor shall be considered to be a Class I, Division 2 location.

(b) For each floor below grade, the entire area up to a level 18 inches above the bottom of outside doors or other openings which are at or above grade level shall be considered to be Class I, Division 2 location. Where adequate positive-pressure ventilation is provided, the authority having jurisdiction may judge that the hazardous location extends up to a level of only 18 inches above each such floor.

(c) Any pit or depression below floor level shall be considered to be a Class I, Division 2 location which shall extend up to said floor level, except that any unventilated pit or depression may be judged by the authority having jurisdiction to be a Class I, Division 1 location.

(d) Adjacent areas in which hazardous vapors are not likely to be released such as stock rooms, switchboard rooms and other similar locations, having floors elevated at least 18 inches above adjacent garage floor, or separated therefrom by tight curbs or partitions at least 18 inches high, shall not be classed as hazardous.

(e) Adjacent areas, which by reason of ventilation, air pressure differentials or physical spacing are such that in the opinion of the authority enforcing this Code no hazard exists, shall be classified as nonhazardous.

▶ *Paragraph a*
Above grade: The hazardous area extends up to **18** inches above each floor.

Paragraph b
Below grade: Where positive-pressure ventilation is provided, the hazardous area extends up to **18** inches above each floor. Where it is not provided, the hazardous area extends from floor to ceiling.

In order to assure positive-pressure ventilation at all times, the authority making this decision may do this on the basis of having suitable interlocking provided between the electrical and ventilating systems. NFPA Standard for Garages, Pamphlet No. **88**, requires ventilation in both repair and storage garages capable of discharging ¾ cubic foot per minute for each square foot of floor area. In addition, discharge openings to the outside shall have air-inlet openings which are perpendicular to the floor with the bottom of the opening extending to the floor. Air velocity through these openings shall be not less than **100** lineal feet per minute. The air-intake openings shall be not more than **50** feet apart.

511-3. Wiring and Equipment in Hazardous Areas. Within hazardous areas as defined in Section 511-2, wiring and equipment shall conform to applicable provisions of Article 501.

511-4. Sealing. Approved seals conforming to the requirements of Section 501-5 shall be provided, and Section 501-5(b-2) shall apply to horizontal as well as to vertical boundaries of the defined hazardous areas. Raceways embedded in a masonry floor or buried beneath a floor shall be considered to be within the hazardous area above the floor if any connections or extensions lead into or through such area.

511-5. Wiring in Spaces Above Hazardous Areas.

(a) All fixed wiring shall be in metallic raceways or shall be Type MI or Type ALS cable. Cellular metal floor raceways may be used only for supplying ceiling outlets or extensions to the area below the floor, but such raceways shall have no connections leading into or through any hazardous area above the floor. No electrical conductor shall be installed in any cell, header or duct which contains a pipe for steam, water, air, gas, drainage, or other service except electrical.

(b) For pendants, flexible cord suitable for the type of service and approved for hard usage shall be used.

(c) For connection of portable lamps, motors or other utilization equipment, flexible cord suitable for the type of service and approved for extra hard usage shall be used.

(d) When a circuit which supplies portables or pendants includes an identified grounded conductor as provided in Article 200, receptacles, attachment plugs, connectors, and similar devices shall be of polarized type, and the identified conductor of the flexible cord shall be connected to the screw shell of any lampholder or to the identified terminal of any utilization equipment supplied.

(e) When a pendant is used to supply a portable lamp or utilization equipment, the female portion of a polarized pin-plug connector or equivalent shall be attached to the lower end of the pendant, and the male portion shall be attached to the cord for the portable. The connector shall be designed to break apart readily in any position, and shall be suspended at a level not less than that specified in Section 511-2. Attachment plug receptacles in fixed position shall be located above the level specified in Section 511-2.

511-6. Equipment Above Hazardous Areas.

(a) Equipment which is less than 12 feet above the floor level, and which may produce arcs, sparks or particles of hot metal, such as cutouts, switches, charging panels, generators, motors or other equipment (excluding receptacles, lamps and lampholders) having make-and-break or sliding contacts, shall be of the totally enclosed type or so constructed as to prevent escape of sparks or hot metal particles.

(b) Lamps and lampholders for fixed lighting which are located over lanes through which vehicles are commonly driven or which may otherwise be exposed to physical damage, shall be located not less than 12 feet above floor level unless of totally enclosed type or so constructed as to prevent escape of sparks or hot metal particles.

(c) Portable lamps shall be equipped with handle, lampholder, hook and substantial guard attached to the lampholder or handle. All exterior surfaces which might come in contact with battery terminals, wiring terminals, or other objects shall be of nonconducting material or shall be effectively protected with insulation. Lampholders shall be of unswitched type, and shall not provide means for plug-in of attachment plugs. Outer shell shall be of moulded composition or other material approved for the purpose, and metal-shell, lined lampholders, either of switched or unswitched type, shall not be used. Unless the lamp and its cord are supported or arranged in such a manner that they cannot be used in the hazardous areas classified in Section 511-2, they shall be of a type approved for such hazardous locations.

511-7. Battery-Charging Equipment. Battery chargers and their control equipment, and batteries being charged shall not be located within hazardous areas classified in Section 511-2. Tables, racks, trays, and wiring shall, in addition, conform to the provisions of Article 480.

511-8. Electric Vehicle Charging.

(a) Flexible cords used for charging shall be suitable for the type of service and approved for extra hard usage. Their ampacity shall be adequate for the charging current.

(b) Connectors shall have a rating not less than the ampacity of the cord, and in no case less than 50 amperes.

(c) Connectors shall be so designed and installed that they will break apart readily at any position of the charging cable, and live parts shall be guarded from accidental contact. No connector shall be located within a hazardous area defined in Section 511-2.

(d) Where plugs are provided for direct connection to vehicles, the point of connection shall not be within a hazardous area as defined in Section 511-2, and where the cord is suspended from overhead, it shall be so arranged that the lowest point of sag is at least 6 inches above the floor. Where the vehicle is equipped with an approved plug which will readily pull apart, and where an automatic arrangement is provided to pull both cord and plug beyond the range of physical damage, no additional connector is required in the cable or at the outlet.

▶   Equipment located in a suitable room or enclosure provided for the purpose or in a showroom separated from the garage proper by a partition which is reasonably tight up to 18 in. need not conform to the requirements of this section. Also, see Section 511-2*e*.

In all garages within the scope of this chapter, because of the possible presence of gasoline vapor near the floor, any equipment which in its normal operation may cause arcs or sparks, if less than 18 in. above the floor, is considered as in a hazardous location.

It is seldom necessary to make use of devices having exposed live parts, but where this is unavoidable, even though the device is 18 in. above the floor, any such device should be well guarded.

The requirements for battery-charging cables and connectors are similar to the requirements for outlets for the connection of portable appliances, except that when hanging free they may hang within 6 in. from the floor. The common form is a plug which is inserted into a receptacle on the vehicle and, since the prongs are alive, they must be covered by a protecting hood.

With reference to the last sentence of the rule, so far as is known there is no such equipment on the market at the present time. The provision was included in anticipation of the development of equipment that will operate as described.

ARTICLE 512. RESIDENTIAL STORAGE GARAGES

512-1. Definition. A residential storage garage is a building or room in which not more than three vehicles of the types described in Section 511-1 are or may be stored, but which will not normally be used for other than minor service or repair operations on such stored vehicles.

512-2. At or Above Grade. Where the lowest floor is at or above adjacent ground or driveway level, and where there is at least one outside door at or below floor level, the garage area shall not be classed as a hazardous location.

512-3. Below Grade. Where the lowest floor is below adjacent ground or driveway level, the following shall apply:

(a) The entire area of the garage or of any enclosed space which includes the garage shall be classified as a Class I, Division 2 location up to a level 18 inches above the garage floor. All electrical equipment and wiring within such hazardous location shall conform to applicable provisions of Article 501.

(b) Wiring and equipment above the defined hazardous location shall conform to the requirements of this Code for nonhazardous locations.

(c) Adjacent areas in which hazardous vapors or gases are not likely to be released, and having floors elevated at least 18 inches above the garage floor, or separated therefrom by tight curbs or partitions at least 18 inches high, shall not be classed as hazardous.

ARTICLE 513. AIRCRAFT HANGARS

513-1. Definition. This occupancy shall include locations used for storage or servicing of aircraft in which gasoline, jet fuels, or other volatile flammable liquids, or flammable gases, are used, but shall not include such locations when used exclusively for aircraft which have never contained such liquids or gases, or which have been drained and properly purged.

513-2. Hazardous Areas. Classification under Article 500.

(a) Any pit or depression below the level of the hangar floor shall be considered to be a Class I, Division 1 location which shall extend up to said floor level.

(b) The entire area of the hangar including any adjacent and communicating areas not suitably cut off from the hangar shall be considered to be a Class I, Division 2 location up to a level 18 inches above the floor.

(c) The area within 5 feet horizontally from aircraft power plants, aircraft fuel tanks or aircraft structures containing fuel shall be considered to be a Class I, Division 2 hazardous location which shall extend upward from the floor to a level 5 feet above the upper surface of wings and of engine enclosures.

(d)   Adjacent areas in which hazardous vapors are not likely to be released such as stock rooms, electrical control rooms, and other similar locations, should not be classed as hazardous when adequately ventilated and when effectively cut off from the hangar itself by walls or partitions.

513-3. Wiring and Equipment in Hazardous Areas.   All fixed and portable wiring and equipment which is or may be installed or operated within any of the hazardous locations defined in Section 513-2 shall conform to applicable provisions of Article 501. All wiring installed in or under the hangar floor shall conform to the requirements for Class I, Division 1. When such wiring is located in vaults, pits, or ducts, adequate drainage shall be provided, and the wiring shall not be placed within the same compartment with any other service except piped compressed air.

Attachment plugs and receptacles in hazardous locations shall be explosion-proof or shall be so designed that they cannot be energized while the connections are being made or broken.

513-4. Wiring Not Within Hazardous Areas.

(a)   All fixed wiring in a hangar, but not within a hazardous area as defined in Section 513-2, shall be installed in metallic raceways or shall be Type MI or Type ALS cable, except that wiring in nonhazardous locations as defined in Section 513-2(d) may be of any type recognized in Chapter 3 of this Code.

(b)   For pendants, flexible cord suitable for the type of service and approved for hard usage shall be used. Each such cord shall include a separate grounding conductor.

(c)   For portable utilization equipment and lamps, flexible cord suitable for the type of service and approved for extra hard usage shall be used. Each such cord shall include a separate grounding conductor.

(d)   Where a circuit which supplies portables or pendants includes an identified grounded conductor as provided in Article 200, receptacles, attachment plugs, connectors, and similar devices shall be of polarized type, and the identified conductor of the flexible cord shall be connected to the screw shell of any lampholder or to the identified terminal of any utilization equipment supplied. Acceptable means shall be provided for maintaining continuity of the grounding conductor between the fixed raceway system and the noncurrent-carrying metallic portions of pendant fixtures, portable lamps, and portable utilization equipment.

513-5. Equipment Not Within Hazardous Areas.

(a)   In locations other than those described in Section 513-2, equipment which is less than 10 feet above wings and engine enclosures of aircraft and which may produce arcs, sparks or particles of hot metal, such as lamps and lampholders for fixed lighting, cutouts, switches, receptacles, charging panels, generators, motors, or other equipment having make-and-break or sliding contacts, shall be of totally enclosed type or so constructed as to prevent escape of sparks or hot metal particles, except that equipment in areas described in Section 513-2(d) may be of general purpose type.

(b)   Lampholders of metal shell, fiber-lined types shall not be used for fixed incandescent lighting.

(c)   Portable lamps which are or may be used within a hangar shall be approved for Class I locations.

(d) Portable utilization equipment which is or may be used within a hangar shall be of a type suitable for use in Class I, Division 2 locations.

513-6. Stanchions, Rostrums and Docks.

(a) Electric wiring, outlets and equipment (including lamps) on or attached to stanchions, rostrums or docks which are located or likely to be located in a hazardous area as defined in Section 513-2(c) shall conform to the requirements for Class I, Division 2 locations.

(b) Where stanchions, rostrums, or docks are not located or likely to be located in a hazardous area as defined in Section 513-2(c), wiring and equipment shall conform to Sections 513-4 and 513-5, except that such wiring and equipment not more than 18 inches above the floor in any position shall conform to Section 513-6(a). Receptacles and attachment plugs shall be of locking type which will not break apart readily.

(c) Mobile stanchions with electrical equipment conforming to Section 513-6(b) shall carry at least one permanently affixed warning sign to read: "WARNING— KEEP 5 FEET CLEAR OF AIRCRAFT ENGINES AND FUEL TANK AREAS."

513-7. Sealing.
Approved seals shall be provided in conformance with Section 501-5 and Section 501-5(a-3) and 501-5(b-2) and shall apply to horizontal as well as to vertical boundaries of the defined hazardous areas. Raceways embedded in a masonry floor or buried beneath a floor shall be considered to be within the hazardous area above the floor when any connections or extensions lead into or through such area.

513-8. Aircraft Electrical Systems.
Aircraft electrical systems should be de-energized when the aircraft is stored in a hangar, and, whenever possible, while the aircraft is undergoing maintenance.

513-9. Aircraft Battery—Charging and Equipment.

(a) Aircraft batteries should not be charged when installed in an aircraft located inside or partially inside a hangar.

(b) Battery chargers and their control equipment shall not be located or operated within any of the hazardous areas defined in Section 513-2, and should preferably be located in a separate building or in an area such as described in Section 513-2(d). Mobile chargers shall carry at least one permanently affixed warning sign to read: "WARNING—KEEP 5 FEET CLEAR OF AIRCRAFT ENGINES AND FUEL TANK AREAS." Tables, racks, trays, and wiring shall not be located within a hazardous area, and shall, in addition, conform to the provisions of Article 480.

513-10. External Power Sources for Energizing Aircraft.

(a) Aircraft energizers shall be so designed and mounted that all electrical equipment and fixed wiring will be at least 18 inches above floor level and shall not be operated in a hazardous area as defined in Section 513-2(c).

(b) Mobile energizers shall carry at least one permanently affixed warning sign to read: "WARNING—KEEP 5 FEET CLEAR OF AIRCRAFT ENGINES AND FUEL TANK AREAS."

(c) Aircraft energizers should be equipped with polarized external power plugs and should have automatic controls to isolate the ground power unit electrically from the aircraft in case excessive voltage is generated by the grounding power unit.

(d) Flexible cords for aircraft energizers and ground support equipment shall be approved for the type of service and extra hard usage and shall include a ground conductor.

513-11. Mobile Servicing Equipment with Electrical Components.

(a) Mobile servicing equipment (such as vacuum cleaners, air compressors, air movers, etc.) having electrical wiring and equipment not suitable for Class I, Division 2 locations shall be so designed and mounted that all such fixed wiring and equipment will be at least 18 inches above the floor. Such mobile equipment shall not be operated within the hazardous areas defined in Section 513-2(c) and shall carry at least one permanently affixed warning sign to read: "WARNING— KEEP 5 FEET CLEAR OF AIRCRAFT ENGINES AND FUEL TANK AREAS."

(b) Flexible cords for mobile equipment shall be suitable for the type of service and approved for extra hard usage, and shall include a grounding conductor. Attachment plugs and receptacles shall be approved for the location in which they are installed, and shall provide for connection of the grounding conductor to the raceway system.

(c) Equipment not of a type suitable for Class I, Division 2 locations should not be operated in areas where maintenance operations likely to release hazardous vapors are in progress.

513-12. Grounding.   All metallic raceways, and all noncurrent-carrying metallic portions of fixed or portable equipment, regardless of voltage, shall be grounded as provided in Article 250.

ARTICLE 514. GASOLINE DISPENSING AND SERVICE STATIONS

514-1. Definitions.   This classification shall include locations where gasoline or other volatile flammable liquids or liquefied flammable gases are transferred to the fuel tanks (including auxiliary fuel tanks) of self-propelled vehicles.

Other areas used as lubritoriums, service rooms and repair rooms, and offices, salesrooms, compressor rooms and similar locations shall conform to Articles 510 and 511 with respect to electrical wiring and equipment.

Where the authority having jurisdiction can satisfactorily determine that flammable liquids having a flash point below 100°F such as gasoline will not be handled, he may classify such an area as nonhazardous.

For further information regarding safeguards for gasoline dispensing and service stations see NFPA Flammable and Combustible Liquids Code (No. 30-1969).

514-2. Hazardous Areas.

(a) The space within the dispenser up to 4 feet from its base and the space within 18 inches extending horizontally from the dispenser up to 4 feet from its base shall be considered a Class I, Division 1 location. This classification shall also apply to any space below the dispenser which may contain electrical wiring or equipment.

(b) In an outside location, any area (excluding Class I, Division 1, but including buildings not suitably cut off) within 20 feet horizontally from the exterior enclosure of any dispensing pump shall be considered a Class I, Division 2 location which will extend to a level 18 inches above driveway or ground level.

(c) In an outside location, any area (excluding Class I, Division 1, but including buildings not suitably cut off) within 10 feet horizontally from any tank fill-pipe shall be considered a Class I, Division 2 location which shall extend upward to a level 18 inches above driveway or ground level.

(d) Electrical wiring and equipment, any portion of which is below the surface of areas defined as Class I, Division 1 or Division 2 in 514-2(a), (b), (c) above shall be considered to be within a Class I, Division 1 location which shall extend at least to the point of emergence above grade.

(e) Where the dispensing unit, including the hose and hose nozzle valve, is suspended from a canopy, ceiling or structural support, the Class I, Division 1 location shall include the volume within the enclosure and shall also extend 18 inches in all directions from the enclosure where not suitably cut off by a ceiling or wall. The Class I, Division 2 location shall extend 2 feet horizontally in all directions beyond the Division 1 classified area and extend to grade below this classified area. In addition, the horizontal area 18 inches above grade for a distance of 20 feet, measured from a point vertically below the edge of any dispenser enclosure, shall be classified Division 2. All electrical equipment integral with the dispensing hose or nozzle shall be suitable for use in a Division 1 location.

(f) The spherical volume within a 3 foot radius from point of discharge of any tank vent-pipe shall be considered a Class I, Division 1 location and the volume between three foot to five foot radius from point of discharge of a vent shall be considered a Class I, Division 2 location. For any vent that does not discharge upward, the cylindrical volume below both the Division 1 and 2 locations extending to the ground shall be considered a Class I, Division 2 location. The hazardous area shall not extend beyond an unpierced wall.

(g) In addition to the requirements of Section 514-1 the area within any pit or space below grade in a lubrication room shall be considered a Class I, Division 1 location. The area within the entire lubrication room up to 18 inches above the floor or grade, and the area within 3 feet measured in any direction from the dispensing point of a hand-operated unit dispensing Class I liquids shall be considered a Class I, Division 2 location.

514-3. Wiring and Equipment Within Hazardous Areas.   All electrical equipment and wiring within the hazardous areas defined in Section 514-2 shall conform to applicable provisions of Article 501.

Exception: Except as permitted in Section 514-8.

For special requirements for conductor insulation, see Section 501-13.

514-4. Wiring and Equipment Above Hazardous Areas.   Wiring and equipment above hazardous areas defined in Section 514-2 shall conform to Sections 511-5 and 511-6.

514-5. Circuit Disconnects.   Each circuit leading to or through a dispensing pump shall be provided with a switch or other acceptable means to disconnect simultaneously from the source of supply all conductors of the circuit including the grounded neutral, if any.

514-6. Sealing.

(a) An approved seal shall be provided in each conduit run entering or leaving a dispenser or any cavities or enclosures in direct communication therewith. The sealing fitting shall be the first fitting after the conduit emerges from the earth or concrete.

(b) Additional seals shall be provided in conformance with Section 501-5 and Sections 501-5(a-3) and 501-5(b-2) shall apply to horizontal as well as to vertical boundaries of the defined hazardous areas.

514-7. Grounding. Metallic portions of dispensing pumps, metallic raceways, and all noncurrent-carrying portions of electrical equipment, regardless of voltage, shall be grounded as provided in Article 250.

514-8. Underground Wiring. Underground wiring shall be installed in rigid metal conduit, or, where buried under not less than 2 feet of earth, may be installed in nonmetallic conduit conforming to the requirements of Article 347. Where nonmetallic conduit is used, a grounding conductor shall be included to provide for metallic continuity of the raceway system and for grounding of noncurrent-carrying metallic parts of equipment.

Exception: Type MI cable may be used when installed in accordance with Article 330.

▶   Article 514 not only covers wiring in the pumps, it also specifies the type of wiring for the areas considered to be hazardous that extend to within 20 ft horizontally from any dispensing pump or 10 ft from any tank fill pipe. It should be noted that sealing is required where the conduit enters the pump and also that additional seals are required in all conduits leaving a hazardous area.

In Fig. 514-1, four seals are shown. Normally panelboards are located in a nonhazardous location so that a seal is shown where the conduit is leaving the hazardous location. According to Section 514-6a there must also be a seal where the conduit enters or leaves the dispenser.

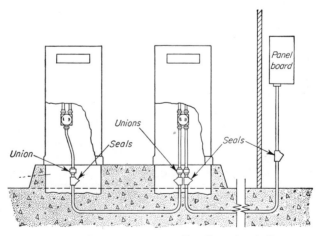

Fɪɢ. 514-1. Installation at a gasoline dispensing station.

When the electrical equipment of a pump is being serviced or repaired, it is very important that there shall be no "hot" wire or wires inside the pump. Since it is always possible that the polarity of the circuit wires may have been accidentally reversed at the panelboard, control switches or circuit breakers must open all conductors. If these circuits are controlled at a panelboard, a special panelboard arrangement is required.

For "gasoline and oil resistant" insulated conductors, see comments following Section 501-13.

Section 514-2e describes the Class I, Division 1 and 2 boundaries for overhead types of gasoline dispensing units.

ARTICLE 515. BULK-STORAGE PLANTS

515-1. Definition. This designation shall include locations where gasoline or other volatile flammable liquids are stored in tanks having an aggregate capacity of one carload or more, and from which such products are distributed (usually by tank truck).

515-2. Hazardous Areas.

(a) Pumps, Bleeders, Withdrawal Fittings, Meters and Similar Devices.

(1) Adequately ventilated indoor areas containing pumps, bleeders, withdrawal fittings, meters and similar devices which are located in pipe lines handling flammable liquids under pressure shall be considered as Class I, Division 2 locations within a 5 foot distance extending in all directions from the exterior surface of such devices. The Class I, Division 2 location shall also extend 25 feet horizontally from any surface of these devices and extend upward to 3 feet above floor or grade level.

See Flammable and Combustible Liquids Code, NFPA No. 30-1969, for discussion of factors influencing adequacy of ventilation required to prevent formation of hazardous vapor-air mixtures.

(2) Inadequately ventilated indoor areas containing pumps, bleeders, withdrawal fittings, meters and similar devices which are located in pipe lines handling flammable liquids under pressure shall be considered as Class I, Division 1 location within a 5 foot distance extending in all directions from the exterior surface of such devices. The Class I, Division 1 location shall also extend 25 feet horizontally from any surface of the devices and extend upward to 3 feet above floor or grade level.

(3) Outdoor areas containing pumps, bleeders, withdrawal fittings, meters and similar devices which are located in pipe lines handling flammable liquids under pressure shall be considered as Class I, Division 2 locations within a 3 foot distance extending in all directions from the exterior surface of such devices. The Class I, Division 2 location shall also extend up to 18 inches above grade level within 10 feet horizontally from any surface of the devices.

(b) Transfer of Flammable Liquids to Individual Containers.

(1) In outdoor areas or where positive and reliable mechanical ventilation is provided in indoor areas in which flammable liquids are transferred to individual containers, such areas shall be considered to be a Class I, Division 1 location within 3 feet of the vent or fill opening extending in all directions and a Class I, Division 2 location within the area extending between a 3 foot and 5 foot radius from the vent or fill opening extending in all directions, and including the area within a horizontal radius of 10 feet from the vent or fill opening and extending to a height of 18 inches above floor or grade levels.

> See Flammable and Combustible Liquids Code, NFPA No. 30-1969, for discussion of factors influencing adequacy and reliability of mechanical ventilation required to prevent formation of hazardous vapor-air mixtures.

(2) When positive and reliable mechanical ventilation is not provided in indoor areas in which flammable liquids are transferred to individual containers, such areas shall be considered to be a Class I, Division 1 location.

(c) Loading and Unloading of Tank Vehicles and Tank Cars in Outside Locations.

(1) The area extending 3 feet in all directions from the dome when loading through an open dome or from the vent when loading through a closed dome with atmospheric venting shall be considered a Class I, Division 1 location.

(2) The area extending between a 3 foot and 5 foot radius from the dome when loading through an open dome or from the vent when loading through a closed dome with atmospheric venting shall be considered a Class I, Division 2 location.

(3) The area extending within 3 feet in all directions from a fixed connection used in bottom loading or unloading, loading through a closed dome with atmospheric venting, or loading through a closed dome with a vapor recovery system, shall be considered a Class I, Division 2 location. In the case of bottom loading or unloading this classification shall also be applied to the area within a 10 foot radius from point of connection and extending 18 inches above grade.

> In deciding upon extent of hazardous area, consideration should be given to the total area within which loading and unloading operation may occur such as racks, platforms, driveways, etc.

(d) Aboveground Tanks.

(1) The area above the roof and within the shell of a floating roof type tank shall be considered a Class I, Division 1 location.

(2) For all types of aboveground tanks the area within 10 feet from the shell, ends and roof of other than a floating roof shall be considered a Class I, Division 2 location. Where dikes are provided the area inside the dike and extending upward to the top of the dike shall be considered to be a Class I, Division 2 location.

(3) The area within 5 feet of a vent opening and extending in all directions shall be considered a Class I, Division 1 location.

(4) The area between 5 and 10 feet of a vent opening and extending in all directions shall be considered a Class I, Division 2 location.

> For underground tanks see Article 514.

(e) Pits.

(1) Any pit or depression, any part of which lies within a Division 1 or Division 2 location as defined herein, shall be considered a Class I, Division 1 location unless provided with positive and reliable mechanical ventilation.

(2) Any such areas when provided with positive and reliable mechanical ventilation shall be considered a Class I, Division 2 location.

See Flammable and Combustible Liquids Code, NFPA No. 30-1969, for discussion of factors pertaining to positive and reliable mechanical ventilation required to prevent formulation of hazardous vapor-air mixtures.

(3) Any pit or depression not within a Division 1 or Division 2 location as defined herein, but which contains piping, valves or fittings shall be classified as a Class I, Division 2 location

(f) Storage and Repair Garages for Tank Vehicles shall be considered to be Class I, Division 2 locations up to 18 inches above floor or grade level unless in the judgment of the authority enforcing this Code conditions warrant more severe classification or a greater extent of the hazardous area.

(g) Office Buildings, Boiler Rooms and Other Similar Locations which are outside the limits of hazardous areas as defined herein, and which are not used for handling or storage of volatile flammable liquids or containers for such liquids, shall not be considered to be hazardous locations.

515-3. Wiring and Equipment Within Hazardous Areas. All electrical wiring and equipment within the hazardous areas defined in Section 515-2 shall conform to applicable provisions of Article 501.

Exception: Except as permitted in Section 515-5.

515-4. Wiring and Equipment Above Hazardous Areas. All fixed wiring above hazardous areas shall be in metallic raceways or shall be Type ALS cable. Fixed equipment which may produce arcs, sparks or particles of hot metal, such as lamps and lampholders for fixed lighting, cutouts, switches, receptacles, motors, or other equipment having make-and-break or sliding contacts, shall be of totally enclosed type or so constructed as to prevent escape of sparks or hot metal particles. Portable lamps or utilization equipment, and their flexible cords shall conform to the provisions of Article 501 for the class of location above which they are connected or used.

515-5. Underground Wiring.

(a) Underground wiring shall be installed in rigid metal conduit, or, where buried under not less than 2 feet of earth, may be installed in nonmetallic conduit or duct, or in the form of cable approved for the purpose. Where cable is used, it shall be enclosed in rigid metal conduit from the point of lowest buried cable level to the point of connection to the aboveground raceway.

(b) Conductor insulation shall conform to Section 501-13.

(c) Where cable with nonmetallic sheath or nonmetallic conduit is used, an additional grounding conductor shall be included to provide for metallic continuity of the raceway system and for grounding of noncurrent-carrying metallic parts of equipment.

515-6. Sealing. Approved seals shall be provided in conformance with Section 501-5 and Sections 501-5(a-3) and 501-5(b-2) shall apply to horizontal as well as to vertical boundaries of the defined hazardous areas. Buried raceways under defined hazardous areas shall be considered to be within such areas.

515-7. Gasoline Dispensing. Where gasoline dispensing is carried on in conjunction with bulk station operations, applicable provisions of Article 514 shall apply.

515-8. Grounding. All metallic raceways, and all noncurrent-carrying metallic portions of electrical equipment shall be grounded as provided in Article 250.

ARTICLE 516. FINISHING PROCESSES

516-1. Definition. This Article shall apply to locations where paints, lacquers or other flammable finishes are regularly or frequently applied by spraying, dipping, brushing or by other means, and where volatile flammable solvents or thinners are used or where readily ignitible deposits or residues from such paints, lacquers or finishes may occur.

> For further information regarding safeguards for finishing processes, such as guarding, fire protection, posting of warning signs, and maintenance, see the NFPA Standard for Spray Finishing Using Flammable and Combustible Materials, No. 33-1969 and NFPA Standard for Dip Tanks Containing Flammable or Combustible Liquids, No. 34-1966. For additional information regarding ventilation, see NFPA Standard for Blower and Exhaust Systems, No. 91-1961.

516-2. Hazardous Areas. Classification is with respect to flammable vapors, some sections of which are also subject to deposits of paint residue. For deposits and residues, see Sections 516-3(b) and (c).

(a) The interiors of spray booths and their exhaust ducts, all space within 20 feet horizontally in any direction from spraying operations more extensive than touch-up spraying and not conducted within spray booths, all space within 20 feet horizontally in any direction from dip tanks and their drain boards, and all other spaces where hazardous concentrations of flammable vapors are likely to occur, shall be considered to be Class I, Division 1 locations.

(b) All space within 20 feet horizontally in any direction from the open face of a spray booth, and all space within the room but beyond the limits for Class I, Division 1 as defined in Section 516-2(a) for extensive open spraying, for dip tanks and drain boards and for other hazardous operations, shall be considered to be Class I, Division 2 locations unless the authority having jurisdiction judges otherwise.

(c) Adjacent areas which are cut off from the defined hazardous areas by tight partitions without communicating openings, and within which hazardous vapors are not likely to be released, shall be classed as nonhazardous unless the authority having jurisdiction judges otherwise.

(d) Areas utilizing drying, curing, or fusion apparatus and provided with positive mechanical ventilation adequate to prevent formation of flammable concentrations of vapors, and provided with effective interlocks to de-energize all electric equipment (other than equipment approved for Class I locations) in case the ventilating equipment is inoperative, may be classed as nonhazardous when the authority having jurisdiction so judges.

> For further information regarding safeguards see NFPA Standard for Ovens and Furnaces, No. 86-A-1969.

516-3. Wiring and Equipment in Hazardous Areas.

(a) All electrical wiring and equipment within the hazardous areas (containing

vapor only—not residues) defined in Section 516-2 shall conform to applicable
provisions of Article 501.

(b) Unless approved for both readily ignitible deposits and the flammable vapor location, no electrical equipment shall be installed or used where it may be subject to hazardous accumulations of readily ignitible deposits or residues, as the susceptibility to spontaneous heating and ignition of some residues may be greatly increased at temperatures above normal. Type MI cable and wiring in threaded rigid conduit may be installed in such locations, if the explosion-proof boxes or fittings contain no taps, splices, or terminal connections which may have the possibility of being loose in service and thereby causing abnormal temperatures on external surfaces of boxes or fittings.

▶ Since there are no fixtures or equipment approved for a location where they may be subject to hazardous accumulations of readily ignitible deposits or residues, only rigid metal conduit and Type MI cable and threaded boxes or fittings containing no taps, splices or terminal connections may be installed in such locations. However, for that part of the hazardous area where the fixtures or equipment may not be subject to readily ignitible deposits or residues, fixtures and equipment approved for Class I, Division 1 locations may be installed. The authority having jurisdiction may decide that because of adequate positive pressure ventilation the possibility of the hazard referred to in paragraph *b* has been eliminated.

(c) Illumination of readily ignitible areas through panels of glass or other transparent or translucent material is permissible only where: (1) fixed lighting units are used as the source of illumination, (2) the panel effectively isolates the hazardous area from the area in which the lighting unit is located, (3) the lighting unit is approved for its specific location, (4) the panel is of a material or is so protected that breakage will be unlikely and (5) the arrangement is such that normal accumulations of hazardous residue on the surface of the panel will not be raised to a dangerous temperature by radiation or conduction from the source of illumination.

(d) Portable electric lamps or other utilization equipment shall not be used within a hazardous area during operation of the finishing process. When such lamps or utilization equipment are used during cleaning or repairing operations, they shall be of a type approved for Class I locations, and all exposed metal parts shall be effectively grounded.

(e) Electrostatic spraying or detearing equipment shall be installed and used only as provided in Section 516-4.

For further information see NFPA Standard, Spray Finishing Using Flammable and Combustible Materials, No. 33-1969.

516-4. Fixed Electrostatic Equipment. Where electrostatic spraying and detearing equipment is installed, such equipment shall be of approved type, and shall conform to the following requirements:

(a) Transformers, power packs, control apparatus, and all other electrical portions of the equipment, with the exception of high-voltage grids, electrodes, electrostatic atomizing heads and their connections, shall be installed outside of the hazardous area as defined in Section 516-2 or be of a type approved for the location.

(b) Electrodes and electrostatic atomizing heads shall be located in suitable noncombustible booths or enclosures provided with adequate mechanical ventilation, shall be adequately supported in permanent locations and shall be effectively insulated from ground. Electrodes and electrostatic atomizing heads, which are permanently attached to their bases, supports, or reciprocators shall be deemed to comply with this Section. Insulators shall be nonporous and noncombustible. Fine-wire elements when used should be under tension at all times and should be of unkinked hardened steel or material of comparable strength.

(c) High-voltage leads to the electrodes shall be properly insulated and protected from mechanical injury or exposure to destructive chemicals. Electrostatic atomizing heads shall be effectively and permanently supported on suitable insulators and shall be effectively guarded against accidental contact or grounding. An automatic means shall be provided for grounding the electrode system when it is electrically de-energized for any reason.

(d) A safe distance shall be maintained between goods being painted and electrodes or electrostatic atomizing heads or conductors of at least twice the sparking distance. A suitable sign indicating this safe distance shall be conspicuously posted near the assembly.

(e) Goods being painted using this process are to be supported on conveyors. The conveyors shall be arranged so as to maintain safe distances between the goods and the electrodes or electrostatic atomizing heads at all times. Any irregularly shaped or other goods subject to possible swinging or movement shall be rigidly supported to prevent such swinging or movement which will reduce the clearance to less than that specified in (d) above.

(f) This process is not approved where goods being coated are manipulated by hand. When finishing materials are applied by electrostatic equipment that is manipulated by hand, see Section 516-5 for applicable requirements.

(g) Electrostatic apparatus shall be equipped with automatic controls which will operate without time delay to disconnect the power supply to the high-voltage transformer and to signal the operator under any of the following conditions: (1) stoppage of ventilating fans or failure of ventilating equipment from any cause; (2) stoppage of the conveyor carrying goods through the high-voltage field; (3) occurrence of a ground or of an imminent ground at any point in the high-voltage system; (4) reduction of clearances below that specified in Section 516-4(d).

(h) All electrically conductive objects within the charging influence of the electrodes shall be adequately grounded. The equipment shall carry a prominent permanently installed warning regarding the necessity for grounding these objects.

(i) Adequate booths, fencing, railings, or guards shall be so placed about the equipment that they, either by their location or character, or both, assure that a safe isolation of the process is maintained from plant storage or personnel. Such railings, fencing, and guards shall be of conducting materials, adequately grounded, and should be at least 5 feet from processing equipment.

516-5. Electrostatic Hand Spraying Equipment. Electrostatic hand spray apparatus and devices used in connection with paint spraying operations shall be of approved types and shall conform to the following requirements:

(a) The equipment shall be so designed that the maximum surface temperature of the equipment in the spraying area cannot exceed 150°F under any condition. The high-voltage circuits shall be so designed as to not produce a spark of sufficient intensity to ignite any vapor-air mixtures, nor result in appreciable shock hazard upon coming in contact with a grounded object under all normal operating conditions. The electrostatically charged exposed elements of the hand gun shall be capable of being energized only by a switch which also controls the paint supply.

(b) Transformers, power packs, control apparatus, and all other electrical portions of the equipment, with the exception of the hand gun itself and its connections to the power supply, shall be located outside of the hazardous area, unless approved for hazardous areas.

(c) The handle of the spraying gun shall be electrically connected to ground by a metallic connection and be so constructed that the operator in normal operating position is in intimate electrical contact with the grounded handle. This requirement is to prevent build-up of a static charge on the operator's body.

(d) All electrically conductive objects in the spraying area shall be adequately grounded. This requirement shall apply to paint containers, wash cans and any other objects or devices in the area. The equipment shall carry a prominent permanently installed warning regarding the necessity for this grounding feature.

(e) Objects being painted shall be maintained in metallic contact with the conveyor or other grounded support. Hooks shall be regularly cleaned to insure this contact and areas of contact shall be sharp points or knife edges where possible. Points of support of the object shall be concealed from random spray where feasible and where the objects being sprayed are supported from a conveyor, the point of attachment to the conveyor shall be so located as to not collect spray material during normal operation.

(f) The spraying operation shall take place within a spray area which is adequately ventilated to remove solvent vapors released from the operation. The electrical equipment shall be so interlocked with the ventilation of spraying area that the equipment cannot be operated unless the ventilation fans are in operation.

516-6. Powder Coating. This Section shall apply to finely ground particles of protective finishing material applied in dry powder form. The hazards associated with combustible dusts are inherent in this process. Generally speaking, the hazard rating of the powders employed is dependent upon the chemical composition of the material, particle size, shape and distribution.

(a) Coating powders are applied by means of: (1) fluidized bed; (2) electrostatic fluidized bed; (3) powder spray guns; or (4) electrostatic powder spray guns.

(b) Electrical equipment and other sources of ignition shall conform to the requirements of Section 516-3(d) and Article 502.

(c) The provisions of Sections 516-4 and 516-6(b) shall apply to fixed electrostatic spraying equipment.

(d) The provisions of Sections 516-5 and 516-6(b) shall apply to electrostatic hand-spraying equipment.

(e) Electrostatic fluidized beds and associated equipment shall be of the approved types. The maximum surface temperature of this equipment in the coating area shall not exceed 150°F. The high-voltage circuits and exposed electrodes shall be so designed as to not produce a spark of sufficient intensity to ignite any powder air mixtures nor result in appreciable shock hazard upon coming in contact with a grounded object under normal operating conditions.

(1) Transformers, power packs, control apparatus and all other electrical portions of the equipment, with the exception of the charging electrodes and their connections to the power supply, shall be located outside of the powder-coating area or shall otherwise conform to the requirements of Section 516-6(b).

(2) All electrically conductive objects within the charging influence of the electrodes shall be adequately grounded. The powder-coating equipment shall carry a prominent, permanently installed warning regarding the necessity for grounding these objects.

(3) Objects being coated shall be maintained in contact with the conveyor or other support in order to insure proper grounding. Hangers shall be regularly cleaned to insure effective contact, and areas of contact shall be sharp points or knife edges where possible.

(4) The electrical equipment shall be so interlocked with a ventilation system that the equipment cannot be operated unless the ventilation fans are in operation.

516-7. Wiring and Equipment Above Hazardous Areas.

(a) All fixed wiring above hazardous areas shall be in metallic raceways or shall be Type MI cable or Type ALS cable. Cellular metal floor raceways may be used only for supplying ceiling outlets or extensions to the area below the floor of a hazardous area, but such raceways shall have no connections leading into or through the hazardous area above the floor unless suitable seals are provided. No electrical conductor shall be installed in any cell, header or duct which contains a pipe for steam, water, air, gas, drainage, or for other service except electrical.

(b) Equipment which may produce arcs, sparks or particles of hot metal, such as lamps and lampholders for fixed lighting, cutouts, switches, receptacles, motors or other equipment having make-and-break or sliding contacts, where installed above a hazardous area or above an area where freshly finished goods are handled, shall be of totally enclosed type or so constructed as to prevent escape of sparks or hot metal particles.

516-8. Grounding. All metallic raceways, and all noncurrent-carrying metallic portions of fixed or portable equipment, regardless of voltage, shall be grounded as provided in Article 250.

▶   The safety of life and property from fire or explosion in the spray application of flammable paints and finishes depends upon the extent, arrangement, maintenance and operation of the process.

An analysis of actual experience in industry demonstrates that largest fire losses and fire frequency have occurred where good practice standards were not observed.

Definitions—See NFPA Standard For Spray Finishing Using Flammable Materials (No. 33).

Spraying Area. Any area in which dangerous quantities of flammable vapors or mists, or combustible residues, dusts or deposits are present due to the operation of spraying processes.

A spraying area includes:

(a) The interior of spray booths (with certain exceptions).

(b) The interior of ducts exhausting from spraying processes.

(c) Any area in the direct path of spray or any area containing dangerous quantities of air-suspended powder or combustible residue, dust, deposits, mists or vapor as a result of spraying operations.

The inspection department having jurisdiction may, for the purpose of this standard, define the limits of the spraying area in any specific case.

Note: The "spraying area" in the vicinity of spraying operations will necessarily vary with the design and arrangement of equipment and method of operation.

When spraying operations are strictly confined to predetermined spaces which are provided with adequate and reliable ventilation, such as a properly constructed spray booth, the "spraying area" should ordinarily not extend beyond the booth enclosure.

When, however, spraying operations are not confined to adequately ventilated spaces the "spraying area" may extend throughout the entire room containing spraying operations.

Spray Booth. A power-ventilated structure provided to enclose or accommodate a spraying operation, to confine and limit the escape of spray, vapor and residue, and to safely conduct or direct them to an exhaust system.

Waterwash Spray Booth. A spray booth equipped with a water washing system designed to minimize dusts or residues entering exhaust ducts and to permit the recovery of overspray finishing material.

Dry Spray Booth. A spray booth not equipped with a water washing system as described above. A dry spray booth may be equipped with (1) distribution or baffle plates to promote an even flow of air through booth or cause deposit of overspray before it enters exhaust duct; or (2) overspray dry filters to minimize dusts or residues entering exhaust ducts; or (3) overspray dry filter rolls designed to minimize dusts or residues entering exhaust ducts; or (4) where dry powders are being sprayed, with powder collection systems arranged in the exhaust to capture oversprayed material.

Notes on Electrical Installations

As stipulated in Definitions the inspection department having jurisdiction may, for any specific installation, determine the extent of the hazardous "spraying area."

From Section 516-3b it will be noted that in general electrical equipment is not permitted inside any spray booth, in the exhaust duct from a spray booth, in the entrained air of an exhaust system from a spraying operation or in the direct path of spray, unless such equipment is specifically approved for both readily ignitible deposits and flammable vapor. At present no such equipment is approved by a nationally recognized laboratory. Electric motors driving exhaust fans are specifically prohibited inside spray booths and exhaust ducts.

From the above, it will be noted that when electrical equipment is installed in locations not subject to deposits of combustible residues but, due to inadequate ventilation, is subject to explosive concentrations of flammable vapors or mists, only approved explosion-proof equipment is permitted.

When spraying operations are confined to adequately ventilated spray booths there should be no dangerous concentrations of flammable vapors or mists, nor deposits of combustible residues outside of the spray booth under normal operation conditions.

In the interest of safety, however, it will be noted that unless separated by partitions, the area within 20 feet of the hazardous "spraying area" is considered Division 2, that is, it should contain no equipment which produces sparks under normal operation. Furthermore, within this 20-foot distance electric lamps must be enclosed to prevent hot particles falling on freshly painted stock or other readily ignitible material and if subject to physical damage must be properly guarded.

Electrical and Other Sources of Ignition

It is obvious that there should be a total absence of open flames or spark producing equipment in any area where, because of inadequate ventilation, explosive vapor-air mixtures or mists are present. Obviously, no open flames or spark producing equipment should be so located that there will be deposited on them highly combustible spray residues. Because some residues may be ignited at very low temperatures, additional consideration must be given to operating temperatures of equipment subject to residue deposits. Many deposits may be ignited at temperatures produced by incandescent light bulbs, even of the explosion-proof type, or low pressure steam pipes.

The area in the vicinity of spraying operations which may contain dangerous quantities of flammable vapors, mists, or residue deposits will vary with design and arrangement of equipment and methods of operation.

For the usual cabinet spray booth it has been generally considered that limited areas not separated by partitions and in the front of a booth may be dangerous. When, however, ventilation is inadequate and spraying is not strictly confined to the inside of the booth, the dangerous area may extend throughout the entire room.

On the other hand, when adequate, reliable, supervised ventilation is provided and spraying operations strictly confined to the predetermined designated spaces, the hazardous areas may not extend beyond the booth enclosure.

When areas of spraying with hazardous quantities of vapor or mists or residue under normal operation have been determined, the unpartitioned-off areas adjacent to hazardous areas which are safe under normal operating conditions but which may become dangerous due to accident or careless operation should be considered. In these adjacent areas, equipment known to produce sparks or flames under normal operating conditions should not be installed.

Sufficient lighting for operations, booth cleaning, and repair should be provided at the time of equipment installation in order to avoid the unjustified use of "temporary" or "emergency" electric lamps connected to ordinary extension cords. A satisfactory and practical method of lighting is the use of ¼ inch thick wired or tempered glass panels in the top or sides of spray booths with electrical light fixtures outside the booth, hence not in the direct path of the spray.

Areas adjacent to a spray booth, particularly where paint stocks are located, should be provided with ventilation sufficiently adequate and reliable to prevent the presence of flammable vapors or deposits. It is nevertheless advisable that electric lamps be totally enclosed to prevent the falling of hot particles in any area where there may be freshly painted stock, accidentally spilled flammable or combustible liquids, or readily ignitible refuse or flammable or combustible liquid containers accidentally left open.

Where electric lamps are in areas subject to atmospheres of flammable vapor, the replacing of lamp bulbs should only be done when electricity is off, otherwise there may be a spark from this source.

The determination of the extent of hazardous areas involved in spray application requires an understanding of the dual hazards of flammable vapors or mists and highly combustible deposits together with intelligent judgment of the objectives, applied to each individual installation.

Automobile undercoating spray operations in garages, conducted in areas having adequate natural or mechanical ventilation, may be exempt from the requirements pertaining to spray finishing operations, when using undercoating materials not more hazardous than kerosene (as listed by Underwriters' Laboratories in respect to fire hazard rating **30–40**) or undercoating materials using only solvents listed as having a flash point in excess of 100°F. There should be no open flames or other sources of ignition within 20 ft while such operations are conducted.

ARTICLE 517. HEALTH CARE FACILITIES

A. General

517-1. Scope. The provisions of this Article shall apply to health care facilities. See Article 660 for medical X-ray equipment and Article 665 for therapeutic high-frequency equipment.

517-2. Definitions.

Alternate Power Source. One or more generator sets intended to provide power during the interruption of the normal electrical service or the public utility electrical service intended to provide power during interruption of service normally provided by the generating facilities on the premises.

Anesthetizing Location. Any area in which it is intended to administer any flammable or nonflammable inhalation anesthetic agents in the course of examination or treatment and includes operating rooms, delivery rooms, emergency rooms, anesthetizing rooms, corridors, utility rooms and other areas when used for induction of anesthesia with flammable or nonflammable anesthetizing agents.

Anesthetizing-Location Receptacle. A receptacle designed to accept the attachment plugs recognized for use in such locations. See Figures 517-2(a) and (b).

These receptacles are of a type for use in nonhazardous areas. There are also compatible receptacles for hazardous areas.

▶ See comments following Section 517-61*d*.

Continuous Power System. An electrical system, independent of the alternate source which supplies power without appreciable interruption (1-cycle or less).

Critical Branch. A sub-system of the emergency system consisting of feeders and branch circuits supplying energy to task illumination and selected receptacles serving areas and functions related to patient care, and which can be connected to alternate power sources by one or more transfer switches.

Critical Patient Care Area. A section (rooms, wards or portions of wards) designated for the treatment of critically ill patients.

Electrically Susceptible Patient. A patient being treated with an externalized electric conductor, such as a probe, catheter, or other electrode connected to the heart.

Electrically Susceptible Patient Area. A location in a health care facility where electrically susceptible patients are cared for collectively.

Emergency System. A system of feeders and branch circuits meeting the requirements of Article 700, connected to alternate power sources by a transfer switch and supplying energy to an extremely limited number of prescribed functions vital to the protection of life and patient safety, with automatic restoration of electrical power within 10 seconds of power interruption.

Equipment System. A system of feeders and branch circuits arranged for delayed, automatic or manual connection to the alternate power source and which serves primarily 3-phase power equipment. See Appendix A of Essential Electrical Systems for Hospitals, NFPA No. 76A-1971.

Essential Electrical Systems. Systems comprised of alternate sources of power, transfer switches, overcurrent protective devices, distribution cabinets, feeders, branch circuits, motor controls, and all connected electrical equipment, designed to provide designated areas with continuity of electrical service during disruption of normal power sources, and also designed to minimize the interruptive effects of disruption within the internal wiring system.

Flammable Anesthetics. Gases or vapors such as fluroxene, cyclopropane, divinyl ether, ethyl chloride, ethyl ether, and ethylene, which may form flammable or explosive mixtures with air, oxygen, or reducing gases such as nitrous oxide.

Flammable Anesthetizing Location. Any operating room, delivery room, anesthetizing room, corridor, utility room, or any other area if used or intended for the application of flammable anesthetics.

Health Care Facilities. Buildings or parts of buildings that contain, but are not limited to, hospitals, nursing homes, extended-care facilities, clinics, and medical and dental offices, whether fixed or mobile.

Immediate Restoration of Service. Automatic restoration of operation with an interruption of not more than 10 seconds as applied to those areas and functions

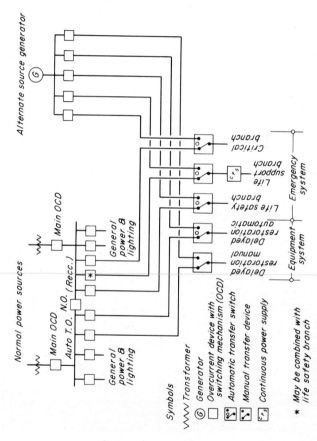

Diagram 517-1. Typical Diagram for Essential Electrical Systems.

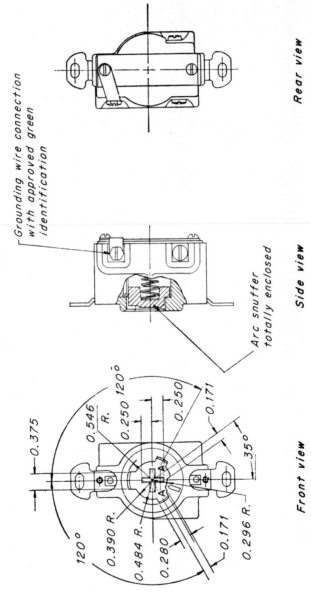

Figure 517-2(a). Two-pole, 20-ampere, 3-wire grounding-type anesthetizing-location receptacle for use in nonhazardous areas for single-phase, 125-volt AC service. See Section 517-62(e).

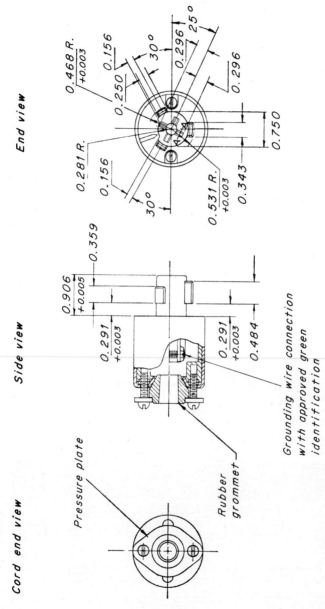

Figure 517-2(b). Two-pole, 20-ampere, 3-wire grounding-type attachment plug for use in nonhazardous areas with the anesthetizing-location receptacle shown in Figure 517-2(a).

served by the emergency system, except for areas and functions for which Article 700 otherwise makes specific provisions.

Intensive Care Units. Groups of beds, rooms, or wards specifically designated to provide intensive care for critically ill patients and intended to be specifically staffed and organized for such service, distinct from surgical or obstetrical recovery units forming a part of a surgical or obstetrical suite.

Life Safety Branch. A sub-system of the emergency system consisting of feeders and branch circuits, meeting the requirements of Article 700 and intended to provide adequate power needs to insure safety to patients and personnel, and which can be connected to alternate power sources by one or more transfer switches.

Life Support Branch. The life support branch of the emergency system supplies power centers in electrically susceptible patient locations.

Line Isolation Monitor. A test instrument designed to continually check the balanced and unbalanced impedance from each line of an isolated circuit to ground and equipped with a built-in test circuit to exercise the alarm without adding to the leakage current hazard.

"Line isolation monitor" was formerly known as "ground contact indicator."

Nurses' Stations. Areas intended to provide a center of nursing activity for a group of nurses working under one nurse supervisor and serving bed patients, where the patient calls are received, nurses are dispatched, nurses' notes written, inpatient charts prepared, and medications prepared for distribution to patients. Where such activities are carried on in more than one location within a nursing unit, all such separate areas are considered a part of the nurses' station.

Probable Failure. One or more failures of the following:

1. Any single component.

2. Any components which might fail without detection during normal use including interruption of the grounding conductor.

3. Any components which might fail as a result of the failure of any or all of the components above.

Reference Grounding Bus, Patient. The terminal grounding bus which serves as the single focus for grounding the electrical equipment connected to an individual patient, or for grounding the metal or conductive furniture or other equipment within reach of the patient or a person who may be touching him.

Reference Grounding Bus, Room. The terminal grounding bus which serves as the single focus for grounding the patient reference grounding buses and all other metal or conductive furniture, equipment, or structural surfaces in the room.

This bus may be located in or outside the room. The room reference grounding bus and the patient reference grounding bus may be a common bus if there is only one patient reference grounding bus in the room.

Task Illumination. Provision for the minimum lighting required to carry out necessary tasks in the described areas, including safe access to supplies and equipment, and access to exits.

▶   It is very important to review the definitions in Section **517-2.** Most of these definitions have been taken from other NFPA Standards that relate to electrical installations in hospitals and other health care facilities. NFPA pamphlets that provide additional details on this subject are NFPA No. 56A, Inhalation Anesthetics, NFPA 76A, Essential Electrical Systems for Hospitals, and NFPA No. 76BM, Safe Use of Electricity in Hospitals (a manual).

B. General Area Wiring Systems

517-3. Grounding. All noncurrent-carrying conductive surfaces and equipment that are likely to become energized and are subject to personal contact shall be grounded by one or more of the methods detailed in Article 250.

517-4. Wiring Methods. Except as modified in this Article, wiring methods shall comply with the applicable requirements of Chapters 1 through 4 of this Code.

C. Essential Electrical Systems

For additional information see Essential Electrical Systems for Hospitals, NFPA 76A-1971 and Installation of Centrifugal Fire Pumps, NFPA No. 20-1971.

517-10. General.

(a) Part C applies to hospitals serving persons. It does not apply to other types of health care facilities.

(b) The essential electrical system consists of two parts: the emergency system and the equipment system. These systems shall be capable of supplying a limited amount of lighting and power service considered essential for life safety, life support and effective operation during the time the normal electrical service is interrupted for any reason. See Diagram 517-1.

(c) Each emergency and equipment system shall have adequate capacity and rating for the operation of all lighting and equipment it serves.

▶   Diagram 517-1 provides a typical layout for essential electrical systems in hospitals. It should be noted that Part C of this Article applies only to hospitals. It does not apply to other types of health care facilities, such as nursing homes or medical or dental offices.

It should be noted that essential electrical systems are required in all hospitals. Acceptable power sources are described in Section 517-30, which, in effect, requires on-site generator(s) to supply the emergency and equipment systems described in Sections 517-11 and 517-20.

The emergency system may consist of three parts: (1) the life safety branch (Section 517-12); (2) the critical branch (Section 517-13); and the life support branch (Section 517-14). These branches are defined in Section 517-2, and their location is described in Diagram 517-1.

517-11. Emergency System.

(a) The emergency system may consist of three parts: the life safety branch, the critical branch, and the life support branch. These branches shall be limited to circuits essential to specified functions.

(b) A life safety branch and a critical branch shall be required in all hospitals.

(1)   The life safety branch shall serve illumination, alarm and alerting equipment which shall be operable at all times for protection of life during emergencies.

(2)   The critical branch shall serve lighting and receptacles in critical patient care areas.

(3)   The life support branch shall serve only power systems, or other equipments meeting the requirements of Section 517-51, in electrically susceptible patient locations. It shall be installed as a separate branch unless combined with the critical branch at the discretion of the hospital administration and with the approval of the authority having jurisdiction.

(c)   The feeders for the emergency system shall be physically separated from the normal wiring or protected in such a way as to minimize the possibility of simultaneous interruption.

(d)   The life safety branch, life support branch, and critical branch of the emergency system shall be run in metal raceways.

These branches shall be kept entirely independent of all other wiring and equipment and shall not enter the same raceways, boxes or cabinets with each other or other wiring.

Exception No. 1: As permitted in 517-11(b)(3).

Exception No. 2: In transfer switches.

Exception No. 3: In exit or emergency lighting fixtures supplied from two sources.

(e)   Only those functions utilizing illumination or equipment which are listed in Sections 517-12, -13, and -14 shall be connected to the emergency system.

(f)   All branches of the emergency system shall be so installed and connected to the alternate source of power that all lighting and equipment will be automatically restored to operation within 10 seconds after interruption of the normal source.

517-12. Life Safety Branch.   The life safety branch of the emergency system shall serve the lighting, receptacles and other equipment which are related to the safety of life as follows:

For additional information see Essential Electrical Systems for Hospitals, NFPA No. 76A-1971.

(1)   Illumination of means of egress, such as lighting required for corridors, passageways, stairways and landings at exit doors, and all necessary ways of approach to exits.

See Life Safety Code, NFPA No. 101-1970, Section 5-10.

(2)   Exit signs and directional signs.

See Life Safety Code, NFPA No. 101-1970, Section 5-11.

(3)   Alarm systems, including: fire alarms actuated at manual stations, electric water-flow alarm devices in connection with sprinkler systems, automatic fire or smoke or products of combustion detection devices.

See Life Safety Code, NFPA No. 101-1970, Sections 6-3211, 10-1362, and 10-2344.

(4)   Alarms required for systems used for the piping of nonflammable medical gases.

See Nonflammable Medical Gas Systems, NFPA No. 56F-1970.

(5) Hospital communication systems when these are intended for issuing instructions during emergency conditions, including local power requirements for the telephone system.

(6) Generator-set location, including task illumination and selected receptacles.

517-13. Critical Branch. The critical branch of the emergency system shall serve only the following areas and functions related to patient care:

(1) Isolating transformers serving anesthetizing locations in existing hospitals only. See Section 517-14 for new hospitals.

(2) Task illumination and selected receptacles in: (a) infant nurseries; (b) medication preparation areas; (c) pharmacy dispensing areas; (d) selected acute nursing areas; (e) psychiatric bed areas (task illumination only); (f) nurses' stations (unless adequately lighted by corridor luminaires); (g) ward treatment rooms; (h) surgical and obstetrical suites; (i) locations such as those listed in Section 517-14.

517-14. Life Support Branch.

(a) The life support branch of the emergency system shall serve only the power systems in electrically susceptible patient locations. These systems may be located in the following areas of the hospital: (1) angiographic labs; (2) cardiac catheterization labs; (3) coronary care units; (4) delivery rooms; (5) dialysis units; (6) emergency room treatment areas; (7) human physiology labs; (8) intensive care units; (9) operating rooms; (10) post-operative recovery rooms.

(b) The power systems in the above locations may be served by an uninterruptible power supply.

517-20. Equipment Systems.

(a) The equipment system shall be so installed and connected to the alternate source that equipment listed in Section 517-20(d) shall be automatically restored to operation at appropriate time-lag intervals following the restoration of the emergency system to operation. This arrangement shall also provide for reconnection of equipment listed in Sections 517-20(e) and (f) by either delayed, automatic, or manual operation.

(b) The equipment systems may be installed in raceways and boxes with general wiring.

(c) The equipment system shall be connected to equipment listed in Sections 517-20(d) and (e). It may be also connected to equipment listed in Section 517-20(f).

(d) The following components of the equipment system shall be arranged for automatic restoration of operation: (1) Central vacuum and medical air systems serving medical and surgical functions; (2) Sump pumps and other equipment including associated control systems and alarms required to operate for the safety of essential apparatus.

(e) The following required components of the equipment system shall be arranged for either automatic or manual connection to the alternate power source:

(1) Heating equipment for heating of operating, delivery, labor, recovery, and patient rooms, and intensive care units and nurseries.

Exception: Patient room heating during disruption of normal source under either of the following conditions:

a. The outside air design temperature is higher than −7°C, (+20°F).

This is based on the median of extremes as shown in the 1967 edition of the American Society of Heating, Air Conditioning and Refrigeration Engineers Handbook of Fundamentals.

b. The hospital is served by at least two utility services, each supplied by separate generating sources or a network distribution system fed by two or more generators. The utility services shall be routed, connected, and protected so that a fault any place between the generators and the hospital will not likely cause an interruption of more than one of the utility services.

(2) Elevator service that will reach every patient floor, ground floors, and floors on which surgical suites and obstetrical delivery suites are located. This shall include connections for cab lighting and control and signal systems.

In instances where interruption of power will result in an elevator stopping between floors, it may be desirable to provide throw-over facilities to allow the temporary operation of any elevator to release patients or other persons who may be trapped between floors.

(3) Supply and exhaust ventilating systems for laboratory fume hoods, and surgical suites, obstetrical suites, infant nurseries, and emergency treatment spaces where such areas contain no windows.

(f) The following components of the equipment system may be arranged for either automatic or manual connection to the alternate source:

(1) Selected autoclaving equipment if electrically heated or controlled.

(2) Other selected equipment in locations such as kitchens, laundries, radiological and central refrigeration rooms.

It is desirable that where heavy interruption currents can be anticipated, the transferred load may be reduced by use of multiple transfer devices. For example, elevator feeders may cause less hazard to electrical continuity if they are fed through individual transfer devices.

517-30. Power Sources.

(a) Essential electrical systems shall have a minimum of two independent sources of power: a normal source generally supplying the entire hospital and an alternate source(s) for use when the normal source is interrupted.

(b) The alternate source of power shall be a generator set(s) driven by some form of prime mover, and located on the premises.

Exception: Where the normal source consists of generating units on the premises, the alternate source shall be either another generating set, or an external utility service.

(c) For the greatest assurance of continuity of electrical service, facilities should be served by two separate full-capacity external services (Section 700-9), connected in such a manner as to pick up the load automatically and so arranged that the load will not be transferred to the generator set(s) if either external service is energized.

(d) All equipment shall be located to minimize the hazards that might cause complete failure of the equipment, such as floods, fires and icing.

(e) Electrical characteristics of the generator set(s) shall be suitable for the operation of all lighting and equipment to be served.

517-40. Switching and Overcurrent Protection.

(a) The emergency system and the equipment system shall be so arranged that in the event of interruption of the normal power source, an alternate power source shall be automatically connected within 10 seconds to the distribution panels connected to the emergency system and to the time-delay and/or manually operated switches connected to the equipment system. Where one or more generators are provided in addition to one or more external services as alternate sources, the automatic connection sequence shall connect either the alternate external service or the generator(s), whichever is arranged for automatic connection.

If the external service and the generator(s) are both arranged for automatic connection, the order of connection to these alternate power sources is an optional design choice.

(b) Automatic switching equipment shall be approved for emergency service and shall be designed and installed with interlocking provisions that will prevent interconnection of normal and alternate sources or any two separate sources of power in any operation of the automatic switching equipment. The equipment shall be so connected that the load will be served by the normal power source, except when the normal source is interrupted. Controls and switching equipment shall be so arranged that interruption of the normal sources will automatically start an alternate source generator, automatically disconnect the interrupted normal source of power, and connect the alternate source of power in proper sequence. If a generator is the only alternate source of power time shall be allowed, but not more than 10 seconds, for the generator to attain rated voltage before its connection. Upon transfer from the normal power source to the alternate power source the loads connected to the emergency system shall be automatically energized immediately. The loads connected onto the equipment system shall be connected either automatically or manually after a time delay in such sequential manner as not to overload the generator.

When the normal power source is restored, the automatic transfer devices shall disconnect the alternate source and restore service connection to the normal power source, permitting the operation of manual switches to reconnect the normal power source.

For automatic operation, a time-delay feature should be provided to avoid short-time re-establishment of the normal source which could cause erratic operation of the transfer switch. This time delay should be set for a minimum of 15 minutes.

(c) The provisions of Section 700-18 shall apply to switches installed in exit lighting circuits.

Exception: As provided in Section 700-20(b) switching arrangements to transfer corridor lighting in patient areas to fixtures designed for night lighting.

For more details, see Life Safety Code, NFPA No. 101-1970.

(d) The provisions of Section 700-18, with respect to the location and installation of switches in lighting circuits other than those controlling exit lighting and exit directional signs, shall apply. Personnel ordinarily assigned to work in an area illuminated by fixtures connected to the emergency system shall be considered as authorized personnel.

This paragraph applies particularly to ungrounded circuits in anesthetizing locations connected to emergency systems.

(e) The life safety branch, the life support branch, the critical branch and the equipment system shall be protected by overcurrent devices so that interruption of service in other wiring systems, due to internal failure, will not interrupt supply to these branches or systems.

Exception: The life safety branch and the life support branch may be supplied through a single transfer device, provided that the life support branch load is smaller than the life safety branch load.

Note 1: Some small hospitals do not have intensive care units and have only a minimum of other connections on the life support branch. The life safety and life support loads may be adequately served through a single transfer device.

Note 2: It is extremely important that the various overcurrent devices in the emergency and equipment systems be coordinated to protect against cascading operation on short-circuit faults. Primary consideration should also be given to prevent overloading of equipment by limiting the possibilities of large current inrushes due to instantaneous re-establishment of connections to heavy loads.

▶ Basically the life safety branch, the life support branch and the critical branch must each be served by separate transfer switches. However, the life safety branch and the life support branch may be served from the same transfer switch if the life support branch load is smaller than the life safety branch load.

According to Section 517-11*b3* the critical branch and the life support branch may be combined at the discretion of the hospital administration and with the approval of the authority having jurisdiction.

(f) The electrical characteristics of the transfer switches shall be suitable for the connected load.

The capacity of transfer switches should be adequate to carry full-load currents and to withstand the thermal and electromagnetic effects of short-circuit currents.

D. Electrically Susceptible Patient Areas

517-50. General. It is the purpose of Part D to specify the performance criteria and/or wiring methods which will minimize the hazard by the maintenance of adequately low-potential differences between conductors which could be contacted by a patient even when pertinent inherent equipment leakage currents exceed 10 microamperes.

In a health care facility, it is not feasible to prevent the occurrence of a conductive or capacitive path from the patient's body to some grounded object, because that path may be established accidentally or through instrumentation directly connected to the patient. All other electrically conductive surfaces which may make an additional contact with the patient, or other instruments which may be connected to the patient, then become possible sources of electrical currents which can traverse the patient's body. When the current path includes a small area of direct contact with the heart, a current in excess of 10 microamperes could be hazardous. Unless special precaution[s] are taken, the power-line-frequency impedance of the patient circuit, which includes the internal conduction path through a small contact area, could be as low as 500 ohms when measured at low-current magnitudes. Under these conditions a voltage difference between the points of patient contact in excess of 5 millivolts also is considered hazardous.

517-51. Performance.

(a) In electrically susceptible patient areas the maximum 60-hertz alternating-current potential difference between any two conducting surfaces within the reach of a patient, or those persons touching the patient, shall not exceed 5 millivolts measured across 500 ohms under normal operating conditions or in case of any probable failure.

▶　　Sections 517-50 and 517-51*a* provide strict performance specifications for systems and equipment in electrically susceptible patient areas; and Part D of Article 517 was introduced in the 1971 National Electrical Code in such a way as to require close attention by hospital personnel, electrical consultants and equipment manufacturers to the potential hazards confronting electrically susceptible patients (see definition in Section 517-2). The fine print note in Section 517-50 appropriately describes the low current and voltage levels (10 microamperes and 5 millivolts) which could cause ventricular fibrillation if electrically susceptible patients contact faulty electrical equipment. An essential part of electrical systems for such areas is an adequate *equipotential* grounding system. Such grounding systems are used to bond all metallic parts within reach of a patient to prevent a difference of potential between metallic components of not more than 5 millivolts.

Bonding can be reduced by using nonmetallic furniture, equipment and similar devices. Where metallic devices are used Section 517-51*b* describes the specific grounding requirements.

Existing standards for hospital safety provide protection against the traditional hazards of electricity, fire and explosion in the design of hospitals, and for the safe operation of specific equipment in hazardous locations. The increasing use of electric appliances and development of surgical and monitoring procedures based on new electric investigative, diagnostic and therapeutic equipment creates additional hazards to the patient. Some procedures require the introduction of electric conductors directly into the heart. These instruments may offer little hazard when used individually, but in conjunction with other devices, their electrical interaction may introduce a unique hazard for the particular patient which is not apparent to the operator.

Some instruments may be hazardous because of prolonged application of pressure, heat, or electric current. Others apply high voltage for their effect, and, like the cardiac defibrillator, are safe only if properly designed and maintained, and used by an operator who is skilled in their use.

At this writing considerable effort is being made to establish appropriate standards for electrical equipment used in electrically susceptible patient areas. An important standard on the subject is Underwriters' Laboratories, Inc. Standard No. 544, Standards for Safety, Medical and Dental Equipment, and revisions to this Standard are being processed to assure compliance of Part D of Article 517. Also, under consideration at this writing are tentative interim amendments to clarify some of the provisions in Part D. A major consideration concerns the status of the isolated power system (ungrounded 120-volt AC power supply with a line isolation monitor).

Under normal operating conditions the isolated power system supplies a high degree of protection, particularly from macroshock conditions (normal line-to-ground shock hazards). It also provides excellent protection from microshock hazards (above 10 microamperes) as long as all grounding conductors are intact. The present question being posed is whether or not to accept a *single* highly reliable equipment ground connection which can be tested frequently. Announcements in this regard should be forthcoming in the near future.

Other approaches for reliable grounding are redundant grounds (more than one for each unit) or monitors to indicate the status of grounds.

Because of numerous advantages the isolation power system and a line isolation monitor are being widely used and specified in electrically susceptible patient areas. Figure 517-3 shows a complete unit, which consists

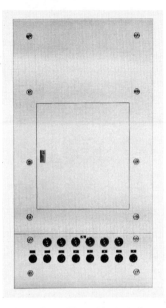

FIG. 517-3. Assembly with isolation transformer, dynamic-type line isolation monitor and reference grounding bus receptacles of the plug-in-jack type. (*Sorgel Electric Corp., Subsidiary of Square D. Co.*)

of a line isolation monitor, and a reference grounding bus, complete with grounding-type receptacles. Figure 517-4 shows equalizer ground bus modules with power receptacles and a plug-in grounding jack.

In addition to isolated power systems a study is underway to develop an adequate grounding system for use with conventional 120-volt grounded systems. Another concept is to completely isolate electrically susceptible patients from all possible grounds, but this is extremely difficult to achieve and maintain.

Fig. 517-4. Module with 120-volt power receptacles (lower) and grounding plugs with one jack inserted. (*Sorgel Electric Corp. Subsidiary of Square D. Co.*)

An important manual, which describes safety criteria, is NFPA No. 76 BM—Safe Use of Electricity in Hospitals. This manual describes the hazards, their acceptable limits, the principles for design and testing for safety of electric services and equipment, and offers suggestions for safe use, inspection, and maintenance. It is not intended to inhibit design, but rather to provide a guide to *minimal* safety criteria. It can be argued that a device which gives wrong information is dangerous; however, performance (except relating to *direct* injury to patient and personnel in patient care areas) is not covered in this manual. While this manual describes the performance requirements for safe operation, it is not intended to be a design manual. Reference is made to good design for illustration only, and where included, indicates one possible way to achieve the desired performance.

The safe use of electricity in hospitals is complex. A safety program must incorporate sufficient redundancy to tolerate the carelessness inherent in human behavior. Purchasing specifications, preventive maintenance schedules, and training programs each contribute. Because they are more amenable to specification and control, primary dependence must be placed on structure and equipment. To attain continued safe operation, greater emphasis must be placed on inspection, maintenance, and training.

Fig. 517-5. Transparent, fused attachment plug for use with biomedical equipment. (*Daniel Woodhead Co.*)

Figure 517-5 shows a transparent, fused attachment plug that permits a constant visual check of wiring connections, and a small fuse, sized according to the rating of an equipment, will disconnect a faulty unit without opening the entire branch circuit. Such attachment plugs have been developed to protect delicate biomedical equipment, which has no internal fuse protection. Figure 517-6 shows a portable field probe that will detect leakage currents as low as 5 microamperes. Equipment such as this is extremely useful in a well-planned hospital preventative maintenance program.

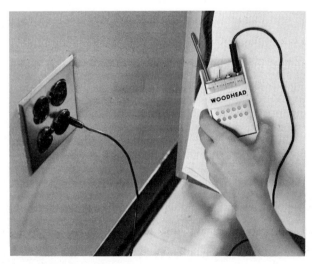

Fig. 517-6. Portable field probe to detect leakage currents, static electricity and open grounds. (*Daniel Woodhead Co.*)

(b) Special Grounding Requirements.

(1) A patient reference grounding bus shall be provided within 5 feet of each patient bed, and shall contain approved connectors for the grounding of all metal or conductive furnishings or other nonelectrical equipment.

The patient reference grounding bus is intended to assure that all electrically conductive surfaces within reach of the patient are at the same electrical potential (within 5 millivolts). Therefore, any such surface, which might become electrically energized, should be connected to it. This requirement is not intended to apply to devices such as bed pans and other small portable nonelectrical devices.

(2) One patient reference grounding bus may serve more than one patient, but one patient shall not be served by more than one patient reference grounding bus.

(3) A separate, insulated, continuous, stranded, copper grounding conductor, not smaller than No. 12 AWG, shall be installed with the circuit conductors in the approved wiring system which connects each patient receptacle including the receptacle grounding terminal to the same patient reference grounding bus. Receptacles grouped in a common enclosure shall be connected by a single grounding conductor to the same patient reference grounding bus.

(4) The grounding conductor connecting any receptacle for that patient and the patient reference grounding bus shall not exceed 15 feet in length.

(5) An approved means of frequent periodic testing for continuity between the patient reference grounding bus and patient-connected equipment shall be provided.

The continuity tester may be either permanently mounted or portable. It should be so designed that the testing does not endanger the patient, even if grounding integrity is lost. The continuity test must include the path through all connections and grounding conductors between each piece of equipment and the patient reference grounding bus.

(6) The patient reference grounding bus and the room reference grounding bus, where separated, shall be interconnected by a continuous, insulated, stranded, copper conductor not smaller than No. 10 AWG.

(7) The room reference grounding bus shall be connected by a continuous, insulated, stranded, copper conductor, not smaller than No. 10 AWG, to the nearest available effectively grounded structural metal member of the building or to the nearest available effectively grounded metal water pipe. The room reference grounding bus may also be connected to the grounding bus in the electrical panelboard, provided that there is an individual grounding conductor, sized in accordance with Table 250-95, connected to the building service grounding point.

(8) All exposed noncurrent-carrying conductive metal surfaces, which may be within reach of the patient or within reach of persons touching the patient (e.g., gas, suction, water, heating, and drain pipes; conduits unrelated to the electrically susceptible patient area electric power distribution system; ducts; portable partitions; structural metal door or window frames), shall be connected to the room reference grounding bus.

(9) Grounding of all metallic raceways shall be assured by means of grounding bushings on all conduit terminations at the panelboard and by means of an insulated, continuous, stranded, copper grounding conductor, not smaller than

No. 12 AWG, extended from the grounding bus in the panelboard to the conduit grounding bushings.

(10) Grounding of metallic switch and receptacle plates shall be provided by means of the mounting-screw connections to the device mounting yokes.

(11) When using a suitable low-voltage transformer and resistor to apply a current of approximately 20 amperes between the room reference grounding bus and each grounding terminal, including each grounding contact of each receptacle, the voltage drop measured between the test points shall not exceed one volt.

For additional information on grounding, including specifications for grounding jacks and plugs, see Inhalation Anesthetics Standard, NFPA No. 56A-1971.

▶   Patient protection is provided primarily by an adequate grounding system. The ungrounded secondary of an isolation transformer permits smaller sizes of the grounding conductors used to protect the patient against a fault-current voltage by reducing the maximum current where a single *line-to-ground fault* occurs.

With such a fault the line isolation monitor provides a warning so that proper corrections can be made. However, the monitor will not indicate an *open* ground.

Excessive current in the grounding conductors will not create a hazard to the patient unless a second fault occurs or an equipment grounding conductor becomes open.

For example, if the current in the grounding system does not exceed 10 milliamperes, even under fault conditions, the voltage across 10 feet of No. 12 copper wire will not exceed 0.2 millivolt, or the voltage across 10 feet of a No. 18 grounding conductor in a flexible cord will not exceed 0.8 millivolt. Assuming 0.1 millivolt across each connector, the voltage between two pieces of patient-connected equipment will not exceed 2 millivolts.

The patient reference grounding bus and the grounding connections to it will assure the detection of any first fault on the isolated system. At the same time the patient and staff will also be protected from excessive voltage if the fault is promptly located and corrected.

The room reference grounding bus will assure proper bonding of all electrically conductive metal surfaces.

Regardless of what system or concept is used, grounding connections must remain intact to provide overall safety to patients and staff personnel.

E. Inhalation Anesthetizing Locations

For further information regarding safeguards for anesthetizing locations, see Inhalation Anesthetics Standard, NFPA No. 56A-1971.

517-60. Hazardous Areas.

(a) Any room or space in which flammable anesthetics or volatile flammable disinfecting agents are stored shall be considered to be a Class I, Division 1 location throughout.

(b) In a flammable anesthetizing location the entire area shall be considered to be a Class I, Division 1 location, which shall extend upward to a level 5 feet above the floor.

517-61. Wiring and Equipment Within Hazardous Areas.

(a) In hazardous areas as defined in Section 517-60, all fixed wiring and equipment, and all portable equipment, including lamps and other utilization equipment, operating at more than 8 volts between conductors, shall conform to the requirements of Sections 501-1 through 501-15 and Sections 501-16(a) and (b) for Class I, Division 1 locations. All such equipment shall be specifically approved for the hazardous atmospheres involved.

(b) Where a box, fitting or enclosure is partially, but not entirely, within a hazardous area, the hazardous area shall be considered to be extended to include the entire box, fitting or enclosure.

(c) Flexible cords, which are or may be used in hazardous areas for connection to portable utilization equipment, including lamps operating at more than 8 volts between conductors, shall be of a type approved for extra-hard usage, shall be of ample length, and shall include an additional conductor for grounding. A storage device for the flexible cord shall be provided, and shall not subject the cord to bending at a radius of less than 3 inches.

(d) Anesthetizing-location receptacles and attachment plugs in hazardous areas shall be of the approved type for services of prescribed voltage, frequency, rating, and number of conductors with provision for the connection of the grounding conductor. The attachment plugs shall be designed for use without adapters in Class I, Group C hazardous locations, and shall be interchangeable with locking-type general-purpose receptacles in nonhazardous areas [See Figures 517-2(a) and (b)]. This requirement shall apply to caps and receptacles of the two-pole, 3-wire grounding-type for single-phase 125-volt AC service.

See Section 24037 of the Inhalation Anesthetics Standard, NFPA 56A-1971, for further information.

▶ The caps and receptacles shown in Figs. 517-2*a* and *b* are for use in nonhazardous areas—above the 5-foot level or in a nonhazardous anesthetizing area. There are receptacles and caps available that may be installed in Class I, Group C hazardous locations, and although the configurations are quite similar to those shown in Figs. 517-2*a* and *b*, they differ in that the hazardous location receptacle will reject the cap shown in Fig. 517-2*b*. A cap suitable for use in the Class I, Group C hazardous location will fit in either the nonhazardous location receptacle shown in Fig. 517-2*a* or a hazardous location receptacle. To avoid complications it is best to install the receptacles shown in Fig. 517-2*a* in the nonhazardous areas of an anesthetizing location.

517-62. Wiring and Equipment in Nonhazardous or Above Hazardous Anesthetizing Areas.

(a) Wiring above a hazardous area as defined in Section 517-60 or in a nonhazardous anesthetizing area shall be installed in metal raceways or shall be Type MI cable, or Type ALS cable.

(b) Equipment which may produce arcs, sparks or particles of hot metal, such as lamps and lampholders for fixed lighting, cutouts, switches, receptacles, generators, motors, or other equipment having make-and-break or sliding contacts, shall be of the totally enclosed type or so constructed as to prevent escape of sparks or hot metal particles.

(c) Surgical and other lighting fixtures shall conform to Section 501-9(b).

Exception No. 1: The surface temperature limitations set forth in Section 501-9(b)(2) shall not apply.

Exception No. 2: Integral or pendant switches which are located above and cannot be lowered into the hazardous area need not be explosion-proof.

(d) Approved seals shall be provided in conformance with Section 501-5, and Section 501-5(a)(3) shall apply to horizontal as well as to vertical boundaries of the defined hazardous areas.

Exception: Seals may be located within 18 inches of the point at which a conduit emerges from a wall forming the boundary of an anesthetizing location if all of the following conditions are met.

a. The junction box, switch or receptacle contains a seal-off device between the arcing contacts and the conduit.

b. The conduit is continuous (without coupling or fitting) between the junction box and the sealing fitting within 18 inches of the point where the conduit emerges from the wall.

(e) Anesthetizing-location receptacles and attachment plugs in nonhazardous or above hazardous anesthetizing areas shall be of the approved type for services of prescribed voltage, frequency, rating, and number of conductors with provision for the connection of the grounding conductor. This requirement shall apply to attachment plugs and receptacles of the two-pole, 3-wire grounding-type for single-phase 125-volt AC service as shown in Figures 517-2(a) and (b).

▶   See comments following Section 517-61*d*.

517-63. Circuits in Anesthetizing Locations.

(a) Except as provided in Section 517-63(f), each circuit within, or partially within, an anesthetizing location as defined in Section 517-60 shall be controlled by a switch having a disconnecting pole in each circuit conductor, and shall be isolated from any distribution system supplying areas other than anesthetizing locations. Such isolation may be obtained by means of one or more transformers having no electrical connection between primary and secondary windings, by means of motor-generator sets, or by means of suitably isolated batteries.

(b) Circuits supplying primaries of isolating transformers shall operate at not more than 300 volts between conductors, and shall be provided with proper overcurrent protection. Secondary voltage of such transformers shall not exceed 300 volts between conductors, and all circuits supplied from such secondaries shall be ungrounded and shall have an approved overcurrent device of proper rating in each conductor. Circuits supplied from batteries or from generators or motor-generator sets shall be ungrounded, and shall be protected against overcurrent in the same manner as transformer-fed secondary circuits.

(c) Transformers, motor-generator sets, batteries and battery chargers, together with their overcurrent devices, shall be installed in nonhazardous locations, and shall conform to the requirements of this Code for such locations.

(d) In addition to the usual control and overcurrent protection the ungrounded system shall be provided with a line isolation monitor so arranged that a green signal lamp, conspicuously visible to persons in the anesthetizing location, remains lighted while the system is isolated from ground. An adjacent red signal lamp and an audible warning signal shall be energized when the total current (consisting of resistive and capacitive leakage currents) from either isolated conductor to ground reads 2 milliamperes under nominal voltage conditions. The line isolation monitor shall not give warning for a total hazard current less than 1.7 ma. The line isolation monitor shall be designed to have sufficient internal impedance so that, when properly connected to the isolated system, the maximum internal current that can flow through the line isolation monitor, when any point of the isolated system is grounded, is 1 ma. An ammeter, calibrated in the total hazard current of the system, shall be mounted in a plainly visible place on the line isolation monitor with the "alarm-on" (total hazard current = 2 ma) zone at approximately the center of the scale.

▶ The line-isolation-monitor meter reading includes the hazard current of its metering circuit, and therefore exceeds the milliammeter reading made during the line-impedance test. Accordingly, it is desirable to limit the size of the isolation transformer to 10 kva or less and to use conductor insulation with low leakage. Short branch-circuit runs and the use of conductor insulation with a dielectric constant less than 3.5 and an insulation resistance constant greater than 20,000 at 60°F will reduce line-to-ground leakage to an acceptable level.

For maintenance tests of the line isolation monitor see Section 3422 of the Inhalation Anesthetics Standard, NFPA No. 56A-1971.

(e) A branch circuit supplying an anesthetizing location shall supply no other location.

(f) Branch circuits supplying only fixed lighting fixtures in nonhazardous areas of anesthetizing locations other than surgical lighting fixtures or supplying only approved permanently installed X-ray equipment may be supplied by a conventional grounded system, provided: (1) wiring for grounded and ungrounded circuits does not occupy the same raceways; (2) the lighting fixtures and the X-ray equipment (except the enclosed X-ray tube and the metal-enclosed high-voltage leads to the tube) are located at least 8 feet above the floor or outside the anesthetizing location; and (3) switches for the grounded circuits are located outside of the anesthetizing location.

Note 1: For a description of approved permanently installed X-ray equipment see Section 24034 of the Inhalation Anesthetics Standard, NFPA No. 56A-1971.

Note 2: Remote-control stations for remote-control switches may be installed in the anesthetizing location if the remote-control circuit is energized from the ungrounded distribution system.

517-64. Low-Voltage Equipment and Instruments.

(a) Low-voltage equipment which is frequently in contact with the bodies of persons or has exposed current-carrying elements shall:

(1) Operate on an electrical potential of 8 volts or less, or

(2) Be approved as intrinsically safe or double-insulated equipment,

(3) Be moisture resistant.

(b) Power shall be supplied to low-voltage equipment from:

(1) An individual isolating transformer (autotransformers shall not be used) connected to an outlet receptacle by means of an anesthetizing location cord and attachment plug, or

(2) A common isolating transformer installed in a nonhazardous location, or

(3) From individual dry-cell batteries, or

(4) From common batteries made up of storage cells located in a nonhazardous location.

(c) Isolating-type transformers for supplying low-voltage circuits shall:

(1) Have approved means for insulating the secondary circuit from the primary circuit, and

(2) Have the core and case grounded in an approved manner.

(d) Resistance or impedance devices may be used to control low-voltage equipment but shall not be used to limit the maximum input voltage.

(e) Battery-powered appliances shall not be capable of being charged while in operation unless their charging circuitry incorporates an integral isolating-type transformer.

(f) Any receptacle or attachment plug used on low-voltage circuits shall be of a type which does not permit interchangeable connection with circuits of higher voltage.

It should be recognized that any interruption of the circuit, even circuits as low as 8 volts, either by any switch, or loose or defective connections anywhere in the circuit, may produce a spark sufficient to ignite flammable anesthetic agents. (See Section 24037 of the Inhalation Anesthetics Standard, NFPA No. 56A-1971).

517-65. Other Equipment.

(a) Suction, pressure, or insufflation equipment involving electrical elements, and located or used within a hazardous area shall be approved for Class I locations.

(b) X-ray equipment installed or operated in an anesthetizing location as defined in Section 517-60 shall be provided with approved means for preventing accumulation of electrostatic charges. All X-ray control devices, switches, relays, meters, and transformers shall be totally enclosed, and where installed or operated within a hazardous area, shall be approved for Class I, Group C locations. High-voltage wiring shall be effectively insulated from ground and adequately guarded against accidental contact. The entire installation shall comply with Article 660.

(c) Equipment for generating high-frequency currents or voltages used in electrocautery, diathermy, television, etc., where installed or used in an anesthetizing location, shall conform to Sections 517-61 and 517-62.

517-66. Grounding. In any anesthetizing area, all metallic raceways, and all noncurrent-carrying conductive portions of fixed or portable equipment including the conductive floor shall be grounded.

Exception: Equipment operating at not more than 8 volts between conductors need not be grounded.

F. Communications, Signaling Systems, and Data Systems

517-80. Electrically Susceptible Patient Areas. Isolation and grounding equivalent to that required for the electrical distribution systems in this Article for these areas shall also be provided. See also Articles 725 and 800.

An acceptable alternate means of providing isolation for patient/nurse call systems is by the use of only nonelectrified signaling, communication or control devices held by the patient or within reach of the patient.

ARTICLE 520. THEATERS AND ASSEMBLY HALLS

A. General

520-1. Scope. The requirements of this Article shall apply to all buildings, or part of a building, designed, intended, or used for dramatic, operatic, motion-picture or other shows, and night clubs, dance halls, armories, sporting arenas, bowling alleys, public auditoriums, television studios and like buildings used for public assembly.

▶ Where only a part of a building is used as a theater, auditorium, or place of public assembly, these special requirements apply only to that part and do not necessarily apply to the entire building. A common example is a school building in which there is an auditorium used for dramatic or other performances. All special requirements of this chapter would apply to the auditorium, stage, dressing rooms, and main corridors leading to the auditorium but not to other parts of the building that do not pertain to the use of the auditorium for performances or entertainments.

520-2. Motion-Picture Projectors. Motion-picture equipment and its installation and use shall comply with Article 540.

520-3. Sound Reproduction. Sound-reproducing equipment and its installation shall comply with Article 640.

520-4. Wiring Method. The wiring method shall be metal raceways, Type ALS cable or Type MI cable except as follows:

Exception No. 1: As provided in Article 640, Sound Reproduction, in Article 800, Communication Circuits, and in Article 725 for Class 2 Remote Control and Signal Circuits.

Exception No. 2: Where the area intended for public assembly has a capacity of less than 200 persons, Type AC metal-clad cable as provided in Article 334 may be used, or for concealed work, concealed knob-and-tube work or nonmetallic sheathed cable as provided in Articles 324 and 336 may also be used.

For recommendations for determination of population capacity, refer to Life Safety Code (NFPA No. 101-1970).

Exception No. 3: The wiring for stage set lighting and stage effects and other wiring which is not fixed as to location shall be done with approved portable cables and approved flexible cords.

▶ Building laws usually require theaters and motion-picture houses to be of fireproof construction, hence practical considerations limit the types of concealed wiring for light and power chiefly to rigid conduit, electrical metallic tubing, and Types ALS and MI cables, except for small auditoriums.

Much of the stage lighting in a modern theater is provided by floodlights and projectors mounted in the ceiling or on the balcony front. In order that the projectors may be adjustable in position, they may be connected by plugs and short cords to suitable receptacles or "pockets."

520-5. Number of Conductors in Raceway.   The number of conductors permitted in any metal conduit or electrical metallic tubing for border or stage pocket circuits or for remote control conductors shall not exceed that shown in Table 1 of Chapter 9. When contained within an auxiliary gutter or a wireway, the sum of the cross sectional areas of all contained conductors at any cross section shall not exceed 20 per cent of the interior cross sectional area of the auxiliary gutter or wireway. The 30 conductor limitation of Section 362-5 or 374-5 shall not apply.

520-6. Enclosing and Guarding Live Parts.   Live parts shall be enclosed or guarded to prevent accidental contact by persons and objects. All switches shall be of the externally operable type. Rheostats shall be placed in approved cases or cabinets which enclose all live parts, having only the operating handles exposed.

B. Fixed Stage Switchboard

520-21. Dead Front.   Stage switchboards shall be of the dead-front type and shall conform to Part C of Article 384 unless approved for the purpose.

520-22. Guarding Back of Switchboard.   Stage switchboards having exposed live parts on the back of such boards shall be enclosed by the building walls, wire mesh grills, or by other approved methods. The entrance to this enclosure shall be by means of a self-closing door.

520-23. Control and Overcurrent Protection of Receptacle Circuits.   Means shall be provided at the stage switchboard for the control and individual overcurrent protection of branch circuits to stage and gallery receptacles used for portable stage equipment.

▶   The term *gallery receptacles* should be understood as including all receptacles, wherever they may be located, that are intended for the connection of stage lighting equipment. Circuits to such receptacles must of necessity be controlled at the same location as other stage lighting circuits.

520-24. Metal Hood.   A stage switchboard that is not completely enclosed dead-front and dead-rear or recessed into a wall shall be provided with a metal hood extending the full length of the board to protect all equipment on the board from falling objects.

▶   Because of the large amount of inflammable material always present on a stage, and because of the crowded space, a stage switchboard must have no live parts on the front, and the back must be so guarded as to keep unauthorized persons away from the space in back of the board. The best form of construction is a sheet-steel enclosure for the space between the back of the board and the wall, with a door at one end of the enclosure.

The more important stage switchboards are commonly of the remote-control type. Pilot switches mounted on the stage board control the operation of contactors installed in any convenient location where space is available, usually below the stage. The contactors in turn control the lighting circuits.

Figure 520-1 is the front view of a small stage switchboard of the partial remote-control type. The small handles at the lower part of the small panels operate 30-amp switches for direct control of all low-capacity circuits. For the control of heavier loads, the same type of switch is used to control magnetically operated contactors located at any convenient point, usually in a special room on a floor below the stage. The egg-shaped handles operate dimmers for individual circuits. The three large levers in a vertical row are for master operation of the dimmers for the three colors, while by means of the single lever at the left all or any desired part of the dimmers may be operated simultaneously.

The stage switchboard is usually built into a recess in the proscenium wall, as shown in the plan view, Fig. 520-2. After passing through the switches and dimmers, many of the main circuits must be subdivided into branch circuits so that no branch circuit will be loaded to more than 20 amp. Where

FIG. 520-1. Small stage switchboard of the partial remote-control type. (*Frank Adam Electric Co.*)

the board is of the remote-control type, the branch-circuit fuses are often mounted on the same panels as the contactors. Where a direct-control type of board is used, and sometimes where the board is remotely controlled, the branch-circuit fuses are mounted on special panelboards known as *magazine panels* which are installed in the space back of the switchboard, usually in the location of the junction box shown in Fig. 520-2.

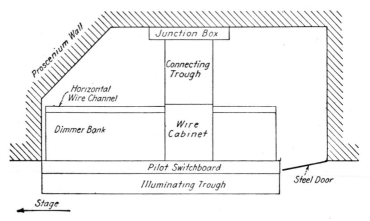

Fig. 520-2. Plan showing location of a stage switchboard in a recess in the proscenium wall.

520-25. Dimmers.   Dimmers shall conform to the following:

(a) Disconnection and Overcurrent Protection.   Where dimmers are installed in ungrounded conductors, each dimmer shall have overcurrent protection not greater than 125 per cent of the dimmer rating, and shall be disconnected from all ungrounded conductors when the master or individual switch or circuit-breaker supplying such dimmer is in the open position.

(b) Resistance or Reactor Type Dimmers.   Resistance or series reactor type dimmers may be placed in either the grounded or the ungrounded conductor of the circuit. Where designed to open either the supply circuit to the dimmer or the circuit controlled by it, the dimmer shall then comply with Section 380-1.

It is recommended that resistance or reactor type dimmers be placed in the grounded neutral conductor of the circuit provided they do not open the circuit.

(c) Autotransformer Type Dimmers.   The circuit supplying an autotransformer type dimmer shall not exceed 150 volts between conductors. The grounded conductor shall be common to the input and output circuits. See Section 200-4.

▶   Figure 520-3 shows typical connections of two branch circuits arranged for control by one switch and one dimmer plate or section. The single-pole switch on the stage switchboard is connected to one of the outside buses, and from this switch a wire runs to a short bus on the magazine panel The magazine panel is similar to an ordinary panelboard, except that it con-

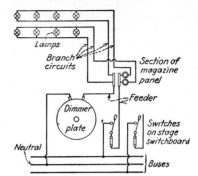

FIG. 520-3. Stage switchboard. Typical connections of control switch, dimmer plate, and one section of magazine panel for the control of two branch circuits.

tains no switches and the circuits are divided into many sections, each section having its own separate buses. One terminal of the dimmer plate, or variable resistor, is connected to the neutral bus at the switchboard and from the other terminal of the dimmer a wire runs to the neutral bus on the magazine panel. This neutral bus must be well insulated from ground and must be separate from other neutral buses on the panel, otherwise the dimmer would be shunted and would fail to control the brightness of the lamps.

While the dimmer is permanently connected to the neutral of the wiring system, this neutral is presumed to be thoroughly grounded and hence the dimmer is dead.

Figure 520-4 shows an autotransformer used as a dimmer. By changing the position of the movable contact, any desired voltage may be supplied to the lamps, from full line voltage to a voltage so low that the lamps are "black out." As compared with a resistance-type dimmer, a dimmer of this type has the advantages that it operates at a much higher efficiency, generates very little heat, and, within its maximum rating, the dimming effect is not dependent upon the wattage of the load it controls.

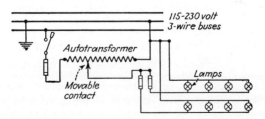

FIG. 520-4. Autotransformer dimmer.

C. Stage Equipment—Fixed

520-41. Circuit Loads. Footlights, border lights, and proscenium side lights shall be so arranged that no branch circuit supplying such equipment will carry a load exceeding 20 amperes; provided that where heavy-duty lampholders only are used, such circuits may conform to the provisions of Article 210 for circuits supplying heavy-duty lampholders.

520-42. Conductor Insulation. Foot, border, proscenium, or portable strip light fixtures shall be wired with conductors having insulation suitable for the temperatures at which the conductors will be operated and not less than 125°C (257°F). See Table 310-2(a).

520-43. Footlights.

(a) Where metal trough construction is employed for footlights, the trough containing the circuit conductors shall be made of sheet metal not lighter than No. 20 MSG treated to prevent oxidation. Lampholder terminals shall be kept at least ½ inch from the metal of the trough. The circuit conductors shall be soldered to the lampholder terminals.

(b) Where the metal trough construction specified in Section 520-43(a) is not used, footlights shall consist of individual outlets with lampholders, wired with rigid or flexible metal conduit, Type ALS cable or Type MI cable. The circuit conductors shall be soldered to the lampholder terminals. Disappearing footlights shall be so arranged that the current supply shall be automatically disconnected when the footlights are replaced in the recess designed therefor.

520-44. Borders and Proscenium Sidelights.

(a) Borders and proscenium sidelights shall be constructed as prescribed in Section 520-43, shall be suitably stayed and supported, and shall be so designed that the flanges of the reflectors or other adequate guards will protect the lamps from mechanical injury and from accidental contact with scenery or other combustible material.

▶   A footlight of the disappearing type might produce so high a temperature as to be a serious fire hazard if the lamps should be left burning after the footlight is closed.

There is no restriction on the number of lamps that may be supplied by one branch circuit. The lamp wattage supplied by one circuit should be such that the current will be slightly less than 20 amp.

Individual outlets as described here are seldom used for footlights as such construction would be much more expensive than the standard trough type.

A modern type of footlight is shown in Fig. 520-5. The wiring is carried in a sheet-iron wire channel in the face of which lamp receptacles are mounted. Each lamp is provided with an individual reflector and glass color screen or "roundel." The circuit wires are usually brought to the wire channel in rigid conduit. In the older type of footlight, still used to some extent, the lamps are placed vertically or nearly so, and an extension of one side of the wire channel is shaped so as to form a reflector to direct the light toward the stage.

(b) Cables for Border Lights. Cables for supply to border lights shall be Type S, SO, or ST flexible cord. See Table 400-11. The cables shall be suitably supported. Such cables shall be employed only where flexible conductors are necessary.

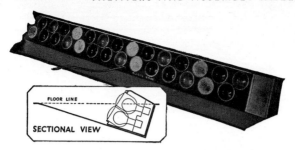

FIG. 520-5. Footlight with individual reflector for each lamp. (*Kliegl Bros.*)

► Figure 520-6 shows a border light of modern type as it appears when installed in place over the stage. Figure 520-7 is a cross section showing the construction of the border. This particular type is intended for the use of 200-watt lamps. An individual reflector is provided for each lamp so as to secure the highest possible efficiency of light utilization. A glass roundel is fitted to each reflector; these may be obtained in any desired color, commonly white, red, and blue for three-color equipment and white, red, blue, and amber for four-color equipment. A splice box is provided on top of the housing for enclosing the connections between the border-light cable and the wiring of the border. From this splice box, the wires are carried to the lamp sockets in a trough extending the entire length of the border.

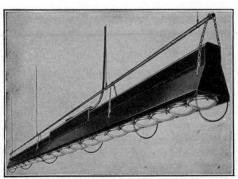

FIG. 520-6. Modern type of border light. (*Major Equipment Co.*)

Border lights are usually hung on steel cables so that their height may be adjusted and so that they may be lowered to the stage for cleaning and replacing lamps and color screens; hence the circuit conductors supplying the lamps must be carried to the border through a flexible cable. The individual conductors of the cable may be of No. 14, though No. 12 is more commonly used.

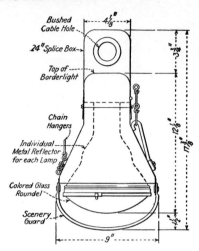

Bushed
Cable Hole

24" Splice Box

Top of
Borderlight

Chain
Hangers

Individual
Metal Reflector
for each Lamp

Colored Glass
Roundel

Scenery
Guard

FIG. 520-7. Construction of border light shown in Fig. 520-6. (*Major Equipment Co.*)

520-45. Receptacles. Receptacles intended for the supply of arc lamps shall have not less than 50 amperes capacity and shall be supplied by conductors not smaller than No. 6. Receptacles intended for the supply of incandescent lamps shall have not less than 20 amperes capacity and shall be supplied by conductors not smaller than No. 12. Plugs for arc and incandescent receptacles shall not be interchangeable.

520-46. Stage Pockets. Receptacles intended for the connection of portable stage lighting equipment shall be mounted in suitable pockets or enclosures, and shall comply with the requirements of Section 520-45.

FIG. 520-8. Stage floor pocket with a single receptacle. (*Kliegl Bros.*)

FIG. 520-9. A four-gang stage wall pocket designed for flush mounting. (*Major Equipment Co.*)

▶   Figure 520-8 shows a common form of stage pocket. A separate circuit of No. 6 should be installed to supply each arc receptacle and a separate circuit of No. 12 or larger to supply each incandescent receptacle.

Figure 520-9 shows a wall pocket designed for flush mounting and equipped with receptacles to receive the standard type of plug, the same as is used with floor pockets.

520-47. Lamps in Scene Docks.   Lamps installed in scene docks shall be so located and guarded as to be free from mechanical injury and provide an air space of not less than 2 inches between such lamps and any combustible material.

520-48. Curtain Motors.   Curtain motors having brushes or sliding contacts shall comply with one of the following conditions:

(a) Be of the totally enclosed, enclosed-fan-cooled, or enclosed-pipe-ventilated types.

(b) Be enclosed in separate rooms or housings built of noncombustible materials so constructed as to exclude flyings or lint, and properly ventilated from a source of clean air.

(c) Have brush or sliding-contact end of motor enclosed by solid metal covers.

(d) Have brushes or sliding contacts enclosed in substantial, tight, metal housings.

(e) Have the upper half of brush or sliding-contact end of the motor enclosed by a wire screen or perforated metal and the lower half enclosed by solid metal covers.

(f) Have wire screens or perforated metal placed at the commutator or brush ends. No dimension of any opening in the wire screen or perforated metal shall exceed .05 inch, regardless of the shape of the opening and of the material used.

520-49. Flue-Damper Control.   Where stage flue dampers are released by an electrical device, the circuit operating the latter shall be normally closed and shall be controlled by at least two externally operable switches, one switch being placed at the electrician's station and the other where designated by the authority having jurisdiction. The device shall be designed for the full voltage of the circuit to which it is connected, no resistance being inserted. The device shall be located in the loft above the scenery and shall be enclosed in a suitable iron box having a tight, self-closing door.

▶   A normally-closed-circuit device has the inherent safety feature that in case the control circuit is accidentally opened by the blowing of a fuse, or in any other way, the device immediately operates to open the flue dampers.

D. Portable Switchboards on Stage

520-51. Supply.   Portable switchboards shall be supplied only from outlets especially provided for this purpose. Such outlets shall include externally operable, enclosed fused switches or circuit breakers mounted on the stage wall or at the switchboard in locations readily accessible from the stage floor.

520-52. Overcurrent Protection.   Circuits from portable switchboards directly supplying equipment containing incandescent lamps of not over 300 watts shall be protected by overcurrent devices having a rating or setting of not more than

20 amperes. Circuits for lampholders over 300 watts may be used where over-current protection conforms to the provisions of Article 210. Other circuits shall be provided with overcurrent devices with a rating or setting not higher than the current required for the connected load.

520-53. Construction.   Portable switchboards for use on stages shall comply with the following:

(a) Enclosure.   Portable switchboards shall be placed within an enclosure of substantial construction which may be so arranged that the enclosure is open during operation. Enclosures of wood shall be completely lined with sheet metal of not less than No. 24 MSG, and shall be well galvanized, enamelled, or otherwise properly coated to prevent corrosion or be of a corrosion-resistant material.

(b) Live Parts.   Except as provided for dimmer faceplates in Section 520-53(e), there shall be no exposed live parts within the enclosure.

(c) Switches and Circuit Breakers.   All switches and circuit breakers shall be of the externally operable, enclosed type.

(d) Circuit Protection.   Overcurrent devices shall be provided in each un-grounded conductor of every circuit supplied through the switchboard. Enclosures shall be provided for all overcurrent devices in addition to the switchboard enclosure.

(e) Dimmers.   The terminals of dimmers shall be provided with enclosures, and dimmer faceplates shall be so arranged that accidental contact cannot be readily made with the faceplate contacts.

(f) Interior Conductors.   All conductors within the switchboard enclosure shall be stranded and, except for cables feeding to or from the switchboard, shall be asbestos-covered Type AA or other types approved for a maximum operating temperature of 200°C (392°F). Each conductor shall have an ampacity at least equal to the rating of the circuit breaker, switch or fuse which it supplies, except for conductors for incandescent lamp circuits having overcurrent protection not exceeding 20 amperes. Conductors shall be enclosed in metal troughs or securely fastened in position and shall be bushed where they pass through metal.

(g) Pilot Light.   A pilot light shall be provided within the enclosure and shall be so connected to the circuit supplying the board that the opening of the master switch will not cut off the supply to the lamp. This lamp shall be on an independent circuit having overcurrent protection of a rating or setting of not more than 15 amperes.

(h) Supply Connections.   The supply to a portable switchboard shall be by means of flexible cord (Type S, SO or ST) terminating within the switchboard enclosure or in an externally operable fused master switch or circuit breaker. The supply cable shall have sufficient ampacity to carry the total load on the switchboard and shall be protected by overcurrent devices.

(i) Cable Arrangement.   Cables shall be protected by bushings where they pass through enclosures and shall be so arranged that tension on the cable will not be transmitted to the connections.

(j) Terminals.   Terminals to which stage cables are connected shall be so located as to permit convenient access to the terminals. At terminals not provided with approved pressure connectors the following construction shall be employed:

(1)   For conductors of No. 10 or larger, solder lugs shall be used.

(2)   For conductors smaller than No. 10, the strands shall be soldered together where connected to clamps or binding screws not specifically approved as pressure connectors.

E. Stage Equipment—Portable

520-61. Arc Lamps. The construction of arc lamps shall be approved by the authorities having jurisdiction.

520-62. Portable Plugging Boxes. Portable plugging boxes shall conform to the following:

(a) Enclosure. The construction shall be such that no current-carrying part will be exposed.

(b) Receptacles and Overcurrent Protection. Each receptacle shall have a rating of not less than 30 amperes, and shall have overcurrent protection which shall be installed in an enclosure equipped with self-closing doors.

(c) Busbars and Terminals. Busbars shall have an ampacity equal to the sum of the ampere ratings of all the receptacles. Lugs shall be provided for the connection of the master cable.

520-63. Lights on Scenery.

(a) Brackets on scenery shall be wired internally and the fixture stem shall be carried through to the back of the scenery where a bushing shall be placed on the end of the stem, except that externally wired brackets or other fixtures may be used when wired with cords designed for hard usage which shall extend through scenery and without joint or splice in canopy of fixture back and terminate in an approved type stage connector located within 18 inches of the fixture, unless such location is impractical.

(b) Fixtures shall be securely fastened in place.

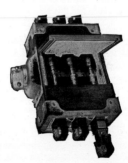

Fig. 520-10. Portable plugging box for stage use. (*Kliegl Bros.*)

520-64. Portable Strips. Portable strips shall be constructed in accordance with the requirements for border lights and proscenium side lights in Section 520-44(a). The supply cable shall be protected by bushings where it passes through metal and shall be so arranged that tension on the cable will not be transmitted to the connections. See Section 520-42 for wiring of portable strips.

520-65. Festoons. Joints in festoon wiring shall be staggered where practicable. Lamps enclosed in lanterns or similar devices of combustible material shall be equipped with approved guards.

▶   "Lanterns or similar devices" are very likely to be made of paper or other inflammable material and the lamps should be prevented from coming in contact with such material.

520-66. Special Effects.   Electrical devices used for simulating lightning, waterfalls, and the like, shall be so constructed and located that flames, sparks, or hot particles cannot come in contact with combustible material.

520-67. Cable Connectors.   Cable connectors for flexible conductors shall be so constructed that tension on the cord or cable will not be transmitted to the connections. See Section 400-10. The female half of the connector shall be attached to the line end of the cord or cable.

520-68. Conductors for Portables.   Flexible conductors used to supply portable stage equipment shall be Type S, SO or ST, except that reinforced cord may be used to supply stand lamps where the cord is not liable to severe physical damage and is protected by an overcurrent protection rated at not over 20 amperes.

F. Dressing Rooms

520-71. Pendant Lampholders.   Pendant lampholders shall not be installed in dressing rooms.

520-72. Lamp Guards.   All incandescent lamps in dressing rooms, where less than 8 feet from the floor, shall be equipped with open-end guards riveted to the outlet box cover or otherwise sealed or locked in place.

▶   Lamps in dressing rooms should be provided with guards that cannot easily be removed to prevent them from coming in contact with inflammable material.

520-73. Switches Required.   All lights and receptacles in dressing rooms shall be controlled by wall switches installed in the dressing rooms. Each switch controlling receptacles shall be provided with a pilot light to indicate when the receptacle or receptacles are energized.

G. Grounding

520-81. Grounding.   All metal raceways shall be grounded. The metal frames and enclosures of equipment including border lights shall be grounded, except the frames and enclosures of portable equipment on grounded circuits operating at not over 150 volts to ground and not within reach of grounded surfaces. Grounding, when employed, shall be done in the manner specified in Article 250.

ARTICLE 530. MOTION-PICTURE STUDIOS AND SIMILAR LOCATIONS

A. General

530-1. Scope. The requirements of this Article shall apply to television studios (except as covered in Section 520-1), motion-picture studios, exchange, factory, laboratory, stage, or a portion of the building in which motion-picture films more than ⅞ inch in width are manufactured, exposed, developed, printed, cut, edited, rewound, repaired or stored.

For the purpose of this Article, a motion-picture studio is one in which photographic film is used to record action. A television studio shall mean one which employs the use of electronic cameras only.

For recommendations for protection against cellulose nitrate film hazards refer to NFPA Standard for the Storage and Handling of Cellulose Nitrate Motion Picture Film (No. 40-1967).

▶ The term *motion-picture studio* is commonly used as meaning a large space, sometimes 100 acres or more in extent, enclosed by walls or fences within which are several "stages," a number of spaces for outdoor setups, warehouses, storage sheds, separate buildings used as dressing rooms, a large substation, a restaurant, and other necessary buildings. The so-called "stages" are large buildings containing numerous temporary and semipermanent setups for both indoor and outdoor views.

The Code rules for motion-picture studios are intended to apply only to those locations where special hazards exist. Such special hazards are confined to the buildings in which films are handled or stored, the stages, and the outdoor spaces where inflammable temporary structures and equipment are used. Some of these special hazards are due to the presence of a considerable quantity of highly inflammable film, otherwise the conditions are much the same as on a theater stage and, in general, the same rules should be observed as in the case of theater stages.

B. Stage or Set

530-11. Permanent Wiring. The permanent wiring shall be Type ALS cable, Type MI cable or in approved metal raceways.

Exception: Communication circuits, and sound recording and reproducing equipment may be wired as permitted by the articles covering those installations. (See Articles 640 and 800).

530-12. Portable Wiring. The wiring for stage set lighting and stage effects, and other wiring which is not fixed as to location, shall be done with approved portable cables and approved flexible cords. This requirement shall not apply to portable lamps or other electrical equipment used as properties in a motion picture set, on a studio stage or lot, or on location.

530-13. Stage Lighting and Effects Control. Switches used for studio stage set lighting and effects (on the stages and lots and on location) shall be of the externally operable type. When contactors are used as the disconnecting means for fuses, an individual externally operable type switch (such as a tumbler switch) for the control of each contactor, shall be located at a distance of not more than six feet from the contactor, in addition to remote control switches.

Exception: A single externally operable switch may be used to simultaneously disconnect all the contactors on any one location board, where located at a distance of not more than 6 feet from the location board.

530-14. Plugging Boxes.   Each receptacle of plugging boxes shall have an ampacity of not less than 30 amperes.

530-15. Enclosing and Guarding Live Parts.

(a)   Live parts shall be enclosed or guarded to prevent accidental contact by persons and objects.

(b)   All switches shall be of the externally operable type.

(c)   Rheostats shall be placed in approved cases or cabinets which enclose all live parts, having only the operating handles exposed.

(d)   Current-carrying parts of "bull-switches," "location boards," "spiders," and plugging boxes shall be so enclosed, guarded, or located that persons cannot accidentally come into contact with them or bring conducting materials into contact with them.

530-16. Portable Lamps.   Portable lamps and work lights shall be equipped with approved portable cords, approved composition or metal-sheathed porcelain sockets and substantial guards.

Exception: The requirements of this Section shall not apply to portable lamps used as properties in a motion picture set or television stage set, on a studio stage or lot, or on location.

530-17. Portable Arc Lamps.   Portable arc lamps shall be substantially constructed. The arc shall be provided with an enclosure designed to retain sparks and carbons and to prevent persons or materials from coming into contact with the arc or bare live parts. The enclosures shall be ventilated. All switches shall be of the externally operable type.

530-18. Overcurrent Protection—Short Time Rating. *

General.   Automatic overcurrent protective devices (circuit breakers or fuses) for motion-picture studio stage set lighting and the stage cables for such stage set lighting, shall be as given in paragraphs (a) through (e) below.

Note: * Special consideration is given to motion-picture studios and similar locations because filming periods are of short duration.

(a) **Stage Cables.**   Stage cables for stage-set lighting shall be protected by means of overcurrent devices set at not more than 400 per cent of the values given in Tables 310-12 through 310-15 and Table 400-9(b).

(b) **Feeders.**   In buildings used primarily for motion-picture production the feeders from the substations to the stages shall be protected by means of overcurrent devices having suitable ampacity (generally located in the substation). The overcurrent devices may be double-pole, or two single-pole gang-operated devices may be used. There need be no pole or overcurrent coil in the neutral conductor. The overcurrent device setting for each feeder shall not exceed 400 per cent of the ampacity of the feeder, as given in Table 310-12 for the kind of insulation used.

(c) "Location Boards." Overcurrent protection (fuses or circuit breakers) shall be provided at the "location boards." The fuses in the "location boards" shall be not larger in rating than 400 per cent of the ampacity of the cables between the "location boards" and the plugging boxes.

(d) Plugging Boxes. Where plugging boxes are not provided with overcurrent protective devices, each cable or cord smaller than No. 8 supplied through a plugging box shall be attached to the plugging box by means of a plug containing two cartridge fuses or a circuit breaker. The rating of the fuses or the setting of the circuit breaker shall be not more than 400 per cent of the safe ampacity of the cables or cords as given in Tables 310-12, 310-13 and 400-9(b) for the kind of insulation used.

(e) Lighting. Work-lights, stand-lamps, and fixtures shall be connected to plugging boxes by means of plugs containing two cartridge fuses not larger than 20 amperes, or they may be connected to special outlets on circuits protected by fuses or circuit-breaker settings of not more than 20 amperes. Plug fuses shall not be used unless they are on the load side of the fuse or circuit breakers on the "location boards."

530-19. Sizing of Feeder Conductors: Television Studio Sets.

(a) General. The demand factors listed in Table 530-19(a) may be applied to that portion of the maximum possible connected load for studio or stage set lighting for all permanently installed feeders between substations and stages and to all permanently installed subfeeders between the main stage switchboard and stage distribution centers or location boards.

Table 530-19(a). Demand Factors for Stage Set Lighting

Total Stage Set Lighting Load (Wattage)	Feeder Demand Factor
First 50,000 or less at	100%
Next 50,001 to 100,000 at	75%
Next 100,001 to 200,000 at	60%
All over 200,000	50%

(b) Portable Feeders. A demand factor of 50 per cent of maximum possible connected load may be applied to all portable feeders.

530-20. Grounding. Conduit, metal-clad cable or metal raceways, and all non-current-carrying metal parts of appliances, devices and equipment shall be grounded as prescribed in Article 250. This shall not apply to pendant and portable lamps, nor to stage lighting and stage sound equipment, nor to other portable or semiportable special stage equipment, operating at not more than 150 volts to ground.

C. Dressing Rooms

530-31. Dressing Rooms. Fixed wiring in dressing rooms shall be installed in accordance with wiring methods covered in Chapter 3. Wiring for portable dressing rooms shall be of an approved type.

D. Viewing, Cutting and Patching Tables

530-41. Lamps at Tables. Only approved composition or metal-sheathed porcelain keyless lampholders, equipped with suitable means to guard lamps from physical damage and from film and film scrap, shall be used at patching, viewing and cutting tables.

E. Film Storage Vaults

530-51. Lamps in Cellulose Nitrate Film Storage Vaults. Lamps in cellulose nitrate film storage vaults shall be rigid fixtures of the glass enclosed and gasketed type. Lamps shall be controlled by a switch having a pole in each ungrounded conductor. This switch shall be located outside of the vault and provided with a pilot light to indicate whether the switch is on or off. This switch shall disconnect from all sources of supply all ungrounded conductors terminating in any outlet in the vault.

530-52. Motors and Other Electrical Equipment in Film Storage Vaults. No electric motors, heaters, portable lights, or other portable electric equipment shall be located in the film storage vaults.

F. Substations

530-61. Substations. Wiring and equipment above 600 volts shall conform to Article 710.

530-62. Low-Voltage Switchboards. On 600 volts or less switchboards shall conform to Article 384.

530-63. Overcurrent Protection of DC Generators. Three-wire DC generators shall have protection consisting of overcurrent devices having current ratings or settings in accordance with the generator rating. The overcurrent protective devices may be single-pole or two-pole and need not have a pole or overcurrent coil in the neutral lead (whether it is grounded or ungrounded).

530-64. Working Space and Guarding. Working space and guarding in permanent fixed substations shall conform to Sections 110-16 and 110-17. For guarding of live parts on motors and generators, see Sections 430-11 and 430-14. Switchboards for voltage of not more than 250 volts DC between conductors when located in substations or switchboard rooms accessible to qualified persons only need not be dead-front.

530-65. Portable Substations. Wiring and equipment in portable substations shall conform to the sections applying to installations in permanent fixed substations, but, due to the limited space available, the working spaces may be reduced, provided that the equipment shall be so arranged that the operator may do his work safely, and so that other persons in the vicinity cannot accidentally come into contact with current-carrying parts or bring conducting objects into contact with them while they are energized.

530-66. Grounding at Substations. Noncurrent-carrying metal parts shall be grounded except the frames of DC circuit breakers installed on switchboards.

ARTICLE 540. MOTION–PICTURE PROJECTORS

A. General

540-1. Scope. This Article applies to motion-picture projectors and associated equipment of the Professional and Nonprofessional Types.

B. Equipment and Projectors of the Professional Type

540-10. Professional Projector—Definition. The professional projector employs a 35-millimeter film which is 1⅜ inch wide and has on each edge 5.4 perforations per inch. Wider film such as 70-millimeter may be employed.

▶   According to the definitions of hazardous locations in Art. 500, a motion-picture booth is not classed as a hazardous location, even though the film is highly inflammable. The film is not volatile at ordinary temperatures and hence no inflammable gases are present, and the wiring installation need not be explosion-proof but should be made with special care to guard against fire hazards.

540-11. Enclosure. The professional type of projector, such as is commonly used in theaters and motion-picture houses, shall be located in an approved enclosure. Such enclosure shall not be considered as a hazardous location as defined in Article 500.

540-12. Motor-Driven Projectors. Motor-driven projectors shall be approved for the purpose as an assembly or shall comply with all of the following conditions:

    (a) An approved projector shall be used.

    (b) An approved projector lamp shall be used.

    (c) Motors shall be so designed or guarded as to prevent ignition of film by sparks or arcs.

    (d) Projectors shall be in charge of a qualified operator.

▶   Figure 540-1 shows the arrangement of the apparatus and wiring in the projection room of a large modern motion-picture theater. This room, or booth, contains three motion-picture projectors P, one stereopticon or "effect machine" L, and two spot machines S.

The light source in each of the six machines is an arc lamp operated on d-c. The d-c supply is obtained from two motor-generator sets which are installed in the basement in order to avoid any possible interference with the sound-reproducing apparatus. The two motor generators are remotely controlled from the generator panel in the projection room. From each generator a feeder consisting of two 500,000-cir mil cables is carried to the d-c panelboard in the projection room.

From the d-c panelboard to each picture machine and to each of the two spot machines a branch circuit is provided consisting of two No. 00 cables. One of these conductors leads directly to the machine; the other side of

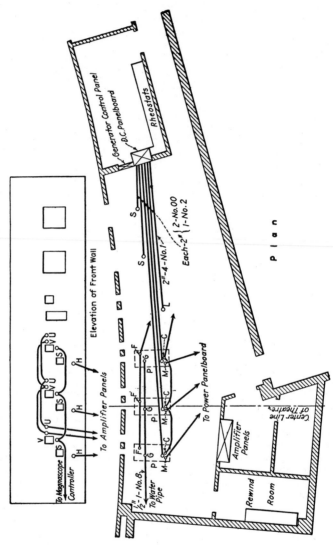

FIG. 540-1. Plan of projection room in a modern motion-picture theater. (*Edwards Electric Construction Co.*)

the circuit is led through the auxiliary gutter to the bank of resistors in the rheostat room and from its rheostat to the machine. The resistors are provided with short-circuiting switches so that the total resistance in series with each arc may be preadjusted to any desired value.

Two circuits consisting of No. 1 conductors are carried to the stereopticon or "effect machine," since this machine contains two arc lamps.

The conduit leading to each machine is brought up through the floor.

It is provided in Section 540-13 that the wires to the projector outlet shall not be smaller than No. 8 but in every case the maximum current drawn by the lamp should be ascertained and conductors should be installed of sufficient size to carry this current. In this case, when suitably adjusted for the large pictures, the arc in each projector takes a current of nearly 150 amp.

In addition to the main outlet for supplying the arc, four other outlets are installed at each projector-machine location for auxiliary circuits.

Outlets F are for foot switches which control the shutters in front of the lenses for change-over from one projector to another.

Outlets G are for a No. 8 grounding conductor which is connected to the frame of each projector and to the water-piping system.

From outlets C a circuit is brought up to each machine for a small incandescent lamp inside the lamp house and a lamp to illuminate the turntable. Outlets M are for power circuits to the motors used to operate the projector machines.

Ventilation is provided by two exhaust fans and two duct systems, one exhausting from the ceiling of the projection room and one connected to the arc-lamp housing of each machine.

A separate room is provided for rewinding films, but as this room opens only into the projection room, it may be considered that the rewinding is performed in the projection room.

540-13. Conductor Size. Conductors supplying outlets for arc projectors of the professional type shall not be smaller than No. 8 and shall be of sufficient size for the projector employed. Conductors for incandescent type projectors shall conform to normal wiring standards as provided in Section 210-25.

540-14. Conductors on Lamps and Hot Equipment. Asbestos covered conductors Type AA or other types of insulated conductors having a maximum operating temperature of 200°C (392°F) shall be used on all lamps or other equipment where the ambient temperature at the conductors as installed will exceed 50°C (122°F).

540-15. Flexible Cords. Cords approved for hard service in Table 400-11 shall be used on portable equipment.

540-16. Lamp Guards. Incandescent lamps in projection rooms or booths shall be provided with an approved lamp guard unless otherwise protected by noncombustible shades or other enclosures.

540-17. Location of Equipment. Motor-generator sets, transformers, rectifiers, rheostats, and similar equipment, for the supply or control of current to arc lamps on projectors shall, if practicable, be located in separate rooms. Where placed in the projector room, they shall be so located or guarded that arcs or sparks cannot come in contact with film, and motor-generator sets shall have the commutator end or ends protected as provided in Section 520-48.

540-18. Construction and Ventilation. It is recommended that the authority having jurisdiction over the construction and ventilation of rooms for professional type projectors refer to the NFPA Standard for the Storage and Handling of Cellulose Nitrate Motion Picture Film (NFPA No. 40-1967).

540-19. Equipment Prohibited. Switches, overcurrent devices, or other equipment not normally required or used for projectors, sound reproduction, flood, or other special effect lamps or other equipment shall not be installed in such booths or rooms.

Exception: Remote-control switches for the control of auditorium lights or a switch for the motor operating the curtain at the motion-picture screen.

▶   All necessary equipment may be located in a projector booth, but equipment which is not necessary in the normal operation of the motion-picture projectors, stage-lighting projectors, and control of the auditorium lighting and stage curtain must be located elsewhere. Equipment such as service equipment and panelboards for the control and protection of circuits for signs, outside lighting, and lighting in the lobby and box office must not be located in the booth.

540-20. Approval. Projectors and enclosures for arc or incandescent lamps, rectifiers, transformers, rheostats, and similar equipment, shall be of an approved type.

540-21. Marking. Projectors and other equipment as set forth in Section 540-20 shall be marked with the name or trademark of the maker and with the voltage and current for which they are designed.

540-22. Rewinding, Examination and Storage of Extra Films. It is recommended that the authority having jurisdiction refer to the NFPA Standard for the Storage and Handling of Cellulose Nitrate Motion Picture Film (NFPA No. 40-1967).

See Sections 530-51 and 530-52. Also see Section 530-41 for viewing tables.

C. Nonprofessional Type Projectors

540-30. Definition. The nonprofessional projector employs film other than that used on professional type projectors.

540-31. Booth Not Required. Projectors of the nonprofessional or miniature type, when employing only approved slow-burning (cellulose acetate or equivalent) film, may be operated without a booth.

540-32. Approval. Projectors, lamp enclosures, and current-controlling devices and similar devices shall be approved as component parts of the projector equipment.

540-33. Source of Illumination. The source of illumination shall be a lamp of a type approved for stereopticon use or for motion-picture projection.

540-34. Marking. Projectors shall be marked with name or trademark of the maker, with the current and voltage for which they are designed, and for projectors of this type using the standard 35-millimeter film, with the wording "For use with slow-burning films only."

540-35. Nonprofessional Film Marking. The slow-burning (cellulose acetate or equivalent) film shall have a permanent distinctive marker for its entire length identifying the manufacturer and the slow-burning character of the film stock.

D. Sound Recording and Reproduction

540-50. Sound Recording and Reproduction. Sound recording and reproduction equipment shall comply with Article 640.

ARTICLE 550. MOBILE HOMES AND MOBILE HOME PARKS

550-1. Scope.

(a) The provisions of this Article cover the electrical conductors and equipment installed within or on mobile homes, the conductors that connect mobile homes to a supply of electricity, and the installation of electrical wiring, fixtures, equipment and appurtenances related to electrical installations within a mobile home park up to the mobile home service-entrance conductors or, if none, the mobile home service equipment.

Wherever the requirements of other Articles of this Code and Article 550 differ, the requirements of Article 550 shall apply.

For requirements on body and frame design, construction, and the installation of plumbing and heating systems in mobile homes refer to Standard for Mobile Homes (NFPA No. 501B-1971).

(b) A mobile home not intended as a dwelling unit, as for example, equipped for sleeping purposes only, contractor's on-site offices, construction job dormitories, mobile studio dressing rooms, banks, clinics, mobile stores or intended for the display or demonstration of merchandise or machinery, shall not be required to meet the provisions of this Article pertaining to the number or capacity of circuits required. It shall, however, meet all other applicable requirements of this Article if provided with an electrical installation intended to be energized from a 115-volt or 115/230-volt AC power supply system.

(c) The provisions of this Article apply to mobile homes intended for connection to a wiring system nominally rated 115/230 volts, 3-wire AC, with grounded neutral.

▶   Several states have laws that require factory inspection of mobile homes by state inspectors. One state requires that mobile homes be inspected by a nationally recognized independent testing laboratory. Underwriters' Laboratories now lists a number of mobile home manufacturers, and such listings are acceptable in many areas of the country.

In setting up any factory inspection program it is in the interest of public safety to adopt the latest edition of NFPA No. 501B—Standard for Mobile Homes. This standard contains electrical requirements identical to those in

Article 550, and in addition, contains requirements on body and frame design, construction, exits, interior-finish flame spread, and the installation of plumbing and heating systems. Inspection of only the wiring will not ensure complete protection for purchasers or users of mobile homes.

550-2. Definitions.

Feeder Assembly. The overhead or under-chassis feeder conductors, including the grounding conductor, together with the necessary fittings and equipment or a power-supply cord approved for mobile home use, designed for the purpose of delivering energy from the source of electrical supply to the distribution panelboard within the mobile home.

Mobile Home. A factory-assembled structure or structures equipped with the necessary service connections and made so as to be readily movable as a unit or units on their own running gear and designed to be used as a dwelling unit(s) without a permanent foundation.

The phrase "without a permanent foundation" indicates that the support system is constructed with the intent that the mobile home placed thereon will be moved from time to time at the convenience of the owner.

Mobile Home Accessory Building or Structure. Any awning, cabana, ramada, storage cabinet, carport, fence, windbreak or porch established for the use of the occupant of the mobile home upon a mobile home lot.

Mobile Home Lot. A designated portion of a mobile home park designed for the accommodation of one mobile home and its accessory buildings or structures for the exclusive use of its occupants.

Mobile Home Park. A contiguous parcel of land which is used for the accommodation of occupied mobile homes.

Mobile Home Service Equipment. The equipment containing the disconnecting means, overcurrent protective devices, and receptacles or other means for connecting a mobile home feeder assembly.

Park Electrical Wiring System. All of the electrical wiring, fixtures, equipment and appurtenances related to electrical installations within a mobile home park, including the mobile home service equipment.

550-3. Power Supply.

(a) The mobile home service equipment shall be located adjacent to the mobile home and not mounted in or on the mobile home. The power supply to the mobile home shall be a feeder assembly consisting of not more than three mobile home supply cords, each rated 50 amperes or a permanently installed circuit.

Exception: A mobile home that is factory-equipped with gas or oil-fired central heating equipment and cooking appliances may be provided with a mobile home power-supply cord rated 40 amperes.

(b) If the mobile home has a power-supply cord, it shall be permanently attached to the distribution panelboard or to a junction box permanently connected to the distribution panelboard, with the free end terminating in an attachment plug cap.

(c) Cords with adapters and pigtail ends, extension cords, and similar items shall not be attached to, or shipped with, a mobile home.

(d) A suitable clamp or the equivalent shall be provided at the distribution panelboard knockout to afford strain relief for the cord to prevent strain from being transmitted to the terminals when the power supply cord is handled in its intended manner.

(e) The cord used shall be of an approved type with four conductors, one of which shall be identified by a continuous green color or a continuous green color with one or more yellow stripes for use as the grounding conductor.

(f) The attachment plug cap shall be 3-pole, 4-wire grounding type, in accordance with American National Standard Dimensions of Caps, Plugs and Receptacles, Grounding Type, General Purpose, 125/250 volts, 50 amperes, 3-pole, 4-wire (ANSI C73.17-1966), intended for use with a receptacle rated 50 amperes, 125/250 volts. It shall be molded of butyl rubber, neoprene, or other approved materials which have been found suitable for the purpose, and shall be molded to the flexible cord so that it adheres tightly to the cord at the point where the cord enters the attachment plug cap. If a right-angle cap is used, the configuration shall be so oriented that the grounding member is farthest from the cord.

▶   See Fig. 550-1 for 50-amp attachment plug configuration.

Receptacle   *Cap*

Fig. 550-1. ANSI C73.17 50-amp 125/250-volt receptacle and attachment-plug-cap configurations, 3-pole 4-wire grounding types, used for mobile homes and mobile home parks.

125 / 250 volt, 50 amp,
3 pole, 4 wire, grounding type

(g) The overall length of a power-supply cord, measured from the end of the cord, including bared leads, to the face of the attachment plug cap shall be no less than 21 feet and shall not exceed 36½ feet. The length of the cord from the face of the attachment plug cap to the point where the outer jacket of the cord is removed shall be at least 20½ feet.

(h) The power-supply cord shall bear the following marking: "For use with mobile homes—40 amperes" or "For use with mobile homes—50 amperes."

(i) The point of entrance of the feeder assembly to the mobile home shall be in the exterior wall, floor, or roof, in the rear third section (away from the coupler) of the mobile home.

(j) Where a separately metered appliance is installed in the mobile home, or where the calculated load of the mobile home is between 50 amperes and 150 amperes, up to three 50-ampere power-supply cords may be installed when permitted by the authority having jurisdiction, or a feeder as provided for in Section 550-3(a) or 550-3(k) may be installed. The additional power-supply cords shall be located not more than 12 inches away from the point of entrance of the main power-supply cord. They shall not be interconnected on either the line side or the load side, except that the grounding means shall be electrically interconnected.

▶ The reason special permission is required to permit two or three 50-amp power supply cords is that most mobile home parks are not presently equipped to handle more than one such power supply cord for each mobile home lot. However, in areas where mobile home parks are being wired with three 50-amp receptacles at each mobile home lot, special permission will usually be permitted to accept mobile homes equipped with two or three 50-amp power supply cords.

In some areas mobile homes are permanently connected as permitted in paragraph *k* below. Accordingly, local requirements must be checked in regard to the approved method of installing feeder assemblies.

(k) Where the calculated load exceeds 150 amperes or where a permanent feeder is used, the supply shall be by means of:

(1) one mast weatherhead installation installed in accordance with Article 230 and shall contain 4 continuous, insulated, color-coded, feeder conductors, one of which shall be a grounding conductor; or,

(2) an approved metal raceway from the disconnecting means in the mobile home to the underside of the mobile home with provisions for the attachment to a suitable junction box or fitting to the raceway on the underside of the mobile home (with or without conductors as in Section 550-3(k)(1)).

▶ Sometimes a raceway is stubbed to the underside of a mobile home from the distribution panelboard. It is optional as to whether the feeder conductors are installed in the raceway by the mobile home manufacturer or by field installers. When installed, four, continuous, insulated, color-coded conductors, as indicated in Section *550-3K1*, are required. The feeder conductors may be spliced in a suitable junction box, but in no case within the raceway proper.

550-4. Disconnecting Means and Branch-Circuit Protective Equipment. The branch-circuit equipment may be combined with the disconnecting means as a single assembly. Such a combination may be designated as a distribution panel. If a fused distribution panel is used, the maximum fuse size for the mains shall be plainly marked as follows, with lettering at least ¼ inch high where visible when fuses are changed: "Maximum Main Fuses 40 (or 50) Amp."

Plug fuses and fuseholders shall be tamper-resistant, Type "S," enclosed in dead-front fuse panels.

(a) Disconnecting Means. A disconnecting means shall be provided in each mobile home, consisting of circuit breakers or a switch and fuses and their accessories installed in a readily accessible location near the point of entrance of the supply cord or conductors into the mobile home. This equipment shall contain a solderless type of grounding connector or bar for the purposes of grounding with sufficient terminals for all grounding conductors. The neutral bar termination of the grounded circuit conductors shall be insulated. The disconnecting equipment shall have a rating suitable for the connected load. The distribution equipment, either circuit breaker or fused type, shall be located a minimum of 24 inches from the bottom of such equipment to the floor level of the mobile home.

Where more than one power-supply cord is installed, disconnecting means shall be provided for each cord and may be combined in a single equipment but without electrical interconnections other than for grounding purposes.

A distribution panel main circuit breaker shall be rated 50 amperes and employ a 2-pole circuit breaker rated 40 amperes for a 40-ampere supply cord, or 50 amperes for a 50-ampere supply cord. A distribution panel employing a disconnect switch and fuses shall be rated 60 amperes and shall employ a single 2-pole 60-ampere fuseholder with 40- or 50-ampere main fuses for 40- or 50-ampere supply cords, respectively. The outside of the distribution panel shall be plainly marked with the fuse size. The main circuit breakers or fuses shall be plainly marked "Main."

The distribution panel may be located with its front just inside a closet entry, or it may be located in a closet above any shelf or floor if the location is such that a clear space of 6 inches is maintained in front of the distribution panel. However, working space shall be provided as required by Section 110-16.

(b) Branch-Circuit Protective Equipment. Branch-circuit distribution equipment shall be installed in each mobile home and shall include overcurrent protection for each branch circuit consisting of either circuit breakers or fuses.

The branch-circuit overcurrent devices shall be rated: (1) not more than the circuit conductors; and (2) not more than 150 per cent of the rating of a single appliance rated 10 amperes or more which is supplied by an individual branch circuit; but (3) not more than the fuse size marked on the air conditioner or other motor-operated appliance.

(c) Two-Pole Circuit Breakers. When circuit breakers are provided for branch-circuit protection, 230-volt circuits shall be protected by 2-pole common or companion trip, or handle-tied paired circuit breakers.

(d) Electrical Nameplates. A metal nameplate on the outside adjacent to the supply cord entrance shall read, "This Mobile Home is Wired for 115/230 Volt, 3-wire, 60 Hertz Supply. Supply Cord 40 (or 50) amp." The voltage marking may read 120/240 Volts instead of 115/230 Volts.

550-5. Branch Circuits. The number of branch circuits required shall be determined in accordance with the following:

(a) Lighting. Based on 3 watts per square foot times outside dimensions of the mobile home (coupler excluded) divided by 115 volts to determine number of 15 or 20 ampere lighting area circuits, e.g.,

$$\frac{3 \times \text{Length} \times \text{Width}}{115 \times 15 \text{ (or 20)}} = \text{No. of 15 (or 20) ampere circuits.}$$

(b) Portable Appliances. For the small appliance load in kitchen, pantry, family room, dining room, and breakfast rooms of mobile homes two or more 20-ampere appliance branch circuits in addition to the branch circuits specified in Section 550-5(a) shall be provided for all receptacle outlets in these rooms, and such circuits shall have no other outlets. Receptacle outlets supplied by at least two appliance receptacle branch circuits shall be installed in the kitchen.

(c) General Appliances. (Including furnace, water heater, range, and central or room air conditioner, etc.) There shall be one or more circuits of adequate rating in accordance with the following:

(1) Ampere rating of fixed appliances not over 50 per cent of circuit rating if lighting outlets (receptacles, other than kitchen, dining area, and laundry, considered as lighting outlets) are on same circuit;

(2) For fixed appliances on a circuit without lighting outlets, the sum of rated amperes shall not exceed the branch-circuit rating for other than motor loads or 80 per cent of the branch-circuit rating for air conditioning or other motor loads;

(3) The rating of a single portable appliance on a circuit having no other outlets shall not exceed 80 per cent of the circuit rating;

(4) The rating of range branch circuit shall be based on the range demand as specified for ranges in Section 550-11 (b) (5).

For the laundry branch circuit, see Section 220-3(b).

550-6. Receptacle Outlets.

(a) All receptacle outlets: (1) shall be of grounding type; (2) shall be installed according to Section 210-7; and (3) except when supplying specific appliances, receptacles shall be parallel blade, 15-ampere, 125-volt, either single or duplex.

(b) There shall be an individual outlet of the grounding type for each cord-connected fixed appliance installed.

(c) Except in the bath and hall areas, receptacle outlets shall be installed at all wall spaces 2 feet wide or more, so that no point along the floor line is more than 6 feet, measured horizontally, from an outlet in that space. Except as explained in the following, receptacle outlets are not required for wall spaces occupied by kitchen or wardrobe cabinets.

In addition, a receptacle outlet shall be installed: (1) Over or adjacent to counter tops in the kitchen (at least one on each side of the sink if counter tops are on each side and 12 inches or more in width); (2) Adjacent to the refrigerator and free-standing gas-range space; (3) At counter top spaces for built-in vanities; (4) At counter top spaces under wall-mounted cabinets.

(d) Receptacle outlets shall not be installed within or adjacent to a shower or bathtub space.

550-7. Fixtures and Appliances.

(a) Electrical materials, devices, appliances, fittings, and other equipment installed, intended for use in, or attached to the mobile home shall be approved for the application and shall be connected in an approved manner when in service. Facilities shall be provided to securely fasten appliances when the mobile home is in transit. (See Section 550-9 for provisions on grounding.)

(b) (1) Specifically approved pendant-type fixtures or pendant cords may be installed in mobile homes.

(2) If a lighting fixture is provided over a bathtub or in a shower stall, it shall be of the approved enclosed and gasketed type.

(3) The switch for shower lighting fixtures and exhaust fans located over a tub or in a shower stall shall be located outside the tub or shower space.

(c) Every appliance shall be accessible for inspection, service, repair, or replacement without removal of permanent construction.

550-8. Wiring Methods and Materials.
Except as specifically limited in this Section the wiring methods and materials included in this Code shall be used in mobile homes.

(a) Nonmetallic outlet boxes are acceptable only with nonmetallic cable.

(b) Nonmetallic cable located 15 inches or less above the floor, if exposed, shall be protected from physical damage by covering boards, guard strips, or conduit. Cable likely to be damaged by stowage shall be so protected in all cases.

(c) Metal-clad and nonmetallic cables may be passed through the centers of the wide side of 2-inch by 4-inch studs. However, they shall be protected where they pass through 2-inch by 2-inch studs or at other studs or frames where the cable or armor would be less than $1\frac{1}{2}$ inches from the inside or outside surface. Steel plates on each side of the cable, or a tube, with not less than No. 16 MSG wall thickness, are required to protect the cable. These plates or tubes shall be securely held in place.

(d) Where metallic faceplates are used they shall be effectively grounded.

(e) If the range, clothes dryer, or similar appliance is connected by metal-clad cable or flexible conduit, a length of free cable or conduit should be provided to permit moving the appliance. The cable or flexible conduit should be adequately secured to the wall. Clearance space behind a range may provide the required protection when a range is connected by Type SE cable. When used, Type SE cable shall have an identified and insulated neutral plus an equipment grounding conductor. Nonmetallic-sheathed cable (Type NM) shall not be used to connect a range or dryer.

This does not prohibit the use of Type NM cable between the branch-circuit overcurrent protective device and a range or dryer receptacle.

(f) Rigid metal conduit shall be provided with a locknut inside and outside the box, and a conduit bushing shall be used on the inside. Inside ends of the conduit shall be reamed.

(g) Switches shall be rated as follows:

(1) For lighting circuits, switches shall have a 10-ampere 125-volt rating; or higher, if needed for the connected load.

(2) For motors or other loads, switches shall have ampere or horsepower ratings or both adequate for loads controlled. (An "AC general use" snap switch may control a motor 2 horsepower or less with full-load current not over 80 per cent of the switch ampere rating.)

(h) At least 4 inches of free conductor shall be left at each outlet box except where conductors are intended to loop without joints.

(i) Under Chassis Wiring. (Exposed to Weather).

(1) When outdoor or under chassis line-voltage wiring is exposed to moisture or physical damage it shall be protected by rigid metal conduit. The conductors shall be suitable for wet locations.

Exception: Electrical metallic tubing may be used when closely routed against frames and equipment enclosures.

(2) The cables or conductors shall be Type NMC, TW, or equivalent.

(j) Outlet boxes of dimensions less than those required in Tables 370-6(a)(1) and 370-6(a)(2) may be used provided the box has been tested and approved for the purpose.

▶ The smaller dimensional boxes mentioned in this rule would usually be a box designed for a special switch or receptacle, or a combination box and wiring device. Such combinations can be properly evaluated and tested with a limited number of conductors and connections and a specific lay of conductors to ensure adequate wiring space in the spirit of the first paragraph in Section 370-6.

(k)   Boxes, fittings and cabinets shall be securely fastened in place.

Exception: Snap-in type boxes or boxes provided with special wall or ceiling brackets that securely fasten boxes in walls or ceilings may be used.

550-9. Grounding.

Grounding of both electrical and nonelectrical metal parts in a mobile home is through connection to a grounding bus in the mobile home distribution panel. The grounding bus is grounded through the green-colored conductor in the supply cord or the feeder wiring to the service ground in the service entrance equipment located adjacent to the mobile home location. Neither the frame of the mobile home nor the frame of any appliance may be connected to the neutral conductor in the mobile home.

▶   **The white (neutral conductor) is required to be run from the "insulated busbar" in the mobile-home panel to the service-entrance equipment where it is connected to the terminal at the point of connection to the grounding electrode conductor.**

The green-colored conductor is required to be run from the "panel grounding bus" in the mobile home to the service-entrance equipment where it is connected to the neutral conductor at the point of connection to the grounding electrode conductor.

The requirements provide that the grounded (white) conductor and the grounding (green) conductor be kept separate within the mobile-home structure in order to secure the maximum protection against electric-shock hazard if the supply neutral conductor should become open.

(a) Insulated Neutral.

(1)   The grounded circuit conductor (neutral) shall be insulated from the grounding conductors and from equipment enclosures and other grounded parts. The grounded (neutral) circuit terminals in the distribution panel and in ranges, clothes dryers, counter-mounted cooking units, and wall-mounted ovens are to be insulated from the equipment enclosure. Bonding screws, straps, or buses in the distribution panel or in appliances are to be removed and discarded.

(2)   Connection of ranges and clothes dryers shall be made with 4 conductor cord and 3-pole, 4-wire grounding type plugs, or by Type AC metal-clad cable or conductors enclosed in flexible steel conduit.

(b) Equipment Grounding Means.

(1)   The green-colored grounding wire in the supply cord or permanent feeder wiring shall be connected to the grounding bus in the distribution panel or disconnecting means.

(2)   In the electrical system, all exposed metal parts, enclosures, frames, lamp fixture canopies, etc. shall be effectively bonded to the grounding terminal or enclosure of the distribution panel.

(3)   Cord-connected appliances, such as washing machines, clothes dryers, refrigerators, and the electrical system of gas ranges, etc. shall be grounded by means of an approved cord with grounding conductor and grounding-type attachment plug.

(c) Bonding of Noncurrent-Carrying Metal Parts.

(1) All exposed noncurrent-carrying metal parts that may become energized shall be effectively bonded to the grounding terminal or enclosure of the distribution panelboard. A bonding conductor shall be connected between each distribution panelboard and an accessible terminal on the chassis.

(2) Grounding terminals shall be of the solderless type and approved as pressure-terminal connectors recognized for the wire size used. The bonding conductor may be solid or stranded, insulated or bare, and shall be No. 8 AWG copper minimum, or equal. The bonding conductor shall be routed so as not to be exposed to physical damage. Protection can be afforded by the configuration of the chassis.

(3) Metallic gas, water, and waste pipes and metallic air circulating ducts are considered bonded if they are connected to the terminal on the chassis (See Section 550-9(c)(1)) by clamps, solderless connectors, or by suitable grounding-type straps.

(4) Any metallic roof and exterior covering are considered bonded if the metal panels overlap one another and are securely attached to the wood or metal frame parts by metallic fasteners and if the lower panel of the metallic exterior covering is secured by metallic fasteners at each cross member of the chassis and the lower panel is bonded to the chassis by a metal strap.

550-10. Testing. Dielectric Strength Test. The wiring of each mobile home shall be subjected to a 1-minute, 900-volt, dielectric strength test (with all switches closed) between live parts (including neutral) and the mobile home ground. Alternatively, the test may be performed at 1,088 volts for 1 second. This test shall be performed after branch circuits are complete and after fixtures or appliances are installed.

Exception: Fixtures or appliances which are approved shall not be required to withstand the dielectric strength test.

550-11. Calculations. The following method is to be employed in computing the supply cord and distribution panel load for each feeder assembly for each mobile home in lieu of the procedure shown in Article 220 and is based on 3-wire, 115/230-volt supply with 115-volt loads balanced between the two legs of the 3-wire system.

(a) Lighting and Small Appliance Load:

Lighting Watts: Length times width of mobile home (outside dimensions, exclusive of coupler) times 3 watts per square foot; e.g.,

Length $\times$ width $\times$ 3 = ... lighting watts.

Small appliance Watts: Number of circuits times 1,500 watts for each 20-ampere appliance receptacle circuit (see definition of Appliance, Portable with note); e.g.,

Number of circuits $\times$ 1,500 = ... small appliance watts.

Total: Lighting watts plus small appliance = ... total watts.

First 3,000 total watts at 100 per cent plus remainder at 35 per cent = ... watts to be divided by 230 volts to obtain current (amperes) per leg.

(b) Total load for determining power supply is the summation of:

(1) Lighting and small appliance load as calculated in Section 550-11(a).

(2)   Nameplate amperes for motors and heater loads (exhaust fans, air conditioners,* electric, gas, or oil heating).**

* Omit smaller of these two, except include blower motor if used as air conditioner evaporator motor.

** When an air conditioner is not installed and a 40-ampere power supply cord is provided, allow 15 amperes per leg for air conditioning.

(3)   25 per cent of current of largest motor in (2).

(4)   Total of nameplate amperes for: disposal, dishwasher, water heater, clothes dryer, wall-mounted oven, cooking units.

Where number of these appliances exceeds three use 75 per cent of total.

(5)   Derive amperes for free standing range (as distinguished from separate ovens and cooking units) by dividing values below by 230 volts.

Nameplate Rating	Use
10,000 watts × or less	80 per cent of rating
10,001–12,500 watts	8,000 watts
12,501–13,500 watts	8,400 watts
13,501–14,500 watts	8,800 watts
14,501–15,500 watts	9,200 watts
15,501–16,500 watts	9,600 watts
16,501–17,500 watts	10,000 watts

(6)   If outlets or circuits are provided for other than factory installed appliances include the anticipated load.

See following Example for illustration of application of this calculation.

Example

A mobile home is 70 × 10 feet and has two portable appliance circuits, a 1000 watt 230 volt heater, a 200 watt 115 volt exhaust fan, a 400 watt 115 volt dishwasher and a 7000 watt electric range.

Lighting and small appliance load

Lighting 70 × 10 × 3 =	2100 watts	
Small appliance 1500 × 2 =	3000 watts	
	5100 watts	
1st 3000 watts at 100%		3000
Remainder (5,100 − 3,000 = 2,100) at 35%		735
		3735

$$\frac{3735}{230} = 16 \text{ amperes per leg}$$

1000 watt (heater) ÷ 230 =	4.4 amp
200 watt (fan) ÷ 115 =	1.7 amp
400 watt (dishwasher) ÷ 115 =	3.5 amp
7000 watt (range) × .8 ÷ 230 =	24. amp

| | Amperes per leg | |
	A	B
Lighting and appliances	16	16
Heater (230 volt)	4	4
Fan (115 volt)	2	—
Dishwasher (115 volt)	—	4
Range	24	24
Totals	46	48

Based on the higher current calculated for either leg, use one 50 ampere supply cord.

550-12. Wiring of Expandable Units and Dual Units.

(a) Expandable or dual-unit mobile homes utilizing permanently installed feeder conductors may use permanent-type wiring methods and materials for connecting such units to each other.

(b) Expandable or dual-unit mobile homes not having permanently installed feeders and which are to be moved from one location to another, may have disconnecting means with branch-circuit protective equipment in each unit when so located that after assembly or joining together of units the requirements of Section 550-3(j) are met.

(c) Expandable or dual-unit mobile homes, which are to be moved from one location to another, may be connected together with cord connections using approved raintight power-supply connectors or approved power-supply connectors installed in protected locations. The cords used shall be as specified in Section 550-3(e). Cord length shall be kept at a minimum with outlet boxes on each unit located where circuit conductors terminate. Such outlet boxes shall be adjacent to each other, as practical, after units are joined together.

550-13. Outdoor Outlets, Fixtures, Air-Cooling Equipment, Etc.

(a) Outdoor fixtures and equipments shall be recognized for outdoor use. Outdoor receptacle or convenience outlets shall be of a gasketed-cover type.

(b) A mobile home provided with a receptacle outlet designed to energize heating and/or air-conditioning equipment located outside the mobile home, shall have permanently affixed, adjacent to the outlet receptacle, a metal tag which reads:

> This Connection is for Air-Conditioning Equipment
> Rated at Not More Than .... Amperes, at
> .... Volts, 60 Hertz.

The correct voltage and ampere rating shall be given. The tag shall be not less than 0.020 inch, etched brass, stainless steel, anodized or alclad aluminum. The tag shall not be less than 3 inches by 1¾ inches minimum size.

B. Mobile Home Parks

550-21. Distribution System.
The mobile home park secondary electrical distribution system to mobile home lots shall be single-phase, nominal 115/230

volts. For the purpose of Part B, where the park service exceeds 240 volts, transformers and secondary distribution panelboards shall be treated as services.

See Table 550-22 for calculation of load.

▶   The mobile home park supply is limited to nominal **115/230** volt single phase three wire to accommodate appliances rated at nominal **230** volts or a combination nominal voltage of **115/230** volts. Accordingly, a three-wire **120/208** supply, derived from a four-wire 208Y/120-volt, would not be acceptable.

While the demand factor for a single mobile home lot is computed at **16,000** watts, it should be noted that Section **550-22**c requires the feeder circuit conductors extending to each mobile home lot to be not less than **100** amps.

550-22. Calculated Load.

(a)   Park electrical wiring systems shall be calculated on the basis of not less than 16,000 watts (at 115/230 volts) per each mobile home service. The demand factors which are set forth in Table 550-22 are the minimum allowable demand factors which may be used in calculating load on feeders and service. No demand factor shall be allowed for any other load, except as provided in this Code.

Table 550-22. Demand Factors for Feeders and Service-Entrance Conductors

Number of Mobile Home Lots	Demand Factor (Per Cent)
1	100
2	55
3	44
4	39
5	33
6	29
7–9	28
10–12	27
13–15	26
16–21	25
22–40	24
41–60	23
61 and over	22

(b)   The demand factor for a given number of lots shall apply to all lots indicated.

Example: 20 lots calculated at 25 per cent of 16,000 watts result in a permissible demand of 4,000 watts per lot or a total of 80,000 watts for 20 lots.

(c)   Mobile home lot feeder circuit conductors shall have adequate capacity for the loads supplied, and shall be rated at not less than 100 amperes at 115/230 volts.

▶   See comments following Section **550-21.**

550-23. Mobile Home Service Equipment.

(a) Mobile home service equipment shall be rated at not less than 100 amperes, and provision shall be made for connecting a mobile home feeder assembly by a permanent wiring method. Mobile home service equipment may also be provided with 50-ampere receptacles conforming to ANSI C73.17-1966.

▶   See Fig. 550-1 for 50-amp receptacle configuration.

(b) Mobile home service equipment may also be provided with a means for connecting a mobile home accessory building or structure or additional electrical equipment located outside a mobile home by a permanent wiring method.

(c) Additional receptacles may be provided for connection of electrical equipment located outside the mobile home

ARTICLE 551. RECREATIONAL VEHICLES AND RECREATIONAL VEHICLE PARKS

A. Recreational Vehicles

551-1. Scope.

(a) The provisions of Part A cover the electrical conductors and equipment installed within or on recreational vehicles and also the conductors that connect them to a supply of electricity. Wherever the requirements of other Articles of this Code and Article 551 differ, the requirements of Article 551 shall apply.

For requirements on the installation of plumbing and heating systems in recreational vehicles, refer to Standard for Recreational Vehicles (NFPA No. 501C-1970).

(b) A recreational vehicle not used for the purposes as defined in Section 551-2 shall not be required to meet the provisions of Part A pertaining to the number or capacity of circuits required. It shall, however, meet all other applicable requirements of this Article if the recreational vehicle is provided with an electrical installation intended to be energized from a 115- or 115/230-volt, AC power-supply system.

(c) Part A covers battery and direct-current power (12-volt or less) systems, combination electrical systems, generator installations, and nominal 115- or 115/230-volt systems.

▶   Some states have laws that require factory inspection of recreational vehicles by state inspectors. Such laws closely follow NFPA 501C, Standard for Recreational Vehicles. This standard contains electrical requirements in accordance with Part A of Art. 551. It also contains requirements for plumbing and heating systems.

551-2. Definitions.   (See Article 100 for other definitions.)

Air-Conditioning or Comfort-Cooling Equipment: All of that equipment intended or installed for the purpose of processing the treatment of air so as to control simultaneously its temperature, humidity, cleanliness and distribution to meet the requirements of the conditioned space.

Camping Trailer: A vehicular portable unit mounted on wheels and constructed with collapsible partial side walls which fold for towing by another vehicle and unfold at the campsite to provide temporary living quarters for recreational, camping, or travel use. (See "Recreational Vehicle.")

Converter: A device which changes electrical energy from one form to another, as from alternating current to direct current.

Dead Front (As applied to switches, circuit breakers, switchboards, and distribution panelboards): So designed, constructed and installed that no current-carrying parts are normally exposed on the front.

Disconnecting Means: The necessary equipment usually consisting of a circuit breaker or switch and fuses, and their accessories, located near the point of entrance of supply conductors in a recreational vehicle and intended to constitute the means of cutoff for the supply to that recreational vehicle.

Receptacles used as disconnecting means shall be accessible (as applied to wiring methods) and capable of interrupting their rated current without hazard to the operator.

Distribution Panelboard: A single panel or group of panel units designed for assembly in the form of a single panel; including buses, and with or without switches and/or automatic overcurrent protective devices for the control of light, heat or power circuits of small individual as well as aggregate capacity; designed to be placed in a cabinet or cutout box placed in or against a wall or partition and accessible only from the front.

Motor Home: A vehicular unit built on a self-propelled motor vehicle chassis, primarily designed to provide temporary living quarters for recreational, camping, or travel use. (See "Recreational Vehicle.")

Power-Supply Assembly: The conductors, including the grounding conductors, insulated from one another, the connectors, attachment plug caps, and all other fittings, grommets, or devices installed for the purpose of delivering energy from the source of electrical supply to the distribution panel within the recreational vehicle.

Recreational Vehicle: A vehicular type unit primarily designed as temporary living quarters for recreational, camping, or travel use, which either has its own motive power or is mounted on or drawn by another vehicle. The basic entities are: travel trailer, camping trailer, truck camper and motor home.

Transformer: A device, which when used, will raise or lower the voltage of alternating current of the original source.

Travel Trailer: A vehicular portable unit, mounted on wheels, of such size or weight as not to require special highway movement permits when drawn by a motorized vehicle; primarily designed and constructed to provide temporary living quarters for recreational, camping, or travel use; and of a body width of no more than 8 feet and a body length of no more than 32 feet when factory equipped for the road. (See "Recreational Vehicle.")

Truck Camper: A portable unit, designed to be loaded onto, or affixed to, the bed or chassis of a truck, constructed to provide temporary living quarters for recreational, camping, or travel use. Truck campers are of two basic types as defined below:

a. Slide-In Camper: A portable unit designed to be loaded onto and unloaded from the bed of a pickup truck, constructed to provide temporary living quarters for recreational, travel, or camping use.

b. Chassis-Mount Camper: A portable unit designed to be affixed to a truck chassis, and constructed to provide temporary living quarters for recreational, travel, or camping use.

551-3. Batteries and Direct-Current (12 volts—Nominal)

▶   Sections **551-3, 551-4,** and **551-5** concern 12-volt systems for running and signal lights similar to those in conventional automobile systems. Also, many recreational vehicles use 12-volt systems for interior lighting or other small loads. The 12-volt system is derived from an on-board battery or through a transfer switch from a 120/12-volt transformer often equipped with a full-wave rectifier.

(a) Battery Circuits. Battery circuits furnished and installed by the recreational vehicle manufacturer, other than those related to braking, are subject to this Code. Circuits supplying lights subject to Federal or State regulations shall be in accordance with applicable government regulations but shall not be lower than provided by this Code.

(b) Low-Voltage Wiring Materials.

(1) Copper conductors shall be used for low-voltage circuits.

(2) The insulation of low-voltage conductors used in battery and direct-current circuits shall be rated at least 60°C.

(3) Conductors furnished and installed by the recreational vehicle manufacturer shall have a minimum of 30 mils thermoplastic insulation or equal.

(4) The insulation of outdoor or under-chassis wire shall be moisture and heat resistant, Type THW or equivalent.

(5) Single-wire, low-voltage conductors shall be of the stranded type.

(c) Low-Voltage Wiring Methods.

(1) Conductors shall be protected against physical damage and shall be adequately supported. Where insulated conductors are clamped to the structure, the conductor insulation shall be supplemented by an additional wrap or layer or equivalent material, except that jacketed cables need not be so protected. Wiring shall be routed away from sharp edges, moving parts or heat sources.

(2) Splices and connections shall be made in accordance with Society of Automotive Engineers (SAE) standards and recommended practices or equivalent.

(3) Battery and direct-current circuits shall be physically separated by at least a ½-inch gap or other approved means, from circuits of a different power source. This may be accomplished by clamping, routing, or equivalent means which ensure permanent total separation.

(d) Battery Installations. Storage batteries subject to the provisions of this Code shall be securely attached to the vehicle and installed in an area which is ventilated directly to the exterior of the vehicle.

(e) Overcurrent Protection.

(1) Battery and direct-current circuit wiring shall be protected by overcurrent protective devices rated not in excess of the ampacity of copper conductors, as follows:

Wire Size	Ampacity	Wire Type
18	3	Stranded only
16	9	Stranded only
14	15	Stranded or solid
12	20	Stranded or solid
10	30	Stranded or solid

For other allowable conductor ampacities, refer to Table 310-12.

(2) Circuit breakers or fuses shall be of an approved type, including automotive types conforming to the requirements of Society of Automotive Engineers (SAE) J554-1968 or Underwriters' Laboratories, Inc., Standard 275b. Fuseholders shall be clearly marked with maximum fuse size.

(3) Higher current-consuming direct-current appliances such as pumps, compressors, heater blowers and similar motor-driven appliances shall be installed in accordance with the manufacturer's instructions.

(4) The overcurrent protective device shall be installed in an accessible location on the vehicle as close as practical to the point where the power supply connects to the vehicle circuits. If located outside the recreational vehicle, the device shall be protected against weather and physical damage.

551-4. Combination Electrical Systems.

(a) General. Vehicle wiring suitable for connection to a battery or direct-current supply source may be connected to a 115-volt source provided that the entire wiring system and equipment are rated and installed in full conformity with Part A requirements covering 115-volt electrical systems. Circuits fed from alternating-current transformers shall not supply direct-current appliances.

(b) Voltage Converters (115-Volt Alternating Current to Low-Voltage Direct Current). The 115-volt alternating current side of voltage converters shall be wired in full conformity with Part A requirements for 115-volt electrical systems. Converters supplied as an integral part of an approved appliance are not subject to the above. All converters and transformers shall be of an approved type.

(c) Dual-Voltage Fixtures or Appliances. Fixtures or appliances having both 115-volt and low-voltage connections shall be approved for dual voltage.

▶   Such fixtures must have barriers to separate 115-volt and 12-volt wiring and connections.

(d) Autotransformers. Autotransformers are prohibited.

(e) Receptacle and Plug Caps. When a recreational vehicle is equipped with separate external connections for a 115-volt alternating current system and a battery or direct-current system, receptacles and plug caps shall be of different configurations.

(f) Identification.

(1) When a vehicle equipped with a battery or direct-current system has an external connection for low-voltage power, the receptacle shall have a configuration that will not accept 120-volt power. The vehicle shall have permanently affixed on the outside wall adjacent to the point of entrance of the power supply conductors a tag which reads:

THIS CONNECTION IS FOR LOW-VOLTAGE BATTERY OR DIRECT CURRENT ONLY. DO NOT CONNECT TO 120 OR 240 VOLTS AC.

(2) The tag shall be 3 inches by $1\frac{3}{4}$ inches minimum size, made of etched, metal-stamped or embossed brass, stainless steel, anodized or alclad aluminum not less than 0.020 inch thick, or other approved material (e.g., 0.005-inch plastic laminates).

551-5. Generator Installations.

(a) Mounting. Generators shall be mounted in such a manner as to be effectively bonded to the recreational vehicle chassis.

(b) Generator Protection. Equipment shall be installed to ensure that the generator is disconnected when the vehicle is energized from an outside source and to ensure that the outside source is disconnected when the vehicle is energized by the generator. The generator field shall be protected by appropriately rated, approved equipment.

(c) Installation of Storage Batteries and Generators. Storage batteries and internal-combustion-driven generator units (subject to the provisions of this Code) shall be secured in place to avoid displacement from vibration and road shock and shall be installed in a compartment which is vaportight to the interior of the vehicle.

(d) Ventilation of Generator Compartments. Compartments accommodating internal-combustion-driven generator units shall be provided with approved ventilation in accordance with instructions provided by the manufacturer of the generator unit.

(e) Location of Internal-Combustion-Engine Generator Exhaust. Exhaust from generator internal-combustion engines shall not terminate adjacent to the vehicle gasoline-tank filler-spout inlet.

551-6. Nominal 115- or 115/230-Volt Systems.

(a) General Requirements. The electrical equipment and material of recreational vehicles indicated for connection to a wiring system nominally rated 115 volts, 2-wire with ground, or a wiring system nominally rated 115/230 volts, 3-wire with ground, shall be approved and installed in accordance with the requirements of Part A.

(b) Materials and Equipment. Electrical materials, devices, appliances, fittings, and other equipment installed, intended for use in, or attached to the recreational vehicle shall be approved for the application.

551-7. Branch Circuits Required.

The branch circuits required in a recreational vehicle shall conform to Section 551-19 and be determined in accordance with subparagraphs (a), (b) and (c) below.

(a) Recreational vehicles with not more than 8 lighting and receptacle outlets combined shall have either:

(1) One 15-ampere general-purpose branch circuit to supply these outlets, provided the total rating of fixed appliances connected to this circuit does not exceed 600 watts, or

(2) One 20-ampere general-purpose branch circuit to supply these outlets, provided the total rating of fixed appliances connected to this circuit does not exceed 1000 watts.

Vehicles wired in accordance with (a)(1) or (a)(2) above shall not be equipped with electrical heating or cooking appliances.

(b) Recreational vehicles with more than 8 lighting and receptacle outlets combined shall have one 20-ampere appliance branch circuit, and either:

(1) One 15-ampere branch circuit to supply these outlets, provided this circuit does not supply receptacles in the cooking and dining area(s) or electrical heating or cooking appliances, and provided the total rating of fixed appliances connected to this circuit does not exceed 600 watts, or

(2) One 20-ampere branch circuit, to supply these outlets, provided this circuit does not supply receptacles in the cooking and dining area(s) or electrical heating or cooking appliances, and provided the total rating of fixed appliances connected to this circuit does not exceed 1000 watts.

(c) Calculations for Lighting and Appliance Load. When Section 551-7(b) (relative to recreational vehicles with more than 8 lighting and receptacle outlets combined) is not applied, the following method shall be employed in computing the power-supply assembly and distribution panel load for the recreational vehicle:

A. Lighting. Length times width of vehicle (outside dimensions, exclusive of hitch and cab) times 3 watts per square foot, e.g.,

Length x width x 3 = _____ lighting watts.

B. Small Appliance. Number of circuits times 1500 watts for each 20-ampere appliance receptacle circuit, e.g.,

Number of Circuits x 1500 _____ small appliance watts.

C. Total. Lighting watts plus small appliance watts = ... total watts.

D. First 3000 total watts at 100 per cent plus remainder at 35 per cent = _____ watts to be divided by voltage to obtain current (amperes) per leg.

	Amperes per Leg	
	A	B
Lighting and small appliance current (amperes) per leg (from D above) =		_____

E. Add nameplate amperes for motors and heater loads (exhaust fans, air conditioners*, electric, gas, or oil heating*) = _____

F. Add 25 per cent of amperes of largest motor in E = _____

G. Add nameplate amperes for:** _____

Disposal	_____	_____
Water Heater	_____	_____
Wall-Mounted Ovens	_____	_____
Cooking Units	_____	_____
TOTAL	_____	_____ = _____

* Omit smaller of these two except include any motor common to both functions.

** When number of appliances is four or more use 75 per cent of total.

H.   Add amperes for free-standing range as distinguished from separate ovens and cooking units. Derive from following table by dividing watts by 230 volts.

Range	Nameplate Rating (watts)	Use (watts)
(Free-standing range	10,000 or less	80 per cent of rating
as distinguished	10,001–12,500	8,000
from separate oven	12,501–13,500	8,400
and cooking units)	13,501–14,500	8,800
	14,501–15,500	9,200
	15,501–16,500	9,600
	16,501–17,500	10,000

	Amperes per Leg
	A B

I.   If outlets or circuits are provided for other than factory-installed major appliances, the anticipated load shall be added for each.

TOTAL = _____

When the total for Legs A and B are unequal, use the larger to determine the distribution panel and supply cord rating. (Service amperes shall not exceed supply cord rating. See Section 551-11.)

551-8. Receptacle Outlets Required.

(a)   Receptacle outlets shall be installed at wall spaces 2 feet wide or more so that no point along the floor line is more than 6 feet, measured horizontally, from an outlet in that space.

Exception No. 1: Bath and hall areas.

Exception No. 2: Wall spaces occupied by kitchen cabinets, wardrobe cabinets, built-in furniture, behind doors which may open fully against a wall surface, or similar facilities.

(b)   Receptacle outlets shall be installed:

(1)   Adjacent to counter tops in the kitchen (at least one on each side of the sink if counter tops are on each side and are 12 inches or over in width).

(2)   Adjacent to the refrigerator and gas range space, except when a gas-fired refrigerator or cooking appliance, requiring no external electrical connection, is factory-installed.

(3)   Adjacent to counter top spaces (and built-in vanities) which cannot be reached from a receptacle required in Section 551-8(b)(1) by a cord of 6 feet without crossing a traffic area, cooking appliance or sink.

(c)   When installed adjacent to a bathroom lavatory, the receptacle outlet shall be a minimum of 30 inches from the floor. The receptacle outlet may be contained in an approved lighting fixture. A receptacle outlet shall not be installed in a tub or combination shower compartment.

551-9. Distribution Panelboard.

(a)   An approved distribution panelboard shall be used. The distribution panelboard shall be of the insulated neutral type, with the grounding bar attached to the metal frame of the panelboard or other approved grounding means.

(b) The distribution panelboard shall be installed in a readily accessible location and may be located in a closet.

(c) The distribution panelboard shall be of the dead-front type and shall consist of one or more circuit breakers or Type S fuseholders. A main disconnecting means shall be provided where fuses are used or where more than two circuit breakers are employed.

551-10. Branch-Circuit Protection.

(a) The branch-circuit overcurrent devices shall be rated:

(1) Not more than the circuit conductors; and

(2) Not more than 150 per cent of the rating of a single appliance rated 10 amperes or more and supplied by an individual branch circuit; but

(3) Not more than the fuse size marked on an air conditioner or other motor-operated appliances.

(b) A 20-ampere fuse or circuit breaker shall be considered adequate protection for fixture leads, cords, or portable appliances, and No. 14 AWG tap conductors, not over 6 feet long for recessed lighting fixtures.

(c) If more than one outlet or load is on a branch circuit, a 15-ampere receptacle shall be considered protected by a 20-ampere fuse or circuit breaker.

551-11. Power-Supply Assembly.

(a) Recreational vehicles wired in accordance with Section 551-7(a)(1) shall use an approved 15-ampere, or larger, main power-supply assembly.

(b) Recreational vehicles wired in accordance with Section 551-7(a)(2) shall use an approved 20-ampere, or larger, main power-supply assembly.

(c) Recreational vehicles wired in accordance with Section 551-7(b) or 551-7(c) shall use an approved 30-ampere, or larger, main power-supply assembly.

(d) In accordance with Section 551-7(c), any recreational vehicle with a rating in excess of 30 amperes, 115 volts, shall use an approved 40-ampere or 50-ampere 115/230-volt power-supply assembly.

Exception: When the calculated load of the recreational vehicle exceeds 30 amperes, 115 volts, a second power-supply cord may be installed. Where a two-cord supply system is installed, they shall not be interconnected on either the line side or the load side. The grounding circuits and grounding means shall be electrically interconnected.

▶   See Fig. 551-1 for attachment plug and receptacle configurations.

551-12. Dual-Supply Source.

(a) Where a dual-supply system, consisting of a generator and a power-supply cord is installed, the feeder from the generator shall be protected by an overcurrent protective device. Installation shall be in accordance with Sections 551-5(a) and 551-5(b).

(b) Calculation of loads shall be in accordance with Section 551-7(c).

(c) The two supply sources need not be of the same capacity.

(d) If the AC generator source exceeds 30 amperes, 115 volts, it may be wired either as a 115-volt system or a 115/230-volt system, providing an overcurrent protective device of the proper rating is installed in the feeder.

(e) The external power-supply assembly may be less than the calculated load

Receptacles   *Caps*

ANSI C73.12, 125 volt, 20 amp, 2 pole, 3 wire, grounding type

ANSI C73.11, 125 volt, 15 amp, 2 pole, 3 wire, grounding type

20 amp — ANSI C73.12 125 volt, 2 pole, 3 wire, grounding type

30 amp

ANSI C73.13
125 volt, 2 pole, 3 wire, grounding type

50 amp

ANSI C73.17
125 / 250 volt, 3 pole, 4 wire, grounding type

Fig. 551-1. ANSI configurations for receptacles and attachment plug caps used for recreational vehicles and recreational vehicle parks.

but not less than 30 amperes and shall have overcurrent protection not greater than the capacity of the external power-supply assembly.

551-13. Means for Connecting to Power Supply.

(a) Assembly. The power-supply assembly or assemblies shall be factory-supplied or factory-installed when of the permanently connected type as specified herein:

(1) Separable. When a separable power-supply assembly consisting of a cord with a female connector and molded attachment plug cap is provided, the vehicle shall be equipped with a permanently mounted, approved, male-recessed-type motor-base receptacle wired directly to the distribution panel by an approved wiring method. The attachment plug cap shall be of an approved type.

(2) Permanently Connected. Each power-supply assembly shall be connected directly to the terminals of the distribution panel or conductors within an approved junction box and provided with means to prevent strain from being transmitted to the terminals. The ampacity of the conductors between each junction box and the terminals of each distribution panel shall be at least equal to the ampacity of the power-supply cord. The supply end of the assembly shall be equipped with an attachment plug of the type described in Section 551-13(c). Where the cord passes through the walls or floors, it shall be protected by means of conduit and bushings or equivalent.

(b) Cord. The cord set shall be approved for use with recreational vehicles. The cord shall be not less than 20 feet as measured from the point of entrance to the recreational vehicle or the face of the motor-base attachment plug nor more than 26½ feet in length overall to the face of the attachment plug at the supply end.

(c) Attachment Plugs.

(1) Recreational vehicles having only one 15-ampere branch circuit as permitted by Section 551-7(a)(1) shall have an attachment plug which shall be 2-pole, 3-wire, grounding-type, rated 15 amperes, 125 volts, conforming to American National Standard C73.11-1966.

(2) Recreational vehicles having only one 20-ampere branch circuit as permitted in Section 551-7(a)(2) shall have an attachment plug which shall be 2-pole, 3-wire, grounding-type, rated 20 amperes, 125 volts, conforming to American National Standard C73.12-1966.

(3) Recreational vehicles wired in accordance with Section 551-7(b) or 551-7(c) shall have an attachment plug which shall be 2-pole, 3-wire, grounding-type, rated 30 amperes, 125 volts, conforming to American National Standard C73.13-1966, intended for use with units rated at 30 amperes, 125 volts.

(4) Recreational vehicles having a power-supply assembly rated 40 amperes or 50 amperes as permitted by Section 551-7(c) shall have a 3-pole, 4-wire, grounding-type attachment plug rated 50 amperes, 125/250 volts, conforming to American National Standard C73.17-1966.

▶ See Fig. 551-1 for 15-, 20-, 30-, and 50-amp attachment plug configurations.

(d) Labeling at Electrical Entrance. Each recreational vehicle shall have permanently affixed to the exterior skin at or near the point of entrance of the power-supply cord(s) a tag 3 inches by 1¾ inches minimum size, made of etched, metal-stamped or embossed brass, stainless steel, anodized or alclad aluminum not less than 0.020 inch thick, or other approved material (e.g., 0.005-inch plastic laminates), which reads, as appropriate, either:

"This connection is for 110-125-volt AC, 60-Hz (Cycles) service. Do not connect to higher voltage" or

"This connection is for 3-wire 120/240-volt AC, 60-Hz (Cycles) ——————— ampere service."

(e) Location. The point of entrance of a power-supply assembly shall be located within 25 feet of the rear, on the left (road) side or at the rear, left of the longitudinal center of the vehicle, within 18 inches of the outside wall.

Exception: A camping trailer not more than 17 feet in length, a motor home or a truck camper may have the electrical point of entrance located on either side, provided the drain outlet and gas connections are located on the same side.

551-14. Wiring Methods.

(a) Electrical metallic tubing, flexible metal conduit, metal-clad cable, and nonmetallic-sheathed cable with a grounding conductor, shall terminate by means of fittings, clamps or connectors approved for the purpose. Flexible metal conduit may be used as a grounding means where both the conduit and the fittings are approved for the purpose.

(b) Rigid metal conduit shall be provided with a locknut inside and outside the box, and a conduit bushing shall be used on the inside. Inside ends of the conduit shall be reamed.

(c) Nonmetallic outlet boxes are acceptable only with nonmetallic-sheathed cable.

(d) In walls and ceilings constructed of wood or other combustible material, outlet boxes and fittings shall be flush with the finished surface or project therefrom.

(e) Wall and ceiling outlets shall be mounted in accordance with Article 370.
Exception: Snap-in type boxes or boxes provided with special wall or ceiling brackets that securely fasten boxes in walls or ceilings may be used.

(f) The sheath of nonmetallic cable or the armor of metal-clad cable shall be continuous between outlet boxes and other enclosures.

(g) Metal-clad and nonmetallic cables may be passed through the centers of the wide side of 2-inch by 4-inch studs. However, they shall be protected where they pass through 2-inch by 2-inch studs or at other studs or frames where the cable would be less than $1\frac{1}{2}$ inches from the inside or outside surface. Steel plates on each side of the cable, or a steel tube, with not less than No. 16 MSG wall thickness, are required to protect the cable. When the thickness of studs or frames makes it impractical or impossible to use metal plates or tubes, particular care shall be exercised in the design and production of the recreational vehicles so as to avoid contacting the cables with nails, screws, or other fasteners. Such care in design shall include appropriate routing of the cables through studs or frames at locations where the likelihood of their being contacted by nails, screws, or other fasteners subsequent to production is remote.

(h) No bend shall have a radius of less than 5 times the cable diameter.

(i) When connected with cable connectors or clamps, cables shall be supported within 12 inches of outlet boxes, distribution panelboards, and splice boxes on appliances. Supports shall be provided every $4\frac{1}{2}$ feet at other places.

(j) Nonmetallic-sheathed cables shall be supported within 8 inches of a nonmetallic outlet box without cable clamps.

(k) Nonmetallic cable, if exposed, shall be protected from physical damage, by covering boards, guard strips or conduit. Cable likely to be damaged shall be so protected in all cases.

(l) Metallic faceplates shall be of ferrous metal not less than 0.030 inch in thickness or of nonferrous metal not less than 0.040 inch in thickness. Nonmetallic faceplates shall be of an approved type.

(m) Where metallic faceplates are used they shall be effectively grounded.

(n) Outdoor or under-chassis wiring (115-volt) exposed to moisture and physical damage shall be protected by rigid metal conduit, or electrical metallic tubing which may be used when closely routed against frames and equipment enclosures. The conductors shall be suitable for wet locations.

551-15. Conductors and Outlet Boxes.

(a)   For requirements for conductors in outlet boxes, see Section 370-6.

Exception: Outlet boxes of dimensions less than those required in Tables 370-6(a)(1) and 370-6(a)(2) of this Code may be used provided that the box has been tested and approved for the purpose.

▶   See comments following Section **550-8***j*.

(b)   At least 4 inches of free conductor shall be left at each outlet box except where conductors are intended to loop without joints.

551-16. Grounded Conductors.   For use of grounded conductors, see Section 200-7.

551-17. Connection of Terminals and Splices.   For connections of terminals and splices, see Section 110-14. If splices of the grounding wire in nonmetallic-sheathed cable are made in outlet boxes, the splices shall be insulated.

551-18. Switches.   Switches shall be rated as follows:

(a)   For lighting circuits, switches shall be rated not less than 10 amperes, 120-125 volts and in no case less than the connected load.

(b)   For motors or other loads, switches shall have ampere or horsepower ratings, or both, adequate for loads controlled. (An AC general-use snap switch may control a motor 2 horsepower or less with full-load current not over 80 per cent of the switch ampere rating.)

551-19. Receptacles.   All receptacle outlets shall be: (1) of the grounding type; and (2) installed in accordance with Sections 210-21 and 210-22.

551-20. Lighting Fixtures.

(a) **General.**   Any combustible wall or ceiling finish exposed between the edge of a fixture canopy, or pan and the outlet box, shall be covered with noncombustible material of either metal equal to the thickness of the fixture or asbestos of 1/16 inch.

(b) **Shower Fixtures.**   If a lighting fixture is provided over a bathtub or in a shower stall, it shall be of the enclosed and gasketed type and approved for the type of installation.

The switch for shower lighting fixtures and exhaust fans, located over a tub or in a shower stall, shall be located outside the tub or shower space.

(c) **Outdoor Outlets, Fixtures, Air-Cooling Equipment, Etc.**   Outdoor fixtures and other equipment shall be approved for outdoor use.

551-21. Grounding.   (See also Section 551-23 on bonding of noncurrent-carrying metal parts.)

(a) **Power-Supply Grounding.**   The grounding conductor in the supply cord or feeder shall be connected to the grounding bus or other approved grounding means in the distribution panelboard.

(b) **Distribution Panelboard.**   The distribution panelboard shall have a grounding bus with sufficient terminals for all grounding conductors or other approved grounding means.

(c) **Insulated Neutral.**

(1)   The grounded circuit conductor (neutral) shall be insulated from the equipment grounding conductors and from equipment enclosures and other grounded parts. The grounded (neutral) circuit terminals in the distribution

panelboard and in ranges, clothes dryers, counter-mounted cooking units, and wall-mounted ovens shall be insulated from the equipment enclosure. Bonding screws, straps or buses in the distribution panelboard or in appliances shall be removed and discarded.

(2) Connection of electric ranges and electric clothes dryers utilizing a grounded (neutral) conductor, if cord-connected, shall be made with 4-conductor cord and 3-pole, 4-wire grounding-type plug caps and receptacles.

551-22. Interior Equipment Grounding.

(a) In the electrical system, all exposed metal parts, enclosures, frames, lighting fixture canopies, etc., shall be effectively bonded to the grounding terminals or enclosure of the distribution panelboard.

(b) Bare wires, green-colored wires, or green wires with yellow stripe(s) shall be used for equipment grounding conductors only.

(c) Where grounding of electrical equipment is specified, it may be accomplished as follows:

(1) Connection by metallic raceway (conduit or electrical metallic tubing) or the sheath of metal-clad cable to metallic outlet boxes.

(2) A connection between the one or more grounding conductors and a metallic box by means of a grounding screw, which shall be used for no other purpose, or an approved grounding device.

(3) The grounding wire in nonmetallic-sheathed cable may be secured under a screw threaded into the fixture canopy other than a mounting screw or cover screw; or may be attached to an approved grounding means (plate) in a nonmetallic outlet box for fixture mounting (grounding means may also be used for fixture attachment screws).

(d) A connection between the one or more grounding conductors brought into a nonmetallic outlet box shall be so arranged that a connection can be made to any fitting or device in that box that requires grounding.

(e) Where more than one equipment grounding conductor of a branch circuit enters a box, all such conductors shall be in good electrical contact with each other, and the arrangement shall be such that the disconnection or removal of a receptacle, fixture, or other device fed from the box will not interfere with or interrupt the grounding continuity.

(f) Cord-connected appliances, such as washing machines, clothes dryers, refrigerators, and the electrical system of gas ranges, etc., shall be grounded by means of an approved cord with grounding conductor and grounding-type attachment plug.

551-23. Bonding of Noncurrent-Carrying Metal Parts.

(a) All exposed noncurrent-carrying metal parts that may become energized shall be effectively bonded to the grounding terminal or enclosure of the distribution panelboard.

(b) A bonding conductor shall be connected between any distribution panelboard and an accessible terminal on the chassis.

Exception: Any recreational vehicle which employs a unitized metal chassis-frame construction to which the distribution panelboard is securely fastened with a bolt(s) and nut(s) or by welding or riveting is considered to be bonded.

(c) Grounding terminals shall be of the solderless type and approved as pressure terminal connectors recognized for the wire size used. The bonding conductor may be solid or stranded, insulated or bare, and shall be No. 8 AWG copper minimum, or equal.

(d) The metallic roof and exterior covering are considered bonded if:

(1) The metal panels overlap one another and are securely attached to the wood or metal frame parts by metallic fasteners, and

(2) The lower panel of the metallic exterior covering is secured by metallic fasteners at each cross member of the chassis, or the lower panel is bonded to the chassis by a metal strap.

(e) The gas, water and waste pipes are considered grounded if they are bonded to the chassis. (See Section 551-23(b) for chassis bonding.)

(f) Furnace and metallic circulating air ducts shall be bonded.

551-24. Appliance Accessibility. Every appliance shall be accessible for inspection, service, repair and replacement without removal of permanent construction.

551-25. Factory Tests (Electrical).

Electrical Factory Test. Each recreational vehicle shall be subjected to the following tests:

(a) Circuits of 115 volts or 115/230 volts. Each recreational vehicle designed with a 115-volt or 115/230-volt electrical system shall withstand the applied potential without electrical breakdown of a one-minute 900-volt dielectric strength test, or a one-second 1080-volt dielectric strength test, with all switches closed between current-carrying conductors, including neutral, and the recreational vehicle ground.

The test transformer shall be adjustable. Starting at zero the applied potential shall be increased gradually in at least four steps until either the test value is reached or breakdown occurs. During the test, all switches and other controls shall be in the "on" position. Fixtures and permanently installed appliances shall not be required to withstand this test.

(b) Battery and Low-Voltage Circuits. The battery or low-voltage circuit conductors in each recreational vehicle shall withstand the applied potential without electrical breakdown of a one-minute 500-volt or a one-second 600-volt dielectric strength test. The test transformer shall be adjustable. The potential shall be applied between live and grounded conductors.

551-26. Examination of Equipment for Safety.

The examination or inspection of equipment for safety should be conducted under uniform conditions and by organizations properly equipped and qualified for experimental testing, inspections of the run of goods at factories, and service-value determinations through field examinations.

B. Recreational Vehicle Parks

551-40. Application and Scope. Part B covers electrical systems on recreational vehicle parks. It does not apply to the electrical systems of recreational vehicles or the conductors that connect them to the park electrical supply facilities. Wherever the requirements of other Articles of this Code and Article 551 differ, the requirements of Article 551 shall apply.

551-41. Definitions.

Lot: The area in a recreational park intended for the connection of one recreational vehicle.

Power-Supply Assembly: The conductors, including the grounding conductors, insulated from one another, the connectors, attachment plug caps, and all other fittings, grommets, or devices installed for the purpose of delivering energy from the source of electrical supply to the distribution panel within the recreational vehicle.

Recreational Vehicle Lot Service Equipment. The necessary equipment usually consisting of a circuit breaker or switch and fuse and their accessories, located near the point of entrance of supply conductors to a recreational vehicle lot and intended to constitute the disconnecting means for the supply to that lot.

551-42. Receptacles Required. A minimum of 75 per cent of all lots with electrical service equipment shall be equipped with both a 20-ampere, 125-volt receptacle conforming to ANSI Standard C73.12-1966, and a 30-ampere, 125-volt receptacle conforming to ANSI Standard C73.13-1966. The remainder of all lots with electrical service equipment shall be equipped with a 20-ampere, 125-volt receptacle conforming to ANSI Standard C73.12-1966.

▶   See Fig. 551-1 for these receptacle configurations.

551-43. Distribution System. The recreational vehicle park secondary electrical distribution system to recreational vehicle lots shall be derived from a single-phase 120/240-volt, 3-wire system.

▶   See comments in first paragraph following Section 550-21.

551-44. Calculated Load.

(a) Electrical service and feeders shall be calculated on the basis of not less than 3600 watts per lot equipped with both 20-ampere and 30-ampere supply facilities and 2400 watts per lot equipped with only 20-ampere supply facilities. The demand factors set forth in Table 551-44 are the minimum allowable demand factors that may be used in calculating load for service and feeders.

(b) For the purpose of this Code, where the park service exceeds 240 volts, transformers and secondary distribution panelboards shall be treated as services.

Table 551-44. Demand Factors for Feeders and Service-Entrance Conductors for Park Lots

Number of Recreational Vehicle Lots	Demand Factor (per cent)	Number of Recreational Vehicle Lots	Demand Factor (per cent)
1	100	10–12	29
2	100	13–15	28
3	70	16–18	27
4	55	19–21	26
5	44	22–40	25
6	39	41–100	24
7–9	33	101 and over	23

(c) The demand factor for a given number of lots shall apply to all lots indicated. For example: 20 lots calculated at 26 per cent of 3600 watts result in a permissible demand of 936 watts per lot or a total of 18,720 watts for 20 lots.

(d) Recreational vehicle lot feeder circuit conductors shall have adequate ampacity for the loads supplied, and shall be rated at not less than 30 amperes.

▶   Each lot requires feeder conductors rated not less than 30 amps.

551-45. Overcurrent Protection. Overcurrent protection shall be provided in accordance with Article 240.

551-46. Grounding. All electrical equipment and installations in recreational vehicle parks shall be grounded as required by Article 250.

551-47. Recreational Vehicle Lot Service Equipment.

(a) Disconnecting Means. A disconnecting switch or circuit breaker shall be provided in the lot service equipment for disconnecting the power supply to the recreational vehicle.

(b) Access. All lot service equipment shall be accessible by an unobstructed entrance or passageway not less than two feet wide and 6½ feet high.

(c) Mounting Height. Lot service equipment shall be located not less than 2 feet nor more than 6½ feet above the ground.

(d) Working Space. Sufficient space shall be provided and maintained about all electrical equipment to permit ready and safe operation, in accordance with Section 110-16.

551-48. Grounding, Recreational Vehicle Lot Equipment.

(a) Exposed noncurrent-carrying metal parts of fixed equipment, metal boxes, cabinets and fittings, which are not electrically connected to grounded equipment shall be grounded by a continuous grounding conductor run with the circuit conductors from the service equipments or from the transformer of a secondary distribution system.

(b) Each secondary distribution system shall be grounded at the transformer.

(c) The neutral conductor shall not be used as an equipment ground for recreational vehicles or equipment within the recreational vehicle park.

(d) No connection to a grounding electrode shall be made to the neutral conductor on the load side of the service disconnecting means or transformer distribution panelboard.

551-49. Protection of Outdoor Equipment.

(a) Wet Locations. All switches, circuit breakers, receptacles, control equipment and metering devices located in wet places or outside of a building shall be rainproof equipment.

(b) Meters. If secondary meters are installed, meter sockets without meters installed shall be blanked off with an approved blanking plate.

551-50. Overhead Conductors.

(a) Vertical Clearance. Open conductors of not over 600 volts shall have a vertical clearance of not less than 18 feet in all areas subject to recreational vehicle movement. In all other areas, vertical clearances shall conform to Section 730-18.

For clearance of conductors of over 600 volts, see National Electrical Safety Code (ANSI C2-1960).

(b) Horizontal Clearance. The horizontal clearance from structures and recreational vehicles for overhead conductors shall be not less than 3 feet for 600 volts or less.

551-51. Underground Service, Feeder, Branch-Circuit and Recreational Vehicle Lot Feeder Circuit Conductors.

(a) General. All direct-burial conductors, including the equipment grounding conductor if of aluminum, shall be insulated and specifically approved for the purpose. All conductors shall be continuous from fitting to fitting. All splices shall be made in approved junction boxes.

(b) Mechanical Protection. Where underground conductors enter or leave a building or trench, they shall have mechanical protection in the form of rigid metal conduit, electrical metallic tubing or other approved mechanical means, extending a minimum of 18 inches into the trench from the finished grade. See Section 310-6 and Article 339.

551-52. Receptacles. A receptacle to supply electric power to a recreational vehicle shall be of one of the following configurations:

(a) ANSI Standard C73.17-1966, 125/250 volts, 50-ampere, 3-pole, 4-wire, grounding-type for 115/230-volt systems.

(b) ANSI Standard C73.13-1966, 125-volt, 30-ampere, 2-pole, 3-wire, grounding-type for 115-volt systems.

(c) ANSI Standard C73.12-1966, 125-volt, 20-ampere, 2-pole, 3-wire, grounding-type for 115-volt systems.

▶   See Fig. 551-1 for these configurations.

ARTICLE 555. MARINAS AND BOATYARDS

555-1. Scope. The provisions of this Article shall apply to the installation of wiring in those areas of marinas, boatyards, boat basins and similar establishments and equipment including floating piers which are used for the construction, repair, storage, launching, berthing and fueling of small craft.

555-2. Voltage Drop. See Section 215-3.

555-3. Receptacles. Receptacles which provide shore power for boats shall be rated not less than 20 amperes and shall be single and of the locking and grounding types conforming to the configurations in ANSI C73-1971.

Ground-fault circuit protection may be provided for these circuits and where used will provide additional protection against line-to-ground shock hazard.

▶   Figure 555-1 shows typical configurations of locking- and grounding-type receptacles and attachment plugs used in marinas and boatyards. A complete chart of these devices can be obtained from the National Electrical Manufacturers Association or various wiring-device manufacturers. Locking-type receptacles and caps are required to provide proper contact and assurance that attachment plugs will not fall out easily and disconnect on-board equipment such as bilge pumps or refrigerators.

Receptacle   *Cap*

125 volt, 2 pole, 3 wire, grounding type

20 amp

30 amp

Receptacle   *Cap*

125 / 250 volt, 3 pole, 4 wire, grounding type

30 amp

FIG. 555-1. Typical configurations for receptacles and attachment plug caps of the locking and grounding types used in marinas and boatyards.

According to Section **555-4** each of these single receptacles must be installed on an individual branch circuit.

555-4. Branch Circuits.   Each single receptacle which supplies shore power for a boat shall be supplied by an individual branch circuit of the voltage class and rating corresponding to the rating of the receptacle.

555-5. Feeder and Service.   The ampacity for feeder and service conductors supplying shore power for boats shall be calculated on the basis of a minimum of 25 watts per lineal foot of slip or dock space for boat outlet circuits plus lighting and other loads. Minimum feeder conductor size shall be No. 10 AWG. Minimum service conductor size shall be No. 8 AWG.

555-6. Wiring Methods.   Wiring methods where exposed to the weather or water shall be rigid nonmetallic conduit approved for the purpose, Type MI cable, nonmetallic cable approved for the purpose, or corrosion-resistant rigid metal conduit approved for the purpose.

Exception No. 1: Open wiring may be installed by special permission.

Factors to be considered would include possible contact with masts, cranes, and other equipment.

Exception No. 2: Underground wiring which conforms to the requirements of this Code.

Exception No. 3: Where flexibility is required, other approved types.

See Fire Protection Standard for Marinas and Boatyards, NFPA No. 303-1969 for further information on wiring methods for various locations.

555-7. Grounding.

(a) Grounding Means. The following items shall be connected to a copper equipment grounding conductor run with circuit conductors in a raceway or cable. Such a conductor shall be insulated and the covering shall be a continuous green color or a continuous green color with one or more yellow stripes:

(1) Boxes, cabinets and all other metallic enclosures.

(2) Metal frames of utilization equipment.

(3) Grounding terminals of grounding-type receptacles.

(b) Size of Equipment Grounding Conductor. The insulated copper equipment grounding conductor shall be sized in accordance with Section 250-95 but not smaller than No. 12 AWG.

(c) Branch-Circuit Equipment Grounding Conductor. The insulated equipment grounding conductor for branch circuits shall terminate at a grounding terminal in a remote panelboard or the grounding terminal in the main service equipment.

(d) Feeder Equipment Grounding Conductors. Where a feeder supplies a remote panelboard an insulated equipment grounding conductor shall extend from a grounding terminal in the service equipment to a grounding terminal in the remote panelboard.

▶   The purpose of Section 555-7 is to require an insulated equipment grounding wire that will ensure a grounding circuit of high integrity. Due to the corrosive influences around marinas and boatyards, metal raceways and boxes are not permitted to serve as equipment grounding conductors.

555-8. Clearance Over Water. Wiring over navigable waterways shall be approved by the authority in charge of the specific waterway.

▶   There are some federal and local agencies that have specific control over navigable waterways. Accordingly, any proposed installations over such waterways should be cleared with the appropriate authorities.

CHAPTER SIX ——————————————————

Special Equipment

ARTICLE 600. ELECTRIC SIGNS AND OUTLINE LIGHTING

A. General

600-1. Scope. The provisions of this Article shall apply to the installation of conductors and equipment for electric signs and outline lighting as defined in Article 100.

▶ In the case of signs that are constructed at a shop or factory and sent out complete and ready for erection, the inspection department can require that every sign shall bear an Underwriters' Laboratories' label. In the case of outline lighting and signs that are constructed at the location where they are installed, the inspection department must make a detailed inspection to make sure that all requirements of this Article are complied with. In some cities, inspection departments inspect signs in local shops.

600-2. Disconnect Required. Each outline lighting installation, and each sign of other than the portable type, shall be controlled by an externally operable switch or breaker which will open all ungrounded conductors and shall be suitable for conditions of installation, such as exposure to the weather.

(a) In Sight of Sign. The switch or breaker required by Section 600-2 shall be within sight of the sign or outline lighting which it controls or may be located elsewhere when capable of being locked in the open position.

▶ For the protection of a workman who may be working on the sign, the control switch, if not within sight of the sign, must be so arranged that it can be locked in the open position.

564

(b) Control Switch Rating. Switches, flashers, and similar devices controlling transformers shall be either of a type approved for the purpose, or have a current rating not less than twice the current rating of the transformers. On alternating-current circuits, general use alternating-current snap switches may be used to control inductive loads other **than** motors, not exceeding the ampere rating of switch. See Section 380-14.

▶   Any switching device controlling the primary of a transformer that supplies a luminous gas tube operates under unusually severe conditions. In order to avoid rapid deterioration of the switch or flasher due to arcing at the contacts, the device must be a general-use a-c snap switch or have a current rating of at least twice the current rating of the transformer it controls.

600-5. Grounding.

(a) Signs, troughs, tube terminal boxes and other metal frames shall be grounded in the manner specified in Article 250 of this Code, unless they are insulated from ground and from other conducting surfaces and are inaccessible to unauthorized persons.

(b) Isolated noncurrent-carrying metal parts of outline lighting may be bonded by No. 14 conductors and grounded in accordance with Article 250.

(c) Signs of the portable incandescent or fluorescent-lamp type in which the open circuit voltage does not exceed 150 volts to ground are not required to be grounded.

600-6. Load of Branch Circuit.
Circuits shall be so arranged that the load imposed by outlets, lamps, and transformers connected to them, shall in no case exceed the rating of the branch circuit.

Circuits which supply lamps, ballasts, and transformers or combinations thereof may be rated not to exceed 20 amperes.

Circuits containing electric discharge lighting transformers exclusively shall not be rated in excess of 30 amperes.

▶   No limit is placed on the number of outlets that may be connected on one circuit on a sign or for outline lighting, except that the total load shall not exceed the rating of the circuit. Where in normal operation the load will continue for 3 hr or more, the load shall not exceed 80 per cent of the branch circuit rating. See Section 210-23*b*.

600-7. Marking.

(a) Signs shall be marked with the maker's name, and for incandescent-lamp signs with the number of lampholders, and for electric discharge signs with input amperes at full load and input voltage. The marking of the sign shall be visible for inspection after installation.

(b) Transformers shall be marked with the maker's name, and transformers for electric discharge signs shall be marked with the input rating in amperes or volt-amperes, the input voltage and the open-circuit high-tension voltage.

600-8. Enclosures.
Enclosures for signs and outline lighting shall conform to the following:

(a) Conductors and Terminals. Conductors and terminals in sign boxes, cabinets, and outline troughs shall be enclosed, except the supply leads.

(b) Cutouts, Flashers, Etc. Cutouts, flashers, and similar devices shall be enclosed in metal boxes the doors of which shall be arranged so that they can be opened without removing obstructions or finished parts of the enclosure.

(c) Strength. Enclosures shall have ample strength and rigidity.

(d) Material. Except for portable signs of the indoor type, signs and outline lighting shall be constructed of metal or other noncombustible material. Wood may be used for external decoration if placed not less than 2 inches from the nearest lampholder or current-carrying part.

(e) Minimum Thickness—Enclosure Metal. Sheet copper shall be at least 20 ounce (0.028 inch). Sheet steel may be of No. 28 MSG except that for outline lighting and for electric discharge signs sheet steel shall be of No. 24 MSG, unless ribbed, corrugated or embossed over its entire surface, when it may be of No. 26 MSG.

(f) Protection of Metal. All steel parts of enclosures shall be galvanized or otherwise protected from corrosion.

(g) Enclosures Exposed to the Weather. Enclosures for outside use shall be weatherproof and shall have an ample number of drain holes, each not larger than ½ inch or smaller than ¼ inch. Wiring connections shall not be made through the bottoms of enclosures exposed to the weather unless the enclosures are of the raintight type.

B. Signs and Outline Lighting—600 Volts or Less

600-21. Installation of Conductors. Conductors shall be installed as follows:

(a) Wiring Method. Conductors shall be installed as open conductors on insulators, in rigid metal conduit, flexible metal conduit, liquidtight flexible metal conduit, electrical metallic tubing, metal-clad cable, metal troughing, Type ALS cable or Type MI cable.

(b) Insulation and Size. Conductors shall be of a type approved for general use and shall be no smaller than No. 14.

Exception No. 1: Conductors in portable signs, short leads permanently attached to lampholders or ballasts, and leads in wiring channels which are permanently attached to electric discharge lampholders or electric discharge ballasts and which are not longer than 8 feet may be smaller than No. 14 but shall not be smaller than No. 18 and shall be of a type approved for the purpose.

Exception No. 2: Conductors, for signs with multiple incandescent lamps requiring one conductor from a control to one or more lamps whose total load does not exceed 250 watts, may be smaller than No. 14 but shall not be smaller than No. 18 if in an approved cable assembly of two or more conductors.

(c) Exposed to the Weather. Conductors in raceways, metal-clad cable or enclosures exposed to the weather, shall be of the lead-covered type or other type specially approved for the conditions, except where rigid conduit, electrical metallic tubing or enclosures are made raintight and arranged to drain.

(d) Number of Conductors in Raceway. Number of conductors in raceway for sign flashers may be in accordance with Table 1 of Chapter 9.

(e) Open Conductors. Open conductors on insulators shall comply with the provisions of Sections 300-2 through 300-22, and, if outdoors, Article 730, except that the separation between conductors need be only 2 inches.

Exception: Open conductors may be supported by lampholders located not more than 1 foot apart.

(f) Conductors Soldered to Terminals. Where the conductors are fastened to lampholders other than of the pin type, they shall be soldered to the terminals and the exposed parts of conductors and terminals shall be treated to prevent corrosion. Where the conductors are fastened to pin-type lampholders which protect the terminals from the entrance of water, and which have been found acceptable for sign use, the conductors shall be of the stranded type but need not be soldered to the terminals.

▶   Portable signs are nearly always small and may be considered as in the same class as portable lighting equipment, and hence No. 16 or 18 wire may be used inside the sign enclosure, provided that the size used shall always have sufficient ampacity for the load.

600-22. Lampholders. Lampholders shall be of the unswitched type having bodies of suitable insulating material and shall be so constructed and installed as to prevent turning. Miniature lampholders shall not be employed for outdoor signs and outline lighting.

C. Signs and Outline Lighting—Exceeding 600 Volts

600-31. Installation of Conductors. Conductors shall be installed as follows:

(a) Wiring Method. Conductors shall be installed as open work, as concealed conductors on insulators, in rigid metal conduit, in flexible metal conduit, in liquidtight flexible metal conduit, or in electrical metallic tubing.

(b) Insulation and Size. Conductors shall be of a type approved for the purpose and for the voltage of the circuit and shall be not smaller than No. 14.

Exception No. 1: Leads in wiring channels which are permanently attached to electric discharge lampholders or electric discharge ballasts and which are not longer than 8 feet may be smaller than No. 14 but shall not be smaller than No. 18 and shall be of a type approved for the purpose.

Exception No. 2: Leads in show-window displays or small portable signs that run from the line ends of the tubing to the secondary windings of the transformer where they are permanently attached within the transformer enclosure and which are not longer than 8 feet may be smaller than No. 14, but shall not be smaller than No. 18 and shall be of a type approved for the purpose.

(c) Bends in Conductors. Sharp bends in the conductors shall be avoided.

(d) Open Conductors—Indoors. Open conductors indoors shall be mounted on noncombustible, nonabsorptive insulators. Insulators of porcelain shall be glazed on all exposed surfaces. A separation of at least 1½ inches shall be maintained between conductors and between conductors and other objects. Conductors shall not be located where subject to physical damage.

(e) Concealed Conductors on Insulators—Indoors. Concealed conductors on insulators shall be separated from each other and from all objects other than the insulators on which they are mounted by a spacing of not less than 1½ inches for voltages above 10,000 volts, and not less than 1 inch for voltages of 10,000 or less. They shall be installed in channels lined with noncombustible material and used for no other purpose, except that the primary circuit conductors may be in the same channel. The insulators shall be of noncombustible, nonabsorptive material.

(f) Conductors in Raceways.   Where the conductors are covered with lead or other metal sheathing, the covering shall extend beyond the end of the raceway, and the surface of the cable shall not be injured where the covering terminates.

(1)   In damp or wet locations, the insulation on all conductors shall extend beyond the metal covering or raceway at least 4 inches for voltages over 10,000, 3 inches for voltages over 5,000 but not exceeding 10,000, and 2 inches for voltages of 5,000 or less.

(2)   In dry locations the insulation shall extend beyond the end of the metal covering or raceways not less than 2½ inches for voltages over 10,000, 2 inches for voltages over 5,000 but not exceeding 10,000, and 1½ inches for voltages of 5,000 or less.

(3)   For conductors at grounded midpoint terminals, no spacing is required.

(4)   A metal raceway containing a single conductor from one secondary terminal of a transformer shall not exceed twenty feet in length.

(g) Open Conductors—Outdoors.   Open conductors outdoors shall be mounted on noncombustible, nonabsorptive insulators. Insulators of porcelain shall be glazed on all exposed surfaces. A separation of at least two inches shall be maintained between conductors, and between conductors and other objects.

Where subject to physical damage, or where within reach from ground, roof, or window, conductors shall be enclosed in raceways or suitably guarded. Where guarded, a spacing of not less than 1½ inches shall be maintained between conductors and the enclosure unless the enclosure is nonconducting and noncombustible.

▶   The conductor insulation should be of the proper quality and thickness to withstand a breakdown test at a voltage considerably higher than the operating voltage.

The heavy insulation required on conductors for gas-tube signs or lighting operating at over 600 volts might be injured by a sharp bend.

Where high-voltage wiring is exposed to physical damage, rigid conduit or electrical metallic tubing should preferably be used, rather than open wiring. The rule permits the use of open wiring guarded by wooden boxing or sheet metal, in which case a clearance of at least 1½ in. from the guard is required, or the conductors may be run through a tube of nonconducting noncombustible material such as bakelite.

Where a cable is run in metal raceway, the conductor of the cable forms one side of a capacitor, with the raceway forming the other side. The capacitor is connected across, i.e., in parallel with, the transformer winding. With the right values of inductance and capacity an excessive voltage will build up between the conductor and the raceway, which may break down the insulation of the cable. The conditions are the same as when a coil in a radio receiver is tuned by means of a capacitor. This condition is not likely to occur if the length of cable in the raceway is limited to 20 ft.

The conduit or tubing should terminate in a bushing and the cable sheath should extend beyond the bushing by the distance specified. The minimum extension specified in the table is the distance from the end of the metal sheath to the point where the insulation is stripped from the cable, if metal-sheathed conductors are used; for conductors that are not metal-sheathed, it is the distance from the end of the raceway to the end of the insulation.

Voltage, kilovolts	Minimum extension, inches	
	In damp or wet locations	In dry locations
Over 10............	4	$2\frac{1}{2}$
5 to 10............	3	2
5 or less...........	2	$1\frac{1}{2}$

(h) Show Windows and Similar Locations. Conductors that hang freely in the air, away from combustible material, and where not subject to physical damage, as in some show-window displays, need not be otherwise protected.

(i) Conductors may be run from the ends of tubing to the grounded midpoint of transformers specifically designed for the purpose and provided with terminals at the midpoint. Where such connections are made to the transformer grounded midpoint, the connections between the high-voltage terminals of the transformer and the line ends of the tubing shall be as short as possible.

600-32. Transformers. Transformers shall comply with the following:

(a) Voltage. The transformer secondary open-circuit voltage shall not exceed 15,000 volts with an allowance on test of 1000 volts additional. In end-grounded transformers the secondary, open-circuit voltage shall not exceed 7,500 volts with an allowance on test of 500 volts additional.

(b) Type. Transformers shall be of a type approved for the purpose and shall be limited in rating to a maximum of 4,500 volt-amperes.

Open core-and-coil type transformers shall be limited to 5,000 volts with an allowance on test of 500 volts, and to indoor applications in small portable signs.

Transformers for outline lighting installations shall have secondary current ratings not in excess of 30 milliamperes except where they and all wiring connected to them are installed in accordance with the provisions of Article 410 for electric discharge lighting of the same voltage.

(c) Exposed to Weather. Transformers used outdoors shall be of the weather-proof type or shall be protected from the weather by enclosure in the sign body or in a separate metal box.

(d) Transformer Secondary Connections. The high-voltage windings of transformers shall not be connected in parallel; and shall not be connected in series, except that two transformers each having one end of its high-voltage winding connected to the metal enclosure may have their high-voltage windings connected in series to form the equivalent of a midpoint grounded transformer. The grounded ends shall be connected by insulated conductors not smaller than No. 14.

Exception: Transformers for small portable signs, show windows, and similar locations that are equipped with leads permanently attached to the secondary winding within the transformer enclosure and that do not extend more than eight feet beyond the enclosure for attaching to the line ends of the tubing may have leads smaller than No. 14, but shall not be smaller than No. 18 and shall be of a type approved for the purpose.

(e) Accessibility. Transformers shall be accessible.

▶ The transformers used to supply luminous gas tubes are, in general, constant-current devices and, up to a certain limit, the voltage delivered by the transformer increases as the impedance of the load increases. The impedance of the tube increases as the length increases and is higher for a tube of small diameter than for one of larger diameter. Hence a transformer should be selected which is designed to deliver the proper current and voltage for the tube; if the tube is too long or of too small a diameter, the voltage of the transformer may rise to too high a value.

600-33. Electric Discharge Tubing. Electric discharge tubing shall conform to the following:

(a) Design. The tubing shall be of such length and design as not to cause a continuous overvoltage on the transformer.

(b) Support. Tubing shall be adequately supported on noncombustible, nonabsorptive supports. Tubing supports should, where practicable, be adjustable.

(c) Contact with Flammable Material and Other Surfaces. The tubing shall be free from contact with flammable material and shall be located where not normally exposed to physical damage. Where operating in excess of 7,500 volts, the tubing shall be supported on noncombustible, nonabsorptive, insulating supports which maintain a spacing of not less than ¼ inch between the tubing and the nearest surface.

▶ See comments following Section 600-34.

600-34. Terminals and Electrode Receptacles for Electric Discharge Tubing. Terminals and electrode receptacles for electric discharge tubing shall comply with the following:

(a) Terminals. Terminals of the tubing shall be inaccessible to unqualified persons and isolated from combustible material and grounded metal or shall be enclosed. Where enclosed they shall be separated from grounded metal and combustible material by noncombustible, nonabsorptive, insulating material approved for the purpose or by 1½ inches of air. Terminals shall be relieved from stress by the independent support of the tubing.

(b) Tube Connections Other Than With Receptacles. Where tubes do not terminate in receptacles designed for the purpose, all live parts of tube terminals and conductors shall be so supported as to maintain a separation of at least 1½ inches between conductors or between conductors and any grounded metal.

(c) Receptacles.   Electrode receptacles for the tubing shall be of noncombustible, nonabsorptive insulating material approved for the purpose.

(d) Bushings.   Where electrodes enter the enclosure of outdoor signs or of an indoor sign operating at a voltage in excess of 7,500 volts, bushings shall be used unless receptacles are provided or the sign is wired with bare wire mounted on approved supports which maintain the tubing in proper position. Bushings shall be of noncombustible, nonabsorptive material. Where bare wiring is used, the conductor shall be not less than No. 14 solid copper, shall be supported so as to prevent sagging and lessening of the spacing required elsewhere in this Article, and electrode terminal assemblies shall be of an approved type and supported not more than 6 inches from the electrode terminals.

(e) Show Windows.   In the exposed type of show-window signs, terminals shall be (1) enclosed by receptacles approved for the purpose or (2) where hanging in air, free from grounded surfaces, enclosed in sleeves of vulcanized fiber, phenolic composition, or other suitable material which overlaps all live parts by at least $\frac{1}{2}$ inch.

(f) Receptacles and Bushing Seals.   A flexible, nonconducting seal may be used to close the opening between the tubing and the receptacle or bushing against the entrance of dust or moisture. This seal shall not be in contact with grounded conductive material and shall not be depended upon for the insulation of the tubing.

(g) Enclosures of Metal.   Enclosures of metal for electrodes shall be of not less than No. 24 MSG sheet metal.

(h) Enclosures of Insulating Material.   Enclosures of insulating material shall be noncombustible, nonabsorptive and approved for the voltage of the circuit.

▶   The component parts of a gas-tube sign or lighting system are:

1. A transformer having a **115-** or **230**-volt primary and a high-voltage secondary. Most primaries are 115 volts.

2. High-voltage leads from the transformer to the tube.

3. The tube terminals, by means of which the leads are connected to the electrodes at the ends of the tube.

4. The tube itself.

Aside from the high-voltage leads and the tube terminals, the tube of a gas-tube system involves little accident hazard except that with high voltages a discharge may take place from the tube to conductive objects. The tube should be kept away from flammable material since such material might be slightly conductive, and the tube should not be located where it is likely to be broken.

In outdoor signs the tube terminals usually project within the sign enclosure. They may, however, be contained in separate enclosures of sheet metal or insulating material or may be without any enclosure if kept away from combustible material and inaccessible to unauthorized persons.

For exposed signs in show windows, the tube terminals must be enclosed in sleeves of insulating material and the high-voltage leads may consist of conductors insulated for the operating voltage and hanging free in air, if kept away from combustible or conductive material and not subject to physical damage.

600-35. Switches on Doors.   Doors or covers giving access to uninsulated parts of indoor signs or outline lighting exceeding 600 volts and accessible to the general public, shall either be provided with interlock switches which on the opening of the doors or covers disconnect the primary circuit, or shall be so fastened that the use of the other than ordinary tools will be necessary to open them.

ARTICLE 610. CRANES AND HOISTS

A. Scope and Use

610-1. Scope.   The provisions of this Article shall apply to the installation of cranes, crane runways, hoists, and monorails.

610-2. Particular Locations.

   (a) Ignitible Material Hazards.   Installations in hazardous locations shall comply with the provisions of Section 503-13.

   (b) Combustible Materials.   Where a crane operates over readily combustible material, the resistors shall be placed in a well-ventilated cabinet composed of noncombustible material so constructed that it will not emit flames or molten metal.

   Exception: Resistors may be located in a cage or cab constructed of noncombustible material which encloses the sides of the cage or cab from the floor to a point at least 6 inches above the top of the resistors.

B. Wiring

610-11. Wiring Method.   Conductors shall be enclosed in raceways or be Type ALS cable or Type MI cable.

   Exception No. 1: Bare conductors used as contact conductors.

   Exception No. 2: Short lengths of open conductors at resistors, collectors, and other equipment.

   Exception No. 3: Where flexible connections are necessary to motors and similar equipment, flexible metal conduit, liquidtight flexible metal conduit, metal-clad cable, multiple-conductor rubber-covered cable or an approved nonmetallic enclosure may be employed.

   Exception No. 4: Where multiple-conductor cable is used with a suspended push-button station, the station must be supported in some satisfactory manner that will protect the electrical conductors against strain.

▶   In general, the wiring on a crane or a hoist should be rigid conduit work or electrical metallic tubing. Short lengths of flexible conduit or metal-clad cable may be used for connections to motors, brake magnets, or other devices where a rigid connection is impracticable because the devices are subject to some movement with respect to the bases to which they are attached. In outdoor or wet locations liquidtight flexible metal conduit should be used for flexible connections.

610-12. Raceway Terminal Fittings.   Conductors leaving raceways shall comply with the provisions of Section 300-16.

610-13. Types of Conductors.   Conductors shall be of the rubber-covered or the thermoplastic type except:

Exception No. 1: Contact conductors along runways, crane bridges and monorails | *may be bare and may be of hard drawn copper, or aluminum, or steel in the form of tees, angles, tee rails, or other stiff shapes.*

Exception No. 2: Flexible conductors may be used to convey current and where | *practicable, cable reels or take-up devices may be employed.*

Exception No. 3: Varnished-cambric conductors (Type V) or asbestos varnished | *cambric (Types AVA and AVB) may be used in dry locations.*

Exception No. 4: Type MI cable may be used in wet or dry locations within its | *specified temperature ratings.*

Exception No. 5: Conductors exposed to external heat or connected to resistors | *shall have an insulation approved for the temperature and location as specified in Section 310-2. Where conductors not having a flame-resistant outer covering are grouped together, the group shall be covered with a flame-resistant tape.*

610-14. Conductors

(a) Ampacity.   The allowable ampacities of conductors shall be as shown in Table 610-14(a). For the ampacities of conductors between controllers and resistors, see Section 430-23.

(b) Minimum.   Conductors shall not be smaller than No. 14.

Exception: No. 16 may be used for crane and hoist motor and control circuits only when the application meets Section 610-14(a) ampacity, and provided the conductors are protected against physical damage.

▶   Crane and hoist motors are rated for "short-time duty." (See definition of "Duty, Short Time," in Art. 100.) These motors seldom operate for more than a few minutes at one time and then remain stationary for several minutes; in other words, the load factor is low. For this reason, the conductors supplying the motors can safely be considerably smaller than would be required for motors of the same horsepower rating that operate continuously.

(c) Contact Conductors.   The size of contact wires shall be not less than the following:

Distance between end strain insulators	Size of wire
0–30 feet	No. 6
31–60 feet	No. 4
over 60 feet	No. 2

(d) Calculation of Motor Load.   The ampacity of the power supply conductors on the crane shall be not less than the combined short time full load ampere rating of the largest motor or group of motors for any single crane motion plus 50 per cent of the combined short time full load ampere rating of the next largest motor or group of motors.

(e) Other Loads.   Additional loads, such as heating, lighting, and air conditioning, shall be provided for by application of the appropriate sections of this Code.

Table 610-14(a). Ampacities of Insulated Conductors in Raceway or Cable Used with Short Time Rated Crane and Hoist Motors

Max. Oper- ating Temp.	60°C		75°C		90°C		110°C	
Size AWG MCM	Type T, TW		Type RH, RHW, THW, THWN, XHHW		Type AVB, FEP, FEPB, RHH, SA, TA, THHN, XHHW*		Type AVA	
	60 min	30 min	60 min	30 min	60 min	30 min	60 min	30 min
16	10	10	10	12	..	..	..	..
14	20	20	25	26	31	32	38	40
12	25	25	30	33	36	40	45	50
10	35	35	40	43	49	52	60	65
8	45	50	55	60	63	69	73	80
6	57	70	76	86	83	94	93	105
5	65	80	85	95	95	106	109	121
4	77	95	100	117	111	130	126	147
3	90	115	120	141	131	153	145	168
2	107	130	137	160	148	173	163	190
1	130	150	143	175	158	192	177	215
0	160	180	190	233	211	259	239	294
00	195	225	222	267	245	294	275	331
000	245	280	280	341	305	372	339	413
0000	295	350	300	369	319	399	352	440
250	350	375	364	420	400	461	447	516
300	410	475	455	582	497	636	554	707
350	460	550	486	646	542	716	616	809
400	515	580	538	688	593	760	666	856
450	565	640	600	765	660	836	740	930
500	620	700	660	847	726	914	815	1004

Other insulations shown in Section 310-2 and approved for the temperatures and location may be substituted for those shown in Table 610-14(a).

The allowable ampacities of conductors used with 15-minute motors shall be the 30-minute ratings increased by 12 per cent.

* For dry locations only. See Table 310-2(a).

610-15. Common Return.   Where a crane or hoist is operated by more than one motor, a common-return conductor of proper ampacity may be used.

C. Contact Conductors

610-21. Installation of Contact Conductors.   Bare contact conductors shall conform to the following:

(a) Contact Wires.   Wires that are used as contact conductors shall be secured at the ends by means of approved strain insulators and shall be so mounted on approved insulators that the extreme limit of displacement of the wire will not bring the latter within less than 1½ inches from the surface wired over.

(b) Supports Along Runways.   Main contact conductors carried along runways shall be supported on insulating supports placed at intervals not exceeding 20 feet, and these supports shall be insulating except for grounded rail conductors as provided in Section 610-21(e). Such conductors shall be separated not less than 6 inches except for monorail hoists where a spacing of not less than 3 inches may be used. Where necessary, intervals between insulating supports may be increased up to 40 feet, the separation between conductors being increased proportionately.

(c) Supports on Bridges.   Bridge contact conductors shall be kept at least 2½ inches apart and, where the span exceeds 80 feet, insulating saddles shall be placed at intervals not exceeding 50 feet.

(d) Supports for Rigid Conductors.   Conductors along runways and crane bridges, which are of the rigid type specified in Section 610-13 Exception No. 1, shall be carried on insulating supports spaced at intervals of not more than 80 times the vertical dimension of the conductor, but in no case greater than 15 feet, and spaced apart sufficiently to give a clear electrical separation of conductors or adjacent collectors of not less than 1 inch.

(e) Track as Circuit Conductor.   Monorail, tramrail or crane-runway tracks may be used as a conductor of current for one phase of a three-phase alternating-current system furnishing power to the carrier, crane or trolley, provided all of the following conditions are fulfilled:

(1)   The conductors for supplying the other two phases of the power supply shall be insulated.

(2)   The power for all phases shall be obtained from an insulating transformer.

(3)   The voltage shall not exceed 300 volts.

(4)   The rail serving as a conductor shall be effectively grounded at the transformer and may also be grounded by the fittings used for the suspension or attachment of the rail to a building or structure.

(f) Electrical Continuity of Contact Conductors.   All sections of bare rigid contact conductors shall be mechanically joined to provide a continuous electrical connection.

(g) Not to Supply Other Equipment.   Contact conductors shall not be used as feeders for any equipment other than the crane or cranes which they are primarily designed to serve.

(h) Locating or Guarding Contact Conductors.   Contact conductors shall be located or guarded in such a manner that unqualified persons cannot inadvertently touch energized current-carrying parts.

▶   In some cases, particularly where a monorail crane or conveyer is used for handling light loads, for the sake of convenience and simplicity it may be desirable to use the track as one conductor of a three-phase system. Where this arrangement is used the power must be supplied through a transformer or bank of transformers so that there will be no electrical connection between the primary power supply and the crane circuit. (See Fig. 610-1.) The secondary voltage would usually be 220 and the primary of

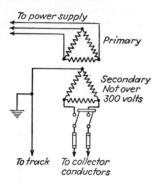

To track   To collector conductors

Fig. 610-1. Three-phase isolating transformer for crane service.

the transformer would usually be connected to the power-distribution system of the building or plant. The leg connected to the track must be grounded at the transformer only, except as permitted in Section 610-21e4.

610-22. Collectors.   Collectors shall be so designed as to reduce to a minimum sparking between them and the contact conductor, and when operated in rooms used for the storage of easily ignitible combustible fibers and materials the requirements of Section 503-13 shall be complied with.

D. Control

610-31. Runway Conductor Disconnecting Means.   A disconnecting means shall be provided between the runway contact conductors and the power supply. Such disconnecting means shall consist of a motor-circuit switch or circuit breaker. This disconnecting means shall be readily accessible and operable from the ground, shall be arranged to be locked in the open position, shall open all ungrounded conductors simultaneously, and shall be placed within sight of the crane or hoist and the runway contact conductors.

▶   The switch required by this rule serves as the disconnecting means required by Section 430-112 for the group of motors on the crane.

610-32. Disconnecting Means for Crane.   A motor-circuit switch or circuit breaker shall be provided in the leads from the runway contact conductors on all bridge cranes. Where this disconnecting means is not readily accessible from the crane operating station, means shall be provided at the crane operating station to open the power circuit to the crane motors.

▶   This switch is an emergency device, provided for use in case trouble develops in any of the electrical equipment on the crane.

610-33. Rating of Disconnecting Means for Crane.   On both alternating-current and direct-current crane protective panels, the continuous ampacity of the switch or circuit breaker required by Section 610-32, and main line contactors, shall be not less than 50 per cent of the combined short-time ampacities of the motors, nor less than 75 per cent of the sum of the short-time ampacities of the motors required for any single crane motion.

▶   It is possible that all the motors on a crane might be in operation at one time, but this condition would continue for only a very short while. A switch or circuit breaker having a current rating not less than 50 per cent of the sum of full-load current rating of all the motors will have ample capacity.

610-34. Limit Switch.   A limit switch shall be provided for upper limit of travel of crane hoists.

E. Overcurrent Protection

610-41. Contact Conductors.   The main contact conductors shall be protected by an overcurrent device.

▶   If the crane or hoist is operated by only one motor, the circuit supplying the contact conductors is a motor branch circuit and the rating of the circuit overcurrent device is governed by Art. **430.**

If the crane or hoist is operated by two or more motors, conductors of the feeder supplying the collector conductors are to be determined in accordance with Sections **430-24** and **430-26,** except that the ampacities given in Section **610-14** may be used, and the rating or setting of the overcurrent device protecting this feeder is to be determined in accordance with Section **430-62.** This device serves also to protect the bare collector conductors.

610-42. Crane Motors.   Where more than one motor is employed on a crane, each motor shall have individual overcurrent protection as provided in Article 430, except that where two motors operate a single hoist, carriage, truck, or bridge, and are controlled as a unit by one controller, the pair of motors with their leads may be protected by a single overcurrent device.

▶   Crane and hoist motors are classified as "short-time duty" motors, hence according to Section **430-33** the only overcurrent protection required is the branch-circuit fuses or circuit breaker; no running protection is required.

Assuming a crane equipped with three motors operating on a d-c system, Figs. **610-2** and **610-3** show two possible circuit arrangements. In order to simplify these diagrams all control devices have been omitted.

Figure 610-2. A two-wire circuit may be run from the panelboard to each motor. Section **430-55** requires a fuse or one pole of a circuit breaker in each conductor, assuming that the d-c system has no grounded conductor. These

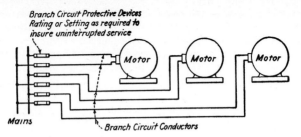

FIG. 610-2. Three crane motors with an individual branch circuit to each motor.

protective devices should be located at the panelboard and their rating or setting should be **150** per cent of the full-load motor current, according to Sections **430-33** and **430-52**.

The size of the conductors is governed by Section **610-14**.

Figure 610-3. Section **610-15** permits a common return conductor to be used for all motors. Where this arrangement is used, it is evidently the intention that single-pole protection for each motor shall be used, since double-pole protection could be provided only by installing a fuse or circuit breaker

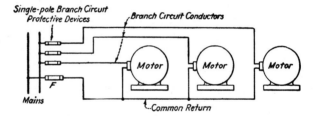

FIG. 610-3. Three crane motors with a single branch-circuit conductor to each motor and a common return conductor.

at each motor and this would be undesirable because devices in such locations would not be readily accessible to the operator.

The common return conductor actually serves as an extension of one conductor of the feeder and is subject to the rules in Art. **240** for the overload protection of conductors. If this common return is protected, in accordance with the rules, by the overcurrent device that protects the feeder supplying the main contact conductors, no additional fuse or circuit breaker is required at the panelboard.

If, on the other hand, the rating or setting of the feeder fuses or circuit breaker is too high to provide proper protection for the common return conductor, a protective device F should be installed.

F. Grounding

610-51. Grounding.   All exposed metal parts of cranes, hoists, and accessories, including pendant controls, shall be metallically joined together into a continuous electrical conductor so that the entire crane or hoist will be grounded on installation in accordance with Article 250. Moving parts, other than removable accessories or attachments having metal-to-metal bearing surfaces, such as bridge wheels running on a track, shall be considered to be electrically connected to each other through the bearing surfaces for grounding purposes.

ARTICLE 620. ELEVATORS, DUMBWAITERS, ESCALATORS, AND MOVING WALKS

A. Scope and General

620-1. Scope. This Article shall apply to electrical equipment and wiring used in connection with elevators, dumbwaiters, escalators, and moving walks.

For further information see ANSI Safety Code for Elevators, Dumbwaiters, Escalators and Moving Walks, A17.1-1965.

▶ These provisions may also be considered as applying to console lifts, equipment for raising and lowering or rotating portions of theater stages, and all similar equipment.

620-2. Voltage Limitations. The nominal voltage used for elevator, dumbwaiter, escalator, and moving walk operating control and signal circuits, operating equipment, driving machine motors, machine brakes, and motor-generator sets shall not exceed the following:

(a) For operating control and signal circuits and related equipment including door operator motors: 300 volts except that higher potentials may be used for frequencies of 25- through 60-hertz alternating current or for direct current provided the current in the system cannot, under any conditions, exceed 8 milliamperes for alternating current or 30 milliamperes for direct current.

(b) Driving machine motors, machine brakes, and motor-generator sets: 600 volts, except that higher potentials may be used for driving motors of motor-generator sets.

620-3. Live Parts Enclosed. All live parts of electrical apparatus in the hoistways, at the landings, or in or on the cars of elevators and dumbwaiters or in the wellways or the landings of escalators or moving walks shall be enclosed to protect against accidental contact.

B. Conductors

620-11. Insulation of Conductors. The insulation of conductors installed in connection with elevators, dumbwaiters, escalators and moving walks, shall comply with the following:

(a) **Control Panel Wiring.** Conductors from panels to main circuit resistors shall be flame-retardant and suitable for a temperature of not less than 90°C. (194°F.). All other wiring on control panels shall be flame-retardant, moisture-resistant.

(b) Traveling Cables. Traveling cables used as flexible connections between the elevator or dumbwaiter car and the raceway shall be of the types of elevator cable listed in Table 400-11 or other approved types.

(c) Other Wiring. All conductors in the raceways and in or on the cars of elevators and dumbwaiters and in the wellways of escalators and moving walks and in the machine room of elevators, dumbwaiters, escalators and moving walks shall have flame-retardant and moisture-resistant insulation.

(d) Thickness of Insulation. The thickness of the insulation of all conductors shall be suitable for the voltage to which the conductors are subjected.

▶ A distinction is made here between the heavy connections carrying the power current and the smaller wires of operating circuits, such as wires connected to the magnet coils of contactors. The operating current passing through the magnet coils may be quite small and a small current leaking through damp slow-burning insulation where two insulated wires are in contact might be sufficient to operate a contactor.

620-12. Minimum Size of Conductors. The minimum size of conductors used for elevator, dumbwaiter, escalator, and moving walk wiring, except for conductors which form an integral part of control equipment, shall be as follows:

(a) Traveling Cables.

(1) For lighting circuits: No. 14.

Exception: No. 20 or larger conductors may be used in parallel provided the ampacity is equivalent to at least that of No. 14 wire.

(2) Operating control and signal circuits: No. 20.

(b) Other Wiring. All operating control and signal circuits: No. 20.

620-13. Motor Circuit Conductors. Conductors supplying elevator, dumbwaiter, escalator, or moving walk motors shall have an ampacity conforming to (a), (b) and (c) below based on the nameplate current rating of the motors. With generator field control, the ampacity shall be based on the nameplate current rating of the driving motor of the motor-generator set which supplies power to the elevator motor.

The heating of conductors depends on root mean square current values which, with generator field control, are reflected by the nameplate current rating of the motor-generator set driving motor rather than by the rating of the elevator motor which represents actual but short time and intermittent full-load current values.

(a) Conductors Supplying a Single Motor. Conductors supplying a single motor shall have an ampacity in conformance with Section 430-22, Table 430-22 (a-Exception).

(b) Conductors Supplying Several Motors. Conductors supplying several motors shall have an ampacity of not less than 125 per cent of the nameplate current rating of the highest rated motor in the group plus the sum of the nameplate current ratings of the remainder of the motors in the group.

(c) Feeder Demand Factor. Feeder conductors of less capacity than required by (b) above may be furnished subject to the requirements of Section 430-26.

▶ Tables 310-12 to 310-15 do not include the ampacity for No. 20 AWG copper conductors. However, it is generally considered that the ampacity for No. 20 conductors up to two conductors in raceways or in cable or cord may safely carry 3 amp.

The development of elevator control equipment, which has been taking place for many years, has resulted in the design and use of equipment including electronic unit contactors requiring very much smaller currents (milliamperes) for their operation.

As a result, the insistence on the use of No. 16 wire for elevator control and operating circuits requires the use of far larger wire than would be required if the size was based, as it should be, on the allowable ampacity of the wires. Even No. 18 wire is considerably larger than is required to safely handle the actual currents involved.

The development of elevator control equipment has also resulted in a very great increase in the number of control and operation circuits between the control equipment in the elevator machine rooms and the car and the equipment in the hoistway which must be pulled in the conduits and carried in the traveling cables. It is important, therefore, not only from the standpoint of cost but particularly from that of the space available in the hoistway, to permit the use of smaller wire with a corresponding reduction in the conduit size. With double wrap traction machines each pound of traveling cable weight adds four (4) pounds to the load on the machine shaft and bearings. The weight of the traveling cables on one of the high rise cars in the Empire State Building exceeded three thousand (3,000) pounds and would be even greater with the modern controls now used for such elevators.

It can be seen, therefore, that the problem has become a serious one and requires relief. As No. 20 wire has ample ampacity and as $\frac{1}{64}$ inch insulation is ample for the 300 volts permitted for the operation and control circuits, they are permitted by the code.

C. Wiring

620-21. Wiring Methods. Conductors located in hoistways and escalators and moving walk wellways, in or on cars and machine and control rooms, not including the traveling cables connecting the car and hoistway wiring, shall be installed in rigid conduit, electrical metallic tubing, metal wireways, Type ALS cable or Type MI cable subject to the following exceptions:

Exception No. 1: Flexible conduit or Type AC metal-clad cable may be used in hoistways and in escalator and moving walk wellways between risers and limit switches, interlocks, operating buttons, and similar devices.

Exception No. 2: Short runs of flexible conduit or Type AC metal-clad cable may be used on cars where so located as to be free from oil and if securely fastened in place.

Exception No. 3: Type S, SO, STO, or ST cords may be used as flexible connections between the fixed wiring on the car and the switches on car doors or gates. Such cords may be used as flexible connections for the top-of-car operating device or the car top work light. These devices or fixtures shall be grounded by means of a grounding conductor run with the circuit conductors.

Exception No. 4: Conductors between control panels and machine motors, machine brakes, and motor generator sets, not exceeding six feet in length, may be grouped together and taped or corded without being installed in a raceway provided the taping or cording is painted with an insulating paint. Such cable groups shall be supported at intervals of not more than three feet and so located as to be free from physical damage.

Where motor generators and machine motors are located adjacent to or underneath control equipment, and are provided with extra length terminal leads not exceeding six feet in length, such leads may be extended to connect directly to controller terminal studs without regard to the carrying capacity requirements of Articles 430 and 445. Auxiliary gutters may be used in machine and control rooms between controllers, starters and similar apparatus.

D. Installation of Conductors

620-31. Raceway Terminal Fittings. Conductors shall comply with the provisions of Section 300-16(b). In locations where conduits project from the floor and terminate in other than a wiring enclosure, they must extend at least 6 inches above the floor.

620-32. Metal Wireways. Section 362-5 shall not apply to wireways. The sum of the cross sectional area of the individual conductors in a metallic wireway shall not be more than 50 per cent of the interior cross sectional area of the wireway.

Vertical runs of wireways shall be securely supported at intervals not exceeding 15 feet and shall have not more than one joint between supports. Adjoining wireway sections shall be securely fastened together to provide a rigid joint.

620-33. Number of Conductors in Other Raceways. The sum of the cross-sectional area of the operating and control circuit conductors in raceways shall not exceed 40 per cent of the interior cross-sectional area of the raceway.

Exception: Wireways as permitted in Section 620-32.

620-34. Supports. Supports for cables or raceways in the hoistway or escalator or moving walk wellway shall be securely fastened to the guide rail or to the hoistway or wellway construction.

620-35. Auxiliary Gutters (Wiring Troughs). Auxiliary gutters shall not be subject to the restrictions of Section 374-2 as to length or of Section 374-5 as to number of conductors.

620-36. Different Systems in One Raceway or Traveling Cable. Conductors for operating, control, power, signal, and light circuits of 600 volts or less may be run in the same traveling cable or raceway system provided that all conductors are insulated for the maximum voltage found in the cables or raceway system and all live parts of the equipment are insulated from ground for this maximum voltage. Such a traveling cable or raceway may also include a pair of telephone conductors for the car telephone provided such conductors are insulated for the maximum voltage found in the cable or raceway system.

▶ It would be difficult, if not practically impossible, to keep the wires of each system completely isolated from the wires of every other system in the case of elevator control and signal circuits, hence such wires may be run in the same conduits and cables if all wires are insulated for the highest voltage used and if all live parts of apparatus are insulated from ground for the highest voltage, provided that the signal system is an integral part of the elevator wiring system.

The characteristics of the current may be changed by using a rectifier or motor generator to change from a-c to d-c. The voltage may be changed by using a transformer or motor generator, or equipment may be provided that will change both the current and the voltage.

620-37. Wiring in Hoistways.   Main feeders for supplying power to elevators and dumbwaiters shall be installed outside the hoistway. Only such electrical wiring, conduit and cable used directly in connection with the elevator or dumbwaiter, including wiring for signals, for communication with the car, for lighting and ventilating the car and wiring for fire-detecting systems for the hoistways, may be installed inside the hoistway.

Exception: In existing structures, feeders for elevators or other purposes may be installed within a hoistway by special permission provided no conductors are spliced within the hoistway.

620-38. Electrical Equipment in Garages and Similar Occupancies.   Electrical equipment and wiring used for elevators, dumbwaiters, escalators, and moving walks in garages shall conform to the requirements of Article 511. Wiring and equipment located on the underside of the car platform shall be considered as being located in the hazardous area.

620-39. Sidewalk Elevators.   Sidewalk elevators with sidewalk doors, located exterior to the building, shall have all electric wiring in rigid metal conduit or electrical metallic tubing and all electrical outlets, switches, junction boxes, and fittings shall be weatherproof.

E. Traveling Cables

620-41. Suspension.   Traveling cables shall be so suspended at the car and hoistway end as to reduce the strain on the individual copper conductors to a minimum.

Cables with an unsupported length exceeding 100 feet shall have steel supporting fillers and shall be suspended directly by the steel supporting fillers.

Where nonmetallic fillers are used, the cables shall be suspended by looping the cables around the supports, or shall be suspended from the support by a means that automatically tightens around the cable when tension is increased.

620-42. Hazardous Locations.   In hazardous locations, traveling cables shall be of a type approved for hazardous locations and shall be secured to explosion proof cabinets as provided in Section 501-11.

620-43. Location of and Protection for Cables.   Traveling cable supports shall be so located as to reduce to a minimum the possibility of damage due to the cables coming in contact with the hoistway construction or equipment in the hoistway. Where necessary, suitable guards shall be provided to protect the cables against damage.

F. Control

620-51. Disconnecting Means.   There shall be in addition to the elevator controller, a means for disconnecting all conductors of the circuit to the elevator motor, or in the case of generator field control, to the motor of the motor-generator set which supplies current to the elevator motor.

(a) Type. The disconnecting means shall be an enclosed externally operable motor circuit switch or circuit breaker arranged to be locked in the open position.

(b) Location. It shall be located adjacent to and be visible from the elevator machine, unless a disconnect switch in the control circuit of the motor-generator set is placed adjacent to and is visible from the elevator machine.

620-53. Phase Protection. Elevators driven by polyphase alternating current machine motors shall be provided with means to prevent starting of the elevator motor when:

(a) The phase rotation is in the wrong direction, or

(b) There is a failure in any phase.

▶ If the connections of any two leads of a three-phase motor are interchanged, or if the connections of the two leads of one phase of a two-phase motor are interchanged, the direction of rotation of the motor will be reversed. This phase reversal is sometimes made unintentionally when repair work is being done on the motor or wiring system and, of course, has the effect of reversing the direction of travel of the car. The reverse-phase relay makes it impossible to operate the controller and start the motor under these conditions.

If one of the leads to the motor is disconnected, leaving the other leads connected, the motor winding that remains connected will draw an excessive current and a burnout will probably result unless the motor is completely disconnected at once.

G. Overcurrent Protection

620-61. Overcurrent Protection. Overcurrent protection shall be provided as follows:

(a) Control and Operating Circuits. Control and operating circuits and signal circuits shall be protected against overcurrent in accordance with the requirements of Section 725-18.

(b) Motors.

(1) Duty on elevator and dumbwaiter driving machine motors and driving motors of motor generators used with generator field control shall be classed as intermittent. Such motors shall be protected against overcurrent in accordance with Section 430-33.

(2) Duty on escalator and moving walk driving machine motors shall be classed as continuous. Such motors shall be protected against overcurrent in accordance with Section 430-32.

(3) Escalator and moving-walk driving machine motors and driving motors of motor-generator sets shall be protected against running overcurrent as provided in Table 430-37.

H. Machine Room

620-71. Guarding Equipment. Elevator, dumbwaiter, escalator, and moving walk driving machines, motor-generator sets, controllers, auxiliary control equipment and disconnecting means shall be installed in a room or enclosure set aside for that purpose. The room or enclosure shall be secured against unauthorized access.

Exception: Dumbwaiter, escalator, or moving-walk controllers may be installed outside the spaces herein specified, provided they are enclosed in cabinets with doors or removable panels capable of being locked in the closed position and the disconnecting means is located adjacent to the controller. Such cabinets may be mounted in the balustrading on the side away from the moving steps or moving treadway.

620-72. Clearance Around Control Panels. There shall be provided sufficient clear working space around control panels to provide safe and convenient access to all live parts of the equipment necessary for maintenance and adjustment. The minimum clear working space about live parts on control panels shall not be less than set forth in Section 110-16.

The minimum working clearance for escalator and moving-walk control panels shall be as specified in Section 110-16, provided that where the control panel is mounted in the same space as the escalator or moving-walk drive machine and the clearances specified cannot be provided, they may be waived where the entire panel is arranged so that it can be readily removed from the machine space and is provided with flexible leads to all external connections.

Where control panels are not located in the same space as the drive machine they shall be so located in cabinets with doors or removable panels capable of being locked in the closed position. Such cabinets may be mounted in the balustrading on the side away from the moving steps or moving treadway.

J. Grounding

620-81. Metal Raceways Attached to Cars. Conduit, Type ALS cable or Type AC metal-clad cable attached to elevator cars shall be bonded to grounded metal parts of the car with which they come in contact.

620-82. Electric Elevators. For electric elevators, the frames of all motors, elevator machines, controllers and the metal enclosures for all electrical devices in or on the car or in the hoistway shall be grounded.

620-83. Nonelectric Elevators. For elevators other than electric, when any electrical conductors are attached to the car, the metal frame of the car, where normally accessible to persons, shall be grounded.

620-85. Inherent Ground. Equipment mounted on members of the structural metal frame of a building shall be deemed to be grounded. Metal car frames supported by metal hoisting cables attached to or running over sheaves or drums of elevator machines shall be deemed to be grounded when the machine is grounded in accordance with Article 250.

K. Overspeed

620-91. Overspeed Protection for Elevators. Under overhauling load conditions, means shall be provided on the load side of each elevator power disconnecting means to prevent the elevator from attaining a speed equal to the governor tripping speed or a speed in excess of 125 per cent of the elevator rated speed, whichever is the lesser.

620-92. Motor-Generator Overspeed Device. Motor-generators driven by direct-current motors and used to supply direct current for the operation of elevator machine motors shall be provided with speed limiting devices as required by Section 430-89(c), which will prevent the elevator from attaining at any time a speed of more than 125 per cent of its rated speed.

ARTICLE 630. ELECTRIC WELDERS

A. General

630-1. Scope. This Article covers electric arc welding, resistance welding apparatus, and other similar welding equipment that is connected to an electrical supply system.

630-2. Other Articles. This Article amplifies or modifies parts of Chapters 1 through 4 of this Code in order to properly cover the operating conditions to which electric welder installations are subjected. Accordingly, the appropriate provisions of Chapters 1 through 4 apply to the component parts of electric welder installations except as otherwise provided in this Article.

▶ There are two general types of electric welding; arc welding and resistance welding. In arc welding, an arc is drawn between the metal parts to be joined together and a metal electrode (a wire or rod), and metal from the electrode is deposited on the joint. In resistance welding, the metal parts to be joined are pressed tightly together between two electrodes, and a heavy current is passed through the electrodes and the plates or other parts to be welded. The electrodes make contact on a small area, thus the current passes through a small cross section of metal having a high resistance, and sufficient heat is generated to raise the parts to be welded to a welding temperature.

In arc welding with a-c, an individual transformer is used for each operator, *i.e.*, a transformer supplies current for one arc only. When d-c is used, there is usually an individual generator for each operator, though there are also "multi-operator" arc-welding generators.

B. AC Transformer and DC Rectifier Arc Welders

630-11. Ampacities of Supply Conductors. The ampacities of conductors for AC transformer and DC rectifier arc welders shall be as follows:

(a) Individual Welders. The rated ampacities of the supply conductors shall be not less than the current values determined by multiplying the rated primary current in amperes, given on the welder nameplate, and the following factor based upon the duty cycle or time rating of the welders:

Rated Per Cent Duty Cycle of Welders	Multiplying Factor
20 or less	0.45
30	0.55
40	0.63
50	0.71
60	0.78
70	0.84
80	0.89
90	0.95
100	1.00

For a welder having a time rating of one hour, the multiplying factor shall be 0.75.

(b) Group of Welders. The rated ampacities of conductors which supply a group of welders may be less than the sum of the currents, as determined in accordance with Section 630-11(a) of the welders supplied. The conductor rating shall be determined in each case according to the welder loading based on the use to be made of each welder and the allowance permissible in the event that all the welders supplied by the conductors will not be in use at the same time. The load value used for each welder shall take into account both the magnitude and the duration of the load while the welder is in use.

Conductor ratings based on 100 per cent of the current, as determined in accordance with Section 630-11(a), of the two largest welders, 85 per cent for the third largest welder, 70 per cent for the fourth largest welder, and 60 per cent for all the remaining welders, should provide an ample margin of safety under high production conditions with respect to the maximum permissible temperature of the conductors. Percentage values lower than those given are permissible in cases where the work is such that a high operating duty cycle for individual welders is impossible.

▶ The term *transformer arc welder* is commonly used in the trade and hence is used in the Code, though the equipment might more properly be described as an *arc-welding transformer*. Reference should be made here to Section **630-31** where the term *duty cycle* is explained.

It is evident that the load on each transformer is intermittent. Where several transformers are supplied by one feeder, the intermittent loading will cause much less heating of the feeder conductors than would result from a continuous load equal to the sum of the full-load current ratings of all the transformers. The ampacity of the feeder conductors may therefore be reduced if the feeder supplies three or more transformers.

630-12. Overcurrent Protection. Overcurrent protection for AC transformer and DC rectifier arc welders shall be as provided in Section 630-12(a) and (b). Where the nearest standard rating of the overcurrent device used is under the value specified in this Section, or where the rating or setting specified results in unnecessary opening of the overcurrent device, the next higher rating or setting may be used.

(a) For Welders. Each welder shall have overcurrent protection rated or set at not more than 200 per cent of the rated primary current of the welder, except that an overcurrent device is not required for a welder having supply conductors protected by an overcurrent device rated or set at not more than 200 per cent of the rated primary current of the welder.

(b) For Conductors. Conductors which supply one or more welders shall be protected by an overcurrent device rated or set at not more than 200 per cent of the conductor rating.

▶   Arc-welding transformers are so designed that as the secondary current increases, the secondary voltage decreases. This characteristic of the transformer greatly reduces the fluctuation of the load on the transformer as the length of the arc, and consequently the secondary current, is varied by the operator.

The rating or setting of the overcurrent devices specified in this Section provides short-circuit protection. It has been stated that with the electrode "frozen" to the work the primary current will in most cases rise to about 170 per cent of the current rating of the transformer. This condition represents the heaviest overload that can occur and of course this condition would never be allowed to continue for more than a very short time.

630-13. Disconnecting Means. A disconnecting means shall be provided in the supply connection of each AC transformer and DC rectifier arc welder which is not equipped with a disconnect mounted as an integral part of the welder.

The disconnecting means shall be a switch or circuit breaker and its rating shall be not less than that necessary to accommodate overcurrent protection as specified under Section 630-12.

▶   Figure 630-1 shows a transformer arc welder complete with its enclosing case and Fig. 630-2 shows the internal construction. Figure 630-3 is a diagram of the connections of the transformer. The lead to the welding electrode is attached to the stud shown in Fig. 630-2 between the upper and lower sets of coils, and is brought out through the large bushed opening in the case. The ground lead for connection to the metal parts to be welded is attached to the stud on the base of the welder. (There is a slight discrepancy between the two illustrations in the position of this stud.) The primary leads, which would usually be in the form of rubber-sheathed cable, are brought in through a bushed opening in the case and connected by means of lugs to studs on a terminal block.

This welder has no integral circuit-opening device, therefore the primary leads must be supplied through a circuit breaker or fused motor-circuit switch.

The upper windings of the transformer serve as a reactor to stabilize the arc. The welding current can be adjusted to any desired value from 50 to 400 amp by changing the position of the movable part of the core. The secondary open-circuit voltage is approximately 80 volts at the 50-amp setting and 70 volts at the 400-amp setting. The maximum primary current at 220 volts is 133 amp.

630-14. Marking. A nameplate giving the following information shall be provided for AC transformer and DC rectifier arc welders: name of manufacturer;

frequency; number of phases; primary voltage; rated primary current; maximum open-circuit voltage; rated secondary current; basis of rating, i.e., the duty cycle, 60-minute rating.

Fig. 630-1. Ampac transformer arc welder. (*Allis-Chalmers Mfg. Co.*)

Fig. 630-2. Ampac transformer arc welder with case removed. (*Allis-Chalmers Mfg. Co.*)

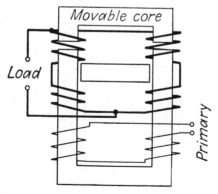

Fig. 630-3. Diagram of connections of transformer arc welder shown in Figs. 630-1 and 630-2.

C. Motor-Generator Arc Welders

630-21. Ampacities of Supply Conductors. The ampacities of conductors for motor-generator arc welders shall be as follows:

(a) Individual Welders. The rated ampacities of the supply conductors shall be not less than the current values determined by multiplying the rated primary current in amperes, given on the welder nameplate, and the following factor based upon the duty cycle or time rating of the welders:

Rated Per cent Duty Cycle of Welders	Multiplying Factor
20 or less	0.55
30	0.62
40	0.69
50	0.75
60	0.81
70	0.86
80	0.91
90	0.96
100	1.00

For a welder having a time rating of one hour, the multiplying factor shall be 0.80.

(b) Group of Welders. The rated ampacities of conductors which supply a group of welders may be less than the sum of the currents, as determined in accordance with Section 630-21(a) of the welders supplied. The conductor rating shall be determined in each case according to the welder loading based on the use to be made of each welder and the allowance permissible in the event that all the welders supplied by the conductors will not be in use at the same time. The load value used for each welder shall take into account both the magnitude and the duration of the load while the welder is in use.

Conductor ratings based on 100 per cent of the current, as determined in accordance with Section 630-21(a), of the two largest welders, 85 per cent for the third largest welder, 70 per cent for the fourth largest welder, and 60 per cent for all the remaining welders, should provide an ample margin of safety under high-production conditions with respect to the maximum permissible temperature of the conductors. Percentage values lower than those given are permissible in cases where the work is such that a high operating duty cycle for individual welders is impossible.

630-22. Overcurrent Protection. Overcurrent protection for motor-generator arc welders shall be as provided in Sections 630-22(a) and (b). Where the nearest standard rating of the overcurrent device used is under the value specified in this Section, or where the rating or setting specified results in unnecessary opening of the overcurrent device, the next higher rating or setting may be used.

(a) For Welders. Each welder shall have overcurrent protection rated or set at not more than 200 per cent of the rated primary current of the welder; except that an overcurrent device is not required for a welder having supply conductors protected by an overcurrent device rated or set at not more than 200 per cent of the rated primary current of the welder.

(b) For Conductors. Conductors which supply one or more welders shall be protected by an overcurrent device rated or set at not more than 200 per cent of the conductor rating.

630-23. Disconnecting Means. A disconnecting means shall be provided in the supply connection of each motor-generator arc welder.

The disconnecting means shall be a circuit breaker or motor-circuit switch and its rating shall be not less than that necessary to accommodate overcurrent protection as specified under Section 630-22.

630-24. Marking. A nameplate giving the following information shall be provided for each motor-generator arc welder: name of manufacturer; rated frequency; number of phases; input voltage; input current; maximum open-circuit voltage; rated output current; basis of rating, i.e., duty cycle, 60-minute rating.

D. Resistance Welders

630-31. Ampacities of Supply Conductors. The ampacities of the supply conductors for resistance welders necessary to limit the voltage drop to a value permissible for the satisfactory performance of the welder are usually greater than that required to prevent overheating as prescribed in Sections 630-32(a and b).

(a) Individual Welders. The rated ampacities for conductors for individual welders shall conform to the following:

(1) Varying Operations. The rated ampacities of the supply conductors for a welder which may be operated at different times at different values of primary current or duty cycle shall be not less than 70 per cent of the rated primary current for seam and automatically fed welders, and 50 per cent of the rated primary current for manually operated nonautomatic welders.

(2) Specific Operation. The rated ampacities of the supply conductors for a welder wired for a specific operation for which the actual primary current and duty cycle are known and remain unchanged shall be not less than the product of the actual primary current and the multiplier given below for the duty cycle at which the welder will be operated.

Duty Cycle (per cent)	50	40	30	25	20	15	10	7.5	5.0 or less
Multiplier	.71	.63	.55	.50	.45	.39	.32	.27	.22

(b) Groups of Welders. The rated ampacities of conductors which supply two or more welders shall be not less than the sum of the value obtained as explained in Section 630-31(a) for the largest welder supplied, and 60 per cent of the values obtained as explained in Section 630-31(a) for all the other welders supplied.

(c) Explanation of Terms. (1) The rated primary current is the rated kva multiplied by 1,000 and divided by the rated primary voltage, using values given on the nameplate. (2) The actual primary current is the current drawn from the supply circuit during each welder operation at the particular heat tap and control setting used. (3) The duty cycle is the percentage of the time during which the welder is loaded. For instance, a spot welder supplied by a 60-hertz system (216,000 cycles per hour) making four hundred 15-cycle welds per hour would have a duty cycle of 2.8 per cent (400 multiplied by 15, divided by 216,000, multiplied by 100). A seam welder operating 2 cycles "on" and 2 cycles "off" would have a duty cycle of 50 per cent.

▶   Subparagraph (a)(1) applies where a resistance welder is intended for a variety of different operations, such as for welding plates of different thicknesses or for welding different metals. In this case the branch-circuit conductors must have an ampacity sufficient for the heaviest demand that may be made upon them. Because the loading is intermittent, the ampacity need not be as high as the rated primary current. A value of 70 per cent is specified for any type of welding machine which is fed automatically. For a manually operated welder, the duty cycle will always be lower and a conductor ampacity of 50 per cent of the rated primary current is considered sufficient.

Example 1

A spot welder supplied by a 60-hertz system makes 400 welds per hour and in making each weld, current flows during 15 cycles.

The number of cycles per hour is 60 × 60 × 60 = 216,000 cycles.

During 1 hr, the time during which the welder is loaded, measured in cycles, is 400 × 15 = 6,000 cycles.

The duty cycle is therefore $\dfrac{6,000}{216,000} \times 100 = 2.8$ per cent.

Example 2

A seam welder operates 2 cycles "on" and 2 cycles "off" or in every 4 cycles the welder is loaded during 2 cycles.

The duty cycle is therefore $\dfrac{2}{4} \times 100 = 50$ per cent.

Transformers for resistance welders are commonly provided with taps by means of which the secondary voltage, and consequently the secondary current, can be adjusted. The rated primary current is the current in the primary when the taps are adjusted for maximum secondary current.

When a resistance welder is set up for a specific operation, the transformer taps are adjusted to provide the exact heat desired for the weld; then in order to apply subparagraph (a)(2) the actual primary current must be measured. A special type of ammeter is required for this measurement because the current impulses are of very short duration, often a small fraction of a second. The duty cycle is controlled by the adjustment of the controller for the welder.

The procedure in determining conductor sizes for an installation consisting of a feeder and two or more branch circuits to supply resistance welders is first to compute the required ampacity for each branch circuit. Then the required feeder ampacity is 100 per cent of the highest ampacity required for any one of the branch circuits, plus 60 per cent of the sum of the ampacities of all the other branch circuits.

Some resistance welders are rated as high as 1,000 kva and may momentarily draw loads of 2,000 kva, or even more. Voltage drop must be held within rather close limits to ensure satisfactory operation.

630-32. Overcurrent Protection.   Overcurrent protection for resistance welders shall be as provided in Sections 630-32(a and b). Where the nearest standard rating of the overcurrent device used is under the value specified in this Section, or where the rating or setting specified results in unnecessary opening of the overcurrent device, the next higher rating or setting may be used.

(a) For Welders. Each welder shall have an overcurrent device rated or set at not more than 300 per cent of the rated primary current of the welder, except that an overcurrent device is not required for a welder having a supply circuit protected by an overcurrent device rated or set at not more than 300 per cent of the rated primary current of the welder.

(b) For Conductors. Conductors which supply one or more welders shall be protected by an overcurrent device rated or set at not more than 300 per cent of the conductor rating.

▶   In this case, as in the case of the overcurrent protection of arc-welding transformers (Section **630-12**), the conductors are protected against short circuits. The conductors of motor branch circuits are protected against short circuits by the branch-circuit overcurrent devices and depend upon the motor-running protective devices for overload protection. Although the resistance welder is not equipped with any device similar to the motor-running protective device, satisfactory operation of the welder is a safeguard against overloading of the conductors. Overheating of the circuit could result only from so operating the welder that either the welds would be imperfect, or parts of the control equipment would be damaged, or both.

630-33. Disconnecting Means. A switch or circuit breaker shall be provided by which each resistance welder and its control equipment can be isolated from the supply circuit. The ampacity of this disconnecting means shall be not less than the supply conductor rating determined as explained in this Article. The supply circuit switch may be used as the welder disconnecting means where the circuit supplies only one welder.

630-34. Marking. A nameplate giving the following information shall be provided for each resistance welder: name of manufacturer, frequency, primary voltage, rated kva at 50 per cent duty cycle, maximum and minimum open-circuit secondary voltage, short-circuit secondary current at maximum secondary voltage and specified throat and gap setting.

ARTICLE 640. SOUND–RECORDING AND SIMILAR EQUIPMENT

640-1. Scope. This Article shall apply to installations of equipment and wiring used for sound-recording and reproduction, centralized distribution of sound, public address, speech-input systems and electronic organs.

▶   Centralized distribution systems consist of one or more radio receivers, the audio-frequency output of which is distributed to a number of reproducers or loud-speakers.

A public-address system includes one or more microphones, an amplifier, and any desired number of reproducers or speakers. A common use of such a system is to render the voice of a speaker clearly audible in all parts of a large assembly room.

640-2. Application of Other Articles.

(a) Except as modified by this Article, wiring and equipment from source of power to and between devices connected to the interior wiring systems shall comply with the requirements of Chapters 1 through 4 of this Code.

(b) Wiring and equipment for public-address, speech-input, radio-frequency, audio-frequency systems, and amplifying equipment associated with radio receiving stations in centralized distribution systems, shall comply with Article 725.

▶   In general the power-supply wiring from the building light or power service to the special equipment named in Section 640-1, and between any parts of this equipment, should be installed as required for light and power systems of the same voltage. Certain variations from the standard requirements are permitted by the following sections. For radio and sound systems the requirements of Art. 810 apply except as otherwise permitted here.

640-3. Number of Conductors in Raceway.   The number of conductors in a conduit or other raceway shall comply with Tables 1 through 7 of Chapter 9 except as follows:

Exception No. 1: Special permission may be granted for the installation of two 2-conductor lead-covered cables in ¾-inch conduit, provided the cross-sectional area of each cable does not exceed .11 square inch.

Exception No. 2: Special permission may be granted for the installation of two 2-conductor No. 19 lead-covered cables in ½-inch conduit, provided the sum of the cross-sectional areas of the cables does not exceed 32 per cent of the internal cross-sectional area of the conduit.

640-4. Wireways and Auxiliary Gutters.

(a) Wireways and auxiliary gutters shall comply with the requirements of Articles 362 and 374.

(b) Where used for sound-recording and reproduction the following exceptions are made:

Exception No. 1: Number of Conductors in Raceway. Conductors in wireways or gutters shall not fill the raceway to more than 75 per cent of its depth.

Exception No. 2: Auxiliary-Gutter Covers. Where the cover of auxiliary gutters is flush with the flooring and is subject to the moving of heavy objects it shall be of steel at least ¼ inch in thickness; where not subject to moving of heavy objects, as in the rear of patch or other equipment panels, the cover shall be at least No. 10 MSG.

Exception No. 3: Metal-Trough Raceways. Metal-trough raceways may be installed in concealed places provided they are run in a straight line between outlets or junction boxes. Covers of boxes must be accessible. Edges of metal must be rounded at outlet or junction boxes and all rough projections smoothed to prevent abrasion of insulation or conductors. Raceways made of sections shall be bonded and grounded as prescribed in Section 250-76.

Exception No. 4: Grounding Wireways and Auxiliary Gutters. Metal wireways and auxiliary gutters shall be grounded in accordance with the requirements of Article 250. Where the wireway or auxiliary gutter does not contain power supply wires, the grounding conductor need not be larger than No. 14 copper or its equivalent. Where the wireway or auxiliary gutter contains power supply wires, the grounding conductor shall not be smaller than the size called for in Section 250-95.

640-5. Conductors.   Amplifier output circuits carrying audio-program signals of 70 volts or less and whose open circuit voltage will not exceed 100 volts, may employ Class 2 wiring as covered in Article 725.

The above is based on amplifiers whose open-circuit voltage will not exceed 100 volts when driven with a signal at any frequency from 60 to 100 hertz sufficient to produce rated output (70.7 volts) into its rated load. This also accepts the known fact that the average program material is 12 db below the amplifier rating—thus the average RMS voltage for an open-circuit 70 volt output would be only 25 volts.

640-6. Grouping of Conductors.   Conductors of different systems grouped in the same conduit or other metallic enclosure, or in portable cords or cables, shall comply with the following requirements:

(a) Power-Supply Conductors.   Power-supply conductors shall be properly indicated and shall be used solely for supplying power to the equipment to which the other conductors are connected.

(b) Leads to Motor-Generator or Rotary Converter.   Input leads to a motor-generator or rotary converter shall be run separately from the output leads.

(c) Conductor Insulation.   The conductors shall be insulated individually, or collectively in groups, by insulation at least equivalent to that on the power-supply and other conductors.

Exception: Where the power-supply and other conductors are separated by a lead sheath or other continuous metallic covering.

640-7. Flexible Cords.   Flexible cords and cables shall be of Types S, SJ, ST, SJO, and SJT or other types specifically approved for the purpose for which they are to be used. The conductors of flexible cords, other than power-supply conductors, may be of a size not smaller than No. 26 provided such conductors are not in direct electrical connection with the power-supply conductors and are equipped with current-limiting means so that the maximum power under any condition will not exceed 150 watts.

640-8. Terminals.   Terminals shall be marked to show their proper connections. Terminals for conductors other than power-supply conductors shall be separated from the terminals of the power-supply conductors by a spacing at least as great as the spacing between power-supply terminals of opposite polarity.

▶   In this class of work, the wires of different systems are in many cases closely associated in the apparatus itself; hence little would be gained by separating them elsewhere.

The input leads to a motor-generator set or to a rotary converter would commonly be 115- or 230-volt power circuits; these wires are not a part of the sound-recording or -reproducing system and should be kept entirely separate from all wires of the sound system.

640-9. Storage Batteries.   Storage batteries shall comply with the following:

(a) Installation.   Storage batteries shall be installed in accordance with Article 480.

(b) Conductor Insulation. Storage-battery leads shall be rubber-covered or thermoplastic-covered.

640-10. Overcurrent Protection of "A," "B" and "C" Circuits. Overcurrent protection shall be provided as follows:

(a) "A" circuit, where supplied by branch-lighting circuits, or by storage batteries of more than 20-ampere-hour capacity, shall have overcurrent protection not exceeding 15 amperes.

(b) "B" circuits shall have overcurrent protection not exceeding one ampere. The overcurrent protection shall be placed in each positive lead.

(c) "C" circuits where supplied from branch lighting circuits or from storage batteries of more than 20 ampere-hour capacity shall have overcurrent protection not exceeding one ampere.

(d) Overcurrent devices shall be located as near as practicable to the battery.

▶   The terms used in the foregoing rule are those that have been adopted by engineers as applying to circuits used in electronics.

A 20 amp-hr battery is capable of delivering a heavy enough current to heat a No. 14 or smaller wire to a dangerously high temperature and overcurrent protection is therefore quite necessary. A storage B battery might be capable of delivering enough current to overheat some part of the equipment. Several different positive connections may be made to the battery in order to obtain different voltages and each such lead must be provided with overcurrent protection.

640-11. Amplifiers and Rectifiers—Type.

(a) They shall be suitably housed and shall be of a type approved for the purpose unless otherwise expressly permitted by the authority having jurisdiction.

(b) Amplifiers and rectifiers shall be so located as to be readily accessible.

(c) Amplifiers and rectifiers shall be so located as to provide sufficient ventilation to prevent undue temperature rise within the housing.

640-12. Hazardous Locations. Equipment used in hazardous locations shall be specifically approved for the purpose.

640-13. Protection Against Physical Damage. Amplifiers, rectifiers, loud-speakers and other equipment shall be so located or protected as to guard against physical damage such as might result in fire or personal hazard.

ARTICLE 645. DATA PROCESSING SYSTEMS

For further information see NFPA Standard for the Protection of Electronic Computer/Data Processing Equipment (No. 75-1968).

645-1. Scope. The provisions of this Article shall apply to equipment, power supply wiring, equipment interconnecting wiring, and grounding of data processing systems including data communications equipment used as a terminal unit.

645-2. Supply Circuits and Interconnecting Cables.

(a) The branch-circuit conductors to which one or more units of a data processing system are connected to a source of supply shall have an ampacity not less than 125 per cent of the total connected load.

(b) The data processing system may be connected by means of computer cable or flexible cord and attachment plug cap or cord set assembly specifically approved as a part of the data processing system. Separate units may be interconnected by means of flexible cords and cables specifically approved as part of the data processing system. When run on the surface of the floor they shall be protected against physical damage.

(c) The power and communication supply cables and interconnecting cables may be installed under a raised floor provided:

(1) The raised floor is of suitable construction. See NFPA No. 75-1968.

(2) The branch-circuit supply conductors to receptacles are in rigid conduit, electrical metallic tubing, flexible metal conduit, Type MI mineral insulated metal sheathed cable, or Type ALS aluminum sheathed cable.

(3) Ventilation in the underfloor area is used for the data processing equipment and data processing area only.

645-3. Disconnecting Means. In addition to any integral individual disconnect switches for components or other units of the data processing system, disconnecting means shall be provided as follows:

(a) In Data Processing Rooms. The disconnecting means shall disconnect the ventilation system serving that room and the power to all electrical equipment in the room except lighting and shall be controlled from locations readily accessible to the operator and at designated exit doors from the data processing room.

(b) In General Building Areas. The disconnecting means shall disconnect all interconnected data processing equipment in the area and shall be controlled from a location readily accessible to the operator.

645-4. Grounding. All exposed noncurrent-carrying metal parts of a data processing system shall be grounded in accordance with Article 250.

645-5. Marking. Each unit of a data processing system which is intended to be supplied by a branch circuit shall be provided with a manufacturer's nameplate, which shall also include the rating in volts, the operating frequency, and the total load in amperes.

ARTICLE 650. ORGANS

650-1. General. This Article shall apply to those electric circuits and parts of electrically operated organs which are employed for the control of the sounding apparatus and keyboards. Electronic organs shall comply with the appropriate provisions of Article 640.

650-2. Source of Energy. The source of energy shall have a potential of not over 15 volts and shall be a self-excited generator, a two-coil transformer type rectifier or a primary battery.

650-3. Insulation—Grounding. The generator shall be effectively insulated from the ground and from the motor driving it, or both the generator and the motor frames shall be grounded in the manner prescribed in Article 250.

▶   Organ control systems are usually supplied from a motor-generator set consisting of a 115- or 230-volt motor driving a generator that operates at about 10 volts. Neither the generator windings nor the control wires are necessarily insulated for the motor voltage. Assume that the frames of the two machines are electrically connected together by being mounted on the same base and that the frames are not grounded. If a wire of the motor winding becomes grounded to the frame of the motor, the frames of both machines may be raised to a potential of 115 or 230 volts above ground, and this voltage may break down the insulation of the generator winding or of the circuit wiring. If the generator is insulated from the motor, or if both frames are well grounded, this trouble cannot occur.

650-4. Conductors.   Conductors shall comply with the following:

   (a) Size.   No conductor shall be smaller than No. 26, and the common-return conductor shall be not smaller than No. 14.

   (b) Insulation.   Conductors shall have rubber, thermoplastic, asbestos, cotton, or silk insulation, except the common-return conductor which shall be rubber-covered, thermoplastic, asbestos-covered (Types AA, AI, or AIA). The cotton or silk may be saturated with paraffin if desired.

   (c) Conductors to Be Cabled.   Except the common-return conductor, and conductors inside the organ proper, the organ sections and the organ console, conductors shall be cabled. The common-return conductor may be placed under an additional covering enclosing both cable and return conductor, or may be installed as a separate conductor and may be in contact with the cable.

   (d) Cable Covering.   The cable shall be provided with one or more braided outer coverings, provided that a tape may be used in place of an inner braid. Where not installed in metal raceways the outer braid shall be flame-retardant or shall be covered with a closely-wound fireproof tape.

▶   The wires of the cable are normally all of the same polarity and hence need not be heavily insulated from one another. The full voltage of the control system exists between the wires in the cable and the common return wire, therefore the common wire must be reasonably well insulated from the cable wires.

650-5. Installation of Conductors.   Cables shall be securely fastened in place and may be attached directly to the organ structure without insulating supports. Cables shall not be placed in contact with other conductors.

▶   A 15-volt system involves very little fire hazard and the cable may be run in any manner desired, but for protection against injury and convenience in making repairs the cable should preferably be installed in a metal raceway.

650-6. Overcurrent Protection.   Circuits shall be so arranged that all conductors, except the main supply conductors and the common-return conductor, shall be protected from overcurrent by an overcurrent device of not greater than 15-ampere rating.

▶   The "main supply conductors" extend from the generator to a convenient
point at which one conductor is connected through 15-amp fuses to as many
circuits as may be necessary, while the other main conductor is connected
to the common return.

ARTICLE 660. X-RAY EQUIPMENT

A. Scope and Installation

660-1. Scope. The provisions of this Article shall apply to all X-ray equipment
operating at any frequency or voltage for medical or industrial use, or for any
other purpose.

Nothing in this Article shall be construed as specifying safeguards against the useful beam or
stray X-ray radiation.

Recommendations for radiation protection by the National Council on Radiation Protection and
Measurements are published as Reports of the National Council on Radiation Protection and
Measurement. These reports are obtainable from NCRP Publications, P.O. Box 4867, Washington
D.C., 20008.

Definitions:

PORTABLE—X-ray equipment designed to be hand-carried.

MOBILE—X-ray equipment mounted on a permanent base with wheels and/or
casters for moving while completely assembled.

TRANSPORTABLE—X-ray equipment to be installed in a vehicle or that may
be readily disassembled for transport in a vehicle.

LONG TIME RATING—A long time rating is the rating based on an operating
interval of five minutes or longer.

MOMENTARY RATING—A momentary rating is the rating based on an operating
interval that does not exceed five seconds.

660-2. Hazardous Locations. Unless approved for the location, X-ray and related equipment shall not be installed or operated in hazardous locations. See
Article 517, Part E.

▶   An X-ray tube of the hot-cathode type, as now commonly used, is a
two-element vacuum tube in which a tungsten filament serves as the
cathode. Current is supplied to the filament at low voltage. In most cases
unidirectional pulsating voltage is applied between the cathode and the
anode. The applied voltage is measured or described in terms of the peak
voltage, which may be anywhere within the range of 10,000 to 1,000,000
volts, or even more. The current flowing in the high-voltage circuit may be
as low as 5 ma or may be as much as 1 amp, depending upon the desired
intensity of radiation. The high voltage is obtained by means of a transformer, usually operating at 230 volts primary, and usually is made unidirectional by means of two-element rectifying vacuum tubes, though in
some cases an a-c is applied to the X-ray tube. The X rays are radiations
of an extremely high frequency (or short wave length) which are the strongest

in a plane at right angles to the electron stream passing between the cathode and the anode in the tube.

As used by physicians and dentists, X rays have three applications: *fluoroscopy,* where a picture or shadow is thrown upon a screen of specially prepared glass by rays passing through some part of the patient's body; *radiography,* which is similar to fluoroscopy except that the picture is thrown upon a photographic film instead of a screen; and *therapy,* in which use is made of the effects of the rays upon the tissues of the human body.

660-3. Connection to Supply Circuit.

(a) Fixed and Stationary Equipment.   Fixed and stationary X-ray equipment shall be connected to the power supply by means of a wiring method meeting the general requirements of this Code.

Exception: Equipment properly supplied by a branch circuit rated at not more than 30 amperes may be supplied through a suitable plug cap and hard-service cable or cord.

(b) Portable, Mobile and Transportable.   Individual branch circuits shall not be required for portable, mobile, and transportable medical X-ray equipment requiring a capacity not exceeding 60 amperes. Receptacles installed on 50- and 60-ampere branch circuits supplying medical X-ray equipment shall be of a configuration as shown in Figure 660-3(b). Portable and mobile types of X-ray equipment of any capacity shall be supplied through a suitable cap and hard-service cable or cord. Transportable X-ray equipment of any capacity may be connected to its power supply by suitable connections and hard-service cable or cord.

(c) More than 600 Volt Supply.   Circuits and equipment operated on a supply circuit of more than 600 volts shall comply with the provisions of Article 710.

660-4. Disconnecting Means.   A disconnecting means of adequate capacity for at least 50 per cent of the input required for the momentary rating or 100 per cent of the input required for the long-time rating of the X-ray equipment whichever is greater shall be provided in the supply circuit and it shall be operable from a location readily accessible from the X-ray control. For equipment connected to a 120-volt branch circuit of 30 amperes or less, a grounding-type cap and receptacle of proper rating may serve as a disconnecting means.

Exception: Portable or mobile X-ray equipment of any capacity which complies with Section 660-11.

660-5. Branch Circuit and Overcurrent Protection Requirements.   Fifty per cent of the momentary rating or 100 per cent of the long-time rating of the X-ray equipment whichever is greater shall be used in determining the rating for branch circuits and overcurrent protective devices.

The ampacities of the branch-circuit conductors and the ratings of disconnecting means and overcurrent protection for X-ray equipment is usually recommended by the manufacturer for the specific installation.

660-6. Wiring Terminals.   Unless provided with a permanently attached cord or a cord set, X-ray equipment shall be provided with suitable wiring terminals or leads for the connection of conductors of at least the size required by the input load corresponding to the long-time rating of the equipment.

660-7. Number of Conductors in Raceway.   The number of control circuit con-

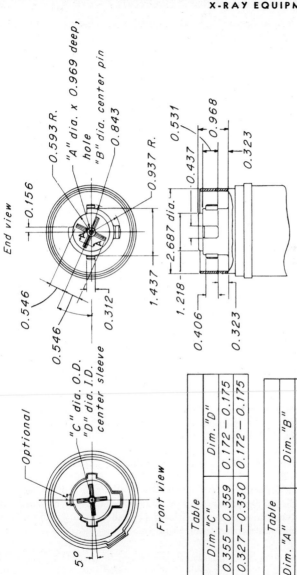

End view

0.593 R.

"A" dia. x 0.969 deep, hole

"B" dia. center pin

0.843

0.937 R.

0.156

0.546

0.546

0.312

1.437

"C" dia. O.D.
"D" dia. I.D.
center sleeve

Optional

5°

Front view

0.531

0.968

0.437

0.323

2.687 dia.

1.218

0.406

0.323

Side view

Table

Receptacle	Dim. "C"	Dim. "D"
50 amp.	0.355 – 0.359	0.172 – 0.175
60 amp.	0.327 – 0.330	0.172 – 0.175

Table

Cap	Dim. "A"	Dim. "B"
50 amp.	0.370 – 0.375	0.164 – 0.168
60 amp.	0.338 – 0.343	0.164 – 0.168

Figure 660-3(b). Medical X-ray, 50- and 60-ampere receptacles and caps, 2-pole, 3-wire, 250-volt AC configurations. The 60-ampere receptacle will receive 50- or 60-ampere caps, but the 50-ampere receptacle will receive only the 50-ampere cap.

ductors installed in a raceway shall be determined in accordance with Section 300-17.

660-8. Minimum Size of Conductors. Sizes No. 18 or 16 fixture wires as specified in Section 725-14 and flexible cords may be used for the control and operating circuits of X-ray and auxiliary equipment when protected by 20-ampere overcurrent devices.

660-9. Equipment Installations. All equipment used on new installations of X-ray equipment, or used or reconditioned equipment moved to and reinstalled at a new location, shall be of the approved type.

B. Control

660-10. Fixed and Stationary Equipment.

(a) Separate Control Device. A separate control device in addition to the disconnecting means, shall be incorporated in the X-ray control supply or in the primary circuit to the high-voltage transformer. This device shall be a part of the X-ray equipment, but may be located in a separate enclosure immediately adjacent to the X-ray control unit.

(b) Protective Device. A protective device which may be incorporated into the separate control device, shall be provided to control the load resulting from failures in the high-voltage circuit.

660-11. Portable and Mobile Equipment. Portable and mobile equipment shall comply with Section 660-10, but the manually controlled device shall be located in or on the equipment.

660-12. Medical Equipment.

(a) Radiographic Type. For each radiographic-type equipment there shall be a timer or automatic exposure terminating device and a manual-hold switch that actuates the timer or automatic exposure terminating device and will interrupt these devices upon release.

(b) Fluoroscopic Type. For each fluoroscopic-type equipment a switch shall be provided which shall be designed to open automatically.

Exception: When held closed by the operator.

(c) Therapeutic Type. For each therapeutic-type equipment a timer or automatic exposure terminating device shall be provided which is not of the repeating type.

660-13. Industrial X-ray Equipment.

(a) Radiographic and Fluoroscopic Types. All radiographic- and fluoroscopic-type equipment shall be effectively enclosed or shall have interlocks that de-energize the equipment automatically to prevent ready access to live current-carrying parts.

(b) Industrial or Laboratory Equipment—Diffraction or Irradiation Types. Diffraction- or irradiation-type equipment shall be provided with positive indication of energization by pilot lights, readable meter deflections or equivalent means.

Exception: Equipment or installations effectively enclosed or provided with interlocks to prevent access to live current-carrying parts during operation.

660-14. Independent Control. Where more than one piece of equipment is operated from the same high-voltage circuit, each piece or each group of equipment as a unit shall be provided with a high-voltage switch or equivalent disconnecting means. This disconnecting means shall be constructed, enclosed, or located so as to avoid contact by persons with its live parts.

▶ In radiography it is important that the exposure be accurately timed, and for this purpose a switch is used which can be set to open the circuit automatically in any desired time after the circuit has been closed.

C. Transformers and Capacitors

660-15. General. Transformers and capacitors which are part of an X-ray equipment shall not be required to conform to the requirements of Articles 450 and 460 of this Code.

▶ A power transformer is usually supplied at a high primary voltage; hence in case of a breakdown of the insulation on the primary winding, a large amount of energy can be delivered to the transformer. An oil-filled X-ray transformer involves much less fire hazard because the primary voltage is low and it is therefore not required that such transformers be placed in vaults of fire-resistance construction.

660-16. Capacitors. Capacitors shall be mounted within enclosures of grounded metal or insulating material.

D. Guarding and Grounding

660-17. General.
(a) High-Voltage Parts. All high-voltage parts, including X-ray tubes, shall be mounted within grounded enclosures. Either air, oil, gas or other suitable insulating media may be used to insulate the high voltage from the grounded enclosure. The connections from the high-voltage equipment to X-ray tubes and other high-voltage components shall be made with high-voltage shielded cables.
(b) Low-Voltage Cables. Low-voltage connecting cables to oil-filled units such as transformers, condensers, oil coolers, and high-voltage switches which are not completely sealed shall be of the oil-resistant type.

▶ This Section definitely requires that all new X-ray equipment shall be so constructed that all high-voltage parts, except leads to the X-ray tube, are in grounded metal enclosures, unless the equipment is in a separate room or enclosure and the circuit to the primary of the transformer is automatically opened by unlocking the door to the enclosure. Conductors leading to the X-ray tube are heavily insulated. This Section repeats requirements of Section 660-8 applying to the installation of exposed high-voltage conductors.

660-18. Grounding. Noncurrent-carrying metal parts of X-ray and associated equipment (controls, tables, X-ray tube stands, transformer tanks, shielded cables, X-ray tube heads, etc.) shall be grounded in the manner prescribed in Article 250.
(a) Portable and Mobile. Portable and mobile equipment shall be provided with an approved grounding-type plug cap.

ARTICLE 665. INDUCTION AND DIELECTRIC HEATING EQUIPMENT

A. Scope and General

665-1. Scope. The provisions of this Article shall apply to the construction and installation of induction and dielectric heating equipment and accessories for industrial, scientific and medical applications, but not for appliances.

665-2. Definitions. The term "heating equipment" as used in this Article includes any equipment used for heating purposes whose heat is generated by induction or dielectric methods.

Induction heating is the heating of a nominally conducting material due to its own I^2R losses when the material is placed in a varying electromagnetic field.

Dielectric heating is the heating of a nominally insulating material due to its own dielectric losses when the material is placed in a varying electric field.

The term "therapeutic high-frequency equipment" as used in this Article shall be understood to mean generating equipment capable of producing alternating currents having frequencies greater than those frequencies which elicit neuromuscular response. In order to comply with the above, the output frequency of the therapeutic high-frequency equipment shall not be less than 2 megahertz.

▶   Induction and dielectric heating are systems wherein a workpiece is heated by means of a rapidly alternating magnetic or electric field.

Induction Heating

Induction heating is used to heat materials that are good electrical conductors, for such purposes as soldering, brazing, hardening, and annealing. Induction heating, in general, involves frequencies ranging from 3 to about 500 kilohertz, and power outputs from a few hundred watts to several thousand kilowatts. In general, motor-generator sets are used for frequencies up to about 30 kHz; spark-gap converters, from 20 to 400 kHz; and vacuum-tube generators, from 100 to 500 kHz. Isolated special jobs may use frequencies as high as 60 to 80 megahertz. Motor-generator sets normally supply power for heating large masses for melting, forging, deep hardening, and the joining of heavy pieces, whereas spark-gap and vacuum-tube generators find their best applications in the joining of smaller pieces and shallow case hardening, with vacuum-tube generators also being used where special high heat concentrations are required.

To heat a workpiece by induction heating, it is placed in a work coil consisting of one or more turns, which is the output circuit of the generator (Fig. 665-1). The high-frequency current which flows through this coil sets up a rapidly alternating magnetic field within it. By inducing a voltage in the workpiece, this field causes a current flow in the piece to be heated. As the current flows through the resistance of the workpiece, it generates heat (I^2R loss) in the piece itself. It is this heat that is utilized in induction heating.

Basic sections of spark gap converter

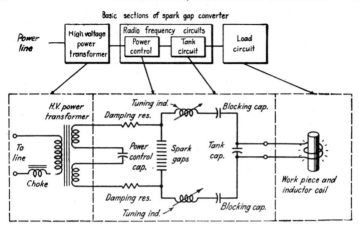

Fig. 665-1. Spark-gap converter for induction heating—simplified basic diagram. (*Westinghouse Electric Corp.*)

Dielectric Heating

In contrast, dielectric heating is used to heat materials that are nonconductors, such as wood, plastic, textiles, rubber, etc., for such purposes as drying, gluing, curing, and baking. It uses frequencies from 1 to 200 megahertz, especially those from 1 to 50 megahertz. Vacuum-tube generators are used exclusively to supply dielectric heating power, with outputs ranging from a few hundred watts to several hundred kilowatts.

Whereas induction heating uses a varying magnetic field, dielectric heating employs a varying electric field. This is done by placing the material to be heated between a pair of metal plates, called electrodes, in the output circuit of the generator. When high-frequency voltage is applied to the electrodes, a rapidly alternating electric field is set up between them, passing through the material to be heated. Because of the electrical charges within the molecules of this material, the field causes the molecules to vibrate in proportion to its frequency. This internal molecular action generates the heat used for dielectric heating.

Generators

In general, both spark-gap and vacuum-tube generators consist of a power-supply circuit, a voltage and/or frequency conversion circuit, a control circuit, and an output circuit. This combination is familiar in motor-generator operation, and can be easily understood in high-frequency generators by referring to Figs. 665-1 through 665-3.

In the spark-gap converter (Fig. 665-1), tank capacitors are alternately charged and discharged, to produce high-frequency oscillations in the output circuit. In vacuum-tube generators, these oscillations are produced by a vacuum-tube oscillator, which is fed by d-c power from a high-voltage power supply. The induction heating generator (Fig. 665-2) and the dielec-

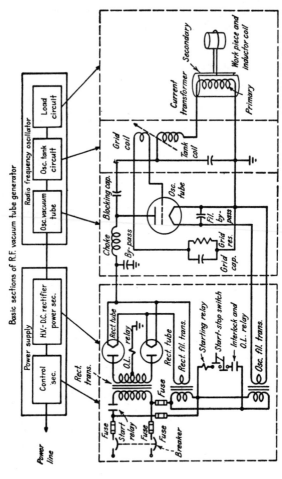

Fig. 665-2. Vacuum-tube generator for induction heating—simplified basic diagram. (*Westinghouse Electric Corp.*)

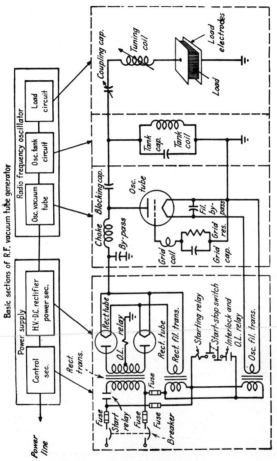

Fig. 665-3. Vacuum-tube generator for dielectric heating—simplified basic diagram. (Westinghouse Electric Corp.)

tric heating generator (Fig. 665-3) differ chiefly in their output circuits. Typical control circuits are shown for each.

The actual work loads are shown disconnected from the rest of the output circuit, emphasizing the fact that external auxiliary equipment is often needed to ensure the most efficient transfer of power from generator to load.

Except in the case of motor-generator sets, low-power generators will probably contain enough control and cooling apparatus for normal operation. However, on installations of over 50 kw, external switchgear and cooling systems are usually required. Such equipment should comply with the appropriate articles of the Code.

665-3. Application of Other Articles. Wiring from the source of power to the heating equipment shall comply with Chapters 1 through 4. Circuits and equipment operating on a supply circuit of more than 600 volts shall comply with the provisions of Article 710.

665-4. Hazardous Locations. Induction and dielectric heating equipment shall not be installed in hazardous locations as defined in Article 500 unless the equipment and wiring is designed and approved for the locations.

B. Motor-Generator Equipment

665-5. Scope. Motor-generator equipment shall include all rotating equipment designed to operate from an AC or DC motor, or by mechanical drive from a prime mover, producing an alternating current of any frequency for induction and/or dielectric heating.

665-6. Ampacities of Supply Conductors. Ampacities of supply conductors shall be determined by Article 430 of this Code.

665-7. Overcurrent Protection. Overcurrent protection shall be provided as specified in Article 430 of this Code for the electrical supply circuit.

665-8. Disconnecting Means. The disconnecting means shall be provided as specified in Article 430 of this Code.

A readily accessible disconnecting means shall be provided by which each heating equipment can be isolated from the supplying circuit. The rating of this disconnecting means shall be not less than the nameplate current rating of the equipment. The supply circuit disconnecting means may be used as a heating equipment disconnecting means where the circuit supplies only one equipment.

665-9. Output Circuit Definition. The output circuit shall include all output components external to the generator, including contactors, transformers, busbars, and other conductors.

665-10. Output Circuits. Output circuits shall conform to the following:

(a) **Generator Output.** The output circuit shall be isolated from ground, except for the capacitive coupling inherent in the generator, which, in effect, causes the generator terminals to have voltages from terminal to ground that are equal.

When rated at more than 500 volts, the output circuit shall incorporate a DC ground protector unit. The DC impressed on the output circuit shall not exceed 30 volts and shall not exceed a current capability of 5 milliamperes.

An isolating transformer for matching the load and the source may be used in the output circuit wherein the secondary is not at DC ground potential.

(b) Component Interconnections.   The various components required for a complete induction heating equipment installation shall be connected by properly protected multiconductor cable, bus-bar, or coaxial cable. Cables shall be installed in nonferrous raceways. Bus-bar shall be protected where required by nonferrous | enclosures.

Fig. 665-4. Two 20-kw, 450-megahertz induction-heating generators used in hardening small wristpins. Note the radio-frequency lines connecting the generators to the work applicator. (*Westinghouse Electric Corp.*)

▶   *RF Lines*

When it is necessary to transmit the high-frequency output of a generator any distance to the work applicator, a radio-frequency line is generally used. This usually consists of a conductor totally enclosed in a grounded metal housing. This central conductor is commonly supported by insulators, mounted in the grounded housing and periodically spaced along its length. Figure 665-4 shows such a line, rectangular in cross section, connecting two induction generators to the load.

While contact with high-voltage radio frequencies may cause severe burns, contact with high-voltage dc could be fatal. Therefore, it is imperative that generator output (directly, capacitively, or inductively coupled) be effectively grounded with respect to dc so that, should generator failure place high-voltage dc in the tank oscillating circuit, there will still be no danger to the operator. This grounding is generally internal in vacuum-tube generators, as shown in the accompanying diagrams. In all types of induction generators, one side of the work coil should usually be externally grounded.

Fᴵɢ. 665-5. A 20-kw, 27-megahertz vacuum-tube dielectric-heating generator used to heat plastic preforms before molding. The protective cage surrounding the electrodes is completely interlocked for the operator's protection. While the cage is open, all voltages are removed from the output circuit. (*Westinghouse Electric Corp.*)

In general, all high-voltage connections to the primary of a current transformer should be enclosed. The primary concern is the operator's safety. Examples would be interlocked cages around small dielectric electrodes, and interlocking safety doors. See Fig. 665-5.

On induction heating jobs, it is not always practical to completely house the work coil and obtain efficient production operation. In these cases, precautions should be taken to minimize the chance of operator contact with the coil.

665-11. Control Enclosures. Low-frequency AC or DC may be used in the control portion of the heating equipment. This shall be limited to a value of 150 volts. Solid or stranded wire, properly sized in No. 18 AWG or larger shall be used.

Sixty-hertz components may be used to control high frequency when properly rated by the induction heating equipment manufacturer. Electronic circuits utilizing solid-state devices and tubes may use printed circuits or wire sizes, properly sized smaller than No. 18 AWG.

665-12. Remote Control

(a) When remote controls are used for applying power, a "Local-Remote" switch shall be provided and interlocked so as to prevent the possibility of applying power from other than one selected control point(s).

(b) Switches operated by foot pressure shall be provided with a shield over the contact button to avoid accidental closing.

C. Equipment Other Than Motor-Generator

665-13. Scope. Equipment other than motor-generators includes all static multipliers and oscillator-type units utilizing vacuum tubes and/or solid-state devices. The equipment shall be capable of converting AC or DC to a frequency suitable for induction and/or dielectric heating.

665-14. Ampacities of Supply Conductors. Ampacities of supply conductors shall be determined as follows:

(a) The ampacity of the circuit conductors shall be not less than the nameplate current rating of the equipment.

(b) The ampacities of conductors supplying two or more equipments shall be not less than the sum of nameplate current ratings on all equipments.

Exception: When simultaneous operation of two or more equipments supplied from the same feeder is not possible, the ampacity of the feeder shall not be less than the sum of the nameplate ratings for the largest group of machines capable of simultaneous operation, plus 100 per cent of the standby currents of the remaining machines supplied.

▶   Quite often where several equipments are operated in a single plant it is possible to conserve on power-line requirements by taking into account the load or use factor of each equipment. The time cycles of operation on various machines may be staggered to allow a minimum of current to be taken from the line. In such cases the Code requires sufficient capacity to carry all full-load currents from those machines which will operate simultaneously, plus the stand-by requirements of all other units.

665-15. Overcurrent Protection. Overcurrent protection shall be provided as specified in Article 240 for the equipment as a whole. This overcurrent protection shall be provided separately or as a part of the equipment.

665-16. Disconnecting Means. A readily accessible disconnecting means shall be provided by which each heating equipment can be isolated from the supplying circuit. The rating of this disconnecting means shall not be less than the nameplate rating of the equipment. The supply circuit disconnecting means may be used for disconnecting the heating equipment where the circuit supplies only one equipment.

665-17. Output Circuit Definition. The output circuit shall include all output components external to the converting device, including contactors, transformers, bus-bars, and other conductors.

665-18. Output Circuits. Output circuits shall conform to the following:

(a) **Converter Output.** The output circuit (direct or coupled) shall be at DC ground potential.

(b) **Converter and Applicator Connection.** When the connections between the converter and the work applicator exceed two feet in length the connections shall be enclosed or guarded with noncombustible material.

665-19. Line Frequency in Converter Equipment Output. Commercial frequencies of 25- to 60-hertz alternating current output may be coupled for control purposes, but shall be limited to a value of 150 volts available only during periods of circuit operation.

665-20. Keying. Where high-speed keying circuits dependent on the effect of "oscillator blocking" are employed, the peak radio-frequency output voltage during the blocked portion of the cycle shall not exceed 100 volts in units employing radio-frequency converters.

▶ Radio-frequency generators are often turned on and off by applying a blocking bias to the grid circuit of the oscillator tube, for the purpose of obtaining fast, accurate control of power. If this keying circuit does not completely block the tube oscillations, high-frequency power will appear at the work applicator, even though the operator thinks it has been turned off. However, if this residual output voltage is limited to a value of 100 volts peak, he will be protected from any serious burns.

665-21. Remote Control.

(a) When remote controls are used for applying power, a "Local Remote" switch shall be provided and interlocked so as to prevent the possibility of applying power from other than one selected control point or points.

(b) Switches operated by foot pressure shall be provided with a shield over the contact button to avoid accidental closing.

▶ If interlocking were not provided, there would be a definite danger to an operator at the remote-control station. It might then be possible, if he had turned off the power and was doing some work in contact with a work coil, for someone else to apply power from another point, seriously injuring the operator.

D. Guarding and Grounding

665-22. Enclosures. The converting apparatus (including the DC line) and high-frequency electrical circuits (excluding the output circuits and remote-control circuits), shall be completely contained in an enclosure or enclosures of noncombustible material.

665-23. Panel Controls. All panel controls shall be of "dead-front" construction.

665-24. Access to Internal Equipment. Doors or detachable panels may be employed for internal access. Where doors are used giving access to voltages from 500 to 1000 volts AC or DC, either door locks shall be provided or interlocking shall be installed with the choice of precaution optional. Where doors are used giving access to voltages above 1000 volts AC or DC, either mechanical lockouts, with a disconnect means to prevent access until voltage is removed from the cubicle, or both door interlocking and mechanical door locks shall be provided. Detachable panels not normally used for access to such parts shall be fastened in a manner which will make them inconvenient to remove.

▶   **This Section allows the manufacturer the option of using interlocked doors or detachable panels. Where panels are used and are not intended as normal access points, they shall be fastened with bolts or screws of sufficient number to discourage removal. They should not be held in place with any type of speed fastener.**

665-25. Warning Labels. "Danger" labels shall be attached on the equipment, and shall be plainly visible even when doors are opened or panels are removed from compartments containing voltages above 250 volts AC or DC.

665-26. Capacitors. When capacitors in excess of 0.1 Mfd. are used in DC circuits, either as rectifier filter components, or suppressors, etc., having circuit voltages exceeding 230 volts above ground, bleeder resistors or grounding switches shall be used as grounding devices. The time of discharge shall be in accordance with Section 460-6.(a).

Where auxiliary rectifiers are used with filter capacitors in the output for bias supplies, tube keyers, etc., bleeder resistors shall be used even though the DC voltage may not exceed 230 volts.

665-27. Work Applicator Shielding. Protective cages or adequate shielding shall be used to guard work applicators other than induction heating coils. Induction heating coils may be protected by insulation and/or refractory materials. Interlock switches shall be used on all hinged access doors, sliding panels or other easy access to the applicator. All interlock switches shall be connected in such a manner as to remove all power from the applicator when any one of the access doors or panels is open. Interlocks on access doors or panels are not required when the applicator is an induction heating coil at DC ground potential or operating at less than 150 volts AC.

▶   **See discussion under Section 665-10. This Section is intended primarily to apply to dielectric-heating installations where it is absolutely essential that the electrodes and associated tuning or matching devices are properly shielded.**

665-28. Grounding and Bonding. Grounding and/or inter-unit bonding shall be used wherever required for circuit operation, for limiting to a safe value radio-frequency potentials between all exposed noncurrent-carrying parts of the equipment and earth ground, between all equipment parts and surrounding objects and between such objects and earth ground. Such grounding and bonding shall be installed in accordance with Article 250.

▶   *Bonding*
At radio frequencies, and especially at dielectric-heating frequencies (1 to 200 megahertz), it is very possible for differences in radio-frequency

potential to exist between the equipment proper and other surrounding metal objects or other units of the complete installation. These potentials exist because of stray currents flowing between units of the equipment or to ground. Bonding is therefore essential and such bonding must take the form of very wide copper or aluminum straps between units and to other surrounding metal objects such as conveyers, presses, etc. The most satisfactory bond is provided by placing all units of the equipment on a flooring or base consisting of copper or aluminum sheet, thoroughly joined where necessary by soldering, welding, or adequate bolting. Such bonding reduces the radio-frequency resistance and reactance between units to a minimum and any stray circulating currents flowing through this bonding will not cause sufficient voltage drop to become dangerous.

Shielding

Shielding at dielectric-heating frequencies is a necessity to provide operator protection from the high radio-frequency potentials involved, and also to prevent possible interference with radio communication systems. Shielding is accomplished by totally enclosing all work circuit components with copper sheet, copper screening, or aluminum sheet.

665-29. Marking.   Each heating equipment shall be provided with a nameplate, giving the manufacturer's name and model identification, and the following input data: line volts, frequency, number of phases, maximum current, full-load kva and full-load power factor.

E. Therapeutic Equipment

665-30. Installation.

(a)   Where portability is not essential, equipment shall be permanently installed in accordance with Chapters 1 to 3 inclusive of this Code.

(b)   Where portability is essential, the power supply cord shall be a three-conductor hard service type with an ampacity not less than the marked rating of the equipment. One conductor having a continuous green color or a continuous green color with a yellow stripe insulation shall be used solely for equipment grounding. The cord shall terminate in an approved grounding-type attachment-plug cap as described in Section 250-59(b).

665-31. Applicators for Therapeutic Equipment.   Application of the high-frequency power to the patient may be made by means of an electric field or of an induction field. Current-carrying parts of applicators shall be so insulated or enclosed that reliable isolation of the patient shall be assured.

665-32. Enclosure.   The converting apparatus including the DC line, and high-frequency electrical circuits, but excluding the line cord for portable units and the output circuits, shall be contained in an enclosure of noncombustible material.

▶   This Section is intended to include all generating equipment except rotating machines, as such machines are normally enclosed according to existing motor-generator set standards. The enclosure referred to is expected to enclose the generating apparatus to protect operating personnel from the high voltages encountered in this type equipment. The enclosure need not comply with Article 100 where the word "cabinet" is defined.

665-33. Panel Controls. All panel controls shall be of "dead-front" construction.
665-34. Access to Internal Equipment. Access shall be through panels not conveniently removable. Panels which need removal for access to fuses, tubes, adjustments, overload reset devices, internal tap switches, and the like, shall be labeled to indicate danger if and when removed, or shall be provided with suitable electrical interlock devices.

ARTICLE 670. METALWORKING MACHINE TOOLS

For further information see NFPA Standard on Metalworking Machine Tools (No. 79-1971).

670-1. Scope. The provisions of this Article apply to the size and overcurrent protection of supply conductors to metalworking machine tools and to the nameplate data required on each such tool.
670-2. Definition of Metalworking Machine Tools. For the purpose of this Article, metalworking machine tools are defined as follows:

A metalworking machine tool is a power-driven machine not portable by hand, used to shape or form metal by cutting, impact, pressure, electrical techniques, or a combination of these processes.

▶ It should be noted that these provisions do not apply to woodworking machines or to any other type of motor-driven machine which is not included in this definition of machine tools. The provisions do not apply to any machine or tool which is not normally used in a fixed location and can be carried from place to place by hand.

670-3. Machine Tool Nameplate Data. A permanent nameplate listing supply voltage, phase, frequency, full-load currents (see note), ampere rating of largest motor, short-circuit interrupting capacity of the machine overcurrent protective device if furnished, and diagram number shall be attached to the control equipment enclosure or machine where plainly visible after installation.

NOTE 1. The full-load current shall be not less than the sum of the full-load currents required for all motors and other equipment which may be in operation at the same time under normal conditions of use. Where unusual type loads, duty cycles, etc., require oversized conductors, the required capacity shall be included in the marked "full-load current."

NOTE 2. Where more than one incoming supply circuit is to be provided, the nameplate shall state the above information for each circuit.

670-4. Conductors Supplying a Machine Tool.
(a) The supply circuit conductor shall have an ampacity of not less than the marked full-load current rating plus 25 per cent of the full-load current rating of

the highest rated motor as indicated on the nameplate. For the protection of supply conductors to the machine tool, refer to Section 240-5.

(b) A machine tool conforming with NFPA No. 79-1971 shall be considered individual unit equipment. It is provided with a disconnecting means and may be supplied by branch circuits protected by either fuses or circuit breakers.

(c) The disconnecting means may or may not incorporate overcurrent protection. Where the machine tool nameplate is marked "Overcurrent protection provided at machine supply terminals," the supply conductors are to be considered either as feeders, or taps as covered by Section 240-15.

"Overcurrent protection provided at machine supply terminals" means that provision has been made in the machine tool for each set of supply conductors to terminate in a single circuit breaker or set of fuses.

▶ NFPA No. 79 states: "The center of the grip of the operating handle of the disconnecting means when in its highest position, shall not be more than 6½ feet above the floor and it is recommended that it be at least **3** feet above the floor. The operating handle shall be so arranged that it may be locked in the "Off" position."

ARTICLE 680. SWIMMING AND WADING POOLS

A. General

680-1. Scope. The provisions of this Article apply to the construction and installation of electric wiring for equipment in or adjacent to all swimming and wading pools, whether permanently installed or storable and to metallic appurtenances in or within 5 feet of the pool, and to the auxiliary equipment such as pumps, filters and similar equipment. No electric appliances or wiring shall be installed in the water or in the enclosing walls of a swimming pool, except as provided for in this Article.

The requirements of Article 680 will add to the safety of decorative and therapeutic pools; however, additional safeguards may be necessary.

▶ Research work conducted by Underwriters' Laboratories, Inc., and others, indicated that an electric shock could be received in two different ways. One of these involved the existence in the water of an electrical potential with respect to ground and the other involved the existence of a potential gradient in the water itself.

A person standing in the pool and touching the energized enclosure of faulty equipment located at poolside would be subject to a severe electrical shock because of the good ground which his body would establish through the water and pool to earth. Accordingly, the provision as given in Section **680-1** is an attempt to insure that all electrical equipment will be located outside a perimeter measured **5** feet away from the edge of the pool unless it has been specifically approved for swimming pool use.

In regard to the fine print note statement, no *additional safeguards* for wiring used in connection with decorative or therapeutic pools have been specified in Article 680. Accordingly, it would appear that in the interest of public safety, all wiring for therapeutic pools *should* be protected by a ground-fault circuit-interrupter. Such a recommendation might also be considered for decorative pools if the installation cannot be made in full compliance with Article 680.

680-2. Approval of Equipment.   All equipment shall be approved for the purpose.

680-3. Application of Other Articles.   Except as modified by this Article, wiring and equipment in or adjacent to swimming pools shall comply with the applicable requirements of Chapters 1 through 4 of this Code. See Section 370-13 for junction boxes, Section 347-3 for rigid nonmetallic conduit and Article 720 for low-voltage lighting.

680-4. Definitions.

(a) Permanently Installed Swimming or Wading Pool.   One that is constructed in the ground, on the ground, or in a building in such a manner that the pool cannot be readily disassembled for storage.

(b) Storable Swimming or Wading Pool.   One that is so constructed that it may be readily disassembled for storage and reassembled to its original integrity.

(c) Forming Shell.   A metal structure designed to support a wet-niche lighting fixture assembly and intended for mounting in a swimming pool structure.

(d) Wet-Niche Lighting Fixture.   A fixture intended for installation in a metallic forming shell mounted in a swimming pool structure where the fixture will be completely surrounded by pool water.

(e) Dry-Niche Lighting Fixture.   A fixture intended for installation in the wall of the pool in a niche which is sealed against the entry of pool water by a fixed lens.

(f) Ground-Fault Circuit-Interrupter.   A device whose function is to interrupt the electric circuit to the load when a fault current to ground exceeds some predetermined value that is less than that required to operate the overcurrent protective device of the supply circuit.

680-5. Transformers and Ground-Fault Circuit-Interrupters.

(a) Transformers.   Transformers used for the supply of fixtures, together with the transformer enclosure, shall be approved for the purpose. The transformer shall be a two-winding type having a grounded metal barrier between the primary and secondary voltage windings.

(b) Wiring.   Conductors on the load side of a ground-fault circuit-interrupter or of a transformer, used to comply with the provisions of Section 680-20(a)(2), shall be kept entirely independent of all other wiring and electrical equipment.

680-6. Location and Protection of Receptacles.   No outdoor receptacles on the property shall be located within 10 feet of the inside walls of the pool. All outdoor receptacles located between 10 feet and 15 feet of the inside walls of the pool shall be protected by a ground-fault circuit-interrupter. See Section 400-4 for prohibited uses of flexible cords. See also Section 210-22(d) for outdoor residential receptacles.

On pools located inside a permanent structure, receptacles within the pool enclosure shall be at least 10 feet from the inside walls of the pool. All receptacles located between 10 feet and 15 feet of the inside walls of the pool shall be protected by a ground-fault circuit-interrupter.

Note: In determining the above dimensions, the distance to be measured is the shortest path which the supply cord of an appliance connected to the receptacle would follow without piercing a building floor, wall, ceiling, or other solid permanent barrier.

▶ The requirements of this Section apply to all types of pools and in all types of occupancies (residential, commercial, etc.). The dimensions mentioned in the first two paragraphs apply only to the property on which the swimming pool is installed. See Figs. 210-1, 210-2, 210-3 and 210-4 and comments on ground-fault circuit-interrupters following Section 210-7. However, unlike Sections 210-7 and 210-22*d* there is no postponed enforcement date for required uses of ground-fault circuit-interrupters specified in Sections **680-6** and **680-31**.

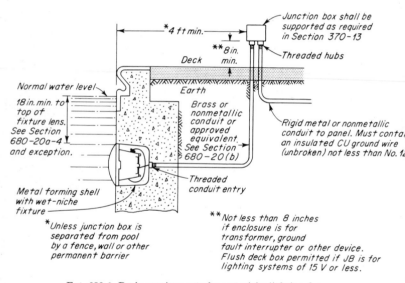

FIG. 680-1. Basic requirements for wet-niche lighting fixtures.

680-7. Cord- and Plug-Connected Equipment. Fixed or stationary equipment rated 20 amperes or less, other than an underwater lighting fixture for a permanently installed pool, may be connected with a flexible cord to facilitate the removal or disconnecting for maintenance or repair. The flexible cord shall not exceed 3 feet in length and shall have a copper equipment grounding conductor not smaller than No. 12 AWG with a grounding-type attachment plug. See Section 680-24(f) for connection with flexible cords.

▶ The three-foot cord limitation mentioned in this rule would not apply to swimming-pool filter pumps used with storable pools under Part C of Art. 680, because these pumps are considered as portable instead of *fixed or stationary*. See comments following Section **680-30**.

680-8. Overhead Conductor Clearances. The following parts of swimming pools shall not be placed under existing service-drop conductors or any other open overhead wiring; nor shall such wiring be installed above the following:

(a) Swimming pool and the area extending 10 feet horizontally from the inside of the walls of the pool.

(b) Diving structure.

(c) Observation stands, towers or platforms.

B. Permanently Installed Pools

680-20. Underwater Lighting Fixtures

(a) General.

(1) The provisions of Section 680-20 apply to all lighting fixtures installed below the normal water level of the pool.

(2) Underwater lighting fixtures supplied either directly from a branch circuit or by a transformer meeting the requirements of Section 680-5(a) shall perform reliably under any likely combination of fault conditions so that there is no shock hazard. Compliance with this requirement shall be assured by one of the following:

a. The design and construction of the fixtures; or

b. The use of a ground-fault circuit-interrupter; or

c. Other acceptable means.

(3) No lighting fixtures shall be installed for operation at more than 150 volts between conductors.

(4) Lighting fixtures mounted in walls shall be installed with the top of the fixture lens at least 18 inches below the normal water level of the pool. A lighting fixture facing upward shall have the lens adequately guarded to prevent contact by any person.

Exception: Lights approved for the purpose may be installed at a depth of at least 4 inches below the normal water level of the pool.

▶ This exception recognizes a type of lighting unit used in shallow wading pools where the 18-inch immersion depth mentioned in subparagraph **4** would not be possible.

(b) Wet-Niche Fixtures.

(1) Approved metal forming shells shall be installed for the mounting of all wet-niche underwater fixtures and shall be equipped with provisions for threaded conduit entries. Rigid metal conduit of brass or other approved corrosion-resistant metal, or rigid nonmetallic conduit, shall extend from the forming shell to a suitable junction box or other enclosure located as provided in Section 680-21. Where rigid nonmetallic conduit is used a No. 8 AWG insulated, solid copper conductor shall be installed in this conduit with provisions for terminating in the forming shell and the junction box or other enclosure. Metal parts of the fixture and forming shell in contact with the pool water shall be of brass or other approved corrosion-resistant metal.

(2) The end of the flexible-cord jacket and the flexible-cord conductor terminations within a fixture shall be covered with or encapsulated in a suitable potting compound to prevent the entry of water into the fixture through the cord or its conductors. In addition, the grounding connection within a fixture shall be similarly treated to protect such connection from the deteriorating effect of pool water in the event of water entry into the fixture.

(3) The fixture shall be bonded to and secured to the forming shell by a positive locking device which will assure a low-resistance contact and which will require a tool to remove the fixture from the forming shell.

(c) Dry-Niche Fixtures. A dry-niche lighting fixture shall be provided with:

(1) provision for drainage of water; and

(2) means for accommodating one equipment grounding conductor for each conduit entry.

Approved rigid metal or rigid nonmetallic conduit shall be installed from the fixture to the service equipment or panelboard. A junction box is not required, but if used, need not be elevated or located as specified in Section 680-21(a)(4) if the fixture is specifically approved for the purpose.

▶ Some approved dry-niche fixtures are provided with an integral flush deck box used to change lamps. Such fixtures have a drain connection at the bottom of the fixture to prevent accumulation of water or moisture.

680-21. Junction Boxes and Enclosures for Transformers and Ground-Fault Circuit-Interrupters.

(a) A junction box connected to a conduit which extends directly to an underwater pool-light forming shell shall be:

(1) equipped with provisions for threaded conduit entries; and

(2) of copper, brass, suitable plastic or other approved corrosion-resistant material; and

(3) provided with electrical continuity between every connected metallic conduit and the grounding terminals by means of copper, brass, or other approved corrosion-resistant metal that is integral with the box; and

(4) located not less than 8 inches, measured from the inside of the bottom of the box, above the ground level, pool deck, or maximum pool water level, whichever provides the greatest elevation, and located not less than 4 feet from the inside wall of the pool unless separated from the pool by a solid fence, wall or other permanent barrier.

Exception: On lighting systems of 15 volts or less, a flush deck box may be used provided:

a. An approved potting compound is used to fill the box to prevent the entrance of moisture, and

b. The flush deck box is located not less than 4 feet from the inside wall of the pool.

(b) An enclosure for a transformer, ground-fault circuit-interrupter, or a similar device connected to a conduit which extends directly to an underwater pool-light forming shell shall be:

(1) equipped with provisions for threaded conduit entries; and

(2) provided with an approved seal, such as duct seal at the conduit connection, that prevents circulation of air between the conduit and the enclosures; and

(3) provided with electrical continuity between every connected metallic

conduit and the grounding terminals by means of copper, brass, or other approved corrosion-resistant metal that is integral with the enclosures; and

(4) located not less than 8 inches, measured from the inside bottom of the enclosure to the ground level, pool deck, or maximum pool water level, whichever provides the greatest elevation; and

(5) located not less than 4 feet from the inside wall of the pool unless separated from the pool by a solid fence, wall or other permanent barrier.

(c) Junction boxes and enclosures mounted above the grade of the finished walkway around the pool shall not be located in the walkway unless afforded additional protection, such as by location under diving boards, adjacent to fixed structures, and the like.

(d) Junction boxes, transformer enclosures and ground-fault circuit-interrupter enclosures shall be provided with a number of grounding terminals which shall be one more than the number of conduit entries.

680-22. Bonding.

(a) The following parts shall be bonded together by a solid copper conductor not smaller than No. 8 AWG:

(1) All metallic parts of the pool structure, including the reinforcing steel.

(2) Forming shell.

(3) All metallic fittings within or attached to the pool structure.

(4) Metal parts of electrical equipment associated with the pool water circulating system, including pump motors.

(5) Metallic conduit and metallic piping within 5 feet of the inside walls of the pool and that are not separated from the pool by a permanent barrier.

(6) All fixed metallic parts that are within 5 feet of the inside walls of the swimming pool and that are not separated from the pool area by a permanent barrier.

Exception No. 1: The usual steel tie wires are considered suitable for bonding the reinforcing steel together, and welding or special clamping will not be required.

Exception No. 2: Structural reinforcing steel or the walls of welded metal pool structures may be used as a common bonding grid for nonelectrical parts wher econnections can be made in accordance with Section 250-113.

(b) For pool water heaters having a rating of more than 50 amperes and having specific instructions regarding the parts of the equipment to be bonded to the other pool components, and the parts of the equipment to be grounded, only those parts designated to be bonded shall be bonded, and only those parts designated to be grounded shall be grounded.

680-23. Grounding.
The following equipment shall be grounded: (1) Wet-niche underwater lighting fixtures; (2) Dry-niche underwater lighting fixtures; (3) All electrical equipment located within 5 feet of the inside wall of the pool; (4) All electrical equipment associated with the recirculating system of the pool; (5) Junction boxes; (6) Transformer enclosures; (7) Panelboards that are not part of the service equipment and that supply any electrical equipment associated with the pool.

680-24. Methods of Grounding.

(a) The following provisions shall apply to the grounding of underwater lighting fixtures, metallic junction boxes, metallic transformer enclosures and other metallic enclosures:

(1) Wet-niche lighting fixtures that are supplied by a flexible cord or cable shall have all exposed noncurrent-carrying metal parts grounded by an insulated, copper equipment grounding conductor that is an integral part of the cord or cable. This grounding conductor shall be connected to a grounding terminal in the supply junction box, transformer enclosure or other enclosure. This grounding conductor shall be equal in size to the supply conductors but not smaller than No. 16 AWG copper.

(2) The junction box, transformer enclosure or other enclosure in the supply circuit to a wet-niche lighting fixture and the field-wiring chamber of a dry-niche lighting fixture shall be grounded to the equipment grounding terminal of the panelboard. This terminal shall be directly connected to the panelboard enclosure. The equipment grounding conductor shall be installed without joint or splice.

Exception No. 1: Where more than one underwater lighting fixture is supplied by the same branch circuit, the equipment grounding conductor, installed between the junction boxes, transformer enclosures or other enclosures in the supply circuit to wet-niche fixtures or between the field-wiring compartments of dry-niche fixtures, may be terminated on approved grounding terminals.

Exception No. 2: Where the underwater lighting fixture is supplied from a transformer, and the transformer is located between the panelboard and a junction box connected to the conduit that extends directly to the underwater lighting fixture, the equipment grounding conductor may terminate on approved grounding terminals in the transformer enclosure.

(b) Other electrical equipment shall be grounded to the equipment grounding terminal of the panelboard.

(c) A panelboard, not part of the service equipment, shall have an equipment grounding conductor installed between its grounding terminal and the grounding terminal of the service equipment.

(d) An equipment grounding conductor shall be sized in accordance with Table 250-95 but not smaller than No. 12 AWG. It shall be an insulated copper conductor and shall be installed with the circuit conductors in an approved rigid metal conduit or rigid nonmetallic conduit.

Exception No. 1: The equipment grounding conductor specified in Section 680-24(a)(1).

Exception No. 2: The equipment grounding conductor between the wiring chamber of the secondary winding of a transformer and a junction box shall be sized in accordance with the overcurrent device in this circuit. See Section 680-24(a)(2), Exception No. 2.

Exception No. 3: The equipment grounding conductor between an existing, remote panelboard and the service equipment need not be in conduit if the interconnection is by means of an approved cable assembly with an insulated or covered copper equipment grounding conductor.

(e) The equipment grounding conductor between a remote panelboard and the service equipment shall be sized in accordance with the overcurrent devices protecting the conductors supplying the panelboard. See Table 250-95.

(f) Where fixed or stationary equipment is connected with a flexible cord to facilitate removal or disconnection for maintenance, repair or storage (see Section 680-7) the equipment grounding conductors specified in Section 680-24(a) shall be connected to a fixed metallic part of the assembly. The removable part shall be mounted on or bonded to the fixed metallic part.

▶ All fixed metallic parts located within this 5-foot area must be effectively bonded and tied together so as to provide a common grounding source with the metal which is otherwise installed in the enclosing walls and floor of the pool and applies whether a grounded or isolated electrical system is used. See Fig. 680-2.

The bonding or interconnecting of circuits or equipment is covered in Section 250-113, and specifically names several commonly recognized means. Because it also recognizes "approved means," it includes any method which is acceptable to the authority having jurisdiction. Where bonding is required between reinforcing bars or wire mesh which is encased in concrete, the use of tie wires tightly applied and used in sufficient number to provide parallel pairs is usually found to have adequate conductivity.

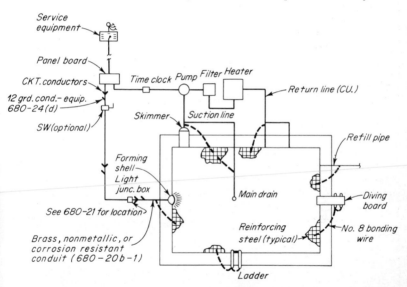

FIG. 680-2. Basic methods of bonding and grounding for swimming pools and associated equipment. See Sections 680-20 through 680-24.

In considering the need to ground metal appurtenances in or within 5 ft of a swimming pool, it should be realized that stray currents in the ground or in piping connected to the swimming pool can be hazardous to persons in the pool. Even where plastic piping is used, water which contains salt or chemicals used to provide sanitation may have a resistance so low as to permit dangerous currents to flow.

A protective ground placed on electrical equipment may be lost in time through corrosion which is normally associated with the wet conditions and dampness usually found around swimming pools so wiring should be checked periodically.

C. Storable Pools

680-30. Pumps.   A cord-connected swimming-pool filter pump shall incorporate an approved system of double insulation or its equivalent, and shall be provided with means for grounding only the internal and nonaccessible noncurrent-carrying metal parts of the appliance.

The means for grounding shall be an equipment grounding conductor run with the power supply conductors in the flexible cord that is properly terminated in a grounding-type attachment plug having a fixed grounding contact member.

680-31. Ground-Fault Circuit-Interrupters Required.   All electrical equipment used with storable swimming pools shall be supplied by circuits protected by ground-fault circuit-interrupters.

▶   There are portable filter pumps listed by Underwriters' Laboratories, Inc. and they comply with Section **680-30**.

Ground-fault circuit interrupters must be installed so that all wiring used with storable pools will be protected. For various types of ground-fault circuit interrupters see Figs. **210-1, 210-2, 210-3** and **210-4** and comments following Sections **210-7, 210-22***d*, and **680-6**.

CHAPTER SEVEN

Special Conditions

ARTICLE 700. EMERGENCY SYSTEMS

A. General

700-1. Scope. The provisions of this Article apply to the installation, operation and maintenance of circuits, systems and equipment intended to supply illumination and power in the event of failure of the normal supply or in the event of accident to elements of a system supplying power and illumination essential for safety to life and property where such systems or circuits are legally required by Municipal, State, Federal or other Codes, or by any governmental agency having jurisdiction.

▶ The placement or location of exit lights is not a function of the National Electrical Code but is covered in the Life Safety Code, NFPA No. 101, (formerly Building Exits Code).

The National Electrical Code indicates how the installation will be made, not where the emergency lighting is required, except as specified in Part C of Art. 517 for essential electrical systems in hospitals.

Emergency systems are generally installed in places of assembly where artificial illumination is required, such as buildings subject to occupancy by large numbers of persons, hotels, theaters, sports arenas, hospitals and similar institutions. Emergency systems may provide power for such functions as essential refrigeration, operation of mechanical breathing apparatus, ventilation when essential to maintain life, illumination and power for hospital operating rooms, fire alarm systems, fire pumps, industrial processes where current interruption would produce serious hazards, public address systems and similar functions.

See NFPA Life Safety Code (NFPA No. 101-1970) for specification of locations where emergency lighting is considered essential to life safety.

▶   An emergency lighting system in a theater or other place of public assemblage includes exit signs, the chief purpose of which is to indicate the location of the exits, and lighting equipment commonly called "emergency lights," the purpose of which is to provide sufficient illumination in the auditorium, corridors, lobbies, passageways, stairways, and fire escapes to enable persons to leave the building safely.

These details, also the various classes of buildings in which emergency lighting is required, are left to be determined by state or municipal codes, and where such codes are in effect the following provisions apply.

700-2. Other Requirements.   All requirements of this Code shall apply to emergency systems, except as modified by this Article.

700-3. Equipment Approval.   All equipment shall be approved for use on emergency systems.

700-4. Tests and Maintenance.

(a)   The authority having jurisdiction shall conduct or witness a test on the complete system upon installation and periodically afterward.

(b)   Systems shall be tested periodically on a schedule acceptable to the authority having jurisdiction to assure their maintenance in proper operating condition.

(c)   Where battery systems or unit equipments are involved, including batteries used for starting or ignition in auxiliary engines, the authority having jurisdiction shall require periodic maintenance.

(d)   A written record shall be kept of such tests and maintenance.

700-5. Capacity.   Emergency systems shall have adequate capacity and rating for the emergency operation of all equipment connected to the system.

▶   It is extremely important that the supply source be of adequate capacity. There are two main reasons for adequate capacity:

1. It is important that power be available for the necessary supply to exit lights, emergency and egress lighting, as well as to operate such equipment as required for elevators and other equipment connected to the emergency system.

2. In such occupancies as hospitals there may be a need for an emergency supply for lighting in hospital operating rooms, also for such equipment as inhalators, iron lungs, incubators, and the like. See Part C of Art. 517 for requirements in hospitals.

B. Sources of Power

700-6. Systems.   Current supply shall be such that in event of failure of the normal supply to or within the building or group of buildings concerned, emergency lighting, or emergency power, or both emergency lighting and power, will be immediately available. The supply system for emergency purposes may comprise one or more of the types of system covered in Sections 700-7 through 700-10. Unit equipments in accordance with Section 700-22 shall satisfy the applicable requirements of this Article.

Consideration must be given to the type of service to be rendered, whether of short time duration, as for exit lights of a theater, or of long duration as for supplying emergency power and lighting due to a long period of current failure from trouble either inside or outside the building, as in the case of a hospital.

Assignment of degree of reliability of the recognized emergency supply system depends upon the careful evaluation of the variables at each particular installation.

700-7. Storage Battery.   One service, in accordance with Article 230, and a storage battery of suitable rating and capacity to supply and maintain at not less than 87½ per cent of system voltage the total load of the circuits supplying emergency lighting and emergency power for a period of at least 1½ hours.

Batteries whether of the acid or alkali type shall be designed and constructed to meet the requirements of emergency service. When of the lead-acid type, this shall include low gravity acid (1.20 to 1.22 SP-GR), relatively thick and rugged plates and separators, and a transparent jar.

▶   **Two separate services brought to different locations in the building are always preferable, and these services should at least receive their supply from separate transformers where this is practicable. In some localities, municipal ordinances require either two services from independent sources of supply, or auxiliary supply for emergency lighting from a storage battery or a generator driven by a steam turbine, internal-combustion engine, or other prime mover.**

700-8. Generator Set.   One service, in accordance with Article 230, and a generator set driven by some form of prime mover and of sufficient capacity and proper rating to supply circuits carrying emergency lighting or lighting and power, with suitable means for automatically starting the prime mover on failure of the normal service. For hospitals, the transition time from instant of failure of the normal power source to the emergency generator source shall not exceed ten seconds.

See Section 700-4.

▶   See comment following Section 700-10.

700-9. Separate Service.   Two services, each in accordance with Article 230, with separate service drops or laterals, widely separated electrically and physically to minimize possibility of simultaneous interruption of supply.

▶   See comment following Section 700-10.

700-10. Connection Ahead of Service Disconnecting Means.   Connections on the line side of the main service disconnecting means if sufficiently separated from the main service disconnecting means to prevent simultaneous interruption of supply through an occurrence within the building or group of buildings served. See Section 230-73.

▶   *General Discussion of Requirements for Emergency Lighting Systems*

Two sources of supply should be provided. These sources may be (1) two services from central-station supply, (2) one service and a storage battery (or battery/inverter), or (3) one service and a generator set.

Either *a single emergency lighting system* may be installed or *two complete systems,* each one of which will, when operated without the other, provide all required emergency illumination.

Single Emergency System.

If a single emergency system is installed, a throw-over switch shall be provided which, in case of failure of the source of supply on which the system is operating, will automatically transfer the emergency system to the other source. Where the two sources of supply are two services, the single emergency system may normally operate on either source. Where the two sources of supply are one service and storage battery, or one service and a generator set, the single emergency system would, as a general rule, be operated normally on the service, using the battery or generator only as a reserve in case of failure of the service.

Two Emergency Systems.

If two emergency lighting systems are installed, each system shall operate on a separate source of supply. Either both systems shall be kept in operation, or switches shall be provided which will automatically place either system in operation upon failure of the other system.

Cases Arising under These Rules

Case 1. Single Emergency System and Two Services.

a. One service to supply emergency lighting only and one service to supply the general lighting and to be capable of supplying the emergency lighting also. The emergency system to be supplied from either service through an automatic throw-over switch.

The service arrangement for Case 1*a* is shown in Fig. 700-1. The emergency-system feeder is small and would not be protected by the fuses or circuit breaker of the general lighting service. Taps to the general lighting

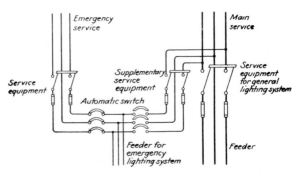

Fig. 700-1. *Case* 1*a*. Service arrangement for single emergency system with two services, one for emergency system only and one for both general lighting and emergency system.

service for supplying the emergency system should be made ahead of the main service equipment and a supplementary service switch and fuses (or circuit breaker) must be installed in this line.

b. Each service to carry a part of the general lighting load, with sufficient additional capacity to carry the emergency system also. The emergency system to be supplied from either service through an automatic throw-over switch.

The service arrangement for this case is shown in Fig. 700-2. For the same

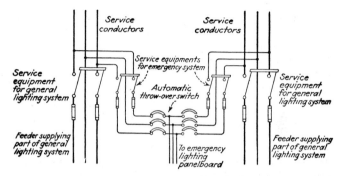

Fɪɢ. 700-2. *Case* 1*b.* Service arrangement for single emergency system with two services, each to supply a part of the general lighting system, with capacity to carry the emergency system also.

reason as in Case 1*a*, as explained above, taps to the two services must be made ahead of the general lighting service switches and two sets of service equipment must be provided for the emergency system.

Case 2. Single Emergency System with One Service and a Storage Battery or Generator Set.

The service to supply the general lighting system and, normally, to supply the emergency system also. The emergency system to be supplied either from the service or from the battery or generator through an automatic throw-over switch.

Figure 700-3 shows the service arrangement for Case 2.

700-11. Auxiliary Source. The requirements of Sections 700-5 and Section 700-6 shall also apply to installations where the entire electrical load on a service or sub-service is arranged to be supplied from a second source. Current supply from a standby power plant shall satisfy the requirements of availability in Section 700-6.

700-12. Derangement Signals. Audible and visual signal devices shall be provided where practicable for the following purposes:

(**a**) To give warning of derangement of the emergency or auxiliary source.

(**b**) To indicate that the battery or generator set is carrying load.

(**c**) To indicate by a visual signal that a battery charger is functioning properly.

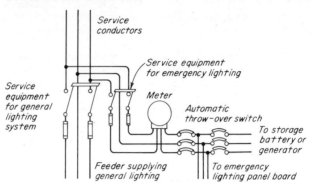

Fig. 700-3. *Case* 2. Service arrangement for single emergency system and a storage battery or generator set as reserve supply.

▶   In order to be effective, the signal devices should be located in some room where an attendant is on duty. Lamps may readily be used as signals to indicate the position of an automatic switching device. An audible signal in any place of public assemblage should not be so located or of such a character that it will cause a general alarm.

The standard signal equipment furnished by the Electric Storage Battery Co. with their 60-cell battery for emergency lighting includes an indicating lamp which is lighted when the charger is operating at the high rate, and a voltmeter marked in three colored sections indicates (1) that the battery is not being charged, or is discharging into the emergency system, (2) that the battery is being trickle charged, or (3) that the battery is being charged at the high rate. This last indication duplicates the indication given by the lamp.

C. Emergency Circuits for Lighting and Power

700-13. Loads on Emergency Branch Circuits.   No appliances and no lamps, other than those specified as required for emergency use shall be supplied by emergency lighting circuits.

700-14. Emergency Illumination.   Emergency illumination shall include all required exit lights and all other lights specified as necessary to provide sufficient illumination.

  Emergency lighting systems should be so designed and installed that the failure of any individual lighting element, such as the burning out of a light bulb, cannot leave any space in total darkness.

700-15. Circuits for Emergency Lighting.   Branch circuits intended to supply emergency lighting shall be so installed as to provide service immediately when the normal supply for lighting is interrupted. Such installations shall provide either one of the following:

(a)   An emergency lighting supply, independent of the general lighting system with provisions for automatically transferring, by means of devices approved for the purpose, the emergency lights upon the event of failure of the general lighting system supply.

(b) Two or more separate and complete systems with independent power supply, each system providing sufficient current for emergency lighting purposes. Unless both systems are used for regular lighting purposes and are both kept lighted, means shall be provided for automatically energizing either system upon failure of the other. Either or both systems may be part of the general lighting system of the protected occupancy if circuits supplying lights for emergency illumination are installed in accordance with other sections of this Article.

▶ *1. Location of Overcurrent Devices*
The installation of an automatic transfer switch does not alter the basic code requirements regarding the location of the overcurrent devices as covered in Section 240-15.

Overcurrent devices must be furnished for both the normal and emergency sources of supply and must be located to conform to Section 240-15.

2. Solid Neutral on A-C and D-C Systems
On a-c to a-c automatic transfer switches, solid neutrals can be used based on the grounding connections specified in Section 250-23. However, in some installations, objectionable ground current flow may occur because of site conditions requiring corrective measures as outlined in Section 250-21.

On a-c to d-c automatic transfer switches, a solid neutral tie between the a-c and d-c neutrals is not permitted where both sources of supply are exterior distribution systems. Section 250-22 regarding location of grounds for d-c exterior systems clearly specifies that the d-c system can be grounded only at the supply station.

Where the d-c system is an interior isolated system, such as a storage battery, solid neutral connection between the a-c system neutral and the d-c source is acceptable.

When the neutrals must be switched on a-c to d-c automatic transfer switches, the required capacity of the neutral switching pole must be properly evaluated on the basis of the service combination. Thus in an installation utilizing a three-phase four-wire normal source and a two-wire d-c emergency source, with the neutral switched, a four-pole double-throw switch would be required. One pole on the d-c emergency source would be required to carry three times the current of the remaining poles.

3. Close Differential Voltage Supervision of Normal Source
Normally adequate voltage supervision of the normal source can be provided by relays adjusted to effect transfer to the emergency source when the normal source voltage is 70 per cent or less on any phase. This value of voltage insures reasonable lighting intensity as well as insuring transfer when the overcurrent device in any branch or phase opens.

Consideration must be given to voltage supervision at close differential for many installations where the load circuits are critical to voltage.

Fig. 700-4. Automatic emergency lighting transfer switch. (*Automatic Switch Co.*)

As an example, starter-type fluorescent lighting is extremely voltage sensitive, starting becoming uncertain at voltages below **105** volts. Close differential relay supervision providing **105** volts transfer and **115** retransfer for a 120-volt system is a requirement for this type of lighting.

Electronic equipment load is frequently voltage critical. Among such installations are television stations, microwave communications, telephone communications, and similar applications. To accommodate the broad requirements of this class of load, the transfer voltage setting should preferably be adjustable over a minimum range of **75** to **93** per cent of normal rated voltage.

Automatic transfer switches applied to motor installations of the polyphase type also require close differential voltage supervision. A polyphase motor operating at partial load will tend to sustain terminal voltages despite the loss of line voltage on one phase. Close differential voltage relays capable of adjustment to within transfer and retransfer values of **2** per cent will insure detection of phase outage over a practical range of motor loading.

4. Automatic Transfer Switches with Emergency Source an Automatically Started Power Plant

In these installations the normal source is usually a utility power line and the emergency source a power plant which starts upon failure of the normal source. To insure maximum reliability, a minimum installation should be arranged to:

a. Initiate starting of the power plant from a contact on relay SE. (See Fig. 700-5.)

b. Sustain connection of load circuits to the normal source during the starting period to provide utilization of any existing service on the normal source.

c. Measure output voltage and frequency of emergency source through use of voltage frequency sensitive LO relay (see Fig. 700-5) and to effect

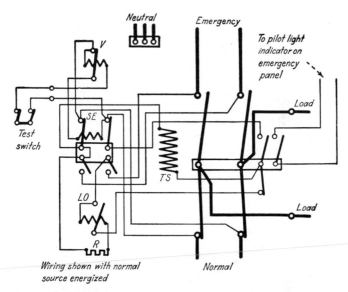

Fig. 700-5. Diagram of connections of the automatic transfer switch shown in Fig. 700-4.

transfer of the load circuits to the power plant only when both voltage and frequency of the power plant are approximately normal.

d. Provide audible or visual signal when power plant is feeding the load.

5. *Time-delay Devices on Automatic Transfer Switches*

All distribution systems are subject to transient conditions which cause outages of the system often of extremely short duration. These momentary outages can usually be ignored, particularly if less than 1 sec duration (field experience indicates that outages less than 1 sec duration are transients and will not be sustained). A desirable addition to automatic transfer switches is the addition of a feature so that outages of less than 1 sec duration will be ignored.

This is readily accomplished by adding the feature to selector relay SE already existing in the transfer panel. (See Fig. 700-5.) The timing feature should be fixed and preferably not longer than 3 sec.

The advantages of this feature are realized in all types of automatic transfer installations. In standby plant installations the reduced number of false starts is especially important to minimize wear on the starting gear, battery, and associated equipment.

A time-delay relay functioning upon retransfer to normal is also a desirable addition to transfer switch installations. The transfer to the emergency source is the result of unstable or outage conditions of the normal source. Obviously some means to determine sustained stability of the normal source is desirable.

A simple and effective means of accomplishing this is to install a time-delay relay, adjustable from 2 to 15 min between relays V and SE. (See Fig. 700-5.) Upon restoration of the normal source, relay V operates to energize the time-delay relay. After the preselected timing period the timer contact closes to energize relay SE to effect the transfer to the normal source. This time delay should be connected so that if the emergency source of supply should fail while it is feeding the load the time delay will be nullified and retransfer to the normal source made instantaneously when normal source is again available.

700-16. Circuits for Emergency Power. For branch circuits which supply equipment classed as emergency, there shall be an emergency supply source to which the load will be transferred automatically and immediately upon the failure of the normal supply.

700-17. Independent Wiring. Emergency circuit wiring shall be kept entirely independent of all other wiring and equipment and shall not enter the same raceway, box or cabinet with other wiring except:

Exception No. 1: In transfer switches.

Exception No. 2: In exit or emergency lighting fixtures supplied from two sources.

Exception No. 3: In a common junction box attached to exit or emergency lighting fixtures supplied from two sources.

▶ This Section requires that the wiring for emergency systems be kept entirely independent of the regular wiring used for lighting and thus it needs to be in separate raceways and boxes. This requirement is to ensure that where faults may occur on the regular wiring, they will not affect the emergency-system wiring as it will be in a separate enclosure.

Exception 1 for transfer switches is intended to permit normal supply conductors to be brought into the transfer-switch enclosure and that these conductors would be the only ones within the transfer-switch enclosure which were not part of the emergency system. Exceptions 2 and 3 permit two sources supplying emergency or exit lighting to enter the fixture and its common junction box.

D. Control

700-18. Switch Requirements. The switch or switches installed in emergency lighting circuits shall be so arranged that only authorized persons will have control of emergency lighting except:

Exception No. 1: Where two or more single-throw switches are connected in parallel to control a single circuit, at least one of these switches shall be accessible only to authorized persons.

Exception No. 2: Additional switches which act only to put emergency lights into operation but not disconnect them are permissible.

Switches connected in series or three and four way switches shall not be used.

700-19. Switch Location.

(a) All manual switches for controlling emergency circuits shall be in locations convenient to authorized persons responsible for their actuation. In places of assembly such as theaters a switch for controlling emergency lighting systems shall be located in the lobby or at a place conveniently accessible thereto.

(b) In no case shall a control switch for emergency lighting in a theater or motion-picture theater be placed in a motion-picture projection booth or on a stage, except that where multiple switches are provided, one such switch may be installed in such location when so arranged that it can energize, but not disconnect, the circuit.

700-20. Other Switches.

(a) Exterior Lights. Those lights on the exterior of the building which are not required for illumination when there is sufficient daylight may be controlled by an automatic light-actuated device approved for the purpose.

(b) Hospital Corridors. Switching arrangements to transfer corridor lighting in patient areas of hospitals from overhead fixtures to fixtures designed to provide night lighting may be permitted, provided the switching system is so designed that switches can only select between two sets of fixtures and cannot extinguish both sets at the same time.

E. Overcurrent Protection

700-21. Accessibility. The branch-circuit overcurrent devices in emergency circuits shall be accessible to authorized persons only.

F. Unit Equipments

700-22. Unit Equipments. Where permitted by the authority having jurisdiction, in lieu of other methods specified elsewhere in this Article, individual unit equipments for emergency illumination shall consist of (a) a rechargeable battery, (b) a battery charging means, (c) provisions for one or more lamps mounted on the equipment and may have terminals for remote lamps, and (d) a relaying device arranged to energize the lamps automatically upon failure of the normal supply to the building. The batteries shall be of suitable rating and capacity to supply and maintain at not less than 87½ per cent of the nominal battery voltage for the total lamp load associated with the unit for a period of at least 1½ hours. Storage batteries whether of the acid or alkali type shall be designed and constructed to meet the requirements of emergency service. When of the lead-acid type the storage battery shall have a transparent jar.

Unit equipments shall be permanently fixed in place (i.e., not portable) and shall have all wiring to each unit installed in accordance with the requirements of any of the wiring methods in Chapter 3. They shall not be connected by flexible cord. The supply circuit between the unit equipment and the service, feeders, or the branch-circuit wiring shall be installed as required by Section 700-17. Emergency illumination fixtures which obtain power from a unit equipment and are not part of the unit equipment shall be wired to the unit equipment as required by Section 700-17 and by one of the wiring methods of Chapter 3.

▶   The intent of the 87½ per cent value is to assure proper *lighting output* from lamps supplied by unit equipment. It is generally considered acceptable to design equipment that will produce acceptable lighting levels for the required 1½ hr even though the 87½ per cent rating of the battery would not be maintained during this period. The objective is adequate light output to permit safe egress from buildings in emergencies.

To clarify this point a tentative interim amendment has been issued. See Tentative Interim Amendment No. 172 in back of book.

ARTICLE 710. OVER 600 VOLTS—GENERAL

A. General

710-1. Scope. This Article applies in general to all circuits and equipment operated at more than 600 volts. For specific installation see the Articles referred to in Section 710-2.

710-2. Installations Covered in Other Articles. Provisions applicable to specific types of installations are included in Article 230, Services; Article 346, Rigid Metal Conduit; Article 347, Rigid Nonmetallic Conduit; Article 365, Cablebus; Article 430, Motors, Motor Circuits and Controllers; Article 450, Transformers and Transformer Vaults; Article 460, Capacitors; Article 730, Outside Branch Circuits and Feeders; Article 410, Lighting Fixtures, Lampholders, Lamps, Receptacles and Rosettes; Article 600, Electric Signs and Outline Lighting; Article 660, X-ray Equipment, and Article 665, Induction and Dielectric Heating Equipment.

710-3. Wiring Methods.

(a) Aboveground Conductors. They shall be installed in rigid metal conduit, in cablebus, in other suitable raceways or as open runs of metal-clad cable suitable for the use and purpose.

In locations accessible to qualified persons only, open runs of nonmetallic sheathed cable, bare conductors and bare bus-bars may also be used.

(b) Underground Conductors. Conductors shall be suitable for the voltage and conditions under which they are installed. Conductors installed in rigid metal conduit or direct burial cable, if of the construction where the energized conductors are surrounded by effectively grounded, multiple, concentric conductors, closely and evenly spaced circumferentially and meeting the requirements of Section 250-51 shall be buried at least 30 inches deep. Where other wiring methods are used the conductors shall be at a minimum depth of 42 inches and preferably at least 6 inches below other utilities.

Exception No. 1: Under streets or roadways—conductor depth may be reduced to 24 inches if installed in rigid metal conduit.

Exception No. 2: Airport runways—in airport runways, including adjacent defined areas where trespass is prohibited, cable may be buried no less than 18 inches deep and without raceways or concrete encasement.

Exception No. 3: Lesser depths for unusual conditions—the above depths may be reduced 12 inches for each additional 2 inches of protective layer of concrete above the conductors.

▶   In locations accessible to qualified persons only there are no restrictions on the types of wiring that may be used. The types more commonly employed are open wiring on insulators with conductors either bare or insulated, and rigid metal conduit or nonmetallic rigid conduit containing lead-covered cable. Figure 710-1 is a summary table of the burial depth requirements contained in Section 710-3*b*, including the exceptions.

Underground Conductors

Wiring methods	Burial depth below grade in inches		
	General applications	Under streets or roadways	Under airport runways & defined adjacent areas
Rigid metal conduit	30	24	18
Direct burial cable (if energized conductors are surrounded by effectively grounded multiple concentric conductors, closely & evenly spaced circumferentially)	30	30	18
Other wiring methods (such as rigid nonmetallic conduit encased in 2 in. of concrete or other types of direct-burial cables)	42	42	18

Note: Above depths may be reduced 12 in. for each additional 2 in. of protective layer of concrete above the conductors.

Fig. 710-1. Summary table for Section 710-3*b* requirements involving underground and direct earth burial of raceways and cables over 600 volts.

710-4. Braid-Covered Insulated Conductors—Open Installation.

Open runs of braid-covered insulated conductors shall have a flame-retardant braid. When the conductors used do not have this protection, a flame-retardant saturant shall be applied to the braid covering after installation. This treated braid covering shall be stripped back a safe distance at conductor terminals, according to the operating voltage. This distance should be not less than one inch for each kilovolt of the conductor-to-ground voltage of the circuit, where practicable.

710-5. Shielding of Solid Dielectric Insulated Conductors.   Where solid dielectric-insulated conductors for permanent installations operate at voltages higher than those indicated in Table 710-5 and under the conditions mentioned, they shall be of a type having shielding for the purpose of confining their dielectric field.

▶   In a solid dielectric insulated conductor, if a slight amount of moisture is present, some moisture will be absorbed by the outer jacket, which then becomes to some extent a conductor. The metal conductor, the insulation, and the jacket then form a capacitor, with the conductor and the jacket as the two electrodes. When a voltage to ground is impressed upon one electrode of a capacitor, a voltage of opposite sign will appear on the other electrode and if this electrode is connected to ground, a current will flow to ground. Thus when a voltage is impressed upon the conductor, a voltage will appear upon the jacket if it has become partially conducting by absorbing some moisture.

Table 710-5. Shielding of Solid Dielectric Insulated Conductors

	Voltage in Kv (L-L) Above which Shielding is Required			
	Neutral Grounded		Neutral Ungrounded	
Method of Installation	Fibrous Covered	Ozone-Resistant Jacket Covering	Fibrous Covered	Ozone-Resistant Jacket Covering
In metallic conduit or trough above grade located indoors and in dry locations				
Single conductor..............	2	5*	2	3
Multi-conductor..............	2	5	2	5
Underground ducts and conduits and other wet locations				
Single conductor.............	2	3**	2	3
Multi-conductor..............	2	5	2	5
On insulators—				
Only multi-conductor..........	Not required under 5 Kv.		3	5
Directly in soil—				
Single conductor.............	—	3	—	3
Multi-conductor..............	—	5	—	5

* It is presumed that installation conditions will be such as to maintain a high level of jacket surface resistivity and so minimize the possibility of destructive discharge. Pulling dry or the use of insulating type pulling lubricants will help attain these conditions. Where surface contamination cannot be prevented and high surface resistivity cannot be maintained, metallic shielding shall be used at over 3 kv.

Note: Sheathed single or 3 conductor cables require no shielding for voltages 5 kv and less. In the case of portable equipment cables it is good practice to specify shielding for all voltages above 2 kv.

** For three single conductor cables, cabled together without overall outer covering the value is 5 kv.

If the cable is in a grounded metal conduit, the voltage appearing on the jacket will discharge to ground at the points where the jacket is in contact with the conduit; in other words, there is a charging current flowing between the conductor and the ground. If the voltage is high enough, the discharge will cause the air to be ionized and ozone will be formed. Ozone is oxygen in such form that it is extremely active in combining with any oxidizable substance. It will attack the jacket and the jacket insulation, and this action may eventually break down the insulation.

The discharge and the consequent formation of ozone can be prevented by surrounding the insulation with a metallic or semiconducting shield which is grounded. Instead of the jacket, the shield then becomes one electrode of the capacitor. Being grounded by a metallic connection to ground, the shield is kept at ground potential and no voltage above ground can appear on the jacket outside of the shield, hence there is no discharge from the jacket and no ionization of the air takes place.

A metallic shield usually consists of a thin ribbon or tape of tinned copper about ⅞ in. or 1 in. wide, wrapped spirally around the insulation. The "semiconducting" shield may consist of conducting fibrous tape, conducting paint, certain types of asbestos coverings, metalized paper, graphite compounds, or similar materials.

Figure 710-2 shows a single-conductor shielded cable and a three-conductor shielded cable.

Fig. 710-2. Single-conductor and three-conductor shielded rubber-insulated cable. (*The Okonite Co.*)

A stress cone consists of an application of insulating tape in conical form, over which the shielding is continued, the purpose being to build up the thickness of the insulation at the point where the shielding ends. The insulating tape may be varnished cambric. The shielding is continued over the cone of tape by means of a spiral wrapping of braided copper tinsel tape which is soldered to the shield on the cable.

Table 710-5 is taken from the Insulated Power Cable Engineers Association (IPCEA) standard. When the 1971 National Electrical Code was adopted, this table was being revised by IPCEA but the changes had not been formalized. Since then the revisions have been made to agree with new Table

310-2e1 of the 1971 National Electrical Code, the latter of which no longer recognizes unshielded *single-conductor* cables at voltages above 2000 volts. In any event, the requirements of Table 310-2e1, which describe the insulation requirements for rubber-covered types from 601 to 5000 volts, govern the construction of such cables. Accordingly, where single-conductor rubber-covered cables (including natural, SBR, and butyl rubbers, and cross-linked polyethylene and ethylene-propylene rubber) are used in other than multi-conductor cables with a common overall covering at over 2 kv, shielding is required. This should help to prevent failures if shielded 5-kv single-conductor cables for a 4160-volt system are installed in raceways. In the past *unshielded* single-conductor 5-kv cable resulted in numerous failures.

Figures 710-3 and 710-4 show a stress cone formed on a single-conductor cable terminating without a pothead and a stress cone inside a pothead.

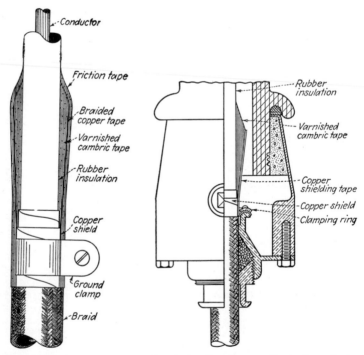

Fig. 710-3. Stress cone on a single-conductor shielded cable terminating without a pothead.

Fig. 710-4. Stress cone on a single-conductor shielded cable terminating in a pothead.

In Fig. 710-3 the shield is grounded by means of a sheet-copper ground clamp which is soldered to the shield. In Fig. 710-4 a clamping ring is provided inside the pothead, and the end of the copper tape is turned out and clamped under the ring, thus grounding the tape and shield to the metallic base of the pothead.

Before proceeding with the installation of any type of high-voltage cable, complete instructions for installation should always be obtained from the manufacturer of the cable. Proper training for making high-voltage terminations is absolutely essential.

710-6. Grounding of Shielding Tape.   The metallic shielding or any other static voltage shields on shielded cable shall be stripped back to a safe distance according to the circuit voltage, at all terminations of the shielding, as in potheads and joints. At such points, suitable methods such as the use of potheads, terminators, stress cones or similar devices shall be employed for stress reduction and the metallic shielding tape shall be grounded.

710-7. Grounding.   Wiring and equipment installations shall conform with the applicable provisions of Article 250.

710-8. Moisture or Mechanical Protection for Metal Sheathed Cables.   Where cable conductors emerge from a metal sheath and where protection against moisture or mechanical injury is necessary, the insulation of the conductors shall be protected by a pothead or other approved means.

B. Equipment—General Provisions

710-10. Indoor Installations.   Indoor electrical equipment installations shall conform with Sections 710-10(a) and (b).

(a) In Places Accessible to Unqualified Persons.   Electrical installations which are open to unqualified persons shall be made with metal enclosed equipments or shall be enclosed in a vault or in an area access to which is controlled by a lock. Metal-enclosed switchgear, unit substations, transformers, pull boxes, connection boxes, and other similar associated equipment shall be marked with appropriate caution signs. Openings in ventilated dry-type transformers or similar openings in other equipment shall be designed so that foreign objects inserted through these openings will be deflected from energized parts.

(b) In Places Accessible to Qualified Persons Only.   Electrical installations shall conform with Sections 710-31 through 710-34.

710-11. Outdoor Installations.

(a) In Places Accessible to Unqualified Persons.   Electrical installations which are open to unqualified persons shall conform with Article 730.

For clearances of conductors over 600 volts see National Electrical Safety Code—ANSI C2-1960.

(b) In Places Accessible to Qualified Persons Only.   Outdoor electrical installations having exposed live parts shall be accessible to qualified persons only and shall conform with Sections 710-31 through 710-34.

710-12. Metal Enclosed Equipments.   Installations consisting of metal enclosed equipments such as metal clad switchgear, transformers, and the like, which have no exposed live parts, need not comply with Section 710-31. Ventilating or similar openings in equipment shall be so designed that foreign objects inserted through these openings will be deflected from energized parts. Where exposed to physical damage from vehicular traffic suitable guards shall be provided. Metal-enclosed equipment located outdoors accessible to the general public shall be designed so that exposed nuts or bolts cannot be readily removed, permitting access to live parts.

C. Equipment—Specific Provisions

See also references to specific types of installations in Section 710-2.

710-21. Circuit Interrupting Devices.

(a) Circuit Breakers.

(1) Indoor installations shall consist of metal-enclosed units or fire-resistant cell-mounted units except that open mounting of circuit breakers is permissible in locations accessible to qualified persons only.

(2) Circuit breakers shall be trip-free in all positions. In every installation the circuit breaker rating in respect to closing, carrying or interrupting capabilities shall not be less than the short-circuit duty at the point of application.

(3) Circuit breakers used to control oil-filled transformers should be located outside the transformer vault.

(4) Circuit breakers shall have a means of indicating the open and closed position of the breaker at the point(s) from which they may be operated.

(5) Oil circuit breakers shall be so arranged or located that adjacent readily combustible structures or materials are safeguarded in an approved manner. Adequate space separation, fire-resistant barriers or enclosures, trenches containing sufficient coarse crushed stone and properly drained oil enclosures such as dikes or basins are recognized as suitable for this purpose.

▶   A typical assembly of metal-clad switchgear is shown in Fig. 710-5. This assembly is designed for a maximum voltage of 5,000. Each unit is equipped with an oil circuit breaker having six contact pockets which, in the operating position, fit corresponding contact posts. When the breaker is in the open position, it can be lowered by means of a crank so that the disconnecting contacts are separated, and the assembly is thus an example of "automatic disconnecting switchgear equipment" for which no separate isolating switch is required. After being lowered, the breaker can be withdrawn from the metal enclosure for inspection or repairs. The circuit breakers are electrically remote-controlled. On the front of each panel are mounted indicating instruments, a wattmeter, two protective relays, and the operating lever of the switch for control of the circuit breaker. This assembly is designed for control of outgoing feeders from a substation.

(b) Fuseholders and Fuses.

(1) Fuses which expel flame in opening the circuit shall be so designed or arranged that they will function properly without hazard to persons or property.

(2) Fuseholders shall be designed so that they can be de-energized while replacing a fuse unless the fuse and fuseholder are designed to permit fuse replacement by qualified persons using equipment designed for the purpose without de-energizing the fuseholder.

Metal-enclosed switchgear and substations which utilize high-voltage fuses shall be provided with a gang-operated disconnecting switch. Isolation of the fuses from the circuit shall be provided by either connecting a switch between the source and the fuses or providing roll-out switch and fuse type of construction. The switch shall be of the load-interrupter type, unless mechanically or electrically interlocked with a load-interrupting device arranged to reduce the load to the interrupting capability of the switch.

(3) When high voltage fused cutouts are installed in a building or a transformer vault, they shall be of a type designed for use in buildings. Where such cutouts are not suitable to interrupt the circuit manually while carrying full load, an approved switch or contactor shall be provided which is capable of interrupting the entire load. In addition, the cutouts shall be interlocked with the approved interrupter or bear a conspicuous sign reading "Do Not Open Cutout Under Load."

The cutouts shall be so located that they may be readily and safely operated and re-fused. Fuses shall be accessible from a clear floor space.

Fɪɢ. 710-5. An assembly of metal-clad switchgear. (*Westinghouse Electric Corp.*)

(c) Load Interrupters. Load interrupter switches may be used providing suitable fuses or circuit breakers are applied in conjunction with these devices to interrupt fault currents. When these devices are used in combination they shall be so coordinated electrically that they will safely withstand the effects of closing, carrying or interrupting all possible currents up to the assigned maximum short-circuit rating.

710-22. Isolating Means. Means shall be provided to completely isolate an item of equipment. The use of isolating switches is not necessary where there are other ways of de-energizing the equipment for inspection and repairs such as metal-enclosed switchgear units, and removable truck panels. Isolating switches should be interlocked with the associated circuit interrupting device to prevent their being opened under load, otherwise signs warning against opening them under load shall be provided. Barriers should be provided on both sides of each pole of indoor open-type isolating switches. A fuseholder and fuse, designed for the purpose, may be used as an isolating switch.

D. Installations Accessible To Qualified Persons Only

710-31. Enclosure for Electrical Installations. Electrical installations in a vault, room, closet or in an area surrounded by a wall, screen or fence, access to which is controlled by lock and key or other approved means, are considered to be accessible to qualified persons only. The height of the wall, screen or fence should not be less than eight feet over-all, unless designed to provide an equivalent degree of isolation. The type of enclosure used in a given case shall be designed and constructed according to the nature and degree of the hazard(s) associated with the installation. Article 450 covers minimum construction requirements for oil-filled transformer vaults.

Isolation by elevation is covered in Sections 710-11 and 710-34.

710-32. Circuit Conductors. They may be installed in conduit; in duct systems; as metal-clad cable; as bare wire, cable and buses, or as nonmetallic-sheathed cables or conductors as provided in Sections 710-3 through 710-6. Bare live conductors shall conform with Sections 710-33 and 710-34.

Insulators, together with their mounting and conductor attachments, when used as supports for wires, single conductor cables and bus-bars, shall be capable of safely withstanding the maximum magnetic forces which would prevail when two or more conductors of a circuit were subjected to short-circuit current.

Open runs of insulated wires and cables, having a bare lead sheath or a braided

Table 710-33. Minimum Air Separation in Inches, Indoors*

Circuit Voltage, kV	Between Bare Live Conductors	Between Bare Live Conductors and Adjacent Surfaces
2.5	5	4
5.0	6	5
7.5	7	6
15.0	12	7
23.0	15	10
34.5	18	13
46.0	21	17
69.0	31	25

* The values given are the minimum permissible space separation under favorable service conditions. They should be increased under unfavorable service conditions or wherever space limitations permit.

outer covering, shall be supported in a manner designed to prevent physical damage to the braid or sheath. Supports for lead covered cables shall be designed to prevent electrolysis of the sheath.

710-33. Minimum Space Separation Between Live Parts and Adjacent Surfaces. The minimum indoor air separation between bare live conductors and between such conductors and adjacent surfaces shall be not less than the values given in Table 710-33. This Section applies to interior wiring design and construction. It does not apply to the space separation provided in electrical apparatus and wiring devices.

710-34. Work Space and Guarding.

(a) **Working Space.** The minimum clear working space in front of electrical equipment, such as switchboards, control panels, switches, circuit breakers, motor controllers, relays and similar equipment shall not be less than set forth in Table 710-34(a) unless otherwise specified in this Code.

Table 710-34(a). Minimum Clear Working Space in Front of Electrical Equipment

Voltage to Ground	Conditions		
	1	2	3
601–2500	3 ft.	4 ft.	5 ft.
2501–7500	4 ft.	5 ft.	6 ft.
over 7500	5 ft.	6 ft.	9 ft.

Where the "Conditions" are as follows:

(1) Exposed live parts on one side and no live or grounded parts on the other side of the working space or exposed live parts on both sides effectively guarded by suitable wood or other insulating materials. Insulated wire or insulated bus-bars operating at not more than 300 volts shall not be considered live parts.

(2) Exposed live parts on one side and grounded parts on the other side. Concrete, brick or tile walls will be considered as grounded surfaces.

(3) Exposed live parts on both sides of the work space (not guarded as provided in Condition 1) with the operator between.

Exception: Working space is not required in back of assemblies such as dead-front switchboards or control assemblies when there are no renewable or adjustable parts such as fuses or switches on the back and when all connections are accessible from other locations than the back.

(b) **Separation from Low-Potential Equipment.** When switches, cutouts or other equipment operating at 600 volts or less are installed in a room or enclosure where there are exposed live parts or exposed wiring operating at more than 600 volts the high potential equipment shall be effectively separated from the space occupied by the low potential equipment by a suitable partition, fence, or screen.

Exception: Switches or other equipment operating at 600 volts or less and serving only equipment within the high-voltage vault, room or enclosure may be installed in the high-voltage enclosure, room or vault if accessible to qualified persons only.

(c) **Locked Rooms or Enclosures.** The entrances to all buildings, rooms or enclosures containing exposed live parts or exposed conductors operating in excess of 600 volts shall be kept locked, except where such entrances are at all times under the observation of a qualified attendant.

Where the voltage exceeds 600 volts permanent and conspicuous warning signs shall be provided, reading substantially as follows: "Warning—High Voltage—Keep Out."

(d) **Illumination.** Adequate illumination shall be provided for all working spaces about electrical equipment. The light outlets shall be so arranged that persons changing lamps or making repairs on the lighting system will not be endangered by live parts or other equipment.

The points of control shall be so located that persons are not liable to come into contact with any live part or moving part of the equipment while turning on the lights.

(e) **Headroom.** The minimum headroom above working spaces about switching equipment where there are live parts exposed at any time shall be not less than 6½ feet.

(f) **Elevation of Unguarded Live Parts.** Unguarded live parts above working space shall be maintained at elevations not less than required by Table 710-34(f).

Table 710-34(f). Elevation of Unguarded Live Parts above the Working Space

Voltage Between Phases	Minimum Vertical Clearance of Unguarded Parts	
	Feet	Inches
601–6600	8	0
6601–11000	9	0
11001–22000	9	3
22001–33000	9	6
33001–44000	9	10
44001–66000	10	5
66001–88000	11	0
88001–110000	11	7
110001–132000	12	2

ARTICLE 720. CIRCUITS AND EQUIPMENT OPERATING AT LESS THAN 50 VOLTS

720-1. Scope. This Article shall apply to installations operating at less than 50 volts, direct current or alternating current, except such as are treated in Articles 650 and 725.

720-2. Hazardous Locations. Circuits or equipment coming within the scope of this Article and installed in hazardous locations shall comply with the appropriate provisions of Articles 500 through 517.

720-3. Larger Current at Lower Voltage. Conductors, devices, and equipment shall have current ratings sufficient for the greater current required to deliver equal power at the lower voltage than at usual voltages.

▶   This rule merely serves as a reminder that at 32 volts the current corresponding to a given wattage is 3.6 times the current for the same wattage at 115 volts. It should also be noted that for a given load in watts and a given size of wire and circuit length, the voltage drop in percentage is about 13 times as great at 32 volts as at 115 volts.

720-4. Conductors. Conductors shall be not smaller than No. 12 AWG copper or equivalent, and for appliance branch circuits supplying more than one appliance, or appliance receptacle, conductors shall be not smaller than No. 10 AWG copper or equivalent.

720-5. Lampholders. Standard lampholders of rating not less than 660 watts shall be used.

720-6. Receptacle Rating. Receptacles shall have a rating not less than 15 amperes.

720-7. Receptacles Required. Receptacles of not less than 20-ampere rating shall be provided in kitchens, laundries, and other locations where portable appliances are likely to be used.

720-8. Overcurrent Protection. Overcurrent protection shall comply with the provisions of Article 240.

720-9. Batteries. See Article 480.

720-10. Grounding. See Sections 250-5(a) and 250-45.

ARTICLE 725. REMOTE-CONTROL, LOW-ENERGY POWER, LOW-VOLTAGE POWER AND SIGNAL CIRCUITS

A. Scope and General

725-1. Scope. Provisions of this Article shall apply to remote-control circuits, including low-voltage relay switching, low-energy power circuits, low-voltage circuits and signal circuits, as defined in Article 100, Definitions.

  The provisions of this Article are not intended to apply to remote-control, low-energy or signal circuits which form an integral part of a device or appliance.

725-2. Hazardous Locations. Circuits or equipment coming within the scope of this Article and installed in hazardous locations shall also comply with the appropriate provisions of Articles 500 through 517.

725-3. Classification. Remote-control and signal circuits shall be classified as follows:

  (a) Class 1 Circuits. Control and signal circuits in which power is not limited in accordance with Section 725-31.

  (b) Class 2 Circuits. Control and signal circuits in which the power is limited in accordance with Section 725-31.

725-4. Low-Energy Power Circuits. Circuits which are neither remote-control nor signal circuits, but which have the power limited in accordance with Section 725-31, shall, for the purpose of this Code, be treated as Class 2 remote-control circuits.

▶   A low-energy power system is a system in which electrical energy is used to operate a signal or other load or to open or close a circuit. A common example is the electric doorlock release, commonly known as a "door opener," though it does not actually open the door.

725-5. Low-Voltage Power Circuits.   Circuits which are neither remote-control nor signal circuits but which operate at not more than 30 volts, where the current is not limited in accordance with Section 725-31, and which are supplied from a source not exceeding 1000 volt-amperes shall for the purpose of this Code be treated as Class 1 remote-control circuits.

725-6. Safety-Control Devices.   Remote-control circuits to safety-control devices, the failure of operation of which would introduce a direct fire or life hazard, shall be considered as Class 1 circuits.

Room thermostats, service hot-water temperature regulating devices, and similar controls used in conjunction with electrically controlled domestic heating equipment, are not considered to be safety-control devices.

725-7. Remote-Control and Signal Circuits in Communication Cables.   Remote-control and signal circuits, which use conductors in the same cable with communication circuits, shall, for the purpose of this Article, be classified as communication circuits and meet the requirements of Article 800 of this Code.

B. Class 1 System

725-11. Wiring Method.   Conductors and equipment of Class 1 remote-control and signal systems and low voltage power circuits shall be installed in accordance with the requirements of the appropriate Articles in Chapter 3 of this Code, except as provided in Sections 725-12 through 725-15.

725-12. Other Articles.   The wiring method required in Section 725-11 does not apply where other Articles of this Code specifically permit or require other methods for remote-control or signal circuits. See Article 620, Elevators, for example.

725-13. Conductor Sizes.   Nos. 18 and 16 AWG conductors may be used provided they are installed in a raceway or a cable approved for the purpose, or in flexible cords in accordance with the provisions of Article 400.

725-14. Conductor Insulation.   Conductors larger than No. 16 shall conform to Article 310. Conductors of sizes No. 18 and No. 16 shall be Types RF-2, FF-2, RFH-2, FFH-2, TF, TFF, TFN, TFFN, PF, PGF, PFF, PGFF, PTF, PTFF, SF-2, SFF-2, or MTW. Conductors with other type and thickness of insulation may be used if approved for the purpose.

725-15. Number and Ampacities of Conductors in Raceways.

(a)   Where only remote control or signal circuits are in a raceway, the number of conductors shall be determined in accordance with Section 300-17. Note 8 to Tables 310-12 through 310-15 shall apply only if such conductors carry continuous loads.

(b)   Where power supply conductors and Class 1 system conductors are permitted in a raceway in accordance with Section 725-16, Note 8 to Tables 310-12 through 310-15 shall apply as follows:

(1) To all conductors when the Class 1 system conductors carry continuous loads and when the total number of conductors are more than three.

(2) To the power supply conductors only, when the Class 1 system conductors do not carry continuous loads and when the number of power supply conductors are more than three.

725-16. Conductors of Different Systems. Conductors of two or more Class 1 remote-control and/or signal circuits may occupy the same enclosure or raceway without regard to whether the individual systems or circuits are alternating current or direct current, provided all conductors are insulated for the maximum voltage of any conductor in the enclosure or raceway. Conductors of remote-control, low-energy power and signal circuits, in which the current is limited as for Class 2 systems, shall be considered as Class 1 system conductors for the purpose of this requirement if insulated and installed in accordance with the provisions for Class 1 system conductors. Power supply conductors may occupy the same enclosure or raceway with Class 1 system conductors when supplying only equipment to which Class 1 system conductors are connected.

▶ **There is seldom any need to bring the conductors of both a Class 1 and a Class 2 system into the same enclosure or to install conductors of both systems in the same raceway; these installation methods are permitted, however, if all the conductors are insulated for the maximum voltage. There might seem to be a conflict with Section 725-42a-2, but Section 725-16 states that even though the current in a system may be limited as required for a Class 2 system, the system is not Class 2 but becomes Class 1 if the conductors are brought into the same enclosure with conductors of a Class 1 system.**

725-17. Mechanical Protection of Remote-Control Circuits. Where damage to a remote-control circuit would introduce a hazard as covered in Section 725-6, all conductors of such remote-control circuits shall be installed in conduit, electrical metallic tubing, Type MI cable or be otherwise suitably protected from physical damage.

725-18. Overcurrent Protection. Conductors shall be protected against overcurrent in accordance with the ampacities of Tables 310-12 through 310-15.

Exception No. 1: Other Articles. Where other Articles of this Code specifically permit or require other overcurrent protection. See Sections 430-72 and 620-61.

Exception No. 2: Conductors of Nos. 18 and 16. Conductors of Nos. 18 and 16 shall be considered as protected by overcurrent devices of 20-ampere rating or setting.

Exception No. 3: Omission of Overcurrent Protection. In remote-control and signal circuits having main and branch circuits, the branch circuits need not be individually protected against overcurrent where the operating voltage does not exceed 30 volts.

725-19. Location of Overcurrent Protection. Overcurrent devices shall be located at the point where the conductor to be protected receives its supply unless the overcurrent device protecting the larger conductor also protects the smaller conductor in accordance with Tables 310-12 through 310-15.

725-20. Circuits Extending Beyond One Building. Class 1 circuits which extend aerially beyond one building shall also meet the requirements of Article 730.

725-21. Grounding. Class 1 remote-control and signal circuits and equipment shall be grounded in accordance with Article 250.

C. Limitation of Low-Voltage Power Circuit

725-22. Overcurrent Protection. Transformer devices supplying low-voltage power circuits shall be provided with overcurrent protection in the secondary circuit rated or set at not more than 250 per cent of the rated secondary current of the transformer. Such protection and mounting shall be approved for the purpose. Overcurrent protection required shall not be interchangeable with protection of a higher rating. The overcurrent protection may be an integral part of a transformer or other power supply device approved for the purpose.

725-23. Transformer Rating. Transformer devices supplying low-voltage power circuits shall be approved for the purpose and be restricted in their rated output to not exceeding 1000 volt-amperes and to not exceeding 30 volts. They shall be marked where plainly visible to show their rated output and the voltage to be applied to the circuit.

A transformer is considered as meeting the 1000 volt-ampere requirement where the approximate temperature limit is reached at 1000 volt-ampere load.

D. Class 2 System Voltage and Current Limits

725-31. Limits of Class 2 Systems. Class 2 remote-control and signal systems, depending on the voltage shall have the current limited as follows:

(a) Maximum 15 Volts: 5 Amperes. Circuits in which the open-circuit voltage does not exceed 15 volts and having overcurrent protection of not more than 5-ampere rating. Where the current supply is from a transformer or other device having energy-limiting characteristics and approved for the purpose, or from primary batteries, the overcurrent protection may be omitted.

(b) 15 to 30 Volts: 3.2 Amperes. Circuits in which the open-circuit voltage exceeds 15 volts but does not exceed 30 volts and having overcurrent protection of not more than 3.2 amperes rating. Where the current supply is from a transformer or other device having energy-limiting characteristics and approved for the purpose, or from primary batteries, the overcurrent protection may be omitted.

(c) 30 to 60 Volts: 1.6 Amperes. Circuits in which open-circuit voltage exceeds 30 volts but does not exceed 60 volts and having overcurrent protection of not more than 1.6 amperes rating. Where the current supply is from a transformer or other device having energy-limiting characteristics and approved for the purpose, the overcurrent protection may be omitted.

(d) 60 to 150 Volts: 1 Ampere. Circuits in which the open-circuit voltage exceeds 60 volts but does not exceed 150 volts, and having overcurrent protection of not more than 1-ampere rating, provided that such circuits are equipped with current-limiting means other than overcurrent protection which will limit the current as a result of a fault to not exceeding 1 ampere.

(e) Maximum 150 Volts: 5 Milliamperes. Circuits in which the open circuit voltage does not exceed 150 volts provided that such circuits are equipped with current-limiting means, other than overcurrent protection, which are approved for the purpose and which will limit the current as a result of a fault to not exceeding 5 milliamperes.

725-32. Overcurrent Protection and Mounting. Where current is limited in Class 2 systems by means of overcurrent protection, such protection and its mounting shall be approved for the purpose. Overcurrent protection required shall not be interchangeable with protection of a higher rating. The overcurrent protection may be an integral part of a transformer or other power supply device approved for the purpose.

725-33. Transformer Rating. Transformer devices supplying Class 2 systems shall be approved for the purpose and be restricted in their rated output to not exceeding 100 volt-amperes. Such devices shall not be paralleled or otherwise interconnected. They shall be marked where plainly visible to show the voltage to be applied to the circuit.

A transformer is considered as meeting the 100 volt-ampere requirement if the approximate temperature limit is reached at a 100-volt-ampere load.

725-34. Transformer Leads. The primary leads of transformers supplying Class 2 remote-control and signal circuits may be smaller than No. 14 but not smaller than No. 18, provided they are not over 12 inches long, have insulation at least equal to Type RF-2 rubber-covered fixture wire, or approved equivalent.

E. Installation of Class 2 Remote-Control and Signal Circuits

725-41. On Supply Side of Overcurrent Protection, Transformers or Current-Limiting Devices. Conductors and equipment on supply side of overcurrent protection, transformers or current-limiting devices shall be installed in accordance with the appropriate requirements of Chapter 3 of this Code. Transformers or other devices supplied from electric light and power circuits shall be protected by an overcurrent device with a rating or setting not exceeding 20 amperes.

725-42. On Load Side of Overcurrent Protection, Transformer or Current-Limiting Devices. Conductors on load side of overcurrent protection, transformers or current-limiting devices shall be insulated and shall comply with the following:

(a) Separation from Other Conductors. Conductors shall be separated from conductors of electric light and power circuits as follows:

(1) Open Conductors. Conductors shall be separated at least two inches from any light or power conductors or Class 1 signal or control circuits not in a raceway nor in metal sheathed, metal-clad, nonmetallic sheathed or Type UF cables unless permanently separated from the conductors of the other system by a continuous and firmly fixed nonconductor, such as porcelain tubes or flexible tubing, additional to the insulation on the wire.

(2) In Raceways and Boxes. Conductors of Class 2 remote-control and signal circuits shall not be placed in any raceway, compartment, outlet box or similar fitting with conductors for either light and power circuits or Class 1 signal and control circuits, unless the conductors of the different systems are separated by a partition; provided that this shall not apply to conductors in outlet boxes, junction boxes or similar fittings or compartments where power supply conductors are introduced solely for supplying power to the remote-control or signal equipment to which the other conductors in the enclosure are connected. See Section 725-16.

(3) In Shafts. Conductors may be run in the same shaft with conductors for light and power where the conductors of the two systems are separated at least

2 inches, or where the conductors of either system are encased in noncombustible tubing. Where the lighting or power conductors are run in a raceway, or in metal sheathed or metal-clad or nonmetallic sheathed or Type UF cables, neither the two-inch separation nor the noncombustible tubing is required. In hoistways conductors shall be installed in rigid conduit or electrical metallic tubing except as provided for in Section 620-21, Exception Nos. 1 and 2.

(b) Vertical Runs. Conductors in a vertical run in a shaft or partition shall have a fire resistant covering capable of preventing the carrying of fire from floor to floor except where conductors are encased in tubing or other outer covering of noncombustible material or are located in a fireproof shaft having fire stops at each floor.

Where 3 or more conductors are used, it is recommended that such conductors be grouped under a common braid or covering.

(c) Conductor Insulation. Conductor insulation shall comply with the following:

(1) 30 Volts or Less. The insulation shall be suitable for the particular application.

The kind of insulation for the conductors is not specified in further detail as reliance is placed on current limitation to stop dangerous currents.

(2) 30 to 150 Volts Maximum Fault Current 5 Milliamperes. The insulation shall be suitable for the particular application.

The kind of insulation for the conductors is not specified in further detail as reliance is placed on current limitation to stop dangerous currents.

(3) 30 to 150 Volts. Greater than 5 Milliamperes. Conductors of a cable shall be of solid or stranded copper not smaller than No. 22 AWG, and shall have thermoplastic insulation of not less than 12 mils nominal (10 mils minimum) thickness. The cable conductors shall have a thermoplastic jacket overall having a nominal thickness of not less than 35 mils (30 mils minimum). Where the number of conductors in a cable exceeds 4, the thickness of the thermoplastic jacket overall shall be increased so as to provide equivalent performance characteristics. Similarly, where the size of conductors in a cable exceeds No. 16 AWG, the thickness of the conductor insulation shall be increased so as to provide equivalent performance characteristics.

Two-conductor assemblies of No. 16 AWG or smaller may be in a flat parallel construction with 30-mil nominal integral-insulation jacket and a 47-mil minimum web. Approved low-energy circuit cable may be used.

Other insulation having equivalent performance characteristics may be acceptable.

Where single conductors are used they shall be not smaller than No. 18 AWG and shall be insulated in conformity with Section 725-14.

▶ Although any type of insulation is permitted for the conductors of Class 2 systems, in order to ensure continuity of service a type of insulation should be selected which is suitable for the conditions, such as the voltage to be employed and possible exposure to moisture.

725-43. Circuits Extending Beyond One Building. Class 2 remote-control and signal circuits which extend beyond one building and are so run as to be subject to accidental contact with light or power conductors operating at a potential exceeding 300 volts, shall also meet the requirements of Sections 800-2, 800-11 and 800-12.

725-44. Grounding. Class 2 remote-control and signal circuits and equipment shall be grounded in accordance with Article 250.

▶ *General Discussion of Signal and Control Systems*

The provisions of the preceding Sections of this chapter divide all signal and control systems into two classes.

Class 1 includes all signal and control systems which do not have the special current limitations of Class 2 systems.

Class 2 systems are those systems in which the current is limited to certain specified low values by fuses or circuit breakers, or by supply through transformers which will deliver only very small currents on short circuit, or by other means which are considered satisfactory. The current values depend upon the voltage at which the system operates and range from 5 ma.

Class 1 Systems

Class 1 systems may operate at any voltage not exceeding 600 volts. They are, in many cases, merely extensions of light and power systems, and, with a few exceptions, are subject to all the installation rules for light and power systems. The following exceptions are made:

1. No. 16 or No. 18 conductors may be used under certain conditions.

2. No. 16 and No. 18 conductors may have special types of insulation.

3. Mechanical protection for the conductors is required in certain cases.

4. In certain cases the general rules for overcurrent protection are modified.

5. Some exceptions are made to the general requirements for system grounding.

A very common example of a Class 1 remote-control system is the circuit wiring and devices used for the operation of a magnetically operated motor controller. Section 430-72 provides that under certain conditions the control-circuit conductors need not have overcurrent protection in accordance with their ampacity; however, Section 240-5a, Exception 2, requires overcurrent protection of not over 20-amp rating or setting if No. 16 or No. 18 conductors are used. Conductors of these sizes are often used where a considerable number of control conductors must be provided between two outlets, as in the case of some printing-press control systems.

The term *remote control switch* is used in various code references to designate a switch or contactor used for the remote control of a feeder or branch circuit. The control conductors and devices are usually Class 1 control systems. As in the case of the circuits of remote-control motor controllers, special provisions apply to the overcurrent protection of the conductors; No. 16 or No. 18 conductors may be used, and for these sizes the overcurrent protection is limited to a maximum of 20 amp.

The signal systems which are included in Class 1 in many cases operate at 115 volts with 20-amp overcurrent protection, though they are not necessarily limited to this voltage and current. Some of the signal systems which may be so operated are some local fire-alarm systems, electric clocks, bank alarm systems, and factory call systems. No. 16 or No. 18 conductors may be used for any of these systems when provided with 20-amp overcurrent protection.

An example of a lower voltage Class 1 signal system is a nurses' call system, as used in hospitals. Such systems commonly operate at not over 25 volts.

Class 2 Systems

Class 2 signal, control, and low-energy power systems are used where the current and voltage requirements are such that it is not necessary to comply with the general requirements for light and power systems.

The limitation of current by means of overcurrent protective devices is an optional method in the first three subclasses and is required for Class 2-*d*. Strict conformity with the requirements would be difficult at the present time because as yet no line of overcurrent devices of the specified ratings is available which meets the requirements of Section 725-32 for noninterchangeability.

For Classes 2-*a* and 2-*b*, current supply from primary batteries is considered as providing satisfactory current limitation. Where batteries are employed to supply small bell, buzzer, or annunciator systems, it is the usual practice to use several No. 6 dry cells in series. One of these cells will deliver 25 to 30 amp on short circuit but the current falls off very rapidly. It would be possible to provide a dry-cell battery that would deliver a fairly heavy current for several hours; however, such batteries are not needed for these systems and it is therefore safe to assume that they will not be installed and that, in any practical case, supply of the system from a primary battery will provide sufficient current limitation.

Wherever a-c service is available, current limitation can be provided by using so-called "current-limiting" transformers. These are transformers having so high a secondary impedance that, even on short circuit, they cannot deliver a current higher than a certain maximum.

It is probable that a doorbell type of transformer will provide the required current limitation for a Class 2-*b* system. In the NEMA Specialty Transformer Standards it is stated that the open-circuit secondary voltage for a doorbell transformer shall not exceed 25 volts and that the maximum input with the secondary short-circuited shall be 50 watts. U/L lists energy-limiting transformers suitable for Class 2 systems.

The NEMA Standards include the following data applying to the type known as signaling transformers.

Output ratings: 50 and 100 va.

Secondary open-circuit voltages for either rating: 4.4, 8.8, 13.2, 17.6, 22.0, and 26.4 volts.

Secondary short-circuit current at maximum voltage: 50-va rating, 2.1 amp, 100-va rating, 4.2 amp. The secondary short-circuit current at any lower voltage is proportional to the voltage.

The great majority of small bell, buzzer, and annunciator systems come under the 2-*a* classification, 0 to 15 volts, 5 amp. This will also include small intercommunicating telephone systems in which the talking circuit is supplied by a primary battery and the ringing circuit by a transformer. Larger and more extensive systems may be in Class 2-*b*.

The classifications 2-*c* and 2-*d* are provided to cover special signal systems which meet the specified voltage and current limitations. The additional current-limiting means required for a Class 2-*d* system may be some device, such as a magnet coil or resistor, included in the circuit at the point where the circuit is connected to its power supply and having an impedance high enough to prevent any excessive flow of current.

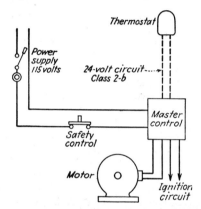

Fig. 725-1. Automatic control for a domestic oil burner.

The application of Section 725-6 is illustrated by Fig. 725-1, which is a simplified diagram of a common type of automatic control for a domestic oil burner. Assuming a steam boiler, the safety control is a switch that opens automatically when the steam pressure reaches a predetermined value and, preferably, also opens if the water level is allowed to fall too low. The master control includes a transformer of the current-limiting type which supplies the thermostat circuit at a voltage of 24 volts. When the thermostat contacts close, a relay closes the circuits to the motor and to the ignition transformer.

Failure to operate of the safety control or ignition would introduce a direct hazard; hence, the circuits to this equipment are Class 1. The thermostat circuit fulfills all requirements of a Class 2-*b* circuit and can be short-circuited or broken without introducing any hazard. The wiring of this circuit can therefore be done with any type of wire or cable that is sufficiently protected from physical damage to ensure serviceability.

ARTICLE 730. OUTSIDE BRANCH CIRCUITS AND FEEDERS

730-1. Scope. This Article applies to electrical equipment and wiring for the supply of utilization equipment located on or attached to the outside of public and private buildings, or run between buildings, structures or poles on other premises served.

For additional information on wiring over 600 volts see the National Electrical Safety Code, ANSI C2-1960 and supplements C-2.2A-1965 and C-2.2B-1967.

730-2. Application of Other Articles. Application of other Articles, including additional requirements to specific cases of equipment and conductors, are as follows:

	Article
Branch Circuits.	210
Communication Circuits.	800
Community Antenna Television and Radio Distribution Systems.	820
Electric Signs and Outline Lighting.	600
Feeders.	215
Fixed Outdoor Electric De-icing and Snow-Melting Equipment.	426
Grounding.	250
Hazardous Locations, General.	500
Hazardous Locations, Specific.	510
Marinas and Boatyards.	555
Over 600 Volts, General.	710
Radio and Television Circuits.	810
Remote-Control, Low-Energy Power, Low-Voltage Power and Signal Circuits.	725
Services.	230
Swimming and Wading Pools.	680
Use and Identification of Grounded Conductors.	200

730-3. Calculation of Load.

(a) Branch Circuits. The load on every outdoor branch circuit is to be determined by the applicable provisions of Article 220.

(b) Feeders. The load to be expected on every outdoor feeder is to be determined by the procedure specified in Article 220.

730-4. Conductor Covering. Where within 10 feet of any building or structure, open conductors supported on insulators shall be insulated or covered. Conductors in cables or raceways, except Type MI cable, shall be of the rubber-covered type or thermoplastic type and in wet locations shall comply with Section 310-5. Conductors for festoon lighting shall be of the rubber-covered or thermoplastic type.

730-5. Size of Conductors. The ampacity of outdoor branch circuits and feeder conductors shall be according to the rating in Tables 310-12 through 310-15 in order to carry the loads determined under Section 730-3.

730-6. Minimum Size of Conductor.

(a) Overhead Spans. Overhead conductors shall not be smaller than No. 10 for spans up to 50 feet in length, and not smaller than No. 8 for longer spans.

(b) Festoon Lighting. Overhead conductors for festoon lighting shall not be smaller than No. 12 unless supported by messenger wires. (See Section 730-25.)

DEFINITION: Festoon lighting is a string of outdoor lights suspended between two points more than 15 feet apart.

(c) Over 600 Volts. Overhead conductors operating at more than 600 volts shall not be smaller than No. 6 when open individual conductors nor smaller than No. 8 when in cable.

730-7. Lighting Equipment on Poles or Other Structures.

(a)   For the supply of lighting equipment installed on a single pole or structure, the branch circuits shall comply with the requirements of Article 210 and paragraph (c) below.

(b)   A common neutral may be used for a multiwire branch circuit consisting of the neutral and not more than 8 ungrounded conductors. The ampacity of the neutral conductor shall be not less than the calculated sum of the currents in all ungrounded conductors connected to any one phase of the circuit.

▶   In installations for the lighting of outdoor athletic fields a large number of floodlights may be mounted on one structure. For example, at one stadium for major-league baseball games there are two structures on each of which 264 floodlights are mounted, constituting for each structure a load of approximately 475 kw. The lamps used are commonly of 1,500-watt rating and are usually operated at 10 per cent overvoltage to provide increased light output, in which case the actual watts per lamp is about 1,800, and at 130 volts the current per lamp is approximately 15 amp.

(c)   The voltage to ground of branch circuits supplying lampholders or lighting fixtures mounted on the outside of buildings or on poles or structures for area illumination of residential, commercial or industrial property shall not exceed 150 volts.

Exception No. 1: The voltage to ground on branch circuits supplying lighting fixtures for illumination of outdoor areas of industrial establishments, office buildings, schools, stores and other commercial or public buildings shall not exceed 300 volts provided:

a. The fixtures are mounted on the outside of buildings or out of doors on poles or other structures.

b. The fixtures are not less than 8 feet above grade or other surface accessible to individuals other than those charged with fixture maintenance and supervision.

c. The fixtures are not less than 3 feet from windows, platforms, fire escapes and the like.

Exception No. 2: The voltage between conductors supplying only ballasts for permanently installed electric-discharge lighting fixtures for area illumination shall not exceed 500 volts provided the fixtures are mounted on poles at a height of not less than 22 feet or on other structures at a height of not less than 18 feet.

730-8. Disconnection.   For branch circuits and feeders see Section 240-18.

730-9. Overcurrent Protection.

(a)   For branch circuits as required in Article 210.

(b)   For feeders as required in Article 215.

730-10. Wiring on Buildings.   Outside wiring on surfaces of buildings may be installed for circuits when not in excess of 600 volts as open conductors on insulating supports, as multiple-conductor cable approved for the purpose, as aluminum sheathed cable or Type MI cable, in rigid metal conduit, in busways as provided in Article 364, or in electrical metallic tubing. Circuits of more than 600 volts shall be installed as provided for services in Section 230-101. Circuits for sign and outline lighting shall be installed as provided in Article 600.

730-11. Circuit Exits and Entrances.   Where outside branch and feeder circuits exit from or enter into buildings the installation shall comply with those requirements of Article 230 which apply to service-entrance conductors.

730-12. Open Conductor Supports.   Open conductors shall be supported on glass or porcelain knobs, racks, brackets, or strain insulators, approved for the purpose.

730-13. Festoon Supports.   In spans exceeding 40 feet the conductors shall be supported by a messenger wire supported by approved strain insulators. Conductors or messenger wires shall not be attached to any fire escape, downspout, or plumbing equipment.

▶   Messenger wires are needed for long strings in order to support the weight and relieve the conductors from strain.

Where the span is over 40 ft long and a messenger wire is used, the wire must be insulated at every point of support by means of a strain insulator, and where no messenger wire is used the wires of the festoon must be secured to their supports through strain insulators.

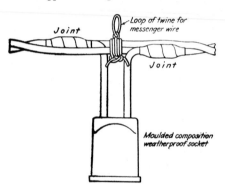

Fig. 730-1. Method of connecting weatherproof socket for festoon lighting.

A downspout does not as a rule provide a sufficiently secure means of support for a festoon. A festoon attached to a fire escape would be accessible; the metal of the fire escape would probably be grounded, and an "unqualified person" standing on the fire escape and tampering with the wire or sockets might receive a severe shock.

730-14. Open Conductor Spacings.   Conductors shall conform to the following spacings:

(a) **Open Conductors Exposed to the Weather.**   As provided in Section 230-47.

(b) **Open Conductors Not Exposed to Weather.**   As provided in Section 230-48.

(c) **Over 600 Volts.**   As provided in Section 230-101(c).

(d) **Separation from Other Circuits.**   Open conductors shall be separated from open conductors of other circuits or systems by not less than 4 inches.

(e) Conductors On Poles. Conductors on poles shall have a separation of not less than 1 foot except when placed on racks or brackets. Conductors supported on poles shall provide a horizontal climbing space not less than the following:

Power conductors, below communication conductors............... 30 inches

Power conductors alone or above communication conductors:

  Less than 300 volts... 24 inches

  Exceeding 300 volts... 30 inches

Communication conductors below power conductors..same as power conductors
Communication conductors alone or above power conductors....no requirement

▶ The climbing space is the distance between the two crossarm pins nearest to the pole that are used to carry wires. Ample climbing space is needed in order to avoid danger to linemen and disturbance of the lower set of wires in climbing through them to reach the upper wires.

730-15. Supports Over Buildings. See Section 230-25.

730-16. Point of Attachment to Buildings. See Section 230-26.

730-17. Means of Attachment to Buildings. See Section 230-27.

730-18. Clearance from Ground. Open conductors of not over 600 volts shall conform to the following:

  10 feet—above finished grade, sidewalks or from any platform or projection from which they might be reached;

  12 feet—over residential driveways and commercial areas such as parking lots and drive-in establishments not subject to truck traffic;

  15 feet—over commercial areas, parking lots, agricultural or other areas subject to truck traffic;

  18 feet—over public streets, alleys, roads, and driveways on other than residential property.

Note: For clearances of conductors of over 600 volts see National Electrical Safety Code, ANSI C2-1960.

730-19. Clearances from Buildings for Conductors Not in Excess of 600 Volts.

(a) Clearance Over Roof. Open conductors shall have a clearance of not less than 8 feet from the highest point of roofs over which they pass with the following exceptions:

Exception No. 1: Where the voltage between conductors does not exceed 300 volts and the roof has a slope of not less than 4 inches in 12 inches, the clearance may be not less than 3 feet.

Exception No. 2: Open conductors of 300 volts or less which do not pass over other than a maximum of 4 feet of the overhang portion of the roof for the purpose of terminating at a through-the-roof raceway or approved support may be maintained at a minimum of 18 inches from any portion of the roof over which they pass.

For service drop conductors see Section 230-22(a).

(b) Horizontal Clearances. Open conductors not attached to a building shall have a minimum horizontal clearance of 36 inches.

(c) Final Spans.   Final spans of feeders or branch circuits to buildings which they supply or from which they are fed may be attached to the building but they shall be kept 3 feet from windows, doors, porches, fire escapes or similar locations.

(d) Zone for Fire Ladders.   Where buildings exceed 3 stories, or 50 feet in height, overhead lines shall be arranged where practicable so that a clear space (or zone) at least 6 feet wide will be left either adjacent to the buildings or beginning not over 8 feet from them, to facilitate the raising of ladders when necessary for fire fighting.

Note: For clearance of conductors over 600 volts, consult National Electrical Safety Code, ANSI C2-1960.

730-20. Mechanical Protection of Conductors.   Mechanical protection of conductors on buildings, structures or poles shall be as provided for services, Section 230-46.

730-21. Conductors Entering Buildings.   Conductors entering buildings shall be as provided for services, Sections 230-44, 230-49, and 230-51.

730-22. Multiple-Conductor Cables on Exterior Surfaces of Buildings.   Multiple-conductor cables on exterior surfaces of buildings shall be as provided for service cable, Section 230-50.

730-23. Raceways on Exterior Surfaces of Buildings.   Raceways on exterior surfaces of buildings shall be made raintight and suitably drained.

▶   Condensation of moisture is very likely to take place in conduit or tubing located outdoors. The conduit or tubing should be considered suitably drained when it is so installed that any moisture condensing inside the raceway or entering from the outside cannot accumulate in the raceway or fittings. This requires that the raceway shall be installed without "pockets," that long runs shall not be truly horizontal but shall always be pitched, and that fittings at low points be provided with drainage openings.

In order to be raintight, all conduit fittings should be provided with threaded hubs, and the joints and connections to fittings must be made up wrench-tight. Couplings and connectors used with electrical metallic tubing shall be of the raintight type. See Section **348-8.**

730-24. Underground Circuits.   Underground circuits shall be as provided for services, Sections 230-32 and 230-33.

730-25. Outdoor Lighting Equipment—Lampholders.   Lampholders shall be of molded composition, or other approved material of the weatherproof type, and where they are attached as pendants shall have the connections to the circuit wires staggered. Where lampholders have terminals of a type which puncture the insulation and make contact with the conductors, they shall be attached only to conductors of the stranded type.

▶   This Section applies particularly to lampholders used in festoons. Where "pigtail" lampholders are used, the splices should be staggered as shown in Fig. 730-1 in order to avoid the possibility of short circuits, in case the taping for any reason should become ineffective.

According to the U/L Standard for Edison-Base Lampholders, "pin-type" terminals shall be employed only in lampholders for temporary lighting or decorations, signs, or specifically approved applications.

730-26. Outdoor Lighting Equipment—Location of Lamps. Location of lamps for outdoor lighting shall be below all live conductors, transformers, or other electrical equipment, unless clearances or other safeguards are provided for relamping operations, or unless the installation is controlled by a disconnecting means which can be locked in the open position.

▶ In some types of outdoor lighting it would be difficult to keep all electrical equipment above the lamps and hence a disconnecting means may be required. A disconnecting means should be provided for the equipment on each individual pole, tower, or other structure if the conditions are such that lamp replacements may be necessary while the lighting system is in use. It may be assumed that grounded metal conduit or tubing extending below the lamps would not constitute a condition requiring that a disconnecting means must be provided.

ARTICLE 750. STAND-BY POWER GENERATION SYSTEMS

750-1. Scope. The provisions of this Article apply to the installation, operation, and maintenance of circuits, systems and equipment intended to supply on-site generated power to selected loads (other than those of Article 700, Emergency Systems), automatically or manually, in the event of failure of the normal source of electrical service.

Stand-by systems are generally installed to provide an alternate source of electrical energy to serve loads, such as heating and refrigeration systems, communications systems, industrial processes which, when stopped during any power outage, could cause discomfort, serious interruption of the process, or damage to the product or process or the like.

The systems covered by this Article shall consist only of those which are permanently installed in their entirety including the prime movers.

▶ The intent here is to recognize a permanently installed stand-by system that is not considered to be an "Emergency System" as covered in Article 517 or 700 of the National Electrical Code, or "Essential Electrical Systems for Hospitals" as covered in NFPA Pamphlet No. 76A.

750-2. Other Requirements. All applicable requirements of this Code shall apply to the stand-by systems, except as modified by this Article.
750-3. Equipment Approval. All equipment shall be approved for the use intended.
750-4. Tests. The complete system after installation should be test operated as directed by the authority having jurisdiction.
750-5. Generator Set. A generator, driven by and connected to a permanently installed prime mover shall comprise the generator set.

750-6. Capacity of the System. The stand-by system shall have adequate capacity and rating for the operation of all equipment to be supplied at one time.

750-7. Controls and Transfer Equipment. Equipment shall be suitable for intended use and be so designed and installed as to prevent the inadvertent interconnection of normal and stand-by sources of supply in any operation of the transfer equipment.

A time delay feature should be provided to avoid short-time operation of the stand-by system.

750-8. Systems Protection. Transfer equipment and wiring associated with the stand-by system shall be provided with suitably rated protective devices.

750-9. Wiring. The stand-by system wiring is not subject to the provisions of Section 700-17, and the wiring of this system may occupy the same raceways, boxes, cabinets, and panelboards with other wiring, except that the wiring shall not occupy the same raceways, boxes or cabinets as wiring for emergency systems.

CHAPTER EIGHT

Communication Systems

ARTICLE 800. COMMUNICATION CIRCUITS

A. General

800-1. Scope. The provisions of this Article shall apply to telephone, telegraph (except radio), district messenger, fire and burglar alarms and similar central station systems and to telephone systems not connected to a central station system but using similar type of equipment, methods of installation and maintenance.

Such protective measures as are essential to safeguard these systems under the various conditions to which they are subjected are outlined in these rules.

For detailed requirements for fire alarm, sprinkler, supervisory, or watchman systems, see the Standards of the National Fire Protection Association.*

▶ The sections of this chapter apply basically to those systems which are connected to a central station and operate as parts of a central-station system.

The paragraph titled "Code Arrangement" of the "Introduction to the Code" states that Chap. 8, which includes Art. 800, Communication Systems, is independent of the preceding chapters except as they are specifically referred to.

B. Protection

800-2. Protective Devices. A protector approved for the purpose shall be provided on each circuit run partly or entirely in aerial wire or aerial cable not confined within a block. Also, a protector approved for the purpose shall be provided

* The NFPA standards on fire alarm and supervisory systems are published by the NFPA in the 1970 National Fire Codes, Vol. 7 and in separate pamphlet form by the NFPA (NFPA Nos. 71-1970, 72A-1967, 72B-1967, 72C-1967, 72D-1967, and 73-1967).

on each circuit, aerial or underground, so located within the block containing the building served as to be exposed to accidental contact with light and power conductors operating at a potential exceeding 300 volts.

The word "block" as used in this Article shall be construed to mean a square or portion of a city, town, or village enclosed by streets and including the alleys so enclosed but not any street.

The word "exposed" as used in this Article means that the circuit is in such a position that in case of failure of supports or insulation, contact with another circuit may result.

(a) Location.   The protector shall be located in, on or immediately adjacent to the structure or building served and as close as practicable to the point at which the exposed conductors enter or attach.

(b) Hazardous Locations.   The protector shall not be located in any hazardous location as defined in Article 500, nor in the vicinity of easily ignitible material.

(c) Protector Requirements.   The protector shall consist of an arrester connected between each line conductor and the ground in an appropriate mounting. Protector terminals shall be marked to indicate line and ground as applicable.

(1)   Fuseless type protectors may be used under any of the following conditions:

a.   Where circuits enter a building through metallic-sheathed cable, or through a nonmetallic-sheathed cable having a metallic grounding shield between the sheath and the conductor assembly, provided the metallic sheath or shield of the cable is effectively grounded and the conductors in the cable shall safely fuse on all currents greater than the ampacity of the protector, and the protector grounding conductor.

b.   Where insulated conductors in accordance with Section 800-11(c)(1) or (c)(2) are used to extend circuits to a building from a metallic-sheathed cable or from a nonmetallic-sheathed cable having a metallic grounding shield between the sheath and the conductor assembly provided the metallic sheath or shield is effectively grounded and the conductors in the cable or cable stub, or the connections between the insulated conductors and the exposed plant, shall safely fuse on all currents greater than the ampacity of the protector, the associated insulated conductors, and the protector grounding conductor.

c.   Where insulated conductors, in accordance with Section 800-11(c)(1) or (c)(2) are used to extend circuits to a building from other than grounded metallic-sheathed or shielded cable, provided (1) the protector is approved for this purpose, and (2) the protector grounding conductor is connected to a water pipe electrode or the grounding conductor or grounding electrode of a multigrounded neutral power system, and (3) the connections of the insulated conductors to the exposed plant, or the conductors of the exposed plant shall safely fuse on all currents greater than the ampacity of the protector, the associated insulated conductors, and the protector grounding conductor.

d.   Where insulated conductors in accordance with Section 800-11(c)(1) or (c)(2) are used to extend circuits aerially to a building from an unexposed buried or underground circuit.

Effectively grounded means permanently connected to earth through a ground connection of sufficiently low impedance and having sufficient ampacity to prevent the building up of voltages which may result in undue hazard to connected equipment or to persons.

(2)   Where the requirements listed under Section 800-2(c)(1a) (1b)(1c) or (1d) are not fulfilled, fused-type protectors shall be used. Fused-type protectors shall consist of an arrester connected between each line conductor and ground, a fuse in series with each line conductor, and an appropriate mounting arrangement. Protector terminals shall be marked to indicate line, instrument, and ground, as applicable.

800-3. Installation of Conductors. Conductors from the protector to the equipment or, where no protector is required, conductors attached to the outside of, or inside the building shall comply with the following:

(a) Separation from Other Conductors. Conductors shall be separated from conductors of electric light and power circuits as follows:

(1) Open Conductors. Conductors shall be separated at least two inches from any light or power conductors or Class 1 signal or control circuits not in a raceway nor in metal-sheathed, metal-clad, nonmetallic-sheathed or Type UF cable unless permanently separated from the conductors of the other system by a continuous and firmly fixed nonconductor, additional to the insulation on the wire, such as porcelain tubes or flexible tubing.

(2) In Raceways and Boxes. Communication conductors shall not be placed in any raceway, compartment, outlet box, junction box or similar fitting with conductors for light and power circuits or Class 1 signal and control circuits unless the conductors of the different systems are separated by a partition; provided that this shall not apply to conductors in outlet boxes, junction boxes or similar fittings or compartments where such conductors are introduced solely for power supply to communication equipment or for connection to remote-control equipment.

(3) In Shafts. Conductors may be run in the same shaft with conductors for light and power provided the conductors of the two systems are separated at least 2 inches, or where the conductors of either system are encased in noncombustible tubing. Where the lighting or power conductors are run in a raceway, or in metal-sheathed or metal-clad or nonmetallic-sheathed or Type UF cables, neither the two-inch separation nor the noncombustible tubing is required.

(b) Vertical Runs. Conductors bunched together in a vertical run in a shaft shall have a fire-resistant covering capable of preventing the carrying of fire from floor to floor, except where conductors are encased in noncombustible tubing or are located in a fireproof shaft having fire stops at each floor.

The conductors referred to in this Section would ordinarily be insulated but the kind of insulation is not specified as reliance is placed on the protective device to stop all dangerous voltages and currents.

(c) Prevention of Spread of Fire. Installations shall be so made that the possible spread of fire through fire walls, fire partitions or fire-resistive floors is reduced to a minimum.

C. Outside Conductors

800-11. Overhead Conductors. Overhead conductors entering buildings shall comply with the following:

(a) On Poles. Where communication conductors and light or power conductors are supported by the same pole, the following conditions shall be met:

(1) Relative Location. The conductors should preferably be located below the light or power conductors.

(2) Attachment to Crossarms. Conductors shall not be attached to a crossarm which carries light or power conductors.

(3) Climbing Space. The climbing space through signal conductors shall comply with the requirements of Section 730-14(e).

(b) On Roofs. Conductors passing over buildings shall be kept at least 8 feet above any roof which may be readily walked upon, except small auxiliary buildings such as garages and the like.

(c) Circuits Requiring Protectors. Circuits which require protectors (see Section 800-2) shall comply with the following:

(1) Insulation, Single or Paired Conductors. Each conductor, from the last outdoor support to the protector, shall have 30-mil rubber insulation, except that when such conductors are entirely within a block the insulation on the conductor may be less than 30 mils, but not less than 25 mils in thickness. In addition, the conductor, either individually or over the pair, shall be covered with a substantial fibrous covering or equivalent protection. Conductors approved for the purpose having rubber insulation of a thickness less than specified above, or having other kinds of insulation may be used.

(2) Insulation, Cables. Conductors within a cable of the metal-sheathed type, or within a cable having a rubber sheath of at least 30-mil thickness and covered with a substantial fibrous covering, may have paper or other suitable insulation. Where the metal or rubber sheath is omitted, each conductor shall be insulated as required in Section 800-11(c-1), and the bunched conductors shall be covered with a substantial fibrous covering or equivalent covering.

(3) On Buildings. Open conductors shall be separated at least 4 inches from light or power conductors not in conduit or cable, unless permanently separated from conductors of the other system by a continuous and firmly fixed nonconductor additional to the insulation on the wires, such as porcelain tubes or flexible tubing. Open conductors exposed to accidental contact with light and power conductors operating at over 300 volts, and attached to buildings, shall be separated from woodwork by being supported on glass, porcelain or other insulating material approved for the purpose except that such separation is not required where fuses are omitted as provided for in Section 800-2(c)(1) or where conductors approved for the purpose are used to extend circuits to a building from a cable having a grounded metal sheath.

(4) Entering Buildings. Where a protector is installed inside the building, the conductors shall enter the building either through a noncombustible, nonabsorptive insulating bushing, or through a metal raceway. The insulating bushing may be omitted where the entering conductors (1) are in metal-sheathed cable, (2) pass through masonry, (3) are approved for the purpose and fuses are omitted as provided for in Section 800-2(c)(1), or (4) are approved for the purpose and are used to extend circuits to a building from a cable having a grounded metal sheath. Raceways or bushings shall slope upward from the outside or, where this cannot be done, drip loops shall be formed in the conductors immediately before they enter the building. Raceways shall be equipped with an approved service head.

More than one conductor may enter through a single raceway or bushing. Conduits or other metallic raceways located ahead of the protector shall be grounded.

800-12. Lightning Conductors. Where practicable, a separation of at least six feet shall be maintained between open conductors of communication systems on buildings and lightning conductors.

D. Underground Circuits

800-21. Underground Circuits. Underground conductors of communication circuits entering buildings shall comply with the following:

(a) With Electric Light or Power Conductors. Underground conductors in a duct, handhole, or manhole containing electric light or power conductors, shall be in a section separated from such conductors by means of brick, concrete, or tile partitions.

(b) Underground Block Distribution. Where the entire street circuit is run underground and the circuit within the block is so placed as to be free from liability of accidental contact with electric light or power circuits of over 300 volts, the insulation requirements of Section 800-11(c-1 and c-4) shall not apply, the conductors need not be placed on insulating supports and no bushings shall be required where the conductors enter the building.

E. Grounding

800-31. Grounding. Equipment shall be grounded as follows:

(a) Cable Sheath. The metal sheath of aerial cables entering buildings which are exposed to contact with electric light or power conductors shall be grounded or shall be interrupted close to the entrance to the building by an insulating joint or equivalent device.

(b) Protector Ground. The protector ground shall comply with the following:

(1) Insulation. The grounding conductor shall have a 30-mil rubber insulation and shall be covered by a substantial fibrous covering. Conductors approved for the purpose having less than 30-mil rubber insulation or having other kinds of insulation may be used.

(2) Size. The grounding conductor shall not be smaller than No. 18 AWG copper or equivalent.

(3) Run in Straight Line. The grounding conductor shall be run in as straight a line as practicable to the grounding electrode.

(4) Physical Damage. Where necessary, the grounding conductor shall be guarded from physical damage.

(5) Electrode. The grounding conductor shall be connected as follows:

a. To an available water pipe electrode, or

b. To the power service conduit, service-equipment enclosure, or grounding electrode conductor where the grounded conductor of the power service is connected to a water-pipe electrode at the building, or

c. Where the grounding means in (a) or (b) above are not available, to the service conduit, service-equipment enclosure, grounding electrode conductor or grounding electrode of the power service of a multigrounded neutral power system, or

d. Where the grounding means in (a), (b) or (c) are not available, to (1) a concrete-encased electrode of not less than 20 feet of bare copper conductor not smaller than No. 4 encased by at least 2 inches of concrete and located within and near the bottom of a concrete foundation footing that is in direct contact with the earth, (2) an effectively grounded metal structure, (3) a continuous and extensive underground gas-piping system where acceptable both to the serving gas supplier and to the authority having jurisdiction, or (4) to a ground rod or pipe driven into permanently damp earth. Steam or hot-water pipes, lightning-rod conductors or pipe or rod electrodes grounding other than multigrounded neutral power circuits shall not be employed as electrodes for protectors.

(6) Electrode Connection. The grounding conductor shall be attached to a pipe electrode by means of a bolted clamp to which the conductor is connected in an effective manner. Where a gas pipe electrode is used, connection shall be made between the gas meter and the street main. In every case the connection to the grounding electrode shall be made as close to the earth as practicable.

(7) Bonding of Electrodes. A bond not smaller than No. 6 copper or equivalent shall be placed between the communication and power grounding electrodes where the requirements of (5) above result in the use of separate electrodes. All separate grounding electrodes may be bonded together. See Section 250-86.

It is recommended that all separate electrodes be bonded together to limit potential differences between them and between their associated wiring systems.

ARTICLE 810. RADIO AND TELEVISION EQUIPMENT

A. General

810-1. Scope. This Article shall apply to radio and television receiving equipment and to amateur radio transmitting and receiving equipment, but shall not apply to equipment and antennas used for coupling carrier current to power line conductors.

It is recommended that the authority having jurisdiction be freely consulted as to the specific methods to be followed in any case of doubt relative to installation of antenna conductors.

▶   For service drops and conductors on the exteriors of buildings, the requirements for insulating covering and methods of installation depend upon the likelihood of crosses occurring between signal conductors and light or power conductors. Where communication wires are run on poles in streets, it is assumed that they are exposed to contact with other wires, and in Section 800-11, 30-mil insulation is required. But where the overhead wires are run in an alley or from building to building and kept away from streets, lighter insulation is permitted.

Where a communication system is connected to a distribution system that is entirely underground except within the block in which the building is located, and any overhead wires in alleys or attached to buildings are not likely to become crossed with light or power wires, nearly all restrictions as to insulating covering and methods of installation are eliminated. The minimum thickness of insulation called for in Section 800-21 and the bushings specified in Section 800-11 are not required under these conditions.

810-2. Application of Other Articles.   Wiring from the source of power to and between devices connected to the interior wiring system shall comply with Chapters 1 to 4, inclusive, except as modified by Sections 640-3, 640-4 and 640-5. Wiring for radio-frequency and audio-frequency equipment and loud speakers shall comply with Article 640.

810-3. Community Television Antenna.   The antenna shall comply with the requirements of this Article. The distribution system shall comply with Article 820.

810-4. Radio Noise Suppressors.   Radio interference eliminators, interference capacitors or radio noise suppressors connected to power supply leads shall be of a type approved for the purpose. They shall not be exposed to physical damage.

B. Receiving Equipment Only

Antenna Systems—General

810-11. Material.   Antenna and lead-in conductors shall be of hard-drawn copper, bronze, aluminum alloy, copper-clad steel or other high-strength, corrosion-resistant material. Soft-drawn or medium-drawn copper may be used for lead-in conductors where the maximum span between points of support is less than 35 feet.

▶   Adequate strength and corrosion-resistant qualities are necessary in all these conductors because of the possibility that a broken wire might come in contact with a light or power wire, also in order to ensure continuity of service.

810-12. Supports.   Outdoor antennas and lead-in conductors shall be securely supported. The antennas shall not be attached to the electrical service mast. They shall not be attached to poles or similar structures carrying electric light or power wires or trolley wires of more than 250 volts between conductors. Insulators supporting the antenna conductors shall have sufficient mechanical strength to safely support the conductors. Lead-in conductors shall be securely attached to the antennas.

810-13. Avoidance of Contacts with Conductors of Other Systems.   Outdoor antennas and lead-in conductors from an antenna to a building shall not cross over electric light or power circuits and shall be kept well away from all such circuits so as to avoid the possibility of accidental contact. Where proximity to electric light and power service conductors of less than 250 volts between conductors cannot be avoided, the installation shall be such as to provide a clearance of at least two feet. It is recommended that antenna conductors be so installed as not to cross under electric light or power conductors.

▶   It is obviously important that all possible precautions be taken to prevent the possibility of a cross between a radio antenna and a light or power conductor.

810-14. Splices.   Splices and joints in antenna spans shall be made with approved splicing devices or by such other means as will not appreciably weaken the conductors.

Soldering may ordinarily be expected to weaken the conductor. Therefore, the joint should be mechanically secure before soldering.

▶   The antenna may unavoidably be so located that in case of a break in the wire it may come in contact with electric light or power wires. For this reason, the wire should be of sufficient size to have considerable mechanical strength and the joints should be as reliable as the wire. Joints will have sufficient mechanical strength if properly made with the standard double tube connectors used in telephone and telegraph work. The intention of the fine-print note is to advise against the use of soldered joints in the main spans of an antenna or counterpoise.

810-15. Grounding.   Masts and metal structures supporting antennas shall be permanently and effectively grounded, without intervening splice or connection.
Antenna Systems—Receiving Station
810-16. Size of Wire-Strung Antenna.
    (a)   Outdoor antenna conductors for receiving stations shall be of a size not less than given in Table 810-16(a).
    (b) Self-Supporting Antennas.   Outdoor antennas, such as vertical rods or dipole structures, shall be of noncorrodible materials and of strength suitable to withstand ice and wind loading conditions, and shall be located well away from overhead conductors of electric light and power circuits of over 150 volts to ground so as to avoid the possibility of the antenna or structure falling into or making accidental contact with such circuits.
810-17. Size of Lead-In.   Lead-in conductors from outside antennas for receiving stations, shall, for various maximum open span lengths, be of such size as to have a tensile strength at least as great as that of the conductors for antennas as specified in Section 810-16. Where the lead-in consists of two or more conductors which are twisted together or are enclosed in the same covering or are concentric, the conductor size shall, for various maximum open span lengths, be such that the tensile strength of the combination will be at least as great as that of the conductors for antennas as specified in Section 810-16.

Table 810-16(a). Size of Receiving-Station Outdoor Antenna Conductors

	Minimum Size of Conductors		
	When Maximum Open Span Length is		
Material	Less than 35 feet	35 feet to 150 feet	Over 150 feet
Aluminum alloy, hard-drawn copper	19	14	12
Copper-clad steel, bronze or other high strength material.......... 20		17	14

For very long span lengths larger conductors will be required, depending on the length of the span and the ice and wind loading.

810-18. Clearances.

(a) On Buildings Outside. Lead-in conductors attached to buildings shall be so installed that they cannot swing closer than two feet to the conductors of circuits of 250 volts or less between conductors, or ten feet to the conductors of circuits of more than 250 volts between conductors, except that in the case of circuits not exceeding 150 volts between conductors, where all conductors involved are supported so as to insure permanent separation, the clearance may be reduced but shall not be less than four inches. The clearance between lead-in conductors and any conductor forming a part of a lightning rod system shall be not less than six feet unless the bonding referred to in Section 250-86 is accomplished.

(b) Antennas and Lead-Ins—Indoors. Indoor antennas and indoor lead-ins shall not be run nearer than two inches to conductors of other wiring systems in the premises unless:

(1)   such other conductors are in metal raceways or cable armor, or

(2)   unless permanently separated from such other conductors by a continuous and firmly fixed nonconductor such as porcelain tubes or flexible tubing.

810-19. Electric Supply Circuits Used in Lieu of Antenna.

Where an electric supply circuit is used in lieu of an antenna, the device by which the radio receiving set is connected to the supply circuit shall be specially approved for the purpose.

▶   The device referred to usually consists of a small fixed condenser connected between one wire of the lighting circuit and the antenna terminal of the receiving set. As most receiving sets are arranged, a breakdown in this condenser would result in a short circuit to ground through the antenna coil of the set and the condenser should therefore be one that is designed for operation at **300** volts or higher in which mica is used as the dielectric so that it will have a high factor of safety.

Antenna Discharge Units

810-20. Antenna Discharge Units—Receiving Stations.

Each conductor of a lead-in from an outdoor antenna shall be provided with an antenna discharge unit approved for the purpose, except that where the lead-in conductors are enclosed in a continuous metallic shield the antenna discharge unit may be installed to protect the shield or may be omitted where the shield is permanently and effectively grounded. Antenna discharge units shall be located outside the building, or inside the building between the point of entrance of the lead-in and the radio set or transformers, and as near as practicable to the entrance of the conductors to the building. The antenna discharge unit shall not be located near combustible material nor in a hazardous location as defined in Article 500.

▶   Where the lead-in is enclosed in a continuous metallic shield, i.e., is run in rigid conduit or electrical metallic tubing, or consists of a lead-covered conductor or pair of conductors, and the metallic enclosure is well grounded, a lightning discharge will usually jump from the lead-in conductor to the metallic shield, because this path to ground offers a much lower impedance than the path through the antenna coil of the receiving set. A lightning arrester is therefore not required where the lead-in is so shielded.

Grounding Conductors—General

810-21. Material. The grounding conductor shall, unless otherwise specified, be of copper, aluminum, copper-clad steel, bronze, or other corrosion-resistant material.

810-22. Insulation. The grounding conductors may be uninsulated.

810-23. Supports. The grounding conductors shall be securely fastened in place and may be directly attached to the surface wired over without the use of insulating supports. Where proper support cannot be provided the size of the grounding conductor shall be increased proportionately.

810-24. Mechanical Protection. The grounding conductor shall be protected where exposed to physical damage or the size of the grounding conductor shall be increased proportionately to compensate for the lack of protection.

810-25. Run in Straight Line. The grounding conductor shall be run in as straight a line as practicable from the antenna mast and/or the antenna discharge unit to the grounding electrode.

810-26. Grounding Electrode. The grounding conductor shall be connected to a metallic underground water piping system as specified in Section 250-81. Where the building is not supplied with a water system the connection shall be made to the metal frame of the building when effectively grounded or to a grounding electrode as specified in Section 250-83. At a penthouse or similar location the ground conductor may be connected to a water pipe or rigid conduit.

▶   In order to avoid potential differences between various masses of metal, in or on buildings, and lead-in conductors, the metal portions of antenna masts should never be grounded to soil pipes, soil vent pipes, metal gutters, downspouts, etc.; in other words, grounding must be done in accordance with Art. 250, and it is required to use the same grounding electrode for the grounding of masts as for the electrical system in the building.

Grounding Conductors—Receiving Stations

810-27. Inside or Outside Building. The grounding conductor may be run either inside or outside the building.

810-28. Size. The grounding conductor shall be not smaller than No. 10 copper or No. 8 aluminum or No. 17 copper-clad steel or bronze.

810-29. Common Ground. A single grounding conductor may be used for both protective and operating purposes.

Where a single conductor is so used, the ground terminal of the equipment should be connected to the ground terminal of the protective device.

C. Amateur Transmitting and Receiving Stations

Antenna System

810-51. Other Sections. In addition to conforming to the requirements of Part C, antenna systems for amateur transmitting and receiving stations shall also comply with Sections 810-11 through 810-15.

810-52. Size of Antenna. Antenna conductors for amateur transmitting and receiving stations shall be of a size not less than given in Table 810-52.

Table 810-52. Size of Amateur-Station Outdoor Antenna Conductors

	Minimum Size of Conductors	
	When Maximum Open Span Length Is	
Material	Less than 150 feet	Over 150 feet
Hard-drawn copper............. 14		10
Copper-clad steel, bronze or other high strength material........ 14		12

For very long span length larger conductors will be required, depending on the span length and the ice and wind loadings.

810-53. Size of Lead-In Conductors. Lead-in conductors for transmitting stations shall, for various maximum span lengths, be of a size at least as great as that of conductors for antennas as specified in Section 810-52.

810-54. Clearance on Building. Antenna conductors for transmitting stations, attached to buildings, shall be firmly mounted at least 3 inches clear of the surface of the building on nonabsorptive insulating supports, such as treated pins or brackets, equipped with insulators having not less than 3-inch creepage and airgap distances. Lead-in conductors attached to buildings shall also conform to these requirements, except when they are enclosed in a continuous metallic shield which is permanently and effectively grounded. In this latter case the metallic shield may also be used as a conductor.

▶   The creepage distance is the distance from the conductor to the building measured on the surface of the supporting insulator. The air gap is the distance measured straight across from the conductor to the building.

810-55. Entrance to Building. Except where protected with a continuous metallic shield which is permanently and effectively grounded, lead-in conductors for transmitting stations shall enter buildings by one of the following methods:

(a) Through a rigid, noncombustible, nonabsorptive insulating tube or bushing.

(b) Through an opening provided for the purpose in which the entrance conductors are firmly secured so as to provide a clearance of at least 2 inches.

(c) Through a drilled window pane.

810-56. Protection Against Accidental Contact. Lead-in conductors to radio transmitters shall be so located or installed as to make accidental contact with them difficult.

810-57. Antenna Discharge Units—Transmitting Stations. Each conductor of a lead-in for outdoor antennas shall be provided with an antenna discharge unit or other suitable means which will drain static charges from the antenna system.

Exception No. 1: Where protected by a continuous metallic shield which is permanently and effectively grounded.

Exception No. 2: Where the antenna is permanently and effectively grounded.

▶   A transmitting station should be protected against lightning, either by an arrester or by a switch that connects the lead-in to ground and is kept closed at all times when the station is not in operation.

Grounding Conductors—General

810-58. Other Sections. All grounding conductors for amateur transmitting and receiving stations shall comply with Sections 810-21 through 810-27.

810-59. Size of Protective Ground. The protective ground conductor for transmitting stations shall be as large as the lead-in, but not smaller than No. 10 copper, bronze, or copper-clad steel.

810-60. Size of Operating Grounding Conductor. The operating grounding conductor for transmitting stations shall be not less than No. 14 copper or its equivalent.

Interior Installation—Transmitting Stations

810-70. Clearance from Other Conductors. Except as provided in Article 640, all conductors inside the building shall be separated at least 4 inches from the conductors of any other light or signal circuit unless separated therefrom by conduit or some firmly fixed nonconductor such as porcelain tubes or flexible tubing.

810-71. General. Transmitters shall comply with the following:

(a) Enclosing. The transmitter shall be enclosed in a metal frame or grille, or separated from the operating space by a barrier or other equivalent means, all metallic parts of which are effectually connected to ground.

(b) Grounding of Controls. All external metallic handles and controls accessible to the operating personnel shall be effectually grounded.

No circuit in excess of 150 volts between conductors should have any parts exposed to direct contact. A complete dead-front type of switchboard is preferred.

(c) Interlocks on Doors. All access doors shall be provided with interlocks which will disconnect all voltages in excess of 350 volts between conductors when any access door is opened.

(d) Audio-Amplifiers. Audio-amplifiers which are located outside the transmitter housing shall be suitably housed and shall be so located as to be readily accessible and adequately ventilated.

ARTICLE 820. COMMUNITY ANTENNA TELEVISION AND RADIO DISTRIBUTION SYSTEMS

A. General

820-1. Scope. The provisions of this Article shall apply to coaxial cable distribution of radio frequency signals typically employed in Community Antenna Television (CATV) systems. Where the wiring system employed is other than coaxial, the provisions of Article 800—Communication Circuits shall apply.

The coaxial cable may be used to deliver low energy power to equipment directly associated with this radio frequency distribution system provided the voltage is not in excess of 60 volts and where the current supply is from a transformer or other device having energy limiting characteristics.

820-2. Material. Coaxial cable used for the radio frequency distribution system shall be suitable for the application.

B. Protection

820-3. Ground of Outer Conductive Shield of a Coaxial Cable. Where coaxial cable is exposed to lightning or to accidental contact with lightning arrester conductors or power conductors operating at a potential exceeding 300 volts, the outer conductive shield of the coaxial cable shall be grounded at the building premises as close to the point of cable entry as practicable.

Where the outer conductive shield of a coaxial cable is grounded, no other protective devices are required.

C. Installation of Cable

Coaxial cable installation for radio frequency distribution shall comply with the following:

820-4. Outside Conductors. Prior to the point of grounding, as defined in Section 820-3.

(a) On Poles. On poles, the conductors should preferably be located below the light and power conductors and shall not be attached to a cross arm which carries light or power conductors.

(b) Lead-in Clearance. Lead-in or aerial drop cables from a pole or other support including the point of initial attachment to a building or structure shall be kept away from electric light or power circuits so as to avoid the possibility of accidental contact. Where proximity to electric light and power service conductors cannot be avoided, the installation shall be such as to provide clearances of not less than 12 inches from light and power service drops.

(c) Over Roofs. Cables passing over buildings shall be at least 8 feet above any roof which is accessible for pedestrian traffic.

(d) Between Buildings. Cables extending between buildings, and also the supports or attachment fixtures shall be acceptable for the purpose, and shall have sufficient strength to withstand the loads to which they may be subjected, except that where cable does not have sufficient strength to be self-supporting, it shall be attached to a supporting messenger cable which together with the attachment fixtures or supports shall be acceptable for the purpose and shall have sufficient strength to withstand the loads to which they may be subjected.

(e) On Buildings. When attached to buildings, cables shall be securely fastened in such a manner that they shall be separated from other conductors as follows:

(1) Light and Power. The coaxial cable shall have a separation of at least 4 inches from light or power conductors not in conduit or cable, unless permanently separated from conductors of the other system by a continuous and firmly fixed nonconductor additional to the insulation on the wires.

(2) Other Communication Systems. Coaxial cable shall be installed so that there will be no unnecessary interference in the maintenance of the separate systems. In no case shall the conductors, cables, messenger strand or equipment of one system cause abrasion to the conductors, cable, messenger strand or equipment of any other system.

(3) Lightning Conductors. Where practicable, a separation of at least 6 feet shall be maintained between any coaxial cable and lightning conductors.

820-5. Entering Buildings. Coaxial cable shall slope upward from the outside where entering a building, or, where this is impracticable, drip loops shall be formed in the cable at the point of entrance.

820-6. Conductors Inside Buildings. Beyond the point of grounding, as defined in Section 820-3, cable installation shall comply with the following:

(a) Light and Power. Coaxial cable shall be separated at least two inches from any light or power conductors or Class 1 signal or control circuits not in a raceway nor in metal-sheathed, metal-clad, nonmetallic sheathed or Type UF cables unless permanently separated from the conductors of the other system by a continuous and firmly fixed nonconductor, additional to the insulation on the wire, such as porcelain tubes or flexible tubing.

(b) In Raceways and Boxes. Coaxial cable shall not be placed in any raceway, compartment, outlet box, junction box or other enclosures with conductors for light and power circuits or Class 1 signal and control circuits unless the conductors of the different systems are separated by a permanent partition; provided that this shall not apply to conductors in outlet boxes, junction boxes or similar fittings or compartments where such conductors are introduced solely for power supply to the coaxial cable system distribution equipment or for power connection to remote control equipment.

(c) In Shafts. Coaxial cable may be installed in the same shaft with conductors for light and power provided the conductors of the two systems are separated at least two inches or where the conductors of either system are encased in noncombustible tubing.

Where the lighting or power conductors are run in a raceway, or in metal sheathed or metal-clad or nonmetallic sheathed or Type UF cables, neither the two-inch separation nor the noncombustible tubing is required.

(d) Vertical Runs. Conductors or coaxial cables bunched together in a vertical run in a shaft shall have a fire resistant covering capable of preventing the carrying of flame from floor to floor except where conductors are encased in noncombustible tubing or are located in a fireproof shaft having fire stops at each floor.

(e) Other Conductors. There is no specific separation requirement between Class 2 signal and control circuits wired distribution system cables and communication cables or conductors other than the clearance necessary to prevent conflict or abrasion.

D. Underground Circuits

820-7. Underground Coaxial Cable. Underground coaxial cable entering buildings shall comply with the following:

(a) With Light and Power Conductors. Underground conductors in a duct, pedestal, handhole, or manhole containing electric light or power conductors shall be in a section permanently separated from such conductors by means of a suitable barrier.

E. Grounding

820-8. Cable Grounding. Coaxial cable shall be grounded as follows:

(a) Ground Circuit. The coaxial cable ground shall comply with the following:

(1) Insulation. The grounding conductor shall have a rubber or other suitable kind of insulation.

(2) Material. The ground conductor shall be copper or other corrosion-resisting conductive material, stranded or solid.

(3) Size. The grounding conductor shall not be smaller than No. 18 AWG; it shall have a conductivity approximately equal to that of the outer conductor of the coaxial cable.

(4) Run. The grounding conductor shall be run in as straight a line as practicable to the grounding electrode.

(5) Physical Protection. Where necessary, the grounding conductor shall be guarded from physical damage.

(6) Electrode. The grounding conductor shall be connected as follows:

a. To an available water pipe electrode, or

b. To the power service conduit, service-equipment enclosure, or grounding electrode conductor where the grounded conductor of the power service is connected to a water-pipe electrode at the building, or

c. Where the grounding means in (a) or (b) above are not available, to the service conduit, service-equipment enclosure, grounding electrode conductor or grounding electrode of the power service of a multigrounded neutral power system, or

d. Where the grounding means in (a), (b) or (c) are not available, to (1) a concrete-encased electrode of not less than 20 feet of bare copper conductor not smaller than No. 4 encased by at least 2 inches of concrete and located within and near the bottom of a concrete foundation footing that is in direct contact with the earth, (2) an effectively grounded metal structure, (3) a continuous and extensive underground gas-piping system where acceptable both to the serving gas supplier and to the authority having jurisdiction, or (4) to a ground rod or pipe driven into permanently damp earth. Steam or hot-water pipes, lightning-rod conductors or pipe or rod electrodes grounding other than multigrounded neutral power circuits shall not be employed as electrodes.

(7) Electrode Connection. It is recommended that the grounding conductor shall be attached to a pipe electrode by means of a bolted clamp to which the conductor is connected in an effective manner. Where a gas pipe electrode is used, connection shall be made between the gas meter and the street main. In every case the connection to the grounding electrode shall be made as close to the earth as practicable.

(8) Bonding of Electrodes. A bond not smaller than No. 6 copper or equivalent shall be placed between the antenna systems and power grounding electrodes where the requirements of (6) above result in the use of separate electrodes. All separate grounding electrodes may be bonded together. See Section 250-86.

820-9. Equipment Grounding. Unpowered equipment and enclosures or equipment powered by the coaxial cable are deemed to be grounded when connected to the metallic cable shield.

F. General

820-10. Prevention of Spread of Fire. Installations shall be so made that the possible spread of fire through fire walls, fire partitions or fire-resistive floors is reduced to a minimum.

CHAPTER NINE _____

Tables and Examples

A. Tables

Notes to Tables

1. Tables 3A, 3B and 3C apply only to complete conduit or tubing systems and are not intended to apply to short sections of conduit or tubing used to protect exposed wiring from physical damage.

2. Equipment grounding conductors, when installed, shall be included when calculating conduit or tubing fill. The actual dimensions of the equipment grounding conductor (insulated or bare) may be used in the calculation.

3. When conduit nipples having a maximum length not to exceed 24 inches are installed between boxes, cabinets, and similar enclosures, the nipple may be filled to 60 per cent of its total cross-sectional area, and Note 8 of Tables 310-12 through 310-15 does not apply to this condition.

4. For conductors not included in Chapter 9 use actual dimensions.

5. See Table 1 for allowable percentage of conduit or tubing fill.

▶   Tables 1, 3A, 3B, and 3C do not apply where short conduit sleeves are used to protect various types of cables from physical damage.

While Note 2 mentions only bare equipment grounding conductors, Note 4 to Table 1 applies to all forms of *bare* conductors (equipment grounding conductors and neutral or grounded conductors). Where any bare conductors are used in conduit or tubing the dimensions given in Table 8 may be used. Since *all* wires utilize space in raceways they must be counted in calculating raceway sizes whether the conductors are insulated or bare. The only exception to this is in Table 350-3 for short lengths of ⅜-in. flexible metal conduit.

In regard to Note 4 there are conductors (particularly high-voltage types) that do not have dimensions listed in Chapter 9. Conduit sizes for such conductors may be determined by computing the cross-sectional area of each conductor as follows:

$D^2 \times 0.7854 = CSA$, where D = outside diameter of conductor, including insulation; CSA = overall cross-sectional area. Then the proper conduit size can be determined by applying Tables 1 and 4 for the appropriate number of conductors.

Example: 3 single-conductor 5-kv cables are to be installed in conduit. The outside diameter (D) of each conductor is 0.750 in. Then $0.750^2 \times 0.7854 \times 3 = 1.3253$ sq in. From Tables 1 and 4 (40 per cent fill) a 2-in. conduit would be required.

Table 1. Per Cent of Cross Section of Conduit and Tubing for Conductors
(See Table 2 for Fixture Wires)

Number of Conductors	1	2	3	4	Over 4
All conductor types except lead-covered (new or rewiring)	53	31	40	40	40
Lead-covered conductors	55	30	40	38	35

Note 1. See Tables 3A, 3B and 3C for number of conductors all of the same size in trade sizes of conduit ½ inch through 6 inch.

Note 2. For conductors larger than 750 MCM or for combinations of conductors of different sizes use Tables 4 through 8, Chapter 9, for dimensions of conductors, conduit and tubing.

Note 3. Where the calculated number of conductors, all of the same size, includes a decimal fraction, the next higher whole number shall be used where this decimal is 0.8 or larger.

Note 4. When bare conductors are permitted by other Sections of this Code, the dimensions for bare conductors in Table 8 of Chapter 9 may be used.

▶ Tables 3A, 3B, and 3C are based on Table 1 allowable percentage fills, and have been provided for the sake of convenience. In any calculation, however, Table 1 is the table to be used where any conflict may occur in Tables 3A, 3B, or 3C.

Table 1 is also used for computing conduit sizes where various sizes of conductors or conductor types are to be used in the same conduit. Tables 1, 3A, 3B, and 3C apply to new work or rewiring, exposed or concealed.

An example of Note 3 would be to determine how many No. 14 Type TW conductors would be permitted in a ½-in. conduit. For 3 or more such conductors Table 1 permits a 40 per cent fill. From Table 4, 40 per cent of the internal cross-sectional area of a ½-in. conduit is 0.12 sq in. From Table 5 (column 5) the cross-sectional area of a No. 14 Type TW conductor is 0.0135 sq in. Thus $0.12/0.0135 = 8.8$ or 9 such conductors would be permitted in a ½-in. conduit. Where the decimal is less than 0.8 (such as 0.7) the decimal would be dropped and the whole number would be the maximum number of equally sized conductors permitted, e.g. 8.7 would be 8 conductors.

The following is an example for computing a conduit size for various conductor sizes:

Number	Wire Size and Type	Table 5 C.S.A. (ea.)	Sub-total C.S.A.
3	No. 10 TW	.0224	.0672
3	No. 12 TW	.0172	.0516
3	No. 6 TW	.0819	.2457
		Total C.S.A.	0.3645

Table 1 permits a 40 per cent fill for three or more conductors. Following the 40 per cent column in Table 4, 1¼-in. conduit or tubing would be required for these nine conductors, which have a combined cross-sectional area of **0.3645** sq in.

Table 2. Maximum Number of Fixture Wires in Trade Size of Conduit or Tubing
(40 Per Cent Fill Based on Individual Diameters)

Conduit Trade Size (Inches)	1/2			3/4			1			1 1/4			1 1/2			2		
Wire Types	18	16	14	18	16	14	18	16	14	18	16	14	18	16	14	18	16	14
PTF, PTFF, PGFF, PGF, PFF, PF	23	18	14	40	31	24	65	50	39	115	90	70	157	122	95	257	200	156
TFFN, TFN	19	15		34	26		55	43		97	76		132	104		216	169	
SF-1	16			29			47			83			114			186		
SFF-1, FF-1, FFH-1	15			26			43			76			104			169		
CF	13	10	8	23	18	14	38	30	23	66	53	40	91	72	55	149	118	90
TF	11	10		20	18		32	30		57	53		79	72		129	118	
RFH-1, RF-1	11			20			32			57			79			129		
TFF	11	10		20	17		32	27		56	49		77	66		126	109	
AF	11	9	7	19	16	12	31	26	20	55	46	36	75	63	49	123	104	81
SFF-2	9	7	6	16	12	10	27	20	17	47	36	30	65	49	42	106	81	68
SF-2	9	8	6	16	14	11	27	23	18	47	40	32	65	55	43	106	90	71
FF-2, FFH-2	9	7		15	12		25	19		44	34		60	46		99	75	
RFH-2	7	5		12	10		20	16		36	28		49	38		80	62	
RF-2	7	6		12	10		20	16		36	29		49	40		80	65	

Table 3A. Maximum Number of Conductors in Trade Sizes of Conduit or Tubing (Based on Table 1, Chapter 9)

Type Letters	Conductor Size AWG, MCM	Conduit Trade Size (Inches) ½	¾	1	1¼	1½	2	2½	3	3½	4	4½	5	6
TW, T, RUH, RUW, XHHW (14 thru 8)	14	9	15	25	44	60	99	142	171					
	12	7	12	19	35	47	78	111	131					
	10	5	9	15	26	36	60	85		176				
	8	3	5	8	14	20	33	47	72	97	124			
RHW and RHH (without outer covering), THW	14	6	10	16	29	40	65	93	143	192				
	12	4	8	13	24	32	53	76	117	157				
	10	4	6	11	19	26	43	61	95	127	163			
	8	1	4	6	11	15	25	36	56	75	96	121	152	
TW, T, THW, RUH (6 thru 2), RUW (6 thru 2)	6	1	2	4	7	10	16	23	36	48	62	78	97	141
	4	1	1	3	5	7	12	17	27	36	47	58	73	106
	3	1	1	2	4	6	10	15	23	31	40	50	63	91
	2	1	1	2	4	5	9	13	20	27	34	43	54	78
	1		1	1	3	4	6	9	14	19	25	31	39	57
FEPB (6 thru 2), RHW and RHH (without outer covering)	0		1	1	2	3	5	8	12	16	21	27	33	49
	00		1	1	1	3	5	7	10	14	18	23	29	41
	000		1	1	1	2	4	6	9	12	15	19	24	35
	0000			1	1	1	3	5	7	10	13	16	20	29
	250			1	1	1	2	4	6	8	10	13	16	23
	300			1	1	1	2	3	5	7	9	11	14	20
	350				1	1	1	3	4	6	8	10	12	18
	400				1	1	1	2	4	5	7	9	11	16
	500				1	1	1	1	3	4	6	7	9	14
	600					1	1	1	3	4	5	6	7	11
	700					1	1	1	2	3	4	5	7	10
	750						1	1						

Type Letters	Conductor Size AWG, MCM	Conduit Trade Size (Inches)												
		½	¾	1	1¼	1½	2	2½	3	3½	4	4½	5	6
THWN,	14	13	24	39	69	94	154							
	12	10	18	29	51	70	114	164						
	10	6	11	18	32	44	73	104	160					
	8	3	6	10	19	26	42	60	93	125	160			
THHN, FEP (14 thru 2), FEPB (14 thru 8),	6	1	4	6	11	15	26	37	57	76	98	125	154	
	4	1	2	4	7	9	16	22	35	47	60	75	94	137
	3	1	1	3	6	8	13	19	29	39	51	64	80	116
	2	1	1	3	5	7	11	16	25	33	43	54	67	97
	1		1	1	3	5	8	12	18	25	32	40	50	72
XHHW (4 thru 500 MCM)	0		1	1	3	4	7	10	15	21	27	33	42	61
	00		1	1	2	3	6	8	13	17	22	28	35	51
	000		1	1	1	3	5	7	11	14	18	23	29	42
	0000		1	1	1	2	4	6	9	12	15	19	24	35
	250			1	1	1	3	4	7	10	12	16	20	28
	300			1	1	1	3	4	6	8	11	13	17	24
	350			1	1	1	2	3	5	7	9	12	15	21
	400				1	1	1	3	5	6	8	10	13	19
	500				1	1	1	2	4	5	7	9	11	16
	600				1	1	1	1	3	4	5	7	9	13
	700					1	1	1	3	4	5	6	8	11
	750					1	1	1	2	3	4	6	7	11
XHHW	6	1	3	5	9	13	21	30	47	63	81	102	128	185
	600				1	1	1	1	3	4	5	7	9	13
	700					1	1	1	3	4	5	6	7	11
	750					1	1	1	2	3	4	6	7	10

Table 3C. Maximum Number of Conductors in Trade Sizes of Conduit or Tubing (Based on Table 1, Chapter 9)

Type Letters	Conductor Size AWG, MCM	6	5	4½	4	3½	3	2½	2	1½	1¼	1	¾	½
RHW,	14				155	121	90	58	41	25	18	10	6	3
	12				132	103	77	50	35	21	15	9	5	3
	10			138	110	86	64	41	29	18	13	7	4	2
	8	152	105	84	67	52	39	25	17	10	8	4	2	1
RHH	6	93	64	51	41	32	24	15	11	6	5	2	1	1
(with	4	72	50	39	31	24	18	12	8	5	3	1	1	1
outer	3	63	44	35	28	22	16	10	7	4	3	1	1	1
covering)	2	56	38	31	24	19	14	9	6	4	3	1	1	
	1	42	29	23	18	14	11	7	5	3	1	1	1	
	0	37	25	20	16	12	9	6	4	2	1	1	1	
	00	32	22	18	14	11	8	5	3	1	1	1		
	000	28	19	15	12	9	7	4	3	1	1	1		
	0000	24	16	13	10	8	6	4	2	1	1	1		
	250	19	13	11	8	6	5	3	1	1	1			
	300	17	11	9	7	5	4	3	1	1	1			
	350	15	10	8	6	5	4	2	1	1	1			
	400	14	9	7	6	4	3	1	1	1	1			
	500	11	8	6	5	4	3	1	1	1	1			
	600	9	6	5	4	3	2	1	1	1				
	700	8	6	4	3	3	1	1	1	1				
	750	8	5	4	3	3	1	1	1					

Conduit Trade Size (Inches)

Tables 4 through 8, Chapter 9. Tables 4 through 8 give the nominal size of conductors and conduit or tubing recommended for use in computing size of conduit or tubing for various combinations of conductors. The dimensions represent average conditions only, and while variations will be found in dimensions of conductors and conduits of different manufacture, these variations will not affect the computation.

Table 4. Dimensions and Per Cent Area of Conduit and of Tubing

Areas of Conduit or Tubing for the Combinations of Wires Permitted in Table 1, Chapter 9.

Trade Size	Internal Diameter Inches	Total 100%	Not Lead Covered			Lead Covered				
			2 Cond. 31%	Over 2 Cond. 40%	1 Cond. 53%	1 Cond. 55%	2 Cond. 30%	3 Cond. 40%	4 Cond. 38%	Over 4 Cond. 35%
½	.622	.30	.09	.12	.16	.17	.09	.12	.11	.11
¾	.824	.53	.16	.21	.28	.29	.16	.21	.20	.19
1	1.049	.86	.27	.34	.46	.47	.26	.34	.33	.30
1¼	1.380	1.50	.47	.60	.80	.83	.45	.60	.57	.53
1½	1.610	2.04	.63	.82	1.08	1.12	.61	.82	.78	.71
2	2.067	3.36	1.04	1.34	1.78	1.85	1.01	1.34	1.28	1.18
2½	2.469	4.79	1.48	1.92	2.54	2.63	1.44	1.92	1.82	1.68
3	3.068	7.38	2.29	2.95	3.91	4.06	2.21	2.95	2.80	2.58
3½	3.548	9.90	3.07	3.96	5.25	5.44	2.97	3.96	3.76	3.47
4	4.026	12.72	3.94	5.09	6.74	7.00	3.82	5.09	4.83	4.45
4½	4.506	15.94	4.94	6.38	8.45	8.77	4.78	6.38	6.06	5.56
5	5.047	20.00	6.20	8.00	10.60	11.00	6.00	8.00	7.60	7.00
6	6.065	28.89	8.96	11.56	15.31	15.89	8.67	11.56	10.98	10.11

Area—Square Inches

Table 5. Dimensions of Rubber-Covered and Thermoplastic-Covered Conductors

Size AWG MCM	Types RF-2, RFH-2, RH, RHH,*** RHW,*** SF-2		Types TF, T, THW,† TW, RUH,** RUW***		Types TFN, THHN, THWN		Types**** FEP, FEPB, TFE, PF, PGF, PTF		Type XHHW	
	Approx. Diam. Inches	Approx. Area Sq. In.	Approx. Diam. Inches	Approx. Area Sq. In.	Approx. Diam. Inches	Approx. Area Sq. In.	Approx. Diam. Inches	Approx. Area Sq. In.	Approx. Diam. Inches	Approx. Area Sq. In.
Col. 1	Col. 2	Col. 3	Col. 4	Col. 5	Col. 6	Col. 7	Col. 8	Col. 9	Col. 10	Col. 11
18	.146	.0167	.106	.0088	.089	.0064	.081	.0052	...	...
16	.158	.0196	.118	.0109	.100	.0079	.092	.0066	...	...
14	30 mils .171	.0230	.131	.0135	.105	.0087	.105 .105	.0087 .0087		
14	45 mils .204*	.0327*	.162†	.0206†	...	...	...	...	.129	.0131
14	... ...		...	...	...	...	...	...		
12	30 mils .188	.0278	.148	.0172	.122	.0117	.121 .121	.0115 .0115		
12	45 mils .221*	.0384*	.179†	.0251†	...	...	...	...	.146	.0167
12	... ...		...	...	...	...	...	...		
10	... .242	.0460	.168	.0224	.153	.0184	.142 .142	.0159 .0159	.166	.0216
10	... ...		.199†	.0311†	...	...	...	...		
8	... .311	.0760	.228	.0408	.201	.0317	.189 .169	.0280 .0225	.224	.0394
8	... ...		.259†	.0526†	...	...	...	...		
6	.397	.1238	.323	.0819	.257	.0519	.244 .302	.0467 .0716	.282	.0625
4	.452	.1605	.372	.1087	.328	.0845	.292 .350	.0669 .0962	.328	.0845
3	.481	.1817	.401	.1263	.356	.0995	.320 .378	.0803 .1122	.356	.0995
2	.513	.2067	.433	.1473	.388	.1182	.352 .410	.0973 .1316	.388	.1182
1	.588	.2715	.508	.2027	.450	.1590	.420	.1385	.450	.1590
0	.629	.3107	.549	.2367	.491	.1893	.462	.1676	.491	.1893
00	.675	.3578	.595	.2781	.537	.2265	.498	.1974	.537	.2265
000	.727	.4151	.647	.3288	.588	.2715	.560	.2463	.588	.2715
0000	.785	.4840	.705	.3904	.646	.3278	.618	.2999	.646	.3278

Table 5—Continued

Size AWG MCM	Types RF-2, RFH-2, RH, RHH,*** RHW,*** SF-2		Types TF, T, THW,† TW, RUH,** RUW**		Types THHN, THWN, TFN, THWN		Types**** FEP, FEPB, TFE, PF, PGF, PTF		Type XHHW	
	Approx. Diam. Inches	Approx. Area Sq. In.	Approx. Diam. Inches	Approx. Area Sq. In.	Approx. Diam. Inches	Approx. Area Sq. In.	Approx. Diam. Inches	Approx. Area Sq. In.	Approx. Diam. Inches	Approx. Area Sq. In.
Col. 1	Col. 2	Col. 3	Col. 4	Col. 5	Col. 6	Col. 7	Col. 8	Col. 9	Col. 10	Col. 11
250	.868	.5917	.788	.4877	.716	.4026	…	…	.716	.4026
300	.933	.6837	.843	.5581	.771	.4669	…	…	.771	.4669
350	.985	.7620	.895	.6291	.822	.5307	…	…	.822	.5307
400	1.032	.8365	.942	.6969	.869	.5931	…	…	.869	.5931
500	1.119	.9834	1.029	.8316	.955	.7163	…	…	.955	.7163
600	1.233	1.1940	1.143	1.0261	1.058	.8792	…	…	1.073	.9043
700	1.304	1.3355	1.214	1.1575	1.129	1.0011	…	…	1.145	1.0297
750	1.339	1.4082	1.249	1.2252	1.163	1.0623	…	…	1.180	1.0936
800	1.372	1.4784	1.282	1.2908	1.196	1.1234	…	…	1.210	1.1499
900	1.435	1.6173	1.345	1.4208	1.259	1.2449	…	…	1.270	1.2668
1000	1.494	1.7531	1.404	1.5482	1.317	1.3623	…	…	1.330	1.3893
1250	1.676	2.2062	1.577	1.9532	…	…	…	…	1.500	1.7672
1500	1.801	2.5475	1.702	2.2748	…	…	…	…	1.620	2.0612
1750	1.916	2.8895	1.817	2.5930	…	…	…	…	1.740	2.3779
2000	2.021	3.2079	1.922	2.9013	…	…	…	…	1.840	2.6590

* The dimensions of Types RHH and RHW.

** No. 14 to No. 2.

† Dimensions of THW in sizes 14 to 8. No. 6 THW and larger is the same dimension as T.

*** Dimensions of RHH and RHW without outer covering are the same as THW.

No. 18 to No. 8, solid; No. 6 and larger, stranded.

**** In Columns 8 and 9 the values shown for sizes No. 1 thru 0000 are for TFE only. The right-hand values in Columns 8 and 9 are for FEPB only.

Table 6. Dimensions of Lead-Covered Conductors
Types RL, RHL, and RUL

Size AWG-MCM	Single Conductor		Two Conductor		Three Conductor	
	Diam. Inches	Area Sq. Ins.	Diam. Inches	Area Sq. Ins.	Diam. Inches	Area Sq. Ins.
14	.28	.062	.28 × .47	.115	.59	.273
12	.29	.066	.31 × .54	.146	.62	.301
10	.35	.096	.35 × .59	.180	.68	.363
8	.41	.132	.41 × .71	.255	.82	.528
6	.49	.188	.49 × .86	.369	.97	.738
4	.55	.237	.54 × .96	.457	1.08	.916
2	.60	.283	.61 × 1.08	.578	1.21	1.146
1	.67	.352	.70 × 1.23	.756	1.38	1.49
0	.71	.396	.74 × 1.32	.859	1.47	1.70
00	.76	.454	.79 × 1.41	.980	1.57	1.94
000	.81	.515	.84 × 1.52	1.123	1.69	2.24
0000	.87	.593	.90 × 1.64	1.302	1.85	2.68
250	.98	.754	....	.....	2.02	3.20
300	1.04	.85	....	.....	2.15	3.62
350	1.10	.95	....	.....	2.26	4.02
400	1.14	1.02	....	.....	2.40	4.52
500	1.23	1.18	....	.....	2.59	5.28

The above cables are limited to straight runs or with nominal offsets equivalent to not more than two quarter bends.

Note—No. 14 to No. 8, solid conductors: No. 6 and larger, stranded conductors. Data for 30-mil insulation not yet compiled.

Table 7. Dimensions of Asbestos-Varnished-Cambric Insulated Conductors

Types AVA, AVB, and AVL

Size AWG MCM	Type AVA		Type AVB		Type AVL	
	Approx. Diam. Inches	Approx. Area Sq. In.	Approx. Diam. Inches	Approx. Area Sq. In.	Approx. Diam. Inches	Approx. Area Sq. In.
14	.245	.047	.205	.033	.320	.080
12	.265	.055	.225	.040	.340	.091
10	.285	.064	.245	.047	.360	.102
8	.310	.075	.270	.057	.390	.119
6	.395	.122	.345	.094	.430	.145
4	.445	.155	.395	.123	.480	.181
2	.505	.200	.460	.166	.570	.255
1	.585	.268	.540	.229	.620	.300
0	.625	.307	.580	.264	.660	.341
00	.670	.353	.625	.307	.705	.390
000	.720	.406	.675	.358	.755	.447
0000	.780	.478	.735	.425	.815	.521
250	.885	.616	.855	.572	.955	.715
300	.940	.692	.910	.649	1.010	.800
350	.995	.778	.965	.731	1.060	.885
400	1.040	.850	1.010	.800	1.105	.960
500	1.125	.995	1.095	.945	1.190	1.118
550	1.165	1.065	1.135	1.01	1.265	1.26
600	1.205	1.140	1.175	1.09	1.305	1.34
650	1.240	1.21	1.210	1.15	1.340	1.41
700	1.275	1.28	1.245	1.22	1.375	1.49
750	1.310	1.35	1.280	1.29	1.410	1.57
800	1.345	1.42	1.315	1.36	1.440	1.63
850	1.375	1.49	1.345	1.43	1.470	1.70
900	1.405	1.55	1.375	1.49	1.505	1.78
950	1.435	1.62	1.405	1.55	1.535	1.85
1000	1.465	1.69	1.435	1.62	1.565	1.93

Note: No. 14 to No. 8, solid, No. 6 and larger, stranded; except AVL where all sizes are stranded

Varnished-Cambric Insulated Conductors
Type V

The insulation thickness for varnished-cambric conductors, Type V, is the same as for rubber-covered conductors, Type RHH, except for No. 8 which has 45-mil insulation for varnished-cambric and 60-mil insulation for rubber-covered conductors. See Table 310-2(b). Table 3C may, therefore, be used for the number of varnished-cambric insulated conductors in a conduit or tubing.

Table 8. Properties of Conductors

Size AWG MCM	Area Cir. Mils	Concentric Lay Stranded Conductors		Bare Conductors		D.C. Resistance Ohms/M Ft. At 25°C. 77°F.		
		No. Wires	Diam. Each Wire Inches	Diam. Inches	*Area Sq. Inches	Copper		Alumi-num
						Bare Cond.	Tin'd. Cond.	
18	1620	Solid	.0403	.0403	.0013	6.51	6.79	10.7
16	2580	Solid	.0508	.0508	.0020	4.10	4.26	6.72
14	4110	Solid	.0641	.0641	.0032	2.57	2.68	4.22
12	6530	Solid	.0808	.0808	.0051	1.62	1.68	2.66
10	10380	Solid	.1019	.1019	.0081	1.018	1.06	1.67
8	16510	Solid	.1285	.1285	.0130	.6404	.659	1.05
6	26240	7	.0612	.184	.027	.410	.427	.674
4	41740	7	.0772	.232	.042	.259	.269	.424
3	52620	7	.0867	.260	.053	.205	.213	.336
2	66360	7	.0974	.292	.067	.162	.169	.266
1	83690	19	.0664	.332	.087	.129	.134	.211
0	105600	19	.0745	.372	.109	.102	.106	.168
00	133100	19	.0837	.418	.137	.0811	.0843	.133
000	167800	19	.0940	.470	.173	.0642	.0668	.105
0000	211600	19	.1055	.528	.219	.0509	.0525	.0836
250	250000	37	.0822	.575	.260	.0431	.0449	.0708
300	300000	37	.0900	.630	.312	.0360	.0374	.0590
350	350000	37	.0973	.681	.364	.0308	.0320	.0505
400	400000	37	.1040	.728	.416	.0270	.0278	.0442
500	500000	37	.1162	.813	.519	.0216	.0222	.0354
600	600000	61	.0992	.893	.626	.0180	.0187	.0295
700	700000	61	.1071	.964	.730	.0154	.0159	.0253
750	750000	61	.1109	.998	.782	.0144	.0148	.0236
800	800000	61	.1145	1.030	.833	.0135	.0139	.0221
900	900000	61	.1215	1.090	.933	.0120	.0123	.0197
1000	1000000	61	.1280	1.150	1.039	.0108	.0111	.0177
1250	1250000	91	.1172	1.289	1.305	.00863	.00888	.0142
1500	1500000	91	.1284	1.410	1.561	.00719	.00740	.0118
1750	1750000	127	.1174	1.526	1.829	.00616	.00634	.0101
2000	2000000	127	.1255	1.630	2.087	.00539	.00555	.00885

* Area given is that of a circle having a diameter equal to the overall diameter of a stranded conductor.

The values given in the Table are those given in Handbook 100 of the National Bureau of Standards except that those shown in the 8th column are those given in Specification B33 of the American Society for Testing and Materials, and those shown in the 9th column are those given in Standard No. S-19-81 of the Insulated Power Cable Engineers Association and Standard No. WC3-1964 of the National Electrical Manufacturers Association.

The resistance values given in the last three columns are applicable only to direct current. When conductors larger than No. 4/0 are used with alternating current the multiplying factors in Table 9, Chapter 9 should be used to compensate for skin effect.

Table 9. Multiplying Factors for Converting D.C. Resistance to 60-Hertz A.C. Resistance

Size	Multiplying Factor			
	For Non-metallic Sheathed Cables in Air or Nonmetallic Conduit		For Metallic Sheathed Cables or all Cables in Metallic Raceways	
	Copper	Aluminum	Copper	Aluminum
Up to 3 AWG	1.	1.	1.	1.
2	1.	1.	1.01	1.00
1	1.	1.	1.01	1.00
0	1.001	1.000	1.02	1.00
00	1.001	1.001	1.03	1.00
000	1.002	1.001	1.04	1.01
0000	1.004	1.002	1.05	1.01
250 MCM	1.005	1.002	1.06	1.02
300 MCM	1.006	1.003	1.07	1.02
350 MCM	1.009	1.004	1.08	1.03
400 MCM	1.011	1.005	1.10	1.04
500 MCM	1.018	1.007	1.13	1.06
600 MCM	1.025	1.010	1.16	1.08
700 MCM	1.034	1.013	1.19	1.11
750 MCM	1.039	1.015	1.21	1.12
800 MCM	1.044	1.017	1.22	1.14
1000 MCM	1.067	1.026	1.30	1.19
1250 MCM	1.102	1.040	1.41	1.27
1500 MCM	1.142	1.058	1.53	1.36
1750 MCM	1.185	1.079	1.67	1.46
2000 MCM	1.233	1.100	1.82	1.56

B. Examples

Selection of Conductors.   In the following examples, the results are generally expressed in amperes. To select conductor sizes refer to Tables 310-12 through 310-15 and the Notes that pertain to such tables.

Voltage.   For uniform application of the provisions of Articles 210, 215 and 220 a nominal voltage of 115 and 230 volts shall be used in computing the ampere load on the conductor.

Fractions of an Ampere.   Except where the computations result in a major fraction of an ampere (larger than 0.5), such fractions may be dropped.

Ranges.   For the computation of the range loads in these examples Column A of Table 220-5 has been used. For optional methods, see Columns B and C of Table 220-5.

▶   It is assumed that the loads in the following examples are properly balanced on the system. If they are not properly balanced on the system, additional feeder capacity may be required.

Example No. 1. Single-Family Dwelling.

Dwelling has a floor area of 1500 sq. ft. exclusive of unoccupied cellar, unfinished attic, and open porches. It has a 12 kw range.

▶   *Example:* A two-story dwelling 30 by 25 ft. First and second floors 30 by 25 ft by 2 = 1500 sq ft. The "floor" area is computed from the "outside" dimensions of the building and multiplied by the number of floors. [Section 220-2a(1).]

Computed Load (see Section 220-4)
General Lighting Load:
1500 sq. ft. at 3 watts per sq. ft. = 4500 watts.
Minimum Number of Branch Circuits Required (see Section 220-3)
General Lighting Load:
4500 ÷ 115 = 39.1 amperes; or three 15 ampere 2-wire circuits; or two 20 ampere 2-wire circuits
Small Appliance Load: Two 2-wire 20 ampere circuits [Section 220-3(b)]
Laundry Load: One 2-wire 20 ampere circuit [Section 220-3(b)]
Minimum Size Feeders Required (see Section 220-4)
Computed Load

General Lighting..................	4500	watts
Small Appl. Load.................	3000	watts
Laundry........................	1500	watts
Total (without range).........	9000	watts
3000 watts at 100%..............	3000	watts
9000 − 3000 = 6000 watts at 35% =	2100	watts
Net computed (without range)..	5100	watts
Range Load (see Table 220-5)......	8000	watts
Net computed (with range)....	13,100	watts

For 115/230 volt 3-wire system feeders, 13,100 ÷ 230 = 57 amperes

Net computed load exceeds 10 kw. so service conductors shall be 100 amperes (see Section 230-41 Exception No. 1).

Example No. 1(a). Single-Family Dwelling.

Same conditions as Example No. 1, plus addition of one 6 ampere 230 volt room air conditioning unit and three 12 ampere 115 volt room air conditioning units. See Article 422, Part F.

From Example No. 1, feeder current is 57 amperes (3 wire, 230 volt)

Line A	Neutral	Line B	
57		57	amperes from Example No. 1
6		6	one 230 volt air cond. motor
12		12	two 115 volt air cond. motors
—		12	one 115 volt air cond. motor
3		3	25% of largest motor (Section 430-24)
78		90	amperes per line

Example No. 1(b). Single-Family Dwelling.
Optional Calculation for Single-Family Dwelling (Section 220-7).

Dwelling has a floor area of 1500 sq. ft. exclusive of unoccupied cellar, unfinished attic and open porches. It has a 12 kw range, a 2.5 kw water heater, a 1.2 kw dishwasher, 9 kw of electric space heating installed in five rooms, a 5.0 kw clothes dryer, and a 6 amp. 230 volt room air conditioning unit.

Air conditioner kw is $6 \times 230 \div 1000 = 1.38$ kw

1.38 kw is less than the connected load of 9 kw of space heating; therefore, the air conditioner load need not be included in the service calculation (see Section 220-4(l)).

1500 sq. ft. at 3 watts......................................	4.5 kw
Two 20 amp. appliance outlet circuits at 1500 watts each........	3.0 kw
Laundry circuit...	1.5 kw
Range (at nameplate rating).................................	12.0 kw
Water heater...	2.5 kw
Dishwasher...	1.2 kw
Space heating..	9.0 kw
Clothes dryer..	5.0 kw
	38.7 kw

First 10 kw at 100% = 10.00 kw
Remainder at 40% (28.7 kw × .4) = 11.48 kw
Calculated load for service size 21.48 kw = 21,480 watts

21,480 ÷ 230 = 93 amperes

Therefore, this dwelling may be served by a 100 ampere service.

Example No. 1(c). Single-Family Dwelling.
Optional Calculation for Single-Family Dwelling (See Section 220-7).

Dwelling has a floor area of 1500 sq. ft. exclusive of unoccupied cellar, unfinished attic and open porches. It has two 20 ampere small appliance circuits, one 20 ampere laundry circuit, two 4 kw wall-mounted ovens, one 5.1 kw counter-mounted cooking unit, a 4.5 kw water heater, a 1.2 kw dishwasher, a 5 kw combination clothes washer and dryer, six 7 ampere 230 volt room air conditioning units and a 1.5 kw permanently installed bathroom space heater.

Air conditioning kw calculation

$$\begin{array}{r} \text{Total amperes } 6 \times 7 = 42.00 \text{ amperes} \\ 25\% \text{ of largest motor } .25 \times 7 = \underline{1.75} \text{ amperes} \\ 43.75 \text{ amperes} \end{array}$$

$$43.75 \times 230 \div 1000 = 10.1 \text{ kw of air conditioner load}$$

Load included at 100%

Air conditioning.................................... 10.1 kw
Space heater (omit, see Section 220-4(l))

Other Load

	kw
1500 sq. ft. at 3 watts......................	4.5
Two 20 amp small appliance circuits at	
1500 watts..............................	3.0
Laundry circuit...........................	1.5
2 ovens..................................	8.
1 cooking unit............................	5.1
Water heater.............................	4.5
Dishwasher..............................	1.2
Washer/dryer............................	5.0
Total other load......................	32.8
1st 10 kw at 100%.......................... 10.0 kw	
Remainder at 40% (22.8 kw × .4)............. 9.12 kw	
Total calculated load..................... 29.22 kw = 29,220 watts	
29,220 ÷ 230 = 127 amperes (service rating)	

▶   All of the air-conditioning load is counted at **100** per cent, as stated in Table **220-7**, and this load as calculated in Example **1c** is figured separately from the "other loads" in order to comply with the requirements.

Example No. 2. Small Roadside Fruitstand With No Show Windows.

A small roadside fruitstand with no show windows has a floor area of 150 square feet. The electrical load consists of general lighting and a 1000 watt floodlight. There are no other outlets.

Computed Load (Section 220-4)
*General Lighting
150 sq. ft. at 3 watts/sq. ft. × 1.25 = 562 watts
(3 watts/sq. ft. for stores)
562 watts ÷ 115 = 4.88 amperes

One 15 ampere 2 wire branch circuit required (Section 220-3)

Minimum Size Service Conductor Required (Section 230-41 Exception No. 2)

Computed load....................	562 watts
Floodlight load....................	1000 watts
Total load................	1562 watts
1562 ÷ 115 = 13.6 amperes	

Use No. 8 service conductor (Section 230-41 Exception No. 2)
Use a 30-ampere service switch or breaker (Section 230-71(a), Exception No. 2)

Example No. 3. Store Building.

A store 50 feet by 60 feet, or 3,000 square feet, has 30 feet of show window.

Computed Load (Section 220-4)
    *General lighting load:
        3,000 square feet at 3 watts per square foot × 1.25 . . . . .   11,250 watts
    **Show window lighting load:
        30 feet at 200 watts per foot . . . .   6,000 watts

Minimum Number of Branch Circuits Required (Section 220-3)
   ***General lighting load: 11,250 ÷ 230 = 49 amperes for 3 wire, 115/230 volts; or 98 amperes for 2 wire, 115 volts:

        Three 30 ampere, 2-wire; and one 15 ampere, 2-wire circuits; or
        Five 20 ampere, 2-wire circuits; or
        Three 20 ampere, 2-wire, and three 15 ampere, 2-wire circuits; or
        Seven 15 ampere, 2-wire, circuits; or
        Three 15 ampere, 3-wire, and one 15 ampere, 2-wire circuits.

Special lighting load (show window): (Sections 220-2 Exception No. 1 and 220-4(c)): 6,000 ÷ 230 = 26 amperes for 3-wire, 115/230 volts; or 52 amperes for 2-wire, 115 volts:

        Four 15 ampere, 2-wire circuits; or
        Three 20 ampere, 2-wire circuits; or
        Two 15 ampere, 3-wire circuits.

Minimum Size Feeders (or Service Conductors) Required (Section 215-2):
    For 115/230 volt, 3-wire system:
        Ampere load: 49 plus 26 = 75 amperes. (Section 220-2):
        Size of each feeder, No. 3
    For 115 volt system:
        Ampere load: 98 plus 52 = 150 amperes. (Section 220-2)

  * The above examples assume that the entire general lighting load is a continuous load and the load is therefore increased by 25 per cent in accordance with Section 220-2. The 25 per cent increase is not applicable to any portion of the load that is not continuous.

  ** If show window load computed as per Section 220-2, the unit load per outlet to be increased 25 per cent.

  *** The load on each general lighting branch circuit shall not exceed 80% of the branch circuit rating (Section 210-23b).

Example No. 4. Multi-Family Dwelling.

Multi-family dwelling having a total floor area of 32,000 square feet with 40 apartments.
Meters in two banks of 20 each and individual sub-feeders to each apartment.
One-half of the apartments are equipped with electric ranges of not exceeding 12 kw each.
Area of each apartment is 800 square feet.
Laundry facilities on premises available to all tenants. Add no circuit to individual apartment. Add 1500 watts for each laundry circuit to house load and add to the example as a "house load."

Computed Load for Each Apartment (Article 220):
    General lighting load:
        800 square feet at 3 watts per square foot . . . .   2,400 watts
    Special appliance load:
        Electric range . . . .   8,000 watts

Minimum Number of Branch Circuits Required for Each Apartment
(Section 220-3):

General lighting load: $2,400 \div 115 = 21$ amperes or two 15 ampere,
2-wire circuits; or two 20 ampere, 2-wire circuits.

Small appliance load: Two 2-wire circuits of No. 12 wire. (See
Section 220-3(b)).

Range Circuit: $8,000 \div 230 = 35$ amperes or a circuit of two
No. 8's and one No. 10 as permitted by Section 210-19(c).

Minimum Size Sub-Feeder Required for Each Apartment (Section 215-2):

Computed load (Article 220):

General lighting load....................................	2,400 watts
Small appliance load, two 20 ampere circuits..............	3,000 watts
Total computed load (without ranges)...............	5,400 watts

Application of Demand Factor:

3,000 watts at 100%...................................	3,000 watts
2,400 watts at 35%....................................	840 watts
Net computed load (without ranges).................	3,840 watts
Range load..	8,000 watts
Net computed load (with ranges)....................	11,840 watts

For 115/230 volt, 3 wire system (without ranges):
Net computed load, $3,840 \div 230 = 16.7$ amperes.
Size of each sub-feeder (see Section 215-2).

For 115/230 volt, 3 wire system (with ranges):
Net computed load, $11,840 \div 230 = 51.5$ amperes.

Sub-Feeder Neutral:

Lighting and small appliance load.......................	3,840 watts
Range load, 8,000 watts at 70% (see Section 220-4(e))......	5,600 watts
Net computed load (neutral)........................	9,440 watts

$9,440 \div 230 = 41$ amperes

Minimum Size Feeders Required from Service Equipment to Meter Bank
(For 20 Apartments—10 with Ranges):

Total Computed Load:

Lighting and small appliance load, $20 \times 5,400$.............	108,000 watts

Application of Demand Factor:

3,000 watts at 100%...................................	3,000 watts
105,000 watts at 35%..................................	36,750 watts
Net computed lighting and small appliance load........	39,750 watts
Range load, 10 ranges (less than 12 kw; Col. A, Table 220-5)..	25,000 watts
Net computed load (with ranges)....................	64,750 watts

For 115/230 volt, 3 wire system:
Net computed load, $64,750 \div 230 = 282$ amperes.

Feeder Neutral:

Lighting and small appliance load.......................	39,750 watts
Range load: 25,000 watts at 70% (see Section 220-4(e)).....	17,500 watts
Computed load (neutral)...........................	57,250 watts

$57,250 \div 230 = 249$ amperes.

Further Demand Factor (Section 220-4(e)):

200 amperes at 100%	= 200 amperes	
49 amperes at 70%	= 34 amperes	

Net computed load (neutral).... 234 amperes

Minimum Size Main Feeder (or Service Conductors) Required
(For 40 Apartments—20 with Ranges):

Total Computed Load:

Lighting and small appliance load, $40 \times 5,400$.............	216,000 watts

Application of Demand Factor:

3,000 watts at 100%..............................	3,000 watts
117,000 watts at 35%..............................	40,950 watts
96,000 watts at 25%..............................	24,000 watts
Net computed lighting and small appliance load........	67,950 watts
Range load, 20 ranges (less than 12 kw, Col. A, Table 220-5)..	35,000 watts
Net computed load..............................	102,950 watts

For 115/230 volt, 3 wire system:

Net computed load, 102,950 ÷ 230 = 448 amperes.

Feeder Neutral:

Lighting and small appliance load........................	67,950 watts
Range load, 35,000 watts at 70% (see Section 220-4(e)).....	24,500 watts
Computed load (neutral)...........................	92,450 watts

92,450 ÷ 230 = 402 amperes.

Further Demand Factor (see Section 220-4(e)):

200 amperes at 100%	= 200 amperes
202 amperes at 70%	= 141 amperes
Net computed load (neutral)....	341 amperes

See Tables 310-12 through 310-15, Notes 8 and 10.

Example No. 4(a). Optional Calculation for Multi-Family Dwelling.

Multi-family dwelling equipped with electric cooking and space heating or air conditioning and having a total floor area of 32,000 square feet with 40 apartments.

Meters in two banks of 20 each plus house metering and individual subfeeders to each apartment.

Each apartment is equipped with an electric range of 8-kw nameplate rating, four 1.5-kw separately controlled 230-volt electric space heaters, and a 2.5-kw 230-volt electric water heater.

A common laundry facility is available to all tenants (Section 210-22(b) Exception No. 1).

Area of each apartment is 800 square feet.

Computed Load for Each Apartment (Article 220)

General lighting load:	
800 square ft. at 3 watts per sq. ft......................	2,400 watts
Electric range..	8,000 watts
Electric heat 6 kw.......................................	6,000 watts
(or air conditioning if larger)	
Electric water heater.......................................	2,500 watts

Minimum Number of Branch Circuits Required for Each Apartment

General lighting load: 2,400 watts ÷ 115 = 21 amp or two 15 ampere 2-wire circuits or two 20 amp 2-wire circuits.

Small appliance load: Two 2-wire circuits of No. 12. (See Section 220-3(b).)

Range circuit: 8,000 watts × 80% ÷ 230 = 28 amperes on a circuit of three No. 10 as permitted in Column C of Table 220-5.

Space heating: 6,000 watts ÷ 230 = 26 amperes.

No. of circuits. (See Sections 210-24, 220-3(a), and 424-3.)

Minimum Size Sub-Feeder Required for Each Apartment (Section 215-2)

Computed load (Article 220)	
General lighting load...................................	2,400 watts

Small appliance load, two 20 amp circuits................. 3,000 watts

Total computed load (without range and space heating). 5,400 watts

Application of Demand Factor

3,000 watts at 100%.................................... 3,000 watts

2,400 watts at 35%.................................... 840 watts

Net computed load (without range and space heating).......... 3,840 watts

Range load... 6,400 watts

Space heating Section 220-4(f)........................... 6,000 watts

Water heater... 2,500 watts

Net computed load for individual apartment.............. 18,740 watts

For 115/230 volt 3 wire system

Net computed load 18,740 ÷ 230 = 81 amperes

Sub-Feeder Neutral (Section 220-4(e))

Lighting and small appliance load...................... 3,840 watts

Range load 6,400 watts at 70% (see Section 220-4(e))....... 4,480 watts

Space and water heating (no neutral) 230 volt............. 0 watts

Net computed load (neutral)........................... 8,320 watts

8,320 ÷ 230 = 36 amperes

Minimum Size Feeder Required from Service Equipment to Meter Bank for 20 Apartments

Total Computed Load:

Lighting and small appliance load 20 × 5,400.............. 108,000 watts

Water and space heating load 20 × 8,500................ 170,000 watts

Range load 20 × 8,000............................... 160,000 watts

Net computed load (20 apartments)..................... 438,000 watts

Net Computed Load using Optional Calculation (Table 220-9)

438,000 × .38.. 166,440 watts

166,440 ÷ 230 = 724 amperes

Feeder Neutral:

Lighting and small appliance load

108,000 × 38% (Table 220-9) =...................... 41,040 watts

Range load 8,000 × 20 = 160,000 watts

160,000 × 38% (Table 220-9)........................ 60,800 watts

Computed load (neutral)............................... 101,840 watts

101,840 ÷ 230 = 443 amperes

Minimum Size Main Feeder Required (less house load)

(For 40 Apartments):

Total Computed Load:

Lighting and small appliance load 40 × 5,400.............. 216,000 watts

Water and space heating 40 × 8,500..................... 340,000 watts

Range load 40 × 8,000............................... 320,000 watts

Net computed load (40 apartments)..................... 876,000 watts

Net computed load using Optional Calculation (Table 220-9)

876,000 × 28%.. 245,280 watts

245,280 ÷ 230 = 1,066 amperes

Feeder Neutral:

Lighting and small appliance load 40 × 5,400 × 28%

(Table 220-9)...................................... 60,480 watts

Range load 8,000 × 40 × 28% (Table 220-9).............. 89,600 watts

Computed load (neutral)............................... 150,080 watts

150,080 ÷ 230 = 653 amperes

Add to obtain size of service conductors, the entire house load including laundry circuit(s) in accordance with applicable Sections of Article 220.

Example No. 5. Calculation of Feeder Neutral.

(See Section 220-4)

The following example illustrates the method of calculating size of a feeder neutral for the computed load of a 5-wire, 2-phase system, where it is desired to modify the load in accordance with provisions of Section 220-4.

An installation consisting of a computed load of 250 amperes connected between the feeder neutral and each ungrounded feeder conductor.

Feeder Neutral (maximum unbalance of load 250 amp. $\times$ 140% = 350 amperes):

200 amperes (first)   at 100% = 200 amperes
150 amperes (excess) at 70% = 105 amperes

Computed load   305 amperes

Example No. 6. Maximum Demand for Range Loads.

Table 220-5, Column A applies to ranges not over 12 kw. The application of Note 1 to ranges over 12 kw (and not over 27 kw) is illustrated in the following examples:

A.   Ranges all of same rating.
Assume 24 ranges each rated 16 kw.
From Column A the maximum demand for 24 ranges of 12 kw rating is 39 kw.
16 kw exceeds 12 kw by 4.
5% $\times$ 4 = 20% (5% increase for each kw in excess of 12).
39 kw $\times$ 20% = 7.8 kw increase.
39 + 7.8 = 46.8 kw: value to be used in selection of feeders.

B.   Ranges of unequal rating.
Assume 5 ranges each rated 11 kw.
2 ranges each rated 12 kw.
20 ranges each rated 13.5 kw.
3 ranges each rated 18 kw.

$$\begin{array}{ll} 5 \times 12 & = 60 \quad \text{Use 12 kw for range rated less than 12.} \\ 2 \times 12 & = 24 \\ 20 \times 13.5 & = 270 \\ \underline{3 \times 18} & = \underline{54} \\ 30 & 408 \text{ kw} \end{array}$$

408 ÷ 30 = 13.6 kw (average to be used for computation)
From Column A the demand for 30 ranges of 12 kw rating is 15 + 30 = 45 kw.
13.6 exceeds 12 by 1.6 (use 2.).
5% $\times$ 2 = 10% (5% increase for each kw in excess of 12).
45 kw $\times$ 10% = 4.5 kw increase.
45 + 4.5 = 49.5 kw = value to be used in selection of feeders.

Example No. 7. Ranges on a 3-Phase System.

(Section 220-4(j))

Thirty ranges rated at 12 kw each are supplied by a 3-phase, 4-wire, 120/208-volt feeder, 10 ranges on each phase.

As there are 20 ranges connected to each ungrounded conductor, the load should be calculated on the basis of 20 ranges (or in case of unbalance, twice the maximum number between any two phase wires) since diversity applies only to the number of ranges connected to adjacent phases and not the total.

The current in any one conductor will be one-half the total watt load of two adjacent phases divided by the line-to-neutral voltage. In this case, 20 ranges, from Table 220-5, will have a total watt load of 35,000 watts for two phases; therefore, the current in the feeder conductor would be:

$$17,500 \div 120 = 146 \text{ amperes.}$$

On a three-phase basis the load would be:

$$3 \times 17,500 = 52,500 \text{ watts}$$

and the current in each feeder conductor—

$$\frac{52,500}{208 \times 1.73} = 146 \text{ amperes}$$

Example No. 8. Motors, Conductors, and Overcurrent Protection.

(See Sections 430-22, 430-24, 430-32, 430-52, 430-62, and Tables 430-150 and 430-152.)

Determine the conductor size, the motor-running overcurrent protection, the branch circuit protection, and the feeder protection, for one 25-h.p. squirrel-cage induction motor (full-voltage starting, service factor 1.15, Code letter F), and two 30-h.p. wound-rotor induction motors (40°C rise), on a 460-volt, 3-phase, 60-hertz supply.

Conductor Loads

The full-load current of the 25-h.p. motor is 34 amperes (Table 430-150). A full-load current of 34 amperes $\times$ 1.25 = 42.5 amperes (Section 430-22). The full-load current of the 30-h.p. motor is 40 amperes (Table 430-150). A full-load current of 40 amperes $\times$ 1.25 = 50 amperes (Section 430-22).

The feeder ampacity will be 125 per cent of 40 plus 40 plus 34, or 124 amperes (Section 430-24).

Overcurrent Protection

Running. The 25-h.p. motor, with full-load current of 34 amperes, must have running overcurrent protection of not over 42.5 amperes. The 30-h.p. motor with full-load current of 40 amperes must have running overcurrent protection of not over 50 amperes.

Branch Circuit. The branch circuit of the 25-h.p. motor must have branch-circuit overcurrent protection of not over 300 per cent for a nontime-delay fuse (Table 430-152) or 3.00 $\times$ 34 = 102 amperes. The next larger size standard fuse is 110 amperes. (See Section 430-52.)

For the 30-h.p. motor the branch circuit overcurrent protection is 150 per cent (Table 430-152) or 1.50 $\times$ 40 = 60 amperes. Where the maximum value of overcurrent protection is not sufficient to start the motor the value for a nontime-delay fuse may be increased to 400 per cent (Section 430-52 Exception (a)).

Feeder Circuit. The maximum rating of the feeder overcurrent protection device is based on the sum of the largest branch circuit protective device (110 ampere fuse) plus the sum of the full-load currents of the other motors or 110 plus 40 plus 40 = 190 amperes. The nearest standard fuse which does not exceed this value is 175 amperes.

Appendix

RULES OF PROCEDURE FOR THE NFPA ELECTRICAL SECTION AND THE NATIONAL ELECTRICAL CODE COMMITTEE

Adopted by the NFPA Board of Directors on January 23, 1964 and Amended June 28, 1967

The National Fire Protection Association is sponsor of the National Electrical Code (ANSI C1, NFPA No. 70) and other standards covering the safe use of electricity. In 1948, the NFPA Board of Directors authorized an Electrical Section of NFPA. The National Electrical Code Committee consists of a Correlating Committee and a number of Code-Making Panels. The Rules of Procedure for these organizations consist of:

Part A—Rules of Procedure for the NFPA Electrical Section

Part B—Rules of Procedure for the National Electrical Code Committee

Part C—Rules of Procedure—Tentative Interim Amendments to the National Electrical Code

Part D—Interpretation Procedure of the National Electrical Code Committee

Part A—Rules of Procedure for the NFPA Electrical Section

Section 10. General

10. There are no dues or fees beyond the regular NFPA membership dues.

11. The Section provides particular opportunity for Section members to become informed and contribute to the development of NFPA electrical standards. It sponsors, for this purpose, open meetings where proposals for revisions or additions to these standards may be discussed.

12. Bulletins and reports on matters affecting the work of NFPA Technical Committees in this field are made available to members of the Section as the need indicates, through its Chairman, Secretary, or the NFPA Executive Office.

Section 20. Activities, Membership, Meetings, Officers

21. Activities, programs, and procedures not covered in these Rules for the NFPA Electrical Section shall be in accordance with the Regulations for NFPA Sections.

22. Membership in the NFPA Electrical Section is open to any Associate Member of the Association and up to four individuals designated by an Organization Member. To become a member of the NFPA Electrical Section, it is necessary to file a special application form with the NFPA Executive Office or the Electrical Section Secretary (forms available on request).

23. The Section shall meet at least annually at the time and place of the National Fire Protection Association Annual Meeting (unless omitted on the request of the Section with the consent of the NFPA Annual Meeting Program Committee). Other meetings of the Section may be held at times and places it may select.

24. The Chairman and Secretary of the National Electrical Code Committee shall be the Chairman and Secretary, respectively, of the Electrical Section. The Secretary of the Section shall keep a record of the membership, notify its members of Section meetings and keep members of the Section informed on matters of interest to them.

25. In order to transact business at any meeting of the Section, there shall be at least fifty members of the Section present. Robert's Rules of Order, Revised, shall govern the transactions of business at all meetings.

26. The Chairman of the National Electrical Code Committee (or his representative) shall report to the Annual Meeting of the Section on the work of that Committee and may take such other steps as he considers desirable to keep the Section informed on Committee matters. The Electrical Section may vote to request further consideration of a specific item by the Correlating Committee. Reports from other existing NFPA Technical Committees may be presented to the Annual Meeting of the Section when such action is considered appropriate by the officers of the Electrical Section.

27. The Section may recommend to the NFPA Board of Directors the establishment of other Technical Committees useful in promoting its objectives, other than as covered by the scope of the National Electrical Code. These Committees, if authorized, shall be organized and operated under the NFPA Regulations Governing Technical Committees or under such special rules as may be authorized by the NFPA Board of Directors. The Chairman of any such Committee so established shall follow the procedures outlined in Paragraph 26.

28. Reports of Technical Committees covering areas that are currently covered by the National Electrical Code, shall be submitted through the Correlating Committee of the National Electrical Code Committee when so directed by the NFPA Board of Directors. (See Paragraphs 54 and 55 of the NFPA Regulations Governing Technical Committees.)

29. The Section does not have authority to commit the Association nor does membership in the Section commit any individual or organization to a course of action.

Part B—Rules of Procedure for the National Electrical Code Committee

Section 30. General

31. The National Electrical Code Committee shall consist of

    a. A Correlating Committee, and

    b. A number of Code-Making Panels.

32. The functions of the National Electrical Code Committee shall be established by the NFPA Board of Directors and shall include

    a. Developing periodically revisions of the National Electrical Code (ANSI C1, NFPA No. 70) on a schedule to be announced to the public following issuance of each successive edition.

    b. Processing proposals for Tentative Interim Amendments of the current edition of the National Electrical Code in accordance with the Rules of Procedure—Tentative Interim Amendments to the National Electrical Code (see Part C of these Rules).

    c. Interpreting provisions of the current edition of the National Electrical Code in accordance with the Interpretation Procedure of the National Electrical Code Committee (see Part D of these Rules).

Section 40. Membership

41. The Chairman of the National Electrical Code Committee shall be the Chairman of the Correlating Committee of the National Electrical Code Committee and shall be appointed by the Board of Directors of the National Fire Protection Association. (See also Paragraph 24 of Part A—Rules of Procedure for the NFPA Electrical Section.)

42. Subject to approval by the Board of Directors of the National Fire Protection Association, the NFPA Electrical Field Engineer serves as the Secretary of the National Electrical Code Committee and as the Secretary of the Correlating Committee of the National Electrical Code Committee. He shall serve in this capacity as a nonvoting member, except as noted in Paragraphs 112 and 121.b. (See also Paragraph 24 of Part A—Rules of Procedure for the NFPA Electrical Section.)

43. Other members of the Correlating Committee shall also be appointed by the NFPA Board of Directors acting on recommendations of the Chairman of the Committee. Alternates for such individuals may be nominated when conditions warrant. The membership of the Correlating Committee shall be restricted to nine voting members (Secretary and other nonvoting members excluded).

44. Groups concerned with various Articles of the Code may nominate qualified individuals to serve on the Code-Making Panels, submitting their recommendations to the Chairman of the Correlating Committee in such form as he may request. Alternates for such individuals may be nominated when conditions warrant. Individuals having an interest in only a portion of the scope of the work of a particular Panel may be nominated to limited membership covering their special field of interest. All appointments of members and alternates shall be made by the Chairman of the Correlating Committee acting with the advice and consent of the members of the Correlating Committee acting in consideration of the items noted in Paragraph 46.

45. The Chairman of the Correlating Committee shall appoint the Chairman of each Code-Making Panel, acting with the advice and consent of the members of the Correlating Committee.

46. All appointments to the Correlating Committee and to the Code-Making Panels shall be based on the technical competence of the individuals selected. Proper balance of all interests concerned shall be made within the desired limits of effective committee size and in accordance with the objectives of the National Fire Protection Association and in accordance with procedures of the American National Standards Institute.

Section 50. Functions of the Correlating Committee

51. The Correlating Committee shall have the following functions:

a. Determine the steps and schedule for each revised edition of the National Electrical Code, subject to approval by the Board of Directors of the National Fire Protection Association.

b. Organize the Code-Making Panels in such a manner as to effectively cover the technical objectives of the National Electrical Code as set forth in Article 90 of the Code. The number of Code-Making Panels and the Code Articles assigned to each shall be determined by the Correlating Committee.

c. Appoint, as needed, Technical Subcommittees to assist in developing the National Electrical Code and such other Codes, Standards or Manuals which the NFPA Board of Directors recommends be handled by the National Electrical Code Committee.

d. Review all reports by the Code-Making Panels that recommend changes or additions to the National Electrical Code; determine whether a consensus exists warranting acceptance of such recommended changes or additions; and determine whether the proposals shall be approved for further processing, rejected, returned to the appropriate Code-Making Panel or Panels for further study, or submitted to a Technical Subcommittee for further consideration. Action to recommend amendments to the National Electrical Code for action at an NFPA Annual

Meeting shall require at least seven affirmative votes by the Correlating Committee provided that, if any absent member subsequently registers disapproval, the action must be reaffirmed by letter ballot or at a later meeting of the Committee.

e. Review all reports of other technical committees of the Electrical Section that normally submit such reports in accordance with Paragraph 28.

f. Establish that no conflict exists and satisfactory correlation is achieved between recommendations of the various Code-Making Panels and with other NFPA Technical Committees having an interest in the subjects under consideration.

g. Report to the Director of Engi-

neering Services of the National Fire Protection Association any proposals for revisions or additions to the National Electrical Code.

h. Determine the Rules of Procedure for Tentative Interim Amendments of the National Electrical Code, subject to approval of the Board of Directors of the National Fire Protection Association (see Part C of these Rules).

i. Establish an Interpretation Procedure for the National Electrical Code, subject to approval of the Board of Directors of the National Fire Protection Association (see Part D of these Rules).

52. Meetings of the Correlating Committee shall be held at the call of the Chairman. Seven members shall constitute a quorum.

Section 60. Functions of the Code-Making Panels

61. A Code-Making Panel shall consider and report its recommendations on all matters referred to it by any of the methods outlined in Paragraph 91 of these Rules.

62. The program of each Code-Making Panel shall be directed by its Chairman as seems most appropriate for the efficient disposition of its business subject to the approval of the Correlating Committee. Code-Making Panel Meeting dates and places shall be coordinated through the Secretary of the National Electrical Code Committee to avoid conflicts of meetings and to assure that the established schedule is adhered to. Within this framework, each Code-Making Panel may develop its own working methods consistent with the objectives of the Association and the National Electrical Code Committee as herein established. A guide outline of "Manual of Procedure for Code-Making Panels" is available from the Secretary of the National Electrical Code Committee. Any proposed revision of the National Electrical Code recommended by a Panel shall represent, to a major degree, the consensus of the membership substantially concerned. (It shall be the responsibility of the Correlating Committee to deter-

mine if such a valid consensus exists.)

63. When reporting recommendations, the vote of each member of a Panel shall be recorded with the Correlating Committee by the Chairman of the Panel. This report shall identify affirmative voters, negative voters, those abstaining, and those whose ballots have not been returned, together with the reasons for negative votes and abstentions.

64. Each Panel shall report the consideration given to each proposal for Code changes that have been referred to it, whether it recommends a specific action, rejects the proposal, votes to retain the item on its docket for further study, refers the proposal to another Code-Making Panel, or takes any other course of action.

65. The various Panels are authorized to solicit from individuals or groups concerned with the scope of an Article such technical assistance and cooperation as will contribute to their work. The Chairman of the National Electrical Code Committee should be kept advised of such actions and those cooperating in this manner shall be mentioned in the report of the Panel to the Correlating Committee.

Section 70. Technical Subcommittees

71. Technical Subcommittees to consider any designated topic shall be appointed by the Chairman of the National Electrical Code Committee. Forming such Technical Subcommittees may result

from a recommendation of the Correlating Committee or a request of a Code-Making Panel following approval by the Correlating Committee. Where the topic to be considered is wholly within a single

Panel, the Chairman of the National Electrical Code Committee may request the Chairman of the Code-Making Panel to appoint the members of the Technical Subcommittee.

72. Those invited to serve on a Technical Subcommittee shall be chosen on the basis of familiarity with the problem or topic and need not be members of the National Electrical Code Committee.

73. Any report from a technical Subcommittee, if containing proposals for changes or additions to the National Electrical Code, shall be referred to the Code-Making Panel or Panels to which the affected Articles of the Code have been assigned. Further processing shall follow the procedures indicated in Sections 91 to 93, inclusive, of these Rules.

Section 80. Revisions, Additions, and Deletions to the National Electrical Code

81. To be approved by the Correlating Committee, a revision of the National Electrical Code shall be either for:

a. A proposed revision for a new Edition of the Code, or

b. A Tentative Interim Amendment (see Part C of these Rules).

82. A new Edition of the National Electrical Code will be planned according to the following conditions:

a. Upon the initiative of the Correlating Committee on a three-year or four-year schedule, or

b. After a shorter interval when requested by the Correlating Committee or the Board of Directors of the National Fire Protection Association.

83. A Tentative Interim Amendment is a revision applied for and processed in accordance with the Rules of Procedure for Tentative Interim Amendments (see Part C of these Rules).

84. A schedule for each revised Edition of the Code shall be published by the Association and announced in suitable news releases to the technical press within six months following the issuance of each revised edition. This schedule shall include dates during which comments or recommendations from the public are to be received.

Section 90. Methods for Handling Proposed Code Revisions

91. The stages through which proposed changes in the Code are to be considered shall be as follows:

a. Proposal is prepared by any member of the National Electrical Code Committee, by any interested person, or by any interested organization and submitted to the Chairman of the National Electrical Code Committee with copies to the Secretary of the National Electrical Code Committee and to the Chairman of the responsible Code-Making Panel. If the submitter is not sure which Code-Making Panel has jurisdiction or if it involves a subject not previously assigned, an extra copy of the proposal should be sent to the Chairman of the National Electrical Code Committee for proper disposition.

b. The proposal is circulated to the members of the Code-Making Panel by its Chairman.

c. The Code-Making Panel considers the proposal and takes one or more of the following steps:

(1) Drafts or prepares a proposed revision or addition to the National Electrical Code, ballots on same, and forwards its recommendations, with a ballot statement (see Paragraphs 63 and 64) to the Correlating Committee for approval as a proposed revision for a new Edition of the Code.

(2) Requests coordination with any other affected Code-Making Panel through the Correlating Committee, looking forward to future submittal in accordance with Paragraph 91.c.(1).

(3) Rejects the proposal, submitting it and a vote statement explaining its action to the Correlating Committee.

(4) Reports to the Correlating Committee that the proposal has been placed on the Panel's docket pending further study.

(5) Refers the recommendation to a Technical Subcommittee for detailed consideration (see Section 70 of these Rules).

d. All proposals for revisions or changes made by the Code-Making Panels and referred to the Correlating Committee are reviewed and processed in accordance with Paragraphs 51.d. and 51.f.

e. For a new Edition of the National Electrical Code, the Committee Secretary prepares for public dissemination through the National Fire Protection Association the "Preprint of the Proposed Amendments for the . . . . .* National Electrical Code" for study and comment, announcing at that time a final date for receipt of such comment in accordance with the prearranged schedule (see Paragraphs 51.a. and 82).

f. Following action specified in Paragraph 91.e., all comments received are referred to the Code-Making Panels for their final consideration and vote. Their proposals are then resubmitted to the Correlating Committee, which reviews them and takes one of the actions indicated in Paragraph 91.d.

g. The Secretary of the National Electrical Code Committee then prepares for publication in the NFPA Technical Committee Reports the proposed . . . . .* National Electrical Code.

h. The Electrical Section (see Part A) is provided with the opportunity of reviewing these amendments or the revised edition at its Annual Meeting prior to Association action on the report. The Electrical Section may vote to request further consideration of a specific item by the Correlating Committee. The Correlating Committee in giving further consideration must either reaffirm its original position or refer the matter back to the Code-Making Panel involved for further study.

i. Following final consideration by the Correlating Committee, the report is submitted to the membership of the National Fire Protection Association in Annual Meeting for action in accordance with the NFPA Regulations Governing Technical Committees.

92. The NFPA submits each edition of the National Electrical Code (NFPA No. 70) to the American National Standards Institute for adoption as a ANSI Standard (ANSI Standard C1).

93. A new edition of the Code is published by the National Fire Protection Association.

* Next date of issue.

Part C—Rules of Procedure—Tentative Interim Amendments to the National Electrical Code

Section 100. Purpose and Scope of Tentative Interim Amendments

101. A Tentative Interim Amendment to the National Electrical Code is an amendment processed and promulgated separate and apart from a revised edition of the Code in accordance with this Part.

102. The purpose of a Tentative Interim Amendment is to correct errors and conflicts or to accomplish recognition of advances in the art of safeguarding of persons and of buildings and their contents as set forth in Section 90-1 of the National Electrical Code.

103. This method of amending the Code shall be resorted to only when action is urgently needed and should not be deferred until the next scheduled revision.

Section 110. Handling Proposals for Tentative Interim Amendments

111. A proposal for such a Tentative Interim Amendment should include a full explanation of the proposal and an exact statement of the suggested solution supported by all pertinent data, together with a specific statement of what new text or amendment of the existing text of the National Electrical Code is recommended. Each proposal must be endorsed by a member of the National Electrical Code Committee and the proposer must be prepared to furnish as many copies of the proposal and supporting data as the Chairman of the National Electrical Code Committee may determine are needed for appropriate consideration.

112. The Chairman of the National Electrical Code Committee shall refer each proposal to a special Subcommittee appointed by him and consisting of two members of the Correlating Committee of the National Electrical Code Committee and the Chairman or Chairmen of the Code-Making Panel(s) concerned with the proposal. The Chairman and Secretary of the National Electrical Code Committee shall be voting members of this special Subcommittee. This special Subcommittee shall determine whether the proposal is within the stated purpose of the Tentative Interim Amendment Procedure set forth in Paragraphs 102 and 103.

a. If the proposal is found not to be within the stated purpose of this procedure, the Chairman of the National Electrical Code Committee shall so notify the submitter.

113. If the proposal is found to be within the stated purpose of this Procedure, the Chairman of the National Electrical Code Committee shall refer the proposal and all supporting data to the appropriate Code-Making Panel or Panels. The Panel or Panels shall report any recommendations to the Correlating Committee of the National Electrical Code Committee, following which the Chairman of the National Electrical Code Committee shall report the proposed Panel action to the submitter. If the submitter is not satisfied with the proposed Panel action, he shall be privileged to withdraw his proposal or submit a revision of the proposed amendment or new data in support of his original proposal. Such a submitter's revision, new data, or both, shall be referred to the Code-Making Panel or Panels for further consideration and report.

a. The Panel is not privileged to revise or amend the proposal as submitted, except for purely editorial content. If it is felt desirable to amend or revise the substantive content of the original proposal, such amendments or revisions shall be subject to the same criteria for handling as a Tentative Interim Amendment, as the original proposal, namely, the criteria specified in Paragraphs 102 and 103.

114. If the Panel recommends against adoption of the proposal and the Correlating Committee determines that the proposal has been processed in accordance with the procedures described herein, the Chairman of the National Electrical Code Committee shall notify the proposer that the National Electrical Code Committee has declined to accept the Tentative Interim Amendment as proposed.

115. If agreement is reached between the interested Panel or Panels and the proposer as to a specific Tentative Interim Amendment of the Code, it shall be submitted to the Correlating Committee for formal approval. If approved by both the Panel and the Correlating Committee with no more than one negative vote by either group, such a Tentative Interim Amendment shall be promulgated for the current edition of the National Electrical Code and will become effective immediately.

a. If the Panel approves the Tentative Interim Amendment by a consensus of voting, but with two or more negative votes or if there is more than one negative vote by the Correlating Committee, the Association shall publish in one of its publications distributed to all members the proposed Amendment with the notice that it is being considered for the current edition of the National Electrical Code, and those persons wishing to comment should file such comments with the Chairman of the National Electrical Code Committee within 60 days after the mailing date of the publication. Any comments so received shall be considered by the Code-Making Panel, which shall make a final report to the Correlating Committee. The latter will then reconsider the amendment, make a final decision regarding it, and notify the submitter of the action taken.

b. A Tentative Interim Amendment, when approved with or without the 60-day waiting period, shall be published by the Association in a manner or manners best designed to notify all interested parties and announced in a suitable NFPA news release to the technical press.

116. All Tentative Interim Amendments are subject to further consideration by the appropriate Code-Making Panel or Panels in preparing recommendations for a subsequent new edition of the National Electrical Code as though originating in accordance with the established regular procedure for revising the National Electrical Code.

Part D—Interpretation Procedure of the National Electrical Code Committee

Section 120. Personnel of Interpretations Committee

121. There shall be a standing committee of the National Electrical Code Committee to be known as the Interpretations Committee. This Committee shall consist of:

a. The Chairman of the Correlating Committee, who shall be the Chairman of the Interpretations Committee and a voting member.

b. The Secretary of the Correlating Committee, who shall be the Secretary of the Interpretations Committee and a voting member.

c. The Chairman of that Code-Making Panel which has charge of the affected Article of the Code for which an interpretation is requested, and

d. At least two other members or alternates of the National Electrical Code Committee selected by the Chairman depending upon the availability, experience, knowledge, and interest of the members. The Code-Making Panel Chairman and the two other members shall be selected for each specific interpretation and shall be discharged upon completion of each.

122. No member or alternate shall be eligible who is directly concerned with a controversial situation to which the specific question for interpretation applies.

Section 130. Method of Applying for Interpretations

131. Those desiring an interpretation shall direct their requests to the Chairman of the Interpretations Committee, National Electrical Code, National Fire Protection Association, 60 Batterymarch Street, Boston, Mass. 02110, supplying five identical copies of a statement in which shall appear specific references to a single problem, Article or Section. Such a statement shall be on the business stationery of the inquirer and shall be duly signed.

132. When applications involve actual field situations, they shall so state and all parties involved shall be named.

Section 140. Forms of Interpretations Recognized

141. Two general forms of findings will be recognized:

a. Those making an interpretation of the literal text.

b. Those making an interpretation of the intent of the National Electrical Code Committee when a particular rule was adopted.

142. There are certain questions which arise in the application of the requirements of the National Electrical Code which are not subject to interpretation under the procedures described herein. These include degree and extent of a hazardous location area, interpretation of suitability of isolation or guarding, interpretation of equivalent protection—and such items which involve an intimate knowledge of the installation rather than a knowledge of the intent and meaning of the requirement.

Section 150. Methods of Handling and Issuing Interpretations

151. The findings of the Interpretations Committee will be in its name and for the National Electrical Code Committee as a whole. In any case, where there is more than one negative vote on any proposed interpretation, the interpretation shall be referred to the Correlating Committee. The Correlating Committee shall then make a judgment on the consensus of voting in the Committee to determine that a consensus does exist. If it is determined that a consensus does not exist, the request shall be referred to the proper Code-Making Panel or Panels.

152. The applicant will be informed of the finding promptly following its having been determined. As soon as feasible, the Interpretation, serially numbered, but not otherwise identified, shall be published by the Association and announced in a suitable NFPA news release to the technical press.

153. When the Committee on Interpretations reports to the Electrical Correlating Committee at its regular meeting, a statement shall be made as to extent of concurrence of the members in the separate findings covered in their report. No other release shall be made of any minority views.

154. Each interpretation will be based on the best judgment of the Committee, but the Committee cannot be responsible for subsequent actions by authorities enforcing the National Electrical Code as to whether they accept or reject the findings.

155. Each Code-Making Panel will be expected to give appropriate consideration to the text of any Article or Section of the National Electrical Code which has produced an Interpretation finding to the end that a suitable revision of the text may be recommended to eliminate the difficulty which prompted the request.

TIME SCHEDULE FOR THE 1974 NATIONAL ELECTRICAL CODE

Adopted by the Correlating Committee of the National Electrical Code Committee, February 11, 1971

Dec. 1, 1972 Final date for receipt of proposals from the public for revision of the 1971 *National Electrical Code* preparatory to the issuance of a 1974 edition. Proposals should be forwarded to the Chairman, the Secretary, and the responsible Code Making Panel Chairmen. (Full names and addresses published on Pages 70-v to 70-xii of the 1971 NEC.)

Dec. 1, 1972 to April 1973 Code Making Panels consider proposals for Code changes and prepare reports for submittal to Correlating Committee.

April 14, 1973 Final Date for Code Making Panel reports to be submitted to the Correlating Committee.

April 15, 1973 to May 1973 Correlating Committee reviews reports submitted by Code Making Panels. Advises Panels with respect to existence of consensus, correlates work among Panels, assigns Panel jurisdiction over new and borderline items. Submits reports of the Panels to the NFPA Executive Office for the *Preprint of the Proposed Amendments for the 1974 National Electrical Code.*

May 1973 Informal report to the NFPA Electrical Section by the Correlating Committee at the 1973 NFPA Annual Meeting.

July 1973 *Preprint of the Proposed Amendments for the 1974 National Electrical Code* published for distribution to the National Electrical Code Committee and other interested parties.

July 1973 to Nov. 15, 1973 Period for study by members of the National Electrical Code Committee, electrical inspectors, industry and others, and submittal of recommendations to Code Making Panel Chairmen* for changes.

Nov. 16, 1973 to Feb. 1, 1974 Code Making Panels reconsider all proposed recommendations for changes and prepare final report for submittal to the Correlating Committee.

Feb. 1, 1974 Final date for Code Making Panel reports to be submitted to the Correlating Committee.

Feb. 1974 Correlating Committee reviews Final Reports of Code Making Panels, accepts or rejects changes, determines existence of consensus, resolves conflicts between Code Making Panel Reports.

March 1, 1974 Final date for Correlating Committee to submit the final proposed changes to NFPA for printing in the *1974 NFPA Technical Committee Reports.*

April 1974 NFPA prints and distributes the *1974 NFPA Technical Committee Reports* containing the proposed 1974 *National Electrical Code* to members of the National Electrical Code Committee and to all other NFPA members who file requests therefor.

May 1974 Review by the NFPA Electrical Section and official action by NFPA Annual Meeting. Submittal by NFPA to American National Standards Institute for approval as ANSI Standard.

Sept. 1974 Publication of the 1974 *National Electrical Code.*

---

* Copies should also be sent to the Chairman and the Secretary.

METHOD OF SUBMITTING PROPOSAL TO REVISE THE NATIONAL ELECTRICAL CODE

A proposal to revise the 1971 Edition of the National Electrical Code must be submitted prior to December 1, 1972 as indicated in the time schedule for the 1974 National Electrical Code. The proposal should be sent to the Chairman and Secretary of the National Electrical Code Committee in the form indicated below. The proposal is to be identified by Section number and paragraph letter, where applicable, and is to state the new or revised Code text. It is essential that the submitter fully understand the intent of an existing requirement before attempting to propose a revision of it.

The submitter is to identify the source of the proposal, indicating whether it is his own or is being submitted by a committee or organization.

The proposal needs to be accompanied by supporting comment explaining the need for the change and should include any available substantiating information or data. Where the submitter believes it imperative that the supporting comment shall provide considerable detailed information that cannot be accommodated on a single page, he is to provide 25 copies of this proposal on plain paper for subsequent use by the Panel Chairman in processing the proposal. An example of a property submitted proposal is as follows:

Section 250-74

Proposal:

Amend Section 250-74 to read:

250-74. Bonding at Grounding-Type Receptacles. Grounding continuity between a grounded outlet box and the grounding circuit of the receptacle shall be established by means of a bonding jumper between the outlet box and the receptacle grounding terminal.

Exception 1: When the box is surface-mounted, direct metal-to-metal contact between the device yoke and the box may be used to establish the grounding circuit.

Exception 2: Contact devices or yokes designed and approved for the purpose may be used in conjunction with the supporting screws to establish the grounding circuit between the device yoke and flush-type boxes installed in walls.

Submitter:

International Association of Electrical Inspectors.

Supporting Comment:

Direct contact between device yokes and boxes is seldom achieved between devices and boxes installed in walls, inasmuch as flush boxes are in practice seldom found flush, despite the provisions of Section 370-10. Screws and yokes currently in use were designed solely for the support of devices rather than as part of the grounding circuit. The intent of the amendment is to encourage the design of either a modified yoke or a supplemental conducting member to augment the supporting screw in the device-to-box grounding circuit.

711

SPECIAL NOTICE

The following tentative interim amendments have been issued subsequent to the publication of the 1971 National Electrical Code (August, 1971). Where the 1971 National Electrical has been adopted by law, all subsequent tentative interim amendments would require similar adoption to be acceptable by the local authority having jurisdiction.

It should also be noted that the tentative interim amendments appearing in this Handbook may not be the only ones issued on the 1971 Code. Other tentative interim amendments may be issued after this Handbook has been completed. Members of the National Fire Protection Association, including members of the Electrical Section, are notified in appropriate issues of the NFPA FIRE NEWS and the ELECTRICAL SECTION NEWS BULLETIN. There are no mailing lists or notifications to non-members of the National Fire Protection Association. However, upon the release of each tentative interim amendment, press releases are sent to major trade publications. In turn, these amendments are published in the various trade and association periodicals.

TENTATIVE INTERIM AMENDMENT NO. 170

Released October 27, 1971

NATIONAL ELECTRICAL CODE, 1971

ARTICLE 334—METAL-CLAD CABLE

Section 334-4(a). Type MC. *Add a new exception as follows:*

Exception: Additional conductors employed for control purposes only in Type MC cable may be of size 14 AWG and larger for copper and 12 AWG and larger for aluminum and copper-clad aluminum.

TENTATIVE INTERIM AMENDMENT NO. 166

Released January 28, 1972

NATIONAL ELECTRICAL CODE, 1971

ARTICLE 501—CLASS I INSTALLATIONS—HAZARDOUS LOCATIONS

Section 501-8(a). Class I, Division 1 (Motors and Generators). *Add a new (4) at end of first sentence, and revise second and third sentences (additions in italics) as follows:*

. . . , *or (4) of a type submerged in natural gas or propane (liquid or gas) which is flammable only when mixed with air and is at a positive pressure and the motor has been purged to exclude air before starting and which is so arranged that the motor will be automatically de-energized if the supply of LNG (liquified natural gas) or propane fails or the pressure is reduced to atmospheric.* Totally enclosed motors of types (2) or (3) *or submerged motors of type (4)* shall have no external surface with an operating temperature in degrees Celsius in excess of 80 per cent of the ignition temperature of the gas or vapor involved, as determined by ASTM test procedure (Designation: D-2155-66.) Appropriate devices shall also be provided to detect any increase in the temperature of the motor beyond design limits and automatically de-energize the equip-

712

ment, *except for a motor submerged in LNG (liquified natural gas) or propane when the temperature is −40°C or less.* Auxiliary equipment shall be of a type approved for the location in which it is installed.

TENTATIVE INTERIM AMENDMENT NO. 172

Released November 8, 1971

NATIONAL ELECTRICAL CODE, 1971

ARTICLE 700—EMERGENCY SYSTEMS

Section 700-22. Unit Equipments.   *Revise the second sentence of the first paragraph by adding the following at the end of the second sentence:*

. . . , or the unit equipment shall supply and maintain not less than 60 per cent of the initial emergency illumination for a period of at least 1½ hours.

Where a subject indexed is treated in detail in a Chapter or Article, this Index refers the reader to the entire Chapter or Article, identified by the abbreviation: "Chap." or "Art."

Where a subject is treated in a Part of an Article, this Index refers to that Part directly, identified by the Article designation and the Part letter, such as "250-J."

Where a subject is treated in a Section or a Paragraph in a Section, this Index refers directly to the Section designation, such as 250-91. This advises the reader to look in Section 250-91 or either of its two Paragraphs, 250-91(a) or 250-91(b).

Index items to the Tables, Diagrams, Exceptions, and Examples are clearly indicated.

Readers are also referred to the Table of Contents in the front of the Code and to Article 100—Definitions.